OUR NATIONAL INCOME ACCOUNTS AND REAL GDP SINCE 1929*

In this table, in which all amounts are in billions of dollars, we see historical data for the various components of nominal GDP. These are given in the first four columns. We then show the rest of the national income accounts going from GDP to NDP to NI to PI to DPI. The last column gives real GDP.

	The Sum of These Expenditures				Equals	Less	Equals	Plus	Less	Equals	Less			Plus	Equals	Less	Equals	
Year	Personal Consumption Expenditures	Gross Private Domestic Investment	Government Purchases of Goods and Services	Net Exports	Gross Domestic Product	Depreciation	Net Domestic Product	Net U.S. Income Earned Abroad	Indirect Business Taxes and Transfers and Other Adjustments	National Income	Undistributed Corporate Profits	Social Security Taxes	Corporate Income Taxes	Transfer Payments and Net Interest Earnings	Personal Income	Personal Income Taxes and Nontax Payments	Disposable Personal Income	Real GDP (2005 Dollars)
1988	3353.6	821.6	1039.0	110.4	5103.8	611.0	4492.8	23.6	33.0	4549.4	155.1	361.5	141.6	362.5	4253.7	505.0	3748.7	7607.4
1989	3598.5	874.9	1099.1	88.2	5484.4	651.5	4832.9	26.2	32.5	4826.6	121.5	385.2	146.1	414.0	4587.8	566.1	4021.7	7879.2
1990	3839.9	861.0	1180.2	78.0	5803.1	691.2	5111.9	34.8	57.6	5089.1	120.0	410.1	145.4	465.0	4878.6	592.8	4285.8	8027.1
1991	3986.1	802.9	1234.4	27.5	5995.9	724.4	5271.5	30.4	74.0	5227.9	138.0	430.2	138.6	529.9	5051.0	586.7	4464.3	8008.3
1992	4235.3	864.8	1271.0	33.2	6337.9	744.4	5593.5	29.7	110.4	5512.8	159.5	455.0	148.7	612.4	5362.0	610.6	4751.4	8280.0
1993	4477.9	953.4	1291.2	65.0	6657.5	778.0	5879.5	31.9	138.0	5773.4	169.7	477.4	171.0	603.2	5558.5	646.6	4911.9	8516.2
1994	4743.3	1097.1	1325.5	93.6	7072.3	819.2	6253.1	26.2	157.0	6122.3	199.4	508.2	193.1	620.9	5842.5	690.7	5151.8	8863.1
1995	4975.8	1144.0	1369.2	91.4	7397.6	869.5	6528.1	35.8	110.0	6453.9	243.9	532.8	217.8	692.9	6152.3	744.1	5408.2	9086.0
1996	5256.8	1240.3	1416.0	96.2	7816.9	912.5	6904.4	35.0	99.3	6840.1	272.3	555.1	231.5	739.4	6520.6	832.1	5688.5	9425.8
1997	5547.4	1389.8	1468.7	101.6	8304.3	963.8	7340.5	33.0	81.3	7292.2	308.2	587.2	245.4	763.7	6915.1	926.3	5988.8	9845.9
1998	5879.5	1509.1	1518.3	159.9	8747.0	1020.5	7726.5	21.3	5.0	7752.8	212.6	624.7	248.4	755.9	7423.0	1027.1	6395.9	10274.7
1999	6342.8	1641.5	1631.3	262.1	9353.5	1094.4	8259.1	33.8	65.1	8358.0	260.1	661.4	258.8	733.1	7910.8	1107.5	6803.3	10770.7
2000	6830.4	1772.2	1731.0	382.1	9951.5	1184.3	8767.2	39.0	132.7	8938.9	176.3	705.8	265.1	767.7	8559.4	1232.2	7327.2	11216.4
2001	7148.8	1661.9	1846.4	371.0	10286.1	1256.2	9029.9	43.6	111.7	9185.2	210.0	733.2	203.3	844.6	8883.3	1234.8	7648.5	11337.5
2002	7439.2	1647.0	1983.3	427.2	10642.3	1305.0	9337.3	30.7	40.5	9408.5	280.6	751.5	192.3	876.0	9060.1	1050.4	8009.7	11543.1
2003	7804.0	1729.7	2112.6	504.1	11142.2	1354.1	9788.1	68.1	16.0	9840.2	309.2	778.9	243.8	869.8	9378.1	1000.3	8377.8	11836.4
2004	8270.6	1968.6	2232.8	618.7	11853.3	1432.8	10420.5	53.7	59.8	10534.0	390.5	827.3	306.1	927.1	9937.2	1047.8	8889.4	12246.9
2005	8803.5	2172.3	2369.9	722.7	12623.0	1541.4	11081.6	68.5	123.7	11273.8	486.4	872.7	412.4	983.6	10485.9	1208.6	9277.3	12623.0
2006	9301.0	2327.1	2518.4	769.3	13377.2	1660.7	11716.5	58.0	256.7	12031.2	430.3	921.8	473.3	1062.3	11268.1	1352.4	9915.7	12958.5
2007	9772.3	2295.2	2674.2	713.0	14028.7	1767.5	12261.2	64.4	122.6	12448.2	270.7	959.5	445.5	1139.8	11912.3	1488.7	10423.6	13206.4
2008	10035.5	2087.6	2878.1	709.7	14291.5	1854.1	12437.4	141.9	131.1	12448.2	152.5	987.3	309.0	1460.8	12460.2	1107.6	11024.5	13161.9
2009	9866.1	1546.8	2917.5	391.4	13939.0	1866.2	12072.8	152.3	77.5	12147.6	469.6	964.1	272.4	1488.7	11930.2	1141.4	10788.8	12703.1
2010	10245.5	1795.1	3002.8	516.9	14526.5	1874.9	12651.6	189.4	0.9	12840.1	651.7	986.8	411.1	1583.0	12373.5	1193.8	11179.7	13088.0
2011[a]	10726.0	1916.2	3030.6	578.7	15094.1	1950.0	13144.1	192.3	100.9	13437.3	677.2	920.1	453.2	1618.5	13005.3	1449.1	11556.2	13315.1
2012[a]	10915.3	1954.0	3439.8	602.2	15706.9	2029.2	13677.7	198.3	106.8	13982.8	704.7	957.5	471.6	1684.2	13533.3	1507.9	12025.4	13597.4
2013[a]	11211.5	2033.3	3726.6	626.7	16344.7	2111.6	14233.1	205.6	111.9	14550.6	733.3	996.3	490.7	1752.6	14082.8	1569.2	12513.6	13858.5

[a]Author's estimates.

*Note: Some notes may not add up due to rounding.

Economics Today

THE MACRO VIEW

Economics Today

THE MACRO VIEW

Seventeenth Edition

Roger LeRoy Miller

Research Professor of Economics
University of Texas–Arlington

PEARSON

Boston Columbus Indianapolis New York San Francisco Upper Saddle River
Amsterdam Cape Town Dubai London Madrid Milan Munich Paris Montréal Toronto
Delhi Mexico City São Paulo Sydney Hong Kong Seoul Singapore Taipei Tokyo

MyEconLab® Provides the Power of Practice

Optimize your study time with **MyEconLab**, the online assessment and tutorial system. When you take a sample test online, **MyEconLab** gives you targeted feedback and a personalized Study Plan to identify the topics you need to review.

Study Plan

The Study Plan shows you the sections you should study next, gives easy access to practice problems, and provides you with an automatically generated quiz to prove mastery of the course material.

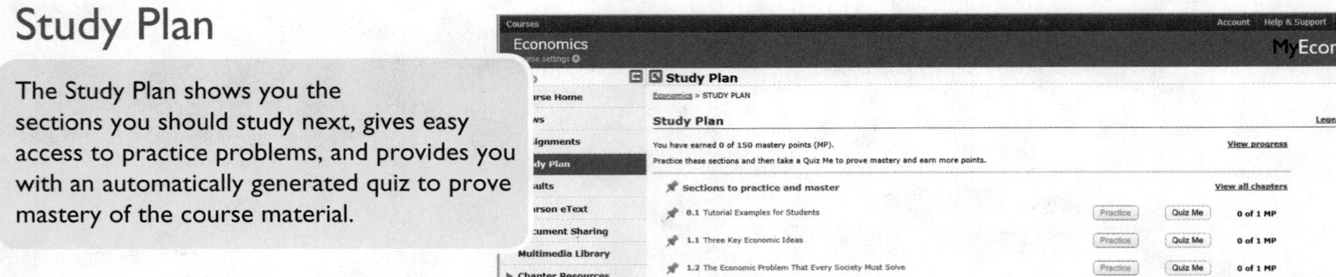

Unlimited Practice

As you work each exercise, instant feedback helps you understand and apply the concepts. Many Study Plan exercises contain algorithmically generated values to ensure that you get as much practice as you need.

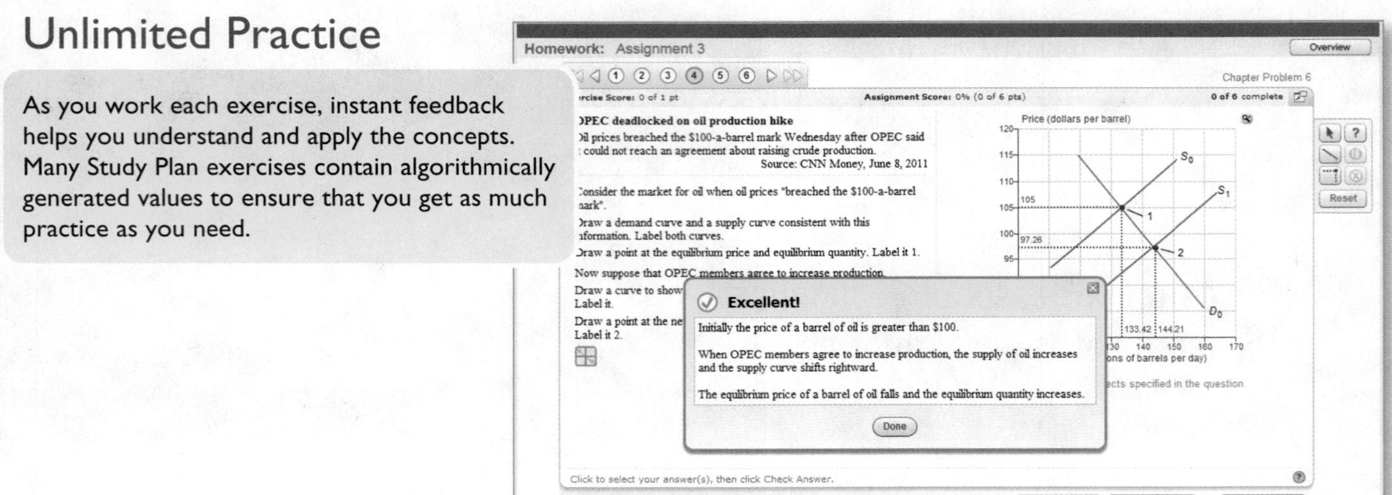

Learning Resources

Study Plan problems link to learning resources that further reinforce concepts you need to master.

- **Help Me Solve This** learning aids help you break down a problem much the same way as an instructor would do during office hours. Help Me Solve This is available for select problems.
- **eText links** are specific to the problem at hand so that related concepts are easy to review just when they are needed.
- A **graphing tool** enables you to build and manipulate graphs to better understand how concepts, numbers, and graphs connect.

Find out more at www.myeconlab.com

Real-Time Data Analysis Exercises

Up-to-date macro data is a great way to engage in and understand the usefulness of macro variables and their impact on the economy. Real-Time Data Analysis exercises communicate directly with the Federal Reserve Bank of St. Louis's FRED site, so every time FRED posts new data, students see new data.

End-of-chapter exercises accompanied by the Real-Time Data Analysis icon include Real-Time Data versions in **MyEconLab**.

Select in-text figures labeled **MyEconLab** Real-Time Data update in the electronic version of the text using FRED data.

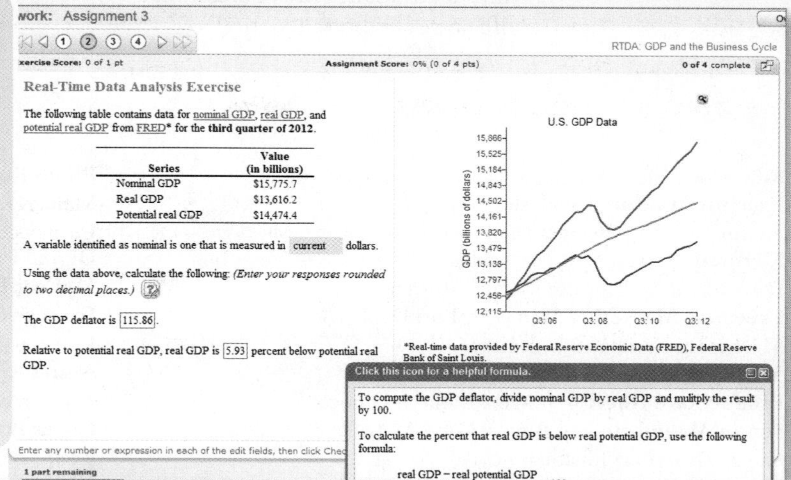

Current News Exercises

Posted weekly, we find the latest microeconomic and macroeconomic news stories, post them, and write auto-graded multi-part exercises that illustrate the economic way of thinking about the news.

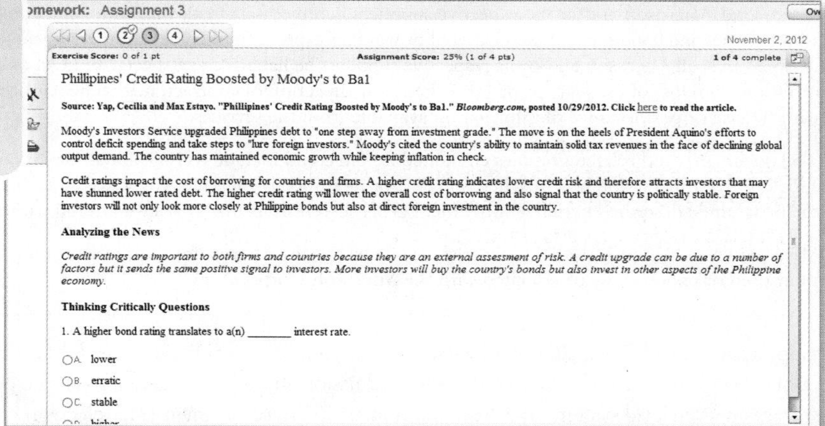

Interactive Homework Exercises

Participate in a fun and engaging activity that helps promote active learning and mastery of important economic concepts.

Pearson's experiments program is flexible and easy for instructors and students to use. For a complete list of available experiments, visit *www.myeconlab.com*.

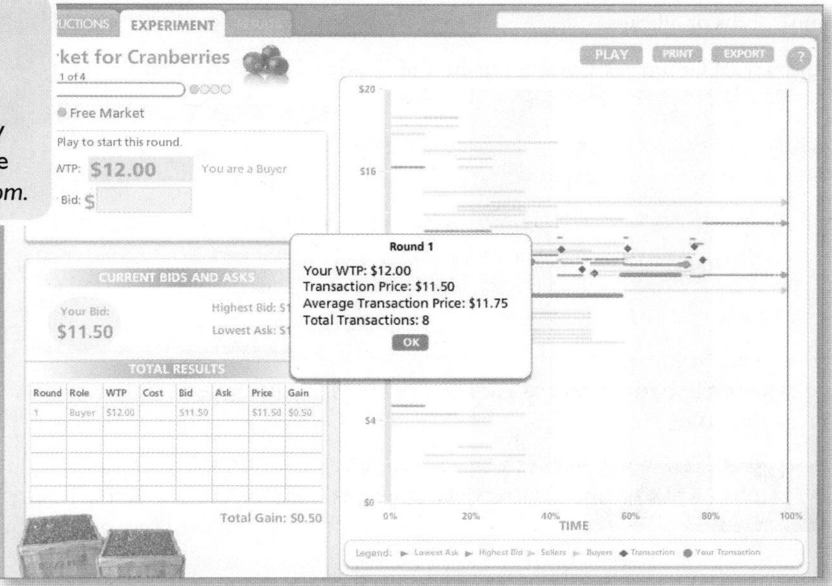

Dedication

To Ann Borman,

Whose commitment to excellence and detail makes my professional life so rewarding

—R.L.M.

Editor in Chief: Donna Battista
Executive Editor: David Alexander
Senior Editorial Project Manager: Carolyn Terbush
Editorial Assistant: Emily Brodeur
Director of Marketing: Maggie Moylan
Executive Marketing Manager: Lori DeShazo
Marketing Assistant: Kim Lovato
Managing Editor: Jeff Holcomb
Production Project Manager: Kathryn Dinovo
Senior Manufacturing Buyer: Carol Melville
Cover Designer: Jonathan Boylan
Manager, Visual Research: Rachel Youdelman
Photo Researcher: Jonathan Yonan
Manager, Rights and Permissions: Michael Joyce
Permissions Specialist/Project Manager: Jill C. Dougan
Digital Publisher, Economics: Denise Clinton
MyEconLab Content Media Leads: Noel Lotz, Courtney Kamauf
Executive Media Producer: Melissa Honig
Full-Service Project Management: Cenveo Publishing Services/ Nesbitt Graphics
Printer/Binder: Courier/Kendallville
Cover Printer: Lehigh-Phoenix Color/Hagerstown
Text Font: Janson Text LT Std.

Credits and acknowledgments borrowed from other sources and reproduced, with permission, in this textbook appear on page xxix.

Library of Congress Cataloging-in-Publication Data is on file.

10 9 8 7 6 5 4 3 2 1

ISBN 10: 0-13-294889-3
ISBN 13: 978-0-13-294889-0

Brief Contents

Contents

PART 8 Global Economics

One-Semester Course Outline

Macroeconomic Emphasis
The Macro View

1. The Nature of Economics
2. Scarcity and the World of Trade-Offs
3. Demand and Supply
4. Extensions of Demand and Supply Analysis
5. Public Spending and Public Choice
6. Funding the Public Sector
7. The Macroeconomy. Unemployment, Inflation, and Deflation
8. Measuring the Economy's Performance
9. Global Economic Growth and Development
10. Real GDP and the Price Level in the Long Run
11. Classical and Keynesian Macro Analyses
12. Consumption, Real GDP, and the Multiplier
13. Fiscal Policy
14. Deficit Spending and the Public Debt
15. Money, Banking, and Central Banking
16. Domestic and International Dimensions of Monetary Policy
17. Stabilization in an Integrated World Economy
18. Policies and Prospects for Global Economic Growth

32. Comparative Advantage and the Open Economy
33. Exchange Rates and the Balance of Payments

Microeconomic Emphasis
The Micro View

1. The Nature of Economics
2. Scarcity and the World of Trade-Offs
3. Demand and Supply
4. Extensions of Demand and Supply Analysis
5. Public Spending and Public Choice
6. Funding the Public Sector

19. Demand and Supply Elasticity
20. Consumer Choice
21. Rents, Profits, and the Financial Environment of Business
22. The Firm: Cost and Output Determination
23. Perfect Competition
24. Monopoly
25. Monopolistic Competition
26. Oligopoly and Strategic Behavior
27. Regulation and Antitrust Policy in a Globalized Economy
28. The Labor Market: Demand, Supply, and Outsourcing
29. Unions and Labor Market Monopoly Power
30. Income, Poverty, and Health Care
31. Environmental Economics
32. Comparative Advantage and the Open Economy
33. Exchange Rates and the Balance of Payments

Balanced Micro-Macro

1. The Nature of Economics
2. Scarcity and the World of Trade-Offs
3. Demand and Supply
4. Extensions of Demand and Supply Analysis
5. Public Spending and Public Choice
6. Funding the Public Sector

20. Consumer Choice
21. Rents, Profits, and the Financial Environment of Business
22. The Firm: Cost and Output Determination
23. Perfect Competition
24. Monopoly

28. The Labor Market: Demand, Supply, and Outsourcing
29. Unions and Labor Market Monopoly Power

7. The Macroeconomy. Unemployment, Inflation, and Deflation

10. Real GDP and the Price Level in the Long Run
11. Classical and Keynesian Macro Analyses
12. Consumption, Real GDP, and the Multiplier
13. Fiscal Policy
14. Deficit Spending and the Public Debt
15. Money, Banking, and Central Banking
16. Domestic and International Dimensions of Monetary Policy

32. Comparative Advantage and the Open Economy
33. Exchange Rates and the Balance of Payments

Preface

Economics Today—Bringing the Real World to Your Students

How do you compete for students' time and attention when their world is so fast paced? How do you get students to focus? How do you present the topics or principles of economics in a way that is both attention grabbing and meaningful? The best way to do so is through real-world examples. I believe in teaching by example. That is why *Economics Today* has always been a textbook filled with international, policy, and domestic examples. This edition is no exception—a total of 110 topics bring your students into the real world, including why it costs so much to go to college, why you should expect to pay more for what you buy on the Internet, why it will cost $700 million to be able to play 3D movies nationwide, and why e-books are upending the publishing business.

In keeping with this approach, I have changed almost every example as well as every Issues & Applications. This chapter-ending feature forms a "bookend" with the introduction presented on the first page of every chapter. Key Concepts are presented along with two Critical Thinking Questions and a Web Resources Project. The *You Are There* features remain student friendly and illustrate how people in the real world respond to changing economic conditions.

"I believe in teaching by example. That is why *Economics Today* has always been a textbook filled with international, policy, and domestic examples."

An engaging new feature called *What If . . . ?* can be found in every chapter. Students new to economics sometimes believe that complex problems can be solved by simple government policies or solutions that require instantaneous changes in human behavior. In the new *What If . . . ?* features I attempt to dispel some of the current notions about how to solve economic issues facing the nation and also encourage students to think like economists. *What If . . . the government were to limit or even ban excessive advertising? What If . . . the government saved U.S. jobs from foreign competition by prohibiting all exports? What If . . . the government required U.S. firms to hire only workers who reside in the United States?* These are just a few examples of this new feature.

"That is one of the underlying goals I have always set for myself when I revise *Economics Today*—to help students recognize the value of the concepts they are learning."

While this edition has been updated throughout, several topics have received special attention. For the macro policy chapters, issues relating to the growing U.S. federal deficit and public debt are covered in even more detail in Chapter 14. This chapter now discusses whether raising taxes on the highest earners can close the deficit gap and whether official measures of the current public debt underestimate promised future benefits. Chapter 16 now provides an analysis of various instruments of credit policy that the Fed appears to have adopted for the foreseeable future as a supplement to traditional monetary policy tools. Along the microeconomic dimension, Chapter 26 extends the coverage of network effects by examining two-sided markets in which intermediary platforms link groups of end users. Finally, Chapter 27 includes discussions of real changes in concentration measures and thresholds used in enforcement of U.S. antitrust policy.

Timely and relevant learning continues with MyEconLab, Pearson's online tutorial and assessment system. You can assign homework, quizzes, and tests that are automatically graded. Students have access to a suite of learning aids that help them at the very moment they might be struggling with the concepts. There are weekly news articles, many experiments, and questions that update in real time with data from the Federal Reserve Bank of St. Louis.

The trained economist sees economics everywhere—we observe people responding to changes in incentives all of the time. We economists would all like to have our students not only understand how powerful economics is but also use their newly acquired skills in their daily and professional lives. That is one of the underlying goals I have always set for myself when I revise *Economics Today*—to help students recognize the value of the concepts they are learning.

—Roger LeRoy Miller

New to This Edition

This new edition of *Economics Today* covers leading-edge issues while lowering barriers to student learning. The text relentlessly pursues the fundamental objective of showing students how economics is front and center in *their* own lives while providing them with many ways to evaluate their understanding of key concepts covered in each chapter.

Modern topics in economic theory and policy are spotlighted throughout the text. These include:

- An appraisal of key questions raised by continuing growth of the **U.S. government deficit and the public debt:** Chapter 14 considers whether the federal government can rely on raising taxes to eliminate its budget deficit and whether official measures of *today's* public debt understate total promises of benefits to be paid in the *future*.
- An evaluation of a new aspect of **Federal Reserve policymaking:** Chapter 16 provides an analysis of various tools of *credit policy* adopted by the Federal Reserve in recent years to supplement its traditional monetary policy instruments.
- Coverage of **two-sided markets:** The discussion of network effects in Chapter 26 now includes consideration of oligopoly pricing complications that arise in markets in which intermediary *platforms* link groups of *end users*.
- An updated exposition of **antitrust guidelines:** Chapter 27 has been revised in light of recent changes in concentration measures and thresholds applied by authorities charged with enforcing U.S. *antitrust policy*.

ISSUES & APPLICATIONS

Have Unemployment Benefits Boosted Unemployment?

CONCEPTS APPLIED

- Unemployment Rate
- Cyclical Unemployment
- Structural Unemployment

Between June 2008 and February 2009, the U.S. unemployment rate rose sharply, from 5.6 percent to more than 8 percent. Although the recession officially ended in June 2009, the unemployment rate ultimately reached a peak of 10.1 percent in October 2009. Since then, the unemployment rate has stayed near 8 percent. Thus, the unemployment rate remained above its prior level by at least 2 percentage points for more than three years. Many economists conclude that structural unemployment has risen. One element contributing to this rise, they suggest, was a substantial increase in the length of time the government paid benefits to unemployed workers.

Additional macro analyses include the following:

- Chapter 7 considers the extent to which lengthening the duration of **unemployment benefits** from 26 weeks to 99 weeks may have contributed to a higher U.S. unemployment rate.
- Chapter 11 explains why an index measure of **financial market fear** is often associated with short-term declines in total production of goods and services.
- Chapter 13 examines why most federal tax dollars recently transmitted to states to spend and thereby provide **stimulus to the U.S. economy** have failed to do so.
- Chapter 15 offers an explanation of why many banks no longer desire to expand **deposits** and indeed now actively discourage customers from depositing more funds.

The micro portion of the text now includes the following:

- Chapter 19 discusses how the concept of **price elasticity of demand** explains why many rock musicians have experienced declining revenues from sales of music recordings and concert tickets, even though the prices of recordings and tickets have increased.
- Chapter 24 examines the economic effects of a substantial expansion of **occupational licensing** requirements that many states impose on their citizens.
- Chapter 28 covers how groundbreaking new technology, such as **robotic apps,** might affect the labor market.
- Chapter 30 explains why the **income gap** between males and females has been shrinking and conceivably could eventually disappear.

Making the Connection—from the Classroom to the Real World

Economics Today provides current examples with critical analysis questions that show students how economic theory applies to their diverse interests and lives. For the Seventeenth Edition, **more than 90 percent** of the examples are new.

DOMESTIC TOPICS AND EVENTS are presented through thought-provoking discussions, such as:

- State University Tuition Rates Jump—Even at the Last Moment
- Price and Revenue Changes and Price Elasticity of Demand for Air Travel

EXAMPLE

Going Online for Credit When Bank Loans Dry Up

Today, a growing number of entrepreneurs who fail to receive loans from banks instead obtain credit from Internet-based companies such as Lending Club and Prosper Marketplace. These firms provide online forums for entrepreneurs to post detailed business plans along with the specific amounts of credit desired to try to achieve success. Individual savers can assess these plans and, if they wish, commit some of their own funds to help fund entrepreneurs' projects.

In exchange for service fees, the online firms pool these individual funding commitments into larger loan packages. For example, if an entrepreneur requests $15,000 in credit and 150 savers provide an average amount of $100 each, the online company collects the savers' funds and extends a loan to the entrepreneur. In this way, firms such as Lending Club and Prosper Marketplace act as financial intermediaries.

FOR CRITICAL THINKING

Why do you suppose that default rates on loans arranged by online firms tend to be substantially higher than default rates on bank loans?

IMPORTANT POLICY QUESTIONS help students understand public debates, such as:

- Federal Indebtedness Is Much Higher Than the Net Public Debt
- The Fed Becomes a Lender of Last Resort for Foreign Banks

POLICY EXAMPLE

A Proposed Wireless Merger Experiences a Dropped Connection

Recently, AT&T and T-Mobile sought to merge their wireless operations into a single firm providing cellular phone and broadband Internet services. The proposed merger would have increased the HHI value for the nationwide wireless market—which the Justice Department's Antitrust Division determined to be the relevant market—by nearly 600. The postmerger level of the HHI would have exceeded 2,800. These amounts were well above thresholds sufficient to raise U.S. antitrust authorities' concerns about potential monopoly capability generated by a horizontal merger. Thus, the Antitrust Division filed a lawsuit seeking to block the merger, based on a claim that if the merger occurred, consumers ultimately would face much higher prices for wireless services. A few weeks later, AT&T and T-Mobile abandoned their merger plans rather than combat the lawsuit in court.

FOR CRITICAL THINKING

By definition, any horizontal merger increases industry concentration. Why might some mergers lead to lower *prices for consumers? (Hint: Recall that mergers might enable firms to experience economies of scale that reduce long-run average cost.)*

INTERNATIONAL EXAMPLE

Why the Value of China's Consumer Price Index Is Rising

In China, food's weight in the CPI is slightly below 35 percent. Food prices have been rising so rapidly, though, that the overall rate of increase in food prices per year has been contributing to 75 percent of China's officially measured annual rate of CPI inflation. Consequently, during a recent 12-month period in which the nation's measured rate of CPI inflation was 6.4 percent, the rate of increase in food prices accounted for 4.8 percentage points

FOR CRITICAL THINKING

Food's weight in the U.S. CPI is about 16 percent. If U.S. food prices rose as rapidly as Chinese food prices, would the U.S. CPI increase as much as the CPI in China? Explain.

INTERNATIONAL POLICY EXAMPLE

African Nations Benefit from Lower U.S. Trade Barriers

In 2000, the U.S. Congress passed the African Growth and Opportunity Act, which reduced substantially the tariffs faced by African companies seeking to export goods and services to the United States. African-U.S. trade has risen considerably since. Earnings that African companies derive from exports are now 500 percent higher than in 2001. Furthermore, estimates indicate that export industries in African nations now employ 300,000 additional workers as a consequence of the increased volume of trade. Thus, slashing trade barriers has generated welfare gains for African residents.

FOR CRITICAL THINKING

How might U.S. residents have benefited from the fact that African countries granted reciprocal reductions in tariffs on imports into their nations from the United States?

GLOBAL AND INTERNATIONAL POLICY EXAMPLES emphasize the continued importance of international perspectives and policy, such as:

- Ireland Experiences Yet Another Big "Brain Drain"
- Utilizing Artificial Intelligence to Try to Beat the Market
- Iran Removes Four Zeroes from Each Unit of Its Currency
- In Greece, "Free" Care Now Includes Substantial Implicit Costs

Helping Students Focus and Think Critically

New and revised pedagogical tools engage students and help them focus on the central ideas in economics today.

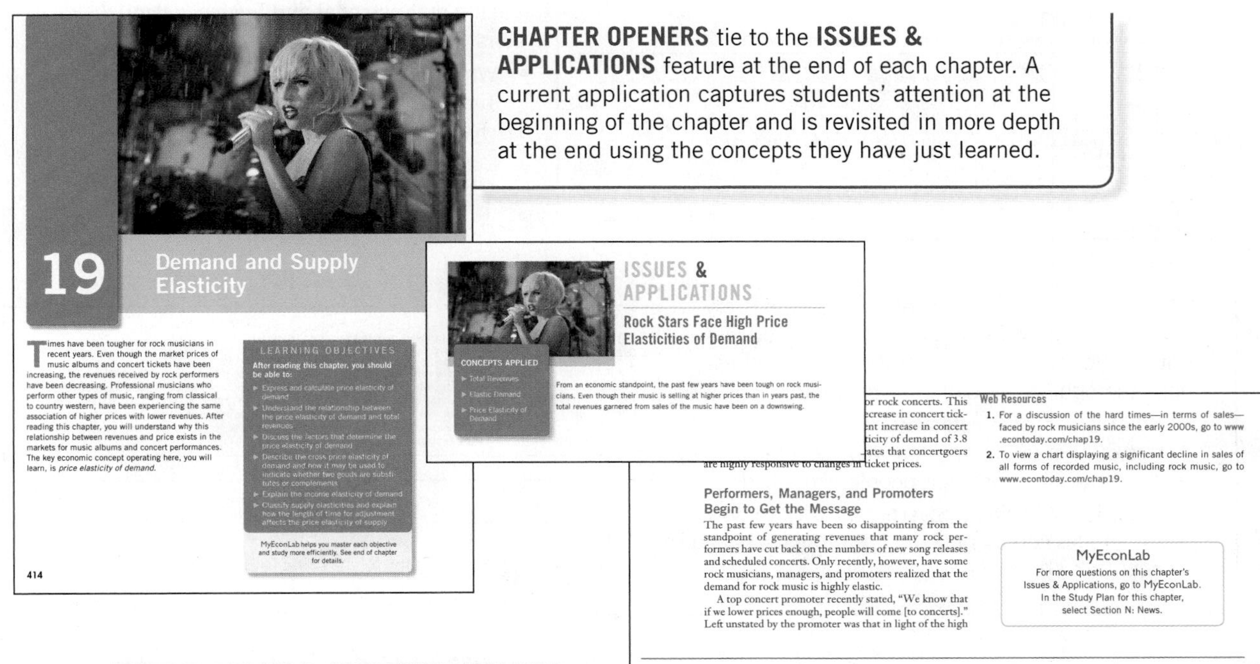

CHAPTER OPENERS tie to the **ISSUES & APPLICATIONS** feature at the end of each chapter. A current application captures students' attention at the beginning of the chapter and is revisited in more depth at the end using the concepts they have just learned.

CRITICAL ANALYSIS QUESTIONS AND WEB RESOURCES provide further opportunities for discussion and exploration. Suggested answers for Critical Analysis questions are in the **INSTRUCTOR'S MANUAL**. Visit MyEconLab for additional practice and assignable questions for each chapter topic.

The **END-OF-CHAPTER SUMMARY** shows students what they need to know and where to go in MyEconLab for more practice.

A VARIETY OF END-OF-CHAPTER PROBLEMS offer students opportunities to test their knowledge and review chapter concepts. Answers for odd-numbered questions are provided in the back of the text, and **ALL QUESTIONS** are assignable in MyEconLab.

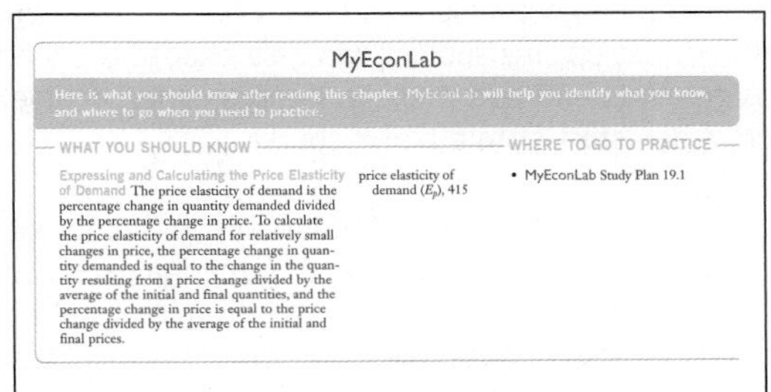

QUICK QUIZZES encourage student interaction and provide an opportunity for them to check their understanding before moving on. Answers are at the end of the chapter, and more practice questions can be found in MyEconLab.

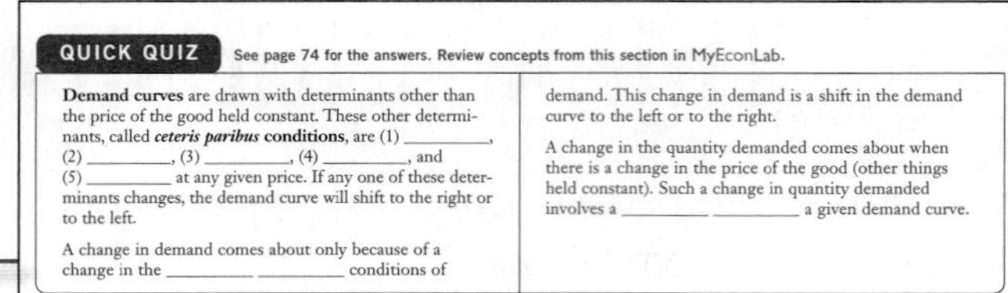

QUICK QUIZ See page 74 for the answers. Review concepts from this section in MyEconLab.

Demand curves are drawn with determinants other than the price of the good held constant. These other determinants, called ***ceteris paribus* conditions**, are (1) ________, (2) ________, (3) ________, (4) ________, and (5) ________ at any given price. If any one of these determinants changes, the demand curve will shift to the right or to the left.

A change in demand comes about only because of a change in the ________ ________ conditions of demand. This change in demand is a shift in the demand curve to the left or to the right.

A change in the quantity demanded comes about when there is a change in the price of the good (other things held constant). Such a change in quantity demanded involves a ________ ________ a given demand curve.

YOU ARE THERE

Implementing a New Patent Framework to Promote Innovation

Senator Patrick Leahy looks on as President Barack Obama signs into law the America Invents Act, a law Leahy had authored with the aim of boosting the rate of U.S. innovation via an overhaul of the nation's patent system. Under the prior law governing patents, property rights to the returns from invention were determined on a "first-to-invent" basis. This meant that if two individuals or companies happened to invent similar products or processes at about the same time, they had to prove in court whose invention was first. Over the years, this requirement had touched off thousands of court fights among patent holders.

The legislation drawn up by Leahy and approved by Congress and the president has established a "first-to-file" rule for patents. Now the property rights associated with any invention are automatically assigned to the first individual or firm to apply for a patent for that invention. Leahy's expectation is that patent holders who once directed financial resources toward funding court battles now will use them to transform more inventions into market innovations. Speeding along the innovation process, Leahy anticipates, will help to fuel economic growth.

Critical Thinking Questions

1. Why are inventions alone insufficient to help boost economic growth?
2. What role do you think that markets perform in determining whether inventions of new products or processes translate into longer-lasting innovations?

YOU ARE THERE discusses real people making real personal and business decisions. Topics include:

- Why a Federal Stimulus Project Took Time to Provide Stimulus
- Using a Smartphone to Attain a Consumer Optimum

NEW! WHAT IF...? boxes can be found in every chapter. This new feature aims to help students think critically about important real-world questions through the eyes of an economist.

- What If... economists were to base their theories of human behavior on what people say they do, rather than on what people actually do?
- What if... a nation's government tries to head off a recession by pushing down the exchange value of the country's currency?

WHAT IF... governments allowed people to own endangered animals as private property?

If all animals of endangered species could be marked and cataloged as private property, some people undoubtedly would mishandle the animals they owned, just as they misuse other resources in their possession. Nevertheless, by definition, animals of endangered species are scarce resources that would have positive values—and sometimes relatively high dollar values—in private markets. This fact would give most self-interested people the incentive to preserve such animal life. Indeed, the most successful programs for preventing "too much" fishing, seal hunting, rhino poaching, and so on have been those that assign property rights. These programs motivate the rights holders to rein in such injurious activities and to preserve endangered species.

MyEconLab: The Power of Practice

MyEconLab is a powerful assessment and tutorial system that works hand-in-hand with *Economics Today.* MyEconLab includes comprehensive homework, quiz, test, and tutorial options, allowing instructors to manage all assessment needs in one program.

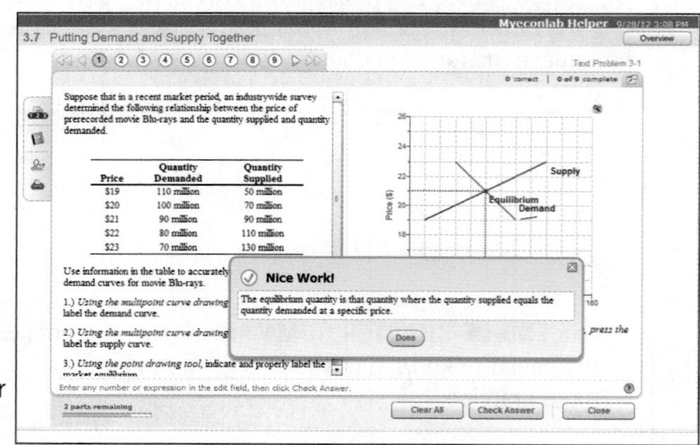

For the Instructor

- Instructors can now select a preloaded course option, which creates a ready-to-go course with homework, quizzes, and tests already set up. Instructors can also choose to create their own assignments and add them to the preloaded course. Or, instructors can start from a blank course.
- All end-of-chapter problems are assignable and automatically graded in MyEconLab, and for most chapters, additional algorithmic, draw-graph, and numerical exercises are available to choose among.
- Instructors can also choose questions from the Test Bank and use the Custom Exercise Builder to create their own problems for assignment.
- The powerful Gradebook records each student's performance and time spent on the Tests and Study Plan, and generates reports by student or by chapter.

MyEconLab *Real-Time Data Analysis*

We now offer new real-time data exercises that students can complete in MyEconLab.

- **Real-Time Data Analysis Exercises** are marked with and allow instructors to assign problems that use up-to-the-minute data. Each RTDA exercise loads the appropriate and most currently available data from FRED, a comprehensive and up-to-date data set maintained by the Federal Reserve Bank of St. Louis. Exercises are graded based on that instance of data, and feedback is provided.

- In the eText available in MyEconLab, select figures labeled MyEconLab Real-Time Data now include a popup graph updated with real-time data from FRED.

- Current News Exercises, new to this edition of the MyEconLab course, provide a turn-key way to assign gradable news-based exercises in MyEconLab. Every week, Pearson scours the news, finds a current article appropriate for the macroeconomics course, creates an exercise around this news article, and then automatically adds it to MyEconLab. Assigning and grading current news-based exercises that deal with the latest macro events and policy issues has never been more convenient.

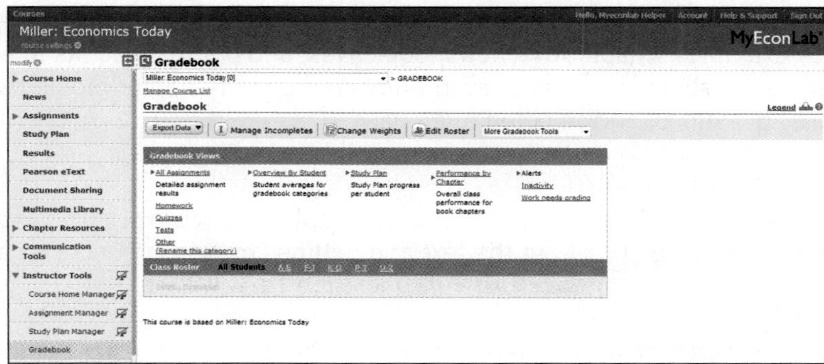

- Economics in the News is a turn-key solution to bringing current news into the classroom. Updated weekly during the academic year, this feature posts news articles with questions for further discussion.

- Experiments in MyEconLab are a fun and engaging way to promote active learning and mastery of important economic concepts. Pearson's experiments program is flexible and easy for instructors and students to use.
  - Single-player experiments allow your students to play an experiment against virtual players from anywhere at any time with an Internet connection.
  - Multiplayer experiments allow you to assign and manage a real-time experiment with your class.

  In both cases, pre- and post-questions for each experiment are available for assignment in MyEconLab.

For the Student

Students are in control of their own learning through a collection of tests, practice, and study tools. Highlights include:

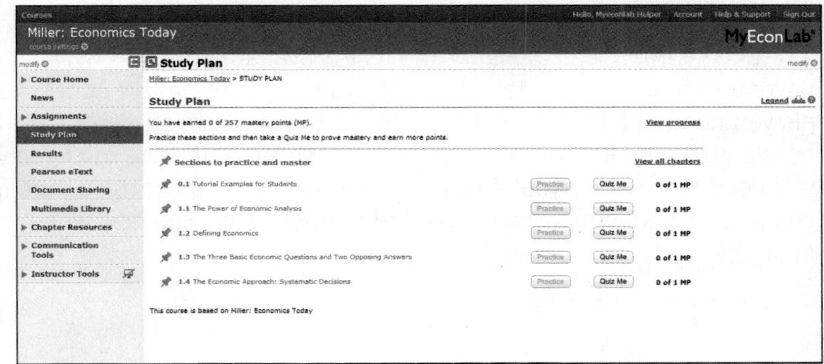

- Two Sample Tests per chapter are preloaded in MyEconLab, enabling students to practice what they have learned, test their understanding, and identify areas for further work.

- Based on each student's performance on homework, quizzes, and tests, MyEconLab generates a Study Plan that shows where the student needs further study.

- Learning Aids, such as step-by-step guided solutions, a graphing tool, content-specific links to the eText, animated graphs, and glossary flashcards, help students master the material.

Please visit www.myeconlab.com for more information.

Supplemental Resources

Student and instructor materials provide tools for success.

Test Banks 1, 2, and 3 offer more than 10,000 multiple choice and short answer questions, all of which are available in computerized format in the TestGen software. The significant revision process by author Jim Lee of Texas A&M University–Corpus Christi and accuracy reviewers Ercument Aksoy of Los Angeles Valley College and Fatma Antar of Manchester Community College ensures the accuracy of problems and solutions in these revised and updated Test Banks. The Test Bank author has connected the questions to the general knowledge and skill guidelines found in the Association to Advance Collegiate Schools of Business (AACSB) assurance of learning standards.

The Instructor's Manual, prepared by Jim Lee of Texas A&M University–Corpus Christi, includes lecture-ready examples; chapter overviews, objectives, and outlines; points to emphasize; answers to all critical analysis questions; answers to even-numbered end-of-chapter problems; suggested answers to "You Are There" questions; and selected references.

PowerPoint lecture presentations for each chapter, revised by Debbie Evercloud of University of Colorado–Denver, include graphs from the text and outline key terms, concepts, and figures from the text.

Clicker PowerPoint slides, prepared by Rick Pretzsch of Lonestar College–CyFair, allow professors to instantly quiz students in class and receive immediate feedback through Clicker Response System technology.

The Instructor's Resource Disk offers all instructor supplements conveniently packaged on a disk.

The Instructor Resource Center puts supplements right at instructors' fingertips. Visit www.pearsonhighered.com/irc to register.

The Study Guide offers the practice and review that students need to excel. Written by Roger LeRoy Miller and updated by David Van Hoose of Baylor University, the Study Guide has been thoroughly revised to take into account changes to the Seventeenth Edition.

The CourseSmart eTextbook for the text is available through www.coursesmart.com. CourseSmart goes beyond traditional expectations by providing instant, online access to the textbooks and course materials you need at a lower cost to students. And, even as students save money, you can save time and hassle with a digital textbook that allows you to search the most relevant content at the very moment you need it. Whether you're evaluating textbooks or creating lecture notes to help students with difficult concepts, CourseSmart can make life a little easier. See how when you visit www.coursesmart.com/instructors.

Acknowledgments

I am the most fortunate of economics textbook writers, for I receive the benefit of literally hundreds of suggestions from those of you who use *Economics Today*. Some professors have been asked by my publisher to participate in a more detailed reviewing process of this edition. I list them below. I hope that each one of you so listed accepts my sincere appreciation for the fine work that you have done.

Hamilton Galloway, *College of Western Idaho*
Frank Garland, *TriCounty Technical College*
Reza G. Hamzaee, *Missouri Western State University*
Ricot Jean, *Valencia College*
Richard W. Kreissle, *Landmark College*
James M. Leaman, *Eastern Mennonite University*
Dr. Larry Olanrewaju, *John Tyler Community College*
Benny E. Overton, *Vance/Granville Community College*
Elizabeth Patch, *Broome Community College*
Van Thi Hong Pham, *Salem State University*
Leila Angelica Rodemann, *Trident Technical College*
Lewis Sage, *Baldwin-Wallace College*
Jonathan Silberman, *Oakland University*
Brian Sommer, *Lynn University*
Manjuri Talukdar, *Northern Illinois University*
Ethel C. Weeks, *Nassau Community College*

I also thank the reviewers of previous editions:

Rebecca Abraham
Cinda J. Adams
Esmond Adams
John Adams
Bill Adamson
Carlos Aguilar
John R. Aidem
Mohammed Akacem
Ercument Aksoy
M. C. Alderfer
John Allen
Ann Al-Yasiri
Charles Anderson
Leslie J. Anderson
Fatma W. Antar
Len Anyanwu
Rebecca Arnold
Mohammad Ashraf
Ali A. Ataiifar
Aliakbar Ataiifar
Leonard Atencio
John Atkins
Glen W. Atkinson
Thomas R. Atkinson
James Q. Aylesworth
John Baffoe-Bonnie
Kevin Baird
Maurice B. Ballabon
Charley Ballard
G. Jeffrey Barbour
Robin L. Barlett
Daniel Barszcz
Kari Battaglia
Robert Becker
Charles Beem
Glen Beeson
Bruce W. Bellner
Daniel K. Benjamin
Emil Berendt
Charles Berry
Abraham Bertisch
John Bethune
R. A. Blewett
Scott Bloom
John Bockino
M. L. Bodnar
Mary Bone
Karl Bonnhi
Thomas W. Bonsor
John M. Booth
Wesley F. Booth
Thomas Borcherding
Melvin Borland
Tom Boston
Barry Boyer
Maryanna Boynton
Ronald Brandolini
Fenton L. Broadhead
Elba Brown
William Brown
Michael Bull
Maureen Burton
Conrad P. Caligaris
Kevin Carey
James Carlson
Robert Carlsson
Dancy R. Carr
Scott Carson
Doris Cash
Thomas H. Cate
Richard J. Cebula
Catherine Chambers
K. Merry Chambers
Richard Chapman
Ronald Cherry
Young Back Choi
Marc Chopin
Carol Cies
Joy L. Clark
Curtis Clarke
Gary Clayton
Marsha Clayton
Dale O. Cloninger
Warren L. Coats
Ed Coen
Pat Conroy
James Cox
Stephen R. Cox
Eleanor D. Craig
Peggy Crane
Jerry Crawford
Patrick M. Crowley
Joanna Cruse
John P. Cullity
Will Cummings
Thomas Curtis
Margaret M. Dalton
Andrew J. Dane
Mahmoud Davoudi
Diana Denison
Edward Dennis
Julia G. Derrick
Sowjanya Dharmasankar
Carol Dimamro
William Dougherty
Barry Duman
Diane Dumont
Floyd Durham
G. B. Duwaji
James A. Dyal
Ishita Edwards
Robert P. Edwards
Alan E. Ellis
Miuke Ellis
Steffany Ellis
Frank Emerson
Carl Enomoto
Zaki Eusufzai
Sandy Evans
John L. Ewing-Smith
Frank Falero
Frank Fato
Abdollah Ferdowsi
Grant Ferguson
Victoria L. Figiel
Mitchell Fisher
David Fletcher
James Foley
John Foreman
Diana Fortier
Ralph G. Fowler
Arthur Friedberg
Peter Frost
Timothy S. Fuerst
Tom Fullerton
E. Gabriel
James Gale
Byron Gangnes
Peter C. Garlick
Steve Garner
Neil Garston
Alexander Garvin
Joe Garwood
Doug Gehrke
Robert Gentenaar
J. P. Gilbert
Otis Gilley
Frank Glesber
Jack Goddard
Michael G. Goode
Allen C. Goodman
Richard J. Gosselin
Paul Graf
Anthony J. Greco
Edward Greenberg
Gary Greene
Peter A. Groothuis
Philip J. Grossman
Nicholas Grunt
William Gunther
Kwabena Gyimah-Brempong
Demos Hadjiyanis
Martin D. Haney
Mehdi Haririan
Ray Harvey
Michael J. Haupert
E. L. Hazlett
Sanford B. Helman
William Henderson
Robert Herman
Gus W. Herring
Charles Hill
John M. Hill
Morton Hirsch
Benjamin Hitchner
Charles W. Hockert
R. Bradley Hoppes
James Horner
Grover Howard
Nancy Howe-Ford
Yu-Mong Hsiao
Yu Hsing
James Hubert
George Hughes
Joseph W. Hunt Jr.
Scott Hunt
John Ifediora
R. Jack Inch
Christopher Inya
Tomotaka Ishimine
E. E. Jarvis
Parvis Jenab
Allan Jenkins
John Jensel
Mark Jensen
S. D. Jevremovic
J. Paul Jewell
Nancy Jianakoplos
Frederick Johnson
David Jones
Lamar B. Jones
Paul A. Joray
Daniel A. Joseph
Craig Justice
M. James Kahiga
Septimus Kai Kai
Devajyoti Kataky
Timothy R. Keely
Ziad Keilany
Norman F. Keiser
Brian Kench
Randall G. Kesselring
Alan Kessler
E. D. Key
Saleem Khan
M. Barbara Killen
Bruce Kimzey
Terrence Kinal
Philip G. King
E. R. Kittrell
David Klingman
Charles Knapp
Jerry Knarr
Tori Knight
Faik Koray
Janet Koscianski
Dennis Lee Kovach
Marie Kratochvil
Peter Kressler
Paul J. Kubik
Michael Kupilik
Margaret Landman
Richard LaNear
Larry Landrum
Keith Langford
Theresa Laughlin
Anthony T. Lee
Jim Lee
Loren Lee
Bozena Leven
Donald Lien
George Lieu
Stephen E. Lile
Lawrence W. Lovick
Marty Ludlum
Laura Maghoney
G. Dirk Mateer
Robert McAuliffe
James C. McBrearty
Howard J. McBride
Bruce McClung
John McDowell
E. S. McKuskey
James J. McLain
Kevin McWoodson
John L. Madden
Mary Lou Madden
John Marangos
Dan Marburger
Glen Marston

John M. Martin
Paul J. Mascotti
James D. Mason
Paul M. Mason
Tom Mathew
Warren Matthews
Akbar Marvasti
Pete Mavrokordatos
Fred May
G. Hartley Mellish
Mike Melvin
Diego Mendez-Carbajo
Dan C. Messerschmidt
Michael Metzger
Herbert C. Milikien
Joel C. Millonzi
Glenn Milner
Daniel Mizak
Khan Mohabbat
Thomas Molloy
William H. Moon
Margaret D. Moore
William E. Morgan
Stephen Morrell
Irving Morrissett
James W. Moser
Thaddeaus Mounkurai
Martin F. Murray
Densel L. Myers
George L. Nagy
Solomon Namala
Ronald M. Nate
Jerome Neadly
James E. Needham
Claron Nelson
Douglas Nettleton
William Nook
Gerald T. O'Boyle
Greg Okoro
Richard E. O'Neill
Lucian T. Orlowski
Diane S. Osborne
Joan Osborne
Melissa A Osborne
James O'Toole
Jan Palmer
Zuohong Pan
Gerald Parker
Ginger Parker
Randall E. Parker
Mohammed Partapurwala
Kenneth Parzych
Norm Paul
Wesley Payne
Raymond A. Pepin
Martin M. Perline
Timothy Perri
Jerry Petr
Maurice Pfannesteil
James Phillips
Raymond J. Phillips
I. James Pickl
Bruce Pietrykowski
Dennis Placone
Mannie Poen
William L. Polvent
Robert Posatko
Greg Pratt
Leila J. Pratt
Steven Pressman
Rick Pretzsch
Reneé Prim
Robert E. Pulsinelli
Rod D. Raehsler
Kambriz Raffiee
Sandra Rahman
Jaishankar Raman
John Rapp
Richard Rawlins
Gautam Raychaudhuri
Ron Reddall
Mitchell Redlo
Charles Reichhelu
Robert S. Rippey
Charles Roberts
Ray C. Roberts
Richard Romano
Judy Roobian-Mohr
Duane Rosa
Richard Rosenberg
Larry Ross
Barbara Ross-Pfeiffer
Marina Rosser
Philip Rothman
John Roufagalas
Stephen Rubb
Henry Ryder
Basel Saleh
Patricia Sanderson
Thomas N. Schaap
William A. Schaeffer
William Schamoe
David Schauer
A. C. Schlenker
David Schlow
Scott J. Schroeder
William Scott
Dan Segebarth
Paul Seidenstat
Swapan Sen
Augustus Shackelford
Richard Sherman Jr.
Liang-rong Shiau
Gail Shields
David Shorow
Vishwa Shukla
R. J. Sidwell
David E. Sisk
Alden Smith
Garvin Smith
Howard F. Smith
Lynn A. Smith
Phil Smith
William Doyle Smith
Lee Spector
George Spiva
Richard L. Sprinkle
Alan Stafford
Amanda Stallings-Wood
Herbert F. Steeper
Diane L. Stehman
Columbus Stephens
William Stine
Allen D. Stone
Osman Suliman
J. M. Sullivan
Rebecca Summary
Terry Sutton
Joseph L. Swaffar
Thomas Swanke
Frank D. Taylor
Daniel Teferra
Lea Templer
Gary Theige
Dave Thiessen
Robert P. Thomas
Deborah Thorsen
Richard Trieff
George Troxler
William T. Trulove
William N. Trumbull
Arianne K. Turner
Kay Unger
Anthony Uremovic
John Vahaly
Jim Van Beek
David Van Hoose
Lee J. Van Scyoc
Roy Van Til
Sharmila Vishwasrao
Craig Walker
Robert F. Wallace
Henry C. Wallich
Milledge Weathers
Ethel Weeks
Roger E. Wehr
Robert G. Welch
Terence West
James Wetzel
Wylie Whalthall
James H. Wheeler
Everett E. White
Michael D. White
Mark A. Wilkening
Raburn M. Williams
James Willis
George Wilson
Travis Wilson
Mark Wohar
Ken Woodward
Tim Wulf
Peter R. Wyman
Whitney Yamamura
Donald Yankovic
Alex Yguado
Paul Young
Shik Young
Mohammed Zaheer
Ed Zajicek
Charles Zalonka
Sourushe Zandvakili
Paul Zarembka
George K. Zestos
William J. Zimmer Jr.

As always, a revision of *Economics Today* requires me to put in the latest data at the last minute. If I did not have such an incredible editorial and production team, I wouldn't be able to do so. I do have a fantastic team both at the publisher—Pearson—and at our production house—Nesbitt (Cenveo Publisher Services), working through them with my long-time Production Manager, John Orr of Orr Book Services. He again did a terrific job. I was fortunate to once more have Kathryn Dinovo, Senior Production Project Manager at Pearson, lead the production team to as perfect a textbook as possible. To be sure, I was pushed hard by my long-time Senior Acquisitions Editor, Noel Seibert, and I was helped greatly by Carolyn Terbush, the Senior Editorial Project Manager on this project. The "pushing" all makes sense now.

I am greatly pleased with the design revision created by Jerilyn Bockorick of Nesbitt Graphics. It is always a challenge to keep the traditional feel of this book, yet make it more exciting for today's students. I think that she succeeded. I am appreciative of the hard work my copy editor, Bonnie Boehme, did. And, of course, the proofreader *par excellence*, Pat Lewis, made sure that everything was perfect. As for the supplements for this edition, I wish to thank the team at Nesbitt for producing them for students and professors. On the marketing side, I appreciate the fine work performed by Lori DeShazo and Kim Lovato.

The online media materials, particularly great improvements in *MyEconLab*, were accomplished by Melissa Honig, Noel Lotz, and Courtney Kamauf.

Jim Lee of Texas A&M University–Corpus Christi, Ercument Aksoy of Los Angeles Valley College, and Fatma Antar of Manchester Community College undertook the vast job of revising and improving the three test banks. David Van Hoose of Baylor University continued to create an accurate *Study Guide*. The *Instructor's Manual* was masterfully revised by Jim Lee of Texas A&M University–Corpus Christi. PowerPoint presentations were updated and improved by Debbie Evercloud of the University of Colorado–Denver. Rick Pretzsch of Lonestar College–Cyfair provided the clicker PowerPoint slides.

As always, my "super reviewer," Professor Dan Benjamin of Clemson University, really kept me honest this time around. And, as always, my long-time assistant, Sue Jasin, did enough typing and retyping to fill a room with paper. I welcome comments and ideas from professors and students alike and hope that you enjoy this latest edition of *Economics Today*.

R. L. M.

Credits

Cover images: Solar power panel array, S.R. Lee Photo Traveller/Shutterstock; Woman riding a bicycle in Vietnam, MJ Prototype/Shutterstock; Eye chart test, Pinkcandy/Shutterstock; Plant sample, Chepko Danil Vitalevich/Shutterstock; Bags in warehouse in shop, Mikhail Zahranichny/Shutterstock; Apple on stack of books and laptop computer, Andreka Photography/Shutterstock; Crowd at a music concert, Alexey Lysenko/Shutterstock; Goalman on the stadium field, Andrey Yurlov/Shutterstock

FRED® is a registered trademark and the FRED® logo and ST. LOUIS FED are trademarks of the Federal Reserve Bank of St Louis, http://research.stlouisfed.org/fred2/

Chapter 1	Alex Hofford/Newscom	1, 12
Chapter 2	Fotolia	26, 42
Chapter 3	Harry Lynch/AP Images	48, 69
Chapter 4	Radius Images/Alamy	75, 90
Chapter 5	Marilyn Humphries/Newscom	100, 116
Chapter 6	Gerald Herbert/AP Images	122, 134
Chapter 7	Rick Bowmer/AP Images	139, 155
Chapter 8	Kin Cheung/AP Images	161, 180
Chapter 9	Filmfoto/Alamy	187, 204
Chapter 10	Shutterstock	210, 223
Chapter 11	Dario Cantatore	229, 245
Chapter 12	Mark Ralston/Newscom	250, 272
Chapter 13	Mark Duncan/AP Images	279, 291
Chapter 14	AP Images	300, 314
Chapter 15	David R. Frazier Photolibrary/Alamy	319, 340
Chapter 16	Susan Walsh/AP Images	346, 363
Chapter 17	John Moore/Getty Images	373, 390
Chapter 18	Newscom	396, 408
Chapter 32	Gallo Images/Alamy	704, 720
Chapter 33	Fotolia	725, 742

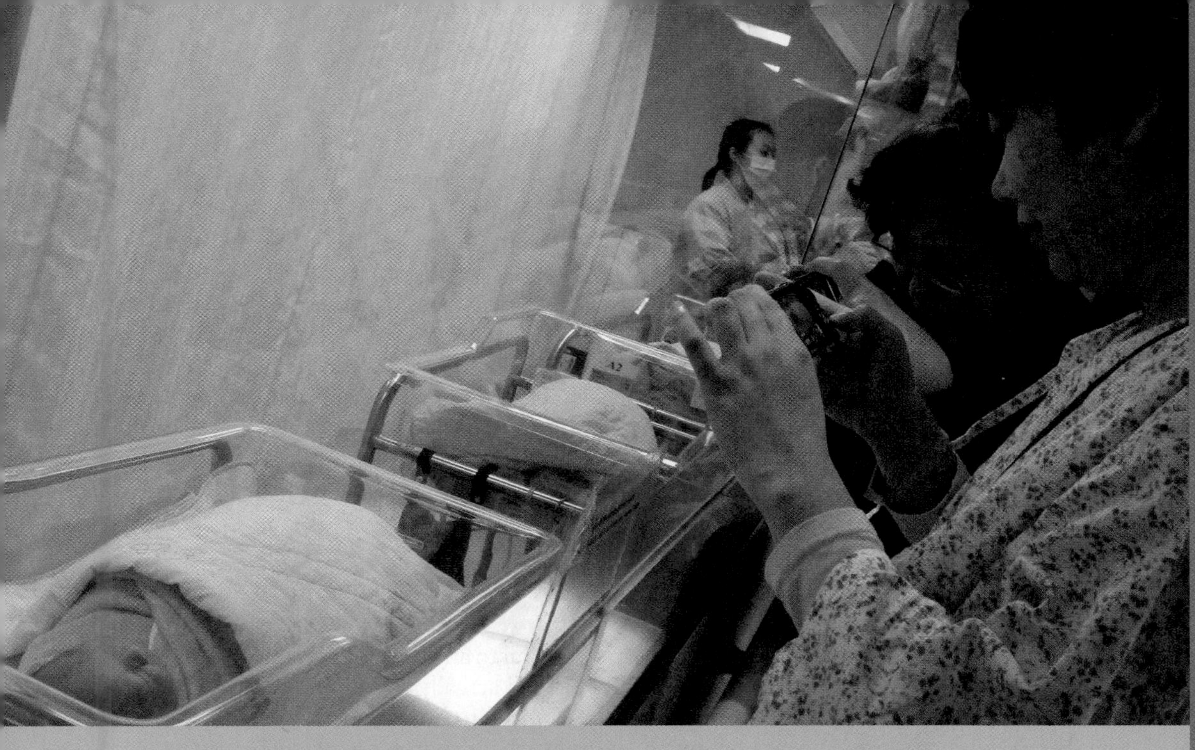

The Nature of Economics

1

LEARNING OBJECTIVES

After reading this chapter, you should be able to:

- Discuss the difference between microeconomics and macroeconomics
- Evaluate the role that rational self-interest plays in economic analysis
- Explain why economics is a science
- Distinguish between positive and normative economics

MyEconLab helps you master each objective and study more efficiently. See end of chapter for details.

Half of the babies delivered in 2011 in a typical Hong Kong hospital maternity ward were born to non–Hong Kong residents. This fact means that these babies were born to women classified as tourists visiting from the Chinese mainland. Why have nearly half of the babies born in Hong Kong hospitals had mothers who are not residents of Hong Kong? To formulate an answer, you must learn more about principles of economics. In particular, you must learn the key concepts discussed in this chapter, such as self-interest.

DID YOU KNOW THAT... the number of college students majoring in economics rose by more than 40 percent during the past decade? One reason that students opt for extensive study of economics is that they find the subject fascinating. Another reason, however, is self-interest. On average, students who major in economics earn 13 percent more than business management majors, 26 percent more than chemistry majors, and 50 percent more than psychology majors. Thus, students have a strong incentive to consider majoring in economics.

In this chapter, you will learn why contemplating the nature of self-interested responses to **incentives** is the starting point for analyzing choices people make in all walks of life. After all, how much time you devote to studying economics in this introductory course depends in part on the incentives established by your instructor's grading system. As you will see, self-interest and incentives are the underpinnings for all the decisions you and others around you make each day.

Incentives
Rewards or penalties for engaging in a particular activity.

The Power of Economic Analysis

Simply knowing that self-interest and incentives are central to any decision-making process is not sufficient for predicting the choices that people will actually make. You also have to develop a framework that will allow you to analyze solutions to each economic problem—whether you are trying to decide how much to study, which courses to take, whether to finish school, or whether the U.S. government should provide more grants to universities or raise taxes. The framework that you will learn in this text is the *economic way of thinking.*

This framework gives you power—the power to reach informed judgments about what is happening in the world. You can, of course, live your life without the power of economic analysis as part of your analytical framework. Indeed, most people do. But economists believe that economic analysis can help you make better decisions concerning your career, your education, financing your home, and other important matters. In the business world, the power of economic analysis can help you increase your competitive edge as an employee or as the owner of a business. As a voter, for the rest of your life you will be asked to make judgments about policies that are advocated by political parties. Many of these policies will deal with questions related to international economics, such as whether the U.S. government should encourage or discourage immigration, prevent foreign residents and firms from investing in port facilities or domestic banks, or restrict other countries from selling their goods here.

Finally, just as taking an art, music, or literature appreciation class increases the pleasure you receive when you view paintings, listen to concerts, or read novels, taking an economics course will increase your understanding and pleasure when watching the news on TV or reading articles on your iPad.

Defining Economics

Economics
The study of how people allocate their limited resources to satisfy their unlimited wants.

Economics is part of the social sciences and, as such, seeks explanations of real events. All social sciences analyze human behavior, as opposed to the physical sciences, which generally analyze the behavior of electrons, atoms, and other nonhuman phenomena.

Economics is the study of how people allocate their limited resources in an attempt to satisfy their unlimited wants. As such, economics is the study of how people make choices.

Resources
Things used to produce goods and services to satisfy people's wants.

Wants
What people would buy if their incomes were unlimited.

To understand this definition fully, two other words need explaining: *resources* and *wants*. **Resources** are things that have value and, more specifically, are used to produce goods and services that satisfy people's wants. **Wants** are all of the items that people would purchase if they had unlimited income.

Whenever an individual, a business, or a nation faces alternatives, a choice must be made, and economics helps us study how those choices are made. For example, you have to choose how to spend your limited income. You also have to choose how to spend your limited time. You may have to choose how many of your company's limited resources to allocate to advertising and how many to allocate to new-product research. In economics, we examine situations in which individuals choose how to do things, when to do things, and with whom to do them. Ultimately, the purpose of economics is to explain choices.

Microeconomics versus Macroeconomics

Economics is typically divided into two types of analysis: **microeconomics** and **macroeconomics.**

Microeconomics
The study of decision making undertaken by individuals (or households) and by firms.

Macroeconomics
The study of the behavior of the economy as a whole, including such economywide phenomena as changes in unemployment, the general price level, and national income.

> ***Microeconomics is the part of economic analysis that studies decision making undertaken by individuals (or households) and by firms. It is like looking through a microscope to focus on the small parts of our economy.***
>
> ***Macroeconomics is the part of economic analysis that studies the behavior of the economy as a whole. It deals with economywide phenomena such as changes in unemployment, in the general price level, and in national income.***

Microeconomic analysis, for example, is concerned with the effects of changes in the price of gasoline relative to that of other energy sources. It examines the effects of new taxes on a specific product or industry. If the government establishes new health care regulations, how individual firms and consumers would react to those regulations would be in the realm of microeconomics. The effects of higher wages brought about by an effective union strike would also be analyzed using the tools of microeconomics.

In contrast, issues such as the rate of inflation, the amount of economywide unemployment, and the yearly growth in the output of goods and services in the nation all fall into the realm of macroeconomic analysis. In other words, macroeconomics deals with **aggregates**, or totals—such as total output in an economy.

Aggregates
Total amounts or quantities. Aggregate demand, for example, is total planned expenditures throughout a nation.

Be aware, however, of the blending of microeconomics and macroeconomics in modern economic theory. Modern economists are increasingly using microeconomic analysis—the study of decision making by individuals and by firms—as the basis of macroeconomic analysis. They do this because even though macroeconomic analysis focuses on aggregates, those aggregates are the result of choices made by individuals and firms.

The Three Basic Economic Questions and Two Opposing Answers

In every nation, three fundamental questions must be addressed irrespective of the form of its government or who heads that government, how rich or how poor the nation may be, or what type of **economic system**—the institutional mechanism through which resources are utilized to satisfy human wants—has been chosen. The three questions concern the problem of how to allocate society's scarce resources:

Economic system
A society's institutional mechanism for determining the way in which scarce resources are used to satisfy human desires.

1. *What and how much will be produced?* Some mechanism must exist for determining which items will be produced while others remain inventors' pipe dreams or individuals' unfulfilled desires.

2. *How will items be produced?* There are many ways to produce a desired item. It is possible to use more labor and less capital, or vice versa. It is possible, for instance, to produce an item with an aim to maximize the number of people employed. Alternatively, an item may be produced with an aim to minimize the total expenses that members of society incur. Somehow, a decision must be made about the mix of resources used in production, the way in which they are organized, and how they are brought together at a particular location.

3. *For whom will items be produced?* Once an item is produced, who should be able to obtain it? People use scarce resources to produce any item, so typically people value access to that item. Thus, determining a mechanism for distributing produced items is a crucial issue for any society.

Now that you know the questions that an economic system must answer, how do current systems actually answer them?

Two Opposing Answers

At any point in time, every nation has its own economic system. How a nation goes about answering the three basic economic questions depends on that nation's economic system.

CENTRALIZED COMMAND AND CONTROL Throughout history, one common type of economic system has been *command and control* (also called *central planning*) by a centralized authority, such as a king or queen, a dictator, a central government, or some other type of authority that assumes responsibility for addressing fundamental economic issues. Under command and control, this authority decides what items to produce and how many, determines how the scarce resources will be organized in the items' production, and identifies who will be able to obtain the items.

For instance, in a command-and-control economic system, a government might decide that particular types of automobiles ought to be produced in certain numbers. The government might issue specific rules for how to marshal resources to produce these vehicles, or it might even establish ownership over those resources so that it can make all such resource allocation decisions directly. Finally, the government will then decide who will be authorized to purchase or otherwise utilize the vehicles.

How is centralized command and control affecting the net cost of constructing a high-speed rail project in California?

POLICY EXAMPLE

The Federal Government Directs New California Train Tracks

The U.S. Department of Transportation recently provided an initial $3 billion in federal tax funds for a 500-mile high-speed rail project stretching between the California cities of Anaheim and San Francisco. Local planners proposed construction of operating rail line segments in phases, starting at the highly populated ends of the route, at a projected total expense of about $18 billion. Planners suggested that opening operating segments at the more heavily populated ends of the line would generate revenues that could assist in financing the building of remaining segments of the multiyear rail construction project.

In reaction, Transportation Department officials mandated the rail line to start in California's less-populated Central Valley region. Of course, train passengers will be far fewer. Why did the U.S. government officials do this? They did so because they consider residents of the Central Valley to be "underserved" by rail transit services. The resulting completion delay will be at least two years and will add more than $1 billion to the project's ultimate net expense to taxpayers.

FOR CRITICAL THINKING

Would Transportation Department officials have made the same decision if they, rather than taxpayers, had to cover the added costs of starting construction in the Central Valley?

THE PRICE SYSTEM The alternative to command and control is the *price system* (also called a *market system*), which is a shorthand term describing an economic system that answers the three basic economic questions via decentralized decision making. Under a pure price system, individuals and families own all of the scarce resources used in production. Consequently, choices about what and how many items to produce are left to private parties to determine on their own initiative, as are decisions about how to go about producing those items. Furthermore, individuals and families choose how to allocate their own incomes to obtain the produced items at prices established via privately organized mechanisms.

In the price system, which you will learn about in considerable detail in Chapters 3 and 4, prices define the terms under which people agree to make exchanges. Prices signal to everyone within a price system which resources are relatively scarce and which resources are relatively abundant. This *signaling* aspect of the price system provides information to individual buyers and sellers about what and how many items should be produced, how production of items should be organized, and who will choose to buy the produced items.

Thus, in a price system, individuals and families own the facilities used to produce automobiles. They decide which types of automobiles to produce, how many of them to produce, and how to bring scarce resources together within their facilities to generate the desired production. Other individuals and families decide how much of their earnings they wish to spend on automobiles.

MIXED ECONOMIC SYSTEMS By and large, the economic systems of the world's nations are mixed economic systems that incorporate aspects of both centralized command and control and a decentralized price system. At any given time, some nations lean toward centralized mechanisms of command and control and allow relatively little scope for decentralized decision making. At the same time, other nations limit the extent to which a central authority dictates answers to the three basic economic questions, leaving people mostly free to utilize a decentralized price system to generate their own answers.

A given country may reach different decisions at different times about how much to rely on command and control versus a price system to answer its three basic economic questions. Until 2008, for instance, the people of the United States preferred to rely mainly on a decentralized price system to decide which and how many automobiles to produce, how to marshal scarce resources to produce those vehicles, and how to decide who should obtain them. Today, the U.S. government owns a substantial fraction of the facilities used to manufacture automobiles and hence has considerable command-and-control authority over U.S. vehicle production.

How has Cuba altered the extent to which it relies on command and control compared with the price system?

INTERNATIONAL POLICY EXAMPLE

Cuba Experiments with Mixing It Up

For more than half of a century, Cuba has been the Western Hemisphere's only Communist nation. The Cuban government sets the prices of most goods and services. For many years, the government also set the wages of about 85 percent of the country's 5.5 million workers who are government-employed. The government permitted the remaining 15 percent of employed individuals to work in 124 "authorized" private occupations, which include farming, teaching music, selling piñatas, and repairing existing items such as furniture and toys.

Today, the government is in the midst of letting go nearly 600,000 public employees, who will have to seek employment at privately determined wages. Although the nation will maintain its heavy reliance on command and control, a larger share of its workers will have their wages determined in the price system. Thus, Cuba's economy is becoming more mixed.

FOR CRITICAL THINKING

When there are fewer public workers and more private workers, will changes in wages be better or worse signals?

The Economic Approach: Systematic Decisions

Economists assume that individuals act *as if* they systematically pursue self-motivated interests and respond predictably to perceived opportunities to attain those interests. This central insight of economics was first clearly articulated by Adam Smith in 1776. Smith wrote in his most famous book, *An Inquiry into the Nature and Causes of the Wealth of Nations*, that "it is not from the benevolence of the butcher, the brewer, or the baker that we expect our dinner, but from their regard to their own interest." Thus, the typical person about whom economists make behavioral predictions is assumed to act *as though* he or she systematically pursues self-motivated interest.

The Rationality Assumption

The **rationality assumption** of economics, simply stated, is as follows:

We assume that individuals do not intentionally make decisions that would leave themselves worse off.

Rationality assumption
The assumption that people do not intentionally make decisions that would leave them worse off.

The distinction here is between what people may think—the realm of psychology and psychiatry and perhaps sociology—and what they do. Economics does *not* involve itself in analyzing individual or group thought processes. Economics looks at what people actually do in life with their limited resources. It does little good to criticize the rationality assumption by stating, "Nobody thinks that way" or "I never think that way" or "How unrealistic! That's as irrational as anyone can get!" In a world in which people can be atypical in countless ways, economists find it useful to concentrate on discovering the baseline. Knowing what happens on average is a good place to start. In this way, we avoid building our thinking on exceptions rather than on reality.

Take the example of driving. When you consider passing another car on a two-lane highway with oncoming traffic, you have to make very quick decisions: You must estimate the speed of the car that you are going to pass, the speed of the oncoming cars, the distance between your car and the oncoming cars, and your car's potential rate of acceleration. If we were to apply a model to your behavior, we would use the rules of calculus. In actual fact, you and most other drivers in such a situation do not actually think of using the rules of calculus, but to predict your behavior, we could make the prediction *as if* you understood those rules.

How are bankers reducing robbery rates by counting on the rationality of would-be thieves?

EXAMPLE

Hello, Bank Robber, I'll Remember You

Until recently, each year since 1979, on average 11 of every 100 U.S. bank branches experienced a robbery. Bankers have worked to bring down this robbery rate by treating prospective robbers as rational people. A would-be bank robber knows that the likelihood of being caught and sentenced to prison increases significantly when someone in the bank gets a good enough look at the robber's face to provide a positive identification.

Consequently, many banks now make a point of having a teller, guard, or branch manager greet each entering customer, look the customer directly in the eye, and say hello. Since banks around the nation have instituted a policy of greeting customers at the doors, the robbery rate has dropped to only 6 of every 100 bank branches.

FOR CRITICAL THINKING

What types of costs and benefits must a prospective criminal rationally weigh before deciding whether to attempt a bank robbery?

Responding to Incentives

YOU ARE THERE

To contemplate how a higher corporate tax rate in the United States relative to other nations is affecting the incentive for U.S. firms to form corporate structures within U.S. borders, take a look at **Why So Many Firms Are Incorporating Outside the United States** on page 11.

If it can be assumed that individuals never intentionally make decisions that would leave them worse off, then almost by definition they will respond to changes in incentives. Indeed, much of human behavior can be explained in terms of how individuals respond to changing incentives over time.

Schoolchildren are motivated to do better by a variety of incentive systems, ranging from gold stars and certificates of achievement when they are young, to better grades with accompanying promises of a "better life" as they get older. Of course, negative incentives affect our behavior, too. Penalties, punishments, and other forms of negative incentives can raise the cost of engaging in various activities.

Defining Self-Interest

Self-interest does not always mean increasing one's wealth measured in dollars and cents. We assume that individuals seek many goals, not just increased wealth measured in monetary terms. Thus, the self-interest part of our economic-person assumption includes goals relating to prestige, friendship, love, power, helping others, creating works of art, and many other matters. We can also think in terms of enlightened self-interest, whereby individuals, in the pursuit of what makes them better off, also achieve the betterment of others around them. In brief, individuals are assumed to want the ability to further their goals by making decisions about how things around them are used. The head of a charitable organization usually will not turn down an additional contribution, because accepting the funds yields control over how they are used, even though it is for other people's benefit.

Thus, self-interest does not rule out doing charitable acts. Giving gifts to relatives can be considered a form of charity that is nonetheless in the self-interest of the giver. But how efficient is such gift giving?

EXAMPLE

The Perceived Value of Gifts

Every holiday season, aunts, uncles, grandparents, mothers, and fathers give gifts to their college-aged loved ones. Joel Waldfogel, an economist at the University of Minnesota, has surveyed several thousand college students after Christmas to find out the value of holiday gifts. He finds that recorded music and outerwear (coats and jackets) have a perceived intrinsic value about equal to their actual cash equivalent. By the time he gets down the list to socks, underwear, and cosmetics, the students' valuation is only about 82 percent of the cash value of the gift. He find that aunts, uncles, and grandparents give the "worst" gifts and friends, siblings, and parents give the "best."

FOR CRITICAL ANALYSIS

What argument could you use against the idea of substituting cash or gift cards for physical gifts?

QUICK QUIZ

See page 16 for the answers. Review concepts from this section in MyEconLab.

Economics is a social science that involves the study of how individuals choose among alternatives to satisfy their__________, which are what people would buy if their incomes were__________.

__________, the study of the decision-making processes of individuals (or households) and firms, and __________, the study of the performance of the economy as a whole, are the two main branches into which the study of economics is divided.

The three basic economic questions ask what and how much will be produced, how will items be produced, and for whom will items be produced. The two opposing answers are provided by the type of economic system: either__________ __________ __________ __________ or the__________ __________.

In economics, we assume that people do not intentionally make decisions that will leave them worse off. This is known as the __________ assumption.

Economics as a Science

Economics is a social science that employs the same kinds of methods used in other sciences, such as biology, physics, and chemistry. Like these other sciences, economics uses models, or theories. Economic **models,** or **theories,** are simplified representations of the real world that we use to help us understand, explain, and predict economic phenomena in the real world. There are, of course, differences between sciences. The social sciences—especially economics—make little use of laboratory experiments in which changes in variables are studied under controlled conditions. Rather, social scientists, and especially economists, usually have to test their models, or theories, by examining what has already happened in the real world.

Models, or **theories**
Simplified representations of the real world used as the basis for predictions or explanations.

Models and Realism

At the outset it must be emphasized that no model in *any* science, and therefore no economic model, is complete in the sense that it captures *every* detail or interrelationship that exists. Indeed, a model, by definition, is an abstraction from reality. It is conceptually impossible to construct a perfectly complete realistic model. For example, in physics we cannot account for every molecule and its position and certainly not for every atom and subatomic particle. Not only is such a model unreasonably expensive to build, but working with it would be impossibly complex.

The nature of scientific model building is that the model should capture only the *essential* relationships that are sufficient to analyze the particular problem or answer the particular question with which we are concerned. *An economic model cannot be faulted as unrealistic simply because it does not represent every detail of the real world.* A map of a city that shows only major streets is not faulty if, in fact, all you need to know is how to pass through the city using major streets. As long as a model is able to shed light on the *central* issue at hand or forces at work, it may be useful.

A map is the quintessential model. It is always a simplified representation. It is always unrealistic. But it is also useful in making predictions about the world. If the model—the map—predicts that when you take Campus Avenue to the north, you always run into the campus, that is a prediction. If a simple model can explain observed behavior in repeated settings just as well as a complex model, the simple model has some value and is probably easier to use.

Assumptions

Every model, or theory, must be based on a set of assumptions. Assumptions define the array of circumstances in which our model is most likely to be applicable. When some people predicted that sailing ships would fall off the edge of the earth, they used the *assumption* that the earth was flat. Columbus did not accept the implications of such a model because he did not accept its assumptions. He assumed that the world was round. The real-world test of his own model refuted the flat-earth model. Indirectly, then, it was a test of the assumption of the flat-earth model.

Is it possible to use our knowledge about assumptions to understand why driving directions sometimes contain very few details?

EXAMPLE

Getting Directions

Assumptions are a shorthand for reality. Imagine that you have decided to drive from your home in San Diego to downtown San Francisco. Because you have never driven this route, you decide to use a travel-planner device such as global-positioning-system equipment.

When you ask for directions, the electronic travel planner could give you a set of detailed maps that shows each city through which you will travel—Oceanside, San Clemente, Irvine, Anaheim, Los Angeles, Bakersfield, Modesto, and so on—with the individual maps showing you exactly how the freeway threads through each of these cities. You would get a nearly complete description of reality because the GPS travel planner will not have used many simplifying assumptions. It is more likely, however, that the travel planner will simply say, "Get on Interstate 5 going north. Stay on it for about 500 miles. Follow the signs for San Francisco. After crossing the toll bridge, take any exit marked 'Downtown.'" By omitting all of the trivial details, the travel planner has told you all that you really need and want to know. The models you will be using in this text are similar to the simplified directions on how to drive from San Diego to San Francisco—they focus on what is relevant to the problem at hand and omit what is not.

FOR CRITICAL ANALYSIS

In what way do small talk and gossip represent the use of simplifying assumptions?

THE *CETERIS PARIBUS* ASSUMPTION: ALL OTHER THINGS BEING EQUAL Everything in the world seems to relate in some way to everything else in the world. It would be impossible to isolate the effects of changes in one variable on another variable if we always had to worry about the many other variables that might also enter the analysis. Similar to other sciences, economics uses the **ceteris paribus assumption.** *Ceteris paribus* means "other things constant" or "other things equal."

***Ceteris paribus* [KAY-ter-us PEAR-uh-bus] assumption**
The assumption that nothing changes except the factor or factors being studied.

Consider an example taken from economics. One of the most important determinants of how much of a particular product a family buys is how expensive that product is relative to other products. We know that in addition to relative prices, other factors influence decisions about making purchases. Some of them have to do with income, others with tastes, and yet others with custom and religious beliefs. Whatever these other factors are, we hold them constant when we look at the relationship between changes in prices and changes in how much of a given product people will purchase.

Deciding on the Usefulness of a Model

We generally do not attempt to determine the usefulness, or "goodness," of a model merely by evaluating how realistic its assumptions are. Rather, we consider a model "good" if it yields usable predictions that are supported by real-world observations. In other words, can we use the model to predict what will happen in the world around us? Does the model provide useful implications about how things happen in our world?

Once we have determined that the model may be useful in predicting real-world phenomena, the scientific approach to the analysis of the world around us requires that we consider evidence. Evidence is used to test the usefulness of a model. This is why we call economics an **empirical** science. *Empirical* means that evidence (data) is looked at to see whether we are right. Economists are often engaged in empirically testing their models.

Empirical
Relying on real-world data in evaluating the usefulness of a model.

Models of Behavior, Not Thought Processes

Take special note of the fact that economists' models do not relate to the way people *think*. Economic models relate to the way people *act*, to what they do in life with their limited resources. Normally, the economist does not attempt to predict how people will think about a particular topic, such as a higher price of oil products, accelerated inflation, or higher taxes. Rather, the task at hand is to predict how people will behave, which may be quite different from what they *say* they will do (much to the consternation of poll takers and market researchers). Thus, people's *declared* preferences are generally of little use in testing economic theories, which aim to explain and predict people's *revealed* preferences. The people involved in examining thought processes are psychologists and psychiatrists, not typically economists.

WHAT IF... economists were to base their theories of human behavior on what people *say* they do, rather than on what people *actually* do?

The task of economists is to try to predict decisions that people will make given the incentives that they face. Consider how people respond when asked by pollsters about whether they will cut back on charitable giving if the government eliminates tax breaks for such donations. Most people state that they will continue to give as much as before, because they suspect this answer will please those who have posed the question. In fact, studies of actual responses to smaller tax breaks for charitable giving reveal that people pursue their own interest. Whether or not their true action might have pleased a pollster, they reduce donations. Thus, if economists were to rely on polls indicating how people claim that they respond to incentives such as diminished tax breaks, economists would persistently make erroneous predictions about the decisions that people actually make.

Behavioral Economics and Bounded Rationality

In recent years, some economists have proposed paying more attention to psychologists and psychiatrists. They have suggested an alternative approach to economic analysis. Their approach, which is known as **behavioral economics,** examines consumer behavior in the face of psychological limitations and complications that may interfere with rational decision making.

Behavioral economics
An approach to the study of consumer behavior that emphasizes psychological limitations and complications that potentially interfere with rational decision making.

BOUNDED RATIONALITY Proponents of behavioral economics suggest that traditional economic models assume that people exhibit three "unrealistic" characteristics:

1. *Unbounded selfishness*. People are interested only in their own satisfaction.
2. *Unbounded willpower*. Their choices are always consistent with their long-term goals.
3. *Unbounded rationality*. They are able to consider every relevant choice.

Bounded rationality
The hypothesis that people are *nearly*, but not fully, rational, so that they cannot examine every possible choice available to them but instead use simple rules of thumb to sort among the alternatives that happen to occur to them.

As an alternative, advocates of behavioral economics have proposed replacing the rationality assumption with the assumption of **bounded rationality,** which assumes that people cannot examine and think through every possible choice they confront. As a consequence, behavioral economists suggest, people cannot always pursue their best long-term personal interests. From time to time, they must also rely on other people and take into account other people's interests as well as their own.

RULES OF THUMB A key behavioral implication of the bounded rationality assumption is that people should use so-called *rules of thumb:* Because every possible choice cannot be considered, an individual will tend to fall back on methods of making decisions that are simpler than trying to sort through every possibility.

A problem confronting advocates of behavioral economics is that people who *appear* to use rules of thumb may in fact behave *as if* they are fully rational. For instance, if a person faces persistently predictable ranges of choices for a time, the individual may rationally settle into repetitive behaviors that an outside observer might conclude to be consistent with a rule of thumb. According to the bounded rationality assumption, the person should continue to rely on a rule of thumb even if there is a major change in the environment that the individual faces. Time and time again, however, economists find that people respond to altered circumstances by fundamentally changing their behaviors. Economists also generally observe that people make decisions that are consistent with their own self-interest and long-term objectives.

BEHAVIORAL ECONOMICS: A WORK IN PROGRESS It remains to be seen whether the application of the assumption of bounded rationality proposed by behavioral economists will truly alter the manner in which economists construct models intended to better predict human decision making. So far, proponents of behavioral economics have not conclusively demonstrated that paying closer attention to psychological thought processes can improve economic predictions.

As a consequence, the bulk of economic analysis continues to rely on the rationality assumption as the basis for constructing economic models. As you will learn in Chapter 20, advocates of behavioral economics continue to explore ways in which psychological elements might improve analysis of decision making by individual consumers.

Positive versus Normative Economics

Economics uses *positive analysis,* a value-free approach to inquiry. No subjective or moral judgments enter into the analysis. Positive analysis relates to statements such as "If A, then B." For example, "If the price of gasoline goes up relative to all other prices, then the amount of it that people buy will fall." That is a positive economic statement. It is a statement of *what is.* It is not a statement of anyone's value judgment or subjective feelings.

Distinguishing between Positive and Normative Economics

Positive economics
Analysis that is *strictly* limited to making either purely descriptive statements or scientific predictions; for example, "If A, then B." A statement of *what is.*

Normative economics
Analysis involving value judgments about economic policies; relates to whether outcomes are good or bad. A statement of *what ought to be.*

For many problems analyzed in the "hard" sciences such as physics and chemistry, the analyses are considered to be virtually value-free. After all, how can someone's values enter into a theory of molecular behavior? But economists face a different problem. They deal with the behavior of individuals, not molecules. That makes it more difficult to stick to what we consider to be value-free or **positive economics** without reference to our feelings.

When our values are interjected into the analysis, we enter the realm of **normative economics,** involving *normative analysis.* A positive economic statement is "If the price of gas rises, people will buy less." If we add to that analysis the statement "so we should not allow the price to go up," we have entered the realm of normative economics—we have expressed a value judgment. In fact, any time you see the word *should,* you will know that values are entering into the discussion. Just remember that positive statements are concerned with *what is,* whereas normative statements are concerned with *what ought to be.*

Each of us has a desire for different things. That means that we have different values. When we express a value judgment, we are simply saying what we prefer, like, or desire. Because individual values are diverse, we expect—and indeed observe—that people express widely varying value judgments about how the world ought to be.

A Warning: Recognize Normative Analysis

It is easy to define positive economics. It is quite another matter to catch all unlabeled normative statements in a textbook, even though an author goes over the manuscript many times before it is printed or electronically created. Therefore, do not get the impression that a textbook author will be able to keep all personal values out of the book. They will slip through. In fact, the very choice of which topics to include in an introductory textbook involves normative economics. There is no value-free way to decide which topics to use in a textbook. The author's values ultimately make a difference when choices have to be made. But from your own standpoint, you might want to be able to recognize when you are engaging in normative as opposed to positive economic analysis. Reading this text will help equip you for that task.

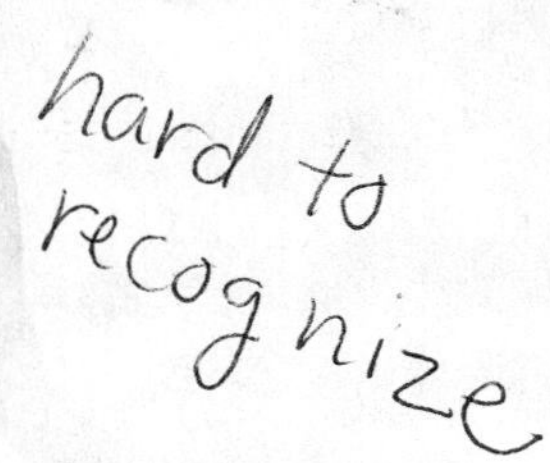

QUICK QUIZ

See page 16 for the answers. Review concepts from this section in MyEconLab.

A __________, or __________, uses assumptions and is by nature a simplification of the real world. The usefulness of a __________ can be evaluated by bringing empirical evidence to bear on its predictions.

Most models use the __________ __________ assumption that all other things are held constant, or equal.

__________ economics emphasizes psychological constraints and complexities that potentially interfere with rational decision making. This approach utilizes the __________ __________ hypothesis that people are not quite rational, because they cannot study every possible alternative but instead use simple rules of thumb to decide among choices.

__________ economics is value-free and relates to statements that can be refuted, such as "If A, then B." __________ economics involves people's values and typically uses the word *should*.

YOU ARE THERE

Why So Many Firms Are Incorporating Outside the United States

Willard Taylor, a tax attorney with Sullivan & Cromwell LLP, is contemplating the latest trend among U.S. firms that have been opting to become corporations. Until recently, it was unusual for U.S. family-owned companies or partnerships to "go public" by incorporating in another nation and selling shares of stock to residents of other nations. A decade ago, only about 1 percent of U.S. companies that became corporations did so outside the United States. During each of the past three years, however, more than 20 percent of U.S. firms choosing corporate structures have decided to incorporate abroad.

As a tax lawyer, Taylor pays close attention to tax rates assessed on corporations based abroad as well as those that apply to U.S. corporations. Most countries' governments, Taylor realizes, have slashed their corporate tax rates in recent years, whereas the U.S. corporate tax rate has remained unchanged at 35 percent. The result, Taylor notes, is that the U.S. corporate tax rate is now second highest in the world, which provides a strong incentive to incorporate elsewhere. Taylor asks, "What are the pluses and minuses of being incorporated in the U.S. versus somewhere else?" He deduces that given the strong incentive provided by lower corporate tax rates abroad, "Very often, depending on what the business is, you'll conclude that there are no pluses to being in the United States."

Critical Thinking Questions

1. How have lower foreign tax rates affected the incentive to incorporate abroad?
2. What do you suppose has happened to federal collections of corporate taxes?

ISSUES & APPLICATIONS

Why So Many Tourists Have Been Giving Birth in Hong Kong

CONCEPTS APPLIED

- Rationality Assumption
- Incentives
- Self-Interest

There has been a significant upswing in the number of babies born in Hong Kong to mothers from China's mainland who officially are visiting Hong Kong as tourists. The number of births to this category of mothers rose from about 13,000 in 2004 to more than 40,000 in 2011—almost half of all Hong Kong births in the latter year. It turns out that this substantial increase in Hong Kong "tourist births" is consistent with the rationality assumption.

Incentives for a Mainland Resident to Desire a Hong Kong Birth

Why are so many more women who are officially in Hong Kong as tourists giving birth instead of visiting the city's sites? The answer is that mothers from mainland China are responding to incentives in a manner consistent with self-interested behavior.

Although the $5,000 price of hospital maternity care is several times higher in Hong Kong than in most hospitals on the mainland, the quality of care is considerably better in Hong Kong. In addition, the benefits for a child born in Hong Kong—and hence for the child's mother—are much greater than those available to a child born on the mainland. These benefits of a Hong Kong birth include twelve years of publicly provided education for the child at no explicit cost and close to zero out-of-pocket health care expenses. Furthermore, tourists who give birth in Hong Kong are exempt from China's "one-child policy," which limits women to bearing a single child. Such an exemption gives pregnant women desiring to raise a second child a strong incentive to "visit" Hong Kong.

Why the "Tourist" Fiction Has Been Rational for Hong Kong

Of course, nearly all tourist mothers who travel to Hong Kong to give birth actually plan to remain there. Why does the Hong Kong government permit these women to remain and to obtain publicly provided health care and education for their children? The answer to this second question also relates to the rationality assumption: The Hong Kong government is responding to incentives.

Since the 1990s, the birth rate among Hong Kong residents has declined by more than 33 percent. Early in the 2000s, government officials realized that unless more people immigrated to Hong Kong, its population would begin to shrink—perhaps eventually by about one-third. The city's leaders did not wish to open its borders to all who desired to immigrate, so they decided to permit more expectant mothers to enter under the tourist classification. Thus, it has been rational for the government of Hong Kong to allow numerous "tourist" births, just as it has been consistent with individual self-interest for "tourists" to give birth there.

For Critical Thinking

1. How have recent improvements in maternity care in mainland China likely affected the incentives to become a "tourist" mother in Hong Kong?
2. How are Hong Kong's incentives to allow "tourist" births affected by the fact that the city pays benefits to older residents from taxes paid by younger residents?

Web Resources

1. To contemplate the sources of pressures within Hong Kong to restrict tourist births, go to **www.econtoday.com/chap01**.
2. Read about the 2011 suspension of Hong Kong's tourist births at **www.econtoday.com/chap01**.

MyEconLab

For more questions on this chapter's Issues & Applications, go to **MyEconLab**. In the Study Plan for this chapter, select Section N: News.

MyEconLab

Here is what you should know after reading this chapter. MyEconLab will help you identify what you know, and where to go when you need to practice.

WHAT YOU SHOULD KNOW		WHERE TO GO TO PRACTICE
Answering the Three Basic Economic Questions Economics is the study of how individuals make choices to satisfy wants. Microeconomics is the study of decision making by individual households and firms, and macroeconomics is the study of nationwide phenomena such as inflation and unemployment. The three basic economic questions ask what and how much will be produced, how items will be produced, and for whom items will be produced. The two opposing answers to these questions are provided by the type of economic system: either centralized command and control or the price system.	incentives, 2 economics, 2 resources, 2 wants, 2 microeconomics, 3 macroeconomics, 3 aggregates, 3 economic system, 3	• MyEconLab Study Plans 1.1, 1.2, 1.3
Self-Interest in Economic Analysis Rational self-interest is the assumption that people never intentionally make decisions that would leave them worse off. Instead, they are motivated mainly by their self-interest, which can relate to monetary and nonmonetary goals, such as love, prestige, and helping others.	rationality assumption, 5	• MyEconLab Study Plan 1.3
Economics as a Science Economic models, or theories, are simplified representations of the real world. Economic models are never completely realistic because by definition they are simplifications using assumptions that are not directly testable. Nevertheless, economists can subject the predictions of economic theories to empirical tests in which real-world data are used to decide whether or not to reject the predictions.	models, or theories, 7 *ceteris paribus* assumption, 8 empirical, 9 behavioral economics, 9 bounded rationality, 10	• MyEconLab Study Plan 1.5
Positive and Normative Economics Positive economics deals with *what is*, whereas normative economics deals with *what ought to be*. Positive economic statements are of the "if . . . then" variety. They are descriptive and predictive. In contrast, statements embodying values are within the realm of normative economics, or how people think things ought to be.	positive economics, 10 normative economics, 10	• MyEconLab Study Plan 1.6

Log in to MyEconLab, take a chapter test, and get a personalized Study Plan that tells you which concepts you understand and which ones you need to review. From there, MyEconLab will give you further practice, tutorials, animations, videos, and guided solutions. For more information, visit www.myeconlab.com

PROBLEMS

All problems are assignable in MyEconLab. *Answers to odd-numbered problems appear at the back of the book.*

1-1. Define economics. Explain briefly how the economic way of thinking—in terms of rational, self-interested people responding to incentives—relates to each of the following situations. (See pages 2, 5–6.)

- **a.** A student deciding whether to purchase a textbook for a particular class
- **b.** Government officials seeking more funding for mass transit through higher taxes
- **c.** A municipality taxing hotel guests to obtain funding for a new sports stadium

1-2. Some people claim that the "economic way of thinking" does not apply to issues such as health care. Explain how economics does apply to this issue by developing a "model" of an individual's choices. (See pages 7–8.)

1-3. Does the phrase "unlimited wants and limited resources" apply to both a low-income household and a middle-income household? Can the same phrase be applied to a very high-income household? (See page 2.)

1-4. In a single sentence, contrast microeconomics and macroeconomics. Next, categorize each of the following issues as a microeconomic issue, a macroeconomic issue, or not an economic issue. (See page 3.)

- **a.** The national unemployment rate
- **b.** The decision of a worker to work overtime or not
- **c.** A family's choice to have a baby
- **d.** The rate of growth of the money supply
- **e.** The national government's budget deficit
- **f.** A student's allocation of study time across two subjects

1-5. One of your classmates, Sally, is a hardworking student, serious about her classes, and conscientious about her grades. Sally is also involved, however, in volunteer activities and an extracurricular sport. Is Sally displaying rational behavior? Based on what you read in this chapter, construct an argument supporting the conclusion that she is. (See pages 5–7.)

1-6. Recently, a bank was trying to decide what fee to charge for "expedited payments"—payments that the bank would transmit extra-speedily to enable customers to avoid late fees on cable TV bills, electric bills, and the like. To try to determine what fee customers were willing to pay for expedited payments, the bank conducted a survey. It was able to determine that many of the people surveyed already paid fees for expedited payment services that *exceeded* the maximum fees that they said they were willing to pay. How does the bank's finding relate to economists' traditional focus on what people do, rather than what they *say* they will do? (See page 9.)

1-7. Explain, in your own words, the rationality assumption, and contrast it with the assumption of bounded rationality proposed by adherents of behavioral economics. (See pages 5–6, 9–10.)

1-8. Why does the assumption of bounded rationality suggest that people might use rules of thumb to guide their decision making instead of considering every possible choice available to them? (See page 10.)

1-9. Under what circumstances might people appear to use rules of thumb, as suggested by the assumption of bounded rationality, even though they really are behaving in a manner suggested by the rationality assumption? (See page 10.)

1-10. For each of the following approaches that an economist might follow in examining a decision-making process, identify whether the approach relies on the rationality assumption or on the assumption of bounded rationality. (See page 10.)

- **a.** To make predictions about how many apps a person will download onto her tablet device, an economist presumes that the individual faces limitations that make it impossible for her to examine every possible choice among relevant apps.
- **b.** In evaluating the price that an individual will be willing to pay for a given quantity of a particular type of health care service, a researcher assumes that the person considers all relevant health care options in pursuit of his own long-term satisfaction with resulting health outcomes.
- **c.** To determine the amount of time that a person will decide to devote to watching online videos each week, an economist makes the assumption that the individual will feel overwhelmed by the sheer volume of videos available online and will respond by using a rule of thumb.

1-11. For each of the following approaches that an economist might follow in examining a decision-making process, identify whether the approach relies on the rationality assumption or on the assumption of bounded rationality. (See page 10.)

- **a.** An economic study of the number of online searches that individuals conduct before selecting a particular item to purchase online presumes that people are interested only in their own satisfaction, pursue their ultimate objectives, and consider every relevant option.

b. An economist seeking to predict the effect that an increase in a state's sales tax rate will have on consumers' purchases of goods and services presumes that people are limited in their ability to process information about how the tax-rate increase will influence the after-tax prices those consumers will pay.

c. To evaluate the impact of an increase in the range of choices that an individual confronts when deciding among devices for accessing the Internet, an economic researcher makes the assumption that the individual is unable to take into account every new Internet-access option available to her.

1-12. Which of the following predictions appear(s) to follow from a model based on the assumption that rational, self-interested individuals respond to incentives? (See pages 6–7.)

a. For every 10 exam points Myrna must earn in order to pass her economics course and meet her graduation requirements, she will study one additional hour for her economics test next week.

b. A coin toss will best predict Leonardo's decision about whether to purchase an expensive business suit or an inexpensive casual outfit to wear next week when he interviews for a high-paying job he is seeking.

c. Celeste, who uses earnings from her regularly scheduled hours of part-time work to pay for her room and board at college, will decide to purchase and download a newly released video this week only if she is able to work two additional hours.

1-13. Consider two models for estimating, in advance of an election, the shares of votes that will go to rival candidates. According to one model, pollsters' surveys of a randomly chosen set of registered voters before an election can be used to forecast the percentage of votes that each candidate will receive. This first model relies on the assumption that unpaid survey respondents will give truthful responses about how they will vote and that they will actually cast a ballot in the election. The other model uses prices of financial assets (legally binding IOUs) issued by the Iowa Electronic Markets, operated by the University of Iowa, to predict electoral outcomes. The final payments received by owners of these assets, which can be bought or sold during the weeks and days preceding an election, depend on the shares of votes the candidates actually end up receiving. This second model assumes that owners of these assets wish to earn the highest possible returns, and it predicts that the market prices of these assets provide an indication of the percentage of votes that each candidate will actually receive on the day of the election. (See pages 8–9.)

a. Which of these two models for forecasting electoral results is more firmly based on the rationality assumption of economics?

b. How would an economist evaluate which is the better model for forecasting electoral outcomes?

1-14. Write a sentence contrasting positive and normative economic analysis. (See pages 10–11.)

1-15. Based on your answer to Problem 1–14, categorize each of the following conclusions as being the result of positive analysis or normative analysis.

a. A higher minimum wage will reduce employment opportunities for minimum wage workers.

b. Increasing the earnings of minimum wage employees is desirable, and raising the minimum wage is the best way to accomplish this.

c. Everyone should enjoy open access to health care at no explicit charge.

d. Heath care subsidies will increase the consumption of health care.

1-16. Consider the following statements, based on a positive economic analysis that assumes that all other things remain constant. For each, list one other thing that might change and thus offset the outcome stated. (See pages 8, 10.)

a. Increased demand for laptop computers will drive up their price.

b. Falling gasoline prices will result in additional vacation travel.

c. A reduction of income tax rates will result in more people working.

ECONOMICS ON THE NET

The Usefulness of Studying Economics This application helps you see how accomplished people benefited from their study of economics. It also explores ways in which these people feel others of all walks of life can gain from learning more about the economics field.

Title: How Taking an Economics Course Can Lead to Becoming an Economist

Navigation: Go to **www.econtoday.com/chap01** to visit the Federal Reserve Bank of Minneapolis publication, *The Region*. Select the last article of the issue, "Economists in *The Region* on Their Student Experiences and the Need for Economic Literacy."

Application Read the interviews of the six economists, and answer the following questions.

1. Based on your reading, which economists do you think other economists regard as influential? What educational institutions do you think are the most influential in economics?
2. Which economists do you think were attracted to microeconomics and which to macroeconomics?

For Group Study and Analysis Divide the class into three groups, and assign the groups the Blinder, Yellen, and Rivlin interviews. Have each group use the content of its assigned interview to develop a statement explaining why the study of economics is important, regardless of a student's chosen major.

ANSWERS TO QUICK QUIZZES

p. 7: (i) wants . . . unlimited; (ii) Microeconomics . . . macroeconomics; (iii) centralized command and control . . . price system; (iv) rationality

p. 11: (i) model . . . theory . . . model; (ii) *ceteris paribus;* (iii) Behavioral . . . bounded rationality; (iv) Positive . . . Normative

APPENDIX A

Reading and Working with Graphs

A graph is a visual representation of the relationship between variables. In this appendix, we'll deal with just two variables: an **independent variable,** which can change in value freely, and a **dependent variable,** which changes as a result of changes in the value of the independent variable. For example, even if nothing else is changing in your life, your weight depends on your intake of calories. The independent variable is caloric intake, and the dependent variable is weight.

Independent variable
A variable whose value is determined independently of, or outside, the equation under study.

Dependent variable
A variable whose value changes according to changes in the value of one or more independent variables.

A table is a list of numerical values showing the relationship between two (or more) variables. Any table can be converted into a graph, which is a visual representation of that list. Once you understand how a table can be converted to a graph, you will understand what graphs are and how to construct and use them.

Consider a practical example. A conservationist may try to convince you that driving at lower highway speeds will help you conserve gas. Table A-1 shows the relationship between speed—the independent variable—and the distance you can go on a gallon of gas at that speed—the dependent variable. This table does show a pattern. As the data in the first column get larger in value, the data in the second column get smaller.

TABLE A-1

Gas Mileage as a Function of Driving Speed

Miles per Hour	Miles per Gallon
45	25
50	24
55	23
60	21
65	19
70	16
75	13

Now let's take a look at the different ways in which variables can be related.

Direct and Inverse Relationships

Two variables can be related in different ways, some simple, others more complex. For example, a person's weight and height are often related. If we measured the height and weight of thousands of people, we would surely find that taller people tend to weigh more than shorter people. That is, we would discover that there is a **direct relationship** between height and weight. By this we simply mean that an *increase* in one variable is usually associated with an *increase* in the related variable. This can easily be seen in panel (a) of Figure A-1 below.

Let's look at another simple way in which two variables can be related. Much evidence indicates that as the price of a specific commodity rises, the amount purchased decreases—there is an **inverse relationship** between the variable's price per unit and quantity purchased. Such a relationship indicates that for higher and higher prices, smaller and smaller quantities will be purchased. We see this relationship in panel (b) of Figure A-1.

Direct relationship
A relationship between two variables that is positive, meaning that an increase in one variable is associated with an increase in the other and a decrease in one variable is associated with a decrease in the other.

Inverse relationship
A relationship between two variables that is negative, meaning that an increase in one variable is associated with a decrease in the other and a decrease in one variable is associated with an increase in the other.

FIGURE A-1 **Direct and Inverse Relationships**

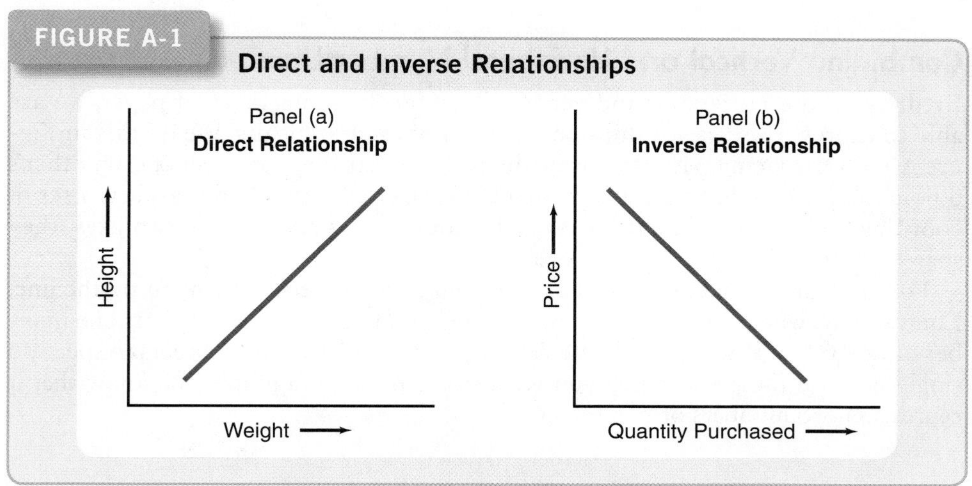

FIGURE A-2

Horizontal Number Line

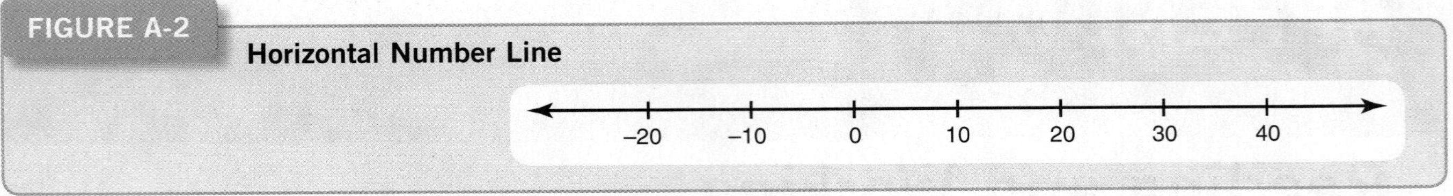

Constructing a Graph

Number line
A line that can be divided into segments of equal length, each associated with a number.

Let us now examine how to construct a graph to illustrate a relationship between two variables.

A Number Line

The first step is to become familiar with what is called a **number line.** One is shown in Figure A-2 above. You should know two things about it:

1. The points on the line divide the line into equal segments.
2. The numbers associated with the points on the line increase in value from left to right. Saying it the other way around, the numbers decrease in value from right to left. However you say it, what you're describing is formally called an *ordered set of points*.

FIGURE A-3

Vertical Number Line

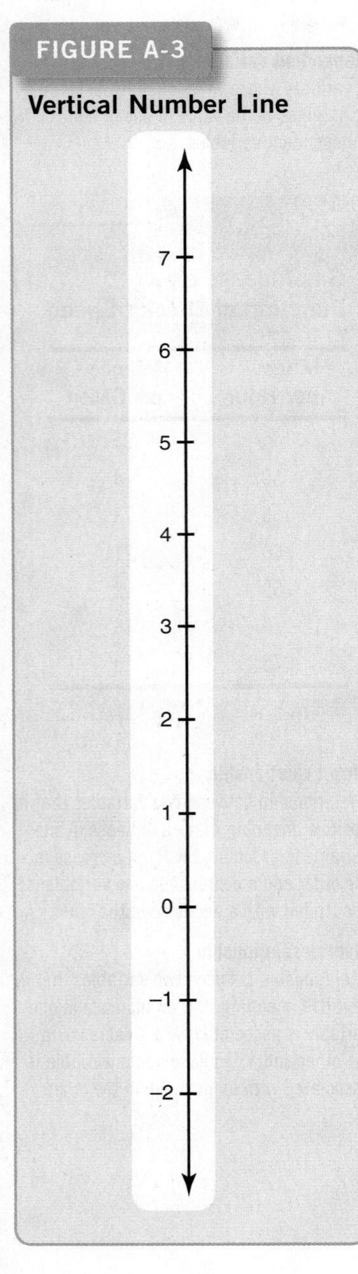

On the number line, we have shown the line segments—that is, the distance from 0 to 10 or the distance between 30 and 40. They all appear to be equal and, indeed, are each equal to $\frac{1}{2}$ inch. When we use a distance to represent a quantity, such as barrels of oil, graphically, we are *scaling* the number line. In the example shown, the distance between 0 and 10 might represent 10 barrels of oil, or the distance from 0 to 40 might represent 40 barrels. Of course, the scale may differ on different number lines. For example, a distance of 1 inch could represent 10 units on one number line but 5,000 units on another. Notice that on our number line, points to the left of 0 correspond to negative numbers and points to the right of 0 correspond to positive numbers.

Of course, we can also construct a vertical number line. Consider the one in Figure A-3 alongside. As we move up this vertical number line, the numbers increase in value; conversely, as we descend, they decrease in value. Below 0 the numbers are negative, and above 0 the numbers are positive. And as on the horizontal number line, all the line segments are equal. This line is divided into segments such that the distance between −2 and −1 is the same as the distance between 0 and 1.

Combining Vertical and Horizontal Number Lines

By drawing the horizontal and vertical lines on the same sheet of paper, we are able to express the relationships between variables graphically. We do this in Figure A-4 on the facing page. We draw them (1) so that they intersect at each other's 0 point and (2) so that they are perpendicular to each other. The result is a set of coordinate axes, where each line is called an *axis*. When we have two axes, they span a *plane*.

For one number line, you need only one number to specify any point on the line. Equivalently, when you see a point on the line, you know that it represents one number or one value. With a coordinate value system, you need two numbers to specify a single point in the plane; when you see a single point on a graph, you know that it represents two numbers or two values.

FIGURE A-4
A Set of Coordinate Axes

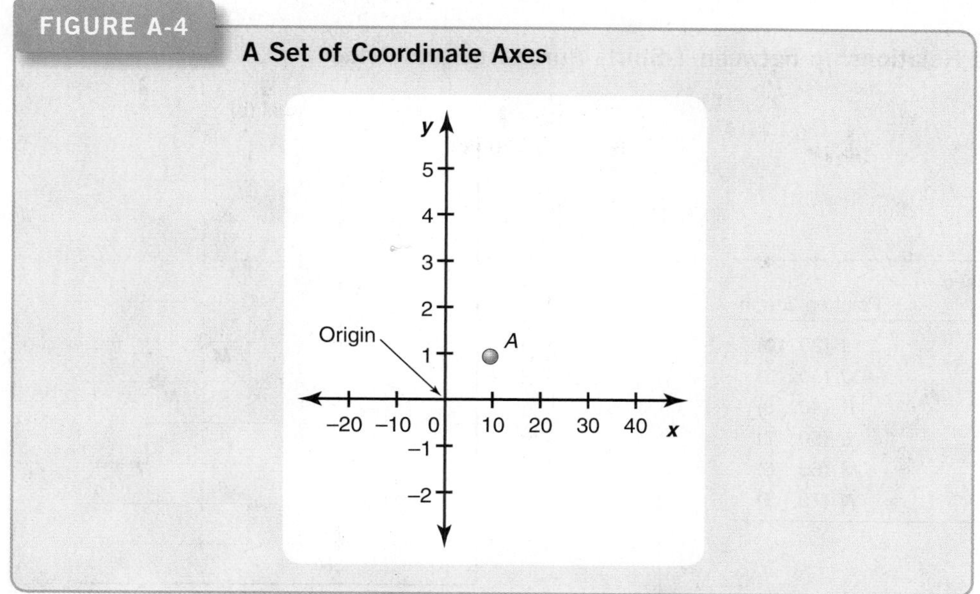

The basic things that you should know about a coordinate number system are that the vertical number line is referred to as the **y axis,** the horizontal number line is referred to as the **x axis,** and the point of intersection of the two lines is referred to as the **origin.**

y axis
The vertical axis in a graph.

x axis
The horizontal axis in a graph.

Origin
The intersection of the y axis and the x axis in a graph.

Any point such as A in Figure A-4 above represents two numbers—a value of x and a value of y. But we know more than that: We also know that point A represents a positive value of y because it is above the x axis, and we know that it represents a positive value of x because it is to the right of the y axis.

Point A represents a "paired observation" of the variables x and y; in particular, in Figure A-4, A represents an observation of the pair of values $x = 10$ and $y = 1$. Every point in the coordinate system corresponds to a paired observation of x and y, which can be simply written (x, y)—the x value is always specified first and then the y value. When we give the values associated with the position of point A in the coordinate number system, we are in effect giving the coordinates of that point. A's coordinates are $x = 10$, $y = 1$, or $(10, 1)$.

Graphing Numbers in a Table

Consider Table A-2 alongside. Column 1 shows different prices for T-shirts, and column 2 gives the number of T-shirts purchased per week at these prices. Notice the pattern of these numbers. As the price of T-shirts falls, the number of T-shirts purchased per week increases. Therefore, an inverse relationship exists between these two variables, and as soon as we represent it on a graph, you will be able to see the relationship. We can graph this relationship using a coordinate number system—a vertical and horizontal number line for each of these two variables. Such a graph is shown in panel (b) of Figure A-5 on the following page.

In economics, it is conventional to put dollar values on the y axis and quantities on the horizontal axis. We therefore construct a vertical number line for price and a horizontal number line, the x axis, for quantity of T-shirts purchased per week. The resulting coordinate system allows the plotting of each of the paired observation points. In panel (a), we repeat Table A-2, with a column added expressing these points in paired-data (x, y) form. For example, point J is the paired observation $(30, 9)$. It indicates that when the price of a T-shirt is \$9, 30 will be purchased per week.

TABLE A-2
T-Shirts Purchased

(1) Price of T-Shirts	(2) Number of T-Shirts Purchased per Week
$10	20
9	30
8	40
7	50
6	60
5	70

FIGURE A-5

Graphing the Relationship between T-Shirts Purchased and Price

Panel (a)

Price per T-Shirt	T-Shirts Purchased per Week	Point on Graph
$10	20	*I* (20, 10)
9	30	*J* (30, 9)
8	40	*K* (40, 8)
7	50	*L* (50, 7)
6	60	*M* (60, 6)
5	70	*N* (70, 5)

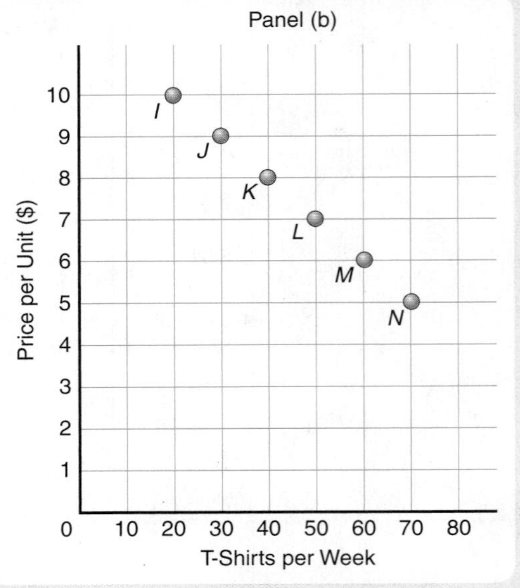

If it were possible to sell parts of a T-shirt ($\frac{1}{2}$ or $\frac{1}{20}$ of a shirt), we would have observations at every possible price. That is, we would be able to connect our paired observations, represented as lettered points. Let's assume that we can make T-shirts perfectly divisible so that the linear relationship shown in Figure A-5 also holds for fractions of dollars and T-shirts. We would then have a line that connects these points, as shown in the graph in Figure A-6 below.

In short, we have now represented the data from the table in the form of a graph. Note that an inverse relationship between two variables shows up on a graph as a line or curve that slopes *downward* from left to right. (You might as well get used to the idea that economists call a straight line a "curve" even though it may not curve at all. Economists' data frequently turn out to be curves, so they refer to everything represented graphically, even straight lines, as curves.)

FIGURE A-6

Connecting the Observation Points

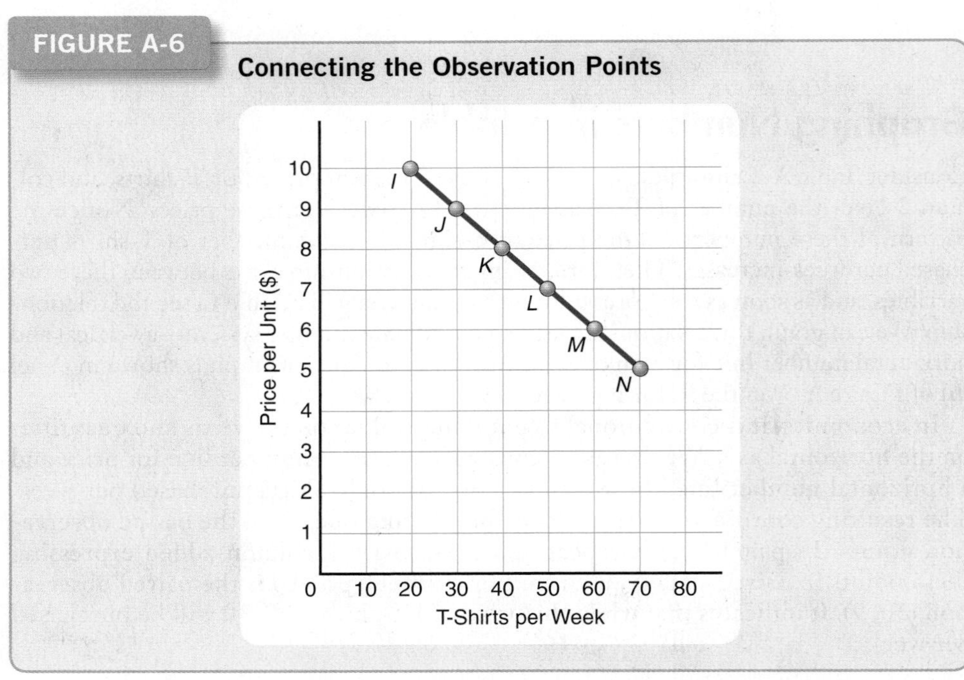

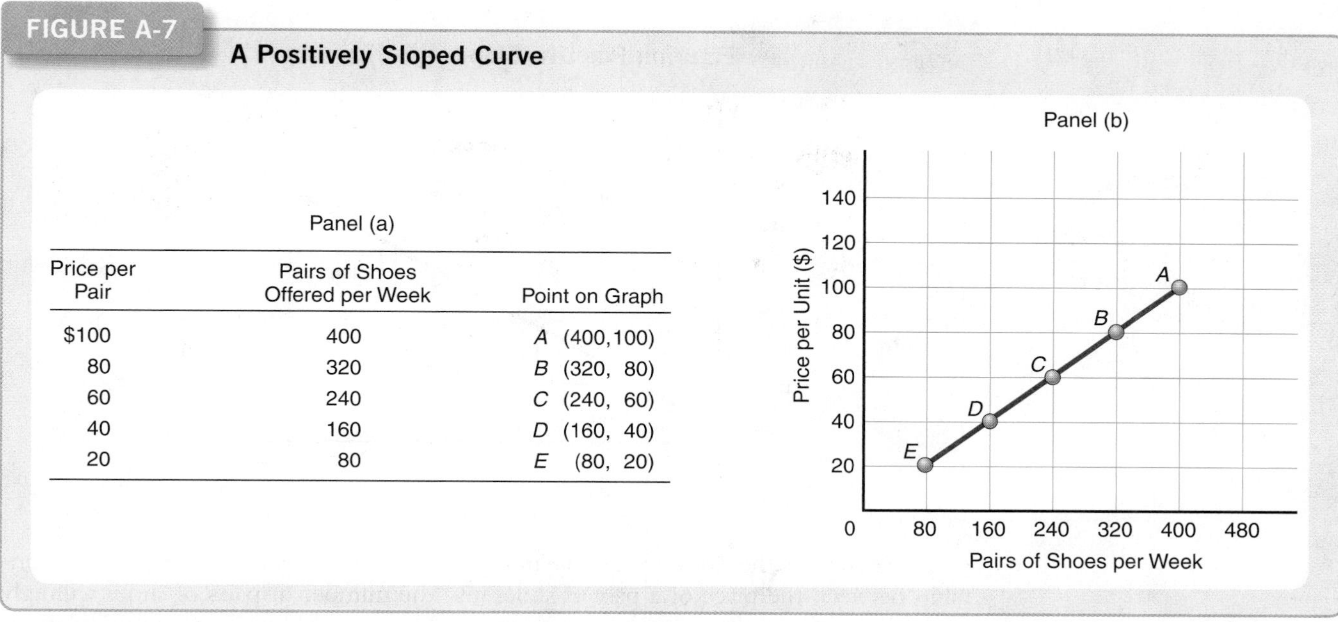

FIGURE A-7
A Positively Sloped Curve

Panel (a)

Price per Pair	Pairs of Shoes Offered per Week	Point on Graph
$100	400	*A* (400,100)
80	320	*B* (320, 80)
60	240	*C* (240, 60)
40	160	*D* (160, 40)
20	80	*E* (80, 20)

The Slope of a Line (A Linear Curve)

An important property of a curve represented on a graph is its *slope*. Consider Figure A-7 above, which represents the quantities of shoes per week that a seller is willing to offer at different prices. Note that in panel (a) of Figure A-7, as in Figure A-5 on page 20, we have expressed the coordinates of the points in parentheses in paired-data form.

Slope
The change in the *y* value divided by the corresponding change in the *x* value of a curve; the "incline" of the curve.

The **slope** of a line is defined as the change in the *y* values divided by the corresponding change in the *x* values as we move along the line. Let's move from point *E* to point *D* in panel (b) of Figure A-7. As we move, we note that the change in the *y* values, which is the change in price, is +20, because we have moved from a price of $20 to a price of $40 per pair. As we move from *E* to *D*, the change in the *x* values is +80; the number of pairs of shoes willingly offered per week rises from 80 to 160 pairs. The slope, calculated as a change in the *y* values divided by the change in the *x* values, is therefore

$$\frac{20}{80} = \frac{1}{4}$$

It may be helpful for you to think of slope as a "rise" (movement in the vertical direction) over a "run" (movement in the horizontal direction). We show this abstractly in Figure A-8 on the following page. The slope is the amount of rise divided by the amount of run. In the example in Figure A-8, and of course in Figure A-7 above, the amount of rise is positive and so is the amount of run. That's because it's a direct relationship. We show an inverse relationship in Figure A-9 on the next page. The slope is still equal to the rise divided by the run, but in this case the rise and the run have opposite signs because the curve slopes downward. That means that the slope is negative and that we are dealing with an inverse relationship.

Now let's calculate the slope for a different part of the curve in panel (b) of Figure A-7. We will find the slope as we move from point *B* to point *A*. Again, we note that the slope, or rise over run, from *B* to *A* equals

$$\frac{20}{80} = \frac{1}{4}$$

A specific property of a straight line is that its slope is the same between any two points. In other words, the slope is constant at all points on a straight line in a graph.

FIGURE A-8
Figuring Positive Slope

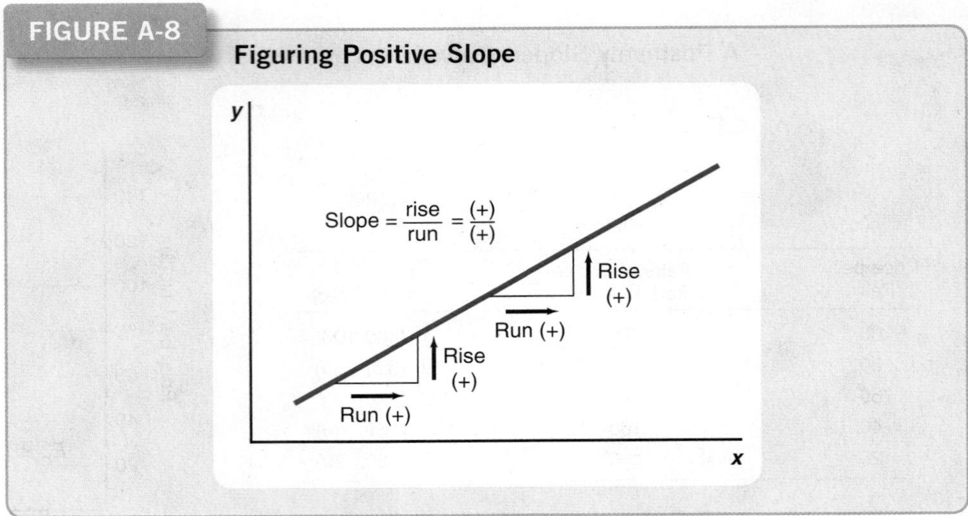

We conclude that for our example in Figure A-7 on the previous page, the relationship between the price of a pair of shoes and the number of pairs of shoes willingly offered per week is *linear*, which simply means "in a straight line," and our calculations indicate a constant slope. Moreover, we calculate a direct relationship between these two variables, which turns out to be an upward-sloping (from left to right) curve. Upward-sloping curves have positive slopes—in this case, the slope is $+\frac{1}{4}$.

We know that an inverse relationship between two variables is a downward-sloping curve—rise over run will be negative because the rise and run have opposite signs, as shown in Figure A-9 below. When we see a negative slope, we know that increases in one variable are associated with decreases in the other. Therefore, we say that downward-sloping curves have negative slopes. Can you verify that the slope of the graph representing the relationship between T-shirt prices and the quantity of T-shirts purchased per week in Figure A-6 on page 20 is $-\frac{1}{10}$?

Slopes of Nonlinear Curves

The graph presented in Figure A-10 on the facing page indicates a *nonlinear* relationship between two variables, total profits and output per unit of time. Inspection of this graph indicates that, at first, increases in output lead to increases in total profits; that is, total profits rise as output increases. But beyond some output level, further increases in output cause decreases in total profits.

FIGURE A-9
Figuring Negative Slope

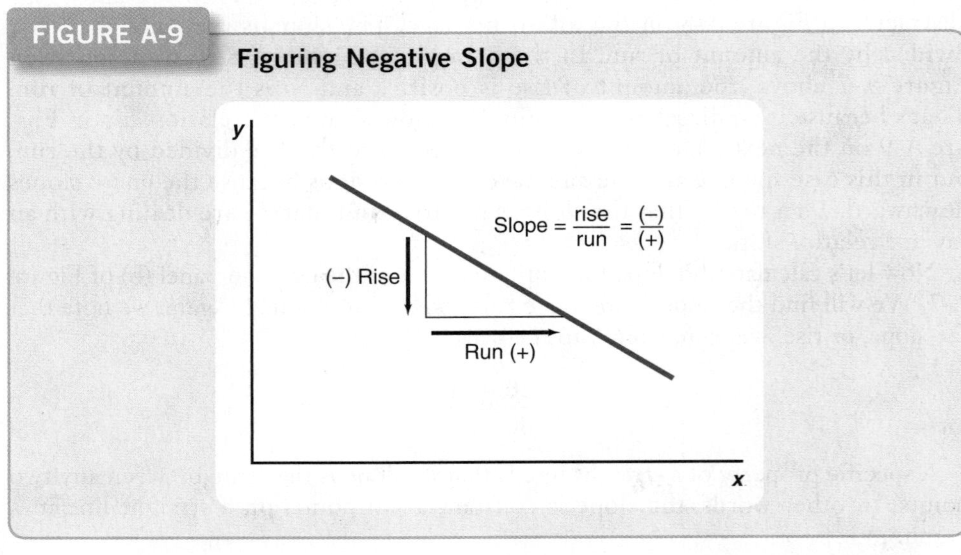

FIGURE A-10

The Slope of a Nonlinear Curve

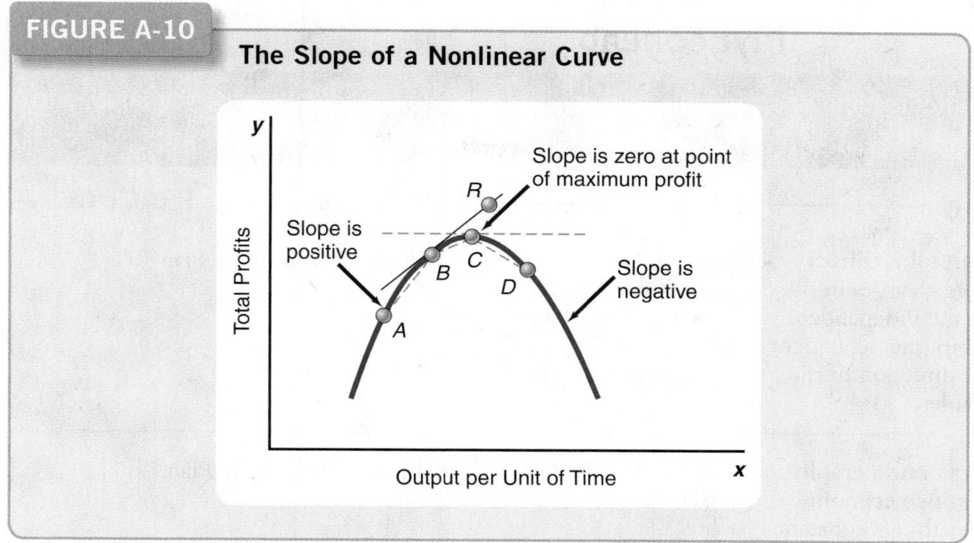

Can you see how this curve rises at first, reaches a peak at point *C*, and then falls? This curve relating total profits to output levels appears mountain-shaped.

Considering that this curve is nonlinear (it is obviously not a straight line), should we expect a constant slope when we compute changes in *y* divided by corresponding changes in *x* in moving from one point to another? A quick inspection, even without specific numbers, should lead us to conclude that the slopes of lines joining different points in this curve, such as between *A* and *B*, *B* and *C*, or *C* and *D*, will *not* be the same. The curve slopes upward (in a positive direction) for some values and downward (in a negative direction) for other values. In fact, the slope of the line between any two points on this curve will be different from the slope of the line between any two other points. Each slope will be different as we move along the curve.

Instead of using a line between two points to discuss slope, mathematicians and economists prefer to discuss the slope *at a particular point*. The slope at a point on the curve, such as point *B* in the graph in Figure A-10 above, is the slope of a line tangent to that point. A tangent line is a straight line that touches a curve at only one point. For example, it might be helpful to think of the tangent at *B* as the straight line that just "kisses" the curve at point *B*.

To calculate the slope of a tangent line, you need to have some additional information besides the two values of the point of tangency. For example, in Figure A-10, if we knew that the point *R* also lay on the tangent line and we knew the two values of that point, we could calculate the slope of the tangent line. We could calculate rise over run between points *B* and *R*, and the result would be the slope of the line tangent to the one point *B* on the curve.

MyEconLab

Here is what you should know after reading this appendix. MyEconLab will help you identify what you know, and where to go when you need to practice.

WHAT YOU SHOULD KNOW		WHERE TO GO TO PRACTICE
Direct and Inverse Relationships In a direct relationship, a dependent variable changes in the same direction as the change in the independent variable. In an inverse relationship, the dependent variable changes in the opposite direction of the change in the independent variable.	independent variable, 17 dependent variable, 17 direct relationship, 17 inverse relationship, 17	• MyEconLab Study Plan 1.7
Constructing a Graph When we draw a graph showing the relationship between two economic variables, we are holding all other things constant (the Latin term for which is *ceteris paribus*).	number line, 18 *y* axis, 19 *x* axis, 19 origin, 19	• MyEconLab Study Plan 1.8
Graphing Numbers We obtain a set of coordinates by putting vertical and horizontal number lines together. The vertical line is called the *y* axis; the horizontal line, the *x* axis.		• MyEconLab Study Plan 1.9
The Slope of a Linear Curve The slope of any linear (straight-line) curve is the change in the *y* values divided by the corresponding change in the *x* values as we move along the line. Otherwise stated, the slope is calculated as the amount of rise over the amount of run, where rise is movement in the vertical direction and run is movement in the horizontal direction.	slope, 21 **Key Figures** Figure A-8, 22 Figure A-9, 22	• MyEconLab Study Plan 1.10 • Animated Figures A-8, A-9
The Slope of a Nonlinear Curve The slope of a nonlinear curve changes; it is positive when the curve is rising and negative when the curve is falling. At a maximum or minimum point, the slope of the nonlinear curve is zero.	**Key Figure** Figure A-10, 23	• MyEconLab Study Plan 1.10 • Animated Figure A-10

Log in to MyEconLab, take an appendix test, and get a personalized Study Plan that tells you which concepts you understand and which ones you need to review. From there, MyEconLab will give you further practice, tutorials, animations, videos, and guided solutions. For more information, visit www.myeconlab.com

PROBLEMS

All problems are assignable in MyEconLab. *Answers to odd-numbered problems appear at the back of the book.*

A-1. Explain which is the independent variable and which is the dependent variable for each of the following examples. (See page 17.)

a. Once you determine the price of a notebook at the college bookstore, you will decide how many notebooks to buy.

b. You will decide how many credit hours to register for this semester once the university tells you how many work-study hours you will be assigned.

c. You anticipate earning a higher grade on your next economics exam because you studied more hours in the weeks preceding the exam.

A-2. For each of the following items, state whether a direct or an inverse relationship is likely to exist. (See page 17.)

a. The number of hours you study for an exam and your exam score

b. The price of pizza and the quantity purchased

c. The number of games the university basketball team won last year and the number of season tickets sold this year

A-3. Review Figure A-4 on page 19, and then state whether each of the following paired observations is on, above, or below the x axis and on, to the left of, or to the right of the y axis. (See page 19.)

a. $(-10, 4)$

b. $(20, -2)$

c. $(10, 0)$

A-4. State whether each of the following functions specifies a direct or an inverse relationship. (See page 17.)

a. $y = 5x$

b. $y = 10 - 2x$

c. $y = 3 + x$

d. $y = -3x$

A-5. Given the function $y = 5x$, complete the following schedule and plot the curve. (See page 20.)

y	x
	−4
	−2
	0
	2
	4

A-6. Given the function $y = 8 - 2x$, complete the following schedule and plot the curve. (See page 21.)

y	x
	−4
	−2
	0
	2
	4

A-7. Calculate the slope of the function you graphed in Problem A-5. (See page 21.)

A-8. Calculate the slope of the function you graphed in Problem A-6. (See page 21.)

2 Scarcity and the World of Trade-Offs

The airliner in which you have been flying will land about an hour earlier than indicated by your formal travel itinerary. As the plane taxis to the gate, you contemplate how to use that extra hour. You might eat a more leisurely dinner at a nicer restaurant, grab an extra hour of sleep, or engage in additional income-generating work. Now you find out the bad news: No empty gates are available for your plane, and you will have to wait at least one hour to exit the plane. Nonetheless, the airline can now report your flight as "on time" because it touched down on the ground earlier than officially scheduled. The result is that you must remain on the plane for the hour you thought would be available for another, most-valued use off the plane. Thus, you will have to give up the alternative use of that hour after all. As you will learn in this chapter, you have incurred an *opportunity cost.*

LEARNING OBJECTIVES

After reading this chapter, you should be able to:

- Evaluate whether even affluent people face the problem of scarcity
- Understand why economics considers individuals' "wants" but not their "needs"
- Explain why the scarcity problem induces individuals to consider opportunity costs
- Discuss why obtaining increasing increments of any particular good typically entails giving up more and more units of other goods
- Explain why the economy faces a trade-off between consumption goods and capital goods
- Distinguish between absolute and comparative advantage

MyEconLab helps you master each objective and study more efficiently. See end of chapter for details.

THAT...

the U.S. Department of Commerce recently published a report concluding ... umers spend about $1.2 trillion, or more than 11 percent of total consumer expenditures, on "non-essential items"? Included among these items were candy, gambling, jewelry, liquor, and pleasure boats. During the weeks that followed, media commentators filled newspaper pages, TV airtime, and the blogosphere with laments about U.S. residents making "poor economic decisions" by paying prices that are "too high" to buy goods and services that "they don't really need."

You will discover in this chapter that economists do not rely on the particularly subjective concept of "needs" to explain people's decisions. What influences individuals' economic choices are their *wants*, which, you learned in the previous chapter, are all of the items that people would purchase if they had unlimited income. In reality, of course, people's incomes *are* limited. Irrespective of normative judgments by U.S. government officials to classify some items as "non-essential," *all* of the items among which consumers allocate their limited incomes are *scarce* goods available only at prices greater than zero.

Scarcity

Whenever individuals or communities cannot obtain everything they desire simultaneously, they must make choices. Choices occur because of *scarcity*. **Scarcity** is the most basic concept in all of economics. Scarcity means that we do not ever have enough of everything, including time, to satisfy our *every* desire. Scarcity exists because human wants always exceed what can be produced with the limited resources and time that nature makes available.

Scarcity
A situation in which the ingredients for producing the things that people desire are insufficient to satisfy all wants at a zero price.

What Scarcity Is Not

Scarcity is not a shortage. After a hurricane hits and cuts off supplies to a community, TV newscasts often show people standing in line to get minimum amounts of cooking fuel and food. A news commentator might say that the line is caused by the "scarcity" of these products. But cooking fuel and food are always scarce—we cannot obtain all that we want at a zero price. Therefore, do not confuse the concept of scarcity, which is general and all-encompassing, with the concept of shortages as evidenced by people waiting in line to obtain a particular product.

Scarcity is not the same thing as poverty. Scarcity occurs among the poor and among the rich. Even the richest person on earth faces scarcity. For instance, even the world's richest person has only limited time available. Low income levels do not create more scarcity. High income levels do not create less scarcity.

Scarcity is a fact of life, like gravity. And just as physicists did not invent gravity, economists did not invent scarcity—it existed well before the first economist ever lived. It has existed at all times in the past and will exist at all times in the future.

Scarcity and Resources

Scarcity exists because resources are insufficient to satisfy our every desire. Resources are the inputs used in the production of the things that we want. **Production** can be defined as virtually any activity that results in the conversion of resources into products that can be used in consumption. Production includes delivering items from one part of the country to another. It includes taking ice from an ice tray to put it in your soft-drink glass. The resources used in production are called *factors of production*, and some economists use the terms *resources* and *factors of production* interchangeably. The total quantity of all resources that an economy has at any one time determines what that economy can produce.

Production
Any activity that results in the conversion of resources into products that can be used in consumption.

Factors of production can be classified in many ways. Here is one such classification:

1. *Land*. **Land** encompasses all the nonhuman gifts of nature, including timber, water, fish, minerals, and the original fertility of land. It is often called the *natural resource*.

Land
The natural resources that are available from nature. Land as a resource includes location, original fertility and mineral deposits, topography, climate, water, and vegetation.

2. *Labor*. **Labor** is the *human resource*, which includes productive contributions made by individuals who work, such as Web page designers, iPad applications creators, and professional football players.

Labor
Productive contributions of humans who work.

How has Japan's energy policy reduced the productive contributions of many individuals who provide labor?

INTERNATIONAL POLICY EXAMPLE

A Lower Productive Contribution of Sweltering Japanese Labor

During the past few years, the Japanese government has established rules aimed at reducing the nation's emissions of carbon dioxide (CO_2) by nearly 3 million tons each summer. To attain this goal, Japan's government has effectively declared war on air conditioning. The government has mandated that thermostats in all government offices be set no lower than 82 degrees during the months spanning June to September. Private Japanese businesses have followed suit with a "Cool Biz" program establishing 82 degrees as the "new office norm" for indoor temperatures.

Of course, 82 degrees is above the temperature at which people in enclosed spaces are most effective at producing goods and services. Consequently, the productive contribution of Japanese labor now declines every summer.

FOR CRITICAL THINKING

What do you suppose happened to the productive contribution of labor when Japan's government temporarily raised the summer target office temperature to 86 degrees?

Physical capital
All manufactured resources, including buildings, equipment, machines, and improvements to land that are used for production.

Human capital
The accumulated training and education of workers.

3. *Physical capital.* **Physical capital** consists of the factories and equipment used in production. It also includes improvements to natural resources, such as irrigation ditches.

4. *Human capital.* **Human capital** is the economic characterization of the education and training of workers. How much the nation produces depends not only on how many hours people work but also on how productive they are, and that in turn depends in part on education and training. To become more educated, individuals have to devote time and resources, just as a business has to devote resources if it wants to increase its physical capital. Whenever a worker's skills increase, human capital has been improved.

Entrepreneurship
The component of human resources that performs the functions of raising capital; organizing, managing, and assembling other factors of production; making basic business policy decisions; and taking risks.

5. *Entrepreneurship.* **Entrepreneurship** (actually a subdivision of labor) is the component of human resources that performs the functions of organizing, managing, and assembling the other factors of production to create and operate business ventures. Entrepreneurship also encompasses taking risks that involve the possibility of losing large sums of wealth. It includes new methods of engaging in common activities and generally experimenting with any type of new thinking that could lead to making more income. Without entrepreneurship, hardly any business organizations could continue to operate.

Goods versus Economic Goods

Goods
All things from which individuals derive satisfaction or happiness.

Economic goods
Goods that are scarce, for which the quantity demanded exceeds the quantity supplied at a zero price.

Services
Mental or physical labor or assistance purchased by consumers. Examples are the assistance of physicians, lawyers, dentists, repair personnel, housecleaners, educators, retailers, and wholesalers; items purchased or used by consumers that do not have physical characteristics.

Goods are defined as all things from which individuals derive satisfaction or happiness. Goods therefore include air to breathe and the beauty of a sunset as well as food, cars, and iPhones.

Economic goods are a subset of all goods—they are scarce goods, about which we must constantly make decisions regarding their best use. By definition, the desired quantity of an economic good exceeds the amount that is available at a zero price. Almost every example we use in economics concerns economic goods—cars, Blu-ray disc players, computers, socks, baseball bats, and corn. Weeds are a good example of *bads*—goods for which the desired quantity is much *less* than what nature provides at a zero price.

Sometimes you will see references to "goods and services." **Services** are tasks that are performed by individuals, often for someone else, such as laundry, Internet access, hospital care, restaurant meal preparation, car polishing, psychological counseling, and teaching. One way of looking at services is to think of them as *intangible goods*.

Wants and Needs

Wants are not the same as needs. Indeed, from the economist's point of view, the term *needs* is objectively undefinable. When someone says, "I need some new clothes," there is no way to know whether that person is stating a vague wish, a want, or a lifesaving requirement. If the individual making the statement were dying of exposure in a northern country during the winter, we might conclude that indeed the person does need clothes—perhaps not new ones, but at least some articles of warm clothing. Typically, however, the term *need* is used very casually in conversation. What people mean, usually, is that they desire something that they do not currently have.

Humans have unlimited wants. Just imagine that every single material want that you might have was satisfied. You could have all of the clothes, cars, houses, downloadable movies, yachts, and other items that you want. Does that mean that nothing else could add to your total level of happiness? Undoubtedly, you might continue to think of new goods and services that you could obtain, particularly as they came to market. You would also still be lacking in fulfilling all of your wants for compassion, friendship, love, affection, prestige, musical abilities, sports abilities, and the like.

In reality, every individual has competing wants but cannot satisfy all of them, given limited resources. This is the reality of scarcity. Each person must therefore make choices. Whenever a choice is made to produce or buy something, something else that is also desired is not produced or not purchased. In other words, in a world of scarcity, every want that ends up being satisfied causes one or more other wants to remain unsatisfied or to be forfeited.

QUICK QUIZ See page 47 for the answers. Review concepts from this section in MyEconLab.

__________ is the situation in which human wants always exceed what can be produced with the limited resources and time that nature makes available.

We use scarce resources, such as __________, __________, __________ and __________ capital, and __________, to produce economic goods—goods that are desired but are not directly obtainable from nature to the extent demanded or desired at a zero price.

__________ are unlimited. They include all material desires and all nonmaterial desires, such as love, affection, power, and prestige.

The concept of __________ is difficult to define objectively for every person. Consequently, we simply consider every person's wants to be unlimited. In a world of **scarcity,** satisfaction of one want necessarily means nonsatisfaction of one or more other wants.

Scarcity, Choice, and Opportunity Cost

The natural fact of scarcity implies that we must make choices. One of the most important results of this fact is that every choice made means that some opportunity must be sacrificed. Every choice involves giving up an opportunity to produce or consume something else.

Valuing Forgone Alternatives

Consider a practical example. Every choice you make to study economics for one more hour requires that you give up the opportunity to choose to engage in any one of the following activities: study more of another subject, listen to music, sleep, browse at a local store, read a novel, or work out at the gym. The most highly valued of these opportunities is forgone if you choose to study economics an additional hour.

Because there were so many alternatives from which to choose, how could you determine the value of what you gave up to engage in that extra hour of studying economics? First of all, no one else can tell you the answer because only *you* can put a value on the alternatives forgone. Only you know the value of another hour of sleep or of an hour looking for the latest digital music downloads—whatever one activity *you* would have chosen if you had not opted to study economics for that hour. That means that only you can determine the highest-valued, next-best alternative that you had to sacrifice in order to study economics one more hour. Only you can determine the value of the next-best alternative.

Opportunity Cost

Opportunity cost
The highest-valued, next-best alternative that must be sacrificed to obtain something or to satisfy a want.

The value of the next-best alternative is called **opportunity cost.** The opportunity cost of any action is the value of what is given up—the next-highest-ranked alternative—because a choice was made. What is important is the choice that you would have made if you hadn't studied one more hour. Your opportunity cost is the *next-highest-ranked* alternative, not *all* alternatives.

YOU ARE THERE

To consider why perceived opportunity costs induce residents of South Korea to work more hours each year than workers in many other countries and, hence, take fewer vacation days, read **The Opportunity Cost of Vacation Time in South Korea** on page 41.

In economics, cost is always a forgone opportunity.

One way to think about opportunity cost is to understand that when you choose to do something, you lose something else. What you lose is being able to engage in your next-highest-valued alternative. The cost of your chosen alternative is what you lose, which is by definition your next-highest-valued alternative. This is your opportunity cost.

What has a decrease in the daily amount of time spent working by a typical U.S. resident revealed about the opportunity cost of approximately a quarter hour of time?

EXAMPLE

The Opportunity Cost of 17 Minutes of Labor in the United States

In the aftermath of the significant economic downturn between 2007 and 2009, the average U.S. resident aged 15 years or older found herself working about 17 fewer minutes per day. The U.S. Labor Department has determined that there were no changes in the amounts of time that the typical resident devoted to engaging in pursuits such as education, volunteering, exercise, or religious activities. Instead, the amount of time per day that the average U.S. resident spent watching TV rose by nearly 12 minutes, and the amount of time she spent sleeping increased by more than 5 minutes. Hence, the implied opportunity cost of the 17 minutes per day that previously had been spent working is the value of passive leisure time that otherwise would have been devoted to TV viewing and sleeping.

FOR CRITICAL THINKING

For someone who could otherwise be working but decides to devote an extra hour per day to obtaining education, what is the opportunity cost of that hour of learning?

The World of Trade-Offs

Whenever you engage in any activity using any resource, even time, you are *trading off* the use of that resource for one or more alternative uses. The extent of the trade-off is represented by the opportunity cost. The opportunity cost of studying economics has already been mentioned—it is the value of the next-best alternative. When you think of *any* alternative, you are thinking of trade-offs.

Let's consider a hypothetical example of a trade-off between the results of spending time studying economics and mathematics. For the sake of this argument, we will assume that additional time studying either economics or mathematics will lead to a higher grade in the subject to which additional study time is allocated. One of the best ways to examine this trade-off is with a graph. (If you would like a refresher on graphical techniques, study Appendix A at the end of Chapter 1 before going on.)

Graphical Analysis

In Figure 2-1 on the facing page, the expected grade in mathematics is measured on the vertical axis of the graph, and the expected grade in economics is measured on the horizontal axis. We simplify the world and assume that you have a maximum of

FIGURE 2-1

Production Possibilities Curve for Grades in Mathematics and Economics (Trade-Offs)

We assume that only 12 hours can be spent per week on studying. If the student is at point *x*, equal time (6 hours a week) is spent on both courses, and equal grades of C will be received. If a higher grade in economics is desired, the student may go to point *y*, thereby receiving a B in economics but a D in mathematics. At point *y*, 3 hours are spent on mathematics and 9 hours on economics.

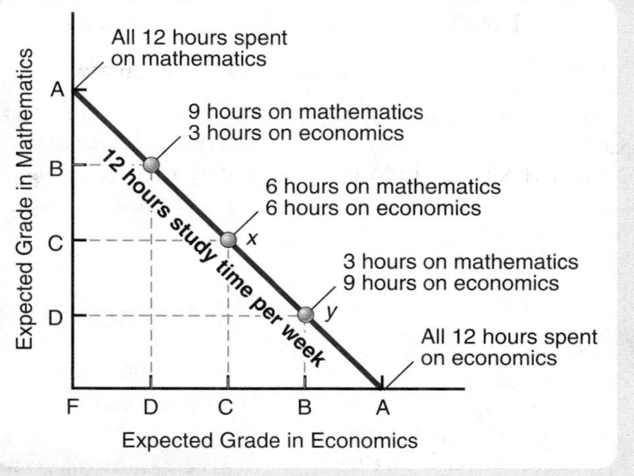

12 hours per week to spend studying these two subjects and that if you spend all 12 hours on economics, you will get an A in the course. You will, however, fail mathematics. Conversely, if you spend all of your 12 hours studying mathematics, you will get an A in that subject, but you will flunk economics. Here the trade-off is a special case: one to one. A one-to-one trade-off means that the opportunity cost of receiving one grade higher in economics (for example, improving from a C to a B) is one grade lower in mathematics (falling from a C to a D).

The Production Possibilities Curve (PPC)

The graph in Figure 2-1 above illustrates the relationship between the possible results that can be produced in each of two activities, depending on how much time you choose to devote to each activity. This graph shows a representation of a **production possibilities curve (PPC).**

Production possibilities curve (PPC) A curve representing all possible combinations of maximum outputs that could be produced, assuming a fixed amount of productive resources of a given quality.

Consider that you are producing a grade in economics when you study economics and a grade in mathematics when you study mathematics. Then the line that goes from A on one axis to A on the other axis therefore becomes a production possibilities curve. It is defined as the maximum quantity of one good or service that can be produced, given that a specific quantity of another is produced. It is a curve that shows the possibilities available for increasing the output of one good or service by reducing the amount of another. In the example in Figure 2-1, your time for studying was limited to 12 hours per week. The two possible outputs were your grade in mathematics and your grade in economics. The particular production possibilities curve presented in Figure 2-1 is a graphical representation of the opportunity cost of studying one more hour in one subject. It is a *straight-line production possibilities curve*, which is a special case. (The more general case will be discussed next.)

If you decide to be at point *x* in Figure 2-1, you will devote 6 hours of study time to mathematics and 6 hours to economics. The expected grade in each course will be a C. If you are more interested in getting a B in economics, you will go to point *y* on the production possibilities curve, spending only 3 hours on mathematics but 9 hours on economics. Your expected grade in mathematics will then drop from a C to a D.

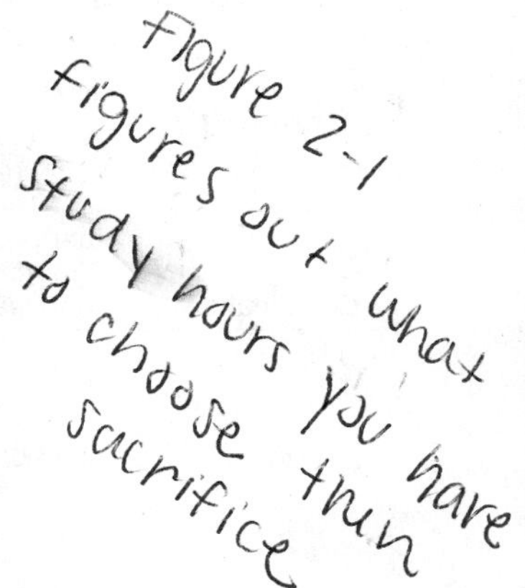

Note that these trade-offs between expected grades in mathematics and economics are the result of *holding constant* total study time as well as all other factors that might influence your ability to learn, such as computerized study aids. Quite clearly, if you were able to spend more total time studying, it would be possible to have higher grades in both economics and mathematics. In that case, however, we would no longer be on the specific production possibilities curve illustrated in Figure 2-1. We would have to draw a new curve, farther to the right, to show the greater total study time and a different set of possible trade-offs.

QUICK QUIZ See page 47 for the answers. Review concepts from this section in MyEconLab.

Scarcity requires us to choose. Whenever we choose, we lose the ________-________-valued alternative.

Cost is always a forgone ________.

Another way to look at **opportunity cost** is the trade-off that occurs when one activity is undertaken rather than the ________-________ alternative activity.

A ________ ________ curve graphically shows the trade-off that occurs when more of one output is obtained at the sacrifice of another. This curve is a graphical representation of, among other things, opportunity cost.

The Choices a Nation's Economy Faces

The straight-line production possibilities curve presented in Figure 2-1 on the previous page can be generalized to demonstrate the related concepts of scarcity, choice, and trade-offs that our entire nation faces. As you will see, the production possibilities curve is a simple but powerful economic model because it can demonstrate these related concepts.

A Two-Good Example

The example we will use is the choice between the production of smartphones and tablet devices. We assume for the moment that these are the only two goods that can be produced in the nation.

Panel (a) of Figure 2-2 below gives the various combinations of smartphones and tablet devices, or tablets, that are possible. If all resources are devoted to smartphone production, 50 million per year can be produced. If all resources are devoted to production of tablets, 60 million per year can be produced. In between are various possible combinations.

FIGURE 2-2

The Trade-Off between Smartphones and Tablet Devices

The production of smartphones and tablet devices is measured in millions of units per year. The various combinations are given in panel (a) and plotted in panel (b). Connecting the points *A*–*G* with a relatively smooth line gives society's production possibilities curve for smartphones and tablets. Point *R* lies outside the production possibilities curve and is therefore unattainable at the point in time for which the graph is drawn. Point *S* lies inside the production possibilities curve and therefore entails unemployed or underemployed resources.

Panel (a)

Combination	Smartphones (millions per year)	Tablets (millions per year)
A	50.0	0
B	48.0	10
C	45.0	20
D	40.0	30
E	33.0	40
F	22.5	50
G	0.0	60

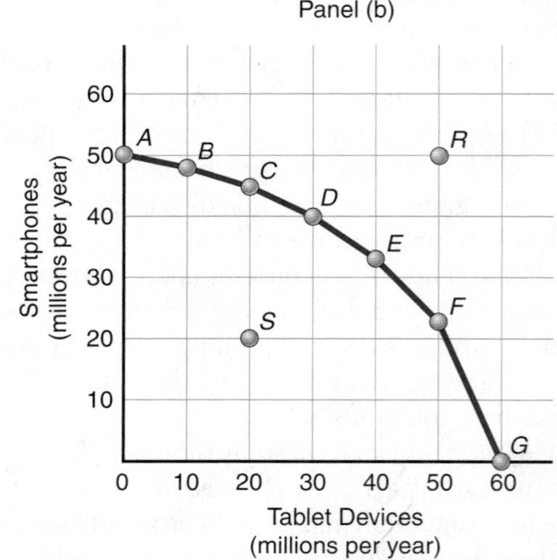

Production Trade-Offs

The nation's production combinations are plotted as points *A*, *B*, *C*, *D*, *E*, *F*, and *G* in panel (b) of Figure 2-2 on the previous page. If these points are connected with a smooth curve, the nation's production possibilities curve (PPC) is shown, demonstrating the trade-off between the production of smartphones and tablets. These trade-offs occur *on* the PPC.

Notice the major difference in the shape of the production possibilities curves in Figure 2-1 on page 31 and Figure 2-2. In Figure 2-1, there is a constant trade-off between grades in economics and in mathematics. In Figure 2-2, the trade-off between production of smartphones and tablet production is not constant, and therefore the PPC is a *bowed* curve. To understand why the production possibilities curve is typically bowed outward, you must understand the assumptions underlying the PPC.

Go to **www.econtoday.com/chap02** for one perspective, offered by the National Center for Policy Analysis, on whether society's production decisions should be publicly or privately coordinated.

How has a trade-off between roads and factories contributed to traffic problems in China?

INTERNATIONAL EXAMPLE

In China, More Factories Mean Fewer Roads—and More Traffic

Recently, a 62-mile section of highway between the Chinese cities of Beijing and Zhangjiakou became ensnarled in a massive traffic jam that took public safety officers nearly two weeks to break up. Traffic experts agree that this stretch of highway, which covers less than 0.7 square mile of area stretched thinly along the 62 miles, is often overburdened with much more traffic than it was designed to handle.

Most observers agree that this state of affairs has arisen because the people of China have allocated resources away from road construction in favor of building new manufacturing facilities. These facilities, though, churn out more products to be shipped by trucks that clog roads. Thus, in China the choice to build more factories to produce goods has entailed an opportunity cost: fewer roads for transporting those goods.

FOR CRITICAL THINKING

What is an example of an opportunity cost that a trucker may have incurred by spending a full day traversing the traffic jam between Beijing and Zhangjiakou?

Assumptions Underlying the Production Possibilities Curve

When we draw the curve that is shown in Figure 2-2, we make the following assumptions:

1. Resources are fully employed.
2. Production takes place over a specific time period—for example, one year.
3. The resource inputs, in both quantity and quality, used to produce smartphones or tablets are fixed over this time period.
4. Technology does not change over this time period.

Technology is defined as the total pool of applied knowledge concerning how goods and services can be produced by managers, workers, engineers, scientists, and artisans, using land, physical and human capital, and entrepreneurship. You can think of technology as the formula or recipe used to combine factors of production. (When better formulas are developed, more production can be obtained from the same amount of resources.) The level of technology sets the limit on the amount and types of goods and services that we can derive from any given amount of resources. The production possibilities curve is drawn under the assumption that we use the best technology that we currently have available and that this technology doesn't change over the time period under study.

Technology
The total pool of applied knowledge concerning how goods and services can be produced.

WHAT IF... **the U.S. government tries to increase total production of all goods by diverting resources to the manufacture of "green" products?**

Some government officials suggest that shifting existing resources away from producing other goods and services to the manufacture of "green" products believed to be safer for the environment will lead to greater overall production of all items. In fact, with a fixed set of available resources and an unchanged technology, shifting resources to making more green products necessarily shifts those resources away from producing other items. As a consequence, production of other goods and services must decrease when the government diverts resources to the manufacture of "green" products.

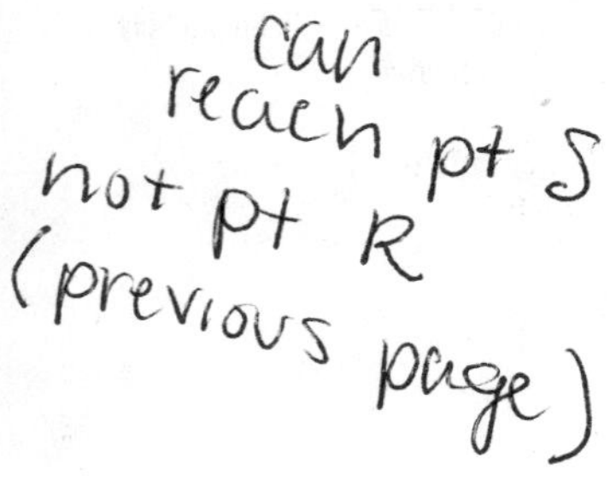

Being off the Production Possibilities Curve

Look again at panel (b) of Figure 2-2 on page 32. Point *R* lies *outside* the production possibilities curve and is *impossible* to achieve during the time period assumed. By definition, the PPC indicates the *maximum* quantity of one good, given the quantity produced of the other good.

It is possible, however, to be at point *S* in Figure 2-2. That point lies beneath the PPC. If the nation is at point *S*, it means that its resources are not being fully utilized. This occurs, for example, during periods of relatively high unemployment. Point *S* and all such points inside the PPC are always attainable but imply unemployed or underemployed resources.

Efficiency

The production possibilities curve can be used to define the notion of efficiency. Whenever the economy is operating on the PPC, at points such as *A*, *B*, *C*, or *D*, we say that its production is efficient. Points such as *S* in Figure 2-2, which lie beneath the PPC, are said to represent production situations that are not efficient.

Efficiency
The case in which a given level of inputs is used to produce the maximum output possible. Alternatively, the situation in which a given output is produced at minimum cost.

Efficiency can mean many things to many people. Even in economics, there are different types of efficiency. Here we are discussing *productive efficiency*. An economy is productively efficient whenever it is producing the maximum output with given technology and resources.

A simple commonsense definition of efficiency is getting the most out of what we have. Clearly, we are not getting the most out of what we have if we are at point *S* in panel (b) of Figure 2-2. We can move from point *S* to, say, point *C*, thereby increasing the total quantity of smartphones produced without any decrease in the total quantity of tablets produced. Alternatively, we can move from point *S* to point *E*, for example, and have both more smartphones and more tablets. Point *S* is called an **inefficient point,** which is defined as any point below the production possibilities curve.

Inefficient point
Any point below the production possibilities curve, at which the use of resources is not generating the maximum possible output.

The Law of Increasing Additional Cost

In the example in Figure 2-1 on page 31, the trade-off between a grade in mathematics and a grade in economics was one to one. The trade-off ratio was constant. That is, the production possibilities curve was a straight line. The curve in Figure 2-2 is a more general case. We have re-created the curve in Figure 2-2 as Figure 2-3 on the facing page. Each combination, *A* through *G*, of smartphones and tablets is represented on the PPC. Starting with the production of zero tablets, the nation can produce 50 million smartphones with its available resources and technology.

INCREASING ADDITIONAL COSTS When we increase production of tablet devices from zero to 10 million per year, the nation has to give up in smartphones an amount shown by that first vertical arrow, *Aa*. From panel (a) of Figure 2-2, you can see that this is 2 million per year (50 million minus 48 million). Again, if we increase production of tablets by another 10 million units per year, we go from *B* to *C*. In order to do so, the nation has to give up the vertical distance *Bb*, or 3 million smartphones per year. By the time we go from 50 million to 60 million tablets, to obtain that 10 million increase, we have to forgo the vertical distance *Ff*, or 22.5 million smartphones.

FIGURE 2-3

The Law of Increasing Additional Cost

Consider equal increments of production of tablets, as measured on the horizontal axis. All of the horizontal arrows—*aB, bC,* and so on—are of equal length (10 million). In contrast, the length of each vertical arrow—*Aa, Bb,* and so on—increases as we move down the production possibilities curve. Hence, the opportunity cost of going from 50 million tablets per year to 60 million (*Ff*) is much greater than going from zero units to 10 million (*Aa*). The opportunity cost of each additional equal increase in production of tablets rises.

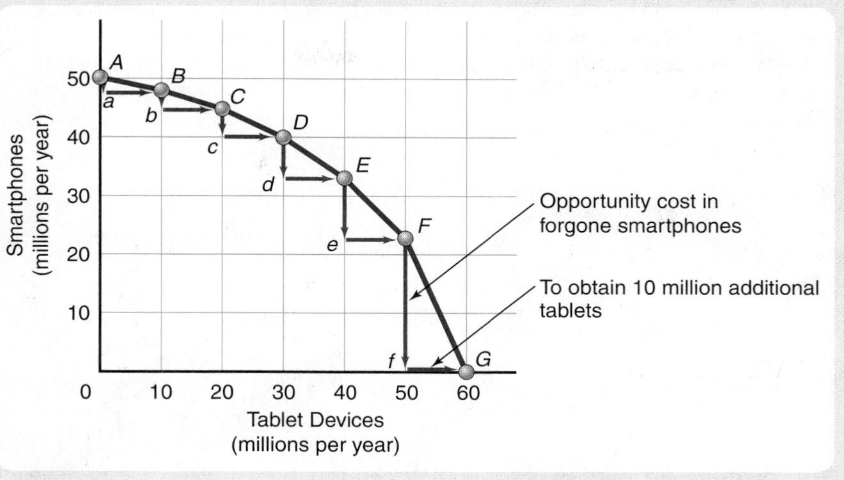

In other words, we see that the opportunity cost of the last 10 million tablets has increased to 22.5 million smartphones, compared to 2 million smartphones for the same increase in tablets when we started with none at all being produced.

What we are observing is called the **law of increasing additional cost.** When people take more resources and applies them to the production of any specific good, the opportunity cost increases for each additional unit produced.

Law of increasing additional cost
The fact that the opportunity cost of additional units of a good generally increases as people attempt to produce more of that good. This accounts for the bowed-out shape of the production possibilities curve.

EXPLAINING THE LAW OF INCREASING ADDITIONAL COST The reason that as a nation we face the law of increasing additional cost (shown as a production possibilities curve that is bowed outward) is that certain resources are better suited for producing some goods than they are for other goods. Generally, resources are not *perfectly* adaptable for alternative uses. When increasing the output of a particular good, producers must use less suitable resources than those already used in order to produce the additional output. Hence, the cost of producing the additional units increases.

With respect to our hypothetical example here, at first the computing specialists at smartphone firms would shift over to producing tablet devices. After a while, though, the workers who normally design and produce smartphones would be asked to help design and manufacture tablet components. Typically, they would be less effective at making tablets than the people who previously specialized in this task.

In general, *the more specialized the resources, the more bowed the production possibilities curve*. At the other extreme, if all resources are equally suitable for smartphone production or production of tablets, the curves in Figures 2-2 (p. 32) and 2-3 above would approach the straight line shown in our first example in Figure 2-1 on page 31.

QUICK QUIZ See page 47 for the answers. Review concepts from this section in MyEconLab.

Trade-offs are represented graphically by a production possibilites curve showing the maximum quantity of one good or service that can be produced, given a specific quantity of another, from a given set of resources over a specified period of time—for example, one year.

A **production possibilities curve** is drawn holding the quantity and quality of all resources fixed over the time period under study.

Points outside the **production possibilities curve** are unattainable. Points inside are attainable but represent an inefficient use or underuse of available resources.

Because many resources are better suited for certain productive tasks than for others, the production possibilities curve is bowed outward, reflecting the **law of increasing additional cost.**

FIGURE 2-4

Economic Growth Allows for More of Everything

If the nation experiences economic growth, the production possibilities curve between smartphones and tablets will move out as shown. This output increase takes time, however, and it does not occur automatically. This means, therefore, that we can have more of both smartphones and tablets only after a period of time during which we have experienced economic growth.

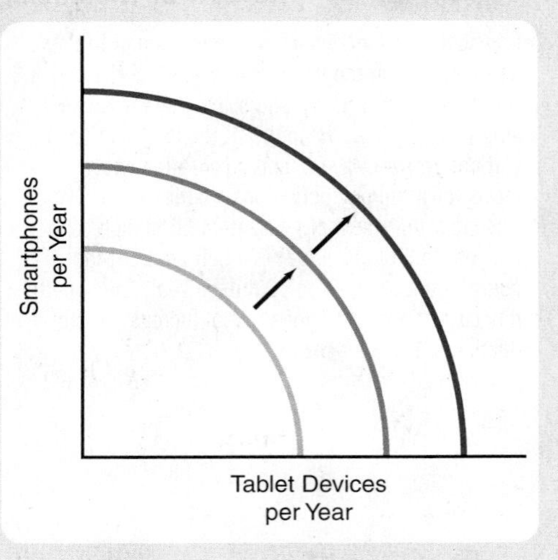

Economic Growth and the Production Possibilities Curve

At any particular point in time, a society cannot be outside the production possibilities curve. *Over time*, however, it is possible to have more of everything. This occurs through economic growth. (An important reason for economic growth, capital accumulation, is discussed next. A more complete discussion of why economic growth occurs appears in Chapter 9.) Figure 2-4 above shows the production possibilities curve for smartphones and tablet devices shifting outward. The two additional curves shown represent new choices open to an economy that has experienced economic growth. Such economic growth occurs for many reasons, including increases in the number of workers and productive investment in equipment.

Scarcity still exists, however, no matter how much economic growth there is. At any point in time, we will always be on some production possibilities curve. Thus, we will always face trade-offs. The more we have of one thing, the less we can have of others.

If economic growth occurs in the nation, the production possibilities curve between smartphones and tablets moves outward, as shown in Figure 2-4. This takes time and does not occur automatically. One reason it will occur involves the choice about how much to consume today.

The Trade-Off between the Present and the Future

Consumption
The use of goods and services for personal satisfaction.

The production possibilities curve and economic growth can be combined to examine the trade-off between present **consumption** and future consumption. When we consume today, we are using up what we call consumption or consumer goods—food and clothes, for example.

Why We Make Capital Goods

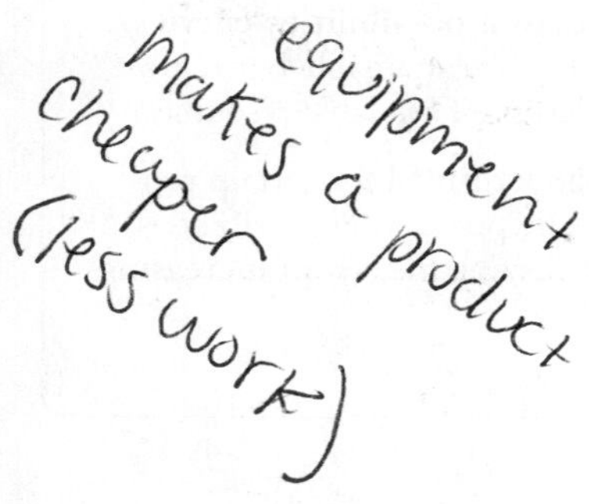

Why would we be willing to use productive resources to make things—capital goods—that we cannot consume directly? The reason is that capital goods enable us to produce larger quantities of consumer goods or to produce them less expensively than we otherwise could. Before fish are "produced" for the market, equipment such as fishing boats, nets, and poles is produced first. Imagine how expensive it would be to obtain fish for market without using these capital goods. Catching fish with one's hands is not an easy task. The cost per fish would be very high if capital goods weren't used.

Forgoing Current Consumption

Whenever we use productive resources to make capital goods, we are implicitly forgoing current consumption. We are waiting for some time in the future to consume the rewards that will be reaped from the use of capital goods. In effect, when we forgo current consumption to invest in capital goods, we are engaging in an economic activity that is forward-looking—we do not get instant utility or satisfaction from our activity.

The Trade-Off between Consumption Goods and Capital Goods

opportunity cost is involved

To have more consumer goods in the future, we must accept fewer consumer goods today, because resources must be used in producing capital goods instead of consumer goods. In other words, an opportunity cost is involved. Every time we make a choice of more goods today, we incur an opportunity cost of fewer goods tomorrow, and every time we make a choice of more goods in the future, we incur an opportunity cost of fewer goods today. With the resources that we don't use to produce consumer goods for today, we invest in capital goods that will produce more consumer goods for us later. The trade-off is shown in Figure 2-5 below. On the left in panel (a), you can see this trade-off depicted as a production possibilities curve between capital goods and consumption goods.

Assume that we are willing to give up $1 trillion worth of consumption today. We will be at point *A* in the left-hand diagram of panel (a). This will allow the economy to grow. We will have more future consumption because we invested in more capital goods today. In the right-hand diagram of panel (a), we see two consumer goods represented, food and entertainment. The production possibilities

FIGURE 2-5

Capital Goods and Growth

In panel (a), people choose not to consume $1 trillion, so they invest that amount in capital goods. As a result, more of all goods may be produced in the future, as shown in the right-hand diagram in panel (a). In panel (b), people choose even more capital goods (point *C*). The result is that the production possibilities curve (PPC) moves even more to the right on the right-hand diagram in panel (b).

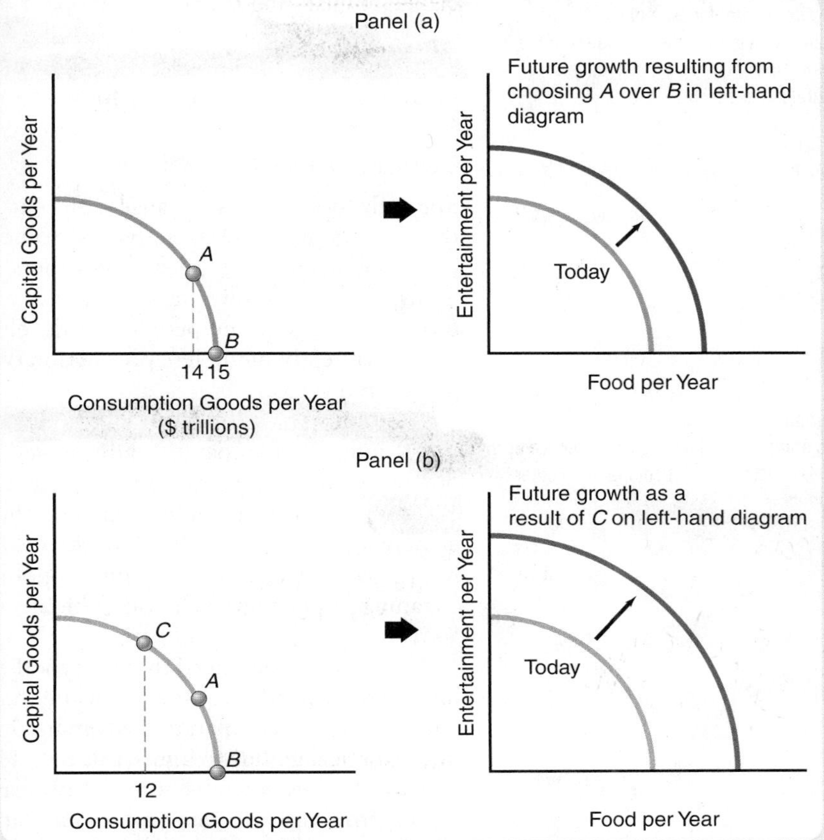

Panel (a)

Capital Goods per Year
A
B
14 15
Consumption Goods per Year ($ trillions)

Future growth resulting from choosing *A* over *B* in left-hand diagram
Entertainment per Year
Today
Food per Year

Panel (b)

Capital Goods per Year
C
A
B
12
Consumption Goods per Year

Future growth as a result of *C* on left-hand diagram
Entertainment per Year
Today
Food per Year

curve will move outward if individuals in the economy decide to restrict consumption now and invest in capital goods.

In panel (b) in Figure 2-5 on the previous page, we show the results of our willingness to forgo even more current consumption. We move from point A to point C in the left-hand side, where we have many fewer consumer goods today but produce many more capital goods. This leads to more future growth in this simplified model, and thus the production possibilities curve in the right-hand side of panel (b) shifts outward more than it did in the right-hand side of panel (a). In other words, the more we give up today, the more we can have tomorrow, provided, of course, that the capital goods are productive in future periods.

QUICK QUIZ See page 47 for the answers. Review concepts from this section in MyEconLab.

_____ goods are goods that will later be used to produce consumer goods.

A trade-off is involved between current consumption and capital goods or, alternatively, between current consumption and future consumption. The _____ we invest in capital goods today, the greater the amount of consumer goods we can produce in the future and the _____ the amount of consumer goods we can produce today.

Specialization and Greater Productivity

Specialization
The organization of economic activity so that what each person (or region) consumes is not identical to what that person (or region) produces. An individual may specialize, for example, in law or medicine. A nation may specialize in the production of coffee, e-book readers, or digital cameras.

Specialization involves working at a relatively well-defined, limited endeavor, such as accounting or teaching. Most individuals do specialize. For example, you could change the oil in your car if you wanted to. Typically, though, you take your car to a garage and let the mechanic change the oil. You benefit by letting the garage mechanic specialize in changing the oil and in doing other repairs on your car.

The specialist normally will get the job finished sooner than you could and has the proper equipment to make the job go more smoothly. Specialization usually leads to greater productivity, not only for each individual but also for the nation.

Comparative Advantage

Specialization occurs because different individuals experience different costs when they engage in the same activities. Some individuals can accurately solve mathematical problems at lower cost than others who might try to solve the same problems. Thus, those who solve math problems at lower cost sacrifice production of fewer alternative items. Some people can develop more high-quality iPad applications than others while giving up less production of other items, such as clean houses and neatly manicured yards.

Comparative advantage
The ability to produce a good or service at a lower opportunity cost compared to other producers.

Comparative advantage is the ability to perform an activity *at a lower opportunity cost*. You have a comparative advantage in one activity whenever you have a lower opportunity cost of performing that activity. Comparative advantage is always a *relative* concept. You may be able to change the oil in your car. You might even be able to change it faster than the local mechanic. But if the opportunity cost you face by changing the oil exceeds the mechanic's opportunity cost, the mechanic has a comparative advantage in changing the oil. The mechanic faces a lower opportunity cost for that activity.

You may be convinced that everybody can do more of everything than you can during the same period of time and using the same resources. In this extreme situation, do you still have a comparative advantage? The answer is yes. You do not have to be a mathematical genius to figure this out. The market tells you so very clearly by offering you the highest income for the job for which you have a comparative advantage. Stated differently, to find your comparative advantage, simply find the job that maximizes your income.

When contemplating how to keep track of balances remaining on gift cards, some people find that doing their own tabulations entails a higher opportunity cost than others face. How has this increased opportunity cost given entrepreneurs an occasion to profit from providing gift-card tracking services?

EXAMPLE

A Comparative Advantage in Watching Gift-Card Balances

Each year, consumers juggle a total of $100 billion in balances on gift cards. Keeping track of these funds and making certain all funds are spent can require considerable time.

Increasingly, people are deciding that taking the time to keep tabs on their gift-card balances is a next-best alternative. These individuals pay others to make sure they are spending all available funds. For instance, a firm called Tango Card uses software to track gift-card balances and provide periodic reports to consumers. The company also sends e-mails warning consumers when unused cards are about to expire before all funds have been spent. The fact that owners of Tango Card have a comparative advantage in keeping tabs on gift-card balances enables its customers to devote extra time to other activities, such as earning additional income.

FOR CRITICAL THINKING

What is the comparative advantage of customers of Tango Cards who devote time to earning income instead of tracking their card balances?

Absolute Advantage

Suppose that you are the president of a firm and are convinced that you have the ability to do every job in that company faster than everyone else who works there. You might be able to enter data into a spreadsheet program faster than any of the other employees, file documents in order in a file cabinet faster than any of the file clerks, and wash windows faster than any of the window washers. Furthermore, you are able to manage the firm in less time more effectively than any other individual in the company.

If all of these self-perceptions were really true, then you would have an **absolute advantage** in all of these endeavors. In other words, if you were to spend a given amount of time in any one of them, you could produce more than anyone else in the company. Nonetheless, you would not spend your time doing these other activities. Why not? Because your time advantage in undertaking the president's managerial duties is even greater. Therefore, you would find yourself specializing in that particular task even though you have an *absolute* advantage in all these other tasks. Indeed, absolute advantage is irrelevant in predicting how you will allocate your time. Only *comparative advantage* matters in determining how you will allocate your time, because it is the relative cost that is important in making this choice.

Absolute advantage
The ability to produce more units of a good or service using a given quantity of labor or resource inputs. Equivalently, the ability to produce the same quantity of a good or service using fewer units of labor or resource inputs.

The coaches of sports teams often have to determine the comparative advantage of an individual player who has an absolute advantage in every aspect of the sport in question. Babe Ruth, who could hit more home runs and pitch more strikeouts per game than other players on the Boston Red Sox, was a pitcher on that professional baseball team. After he was traded to the New York Yankees, the owner and the manager decided to make him an outfielder, even though he could also pitch more strikeouts per game than other Yankees. They wanted "The Babe" to concentrate on his hitting because a home-run king would bring in more paying fans than a good pitcher would. Babe Ruth had an absolute advantage in both aspects of the game of baseball, but his comparative advantage was clearly in hitting homers rather than in practicing and developing his pitching game.

Scarcity, Self-Interest, and Specialization

In Chapter 1, you learned about the assumption of rational self-interest. To repeat, for the purposes of our analyses we assume that individuals are rational in that they will do what is in their own self-interest. They will not consciously carry out actions that will make them worse off. In this chapter, you learned that scarcity requires people to make choices. We *assume* that they make choices based on their self-interest. When people make choices, they attempt to maximize benefits net of opportunity cost. In so doing, individuals choose their comparative advantage and end up specializing.

The Division of Labor

Division of labor
The segregation of resources into different specific tasks. For instance, one automobile worker puts on bumpers, another doors, and so on.

In any firm that includes specialized human and nonhuman resources, there is a **division of labor** among those resources. The best-known example comes from Adam Smith (1723–1790), who in *The Wealth of Nations* illustrated the benefits of a division of labor in the making of pins, as depicted in the following example:

> One man draws out the wire, another straightens it, a third cuts it, a fourth points it, a fifth grinds it at the top for receiving the head; to make the head requires two or three distinct operations; to put it on is a peculiar business, to whiten the pins is another; it is even a trade by itself to put them into the paper.

Making pins this way allowed 10 workers without very much skill to make almost 48,000 pins "of a middling size" in a day. One worker, toiling alone, could have made perhaps 20 pins a day. Therefore, 10 workers could have produced 200. Division of labor allowed for an increase in the daily output of the pin factory from 200 to 48,000! (Smith did not attribute all of the gain to the division of labor but credited also the use of machinery and the fact that less time was spent shifting from task to task.)

What we are discussing here involves a division of the resource called labor into different uses of labor. The different uses of labor are organized in such a way as to increase the amount of output possible from the fixed resources available. We can therefore talk about an organized division of labor within a firm leading to increased output.

Comparative Advantage and Trade among Nations

Most of our analysis of absolute advantage, comparative advantage, and specialization has dealt with individuals. Nevertheless, it is equally applicable to groups of people.

Trade among Regions

Consider the United States. The Plains states have a comparative advantage in the production of grains and other agricultural goods. Relative to the Plains states, the states to the east tend to specialize in industrialized production, such as automobiles. Not surprisingly, grains are shipped from the Plains states to the eastern states, and automobiles are shipped in the reverse direction. Such specialization and trade allow for higher incomes and standards of living.

If both the Plains states and the eastern states were separate nations, the same analysis would still hold, but we would call it international trade. Indeed, the European Union (EU) is comparable to the United States in area and population, but instead of one nation, the EU has 27. What U.S. residents call *interstate* trade, Europeans call *international* trade. There is no difference, however, in the economic results—both yield greater economic efficiency and higher average incomes.

International Aspects of Trade

Political problems that normally do not occur within a particular nation often arise between nations. For example, if California avocado growers develop a cheaper method of producing avocados than growers in southern Florida use, the Florida growers will lose out. They cannot do much about the situation except try to lower their own costs of production or improve their product.

If avocado growers in Mexico, however, develop a cheaper method of producing avocados, both California and Florida growers can (and likely will) try to raise political barriers that will prevent Mexican avocado growers from freely selling their product in the United States. U.S. avocado growers will use such arguments as "unfair" competition and loss of U.S. jobs. Certainly, avocado-growing jobs may decline in the United States, but there is no reason to believe that U.S. jobs will decline overall. Instead, former U.S. avocado workers will move into alternative employment—something that 1 million people do every *week* in the United States. If the argument of U.S. avocado growers had any validity, every time a region in the United States developed a better way to produce a product manufactured somewhere else in the country, U.S. employment would decline. That has never happened and never will.

When nations specialize in an area of comparative advantage and then trade with the rest of the world, the average standard of living in the world rises. In effect, international trade allows the world to move from inside the global production possibilities curve toward the curve itself, thereby improving worldwide economic efficiency. Thus, all countries that engage in trade can benefit from comparative advantage, just as regions in the United States benefit from interregional trade.

Go to **www.econtoday.com/chap02** to find out from the World Trade Organization how much international trade takes place. Under "Resources," click on "Trade statistics" and then click on "International Trade Statistics" for the most recent year.

QUICK QUIZ See page 47 for the answers. Review concepts from this section in MyEconLab.

With a given set of resources, specialization results in __________ output. In other words, there are gains to specialization in terms of greater material well-being.

Individuals and nations specialize in their areas of __________ advantage in order to reap the gains of specialization.

Comparative advantages are found by determining which activities have the __________ opportunity costs—that is, which activities yield the highest return for the time and resources used.

A __________ of labor occurs when different workers are assigned different tasks. Together, the workers produce a desired product.

YOU ARE THERE

The Opportunity Cost of Vacation Time in South Korea

Lee Charm recently became head of the South Korean government's Korea Tourism Organization (KTO), which develops and promotes vacation tours for South Koreans. Shortly after assuming this position, Charm discovered that the agency's 550 employees were allocating only about five days to vacations each year, one fewer than for the average Korean.

Charm was rebuffed when he tried to convince KTO employees to take more vacation days each year voluntarily. A key reason for the unwillingness of KTO's employees to take off additional days for vacations was that KTO, like other government agencies and private firms in South Korea, rewards both workers and managers with extra pay for unused vacation days. Thus, if KTO employees had expanded their number of vacation days, they would have forgone income that could be allocated to other purposes. They viewed the opportunity cost of any additional time spent on vacations as too high to justify taking more time off.

Critical Thinking Questions

1. Why do you suppose KTO employees were displeased when Charm required them to take more vacation days each year to "set a good example" for other workers?
2. During his first year as KTO's manager, what did Charm himself gain from taking one less day off than the average KTO employee's five vacation days?

ISSUES & APPLICATIONS

The Rising Opportunity Cost of Airlines' "Block Times"

CONCEPTS APPLIED

- Scarcity
- Opportunity Cost
- Trade-Offs

Average published durations of airline flights increased by about ten minutes between the late 1990s and early 2010s. Time is scarce for everyone, including air travelers, who are experiencing increases in opportunity costs equal to the values of alternative uses for which they could spend these extra minutes now allocated to air travel.

Why Published Flight Times Are Longer Than They Used to Be

For about fifteen years, airlines lengthened their *block times*—intervals of time for flight schedules. Block times include the sum of estimated times required to taxi out onto the runway, to travel in the air, to taxi to the destination terminal, and to pull into a gate. In addition, block times typically include a *buffer*, which is a period that can range from just a few minutes to more than an hour.

Airlines have long built buffer minutes into block times for flights, to allow for contrary winds and other weather-related factors that can lengthen time in the air. Figure 2-6 below displays buffer periods for a number of airlines' flights on a recent day and shows that airlines tend to set longer buffers for flights of greater duration.

Fewer than two of the ten extra minutes that airlines for a time added to the average per-flight block time reflected increased time spent taxiing at airports. What accounted for the additional eight minutes? Airlines lengthened buf-

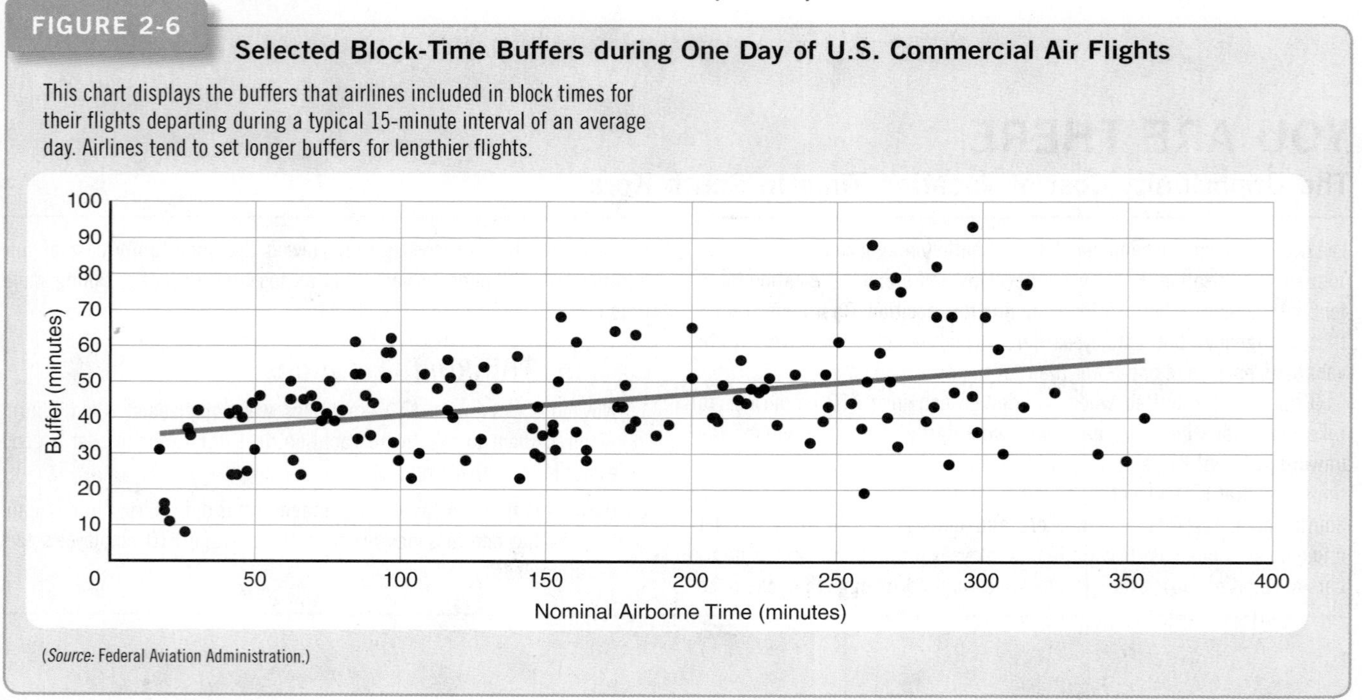

FIGURE 2-6 **Selected Block-Time Buffers during One Day of U.S. Commercial Air Flights**

This chart displays the buffers that airlines included in block times for their flights departing during a typical 15-minute interval of an average day. Airlines tend to set longer buffers for lengthier flights.

(*Source:* Federal Aviation Administration.)

fers to ensure that many flights that previously would have been marked a few minutes late instead would be listed as "on time." Being classified as consistently "on time" has considerable value to an airline company, because it helps the company sell more tickets.

A Higher Opportunity Cost of Air Travel Time

Traveling by air entails incurring both explicit and implicit costs. The explicit cost is the price of the plane ticket. A key implicit-cost component is the time that a person spends at and between airports instead of being able to allocate the time to the next-highest-valued activity—that is, the opportunity cost of the time.

For everyone who flies, the terms of the trade-off associated with flying worsened slightly between the late 1990s and early 2010s. Consider each individual who otherwise could have been earning the average U.S. hourly wage, for whom ten extra minutes devoted to a flight translates into approximately $3 of lost wages. Suppose that we use this figure to place a dollar value on each passenger's opportunity cost, and consider a "slow day" in which only 500,000 U.S. residents otherwise could have been earning hourly wages fly on airliners. Under these assumptions, the extra ten minutes of block time per passenger yielded an estimated additional $1.5 million total *daily* opportunity cost.

For Critical Thinking

1. Why might it prove difficult to measure the aggregate additional opportunity cost of ten extra minutes of airlines' block time across *all* individuals? (Hint: Not everyone works.)
2. Why did the extra ten minutes of block time constitute an opportunity cost even for an airline passenger who were on vacation from a job that pays hourly wages?

Web Resources

1. Learn about block time and other economic issues that airlines face in scheduling flights at **www.econtoday.com/chap02.**
2. To contemplate how adding block time can potentially boost airlines' own explicit labor costs, go to **www.econtoday.com/chap02.**

MyEconLab

For more questions on this chapter's Issues & Applications, go to MyEconLab. In the Study Plan for this chapter, select Section N: News.

MyEconLab

Here is what you should know after reading this chapter. MyEconLab will help you identify what you know, and where to go when you need to practice.

WHAT YOU SHOULD KNOW		WHERE TO GO TO PRACTICE
The Problem of Scarcity, Even for the Affluent Even the richest people face scarcity because they have to make choices among alternatives. Despite their high levels of income or wealth, affluent people, like everyone else, want more than they can have (in terms of goods, power, prestige, and so on).	scarcity, 27 production, 27 land, 27 labor, 27 physical capital, 28 human capital, 28 entrepreneurship, 28 goods, 28 economic goods, 28 services, 28	• MyEconLab Study Plan 2.1
Why Economists Consider Individuals' Wants but Not Their "Needs" Goods are all things from which individuals derive satisfaction. Economic goods are those for which the desired quantity exceeds the amount that is available at a zero price. The term *need* is undefinable, whereas humans have unlimited *wants*, which are the items on which we place a positive value.		• MyEconLab Study Plan 2.2

MyEconLab *continued*

WHAT YOU SHOULD KNOW		WHERE TO GO TO PRACTICE
Why Scarcity Leads People to Evaluate Opportunity Costs Opportunity cost is the highest-valued alternative that one must give up to obtain an item. The trade-offs people face can be represented by a production possibilities curve (PPC). Moving along a PPC from one point to another entails incurring an opportunity cost of allocating scarce resources toward the production of one good instead of another good.	opportunity cost, 30 production possibilities curve (PPC), 31 **Key Figure** Figure 2-1, 31	• MyEconLab Study Plans 2.3, 2.4
Why Obtaining Increasing Increments of a Good Requires Giving Up More and More Units of Other Goods When people allocate additional resources to producing more units of a good, it must increasingly employ resources that would be better suited for producing other goods. As a result, the law of increasing additional cost holds. Each additional unit of a good can be obtained only by giving up more and more of other goods. Hence, the production possibilities curve is bowed outward.	technology, 33 efficiency, 34 inefficient point, 34 law of increasing additional cost, 35 **Key Figures** Figure 2-3, 35 Figure 2-4, 36	• MyEconLab Study Plan 2.5 • Animated Figures 2-3, 2-4
The Trade-Off between Consumption Goods and Capital Goods If we allocate more resources to producing capital goods today, then the production possibilities curve will shift outward by more in the future, which means that we can have additional future consumption goods. The trade-off is that producing more capital goods today entails giving up consumption goods today.	consumption, 36	• MyEconLab Study Plans 2.6, 2.7
Absolute Advantage versus Comparative Advantage A person has an absolute advantage if she can produce more of a good than someone else who uses the same amount of resources. An individual can gain from specializing in producing a good if she has a comparative advantage in producing that good, meaning that she can produce the good at a lower opportunity cost than someone else.	specialization, 38 comparative advantage, 38 absolute advantage, 39 division of labor, 40	• MyEconLab Study Plans 2.8, 2.9

Log in to MyEconLab, take a chapter test, and get a personalized Study Plan that tells you which concepts you understand and which ones you need to review. From there, MyEconLab will give you further practice, tutorials, animations, videos, and guided solutions. For more information, visit www.myeconlab.com

PROBLEMS

All problems are assignable in MyEconLab. *Answers to odd-numbered problems appear at the back of the book.*

2-1. Define opportunity cost. What is your opportunity cost of attending a class at 11:00 a.m.? How does it differ from your opportunity cost of attending a class at 8:00 a.m.? (See page 30.)

2-2. If you receive a ticket to a concert at no charge, what, if anything, is your opportunity cost of attending the concert? How does your opportunity cost change if miserable weather on the night of the concert requires you to leave much earlier for the concert hall and greatly extends the time it takes to get home afterward? (See page 30.)

2-3. You and a friend decide to spend $100 each on concert tickets. Each of you alternatively could have spent the $100 to purchase a textbook, a meal at a highly rated local restaurant, or several Internet movie downloads. As you are on the way to the concert, your friend tells you that if she had not bought the concert ticket, she would have opted for a restaurant meal, and you reply that you otherwise would have downloaded several movies. Identify the relevant opportunity costs for you and your friend of the concert tickets that you purchased. Explain briefly. (See page 30.)

2-4. After the concert discussed in Problem 2-3 is over and you and your friend are traveling home, you discuss how each of you might otherwise have used the four hours devoted to attending the concert. The four hours could have been used to study, to watch a sporting event on TV, or to get some extra sleep. Your friend decides that if she had not spent four hours attending the concert, she would have chosen to study, and you reply that you otherwise would have watched the televised sporting event. Identify the relevant opportunity costs for you and your friend for allocating your four hours to attending the concert. Explain briefly. (See page 30.)

2-5. Recently, a woman named Mary Krawiec attended an auction in Troy, New York. At the auction, a bank was seeking to sell a foreclosed property: a large Victorian house suffering from years of neglect in a neighborhood in which many properties had been on the market for years yet remained unsold. Her $10 offer was the highest bid in the auction, and she handed over a $10 bill for a title to ownership. Once she acquired the house, however, she became responsible for all taxes on the property and for an overdue water bill of $2,000. In addition, to make the house habitable, she and her husband devoted months of time and unpaid labor to renovating the property. In the process, they incurred explicit expenses totaling $65,000. Why do you suppose that the bank was willing to sell the house to Ms. Krawiec for only $10? (Hint: Contemplate the bank's expected gain, net of all explicit and opportunity costs, if it had attempted to make the house habitable. See page 30.)

2-6. The following table illustrates the points a student can earn on examinations in economics and biology if the student uses all available hours for study.

Economics	Biology
100	40
90	50
80	60
70	70
60	80
50	90
40	100

Plot this student's production possibilities curve. Does the PPC illustrate the law of increasing additional cost? (See page 31.)

2-7. Based on the information provided in Problem 2-6, what is the opportunity cost to this student of allocating enough additional study time on economics to move her grade up from a 90 to a 100?

2-8. Consider a change in the table in Problem 2-6. The student's set of opportunities is now as follows:

Economics	Biology
100	40
90	60
80	75
70	85
60	93
50	98
40	100

Does the PPC illustrate the law of increasing additional cost? What is the opportunity cost to this student for the additional amount of study time on economics required to move her grade from 60 to 70? From 90 to 100? (See page 35.)

2-9. Construct a production possibilities curve for a nation facing increasing opportunity costs for producing food and video games. Show how the PPC changes given the following events. (See page 37.)

a. A new and better fertilizer is invented.

b. Immigration occurs, and immigrants' labor can be employed in both the agricultural sector and the video game sector.

c. People invent a new programming language that is much less costly to code and is more memory-efficient.

d. A heat wave and drought result in a 10 percent decrease in usable farmland.

Consider the following diagram when answering Problems 2-10, 2-11, and 2-12.

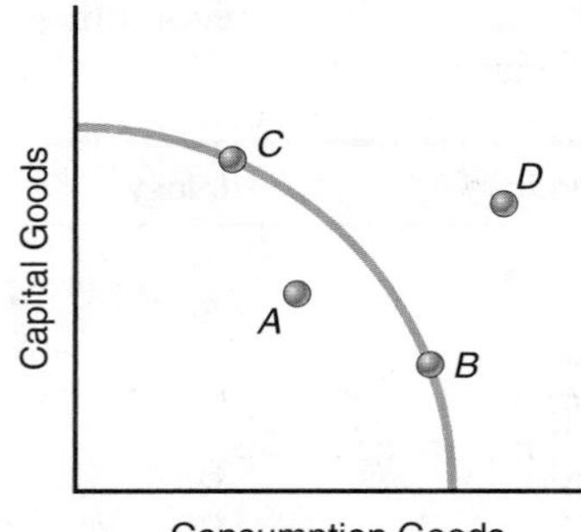

2-10. During a debate on the floor of the U.S. Senate, Senator Creighton states, "Our nation should not devote so many of its fully employed resources to producing capital goods because we already are not producing enough consumption goods for our citizens." Compared with the other labeled points on the diagram, which one could be consistent with the *current* production combination choice that Senator Creighton believes the nation has made? (See page 34.)

2-11. In response to Senator Creighton's statement reported in Problem 2-10, Senator Long replies, "We must remain at our current production combination if we want to be able to produce more consumption goods in the future." Of the labeled points on the diagram, which one could depict the *future* production combination Senator Long has in mind? (See page 34.)

2-12. Senator Borman interjects the following comment after the statements by Senators Creighton and Long reported in Problems 2-10 and 2-11: "In fact, both of my esteemed colleagues are wrong, because an unacceptably large portion of our nation's resources is currently unemployed." Of the labeled points on the diagram, which one is consistent with Senator Borman's position? (See page 34.)

2-13. A nation's residents can allocate their scarce resources either to producing consumption goods or to producing human capital—that is, providing themselves with training and education. (See page 35.) The table at the top of next column displays the production possibilities for this nation:

Production Combination	Units of Consumption Goods	Units of Human Capital
A	0	100
B	10	97
C	20	90
D	30	75
E	40	55
F	50	30
G	60	0

a. Suppose that the nation's residents currently produce combination A. What is the opportunity cost of increasing production of consumption goods by 10 units? By 60 units?

b. Does the law of increasing additional cost hold true for this nation? Why or why not?

2-14. Like physical capital, human capital produced in the present can be applied to the production of future goods and services. Consider the table in Problem 2-13, and suppose that the nation's residents are trying to choose between combination C and combination F. Other things being equal, will the future production possibilities curve for this nation be located farther outward if the nation chooses combination F instead of combination C? Explain. (See page 35.)

2-15. You can wash, fold, and iron a basket of laundry in two hours and prepare a meal in one hour. Your roommate can wash, fold, and iron a basket of laundry in three hours and prepare a meal in one hour. Who has the absolute advantage in laundry, and who has an absolute advantage in meal preparation? Who has the comparative advantage in laundry, and who has a comparative advantage in meal preparation? (See page 38.)

2-16. Based on the information in Problem 2-15, should you and your roommate specialize in a particular task? Why? And if so, who should specialize in which task? Show how much labor time you save if you choose to "trade" an appropriate task with your roommate as opposed to doing it yourself. (See page 38.)

2-17. Using only the concept of comparative advantage, evaluate this statement: "A professor with a Ph.D. in physics should never mow his or her own lawn, because this would fail to take into account the professor's comparative advantage." (See page 38.)

2-18. Country A and country B produce the same consumption goods and capital goods and currently have *identical* production possibilities curves. They also have the same resources at present, and they have access to the same technology. (See page 38.)

a. At present, does either country have a comparative advantage in producing capital goods? Consumption goods?

b. Currently, country A has chosen to produce more consumption goods, compared with country B. Other things being equal, which country will experience the larger outward shift of its PPC during the next year?

ECONOMICS ON THE NET

Opportunity Cost and Labor Force Participation Many students choose to forgo full-time employment to concentrate on their studies, thereby incurring a sizable opportunity cost. This application explores the nature of this opportunity cost.

Title: College Enrollment and Work Activity of High School Graduates

Navigation: Go to **www.econtoday.com/chap02** to visit the Bureau of Labor Statistics (BLS) home page. Select A–Z Index and then click on *Educational attainment (Statistics)*. Under "School Enrollment," click on *Recent High School Graduates and Labor Force Participation*.

Application Read the abbreviated report on college enrollment and work activity of high school graduates. Then answer the following questions.

1. Based on the article, explain who the BLS considers to be in the labor force and who it does not view as part of the labor force.
2. What is the difference in labor force participation rates between high school students entering four-year universities and those entering two-year universities? Using the concept of opportunity cost, explain the difference.
3. What is the difference in labor force participation rates between part-time college students and full-time college students? Using the concept of opportunity cost, explain the difference.

For Group Study and Analysis Read the last paragraph of the article. Then divide the class into two groups. The first group should explain, based on the concept of opportunity cost, the difference in labor force participation rates between youths not in school but with a high school diploma and youths not in school and without a high school diploma. The second group should explain, based on opportunity cost, the difference in labor force participation rates between men and women not in school but with a high school diploma and men and women not in school and without a high school diploma.

ANSWERS TO QUICK QUIZZES

p. 29: (i) Scarcity; (ii) land . . . labor . . . physical . . . human . . . entrepreneurship; (iii) Wants; (iv) need

p. 32: (i) next-highest; (ii) opportunity; (iii) next-best; (iv) production possibilities

p. 35: (i) production possibilities; (ii) fixed; (iii) outside . . . inside; (iv) outward

p. 38: (i) Capital; (ii) more . . . smaller

p. 41: (i) higher; (ii) comparative; (iii) lowest; (iv) division

3 Demand and Supply

At the time that your parents might have attended college, average tuition and fees were more than 90 percent lower than their current levels. In addition, the prices of textbooks and supplies were more than 80 percent lower than current prices. For example, in comparison with a college student who pays $20,000 in annual tuition and fees today, a student in the 1980s would have paid not much over $1,600 in inflation-adjusted dollars. Compared with a student who spends $1,000 per year for textbooks and other supplies, a student in the 1980s would have spent about $110 in inflation-adjusted dollars. Why have these prices risen so much? In this chapter, you will learn the answer.

LEARNING OBJECTIVES

After reading this chapter, you should be able to:

- Explain the law of demand
- Discuss the difference between money prices and relative prices
- Distinguish between changes in demand and changes in quantity demanded
- Explain the law of supply
- Distinguish between changes in supply and changes in quantity supplied
- Understand how the interaction of the demand for and supply of a commodity determines the market price of the commodity and the equilibrium quantity of the commodity that is produced and consumed

MyEconLab helps you master each objective and study more efficiently. See end of chapter for details.

T...

after truck freight-hauling prices jumped substantially in the early 2010s, ntainers rose by more than 10 percent? Higher truck-transportation prices induced many companies to substitute away from having their products moved by trucks in favor of rail transportation.

If we use the economist's primary set of tools, *demand* and *supply*, we can develop a better understanding of why we sometimes observe relatively large increases in the purchase, or consumption, of items such as rail freight services. We can also better understand why a persistent increase in the price of an item such as truck-hauling services ultimately induces an increase in consumption of rail freight services. Demand and supply are two ways of categorizing the influences on the prices of goods that you buy and the quantities available. Indeed, demand and supply characterize much economic analysis of the world around us.

As you will see throughout this text, the operation of the forces of demand and supply takes place in *markets*. A **market** is an abstract concept summarizing all of the arrangements individuals have for exchanging with one another. Goods and services are sold in markets, such as the automobile market, the health care market, and the market for high-speed Internet access. Workers offer their services in the labor market. Companies, or firms, buy workers' labor services in the labor market. Firms also buy other inputs to produce the goods and services that you buy as a consumer. Firms purchase machines, buildings, and land. These markets are in operation at all times. One of the most important activities in these markets is the determination of the prices of all of the inputs and outputs that are bought and sold in our complicated economy. To understand the determination of prices, you first need to look at the law of demand.

Market
All of the arrangements that individuals have for exchanging with one another. Thus, for example, we can speak of the labor market, the automobile market, and the credit market.

Demand

Demand has a special meaning in economics. It refers to the quantities of specific goods or services that individuals, taken singly or as a group, will purchase at various possible prices, other things being constant. We can therefore talk about the demand for microprocessor chips, french fries, multifunction digital devices, children, and criminal activities.

Demand
A schedule showing how much of a good or service people will purchase at any price during a specified time period, other things being constant.

The Law of Demand

Associated with the concept of demand is the **law of demand,** which can be stated as follows:

> ***When the price of a good goes up, people buy less of it, other things being equal. When the price of a good goes down, people buy more of it, other things being equal.***

Law of demand
The observation that there is a negative, or inverse, relationship between the price of any good or service and the quantity demanded, holding other factors constant.

The law of demand tells us that the quantity demanded of any commodity is inversely related to its price, other things being equal. In an inverse relationship, one variable moves up in value when the other moves down. The law of demand states that a change in price causes a change in the quantity demanded in the *opposite* direction.

Notice that we tacked on to the end of the law of demand the statement "other things being equal." We referred to this in Chapter 1 as the *ceteris paribus* assumption. It means, for example, that when we predict that people will buy fewer digital devices if their price goes up, we are holding constant the price of all other goods in the economy as well as people's incomes. Implicitly, therefore, if we are assuming that no other prices change when we examine the price behavior of digital devices, we are looking at the *relative* price of digital devices.

The law of demand is supported by millions of observations of people's behavior in the marketplace. Theoretically, it can be derived from an economic model based on rational behavior, as was discussed in Chapter 1. Basically, if nothing else changes and the price of a good falls, the lower price induces us to buy more because we can enjoy additional net gains that were unavailable at the higher price. If you examine your own behavior, you will see that it generally follows the law of demand.

Relative price
The money price of one commodity divided by the money price of another commodity; the number of units of one commodity that must be sacrificed to purchase one unit of another commodity.

Relative Prices versus Money Prices

The **relative price** of any commodity is its price in terms of another commodity. The price that you pay in dollars and cents for any good or service at any point in time is called its **money price.** You might hear from your grandparents, "My first new car cost only

Money price
The price expressed in today's dollars; also called the *absolute* or *nominal price.*

Table 3-1

Money Price versus Relative Price

The money prices of both 350-gigabyte flash memory drives and 350-gigabyte external hard drives have fallen. But the relative price of external hard drives has risen (or conversely, the relative price of flash memory drives has fallen).

	Money Price		Relative Price	
	Price Last Year	**Price This Year**	**Price Last Year**	**Price This Year**
Flash memory drives	\$300	\$210	$\frac{\$300}{\$150} = 2.0$	$\frac{\$210}{\$140} = 1.50$
External hard drives	\$150	\$140	$\frac{\$150}{\$300} = 0.50$	$\frac{\$140}{\$210} = 0.67$

fifteen hundred dollars." The implication, of course, is that the price of cars today is outrageously high because the average new car may cost \$32,000. But that is not an accurate comparison. What was the price of the average house during that same year? Perhaps it was only \$12,000. By comparison, then, given that the average price of houses today is close to \$180,000, the price of a new car today doesn't sound so far out of line, does it?

The point is that money prices during different time periods don't tell you much. You have to calculate relative prices. Consider an example of the price of 350-gigabyte flash memory drives versus the price of 350-gigabyte external hard drives from last year and this year. In Table 3-1 above, we show the money prices of flash memory drives and external hard drives for two years during which they have both gone down.

That means that in today's dollars we have to pay out less for both flash memory drives and external hard drives. If we look, though, at the relative prices of flash memory drives and external hard drives, we find that last year, flash memory drives were twice as expensive as external hard drives, whereas this year they are only one and a half times as expensive. Conversely, if we compare external hard drives to flash memory drives, last year the price of external hard drives was 50 percent of the price of external hard drives, but today the price of external hard drives is about 67 percent of the price of flash memory drives. In the one-year period, although both prices have declined in money terms, the relative price of external hard drives has risen in relation to that of flash memory drives.

Sometimes relative price changes occur because the quality of a product improves, thereby bringing about a decrease in the item's effective *price per constant-quality unit*. Or the price of an item may decrease simply because producers have reduced the item's quality. Thus, when evaluating the effects of price changes, we must always compare *price per constant-quality unit*.

Why is it that for most drivers, the quality-adjusted price of electric vehicles is higher than the posted price?

EXAMPLE

Why Sales of Electric Cars Are Stuck in Low Gear

Prices of solely battery-operated, "electric" autos exceed prices of hybrid (combined gasoline and battery-powered) versions of the same vehicles by at least 30 percent and of all-gasoline-powered versions by at least 50 percent. Nevertheless, the quality-adjusted prices of electric vehicles are even higher.

Not everyone uses an auto just for traveling short, local distances between home and schools, retail stores, and places of employment. Many people commonly desire to drive vehicles farther out than the roughly 250-mile range beyond which the batteries in electric autos cease to function. The absence of networks of battery-charging or battery-swapping stations limits the usefulness of the vehicles, thereby increasing their quality-adjusted prices. This fact helps to explain why purchases of these vehicles have been trivial since the early 2010s.

FOR CRITICAL THINKING

As the prices of digital devices have declined over time—even as these devices have performed more functions—what has happened to their quality-adjusted prices?

QUICK QUIZ See page 74 for the answers. Review concepts from this section in MyEconLab.

The **law of demand** posits an __________ relationship between the quantity demanded of a good and its price, other things being equal.	The law of __________ applies when other things, such as income and the prices of all other goods and services, are held constant.

The Demand Schedule

Let's take a hypothetical demand situation to see how the inverse relationship between the price and the quantity demanded looks (holding other things equal). We will consider the quantity of magneto optical (MO) disks—utilized for digital data storage—demanded *per year*. Without stating the *time dimension*, we could not make sense out of this demand relationship because the numbers would be different if we were talking about the quantity demanded per month or the quantity demanded per decade.

In addition to implicitly or explicitly stating a time dimension for a demand relationship, we are also implicitly referring to *constant-quality units* of the good or service in question. Prices are always expressed in constant-quality units in order to avoid the problem of comparing commodities that are in fact not truly comparable.

In panel (a) of Figure 3-1 below, we see that if the price is $1 apiece, 50 magneto optical (MO) disks will be bought each year by our representative individual, but if the price is $5 apiece, only 10 MO disks will be bought each year. This reflects the law of demand. Panel (a) is also called simply demand, or a *demand schedule*, because it gives a schedule of alternative quantities demanded per year at different possible prices.

FIGURE 3-1

The Individual Demand Schedule and the Individual Demand Curve

In panel (a), we show combinations *A* through *E* of the quantities of magneto optical disks demanded, measured in constant-quality units at prices ranging from $5 down to $1 apiece. These combinations are points on the demand schedule. In panel (b), we plot combinations *A* through *E* on a grid. The result is the individual demand curve for MO disks.

Panel (a)

Combination	Price per Constant-Quality Magneto Optical Disk	Quantity of Constant-Quality Titanium Batteries per Year
A	$5	10
B	4	20
C	3	30
D	2	40
E	1	50

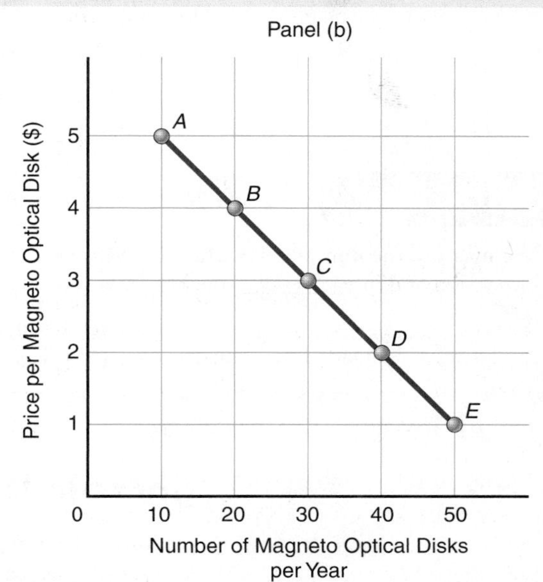

The Demand Curve

Tables expressing relationships between two variables can be represented in graphical terms. To do this, we need only construct a graph that has the price per constant-quality magneto optical disk on the vertical axis and the quantity measured in constant-quality MO disks per year on the horizontal axis. All we have to do is take combinations A through E from panel (a) of Figure 3-1 on the previous page and plot those points in panel (b). Now we connect the points with a smooth line, and *voilà*, we have a **demand curve.** It is downward sloping (from left to right) to indicate the inverse relationship between the price of MO disks and the quantity demanded per year.

Demand curve
A graphical representation of the demand schedule. It is a negatively sloped line showing the inverse relationship between the price and the quantity demanded (other things being equal).

Our presentation of demand schedules and curves applies equally well to all commodities, including dental floss, bagels, textbooks, credit, and labor. Remember, the demand curve is simply a graphical representation of the law of demand.

Individual versus Market Demand Curves

The demand schedule shown in panel (a) of Figure 3-1 and the resulting demand curve shown in panel (b) are both given for an individual. As we shall see, the determination of price in the marketplace depends on, among other things, the **market demand** for a particular commodity. The way in which we measure a market demand schedule and derive a market demand curve for magneto optical disks or any other good or service is by summing (at each price) the individual quantities demanded by all buyers in the market. Suppose that the market demand for MO disks consists of only two buyers: buyer 1, for whom we've already shown the demand schedule, and buyer 2, whose demand schedule is displayed in column 3 of panel (a) of Figure 3-2 on the facing page. Column 1 shows the price, and column 2 shows the quantity demanded by buyer 1 at each price. These data are taken directly from Figure 3-1. In column 3, we show the quantity demanded by buyer 2. Column 4 shows the total quantity demanded at each price, which is obtained by simply adding columns 2 and 3. Graphically, in panel (d) of Figure 3-2, we add the demand curves of buyer 1 [panel (b)] and buyer 2 [panel (c)] to derive the market demand curve.

Market demand
The demand of all consumers in the marketplace for a particular good or service. The summation at each price of the quantity demanded by each individual.

There are, of course, numerous potential consumers of MO disks. We'll simply assume that the summation of all of the consumers in the market results in a demand schedule, given in panel (a) of Figure 3-3 on page 54, and a demand curve, given in panel (b). The quantity demanded is now measured in millions of units per year. Remember, panel (b) in Figure 3-3 shows the market demand curve for the millions of buyers of MO disks. The "market" demand curve that we derived in Figure 3-2 on the facing page was undertaken assuming that there were only two buyers in the entire market. That's why we assume that the "market" demand curve for two buyers in panel (d) of Figure 3-2 is not a smooth line, whereas the true market demand curve in panel (b) of Figure 3-3 is a smooth line with no kinks.

QUICK QUIZ See page 74 for the answers. Review concepts from this section in MyEconLab.

We measure the **demand schedule** in terms of a time dimension and in __________-quality units.

The __________ __________ curve is derived by summing the quantity demanded by individuals at each price.

Graphically, we add the individual demand curves horizontally to derive the total, or market, demand curve.

Shifts in Demand

Assume that the federal government gives every student registered in a college, university, or technical school in the United States a magneto optical disk drive. The demand curve presented in panel (b) of Figure 3-3 on page 54 would no longer

FIGURE 3-2

The Horizontal Summation of Two Demand Curves

Panel (a) shows how to sum the demand schedule for one buyer with that of another buyer. In column 2 is the quantity demanded by buyer 1, taken from panel (a) of Figure 3-1 on page 51. Column 4 is the sum of columns 2 and 3. We plot the demand curve for buyer 1 in panel (b) and the demand curve for buyer 2 in panel (c). When we add those two demand curves horizontally, we get the market demand curve for two buyers, shown in panel (d).

Panel (a)

(1) Price per Magneto Optical Disk	(2) Buyer 1's Quantity Demanded	(3) Buyer 2's Quantity Demanded	(4) = (2) + (3) Combined Quantity Demanded per Year
$5	10	10	20
4	20	20	40
3	30	40	70
2	40	50	90
1	50	60	110

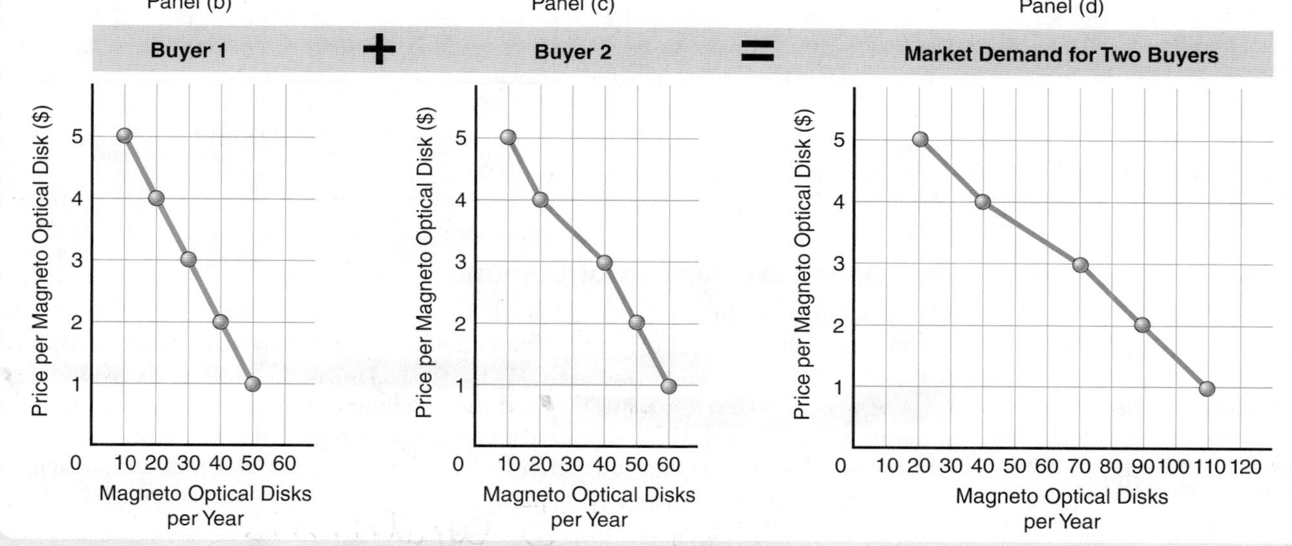

be an accurate representation of total market demand for MO disks. What we have to do is shift the curve outward, or to the right, to represent the rise in demand that would result from this program. There will now be an increase in the number of MO disks demanded at *each and every possible price*. The demand curve shown in Figure 3-4 on the following page will shift from D_1 to D_2. Take any price, say, $3 per MO disk. Originally, before the federal government giveaway of MO disk drives, the amount demanded at $3 was 6 million MO disks per year. After the government giveaway of MO disk drives, however, the new amount demanded at the $3 price is 10 million MO disks per year. What we have seen is a shift in the demand for MO disks.

Under different circumstances, the shift can also go in the opposite direction. What if colleges uniformly prohibited the use of magneto optical disk drives by any of their students? Such a regulation would cause a shift inward—to the left—of the demand curve for MO disks. In Figure 3-4 on the following page, the demand curve would shift to D_3. The quantity demanded would now be less at each and every possible price.

FIGURE 3-3

The Market Demand Schedule for Magneto Optical Disks

In panel (a), we add up the existing demand schedules for magneto optical disks. In panel (b), we plot the quantities from panel (a) on a grid. Connecting them produces the market demand curve for MO disks.

Panel (a)

Price per Constant-Quality Magneto Optical Disk	Total Quantity Demanded of Constant-Quality Magneto Optical Disks per Year (millions)
$5	2
4	4
3	6
2	8
1	10

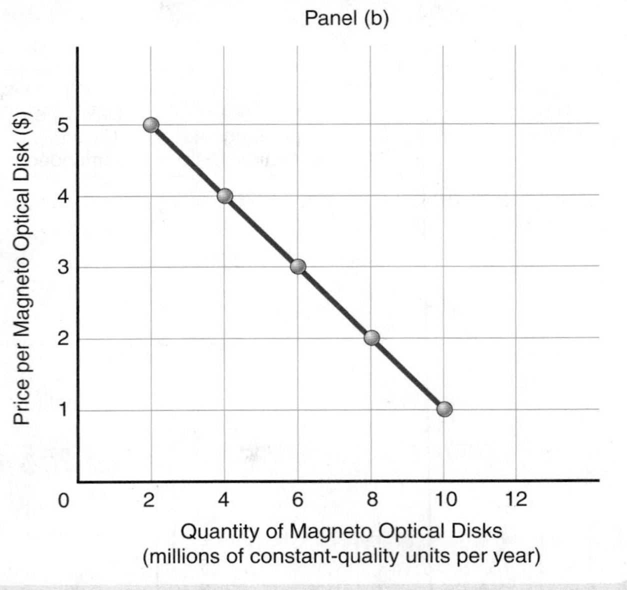

The Other Determinants of Demand

The demand curve in panel (b) of Figure 3-3 above is drawn with other things held constant, specifically all of the other factors that determine how many magneto optical disks will be bought. There are many such determinants. We refer to these determinants as ***ceteris paribus* conditions,** and they include consumers' income; tastes and preferences; the prices of related goods; expectations regarding future prices and future incomes; and market size (number of potential buyers). Let's examine each of these determinants more closely.

***Ceteris paribus* conditions**
Determinants of the relationship between price and quantity that are unchanged along a curve. Changes in these factors cause the curve to shift.

FIGURE 3-4

Shifts in the Demand Curve

If some factor other than price changes, we can show its effect by moving the entire demand curve, say, from D_1 to D_2. We have assumed in our example that this move was precipitated by the government's giving a magneto optical disk drive to every registered college student in the United States. Thus, at *all* prices, a larger number of MO disks would be demanded than before. Curve D_3 represents reduced demand compared to curve D_1, caused by a prohibition of MO disk drives on campus.

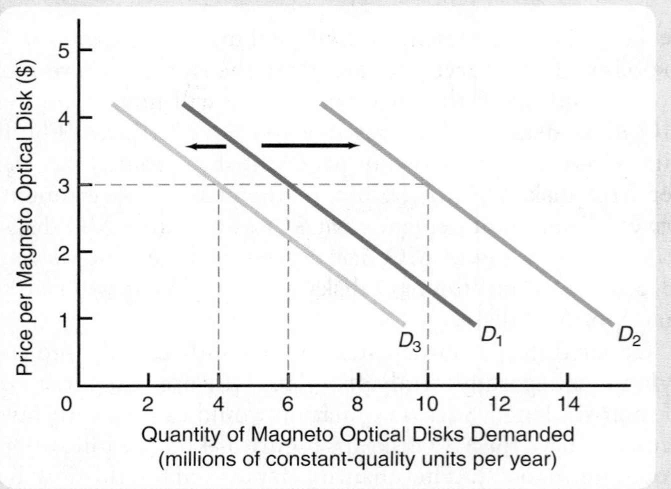

INCOME For most goods, an increase in income will lead to an increase in demand. That is, an increase in income will lead to a rightward shift in the position of the demand curve from, say, D_1 to D_2 in Figure 3-4 on the facing page. You can avoid confusion about shifts in curves by always relating a rise in demand to a rightward shift in the demand curve and a fall in demand to a leftward shift in the demand curve. Goods for which the demand rises when consumer income rises are called **normal goods.** Most goods, such as shoes, computers, and flash memory drives, are "normal goods." For some goods, however, demand *falls* as income rises. These are called **inferior goods.** Beans might be an example. As households get richer, they tend to purchase fewer and fewer beans and purchase more and more fish. (The terms *normal* and *inferior* are merely part of the economist's lexicon. No value judgments are associated with them.)

Normal goods
Goods for which demand rises as income rises. Most goods are normal goods.

Inferior goods
Goods for which demand falls as income rises.

Remember, a shift to the left in the demand curve represents a decrease in demand, and a shift to the right represents an increase in demand.

How have recent declines in incomes for a large share of U.S. consumers affected the demand for used cell phones that specialty firms recondition and resell?

EXAMPLE

Lower Incomes Boost the Demand for Reconditioned Cell Phones

The more than 15 percent of U.S. residents who either have been out of work or are classified by the government as discouraged workers who have given up looking for jobs. These people are earning much lower incomes than they did a few years ago. Many of these people are customers of companies such as ReCellular and Second Rotation, firms that obtain used cell phones from previous owners, recondition the devices, and resell them. Since the economy slipped into its dampened state, sales of reconditioned cell phones have increased by more than 150 percent. Thus, as incomes have fallen for a significant percentage of U.S. consumers, the amount of reconditioned cell phones demanded has increased, indicating that reconditioned cell phones are an inferior good.

FOR CRITICAL THINKING

What is your prediction about the likely effect on the amount of reconditioned cell phones demanded if the U.S. economy were to rebound?

TASTES AND PREFERENCES A change in consumer tastes in favor of a good can shift its demand curve outward to the right. When Pokémon trading cards became the rage, the demand curve for them shifted outward to the right. When the rage died out, the demand curve shifted inward to the left. Fashions depend to a large extent on people's tastes and preferences. Economists have little to say about the determination of tastes. That is, they don't have any "good" theories of taste determination or why people buy one brand of product rather than others. (Advertisers, however, have various theories that they use to try to make consumers prefer their products over those of competitors.)

PRICES OF RELATED GOODS: SUBSTITUTES AND COMPLEMENTS Demand schedules are always drawn with the prices of all other commodities held constant. That is to say, when deriving a given demand curve, we assume that only the price of the good under study changes. For example, when we draw the demand curve for laptop computers, we assume that the price of tablet devices is held constant. When we draw the demand curve for home cinema speakers, we assume that the price of surround-sound amplifiers is held constant. When we refer to *related goods*, we are talking about goods for which demand is interdependent. If a change in the price of one good shifts the demand for another good, those two goods have interdependent demands.

There are two types of demand interdependencies: those in which goods are *substitutes* and those in which goods are *complements*. We can define and distinguish between substitutes and complements in terms of how the change in price of one commodity affects the demand for its related commodity.

YOU ARE THERE

To contemplate how a widening spread between the price of an item and the price of another good that is a close substitute can affect the industry producing the item, take a look at **Why the Casket Industry Is on Life Support**, on page 69.

Substitutes
Two goods are substitutes when a change in the price of one causes a shift in demand for the other in the same direction as the price change.

Butter and margarine are **substitutes.** Either can be consumed to satisfy the same basic want. Let's assume that both products originally cost $2 per pound. If the price of butter remains the same and the price of margarine falls from $2 per pound to $1 per pound, people will buy more margarine and less butter. The demand curve for butter shifts inward to the left. If, conversely, the price of margarine rises from $2 per pound to $3 per pound, people will buy more butter and less margarine. The demand curve for butter shifts outward to the right. In other words, an increase in the price of margarine will lead to an increase in the demand for butter, and an increase in the price of butter will lead to an increase in the demand for margarine. For substitutes, a change in the price of a substitute will cause a change in demand *in the same direction.*

How has the availability of lower-priced plastic substitutes affected the market demand for natural cork stoppers for wine bottles?

EXAMPLE

Why Fewer Wine Bottles Have Natural Cork Stoppers

In the late 1600s, a French monk discovered that natural cork bottle stoppers seal wine into a bottle while allowing the wine to indirectly "breathe" air via the porous characteristics of natural cork's cell structure. Nevertheless, many of today's wine sellers utilize plastic stoppers. These plastic stoppers add to the overall price of a bottle of wine an amount ranging from $0.02 for screw-on stoppers to $0.20 for stoppers composed of extruded plastic that replicates the sponginess of natural cork.

Since the early 2000s, prices of natural cork stoppers have risen above those of plastic stoppers, to levels from about $0.03 for low-quality stoppers to as much as $2 for stoppers of the highest quality. Wine consumers have responded to higher prices of wines bottled with natural cork stoppers by substituting in favor of wines bottled with plastic stoppers. During the past decade, purchases of wine bottled with plastic stoppers have increased by more than 50 percent.

FOR CRITICAL THINKING

Natural cork producers advertise that plastic stoppers harm the environment. If such ads shift the preferences of wine producers and consumers back in favor of natural cork stoppers, what will happen to the market demand for plastic *stoppers?*

Complements
Two goods are complements when a change in the price of one causes an opposite shift in the demand for the other.

For **complements,** goods typically consumed together, the situation is reversed. Consider digital devices and online applications (apps). We draw the demand curve for apps with the price of digital devices held constant. If the price per constant-quality unit of digital devices decreases from, say, $500 to $300, that will encourage more people to purchase apps. They will now buy more apps, at any given app price, than before. The demand curve for apps will shift outward to the right. If, by contrast, the price of digital devices increases from $250 to $450, fewer people will purchase downloadable applications. The demand curve for apps will shift inward to the left.

To summarize, a decrease in the price of digital devices leads to an increase in the demand for apps. An increase in the price of digital devices leads to a decrease in the demand for apps. Thus, for complements, a change in the price of a product will cause a change in demand *in the opposite direction* for the other good.

EXPECTATIONS Consumers' expectations regarding future prices and future incomes will prompt them to buy more or less of a particular good without a change in its current money price. For example, consumers getting wind of a scheduled 100 percent increase in the price of magneto optical disks next month will buy more of them today at today's prices. Today's demand curve for MO disks will shift from D_1 to D_2 in Figure 3-4 on page 54. The opposite would occur if a decrease in the price of MO disks was scheduled for next month (from D_1 to D_3).

Expectations of a rise in income may cause consumers to want to purchase more of everything today at today's prices. Again, such a change in expectations of higher future income will cause a shift in the demand curve from D_1 to D_2 in Figure 3-4.

Finally, expectations that goods will not be available at any price will induce consumers to stock up now, increasing current demand.

In what ways did recent policy actions by several nations' governments regarding the use of nuclear power affect expectations of the future price of uranium and, as a result, the current market demand for uranium?

POLICY EXAMPLE

An Expected Uranium Price Implosion Cuts Current Uranium Demand

Following the meltdown of a Japanese nuclear reactor in the wake of that nation's disastrous earthquake and tsunami in 2011, governments of a number of countries announced that they planned to decrease their reliance on nuclear power as a source of energy. These policy actions led participants in the uranium market to anticipate a decrease in the future price of uranium. In turn, this expectation of a lower *future* uranium price induced consumers of the nuclear fuel to postpone *current* purchases to the future, when they expected lower prices to prevail. As a consequence, the expected drop in the future price of uranium generated a nearly 10 percent decrease in the contemporaneous market demand for uranium.

FOR CRITICAL THINKING

What would happen to the market demand for uranium if a different current event induced people to anticipate higher future uranium prices?

MARKET SIZE (NUMBER OF POTENTIAL BUYERS) An increase in the number of potential buyers (holding buyers' incomes constant) at any given price shifts the market demand curve outward. Conversely, a reduction in the number of potential buyers at any given price shifts the market demand curve inward.

Changes in Demand versus Changes in Quantity Demanded

We have made repeated references to demand and to quantity demanded. It is important to realize that there is a difference between a *change in demand* and a *change in quantity demanded.*

Demand refers to a schedule of planned rates of purchase and depends on a great many *ceteris paribus* conditions, such as incomes, expectations, and the prices of substitutes or complements. Whenever there is a change in a *ceteris paribus* condition, there will be a change in demand—a shift in the entire demand curve to the right or to the left.

A *quantity demanded* is a specific quantity at a specific price, represented by a single point on a demand curve. When price changes, quantity demanded changes according to the law of demand, and there will be a movement from one point to another along the same demand curve. Look at Figure 3-5 on the following page. At a price of $3 per magneto optical disk, 6 million MO disks per year are demanded. If the price falls to $1, quantity demanded increases to 10 million per year. This movement occurs because the current market price for the product changes. In Figure 3-5, you can see the arrow pointing down the given demand curve *D*.

When you think of demand, think of the entire curve. Quantity demanded, in contrast, is represented by a single point on the demand curve.

***A change or shift in demand is a movement of the entire curve. The* only *thing that can cause the entire curve to move is a change in a determinant* other than the good's own price.**

In economic analysis, we cannot emphasize too much the following distinction that must constantly be made:

A change in a good's own price leads to a change in quantity demanded for any given demand curve, other things held constant. This is a movement* along *the curve.

A change in any of the* ceteris paribus *conditions for demand leads to a change in demand. This causes a* shift *of the curve.

FIGURE 3-5

Movement along a Given Demand Curve

A change in price changes the quantity of a good demanded. This can be represented as movement along a given demand schedule. If, in our example, the price of magneto optical disks falls from $3 to $1 apiece, the quantity demanded will increase from 6 million to 10 million MO disks per year.

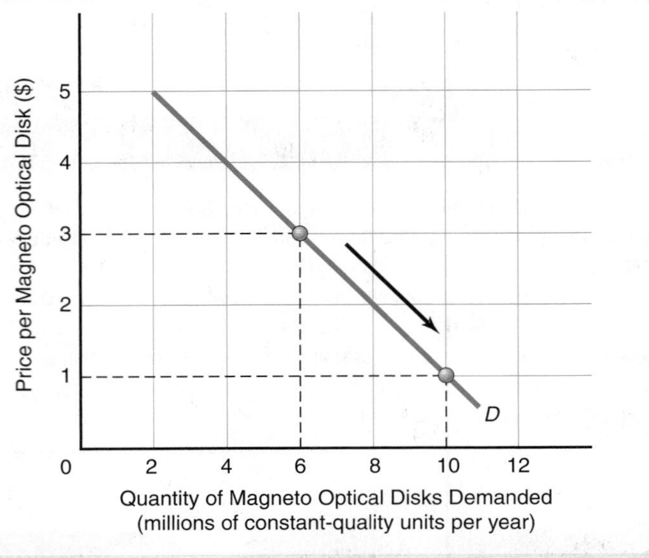

QUICK QUIZ See page 74 for the answers. Review concepts from this section in MyEconLab.

Demand curves are drawn with determinants other than the price of the good held constant. These other determinants, called ***ceteris paribus* conditions**, are (1) __________, (2) __________, (3) __________, (4) __________, and (5) __________ at any given price. If any one of these determinants changes, the demand curve will shift to the right or to the left.

A change in demand comes about only because of a change in the __________ __________ conditions of demand. This change in demand is a shift in the demand curve to the left or to the right.

A change in the quantity demanded comes about when there is a change in the price of the good (other things held constant). Such a change in quantity demanded involves a __________ __________ a given demand curve.

The Law of Supply

Supply
A schedule showing the relationship between price and quantity supplied for a specified period of time, other things being equal.

Law of supply
The observation that the higher the price of a good, the more of that good sellers will make available over a specified time period, other things being equal.

The other side of the basic model in economics involves the quantities of goods and services that firms will offer for sale to the market. The **supply** of any good or service is the amount that firms will produce and offer for sale under certain conditions during a specified time period. The relationship between price and quantity supplied, called the **law of supply,** can be summarized as follows:

> ***At higher prices, a larger quantity will generally be supplied than at lower prices, all other things held constant. At lower prices, a smaller quantity will generally be supplied than at higher prices, all other things held constant.***

There is generally a direct relationship between price and quantity supplied. As the price rises, the quantity supplied rises. As the price falls, the quantity supplied also falls. Producers are normally willing to produce and sell more of their product at a higher price than at a lower price, other things being constant. At $5 per magneto optical disk, manufacturers would almost certainly be willing to supply a larger quantity than at $1 per MO disk, assuming, of course, that no other prices in the economy had changed.

As with the law of demand, millions of instances in the real world have given us confidence in the law of supply. On a theoretical level, the law of supply is based on a model in which producers and sellers seek to make the most gain possible from their activities. For example, as a manufacturer attempts to produce more and more MO disks over the same time period, it will eventually have to hire more workers, pay overtime wages (which are higher), and overutilize its machines. Only if offered a higher price per MO disk will the manufacturer be willing to incur these higher costs. That is why the law of supply implies a direct relationship between price and quantity supplied.

Have steel manufacturers' responses to a decline in the price of steel been consistent with the law of supply?

EXAMPLE

Steel Producers Reduce Production When the Price of Steel Falls

Recently, the market price of steel declined from $660 per ton to below $625 per ton. Steel-producing firms responded by cutting back on their production of steel. Thus, as predicted by the law of supply, a decrease in the price of steel resulted in a decrease in the quantity of steel supplied. This direct relationship between price and quantity supplied is consistent with an upward-sloping supply curve for steel.

FOR CRITICAL THINKING

After the price of steel declined, which direction did each steel manufacturer move along its supply curve?

The Supply Schedule

Just as we were able to construct a demand schedule, we can construct a *supply schedule*, which is a table relating prices to the quantity supplied at each price. A supply schedule can also be referred to simply as *supply*. It is a set of planned production rates that depends on the price of the product. We show the individual supply schedule for a hypothetical producer in panel (a) of Figure 3-6 below. At a price of $1 per MO disk, for example, this producer will supply 20,000 MO disks per year. At a price of $5 per MO disk, this producer will supply 55,000 MO disks per year.

FIGURE 3-6

The Individual Producer's Supply Schedule and Supply Curve for Magneto Optical Disks

Panel (a) shows that at higher prices, a hypothetical supplier will be willing to provide a greater quantity of magneto optical disks. We plot the various price-quantity combinations in panel (a) on the grid in panel (b). When we connect these points, we create the individual supply curve for MO disks. It is positively sloped.

Panel (a)

Combination	Price per Constant-Quality Magneto Optical Disk	Quantity of Magneto Optical Disks Supplied (thousands of constant-quality units per year)
F	$5	55
G	4	40
H	3	35
I	2	25
J	1	20

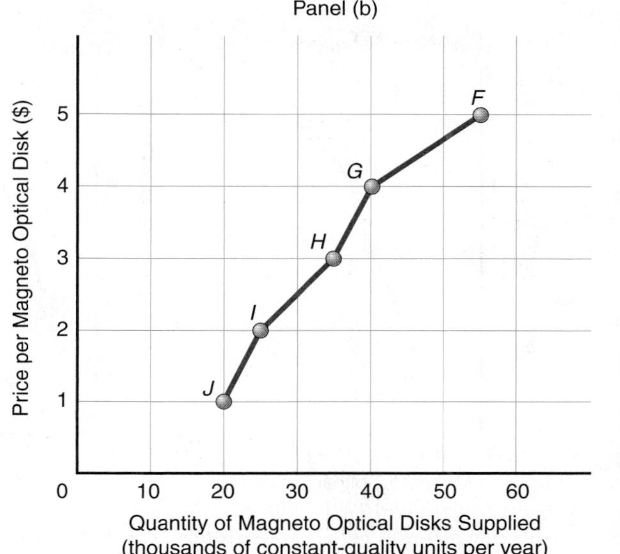

The Supply Curve

Supply curve
The graphical representation of the supply schedule; a line (curve) showing the supply schedule, which generally slopes upward (has a positive slope), other things being equal.

We can convert the supply schedule from panel (a) of Figure 3-6 on the previous page into a **supply curve,** just as we earlier created a demand curve in Figure 3-1 on page 51. All we do is take the price-quantity combinations from panel (a) of Figure 3-6 and plot them in panel (b). We have labeled these combinations *F* through *J*. Connecting these points, we obtain an upward-sloping curve that shows the typically direct relationship between price and quantity supplied. Again, we have to remember that we are talking about quantity supplied *per year*, measured in constant-quality units.

The Market Supply Curve

Just as we summed the individual demand curves to obtain the market demand curve, we sum the individual producers' supply curves to obtain the market supply curve. Look at Figure 3-7 below, in which we horizontally sum two typical supply curves for manufacturers of magneto optical disks. Supplier 1's data are taken from Figure 3-6 on the previous page. Supplier 2 is added. The numbers are presented in panel (a). The graphical representation of supplier 1 is in panel (b), of supplier 2 in panel (c), and of the summation in panel (d). The result, then, is the supply curve for magneto optical

FIGURE 3-7

Horizontal Summation of Supply Curves

In panel (a), we show the data for two individual suppliers of magneto optical disks. Adding how much each is willing to supply at different prices, we come up with the combined quantities supplied in column 4. When we plot the values in columns 2 and 3 on grids from panels (b) and (c) and add them horizontally, we obtain the combined supply curve for the two suppliers in question, shown in panel (d).

Panel (a)

(1) Price per Magneto Optical Disk	(2) Supplier 1's Quantity Supplied (thousands)	(3) Supplier 2's Quantity Supplied (thousands)	(4) = (2) + (3) Combined Quantity Supplied per Year (thousands)
$5	55	35	90
4	40	30	70
3	35	20	55
2	25	15	40
1	20	10	30

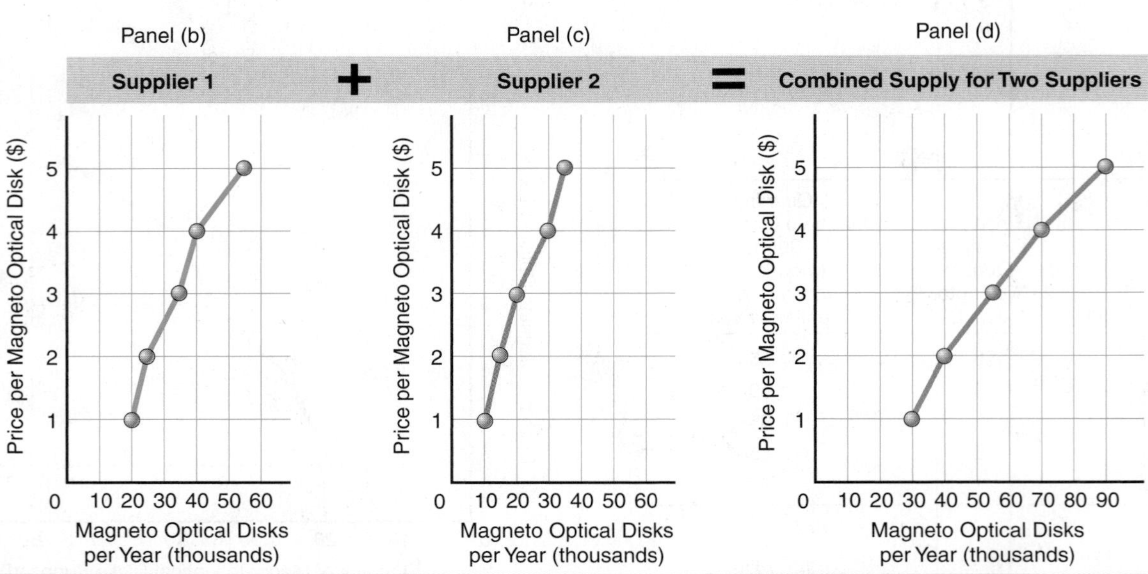

disks for suppliers 1 and 2. We assume that there are more suppliers of MO disks, however. The total market supply schedule and total market supply curve for MO disks are represented in Figure 3-8 below, with the curve in panel (b) obtained by adding all of the supply curves, such as those shown in panels (b) and (c) of Figure 3-7 on the facing page. Notice the difference between the market supply curve with only two suppliers in Figure 3-7 and the one with many suppliers—the entire true market—in panel (b) of Figure 3-8. (For simplicity, we assume that the true total market supply curve is a straight line.)

Note what happens at the market level when price changes. If the price is $3, the quantity supplied is 6 million. If the price goes up to $4, the quantity supplied increases to 8 million per year. If the price falls to $2, the quantity supplied decreases to 4 million per year. Changes in quantity supplied are represented by movements along the supply curve in panel (b) of Figure 3-8.

QUICK QUIZ See page 74 for the answers. Review concepts from this section in MyEconLab.

There is normally a __________ relationship between price and quantity of a good supplied, other things held constant.

The __________ curve normally shows a direct relationship between price and quantity supplied. The __________ __________ curve is obtained by horizontally adding individual supply curves in the market.

Shifts in Supply

When we looked at demand, we found out that any change in anything relevant besides the price of the good or service caused the demand curve to shift inward or outward. The same is true for the supply curve. If something besides price changes and alters the willingness of suppliers to produce a good or service, we will see the entire supply curve shift.

FIGURE 3-8

The Market Supply Schedule and the Market Supply Curve for Magneto Optical Disks

In panel (a), we show the summation of all the individual producers' supply schedules. In panel (b), we graph the resulting supply curve. It represents the market supply curve for MO disks and is upward sloping.

Panel (a)

Price per Constant-Quality Magneto Optical Disk	Quantity of Magneto Optical Disks Supplied (millions of constant-quality units per year)
$5	10
4	8
3	6
2	4
1	2

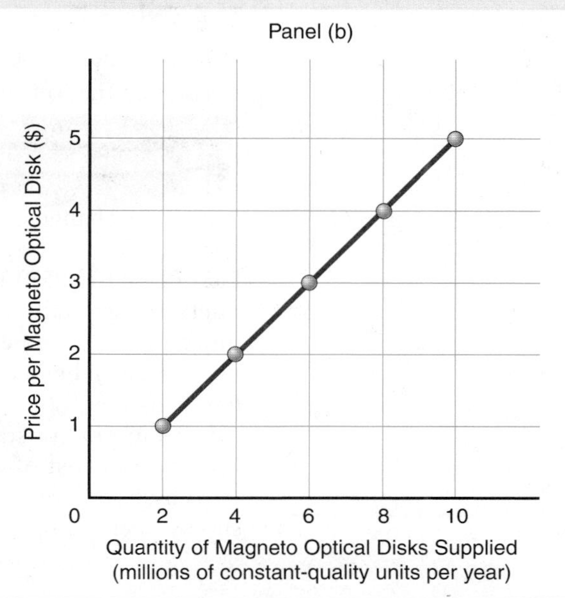

FIGURE 3-9

Shifts in the Supply Curve

If the cost of producing magneto optical disks were to fall dramatically, the supply curve would shift rightward from S_1 to S_2 such that at all prices, a larger quantity would be forthcoming from suppliers. Conversely, if the cost of production rose, the supply curve would shift leftward to S_3.

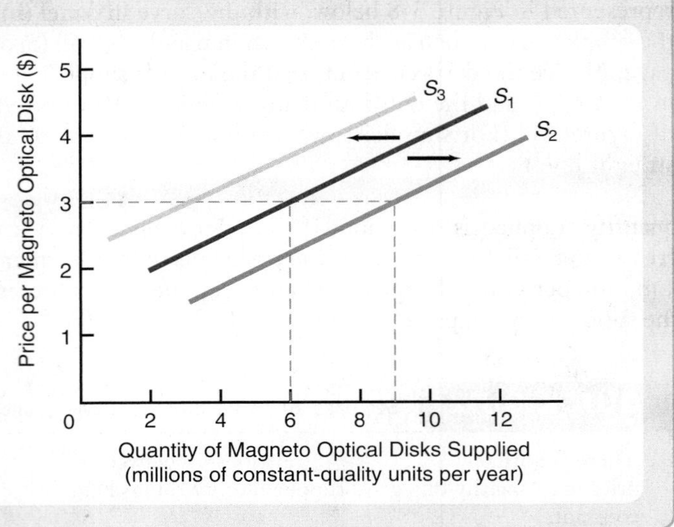

Consider an example. There is a new method of manufacturing magneto optical disks that significantly reduces the cost of production. In this situation, producers of MO disks will supply more product at *all* prices because their cost of so doing has fallen dramatically. Competition among manufacturers to produce more at each and every price will shift the supply curve outward to the right from S_1 to S_2 in Figure 3-9 above. At a price of $3, the number supplied was originally 6 million per year, but now the amount supplied (after the reduction in the costs of production) at $3 per MO disk will be 9 million a year. (This is similar to what has happened to the supply curve of digital devices in recent years as memory chip prices have fallen.)

Consider the opposite case. If the price of raw materials used in manufacturing magneto optical disks increases, the supply curve in Figure 3-9 will shift from S_1 to S_3. At each and every price, the quantity of MO disks supplied will fall due to the increase in the price of raw materials.

The Other Determinants of Supply

When supply curves are drawn, only the price of the good in question changes, and it is assumed that other things remain constant. The other things assumed constant are the *ceteris paribus* conditions of supply. They include the prices of resources (inputs) used to produce the product, technology and productivity, taxes and subsidies, producers' price expectations, and the number of firms in the industry. If *any* of these *ceteris paribus* conditions changes, there will be a shift in the supply curve.

COST OF INPUTS USED TO PRODUCE THE PRODUCT If one or more input prices fall, production costs fall, and the supply curve will shift outward to the right. That is, more will be supplied at each and every price. The opposite will be true if one or more inputs become more expensive. For example, when we draw the supply curve of new tablet devices, we are holding the price of microprocessors (and other inputs) constant. When we draw the supply curve of blue jeans, we are holding the cost of cotton fabric fixed.

Why have large swings in the price of cotton generated variations in the market supply of clothing?

EXAMPLE

Cotton Price Movements Squeeze and Stretch Clothing Supply

Between 2009 and 2010, the price of cotton, a key input cost in the production of many articles of clothing, increased by 55 percent. Clothing manufacturers responded by reducing the amount of clothing supplied at any given price of clothing, so the market supply of clothing decreased.

During 2011, the price of cotton decreased by 53 percent, to nearly its 2009 level. This cotton-price reversal induced clothing-producing firms to increase the amount of clothing supplied at each possible clothing price. Thus, the market supply of clothing increased.

FOR CRITICAL THINKING

What do you think happened to the market supply of clothing when cotton prices rose somewhat again in 2012?

TECHNOLOGY AND PRODUCTIVITY Supply curves are drawn by assuming a given technology, or "state of the art." When the available production techniques change, the supply curve will shift. For example, when a better production technique for magneto optical disks becomes available, production costs decrease, and the supply curve will shift to the right. A larger quantity will be forthcoming at each and every price because the cost of production is lower.

TAXES AND SUBSIDIES Certain taxes, such as a per-unit tax, are effectively an addition to production costs and therefore reduce the supply. If the supply curve is S_1 in Figure 3-9 on the facing page, a per-unit tax increase would shift it to S_3. A per-unit **subsidy** would do the opposite. Every producer would get a "gift" from the government for each unit produced. This per-unit subsidy would shift the curve to S_2.

Subsidy
A negative tax; a payment to a producer from the government, usually in the form of a cash grant per unit.

WHAT IF... politicians simultaneously oppose a higher price for the current quantity of gasoline supplied yet favor higher taxes on the fuel?

A decrease in the market supply of gasoline implies that producers require a higher price to continue providing the same quantity of this fuel. When this occurs, media reports typically feature members of Congress complaining about gasoline sellers insisting on prices that are "too high." Voting records, though, often reveal that many of the politicians who make these complaints have voted to boost federal fuel taxes. Such tax hikes generate decreases in the supply of gasoline and hence contribute to sellers' desires to receive a higher price for any given quantity. Thus, when politicians join congressional majorities to impose higher federal gasoline taxes, what results is the fuel supply reductions that these politicians criticize.

PRICE EXPECTATIONS A change in the expectation of a future relative price of a product can affect a producer's current willingness to supply, just as price expectations affect a consumer's current willingness to purchase. For example, suppliers of magneto optical disks may withhold from the market part of their current supply if they anticipate higher prices in the future. The current amount supplied at each and every price will decrease.

NUMBER OF FIRMS IN THE INDUSTRY In the short run, when firms can change only the number of employees they use, we hold the number of firms in the industry constant. In the long run, the number of firms may change. If the number of firms increases, supply will increase, and the supply curve will shift outward to the right. If the number of firms decreases, supply will decrease, and the supply curve will shift inward to the left.

How did a rash of tornadoes affect the supply curve in the U.S. poultry market?

EXAMPLE

How Deadly Southern Twisters Pummeled the U.S. Poultry Supply

During the course of the deadliest U.S. tornado season in decades, 278 tornadoes swept across the United States between April 26 and 28, 2011. Most of the twisters struck southern states. Particularly hard hit was Alabama, whose farmers typically contribute just over 1 billion chickens to the nation's production of poultry—about 12 percent of the total. Tornadoes damaged numerous feed mills and chicken-processing plants so severely that many poultry-producing companies were unable to supply poultry for a few months. This reduction in the number of chicken-producing firms in operation caused a decrease in the amount of poultry supplied at any given poultry price. That is, the U.S. market poultry supply decreased temporarily in 2011.

FOR CRITICAL THINKING

How did the outright destruction of millions of chickens by the April 2011 tornadoes affect the position of the market poultry supply curve?

Changes in Supply versus Changes in Quantity Supplied

We cannot overstress the importance of distinguishing between a movement along the supply curve—which occurs only when the price changes for a given supply curve—and a shift in the supply curve—which occurs only with changes in *ceteris paribus* conditions. A change in the price of the good in question always (and only) brings about a change in the quantity supplied along a given supply curve. We move to a different point on the existing supply curve. This is specifically called a *change in quantity supplied.* When price changes, quantity supplied changes—there is a movement from one point to another along the same supply curve.

When you think of *supply,* think of the entire curve. Quantity supplied is represented by a single point on the supply curve.

> ***A change, or shift, in supply is a movement of the entire curve. The* only *thing that can cause the entire curve to move is a change in one of the* ceteris paribus *conditions.***

Consequently,

> ***A change in price leads to a change in the quantity supplied, other things being constant. This is a movement* along *the curve.***

> ***A change in any* ceteris paribus *condition for supply leads to a change in supply. This causes a* shift *of the curve.***

QUICK QUIZ See page 74 for the answers. Review concepts from this section in MyEconLab.

If the price changes, we __________ __________ a curve—there is a change in quantity demanded or supplied. If some other determinant changes, we __________ a curve—there is a change in demand or supply.

The **supply curve** is drawn with other things held constant. If these *ceteris paribus* conditions of supply change, the supply curve will shift. The major *ceteris paribus* conditions are (1) __________, (2) __________, (3) __________, (4) __________, and (5) __________.

Putting Demand and Supply Together

In the sections on demand and supply, we tried to confine each discussion to demand or supply only. But you have probably already realized that we can't view the world just from the demand side or just from the supply side. There is interaction between the two. In this section, we will discuss how they interact and how that interaction determines the prices that prevail in our economy and other economies in which the forces of demand and supply are allowed to work.

Go to www.econtoday.com/chap03 to see how the U.S. Department of Agriculture seeks to estimate demand and supply conditions for major agricultural products.

Let's first combine the demand and supply schedules and then combine the curves.

Demand and Supply Schedules Combined

Let's place panel (a) from Figure 3-3 (the market demand schedule) on page 54 and panel (a) from Figure 3-8 (the market supply schedule) on page 61 together in panel (a) of Figure 3-10 on the following page. Column 1 displays the price. Column 2 shows the quantity supplied per year at any given price. Column 3 displays the quantity demanded. Column 4 is the difference between columns 2 and 3, or the difference between the quantity supplied and the quantity demanded. In column 5, we label those differences as either excess quantity supplied (called a *surplus*, which we shall discuss shortly) or excess quantity demanded (commonly known as a *shortage*, also discussed shortly). For example, at a price of $1, only 2 million magneto optical disks would be supplied, but the quantity demanded would be 10 million. The difference would be −8 million, which we label excess quantity demanded (a shortage). At the other end, a price of $5 would elicit 10 million in quantity supplied. Quantity demanded would drop to 2 million, leaving a difference of +8 million units, which we call excess quantity supplied (a surplus).

Now, do you notice something special about the price of $3? At that price, both the quantity supplied and the quantity demanded per year are 6 million. The difference then is zero. There is neither excess quantity demanded (shortage) nor excess quantity supplied (surplus). Hence the price of $3 is very special. It is called the **market clearing price**—it clears the market of all excess quantities demanded or supplied. There are no willing consumers who want to pay $3 per MO disk but are turned away by sellers, and there are no willing suppliers who want to sell MO disks at $3 who cannot sell all they want at that price. Another term for the market clearing price is the **equilibrium price,** the price at which there is no tendency for change. Consumers are able to get all they want at that price, and suppliers are able to sell all they want at that price.

Market clearing, or **equilibrium, price**
The price that clears the market, at which quantity demanded equals quantity supplied; the price where the demand curve intersects the supply curve.

Equilibrium

We can define **equilibrium** in general as a point at which quantity demanded equals quantity supplied at a particular price. There tends to be no movement of the price or the quantity away from this point unless demand or supply changes. Any movement away from this point will set into motion forces that will cause movement back to it. Therefore, equilibrium is a stable point. Any point that is not an equilibrium is unstable and will not persist.

Equilibrium
The situation when quantity supplied equals quantity demanded at a particular price.

The equilibrium point occurs where the supply and demand curves intersect. The equilibrium price is given on the vertical axis directly to the left of where the supply and demand curves cross. The equilibrium quantity is given on the horizontal axis directly underneath the intersection of the demand and supply curves.

Panel (b) in Figure 3-3 (p. 54) and panel (b) in Figure 3-8 (p. 61) are combined as panel (b) in Figure 3-10 on the next page. The demand curve is labeled D, the supply curve S. We have labeled the intersection of the supply curve with the demand curve as point E, for equilibrium. That corresponds to a market clearing price of $3, at which both the quantity supplied and the quantity demanded are 6 million units per year. There is neither excess quantity supplied nor excess quantity demanded. Point E, the equilibrium point, always occurs at the intersection of the supply and demand curves. This is the price *toward which* the market price will automatically tend to gravitate, because there is no outcome more advantageous than this price for both consumers and producers.

FIGURE 3-10

Putting Demand and Supply Together

In panel (a), we see that at the price of $3, the quantity supplied and the quantity demanded are equal, resulting in neither an excess quantity demanded nor an excess quantity supplied. We call this price the equilibrium, or market clearing, price. In panel (b), the intersection of the supply and demand curves is at *E*, at a price of $3 and a quantity of 6 million per year. At point *E*, there is neither an excess quantity demanded nor an excess quantity supplied. At a price of $1, the quantity supplied will be only 2 million per year, but the quantity demanded will be 10 million. The difference is excess quantity demanded at a price of $1. The price will rise, so we will move from point *A* up the supply curve and from point *B* up the demand curve to point *E*. At the other extreme, a price of $5 elicits a quantity supplied of 10 million but a quantity demanded of only 2 million. The difference is excess quantity supplied at a price of $5. The price will fall, so we will move down the demand curve and the supply curve to the equilibrium price, $3 per magneto optical disk.

Panel (a)

(1) Price per Constant-Quality Magneto Optical Disk	(2) Quantity Supplied (magneto optical disks per year)	(3) Quantity Demanded (magneto optical disks per year)	(4) Difference (2) − (3) (magneto optical disks per year)	(5) Condition
$5	10 million	2 million	8 million	Excess quantity supplied (surplus)
4	8 million	4 million	4 million	Excess quantity supplied (surplus)
3	6 million	6 million	0	Market clearing price—equilibrium (no surplus, no shortage)
2	4 million	8 million	–4 million	Excess quantity demanded (shortage)
1	2 million	10 million	–8 million	Excess quantity demanded (shortage)

Panel (b)

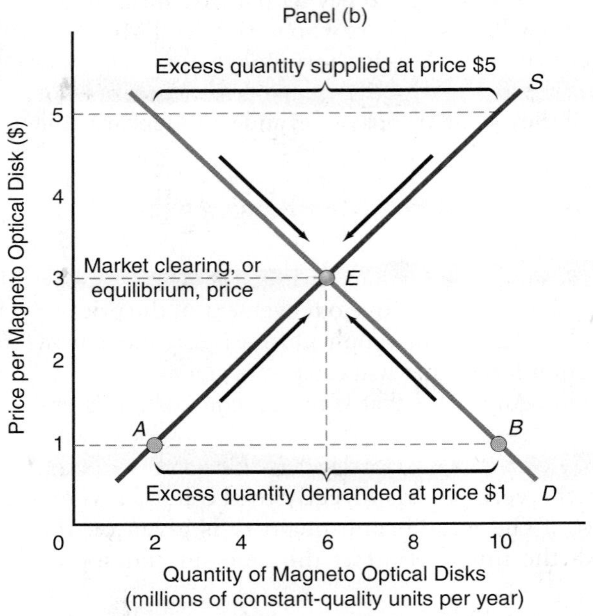

Shortages

The price of $3 depicted in Figure 3-10 above represents a situation of equilibrium. If there were a non-market-clearing, or disequilibrium, price, this price would put into play forces that would cause the price to change toward the market clearing price, at which equilibrium would again be sustained. Look again at panel (b) in Figure 3-10. Suppose that instead of being at the equilibrium price of $3, for some reason the market price is $1. At this price, the quantity demanded of 10 million per year exceeds the quantity supplied of 2 million per year. We have a situation of excess quantity demanded at the price of $1. This is usually called a **shortage.** Consumers of magneto optical disks would find that they could not buy all that they wished at $1 apiece. But forces will cause the price to rise: Competing consumers will bid up the price, and suppliers will increase output in response. (Remember, some buyers would pay $5 or more rather than do without MO disks.) We would move from points *A* and *B* toward point *E*. The process would stop when the price again reached $3 per MO disk.

Shortage
A situation in which quantity demanded is greater than quantity supplied at a price below the market clearing price.

At this point, it is important to recall a distinction made in Chapter 2:

Shortages and scarcity are not the same thing.

A shortage is a situation in which the quantity demanded exceeds the quantity supplied at a price that is somehow kept *below* the market clearing price. Our definition of scarcity was much more general and all-encompassing: a situation in which the resources available for producing output are insufficient to satisfy all wants. Any choice necessarily costs an opportunity, and the opportunity is lost. Hence, we will always live in a world of scarcity because we must constantly make choices, but we do not necessarily have to live in a world of shortages.

What has caused a shortage of a key drug used to treat victims of a common form of leukemia?

EXAMPLE

Production Breakdowns Create a Shortage of a Life-Saving Drug

Each year, physicians diagnose more than 20,000 new cases of acute lymphoblastic leukemia. Recently, all of the companies that manufacture cytarabine, a drug commonly used in treatment regimens for this disease, experienced problems that slowed or halted production of the drug. As a consequence, the quantity of cytarabine supplied fell well below the quantity demanded for treatments at the prevailing price.

In response to the shortage, hospitals and clinics began limiting available cytarabine doses to children and to only a few adults judged most likely to benefit from treatment with that drug. Other adults had to switch to different drugs even if they were unlikely to be as effective. Physicians hope that eventually more adults will be able to undergo treatment with this drug, after resolution of production problems, albeit at a market clearing price that probably will be higher.

FOR CRITICAL THINKING

Why is the market clearing price of cytarabine likely to increase, and why might an increase in that price be required to eliminate the shortage of the drug?

Surpluses

Now let's repeat the experiment with the market price at $5 rather than at the market clearing price of $3. Clearly, the quantity supplied will exceed the quantity demanded at that price. The result will be an excess quantity supplied at $5 per unit. This excess quantity supplied is often called a **surplus.** Given the curves in panel (b) in Figure 3-10 on the facing page, however, there will be forces pushing the price back down toward $3 per magneto optical disk. Competing suppliers will cut prices and reduce output, and consumers will purchase more at these new lower prices. If the two forces of supply and demand are unrestricted, they will bring the price back to $3 per MO disk.

Surplus
A situation in which quantity supplied is greater than quantity demanded at a price above the market clearing price.

Shortages and surpluses are resolved in unfettered markets—markets in which price changes are free to occur. The forces that resolve them are those of competition: In the case of shortages, consumers competing for a limited quantity supplied drive up the price; in the case of surpluses, sellers compete for the limited quantity demanded, thus driving prices down to equilibrium. The equilibrium price is the only stable price, and the (unrestricted) market price tends to gravitate toward it.

What happens when the price is set below the equilibrium price? Here come the scalpers.

POLICY EXAMPLE

Should Shortages in the Ticket Market Be Solved by Scalpers?

If you have ever tried to get tickets to a playoff game in sports, a popular Broadway play, or a superstar's rap concert, you know about "shortages." The standard Super Bowl ticket situation is shown in Figure 3-11 below. At the face-value price of Super Bowl tickets ($800), the quantity demanded (175,000) greatly exceeds the quantity supplied (80,000). Because shortages last only as long as prices and quantities do not change, markets tend to exhibit a movement out of this disequilibrium toward equilibrium. Obviously, the quantity of Super Bowl tickets cannot change, but the price can go as high as $6,000.

Enter the scalper. This colorful term is used because when you purchase a ticket that is being resold at a price higher than face value, the seller is skimming profit off the top ("taking your scalp"). If an event sells out and people who wished to purchase tickets at current prices were unable to do so, ticket prices by definition were lower than market clearing prices. People without tickets may be willing to buy high-priced tickets because they place a greater value on the entertainment event than the face value of the ticket. Without scalpers, those individuals would not be able to attend the event. In the case of the Super Bowl, various forms of scalping occur nationwide. Tickets for a seat on the 50-yard line have been sold for as much as $6,000 apiece. In front of every Super Bowl arena, you can find ticket scalpers hawking their wares.

In most states, scalping is illegal. In Pennsylvania, convicted scalpers are either fined $5,000 or sentenced to two years behind bars. For an economist, such legislation seems strange. As one New York ticket broker said, "I look at scalping like working as a stockbroker, buying low and selling high. If people are willing to pay me the money, what kind of problem is that?"

FOR CRITICAL ANALYSIS

What happens to ticket scalpers who are still holding tickets after an event has started?

FIGURE 3-11

Shortages of Super Bowl Tickets

The quantity of tickets for a Super Bowl game is fixed at 80,000. At the price per ticket of $800, the quantity demanded is 175,000. Consequently, there is an excess quantity demanded at the below-market clearing price. In this example, prices can go as high as $6,000 in the scalpers' market.

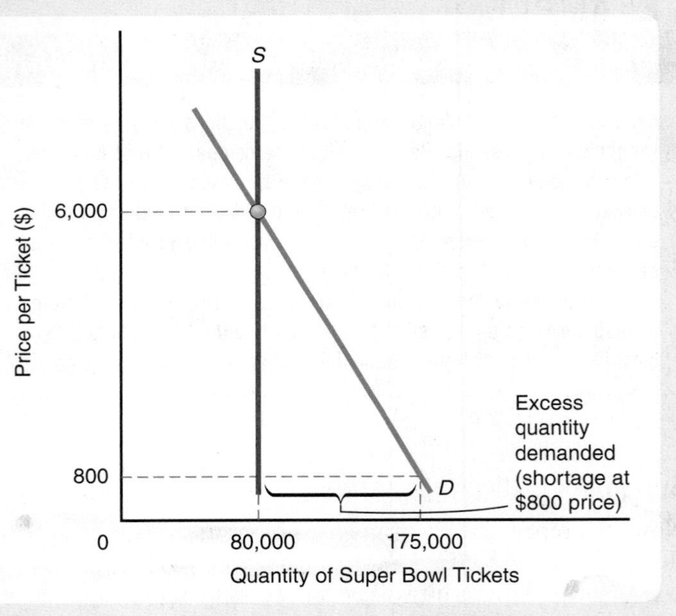

QUICK QUIZ See page 74 for the answers. Review concepts from this section in MyEconLab.

The market clearing price occurs at the __________ of the market demand curve and the market supply curve. It is also called the __________ price, the price from which there is no tendency to change unless there is a change in demand or supply.

Whenever the price is __________ than the equilibrium price, there is an excess quantity supplied (a **surplus**).

Whenever the price is __________ than the equilibrium price, there is an excess quantity demanded (a **shortage**).

YOU ARE THERE

Why the Casket Industry Is on Life Support

Ken Camp, the chief executive officer of Hillenbrand, Inc., has succinctly summed up his company's situation: "We are a very significant player in an industry that isn't growing." Hillenbrand is part of the casket industry, which is facing tough times as a consequence of the falling price of cremations, which are substitutes for casket burials of deceased individuals. The overall price of a traditional casket burial exceeds $7,200. In contrast, the price of a cremation service has recently fallen to about $1,300.

The widening differential between the price of traditional casket burials and the price of cremation services has induced many people to substitute away from purchasing caskets. Today, nearly 400,000 fewer caskets are purchased per year in the United States than were purchased in 2008. Thus, the demand for caskets has declined in response to a decrease in the price of an already lower-priced substitute—cremation. This fact explains why Camp has concluded that the casket industry "isn't growing."

Critical Thinking Questions

1. What impact do you think that the decline in demand for caskets has had on sellers' total revenues, which equal price multiplied by quantity sold?
2. How have technological improvements in the cremation-services industry likely affected the supply curve for these services?

ISSUES & APPLICATIONS

Your Higher Education Bills Really Are Increasing

CONCEPTS APPLIED

- Money Price
- Relative Price
- Market Clearing Price

Undoubtedly, you have noticed that your college expenses have been rising. The reason is that the prices of goods and services that students must purchase to obtain higher education have been increasing persistently for more than three decades.

A Tale of Upward Trends in Two Sets of Money Prices

Figure 3-12 on the following page displays index measures of two sets of money prices that are important to current U.S. college students. One is an index measure of U.S. college tuition and fees. The other is an index measure of the prices of U.S. educational books and supplies.

Clearly, the figure indicates that both indexes of these money prices have increased substantially in recent years. The money value of tuition and fees that college students pay is about thirteen times greater today than in the late 1970s, and the money prices of educational books and supplies are more than nine times higher.

Relative Prices of Higher Education Are Also Rising

Have prices of higher education been rising faster than the average level of prices of all good and services? Figure 3-12 also shows an index measure of the level of prices of all goods and services purchased in the United States. Taking into account the significant increase in the prices of all goods and services during the past four decades indicates that *relative* prices of educational books and supplies have more than doubled. *Relative* tuition-and-fee prices have more than tripled.

Continuing increases in the relative prices of tuition and fees and of educational books and supplies reflect higher market clearing prices of college enrollment, books, and

FIGURE 3-12

Indexes of Prices for Higher-Education-Related Items and All Goods and Services since 1978

The rise in the index of U.S. tuition and fees from 100 in 1978 to the current level of just over 1,300 indicates that the money price of college enrollment is now thirteen times higher. Money prices of educational books and supplies are now more than nine times higher, and money prices of all goods and services are about four times higher.

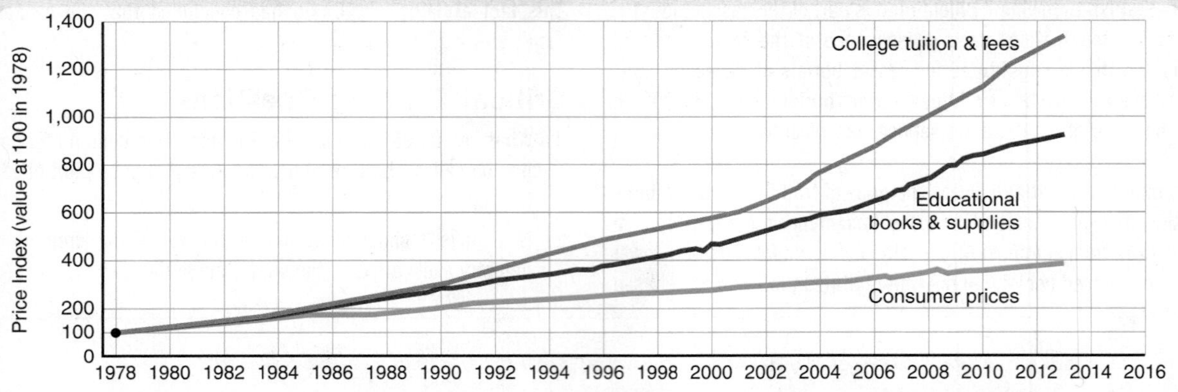

Sources: Bureau of Labor Statistics; author's estimates.

supplies. These are the prices at which the demand and supply curves for these items cross in the relevant markets—prices at intersections that have continued drifting upward over time.

For Critical Thinking

1. In relation to higher education, what has happened to the relative prices of other goods and services?
2. Given that market supply has increased steadily during the past four decades, what must account for rising money and relative prices of higher education?

Web Resources

1. Review a list of the highest-priced U.S. colleges at **www.econtoday.com/chap03**.
2. Compare the money prices of college enrollment in the United States to the lower money prices prevailing in the United Kingdom at **www.econtoday.com/chap03**.

MyEconLab

For more questions on this chapter's Issues & Applications, go to **MyEconLab**. In the Study Plan for this chapter, select Section N: News.

MyEconLab

Here is what you should know after reading this chapter. MyEconLab will help you identify what you know, and where to go when you need to practice.

WHAT YOU SHOULD KNOW		WHERE TO GO TO PRACTICE
The Law of Demand Other things being equal, individuals will purchase fewer units of a good at a higher price and will purchase more units at a lower price.	market, 49 demand, 49 law of demand, 49	• MyEconLab Study Plan 3.1

MyEconLab *continued*

WHAT YOU SHOULD KNOW		WHERE TO GO TO PRACTICE
Relative Prices versus Money Prices The relative price is the price of the good in terms of other goods. In a world of generally rising prices, people compare the price of one good with the general level of prices of other goods in order to decide whether the relative price of that one good has gone up, gone down, or stayed the same.	relative price, 49 money price, 49	• MyEconLab Study Plan 3.1
A Change in Quantity Demanded versus a Change in Demand The demand schedule shows quantities purchased per unit of time at various possible prices. Graphically, the demand schedule is a downward-sloping demand curve. A change in the price of the good generates a change in the quantity demanded, which is a movement along the demand curve. Factors other than the price of the good that affect the amount demanded are (1) income, (2) tastes and preferences, (3) the prices of related goods, (4) expectations, and (5) market size (the number of potential buyers). If any of these *ceteris paribus* conditions of demand changes, there is a change in demand, and the demand curve shifts to a new position.	demand curve, 52 market demand, 52 *ceteris paribus* conditions, 54 normal goods, 55 inferior goods, 55 substitutes, 56 complements, 56 **Key Figures** Figure 3-2, 53 Figure 3-4, 54 Figure 3-5, 58	• MyEconLab Study Plans 3.2, 3.3 • Animated Figures 3-2, 3-4, 3-5
The Law of Supply According to the law of supply, sellers will produce and offer for sale more units of a good at a higher price, and they will produce and offer for sale fewer units of the good at a lower price.	supply, 58 law of supply, 58	• MyEconLab Study Plan 3.4
A Change in Quantity Supplied versus a Change in Supply The supply schedule shows quantities produced and sold per unit of time at various possible prices. On a graph, the supply schedule is a supply curve that slopes upward. A change in the price of the good generates a change in the quantity supplied, which is a movement along the supply curve. Factors other than the price of the good that affect the amount supplied are (1) input prices, (2) technology and productivity, (3) taxes and subsidies, (4) price expectations, and (5) the number of sellers. If any of these *ceteris paribus* conditions changes, there is a change in supply, and the supply curve shifts to a new position.	supply curve, 60 subsidy, 63 **Key Figures** Figure 3-6, 59 Figure 3-7, 60 Figure 3-9, 62	• MyEconLab Study Plans 3.5, 3.6 • Animated Figures 3-6, 3-7, 3-9

MyEconLab *continued*

WHAT YOU SHOULD KNOW		WHERE TO GO TO PRACTICE
Determining the Market Price and the Equilibrium Quantity The equilibrium price of a good and the equilibrium quantity of the good that is produced and sold are determined by the intersection of the demand and supply curves. At this intersection point, the quantity demanded by buyers of the good just equals the quantity supplied by sellers, so there is neither an excess quantity of the good supplied (surplus) nor an excess quantity of the good demanded (shortage).	market clearing, or equilibrium, price, 65 equilibrium, 65 shortage, 67 surplus, 67 **Key Figure** Figure 3-11, 68	• MyEconLab Study Plan 3.7 • Animated Figure 3-11

Log in to MyEconLab, take a chapter test, and get a personalized Study Plan that tells you which concepts you understand and which ones you need to review. From there, MyEconLab will give you further practice, tutorials, animations, videos, and guided solutions. For more information, visit www.myeconlab.com

PROBLEMS

All problems are assignable in MyEconLab. *Answers to odd-numbered problems appear at the back of the book.*

3-1. Suppose that in a recent market period, the following relationship existed between the price of tablet devices and the quantity supplied and quantity demanded.

Price	Quantity Demanded	Quantity Supplied
$390	100 million	40 million
$400	90 million	60 million
$410	80 million	80 million
$420	70 million	100 million
$430	60 million	120 million

Graph the supply and demand curves for tablet devices using the information in the table. What are the equilibrium price and quantity? If the industry price is $400, is there a shortage or surplus of tablet devices? How much is the shortage or surplus? (See pages 66–67.)

3-2. Suppose that in a later market period, the quantities supplied in the table in Problem 3-1 are unchanged. The amount demanded, however, has increased by 30 million at each price. Construct the resulting demand curve in the illustration you made for Problem 3-1. Is this an increase or a decrease in demand? What are the new equilibrium quantity and the new market price? Give two examples of changes in *ceteris paribus* conditions that might cause such a change. (See page 54.)

3-3. Consider the market for cable-based Internet access service, which is a normal good. Explain whether the following events would cause an increase or a decrease in demand or an increase or a decrease in the quantity demanded. (See page 57.)

a. Firms providing wireless (an alternative to cable) Internet access services reduce their prices.

b. Firms providing cable-based Internet access services reduce their prices.

c. There is a decrease in the incomes earned by consumers of cable-based Internet access services.

d. Consumers' tastes shift away from using wireless Internet access in favor of cable-based Internet access services.

3-4. In the market for flash memory drives (a normal good), explain whether the following events would cause an increase or a decrease in demand or an increase or a decrease in the quantity demanded. Also explain what happens to the equilibrium quantity and the market clearing price. (See page 54.)

a. There are increases in the prices of storage racks for flash memory drives.

b. There is a decrease in the price of computer drives that read the information contained on flash memory drives.

c. There is a dramatic increase in the price of secure digital cards that, like flash memory drives, can be used to store digital data.

d. A booming economy increases the income of the typical buyer of flash memory drives.

e. Consumers of flash memory drives anticipate that the price of this good will decline in the future.

3-5. Give an example of a complement and a substitute in consumption for each of the following items. (See pages 55–56.)

a. Bacon

b. Tennis racquets

c. Coffee

d. Automobiles

3-6. For each of the following shifts in the demand curve and associated price change of a complement or substitute item, explain whether the change in the price of the complement or substitute must have been an increase or a decrease. (See page 56.)

a. A rise in the demand for a dashboard global-positioning-system device follows a change in the price of automobiles, which are complements.

b. A fall in the demand for e-book readers follows a change in the price of e-books, which are complements.

c. A rise in the demand for tablet devices follows a change in the price of ultrathin laptop computers, which are substitutes.

d. A fall in the demand for physical books follows a change in the price of e-books, which are substitutes.

3-7. Identify which of the following would generate an increase in the market demand for tablet devices, which are a normal good. (See pages 54–57.)

a. A decrease in the incomes of consumers of tablet devices

b. An increase in the price of ultrathin computers, which are substitutes

c. An increase in the price of online apps, which are complements

d. An increase in the number of consumers in the market for tablet devices

3-8. Identify which of the following would generate a decrease in the market demand for e-book readers, which are a normal good. (See pages 54–57.)

a. An increase in the price of downloadable apps utilized to enhance the e-book reading experience, which are complements

b. An increase in the number of consumers in the market for e-book readers

c. A decrease in the price of tablet devices, which are substitutes

d. A reduction in the incomes of consumers of e-book readers

3-9. Consider the following diagram of a market for one-bedroom rental apartments in a college community. (See pages 66–67.)

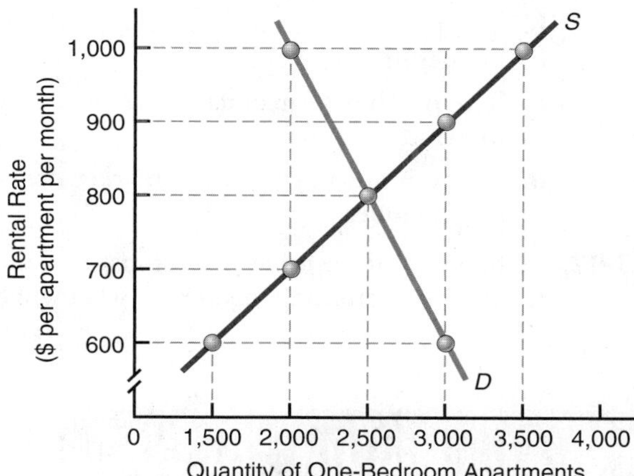

a. At a rental rate of $1,000 per month, is there an excess quantity supplied, or is there an excess quantity demanded? What is the amount of the excess quantity supplied or demanded?

b. If the present rental rate of one-bedroom apartments is $1,000 per month, through what mechanism will the rental rate adjust to the equilibrium rental rate of $800?

c. At a rental rate of $600 per month, is there an excess quantity supplied, or is there an excess quantity demanded? What is the amount of the excess quantity supplied or demanded?

d. If the present rental rate of one-bedroom apartments is $600 per month, through what mechanism will the rental rate adjust to the equilibrium rental rate of $800?

3-10. Consider the market for paperbound economics textbooks. Explain whether the following events would cause an increase or a decrease in supply or an increase or a decrease in the quantity supplied. (See page 64.)

a. The market price of paper increases.

b. The market price of economics textbooks increases.

c. The number of publishers of economics textbooks increases.

d. Publishers expect that the market price of economics textbooks will increase next month.

3-11. Consider the market for smartphones. Explain whether the following events would cause an increase or a decrease in supply or an increase or a decrease in the quantity supplied. Illustrate each, and show what would happen to the equilibrium quantity and the market price. (See page 64.)

a. The price of touch screens used in smartphones declines.

b. The price of machinery used to produce smartphones increases.

c. The number of manufacturers of smartphones increases.

d. There is a decrease in the market demand for smartphones.

3-12. If the price of flash memory chips used in manufacturing smartphones decreases, what will happen in the market for smartphones? How will the equilibrium price and equilibrium quantity of smartphones change? (See page 56.)

3-13. Assume that the cost of aluminum used by soft-drink companies increases. Which of the following correctly describes the resulting effects in the market for soft drinks distributed in aluminum cans? (More than one statement may be correct. See page 56.)

a. The demand for soft drinks decreases.

b. The quantity of soft drinks demanded decreases.

c. The supply of soft drinks decreases.

d. The quantity of soft drinks supplied decreases.

ECONOMICS ON THE NET

The U.S. Nursing Shortage For some years media stories have discussed a shortage of qualified nurses in the United States. This application explores some of the factors that have caused the quantity of newly trained nurses demanded to tend to exceed the quantity of newly trained nurses supplied.

Title: Nursing Shortage Resource Web Link

Navigation: Go to the Nursing Shortage Resource Web Link at www.econtoday.com/chap03, and click on *Nursing Shortage Fact Sheet*.

Application Read the discussion, and answer the following questions.

1. What has happened to the demand for new nurses in the United States? What has happened to the supply of new nurses? Why has the result been a shortage?

2. If there is a free market for the skills of new nurses, what can you predict is likely to happen to the wage rate earned by individuals who have just completed their nursing training?

For Group Study and Analysis Discuss the pros and cons of high schools and colleges trying to factor predictions about future wages into student career counseling. How might this potentially benefit students? What problems might high schools and colleges face in trying to assist students in evaluating the future earnings prospects of various jobs?

ANSWERS TO QUICK QUIZZES

p. 51: (i) inverse; (ii) demand

p. 52: (i) constant; (ii) market demand

p. 58: (i) income . . . tastes and preferences . . . prices of related goods . . . expectations about future prices and incomes . . . market size (the number of potential buyers in the market); (ii) *ceteris paribus;* (iii) movement along

p. 61: (i) direct; (ii) supply; (iii) market supply

p. 64: (i) move along . . . shift; (ii) input prices . . . technology and productivity . . . taxes and subsidies . . . expectations of future relative prices . . . the number of firms in the industry

p. 68: (i) intersection . . . equilibrium; (ii) greater; (iii) less

4 Extensions of Demand and Supply Analysis

LEARNING OBJECTIVES

After reading this chapter, you should be able to:

- Discuss the essential features of the price system
- Evaluate the effects of changes in demand and supply on the market price and equilibrium quantity
- Understand the rationing function of prices
- Explain the effects of price ceilings
- Explain the effects of price floors
- Describe various types of government-imposed quantity restrictions on markets

MyEconLab helps you master each objective and study more efficiently. See end of chapter for details.

During the past couple of years, people shopping for cars have confronted an unusual type of "sticker shock": As the prices of new vehicles have increased, the prices of used models have risen even faster. Today, the prices of a number of used vehicles are only a few hundred dollars lower than those of newly produced versions of the same cars. To understand why this situation exists in the used-car market, you must learn more about the effects of changes in market demand and supply on equilibrium prices and quantities—one key topic of this chapter. Indeed, you must develop an ability to consider the effects of *simultaneous* changes in market demand and supply, because such variations have occurred in the market for used cars.

DID YOU KNOW THAT... in Venezuela, in which substantial quantities of coffee once were produced and consumed year after year, so little coffee is now produced that persistent coffee *shortages* exist? As you learned in Chapter 3, normally we would anticipate that in the face of a shortage in which quantity supplied is less than the quantity demanded, the price of coffee would increase. A rise in the price to its market clearing level, you learned, would bring quantities demanded and supplied back into equality. Since 2003, however, Venezuela's government has maintained a *price ceiling* in the coffee market. This means that it is illegal in Venezuela for the price of coffee to increase in order to eliminate a shortage.

What effects can a price ceiling have on the availability and consumption of a good or service? As you will learn in this chapter, we can use the supply and demand analysis developed in Chapter 3 to answer this question. You will find that when a government sets a ceiling below the equilibrium price, the result will be a shortage. Similarly, you will learn how we can use supply and demand analysis to examine the "surplus" of various agricultural products, the "shortage" of apartments in certain cities, and many other phenomena. All of these examples are part of our economy, which we characterize as a *price system*.

The Price System and Markets

Price system
An economic system in which relative prices are constantly changing to reflect changes in supply and demand for different commodities. The prices of those commodities are signals to everyone within the system as to what is relatively scarce and what is relatively abundant.

In a **price system,** otherwise known as a *market system,* relative prices are constantly changing to reflect changes in supply and demand for different commodities. The prices of those commodities are the signals to everyone within the price system as to what is relatively scarce and what is relatively abundant. In this sense, prices provide information.

Indeed, it is the *signaling* aspect of the price system that provides the information to buyers and sellers about what should be bought and what should be produced. In a price system, there is a clear-cut chain of events in which any changes in demand and supply cause changes in prices that in turn affect the opportunities that businesses and individuals have for profit and personal gain. Such changes influence our use of resources.

Exchange and Markets

Voluntary exchange
An act of trading, done on an elective basis, in which both parties to the trade expect to be better off after the exchange.

The price system features **voluntary exchange,** acts of trading between individuals that make both parties to the trade subjectively better off. The prices we pay for the desired items are determined by the interaction of the forces underlying supply and demand. In our economy, exchanges take place voluntarily in markets. A market encompasses the exchange arrangements of both buyers and sellers that underlie the forces of supply and demand. Indeed, one definition of a market is that it is a low-cost institution for facilitating exchange. A market increases incomes by helping resources move to their highest-valued uses.

Transaction Costs

Transaction costs
All of the costs associated with exchange, including the informational costs of finding out the price and quality, service record, and durability of a product, plus the cost of contracting and enforcing that contract.

Individuals turn to markets because markets reduce the cost of exchanges. These costs are sometimes referred to as **transaction costs,** which are broadly defined as the costs associated with finding out exactly what is being transacted as well as the cost of enforcing contracts. If you were Robinson Crusoe and lived alone on an island, you would never incur a transaction cost. For everyone else, transaction costs are just as real as the costs of production. Today, high-speed computers have allowed us to reduce transaction costs by increasing our ability to process information and keep records.

Consider some simple examples of transaction costs. A club warehouse such as Sam's Club or Costco reduces the transaction costs of having to go to numerous specialty stores to obtain the items you desire. Financial institutions, such as commercial banks, have reduced the transaction costs of directing funds from savers to borrowers. In general, the more organized the market, the lower the transaction costs. Among those who constantly attempt to lower transaction costs are the much maligned middlemen.

The Role of Middlemen

As long as there are costs of bringing together buyers and sellers, there will be an incentive for intermediaries linking ultimate sellers and buyers, normally called middlemen, to lower those costs. This means that middlemen specialize in lowering transaction costs. Whenever producers do not sell their products directly to the final consumer, by definition, one or more middlemen are involved. Farmers typically sell their output to distributors, who are usually called wholesalers, who then sell those products to retailers such as supermarkets.

How have companies that offer downloadable apps altered the transaction costs of firms seeking to sell products to mobile consumers?

EXAMPLE

Linking Businesses to Customers on the Go via QR Apps

In recent years, firms seeking to simplify the process of selling their products to busy customers have been turning to online apps, or Web-based application programs. One increasingly useful type of app for many small businesses is the quick-response (QR) app. These apps are offered by middlemen companies, such as Kaywa AT and Scanbuy, Inc. The apps enable sellers to create codes that they can place on poster ads. Consumers can scan the ads with their smartphones to place orders for the firms' products.

For instance, an individual who is about to board a commuter train can use a smartphone to scan a code from the ad of a coffee shop near the train's destination. The code enables the smartphone to acquire the QR app, which in turn displays the coffee shop's menu, from which the individual can choose items to purchase remotely. The individual can then pick up those items at the coffee shop upon arrival—hence completing a mobile purchase made possible by a middlemen company that offers the QR app linking the individual to the coffee shop.

FOR CRITICAL THINKING

Why do you suppose that firms such as coffee shops are willing to pay fees to middlemen for ad codes to be used with QR apps?

Changes in Demand and Supply

A key function of middlemen is to reduce transaction costs of buyers and sellers in markets for goods and services, and it is in markets that we see the results of changes in demand and supply. Market equilibrium can change whenever there is a *shock* caused by a change in a *ceteris paribus* condition for demand or supply. A shock to the supply and demand system can be represented by a shift in the supply curve, a shift in the demand curve, or a shift in both curves. Any shock to the system will result in a new set of supply and demand relationships and a new equilibrium. Forces will come into play to move the system from the old price-quantity equilibrium (now a disequilibrium situation) to the new equilibrium, where the new demand and supply curves intersect.

Effects of Changes in Either Demand or Supply

In many situations, it is possible to predict what will happen to both equilibrium price and equilibrium quantity when demand or supply changes. Specifically, whenever one curve is stable while the other curve shifts, we can tell what will happen to both price and quantity. Consider the possibilities in Figure 4-1 on the following page. In panel (a), the supply curve remains unchanged, but demand increases from D_1 to D_2. Note that the results are an increase in the market clearing price from P_1 to P_2 and an increase in the equilibrium quantity from Q_1 to Q_2.

In panel (b) in Figure 4-1, there is a decrease in demand from D_1 to D_3. This results in a decrease in both the equilibrium price of the good and the equilibrium quantity. Panels (c) and (d) show the effects of a shift in the supply curve while the demand curve is unchanged. In panel (c), the supply curve has shifted rightward. The equilibrium price of the product falls, and the equilibrium quantity increases. In panel (d), supply has shifted leftward—there has been a supply decrease. The product's equilibrium price increases, and the equilibrium quantity decreases.

FIGURE 4-1

Shifts in Demand and in Supply: Determinate Results

In panel (a), the supply curve is unchanged at S. The demand curve shifts outward from D_1 to D_2. The equilibrium price and quantity rise from P_1, Q_1 to P_2, Q_2, respectively. In panel (b), again the supply curve is unchanged at S. The demand curve shifts inward to the left, showing a decrease in demand from D_1 to D_3. Both equilibrium price and equilibrium quantity fall. In panel (c), the demand curve now remains unchanged at D. The supply curve shifts from S_1 to S_2. The equilibrium price falls from P_1 to P_2. The equilibrium quantity increases, however, from Q_1 to Q_2. In panel (d), the demand curve is unchanged at D. Supply decreases as shown by a leftward shift of the supply curve from S_1 to S_3. The market clearing price increases from P_1 to P_3. The equilibrium quantity falls from Q_1 to Q_3.

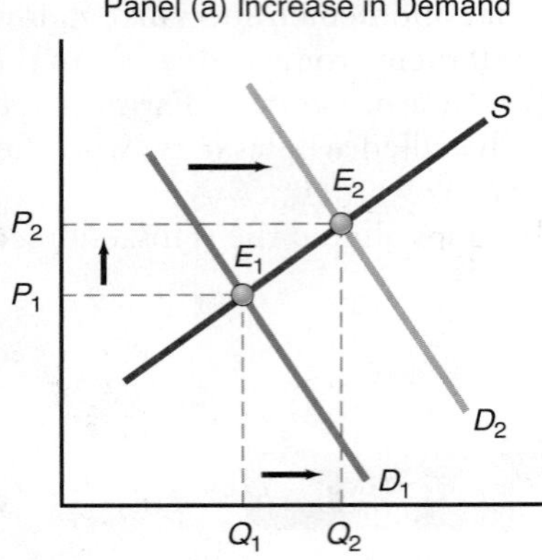

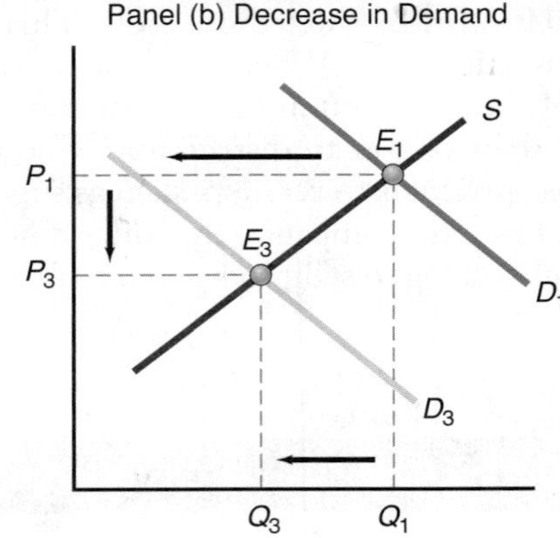

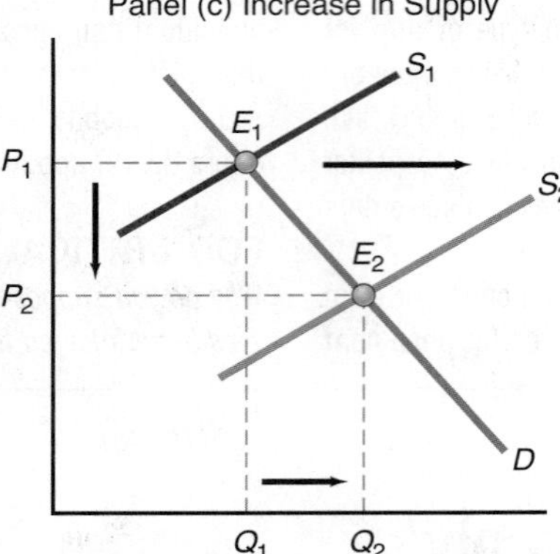

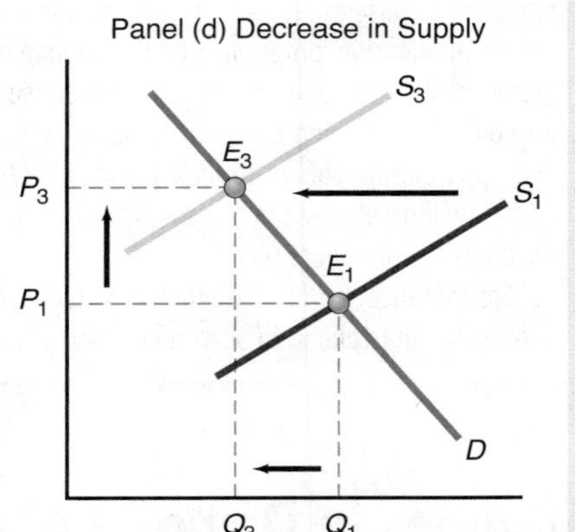

Situations in Which Both Demand and Supply Shift

The examples in Figure 4-1 above show a theoretically determinate outcome of a shift either in the demand curve, holding the supply curve constant, or in the supply curve, holding the demand curve constant. When both the supply and demand curves change, the outcome is indeterminate for either equilibrium price or equilibrium quantity.

When both demand and supply increase, the equilibrium quantity unambiguously rises, because the increase in demand and the increase in supply *both* tend to generate a rise in quantity. The change in the equilibrium price is uncertain without more information, because the increase in demand tends to increase the equilibrium price, whereas the increase in supply tends to decrease the equilibrium price.

Decreases in both demand and supply tend to generate a fall in quantity, so the equilibrium quantity falls. Again, the effect on the equilibrium price is uncertain without additional information, because a decrease in demand tends to reduce the equilibrium price, whereas a decrease in supply tends to increase the equilibrium price.

We can be certain that when demand decreases and supply increases at the same time, the equilibrium price will fall, because *both* the decrease in demand and the increase in supply tend to push down the equilibrium price. The change in the equilibrium quantity is uncertain without more information, because the decrease in demand tends to reduce the equilibrium quantity, whereas the increase in supply tends to increase the equilibrium quantity. If demand increases and supply decreases at the same time, both occurrences tend to push up the equilibrium price, so the equilibrium price definitely rises. The change in the equilibrium quantity cannot be determined without more information, because the increase in demand tends to raise the equilibrium quantity, whereas the decrease in supply tends to reduce the equilibrium quantity.

How have simultaneous shifts in demand and supply affected the equilibrium global price of shipping containers?

INTERNATIONAL EXAMPLE

What Accounts for the Rising Price of Shipping Containers?

Since 2011, shipping-container prices have surged. Several reasons account for the jump in the equilibrium price. One is that companies using the containers, which typically last no longer than 8 to 10 years, bought large quantities during a five-year period that began in 2001, and many of these containers now must be replaced to maintain shipping volumes. Hence, as shown in Figure 4-2 below, the demand curve for shipping containers has shifted rightward.

In addition, the massive tsunami that struck Japan in 2011 washed thousands of containers out to sea. Furthermore, the price of steel that serves as the primary input for the containers has increased by 7 percent. These events have contributed to a reduction in the supply of shipping containers. On net, the equilibrium quantity of shipping containers produced and purchased has risen, and the market clearing price of shipping containers has increased.

FOR CRITICAL THINKING

How do you suppose that a rise in the price of truck trailers that are substitutes for shipping containers has affected the market clearing price of shipping containers?

FIGURE 4-2

The Effects of a Simultaneous Decrease in Shipping-Container Supply and Increase in Shipping-Container Demand

Since 2011, various factors have contributed to a reduction in the supply of shipping containers, depicted by the leftward shift in the supply curve from S_1 to S_2. At the same time, there was an increase in the demand for shipping containers, as shown by the shift in the demand curve from D_1 to D_2. On net, the equilibrium quantity of shipping containers produced and purchased rose, from 750,000 containers per year at point E_1 to 900,000 containers per year at point E_2, and the equilibrium price of shipping containers increased from about $3,000 per container to about $3,500 per container.

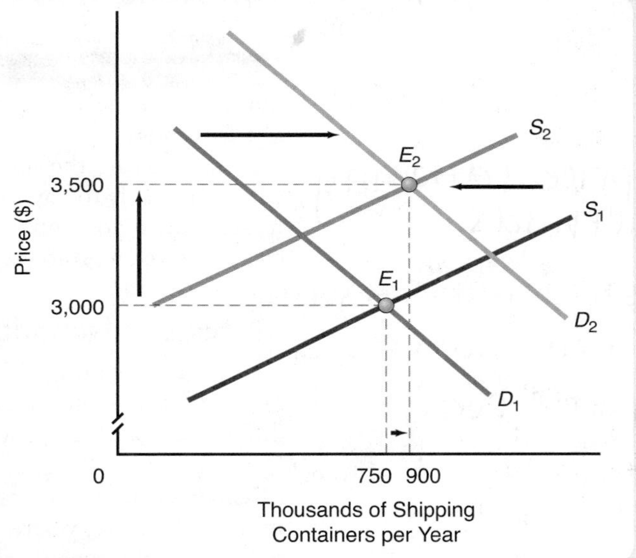

Price Flexibility and Adjustment Speed

We have used as an illustration for our analysis a market in which prices are quite flexible. Some markets are indeed like that. In others, however, price flexibility may take the form of subtle adjustments such as hidden payments or quality changes. For example, although the published price of bouquets of flowers may stay the same, the freshness of the flowers may change, meaning that the price per constant-quality unit changes. The published price of French bread might stay the same, but the quality could go up or down, perhaps through use of a different recipe, thereby changing the price per constant-quality unit. There are many ways to implicitly change prices without actually changing the published price for a *nominal* unit of a product or service.

We must also note that markets do not always return to equilibrium immediately. There may be a significant adjustment time. A shock to the economy in the form of an oil embargo, a drought, or a long strike will not be absorbed overnight. This means that even in unfettered market situations, in which there are no restrictions on changes in prices and quantities, temporary excess quantities supplied or excess quantities demanded may appear. Our analysis simply indicates what the market clearing price and equilibrium quantity ultimately will be, given a demand curve and a supply curve.

Nowhere in the analysis is there any indication of the speed with which a market will get to a new equilibrium after a shock. The price may even temporarily overshoot the new equilibrium level. Remember this warning when we examine changes in demand and in supply due to changes in their *ceteris paribus* conditions.

QUICK QUIZ **See page 95 for the answers. Review concepts from this section in MyEconLab.**

When the __________ curve shifts outward or inward with an unchanged __________ curve, equilibrium price and quantity increase or decrease, respectively. When the __________ curve shifts outward or inward given an unchanged __________ curve, equilibrium price moves in the direction opposite to equilibrium quantity.

When there is a shift in demand or supply, the new equilibrium price is not obtained __________. Adjustment takes __________.

The Rationing Function of Prices

The synchronization of decisions by buyers and sellers that leads to equilibrium is called the *rationing function of prices.* Prices are indicators of relative scarcity. An equilibrium price clears the market. The plans of buyers and sellers, given the price, are not frustrated. It is the free interaction of buyers and sellers that sets the price that eventually clears the market. Price, in effect, rations a good to demanders who are willing and able to pay the highest price. Whenever the rationing function of prices is frustrated by government-enforced price ceilings that set prices below the market clearing level, a prolonged shortage results.

Methods of Nonprice Rationing

There are ways other than price to ration goods. *First come, first served* is one method. *Political power* is another. *Physical force* is yet another. Cultural, religious, and physical differences have been and are used as rationing devices throughout the world.

RATIONING BY WAITING Consider first come, first served as a rationing device. We call this *rationing by queues,* where *queue* means "line." Whoever is willing to wait in line the longest obtains the good that is being sold at less than the market clearing price. All who wait in line are paying a higher *total outlay* than the money price paid for the good. Personal time has an opportunity cost. To calculate the total outlay expended on the good, we must add up the money price plus the opportunity cost of the time spent waiting.

Rationing by waiting may occur in situations in which entrepreneurs are free to change prices to equate quantity demanded with quantity supplied but choose not to do so. This results in queues of potential buyers. It may seem that the price in the market is being held below equilibrium by some noncompetitive force. That is not true, however. Such queuing may arise in a free market when the demand for a good is subject to large or unpredictable fluctuations, and the additional costs to firms (and ultimately to consumers) of constantly changing prices or of holding sufficient inventories or providing sufficient excess capacity to cover peak demands are greater than the costs to consumers of waiting for the good.

Common examples are waiting in line to purchase a fast-food lunch and queuing to purchase a movie ticket a few minutes before the next showing.

RATIONING BY RANDOM ASSIGNMENT OR COUPONS *Random assignment* is another way to ration goods. You may have been involved in a rationing-by-random-assignment scheme in college if you were assigned a housing unit. Sometimes rationing by random assignment is used to fill slots in popular classes.

Rationing by *coupons* has also been used, particularly during wartime. In the United States during World War II, families were allotted coupons that allowed them to purchase specified quantities of rationed goods, such as meat and gasoline. To purchase such goods, they had to pay a specified price *and* give up a coupon.

Why has American Airlines been randomly assigning its coach passengers to boarding groups?

EXAMPLE

An Airline Boarding Lottery

For several years now, U.S. airlines have charged coach passengers to transport bags as separate cargo. This practice has induced many passengers to pack more items into carry-on bags that they stuff under seats or into overhead compartments.

American Airlines has been assigning coach boarding-group numbers randomly, rather than by groups of rows starting with the rear of the plane and ending with the front coach rows. Under the latter boarding method, many people with seats at the rear of a plane tend to place their carry-on bags in compartments near the front of the plane. Then people arriving in the front at the end of the boarding process spend time scrambling to find places to stow their carry-ons. In contrast, under a randomized boarding process that ignores row locations, coach passengers are more likely to stow their bags near their seats. This mode of passenger behavior speeds the overall boarding process by several minutes, thereby ensuring that more flights depart on time.

FOR CRITICAL THINKING

Suppose the airline has established a system of boarding fees in which passengers wishing to be among the first to board a plane pay the highest fees. Would such a system likely reduce or lengthen boarding times? Why?

The Essential Role of Rationing

In a world of scarcity, there is, by definition, competition for what is scarce. After all, any resources that are not scarce can be obtained by everyone at a zero price in as large a quantity as everyone wants, such as air to burn in internal combustion engines. Once scarcity arises, there has to be some method to ration the available resources, goods, and services. The price system is one form of rationing. The others that we mentioned are alternatives. Economists cannot say which system of rationing is "best." They can, however, say that rationing via the price system leads to the most efficient use of available resources. As explained in Appendix B, this means that generally in a freely functioning price system, all of the gains from mutually beneficial trade will be captured.

QUICK QUIZ

See page 95 for the answers. Review concepts from this section in MyEconLab.

Prices in a market economy perform a rationing function because they reflect relative scarcity, allowing the market to clear. Other ways to ration goods include __________ __________, __________ __________, __________ __________, __________ __________, __________ __________, and __________.

Even when businesspeople can change prices, some rationing by waiting may occur. Such __________ arises when there are large changes in demand coupled with high costs of satisfying those changes immediately.

Price controls
Government-mandated minimum or maximum prices that may be charged for goods and services.

Price ceiling
A legal maximum price that may be charged for a particular good or service.

The Policy of Government-Imposed Price Controls

The rationing function of prices is prevented when governments impose price controls. **Price controls** often involve setting a **price ceiling**—the maximum price that may be allowed in an exchange. The world has had a long history of price ceilings

Price floor
A legal minimum price below which a good or service may not be sold. Legal minimum wages are an example.

applied to product prices, wages, rents, and interest rates. Occasionally, a government will set a **price floor**—a minimum price below which a good or service may not be sold. Price floors have most often been applied to wages and agricultural products. Let's first consider price ceilings.

YOU ARE THERE

To learn about how government controls of prices of life-saving medications are creating situations in which quantities demanded exceed quantities supplied year after year, read **Explaining the "Crisis" of Persistent Drug Shortages** on page 89.

Price Ceilings and Black Markets

As long as a price ceiling is below the market clearing price, imposing a price ceiling creates a shortage, as can be seen in Figure 4-3 below. At any price below the market clearing, or equilibrium, price of $1,000, there will always be a larger quantity demanded than quantity supplied—a shortage, as you will recall from Chapter 3. Normally, whenever quantity demanded exceeds quantity supplied—that is, when a shortage exists—there is a tendency for the price to rise to its equilibrium level. But with a price ceiling, this tendency cannot be fully realized because everyone is forbidden to trade at the equilibrium price.

Nonprice rationing devices
All methods used to ration scarce goods that are price-controlled. Whenever the price system is not allowed to work, nonprice rationing devices will evolve to ration the affected goods and services.

The result is fewer exchanges and **nonprice rationing devices.** Figure 4-3 shows the situation for portable electric generators after a natural disaster: The equilibrium quantity of portable generators demanded and supplied (or traded) would be 10,000 units, and the market clearing price would be $1,000 per generator. But, if the government essentially imposes a price ceiling by requiring the price of portable generators to remain at the predisaster level, which the government determines was a price of $600, the equilibrium quantity offered is only 5,000.

Because frustrated consumers will be able to purchase only 5,000 units, there is a shortage. The most obvious nonprice rationing device to help clear the market is queuing, or physical lines, which we have already discussed. To avoid physical lines, waiting lists may be established.

Black market
A market in which goods are traded at prices above their legal maximum prices or in which illegal goods are sold.

Typically, an effective price ceiling leads to a **black market.** A black market is a market in which the price-controlled good is sold at an illegally high price through various methods. For example, if the price of gasoline is controlled at lower than the market clearing price, drivers who wish to fill up their cars may offer the gas station attendant a cash payment on the side (as happened in the United States in the 1970s and in China and India in the mid-2000s during price controls on gasoline). If the price of beef is controlled at below its market clearing price, a customer who offers the butcher tickets for good seats to an upcoming football game may be allocated otherwise

FIGURE 4-3
Black Markets for Portable Electric Generators

The demand curve is *D*. The supply curve is *S*. The equilibrium price is $1,000. The government, however, steps in and imposes a maximum price of $600. At that lower price, the quantity demanded will be 15,000, but the quantity supplied will be only 5,000. There is a "shortage." The implicit price (including time costs) tends to increase to $1,400. If black markets arise, as they generally will, the equilibrium black market price will end up somewhere between $600 and $1,400. The actual quantity transacted will be between 5,000 and 10,000.

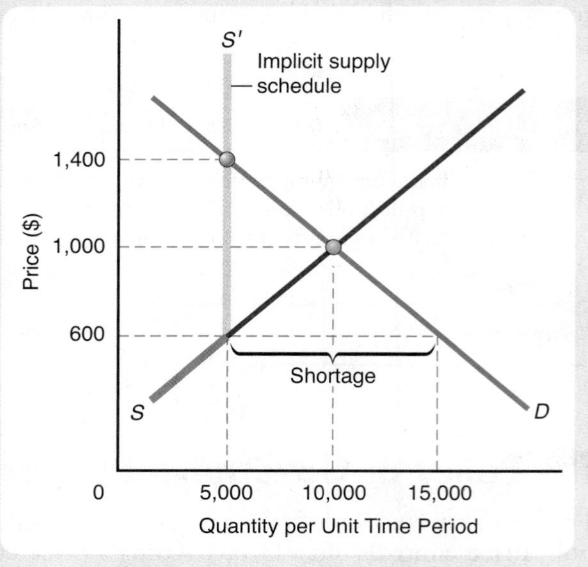

unavailable beef. Indeed, the true implicit price of a price-controlled good or service can be increased in an infinite number of ways, limited only by the imagination. (Black markets also occur when goods are made illegal.)

How have multiple price ceilings magnified electricity shortages in China?

INTERNATIONAL POLICY EXAMPLE

Multiple Price Ceilings Lead to Electricity Rationing in China

In China, two key sources of electricity are coal and diesel fuel that power generators. Sellers of both items, however, confront ceiling prices that are below market clearing levels. Hence, firms operating power generators often struggle to obtain enough coal and diesel fuel to provide as much electricity as they wish to produce. Power companies do not desire to sell as much electricity as many Chinese residents want to use, though, because China's government has also placed ceilings on electricity prices in a number of regional electricity markets.

These multiple price ceilings help to explain why most of the nation commonly faces electricity rationing in the form of "brownouts," or reductions in power flow. Shortages created by the ceiling prices also explain why businesses in more than one-third of China's provinces often have their power completely shut off for days at a time during the coldest weeks of winter and the warmest weeks of summer.

FOR CRITICAL THINKING

Given that China's electricity demand is growing at 13 percent per year, why do you suppose that electricity shortages likely will worsen in the future?

QUICK QUIZ

See page 95 for the answers. Review concepts from this section in MyEconLab.

Governments sometimes impose **price controls** in the form of price __________ and price __________.

An effective price __________ is one that sets the legal price below the market clearing price and is enforced.

Effective price __________ lead to nonprice rationing devices and black markets.

The Policy of Controlling Rents

More than 200 U.S. cities and towns, including Berkeley, California, and New York City, operate under some kind of rent control. **Rent control** is a system under which the local government tells building owners how much they can charge their tenants for rent. In the United States, rent controls date back to at least World War II. The objective of rent control is to keep rents below levels that would be observed in a freely competitive market.

Rent control
Price ceilings on rents.

The Functions of Rental Prices

In any housing market, rental prices serve three functions: (1) to promote the efficient maintenance of existing housing and to stimulate the construction of new housing, (2) to allocate existing scarce housing among competing claimants, and (3) to ration the use of existing housing by current demanders. Rent controls interfere with all of these functions.

RENT CONTROLS AND CONSTRUCTION Rent controls discourage the construction of new rental units. Rents are the most important long-term determinant of profitability, and rent controls artificially depress them. Consider some examples. In a recent year in Dallas, Texas, with a 16 percent rental vacancy rate but no rent control laws, 11,000 new rental housing units were built. In the same year in San Francisco, California, only 2,000 units were built, despite a mere 1.6 percent vacancy rate. The major difference? San Francisco has had stringent rent control laws. In New York City, most rental units being built are luxury units, which are exempt from controls.

EFFECTS ON THE EXISTING SUPPLY OF HOUSING When rental rates are held below equilibrium levels, property owners cannot recover the cost of maintenance, repairs, and capital improvements through higher rents. Hence, they curtail these activities. In the extreme situation, taxes, utilities, and the expenses of basic repairs exceed rental receipts. The result has been abandoned buildings from Santa Monica, California, to New York City. Some owners have resorted to arson, hoping to collect the insurance on their empty buildings before the city claims them to pay back taxes.

RATIONING THE CURRENT USE OF HOUSING Rent controls also affect the current use of housing because they restrict tenant mobility. Consider a family whose children have gone off to college. That family might want to live in a smaller apartment. But in a rent-controlled environment, giving up a rent-controlled unit can entail a substantial cost. In most rent-controlled cities, rents can be adjusted only when a tenant leaves. That means that a move from a long-occupied rent-controlled apartment to a smaller apartment can involve a hefty rent hike. In New York, this artificial preservation of the status quo came to be known as "housing gridlock."

Attempts to Evade Rent Controls

Go to **www.econtoday.com/chap04** to learn more about New York City's rent controls from Tenant.net.

The distortions produced by rent controls lead to efforts by both property owners and tenants to evade the rules. These efforts lead to the growth of expensive government bureaucracies whose job it is to make sure that rent controls aren't evaded. In New York City, because rent on a rent-controlled apartment can be raised only if the tenant leaves, property owners have had an incentive to make life unpleasant for tenants in order to drive them out or to evict them on the slightest pretext. The city has responded by making evictions extremely costly for property owners. Eviction requires a tedious and expensive judicial proceeding.

Tenants, for their part, routinely try to sublet all or part of their rent-controlled apartments at fees substantially above the rent they pay to the owner. Both the city and the property owners try to prohibit subletting and often end up in the city's housing courts—an entire judicial system developed to deal with disputes involving rent-controlled apartments. The overflow and appeals from the city's housing courts sometimes clog the rest of New York's judicial system.

Who Gains and Who Loses from Rent Controls?

The big losers from rent controls are clearly property owners. But there is another group of losers—low-income individuals, especially single mothers, trying to find apartments. Some observers now believe that rent controls have worsened the problem of homelessness in cities such as New York.

Often, owners of rent-controlled apartments charge "key money" before allowing a new tenant to move in. This is a large up-front cash payment, usually illegal but demanded nonetheless—just one aspect of the black market in rent-controlled apartments. Poor individuals have insufficient income to pay the hefty key money payment, nor can they assure the owner that their rent will be on time or even paid each month.

Because controlled rents are usually below market clearing levels, apartment owners have little incentive to take any risk on low-income individuals as tenants. This is particularly true when a prospective tenant's chief source of income is a welfare check. Indeed, a large number of the litigants in the New York housing courts are welfare mothers who have missed their rent payments due to emergency expenses or delayed welfare checks. Their appeals often end in evictions and a new home in a temporary public shelter—or on the streets.

Who benefits from rent control? Ample evidence indicates that upper-income professionals benefit the most. These people can use their mastery of the bureaucracy and their large network of friends and connections to exploit the rent control system. Consider that in New York, actresses Mia Farrow and Cicely Tyson live in rent-controlled apartments, paying well below market rates. So do the former director of the Metropolitan Museum of Art and singer and children's book author Carly Simon.

QUICK QUIZ See page 95 for the answers. Review concepts from this section in MyEconLab.

__________ prices perform three functions: (1) allocating existing scarce housing among competing claimants, (2) promoting efficient maintenance of existing houses and stimulating new housing construction, and (3) rationing the use of existing houses by current demanders.

Effective rent __________ impede the functioning of rental prices. Construction of new rental units is discouraged.

Rent __________ decrease spending on maintenance of existing ones and also lead to "housing gridlock."

There are numerous ways to evade rent controls. __________ __________ is one.

Price Floors in Agriculture

Another way that government can affect markets is by imposing price floors or price supports. In the United States, price supports are most often associated with agricultural products.

Price Supports

During the Great Depression, the federal government swung into action to help farmers. In 1933, it established a system of price supports for many agricultural products. Since then, there have been price supports for wheat, feed grains, cotton, rice, soybeans, sorghum, and dairy products, among other foodstuffs. The nature of the supports is quite simple: The government simply chooses a *support price* for an agricultural product and then acts to ensure that the price of the product never falls below the support level. Figure 4-4 below shows the market demand for and supply of milk. Without a price-support program, competitive forces would yield an equilibrium price of $0.08 per pound and an equilibrium quantity of 15.4 billion pounds per year. Clearly, if the government were to set the support price at or below $0.08 per pound, the quantity of milk demanded would equal the quantity of milk supplied at point *E*, because farmers could sell all they wanted at the market clearing price of $0.08 per pound.

FIGURE 4-4

Agricultural Price Supports

Free market equilibrium occurs at *E*, with an equilibrium price of $0.08 per pound and an equilibrium quantity of 15.4 billion pounds. When the government sets a support price at $0.10 per pound, the quantity demanded is 15 billion pounds and the quantity supplied is 16 billion pounds. The difference is the surplus, which the government buys. Farmers' income from consumers equals $0.10 per pound × 1 billion pounds = $100 million.

But what happens when the government sets the support price *above* the market clearing price, at $0.10 per pound? At a support price of $0.10 per pound, the quantity demanded is only 15 billion pounds, but the quantity supplied is 16 billion pounds. The 1-billion-pound difference between them is called the *excess quantity supplied*, or *surplus*. As simple as this program seems, its existence creates a fundamental question: How can the government agency charged with administering the price-support program prevent market forces from pushing the actual price down to $0.08 per pound?

If production exceeds the amount that consumers want to buy at the support price, what happens to the surplus? Quite simply, if the price-support program is to work, the government has to buy the surplus—the 1-billion-pound difference. As a practical matter, the government acquires the 1-billion-pound surplus indirectly through a government agency. The government either stores the surplus or sells it to foreign countries at a greatly reduced price (or gives it away free of charge) under the Food for Peace program.

Who Benefits from Agricultural Price Supports?

Although agricultural price supports have traditionally been promoted as a way to guarantee "decent" earnings for low-income farmers, most of the benefits have in fact gone to the owners of very large farms. Price-support payments are made on a per-pound basis, not on a per-farm basis. Thus, traditionally, the larger the farm, the bigger the benefit from agricultural price supports. In addition, *all* of the benefits from price supports ultimately accrue to *landowners* on whose land price-supported crops grow.

KEEPING PRICE SUPPORTS ALIVE UNDER A NEW NAME Back in the early 1990s, Congress indicated an intention to phase out most agricultural subsidies by the early 2000s. What Congress actually *did* throughout the 1990s, however, was to pass a series of "emergency laws" keeping farm subsidies alive. Some of these laws aimed to replace agricultural price supports with payments to many farmers for growing no crops at all, thereby boosting the market prices of crops by reducing supply. Nevertheless, the federal government and several state governments have continued to support prices of a number of agricultural products, such as peanuts, through "marketing loan" programs. These programs advance funds to farmers to help them finance the storage of some or all of their crops. The farmers can then use the stored produce as collateral for borrowing or sell it to the government and use the proceeds to repay debts.

Marketing loan programs raise the effective price that farmers receive for their crops and commit federal and state governments to purchasing surplus production. Consequently, they lead to outcomes similar to those of traditional price-support programs.

THE MAIN BENEFICIARIES OF AGRICULTURAL SUBSIDIES In 2002, Congress enacted the Farm Security Act, which has perpetuated marketing loan programs and other subsidy and price-support arrangements for such farm products as wheat, corn, rice, peanuts, and soybeans. All told, the more than $9 billion in U.S. government payments for these and other products amounts to about 25 percent of the annual market value of all U.S. farm production.

The government seeks to cap the annual subsidy payment that an individual farmer can receive at $360,000 per year, but some farmers are able to garner higher annual amounts by exploiting regulatory loopholes. The greatest share of total agricultural subsidies goes to the owners of the largest farming operations. At present, 10 percent of U.S. farmers receive more than 70 percent of agricultural subsidies.

The 2008 Food, Conservation, and Energy Act expanded on the 2002 legislation by giving farmers raising any of a number of crops a choice between subsidy programs. On the one hand, farmers can opt to participate in traditional programs involving a mix of direct payments and marketing loan programs. On the other hand, farmers can choose a program offering guaranteed revenues. If market clearing crop prices end up higher than those associated with the government's revenue guarantee, farmers sell their crops at the higher prices instead of collecting government subsidies. But if equilibrium crop prices end up below a level consistent with the government guarantee, farmers receive direct subsidies to bring their total revenues up to the guaranteed level.

WHAT IF... the government decides to "help dairy farmers" by imposing a floor price in the market for milk that is above the equilibrium price?

The floor price above the equilibrium level would cause the quantity of milk supplied by dairy farmers to rise above the quantity demanded by consumers. The government would have to purchase the surplus milk, which would indeed "help" the dairy farmers from whom the milk would be purchased. As a result, consumers, such as parents of young children, would have to pay a higher price for each unit of the smaller quantity of milk that they will choose to buy. Thus, the government's price-support program would necessarily "help dairy farmers" at the expense of milk consumers.

Price Floors in the Labor Market

The **minimum wage** is the lowest hourly wage rate that firms may legally pay their workers. Proponents favor higher minimum wages to ensure low-income workers a "decent" standard of living. Opponents counter that higher minimum wages cause increased unemployment, particularly among unskilled minority teenagers.

Minimum wage
A wage floor, legislated by government, setting the lowest hourly rate that firms may legally pay workers.

Minimum Wages in the United States

The federal minimum wage started in 1938 at 25 cents an hour, about 40 percent of the average manufacturing wage at the time. Typically, its level has stayed at about 40 to 50 percent of average manufacturing wages. After holding the minimum wage at $5.15 per hour from 1997 to 2007, Congress enacted a series of phased increases in the hourly minimum wage, effective on July 24 of each year, to $5.85 in 2007, $6.55 in 2008, and $7.25 in 2009.

Go to www.econtoday.com/chap04 for information from the U.S. Department of Labor about recent developments concerning the federal minimum wage.

Many states and cities have their own minimum wage laws that exceed the federal minimum. A number of municipalities refer to their minimum wage rules as "living wage" laws. Governments of these municipalities seek to set minimum wages consistent with living standards they deem to be socially acceptable—that is, overall wage income judged to be sufficient to purchase basic items such as housing and food.

Economic Effects of a Minimum Wage

What happens when the government establishes a floor on wages? The effects can be seen in Figure 4-5 on the following page. We start off in equilibrium with the equilibrium wage rate of W_e and the equilibrium quantity of labor equal to Q_e. A minimum wage, W_m, higher than W_e, is imposed. At W_m, the quantity demanded for labor is reduced to Q_d, and some workers now become unemployed. Certain workers will become unemployed as a result of the minimum wage, but others will move to sectors where minimum wage laws do not apply. Wages will be pushed down in these uncovered sectors.

Note that the reduction in employment from Q_e to Q_d, or the distance from B to A, is less than the excess quantity of labor supplied at wage rate W_m. This excess quantity supplied is the distance between A and C, or the distance between Q_d and Q_s. The reason the reduction in employment is smaller than the excess quantity of

FIGURE 4-5

The Effect of Minimum Wages

The market clearing wage rate is W_e. The market clearing quantity of employment is Q_e, determined by the intersection of supply and demand at point *E*. A minimum wage equal to W_m is established. The quantity of labor demanded is reduced to Q_d. The reduction in employment from Q_e to Q_d is equal to the distance between *B* and *A*. That distance is smaller than the excess quantity of labor supplied at wage rate W_m. The distance between *B* and *C* is the increase in the quantity of labor supplied that results from the higher minimum wage rate.

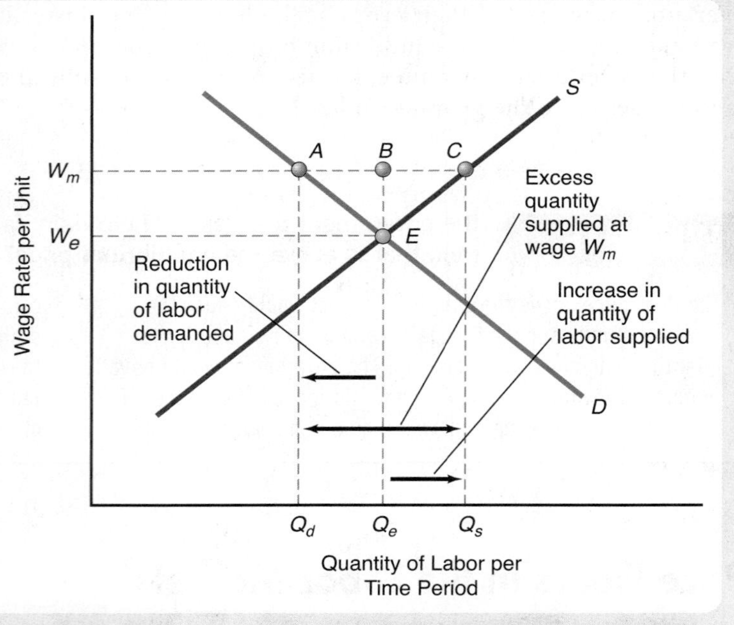

labor supplied at the minimum wage is that the excess quantity of labor supplied also includes the *additional* workers who would like to work more hours at the new, higher minimum wage.

In the long run (a time period that is long enough to allow for full adjustment by workers and firms), some of the reduction in the quantity of labor demanded will result from a reduction in the number of firms, and some will result from changes in the number of workers employed by each firm. Economists estimate that a 10 percent increase in the inflation-adjusted minimum wage decreases total employment of those affected by 1 to 2 percent.

We can conclude from the application of demand and supply analysis that a minimum wage established above the equilibrium wage rate typically has two fundamental effects. On the one hand, it boosts the wage earnings of those people who obtain employment. On the other hand, the minimum wage results in unemployment for other individuals. Thus, demand and supply analysis implies that the minimum wage makes some people better off while making others worse off.

How have teenagers fared following successive increases in the minimum wage in 2007, 2008, and 2009?

POLICY EXAMPLE

A Higher Minimum Wage Translates into Fewer Employed Teens

In three steps between 2007 and 2009, the federal government boosted the minimum wage rate faced by all employers in the 50 states from \$5.15 per hour to \$7.25 per hour. The legislation had almost no effects in 18 states in which market wages were generally already higher than \$7.25 per hour. In the other 32 states, though, the three-stage hike in the minimum wage reduced total employment of teens by an estimated 2.5 percentage points. The result for these states was an estimated reduction in the number of employed teens totaling more than 114,000 teens, who consequently joined the ranks of the nation's unemployed.

FOR CRITICAL THINKING

What do you suppose has happened to the teen unemployment rate as the demand for labor has fallen and remained dampened since the 2008–2009 economic downturn?

Quantity Restrictions

Governments can impose quantity restrictions on a market. The most obvious restriction is an outright ban on the ownership or trading of a good. It is currently illegal to buy and sell human organs. It is also currently illegal to buy and sell certain psychoactive drugs such as cocaine, heroin, and methamphetamine. In some states, it is illegal to start a new hospital without obtaining a license for a particular number of beds to be offered to patients. This licensing requirement effectively limits the quantity of hospital beds in some states. From 1933 to 1973, it was illegal for U.S. citizens to own gold except for manufacturing, medicinal, or jewelry purposes.

Some of the most common quantity restrictions exist in the area of international trade. The U.S. government, as well as many foreign governments, imposes import quotas on a variety of goods. An **import quota** is a supply restriction that prohibits the importation of more than a specified quantity of a particular good in a one-year period. The United States has had import quotas on tobacco, sugar, and immigrant labor. For many years, there were import quotas on oil coming into the United States. There are also "voluntary" import quotas on certain goods. For instance, since the mid-2000s, the Chinese government has agreed to "voluntarily" restrict the amount of textile products China sends to the United States and the European Union.

Import quota
A physical supply restriction on imports of a particular good, such as sugar. Foreign exporters are unable to sell in the United States more than the quantity specified in the import quota.

QUICK QUIZ See page 95 for the answers. Review concepts from this section in MyEconLab.

With a price-__________ system, the government sets a minimum price at which, say, qualifying farm products can be sold. Any farmers who cannot sell at that price in the market can "sell" their surplus to the government. The only way a price-__________ system can survive is for the government or some other entity to buy up the excess quantity supplied at the support price.

When a __________ is placed on wages at a rate that is above market equilibrium, the result is an excess quantity of labor supplied at that minimum wage.

Quantity restrictions may take the form of __________ __________, which are limits on the quantity of specific foreign goods that can be brought into the United States for resale purposes.

YOU ARE THERE

Explaining the "Crisis" of Persistent Drug Shortages

According to Bona Benjamin of the American Society of Health-System Pharmacists, "We are in a crisis situation" in terms of shortages of many drugs used to treat a variety of diseases, including cancer. In 2006, the U.S. Food and Drug Administration (FDA) identified persistent shortages of 55 drugs. Today, there are shortages of about 300 drugs.

Benjamin and others involved in the markets for pharmaceuticals suggest that the persistent shortages of many drugs result from government price restrictions. The FDA can place limits on the percentage increase in a drug's price during a given year. Such a limitation often causes the allowed level of a drug's price in a given year to be lower than the market clearing price. Thus, the FDA's restraint on allowed price growth creates a shortage. If the FDA continues imposing limits on annual percentage increases in the price that are too low in relation to the rate of increase in the market clearing price, then the result is a persistent shortage.

Each year, the FDA has also broadened the list of medications for which limits on annual rates of allowed percentage price increases apply. This is why the number of drugs experiencing persistent shortages has increased.

Critical Thinking Questions

1. What would happen to the magnitudes of drug shortages if the FDA allowed higher annual price increases?
2. Would drug shortages be likely to persist if price controls were lifted? Explain.

ISSUES & APPLICATIONS

Why Prices of Used Cars Are So High

CONCEPTS APPLIED

- Supply
- Demand
- Market Clearing Price

Since 2009, the average price of a used car has increased by nearly 10 percent. Prices of a number of used models have risen by more than 30 percent. In some cases, prices of used cars are within a few hundred dollars of the prices of newly produced versions of the same models. These significant price increases can be explained by simultaneous changes in the supply of and demand for used cars.

"Cash for Clunkers" and a Decreased Supply of Used Cars

During the summer of 2009, the federal government implemented a program that became widely known as "cash for clunkers." Under this program, the government provided owners of specific low-fuel-economy vehicles with vouchers that the owners could apply toward purchases of new, more fuel-efficient vehicles. Ultimately, the government expended nearly $3 billion to purchase and crush (or shred) almost 700,000 used vehicles.

In the years since 2009, many of the vehicles destroyed under the program would have been available for sale in the used-car market. Their absence reduced the market supply of used vehicles: Fewer used vehicles were offered for sale at any given used-car price. Consequently, as shown in Figure 4-6 below, the market supply curve for used cars shifted leftward.

FIGURE 4-6

The Effects of a Decrease in the Supply of Used Cars in Conjunction with an Increase in the Demand for Used Cars

The federal government's cash-for-clunkers program removed hundreds of thousands of used cars from the used-car market, resulting in a decrease in supply, depicted by the leftward shift in the supply curve from S_1 to S_2. In addition, higher new-car prices induced consumers to substitute in favor of used cars, resulting in an increase in demand, shown by the rightward shift in the demand curve from D_1 to D_2. The market clearing price of used cars increased, from P_1 to P_2, and the equilibrium quantity of used cars decreased, from Q_1 to Q_2.

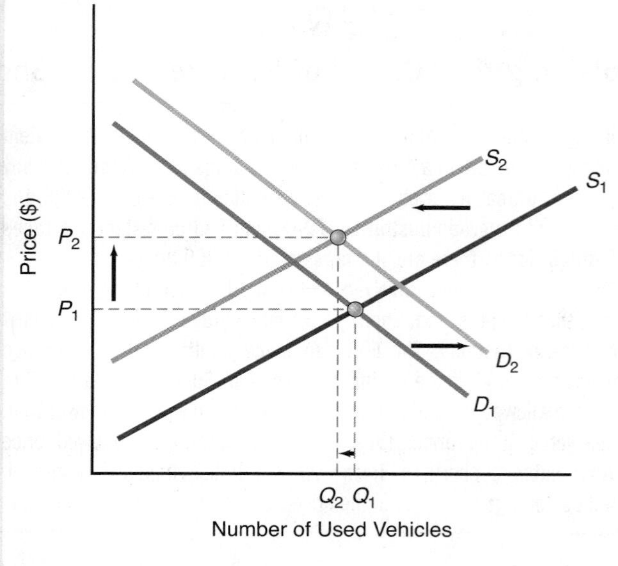

Higher Prices of New Cars Boost the Demand for Used Cars

Then, in 2011, northeastern Japan was struck both by destructive earthquakes and by a massive tsunami. Manufacturers based in Japan supply one of every four newly produced autos sold in the United States. For months following the disaster, exports of vehicles produced in Japan and shipments of Japanese-produced vehicle parts to U.S.-based assembly facilities of Japanese automakers were halted or delayed. The result was a fall in the supply of *new* vehicles, which led to an increase in the market clearing price of *new* cars.

Because new cars are a substitute for used vehicles, the rise in the price of new cars generated an increase in the demand for *used* vehicles: People desired to purchase more used vehicles at any given used-car price. Thus, as shown in Figure 4-6, the demand curve for used cars shifted rightward.

Taken together, the reduction in the supply of used cars caused by the cash-for-clunkers program and the increase in demand caused by higher new-car prices generated an increase in the market clearing price of used cars. The observed equilibrium-quantity outcome in the used-car market has been a slight decrease, as displayed in the figure.

For Critical Thinking

1. If used cars are a normal good and consumers' incomes were to fall during the next few years, what would happen to the market clearing price of used cars?
2. If the price change discussed in Question 1 were to occur, would this cause a change in the supply of used cars or in the quantity supplied? Explain.

Web Resources

1. Learn more about the federal government's cash-for-clunkers program at **www.econtoday.com/chap04**.
2. For a discussion of the lengthy production delays faced by Japanese automakers for an extended period following the earthquake and tsunami disaster, go to **www.econtoday.com/chap04**.

> **MyEconLab**
>
> For more questions on this chapter's Issues & Applications, go to MyEconLab. In the Study Plan for this chapter, select Section N: News.

MyEconLab

Here is what you should know after reading this chapter. MyEconLab will help you identify what you know, and where to go when you need to practice.

WHAT YOU SHOULD KNOW		WHERE TO GO TO PRACTICE
Essential Features of the Price System In the price system, prices respond to changes in supply and demand. Decisions on resource use depend on what happens to prices. Middlemen reduce transaction costs by bringing buyers and sellers together.	price system, 76 voluntary exchange, 76 transaction costs, 76	• MyEconLab Study Plan 4.1
How Changes in Demand and Supply Affect the Market Price and Equilibrium Quantity With a given supply curve, an increase in demand causes increases in the market price and equilibrium quantity, and a decrease in demand induces decreases in the market price and equilibrium quantity. With a given demand curve, an increase in supply causes a fall in the market price and an increase in the equilibrium quantity, and a decrease in supply causes a rise in the market price and a decline in the equilibrium quantity. When both demand and supply shift at the same time, we must know the direction and amount of each shift in order to predict changes in the market price and the equilibrium quantity.	**Key Figure** Figure 4-1, 78	• MyEconLab Study Plan 4.2 • Animated Figure 4-1

MyEconLab *continued*

WHAT YOU SHOULD KNOW		WHERE TO GO TO PRACTICE
The Rationing Function of Prices In the price system, prices ration scarce goods and services. Other ways of rationing include first come, first served; political power; physical force; random assignment; and coupons.		• MyEconLab Study Plan 4.3
The Effects of Price Ceilings Government-imposed price controls that require prices to be no higher than a certain level are price ceilings. If a government sets a price ceiling below the market price, then at the ceiling price the quantity of the good demanded will exceed the quantity supplied. There will be a shortage at the ceiling price. Price ceilings can lead to nonprice rationing devices and black markets.	price controls, 81 price ceiling, 81 price floor, 82 nonprice rationing devices, 82 black market, 82 rent control, 83 **Key Figure** Figure 4-3, 82	• MyEconLab Study Plans 4.4, 4.5 • Animated Figure 4-3
The Effects of Price Floors Government-mandated price controls that require prices to be no lower than a certain level are price floors. If a government sets a price floor above the market price, then at the floor price the quantity of the good supplied will exceed the quantity demanded. There will be a surplus at the floor price.	minimum wage, 87 **Key Figures** Figure 4-4, 85 Figure 4-5, 88	• MyEconLab Study Plans 4.6, 4.7 • Animated Figures 4-4, 4-5
Government-Imposed Restrictions on Market Quantities Quantity restrictions can take the form of outright government bans on the sale of certain goods. They can also arise from licensing and import restrictions that limit the number of sellers and thereby restrict the amount supplied.	import quota, 89	• MyEconLab Study Plan 4.8

Log in to MyEconLab, take a chapter test, and get a personalized Study Plan that tells you which concepts you understand and which ones you need to review. From there, MyEconLab will give you further practice, tutorials, animations, videos, and guided solutions. For more information, visit www.myeconlab.com

PROBLEMS

All problems are assignable in MyEconLab. *Answers to odd-numbered problems appear at the back of the book.*

4-1. In recent years, technological improvements have greatly reduced the costs of producing basic cell phones, and a number of new firms have entered the cell phone industry. At the same time, prices of substitutes for cell phones, such as smartphones and some tablet devices, have declined considerably. Construct a supply and demand diagram of the market for cell phones. Illustrate the impacts of these developments, and evaluate the effects on the market price and equilibrium quantity. (See page 78.)

4-2. Advances in research and development in the pharmaceutical industry have enabled manufacturers to identify potential cures more quickly and therefore at lower cost. At the same time, the aging of our society has increased the demand for new drugs. Construct a supply and demand diagram of the market for pharmaceutical drugs. Illustrate the impacts of these developments, and evaluate the effects on the market price and the equilibrium quantity. (See page 78.)

4-3. There are simultaneous changes in the demand for and supply of global-positioning-system (GPS) devices, with the consequences being an unambiguous increase in the market clearing price of these devices but no change in the equilibrium quantity. What changes in the demand for and supply of GPS devices could have generated these outcomes? Explain. (See pages 78–79.)

4-4. There are simultaneous changes in the demand for and supply of tablet devices, with the consequences being an unambiguous decrease in the equilibrium quantity of these devices but no change in the market clearing price. What changes in the demand for and supply of tablet devices could have generated these outcomes? Explain. (See pages 78–79.)

4-5. The following table depicts the quantity demanded and quantity supplied of studio apartments in a small college town.

Monthly Rent	Quantity Demanded	Quantity Supplied
$600	3,000	1,600
$650	2,500	1,800
$700	2,000	2,000
$750	1,500	2,200
$800	1,000	2,400

What are the market price and equilibrium quantity of apartments in this town? If this town imposes a rent control of $650 per month, how many studio apartments will be rented? (See pages 83–84.)

4-6. Suppose that the government places a ceiling on the price of a medical drug below the equilibrium price. (See page 82.)

a. Show why there is a shortage of the medical drug at the new ceiling price.

b. Suppose that a black market for the medical drug arises, with pharmaceutical firms secretly selling the drug at higher prices. Illustrate the black market for this medical drug, including the implicit supply schedule, the ceiling price, the black market supply and demand, and the highest feasible black market price.

4-7. The table below illustrates the demand and supply schedules for seats on air flights between two cities:

Price	Quantity Demanded	Quantity Supplied
$200	2,000	1,200
$300	1,800	1,400
$400	1,600	1,600
$500	1,400	1,800
$600	1,200	2,000

What are the market price and equilibrium quantity in this market? Now suppose that federal authorities limit the number of flights between the two cities to ensure that no more than 1,200 passengers can be flown. Evaluate the effects of this quota if price adjusts. (Hint: What price per flight are the 1,200 passengers willing to pay? See page 89.)

4-8. The consequences of decriminalizing illegal drugs have long been debated. Some claim that legalization will lower the price of these drugs and reduce related crime and that more people will use these drugs. Suppose that some of these drugs are legalized so that anyone may sell them and use them. Now consider the two claims—that price will fall and quantity demanded will increase. Based on positive economic analysis, are these claims sound? (See page 89.)

4-9. In recent years, the government of Pakistan has established a support price for wheat of about $0.20 per kilogram of wheat. At this price, consumers are willing to purchase 10 billion kilograms of wheat per year, while Pakistani farmers are willing to grow and harvest 18 billion kilograms of wheat per year. The government purchases and stores all surplus wheat. (See page 85.)

a. What are annual consumer expenditures on the Pakistani wheat crop?

b. What are annual government expenditures on the Pakistani wheat crop?

c. How much, in total, do Pakistani wheat farmers receive for the wheat they produce?

4-10. Consider the information in Problem 4-9 and your answers to that question. Suppose that the market clearing price of Pakistani wheat in the absence of price supports is equal to $0.10 per kilogram. At this price, the quantity of wheat demanded is 12 billion kilograms. Under the government wheat price-support program, how much more is spent each year on wheat harvested in Pakistan than otherwise would have been spent in an unregulated market for Pakistani wheat? (See page 85.)

4-11. Consider the diagram below, which depicts the labor market in a city that has adopted a "living wage law" requiring employers to pay a minimum wage rate of $11 per hour. Answer the questions that follow. (See page 88.)

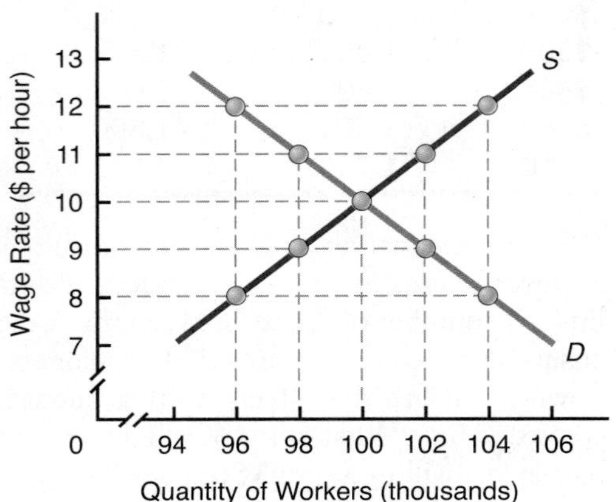

a. What condition exists in this city's labor market at the present minimum wage of $11 per hour? How many people are unemployed at this wage?

b. A city councilwoman has proposed amending the living wage law. She suggests reducing the minimum wage to $9 per hour. Assuming that the labor demand and supply curves were to remain in their present positions, how many people would be unemployed at a new $9 minimum wage?

c. A councilman has offered a counterproposal. In his view, the current minimum wage is too low and should be increased to $12 per hour. Assuming that the labor demand and supply curves remain in their present positions, how many people would be unemployed at a new $12 minimum wage?

4-12. A city has decided to impose rent controls, and it has established a rent ceiling below the previous equilibrium rental rate for offices throughout the city. How will the quantity of offices leased by building owners change? (See page 83.)

4-13. In 2011, the government of a nation established a price support for wheat. The government's support price has been above the equilibrium price each year since, and the government has purchased all wheat over and above the amounts that consumers have bought at the support price. Every year since 2011, there has been an increase in the number of wheat producers in the market. No other factors affecting the market for wheat have changed. Predict what has happened every year since 2011, to each of the following (see page 85):

a. Amount of wheat supplied by wheat producers

b. Amount of wheat demanded by all wheat consumers

c. Amount of wheat purchased by the government

4-14. In advance of the recent increase in the U.S. minimum wage rate, the government of the state of Arizona decided to boost its own minimum wage by an additional $1.60 per hour. This pushed the wage rate earned by Arizona teenagers above the equilibrium wage rate in the teen labor market. What is the predicted effect of this action by Arizona's government on each of the following? (See page 88.)

a. The quantity of labor supplied by Arizona teenagers

b. The quantity of labor demanded by employers of Arizona teenagers

c. The number of unemployed Arizona teenagers

ECONOMICS ON THE NET

The Floor on Milk Prices At various times, the U.S. government has established price floors for milk. This application gives you an opportunity to apply what you have learned in this chapter to this real-world issue.

Title: Northeast Dairy Compact Commission

Navigation: Go to **www.econtoday.com/chap04** to visit the Web site of the Northeast Dairy Compact Commission.

Application Read the contents and answer these questions.

1. Based on the government-set price control concepts discussed in Chapter 4, explain the Northeast Dairy Compact that was once in place in the northeastern United States.

2. Draw a diagram illustrating the supply of and demand for milk in the Northeast Dairy Compact and the supply of and demand for milk outside the Northeast

Dairy Compact. Illustrate how the compact affected the quantities demanded and supplied for participants in the compact. In addition, show how this affected the market for milk produced by those producers outside the dairy compact.

3. Economists have found that while the Northeast Dairy Compact functioned, midwestern dairy farmers lost their dominance of milk production and sales. In light of your answer to Question 2, explain how this occurred.

For Group Discussion and Analysis Discuss the impact of congressional failure to reauthorize the compact based on your above answers. Identify which arguments in your debate are based on positive economic analysis and which are normative arguments.

ANSWERS TO QUICK QUIZZES

p. 80: (i) demand . . . supply . . . supply . . . demand; (ii) immediately . . . time

p. 81: (i) first come, first served . . . political power . . . physical force . . . random assignment . . . coupons; (ii) queuing

p. 83: (i) ceilings . . . floors; (ii) ceiling . . . controls

p. 85: (i) Rental; (ii) controls . . . controls; (iii) Key money

p. 89: (i) support . . . support; (ii) floor; (iii) import quotas

APPENDIX B

Consumer Surplus, Producer Surplus, and Gains from Trade within a Price System

A key principle of economics is that the price system enables people to benefit from the voluntary exchange of goods and services. Economists measure the benefits from trade by applying the concepts of *consumer surplus* and *producer surplus*, which are defined in the sections that follow.

Consumer Surplus

Let's first examine how economists measure the benefits that consumers gain from engaging in market transactions in the price system. Consider Figure B-1 below, which displays a market demand curve, D. We begin by assuming that consumers face a per-unit price of this item given by P_A. Thus, the quantity demanded of this particular product is equal to Q_A at point A on the demand curve.

FIGURE B-1

Consumer Surplus

If the per-unit price is P_A, then at point A on the demand curve D, consumers desire to purchase Q_A units. To purchase Q_1 units of this item, consumers would have been willing to pay the price P_1 for the last unit purchased, but they have to pay only the per-unit price P_A, so they gain a surplus equal to $P_1 - P_A$ for the last of the Q_1 units purchased. Likewise, to buy the last of the Q_2 units, consumers would have been willing to pay the price P_2, so they gain the surplus equal to $P_2 - P_A$ for the last of the Q_2 units purchased. Summing these and all other surpluses that consumers receive from purchasing each of the Q_A units at the price P_A yields the total consumer surplus at this price, shown by the blue-shaded area.

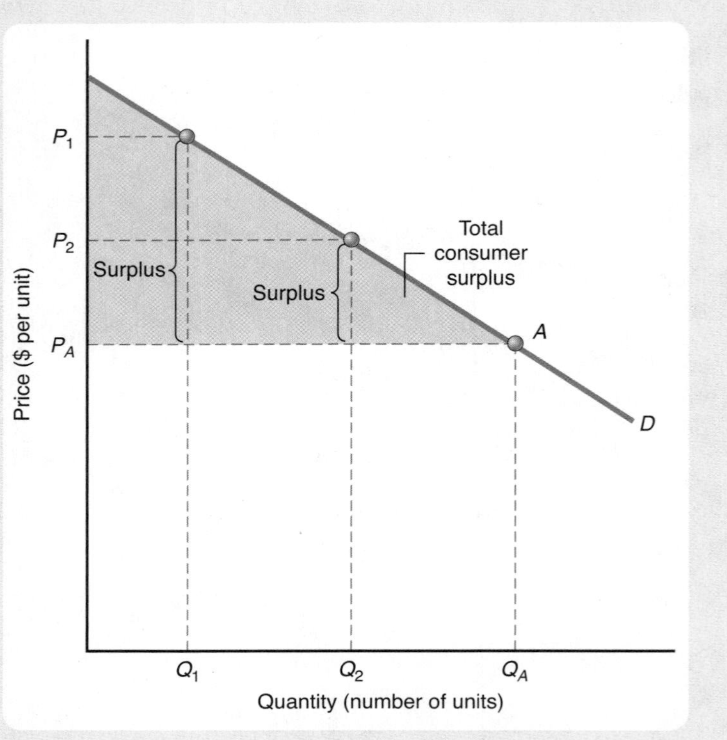

Typically, we visualize the market demand curve as indicating the quantities that all consumers are willing to purchase at each possible price. But the demand curve also tells us the price that consumers are willing to pay for a unit of output at various possible quantities. For instance, if consumers buy Q_1 units of this good, they will be willing to pay a price equal to P_1 for the last unit purchased. If they have to pay only the price P_A for each unit they buy, however, consumers gain an amount equal to $P_1 - P_A$ for the last of the Q_1 units purchased. This benefit to consumers equals the vertical distance between the demand curve and the level of the market clearing price. Economists call this vertical distance a *surplus* value to consumers from being able to consume the last of the Q_1 units at the lower, market clearing price.

Likewise, if consumers purchase Q_2 units of this good, they will be willing to pay a price equal to P_2 for the last unit. Nevertheless, because they have to pay only the price P_A for each unit purchased, consumers gain an amount equal to $P_2 - P_A$. Hence, this is the surplus associated with the last of the Q_2 units that consumers buy.

Of course, when consumers pay the same per-unit price P_A for every unit of this product that they purchase at point A, they obtain Q_A units. Thus, consumers gain surplus values—all of the vertical distances between the demand curve and the level of the market clearing price—for each unit consumed, up to the total of Q_A units. Graphically, this is equivalent to the blue-shaded *area under the demand curve but above the market clearing price* in Figure B-1 on the facing page. This entire area equals the total **consumer surplus,** which is the difference between the total amount that consumers *would have been willing to pay* for an item and the total amount that they actually pay.

Consumer surplus
The difference between the total amount that consumers would have been willing to pay for an item and the total amount that they actually pay.

Producer Surplus

Consumers are not the only ones who gain from exchange. Producers (suppliers) gain as well. To consider how economists measure the benefits to producers from supplying goods and services in exchange, look at Figure B-2 below, which displays a market supply curve, S. Let's begin by assuming that suppliers face a per-unit price of this item given by P_B. Thus, the quantity supplied of this particular product is equal to Q_B at point B on the supply curve.

FIGURE B-2

Producer Surplus

If the per-unit price is P_B, then at point B on the supply curve S, producers are willing to supply Q_B units. To sell Q_3 units of this item, producers would have been willing to receive the price P_3 for the last unit sold, but instead they accept the higher per-unit price P_B, so they gain a surplus equal to $P_B - P_3$ for the last of the Q_3 units sold. Similarly, producers would have been willing to accept P_4 to provide Q_4 units, so they gain the surplus equal to $P_B - P_4$ for the last of the Q_4 units sold. Summing these and all other surpluses that producers receive from supplying each of the Q_B units at the price P_B yields the total producer surplus at this price, shown by the red-shaded area.

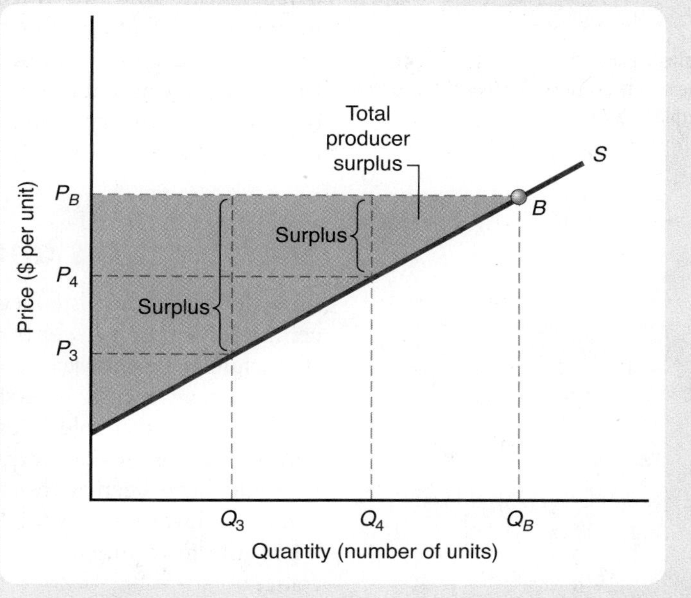

The market supply curve tells us the quantities that all producers are willing to to sell at each possible price. At the same time, the supply curve also indicates the price that producers are willing to accept to sell a unit of output at various possible quantities. For example, if producers sell Q_3 units of this good, they will be willing to accept a price equal to P_3 for the last unit sold. If they receive the price P_B for each unit that they supply, however, producers gain an amount equal to $P_B - P_3$ for the last of the Q_3 units sold. This benefit to producers equals the vertical distance between the supply curve and the market clearing price, which is a *surplus* value from being able to provide the last of the Q_3 units at the higher, market clearing price.

Similarly, if producers supply Q_4 units of this good, they will be willing to accept a price equal to P_4 for the last unit. Producers actually receive the price P_B for each unit supplied, however, so they gain an amount equal to $P_B - P_4$. Hence, this is the surplus gained from supplying the last of the Q_4 units.

Naturally, when producers receive the same per-unit price P_B for each unit supplied at point B, producers sell Q_B units. Consequently, producers gain surplus values—all of the vertical distances between the level of the market clearing price and the supply curve—for each unit supplied, up to the total of Q_B units. In Figure B-2 on the previous page, this is equivalent to the red-shaded *area above the supply curve but below the market clearing price*. This area is the total **producer surplus,** which is the difference between the total amount that producers actually receive for an item and the total amount that they *would have been willing to accept* for supplying that item.

Producer surplus
The difference between the total amount that producers actually receive for an item and the total amount that they would have been willing to accept for supplying that item.

Gains from Trade within a Price System

The concepts of consumer surplus and producer surplus can be combined to measure the gains realized by consumers and producers from engaging in voluntary exchange. To see how, take a look at Figure B-3 on the facing page. The market demand and supply curves intersect at point E, and as you have learned, at this point, the equilibrium quantity is Q_E. At the market clearing price P_E, this is both the quantity that consumers are willing to purchase and the quantity that producers are willing to supply.

In addition, at the market clearing price P_E and the equilibrium quantity Q_E, the blue-shaded area under the demand curve but above the market clearing price is the amount of consumer surplus. Furthermore, the red-shaded area under the market clearing price but above the supply curve is the amount of producer surplus. The sum of *both* areas is the total value of the **gains from trade**—the sum of consumer surplus and producer surplus—generated by the mutually beneficial voluntary exchange of the equilibrium quantity Q_E at the market clearing price P_E.

Gains from trade
The sum of consumer surplus and producer surplus.

Price Controls and Gains from Trade

How do price controls affect gains from trade? Consider first the effects of imposing a ceiling price that is lower than the market clearing price. As you learned in Chapter 4, the results are an increase in quantity demanded and a decrease in quantity supplied, so a shortage occurs. The smaller quantity supplied by firms is the amount actually produced and available in the market for the item in question. Thus, consumers are able to purchase fewer units, and this means that consumer surplus may be lower than it would have been without the government's price ceiling. Furthermore, because firms sell fewer units at the lower ceiling price, producer surplus definitely decreases. Thus, the government's imposition of the price ceiling tends to reduce gains from trade.

FIGURE B-3

Consumer Surplus, Producer Surplus, and Gains from Trade

At point *E*, the demand and supply curves intersect at the equilibrium quantity Q_E and the market clearing price P_E. Total consumer surplus at the market clearing price is the blue-shaded area under the demand curve but above the market clearing price. Total producer surplus is the red-shaded area below the market clearing price but above the supply curve. The sum of consumer surplus and producer surplus at the market clearing price constitutes the total gain to society from voluntary exchange of the quantity Q_E at the market clearing price P_E.

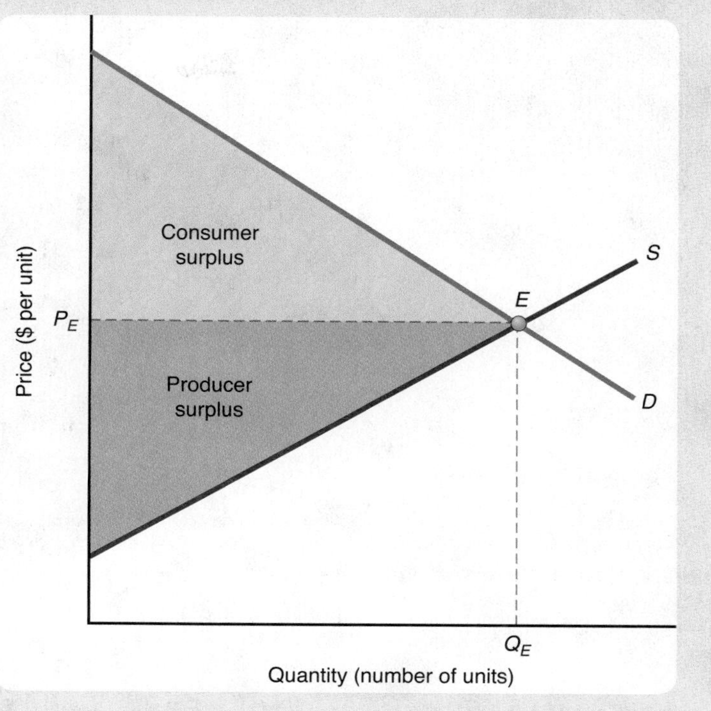

Now consider the effects of the establishment of a price floor above the market clearing price of a good. As discussed in Chapter 4, the effects of imposing such a floor price are an increase in the quantity supplied and a decrease in the quantity demanded. The smaller quantity demanded by consumers is the amount actually traded in the market. Thus, consumers purchase fewer units of the good, resulting in a reduction in consumer surplus. In addition, firms sell fewer units, so producer surplus may decrease. Thus, the establishment of a price floor also tends to reduce gains from trade.

5 Public Spending and Public Choice

The U.S. Postal Service (USPS) delivers nearly 40 percent of the world's mail. Nevertheless, its annual volume of delivered mail has declined by more than 20 percent since 2006. Even though the USPS commonly refers to itself as a private enterprise, economists classify it as *government-sponsored*. Government sponsorship of the USPS is evidenced by the fact that the USPS now receives more than $15 billion in U.S. government loans. Without these funds, the USPS would have to shut down many of its operations. Why does the government sponsor the provision of certain items, such as mail delivery services, even though private firms otherwise could provide them? This is among the several questions relating to government's economic role that are addressed in the present chapter.

LEARNING OBJECTIVES

After reading this chapter, you should be able to:

- Explain how market failures such as externalities might justify economic functions of government
- Distinguish between private goods and public goods and explain the nature of the free-rider problem
- Describe political functions of government that entail its involvement in the economy
- Analyze how Medicare affects the incentives to consume medical services
- Explain why increases in government spending on public education have not been associated with improvements in measures of student performance
- Discuss the central elements of the theory of public choice

MyEconLab helps you master each objective and study more efficiently. See end of chapter for details.

a 75-year-old woman accidentally managed to halt all Internet traffic to the entire country of Armenia? The woman was shoveling for scrap metal in the Eastern European nation of Georgia, when she sliced through the single fiber optic cable routing all of Armenia's Web transmissions. In her defense, the woman stated that a jump in the market price of scrap metals had induced her to search beneath the ground for old, unused wires that might contain copper. She was only pursuing her own self-interest with an aim to profit from selling items in the scrap-metals market, she contended. She had not, she insisted, intended to cut off Internet access for thousands of people. This event was an example of how people interacting in markets, including the market for scrap metal, can create negative spillovers, such as interrupted Internet traffic, for people outside those markets. As you will learn in this chapter, economists classify such third-party spillovers, which they refer to as *externalities*, among flaws in the price system called *market failures*.

What a Price System Can and Cannot Do

Throughout the book so far, we have alluded to the advantages of a price system. High on the list is economic efficiency. In its ideal form, a price system allows all resources to move from lower-valued uses to higher-valued uses via voluntary exchange, by which mutually advantageous trades take place. In a price system, consumers are sovereign. That is to say, they have the individual freedom to decide what they wish to purchase. Politicians and even business managers do not ultimately decide what is produced. Consumers decide. Some proponents of the price system argue that this is its most important characteristic. Competition among sellers protects consumers from coercion by one seller, and sellers are protected from coercion by one consumer because other consumers are available.

Sometimes, though, the price system does not generate these results, and too few or too many resources go to specific economic activities. Such situations are **market failures.** Market failures prevent the price system from attaining economic efficiency and individual freedom. Market failures offer one of the strongest arguments in favor of certain economic functions of government, which we now examine.

Market failure
A situation in which the market economy leads to too few or too many resources going to a specific economic activity.

Correcting for Externalities

In a pure market system, competition generates economic efficiency only when individuals know and must bear the true opportunity cost of their actions. In some circumstances, the price that someone actually pays for a resource, good, or service is higher or lower than the opportunity cost that all of society pays for that same resource, good, or service.

Externalities

Consider a hypothetical world in which there is no government regulation against pollution. You are living in a town that until now has had clean air. A steel mill moves into town. It produces steel and has paid for the inputs—land, labor, capital, and entrepreneurship. The price the mill charges for the steel reflects, in this example, only the costs that it incurs. In the course of production, however, the mill utilizes one input—clean air—by simply using it. This is indeed an input because in making steel, the furnaces emit smoke. The steel mill doesn't have to pay the cost of dirtying the air. Rather, it is the people in the community who incur that cost in the form of dirtier clothes, dirtier cars and houses, and more respiratory illnesses.

The effect is similar to what would happen if the steel mill could take coal or oil or workers' services without paying for them. There is an **externality,** an external cost. Some of the costs associated with the production of the steel have "spilled over" to affect **third parties,** parties other than the buyer and the seller of the steel.

Externality
A consequence of an economic activity that spills over to affect third parties. Pollution is an externality.

Third parties
Parties who are not directly involved in a given activity or transaction.

Property rights
The rights of an owner to use and to exchange property.

A fundamental reason that air pollution creates external costs is that the air belongs to everyone and hence to no one in particular. Lack of clearly assigned **property rights,** or the rights of an owner to use and exchange property, prevents market prices from reflecting all the costs created by activities that generate spillovers onto third parties.

External Costs in Graphical Form

To consider how market prices fail to take into account external costs in situations in which third-party spillovers exist without a clear assignment of property rights, look at panel (a) in Figure 5-1 below. Here we show the demand curve for steel as D. The supply curve is S_1. The supply curve includes only the costs that the firms in the market have to pay. Equilibrium occurs at point E, with a price of $800 per ton and a quantity equal to 110 million tons per year.

But producing steel also involves externalities—the external costs that you and your neighbors pay in the form of dirtier clothes, cars, and houses and increased respiratory disease due to the air pollution emitted from the steel mill. In this case, the producers of steel use clean air without having to pay for it. Let's include these external costs in our graph to find out what the full cost of steel production would really be if property rights to the air around the steel mill could generate payments for "owners" of that air. We do this by imagining that steel producers have to pay the "owners" of the air for the input—clean air—that the producers previously used at a zero price.

Recall from Chapter 3 that an increase in input prices shifts the supply curve up and to the left. Thus, in panel (a) of the figure, the supply curve shifts from S_1 to S_2. External costs equal the vertical distance between A and E_1. In this example, if steel firms had to take into account these external costs, the equilibrium quantity would

FIGURE 5-1
External Costs and Benefits

Panel (a) shows a situation in which production of steel generates external costs. If the steel mills ignore pollution, at equilibrium the quantity of steel will be 110 million tons. If the steel mills had to pay external costs caused by the mills' production but currently borne by nearby residents, the supply curve would shift the vertical distance A–E_1, to S_2. If consumers of steel were forced to pay a price that reflected the spillover costs, the quantity demanded would fall to 100 million tons. Panel (b) shows a situation in which inoculations against communicable diseases generate external benefits to those individuals who may not be inoculated but who will benefit because epidemics will not occur. If each individual ignores the external benefit of inoculations, the market clearing quantity will be 150 million. If external benefits were taken into account by purchasers of inoculations, however, the demand curve would shift to D_2. The new equilibrium quantity would be 200 million inoculations, and the price of an inoculation would rise from $10 to $15.

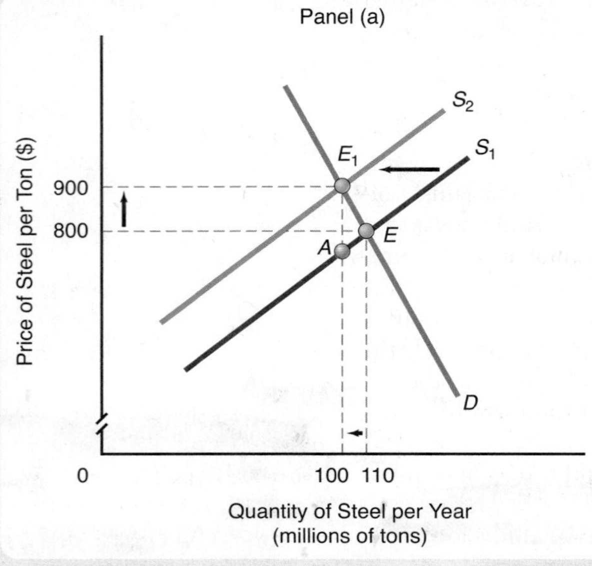

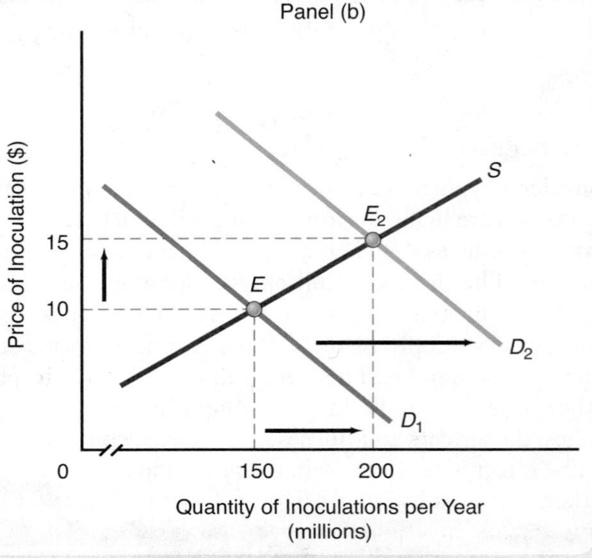

fall to 100 million tons per year, and the price would rise to $900 per ton. Equilibrium would shift from E to E_1. In contrast, if the price of steel does not account for external costs, third parties bear those costs—represented by the distance between A and E_1—in the form of dirtier clothes, houses, and cars and increased respiratory illnesses.

External Benefits in Graphical Form

Externalities can also be positive. To demonstrate external benefits in graphical form, we will use the example of inoculations against communicable disease. In panel (b) of Figure 5-1 on the facing page, we show the demand curve as D_1 (without taking account of any external benefits) and the supply curve as S. The equilibrium price is $10 per inoculation, and the equilibrium quantity is 150 million inoculations.

We assume, however, that inoculations against communicable diseases generate external benefits to individuals who may not be inoculated but will benefit nevertheless because epidemics will not break out. If such external benefits were taken into account by those who purchase inoculations, the demand curve would shift from D_1 to D_2.

As a consequence of this shift in demand at point E_2, the new equilibrium quantity would be 200 million inoculations, and the new equilibrium price would be $15 per inoculation. If people who consider getting inoculations fail to take external benefits into account, individuals in society are not devoting enough resources to inoculations against communicable diseases.

Resource Misallocations of Externalities

When there are external costs, the market will tend to *overallocate* resources to the production of the good or service in question, for those goods or services are implicitly priced deceptively low. In the steel example, too many resources will be allocated to steel production, because the steel mill owners and managers are not required to take account of the external cost that steel production is imposing on other individuals. In essence, the full cost of production is not borne by the owners and managers, so the price they charge the public for steel is lower than it would otherwise be. And, of course, the lower price means that buyers are willing and able to buy more. More steel is produced and consumed than if the sellers and buyers were to bear external costs.

In contrast, when there are external benefits, the price is too low to induce suppliers to allocate resources to the production of that good or service (because the demand, which fails to reflect the external benefits, is relatively too low). Thus, the market *underallocates* resources to producing the good or service. Hence, in a market system, too many of the goods that generate external costs are produced, and too few of the goods that generate external benefits are produced.

How the Government Can Correct Negative Externalities

In theory, the government can take action to try to correct situations in which a lack of property rights allows third-party spillovers to create an externality. In the case of negative externalities, at least two avenues are open to the government: special taxes and legislative regulation or prohibition.

SPECIAL TAXES In our example of the steel mill, the externality problem arises because using the air for waste disposal is costless to the firm but not to society. The government could attempt to tax the steel mill commensurate with the cost to third parties from smoke in the air. This, in effect, would be a pollution tax or an **effluent fee.** The ultimate effect would be to reduce the supply of steel and raise the price to consumers, ideally making the price equal to the full cost of production to society.

Effluent fee
A charge to a polluter that gives the right to discharge into the air or water a certain amount of pollution; also called a *pollution tax.*

Why has Hungary's government imposed taxes on foods that it has determined to be detrimental to the health of that nation's residents?

INTERNATIONAL POLICY EXAMPLE

Hungary's Tax on Prepackaged Snacks

The government of Hungary has determined that the nation's health care system experiences external spillovers from the snack food market. People who consume too many chips, salted nuts, sweets, ice creams, instant soups, and energy drinks are, the government has concluded, experiencing worse health. As these people seek treatment for their health problems, they are clogging the nation's physicians' offices and hospitals. Thus, Hungary's government is seeking to induce producers of certain snack foods and beverages to cut back on an overallocation of resources that the government perceives to be creating a negative externality.

Toward this end, the government is placing special taxes on foodstuffs with high sugar, salt, and carbohydrate content and on fluid products containing more than 20 milligrams of caffeine per 100 milliliters. By imposing these taxes, it intends to reduce the supply of each of these items and thereby raise its price toward equality with the full cost of its production to society as a whole.

FOR CRITICAL THINKING

If untaxed bakery sweets and fast food are close substitutes for snack foods, could Hungary's tax on snack foods boost consumption of the untaxed items? Explain.

Go to **www.econtoday.com/chap05** to learn more about how the Environmental Protection Agency uses regulations to try to protect the environment.

REGULATION Alternatively, to correct a negative externality arising from steel production, the government could specify a maximum allowable rate of pollution. This regulation would require that the steel mill install pollution abatement equipment at its facilities, reduce its rate of output, or some combination of the two. Note that the government's job would not be simple, for it would have to determine the appropriate level of pollution, which would require extensive knowledge of both the benefits and the costs of pollution control.

How the Government Can Correct Positive Externalities

What can the government do when the production of one good spills *benefits* over to third parties? It has several policy options: financing the production of the good or producing the good itself, subsidies (negative taxes), and regulation.

GOVERNMENT FINANCING AND PRODUCTION If the positive externalities seem extremely large, the government has the option of financing the desired additional production facilities so that the "right" amount of the good will be produced. Again consider inoculations against communicable diseases. The government could—and often does—finance campaigns to inoculate the population. It could (and does) even produce and operate inoculation centers where inoculations are given at no charge.

SUBSIDIES A subsidy is a negative tax. A subsidy is a per-unit payment made either to a business or to a consumer when the business produces or the consumer buys a good or a service. To generate more inoculations against communicable diseases, the government could subsidize everyone who obtains an inoculation by directly reimbursing those inoculated or by making per-unit payments to private firms that provide inoculations. Subsidies reduce the net price to consumers, thereby causing a larger quantity to be demanded.

How are some state governments seeking to help society capture external benefits that the governments suggest society derives from being kept informed?

POLICY EXAMPLE

Stop the Presses for Subsidies!

Since the late 2000s, total physical newspaper circulation to paid subscribers has declined by more than 5 percent per year. The cumulative reduction in readership of paper editions since 2000 has exceeded 50 percent.

Some state government officials suggest that local newspapers provide positive externalities. Making readers better informed, they argue, improves people's lives and in some cases saves lives. On the basis of this logic, several state governments are now providing subsidies to newspapers. For example, Minnesota's state government has provided hundreds of thousands of dollars to newspapers in Duluth and St. Paul. These newspapers have used the funds to train their staffs to post content and ads online instead of relying solely on physical print editions to generate revenues. In this way, the Minnesota state government seeks to help local newspapers keep operating.

FOR CRITICAL THINKING

How does the provision of subsidies to local newspapers likely affect the supply of news content at each possible price?

REGULATION In some cases involving positive externalities, the government can require by law that individuals in the society undertake a certain action. For example, regulations require that all school-age children be inoculated before entering public and private schools. Some people believe that a basic school education itself generates positive externalities. Perhaps as a result of this belief, we have regulations—laws—that require all school-age children to be enrolled in a public or private school.

QUICK QUIZ See page 121 for the answers. Review concepts from this section in MyEconLab.

External __________ lead to an overallocation of resources to the specific economic activity. Two possible ways of correcting these spillovers are __________ and __________.

External __________ result in an underallocation of resources to the specific activity. Three possible government corrections are __________ the production of the activity, __________ private firms or consumers to engage in the activity, and __________.

The Other Economic Functions of Government

Besides correcting for externalities, the government performs many other economic functions that affect the way exchange is carried out. In contrast, the political functions of government have to do with deciding how income should be redistributed among households and selecting which goods and services have special merits and should therefore be treated differently. The economic and political functions of government can and do overlap.

Let's look at four more economic functions of government.

Providing a Legal System

The courts and the police may not at first seem like economic functions of government. Their activities nonetheless have important consequences for economic activities in any country. You and I enter into contracts constantly, whether they be oral or written, expressed or implied. When we believe that we have been wronged, we seek redress of our grievances through our legal institutions. Moreover, consider the legal system that is necessary for the smooth functioning of our economic system. Our system has defined quite explicitly the legal status of businesses, the rights of private ownership, and a method of enforcing contracts. All relationships among consumers and businesses are governed by the legal rules of the game.

In its judicial function, then, the government serves as the referee for settling disputes in the economic arena. In this role, the government often imposes penalties for violations of legal rules.

Much of our legal system is involved with defining and protecting property rights. One might say that property rights are really the rules of our economic game. When property rights are well defined, owners of property have an incentive to use that property efficiently. Any mistakes in their decisions about the use of property have negative consequences that the owners suffer. Furthermore, when property rights are well defined, owners of property have an incentive to maintain that property so that if they ever desire to sell it, it will fetch a better price.

What happens when the government fails to establish clear rights to private property and fails to enforce owners' rights fully? In such situations, individuals and firms are more likely to be willing to engage in activities that create spillover effects for other individuals. Thus, externalities will result. In such cases, however, these externalities result from ambiguously assigned and weakly enforced property rights. The government, rather than the market, is at fault.

Promoting Competition

Antitrust legislation
Laws that restrict the formation of monopolies and regulate certain anticompetitive business practices.

Monopoly
A firm that can determine the market price of a good. In the extreme case, a monopoly is the only seller of a good or service.

Many economists argue that the only way to attain economic efficiency is through competition. One of the roles of government is to serve as the protector of a competitive economic system. Congress and the various state governments have passed **antitrust legislation.** Such legislation makes illegal certain (but not all) economic activities that might restrain trade—that is, that might prevent free competition among actual and potential rival firms in the marketplace. The avowed aim of antitrust legislation is to reduce the power of **monopolies**—firms that can determine the market price of the goods they sell. A large number of antitrust laws have been passed that prohibit specific anticompetitive actions. Both the Antitrust Division of the U.S. Department of Justice and the Federal Trade Commission attempt to enforce these antitrust laws. Various state judicial agencies also expend efforts at maintaining competition.

Providing Public Goods

Private goods
Goods that can be consumed by only one individual at a time. Private goods are subject to the principle of rival consumption.

Principle of rival consumption
The recognition that individuals are rivals in consuming private goods because one person's consumption reduces the amount available for others to consume.

The goods used in our examples up to this point have been **private goods.** When I eat a cheeseburger, you cannot eat the same one. So you and I are rivals for that cheeseburger, just as much as contenders for the title of world champion are. When I use the services of an auto mechanic, that person cannot work at the same time for you. That is the distinguishing feature of private goods—their use is exclusive to the people who purchase them. The **principle of rival consumption** applies to most private goods. Rival consumption is easy to understand. Either you use such a private good or I use it.

Of course, private firms provide some goods and services that are not fully subject to the principle of rival consumption. For instance, you and a friend can both purchase tickets providing the two of you with the right to sit in a musical facility and listen to a concert during a specified period of time. Your friend's presence does not prohibit you from enjoying the music, nor does your presence prevent him from appreciating the concert. Nevertheless, the owner of the musical facility can prevent others who have not purchased tickets from entering the facility during the concert. Consequently, as long as nonpayers can be excluded from consuming an item, that item can also be produced and sold as a private good.

Public goods
Goods for which the principle of rival consumption does not apply and for which exclusion of nonpaying consumers is too costly to be feasible. They can be jointly consumed by many individuals simultaneously at no additional cost and with no reduction in quality or quantity. Furthermore, no one who fails to help pay for the good can be denied the benefit of the good.

There is an entire class of goods that are not private goods. These are called **public goods.** Like musical concerts, public goods are items to which the principle of rival consumption does not apply. Hence, many individuals simultaneously can consume public goods *jointly*. What truly distinguishes public goods from all private goods is that the costs required to exclude nonpayers from consuming public goods are so high that doing so is infeasible. National defense and police protection are examples. Suppose that your next-door neighbor were to pay for protection from a terrorist effort to explode a large bomb. If so, your neighbor's life and property could not be defended from such a threat without your life and property also receiving the same defense, even if you had failed to provide any payment for protection. Finding a way to avoid protecting you while still protecting your neighbor would be so expensive that such exclusion of defense for you and your property would be difficult.

CHARACTERISTICS OF PUBLIC GOODS Two fundamental characteristics of public goods set them apart from all other goods:

1. *Public goods can be used by more and more people at no additional opportunity cost and without depriving others of any of the services of the goods.*Once funds have been spent on national defense, the defense protection you receive does not reduce the amount of protection bestowed on anyone else. The opportunity cost of your receiving national defense once it is in place is zero because once national defense is in place to protect you, it also protects others.

2. *It is difficult to design a collection system for a public good on the basis of how much individuals use it.*Nonpayers can often utilize a public good without incurring any monetary cost, because the cost of excluding them from using the good is so high. Those

who provide the public good find that it is not cost-effective to prevent nonpayers from utilizing it. For instance, taxpayers who pay to provide national defense typically do not incur the costs that would be entailed in excluding nonpayers from benefiting from national defense.

The fundamental problem of public goods is that the private sector has a difficult, if not impossible, time providing them. Individuals in the private sector have little or no incentive to offer public goods. It is difficult for them to make a profit doing so, because it is too costly and, hence, infeasible to exclude nonpayers. Consequently, true public goods must necessarily be provided by government. (Note, though, that economists do not categorize something as a public good simply because the government provides it.)

Governments traditionally have operated facilities for space flight, so why are private firms now involved in placing humans beyond the earth's atmosphere?

EXAMPLE

Private Companies Look to Place Humans in Orbit—and Beyond

Would you like to live in earth orbit, or would you prefer landing on the moon? If you wish to go no farther than 228 miles above the earth, Bigelow Aerospace has developed, constructed, and tested low-cost inflatable space stations in which humans can reside. The company has already established a rental rate of $28,750,000 per astronaut per month. If your objective is to go to the moon—say, to mine platinum—then you could contact another firm called Moon Express. That company has developed a new technology for landing people on the moon at a cost 90 percent below that at which the U.S. government could manage to do it.

In both cases, the only catch is that you would have to find another company that could send you into orbit about the earth or take you to the moon. In fact, several private firms are working on developing rocket propulsion systems for transporting humans to and beyond earth orbit.

FOR CRITICAL THINKING

Do the services of transporting people to or beyond the earth's orbit or providing them with places to reside in space possess the characteristics of public or private goods?

FREE RIDERS The nature of public goods leads to the **free-rider problem,** a situation in which some individuals take advantage of the fact that others will assume the burden of paying for public goods such as national defense. Suppose that citizens were taxed directly in proportion to how much they tell an interviewer that they value national defense. Some people who actually value national defense will probably tell interviewers that it has no value to them—they don't want any of it. Such people are trying to be free riders. We may all want to be free riders if we believe that someone else will provide the commodity in question that we actually value.

Free-rider problem
A problem that arises when individuals presume that others will pay for public goods so that, individually, they can escape paying for their portion without causing a reduction in production.

The free-rider problem often arises in connection with sharing the burden of international defense. A country may choose to belong to a multilateral defense organization, such as the North Atlantic Treaty Organization (NATO), but then consistently attempt to avoid contributing funds to the organization. The nation knows it would be defended by others in NATO if it were attacked but would rather not pay for such defense. In short, it seeks a free ride.

Ensuring Economywide Stability

Our economy sometimes faces the problems of undesired unemployment and rising prices. The government, especially the federal government, has made an attempt to solve these problems by trying to stabilize the economy by smoothing out the ups and downs in overall business activity. The notion that the federal government should undertake actions to stabilize business activity is a relatively new idea in the United States, encouraged by high unemployment rates during the Great Depression of the 1930s and subsequent theories about possible ways that government could reduce unemployment. In 1946, Congress passed the Full-Employment Act, a landmark law concerning government responsibility for economic performance. It established three goals for government stabilization policy: full employment, price stability, and economic growth. These goals have provided the justification for many government economic programs during the post–World War II period.

The Political Functions of Government

At least two functions of government are political or normative functions rather than economic ones like those discussed in the first part of this chapter. These two areas are (1) the provision and regulation of government-sponsored and government-inhibited goods and (2) income redistribution.

Government-Sponsored and Government-Inhibited Goods

Government-sponsored good
A good that has been deemed socially desirable through the political process. Museums are an example.

Through political processes, governments often determine that certain goods possess special merit and seek to promote their production and consumption. A **government-sponsored good** is defined as any good that the political process has deemed socially desirable. (Note that nothing inherent in any particular good makes that item a government-sponsored good. The designation is entirely subjective.) Examples of government-sponsored goods in our society are sports stadiums, museums, ballets, plays, and concerts. In these areas, the government's role is the provision of these goods to the people in society who would not otherwise purchase them at market clearing prices or who would not purchase an amount of them judged to be sufficient. This provision may take the form of government production and distribution of the goods. It can also take the form of reimbursement for spending on government-sponsored goods or subsidies to producers or consumers for part of the goods' costs.

Governments do indeed subsidize such goods as professional sports, concerts, ballets, museums, and plays. In most cases, those goods would not be so numerous without subsidization.

Government-inhibited good
A good that has been deemed socially undesirable through the political process. Heroin is an example.

Government-inhibited goods are the opposite of government-sponsored goods. They are goods that, through the political process, have been deemed socially undesirable. Heroin, cigarettes, gambling, and cocaine are examples. The government exercises its role with respect to these goods by taxing, regulating, or prohibiting their manufacture, sale, and use. Governments justify the relatively high taxes on alcohol and tobacco by declaring that they are socially undesirable. The best-known example of governmental exercise of power in this area is the stance against certain psychoactive drugs. Most psychoactives (except nicotine, caffeine, and alcohol) are either expressly prohibited, as is the case for heroin, cocaine, and opium, or heavily regulated, as in the case of prescription psychoactives.

Income Redistribution

Transfer payments
Money payments made by governments to individuals for which no services or goods are rendered in return. Examples are Social Security old-age and disability benefits and unemployment insurance benefits.

Transfers in kind
Payments that are in the form of actual goods and services, such as food stamps, subsidized public housing, and medical care, and for which no goods or services are rendered in return.

Another relatively recent political function of government has been the explicit redistribution of income. This redistribution uses two systems: the progressive income tax (described in Chapter 6) and transfer payments. **Transfer payments** are payments made to individuals for which no services or goods are rendered in return. The two primary money transfer payments in our system are Social Security old-age and disability benefits and unemployment insurance benefits. Income redistribution also includes a large amount of income **transfers in kind,** rather than money transfers. Some income transfers in kind are food stamps, Medicare and Medicaid, government health care services, and subsidized public housing.

The government has also engaged in other activities as a form of redistribution of income. For example, the provision of public education is at least in part an attempt to redistribute income by making sure that the poor have access to education.

QUICK QUIZ See page 121 for the answers. Review concepts from this section in MyEconLab.

The economic activities of government include (1) correcting for __________, (2) providing a __________ __________, (3) promoting __________, (4) producing __________ goods, and (5) ensuring __________ __________.

The principle of __________ __________ does not apply to public goods as it does to private goods.

Public goods have two characteristics: (1) Once they are produced, there is no additional __________ __________ when additional consumers use them, because your use of a public good does not deprive others of its simultaneous use; and (2) consumers cannot conveniently be __________ on the basis of use.

Political, or normative, activities of the government include the provision and regulation of __________-__________ and __________-__________ goods and __________ redistribution.

Public Spending and Transfer Programs

The size of the public sector can be measured in many different ways. One way is to count the number of public employees. Another is to look at total government outlays. Government outlays include all government expenditures on employees, rent, electricity, and the like. In addition, total government outlays include transfer payments, such as welfare and Social Security. In Figure 5-2 below, you see that government outlays prior to World War I did not exceed 10 percent of annual national income. There was a spike during World War I, a general increase during the Great Depression, and then a huge spike during World War II. After World War II, government outlays as a percentage of total national income rose steadily before dropping in the 1990s, rising again in the early 2000s, and then jumping sharply beginning in 2008.

How do federal and state governments allocate their spending? A typical federal government budget is shown in panel (a) of Figure 5-3 on the following page. The three largest categories are Medicare and other health-related spending, Social Security and other income-security programs, and national defense, which together constitute 79.7 percent of the total federal budget.

The makeup of state and local expenditures is quite different. As panel (b) shows, education is the biggest category, accounting for 34.3 percent of all expenditures.

FIGURE 5-2

Total Government Outlays over Time

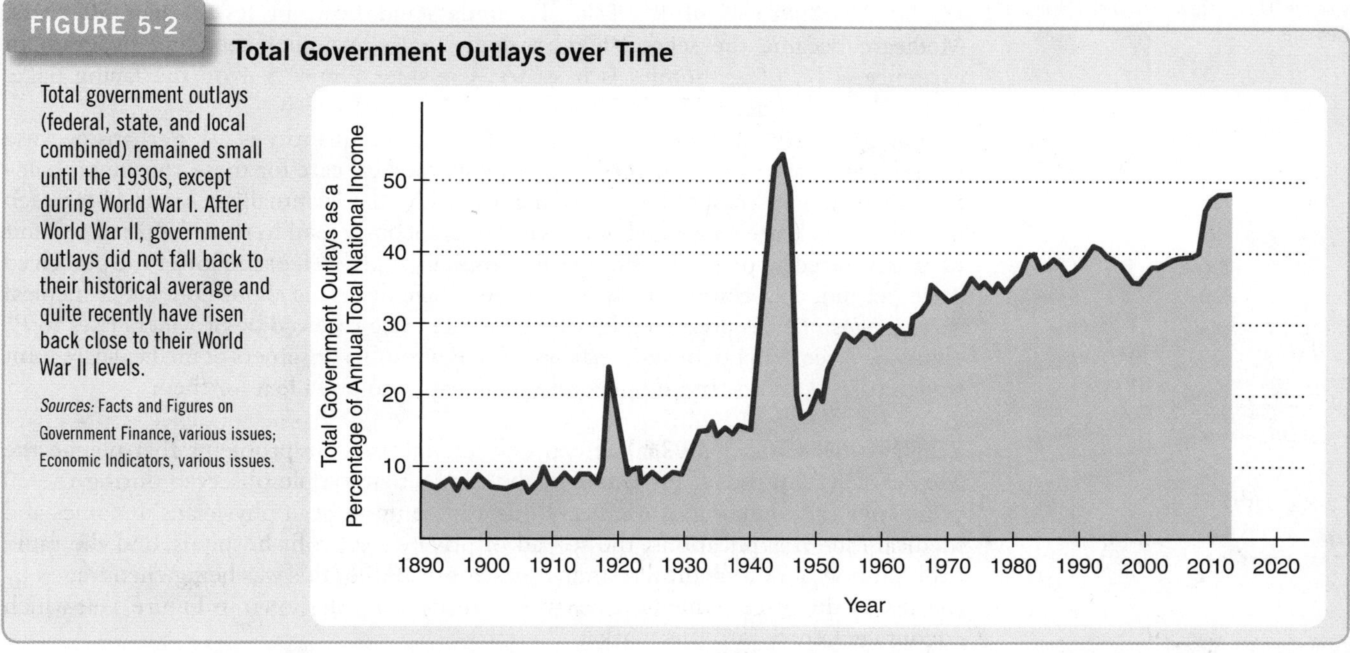

Total government outlays (federal, state, and local combined) remained small until the 1930s, except during World War I. After World War II, government outlays did not fall back to their historical average and quite recently have risen back close to their World War II levels.

Sources: Facts and Figures on Government Finance, various issues; Economic Indicators, various issues.

FIGURE 5-3

Federal Government Spending Compared to State and Local Spending

The federal government's spending habits are quite different from those of the states and cities. In panel (a), you can see that the most important categories in the federal budget are Medicare and other health-related spending, Social Security and other income-security programs, and national defense, which make up 79.7 percent. In panel (b), the most important category at the state and local level is education, which makes up 34.3 percent. "Other" includes expenditures in such areas as waste treatment, garbage collection, mosquito abatement, and the judicial system.

Sources: Economic Report of the President, Economic Indicators.

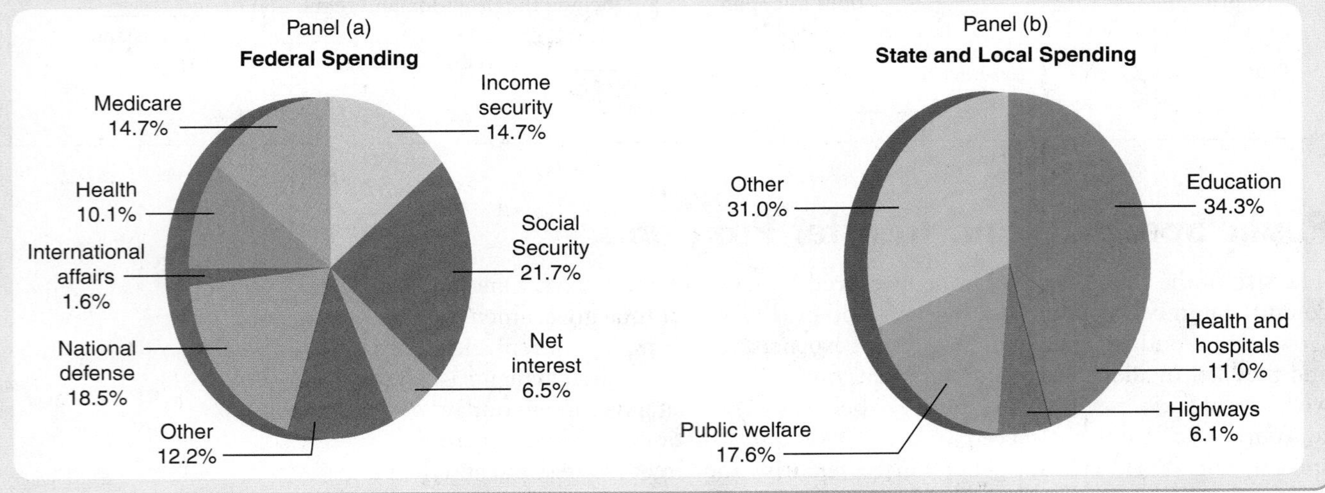

Publicly Subsidized Health Care: Medicare

Figure 5-3 above shows that health-related spending is a significant portion of total government expenditures. Certainly, medical expenses are a major concern for many elderly people. Since 1965, that concern has been reflected in the existence of the Medicare program, which pays hospital and physicians' bills for U.S. residents over the age of 65 (and for those younger than 65 in some instances). In return for paying a tax on their earnings while in the workforce (2.9 percent of wages and salaries, plus 3.8 percent on certain income for high-income households), retirees are assured that the majority of their hospital and physicians' bills will be paid for with public monies.

Go to **www.econtoday.com/chap05** to visit the U.S. government's official Medicare Web site.

THE SIMPLE ECONOMICS OF MEDICARE To understand how, in fewer than 50 years, Medicare became the second-biggest domestic government spending program in existence, a bit of economics is in order. Consider Figure 5-4 on the facing page, which shows the demand for and supply of medical care.

The initial equilibrium price is P_0 and equilibrium quantity is Q_0. Perhaps because the government believes that Q_0 is not enough medical care for these consumers, suppose that the government begins paying a subsidy that eventually is set at M for each unit of medical care consumed. This will simultaneously tend to raise the price per unit of care received by providers (physicians, hospitals, and the like) and lower the perceived price per unit that consumers see when they make decisions about how much medical care to consume. As presented in the figure, the price received by providers rises to P_s, while the price paid by consumers falls to P_d. As a result, consumers of medical care want to purchase Q_m units, and suppliers are quite happy to provide it for them.

MEDICARE INCENTIVES AT WORK We can now understand the problems that plague the Medicare system today. First, one of the things that people observed during the 20 years after the founding of Medicare was a huge upsurge in physicians' incomes and medical school applications, the spread of private for-profit hospitals, and the rapid proliferation of new medical tests and procedures. All of this was being encouraged by the rise in the price of medical services from P_0 to P_s, as shown in Figure 5-4, which encouraged entry into this market.

FIGURE 5-4

The Economic Effects of Medicare Subsidies

When the government pays a per-unit subsidy M for medical care, consumers pay the price of services P_d for the quantity of services Q_m. Providers receive the price P_s for supplying this quantity. Originally, the federal government projected that its total spending on Medicare would equal an amount such as the area $Q_0 \times (P_0 - P_d)$. Because actual consumption equals Q_m, however, the government's total expenditures equal $Q_m \times M$.

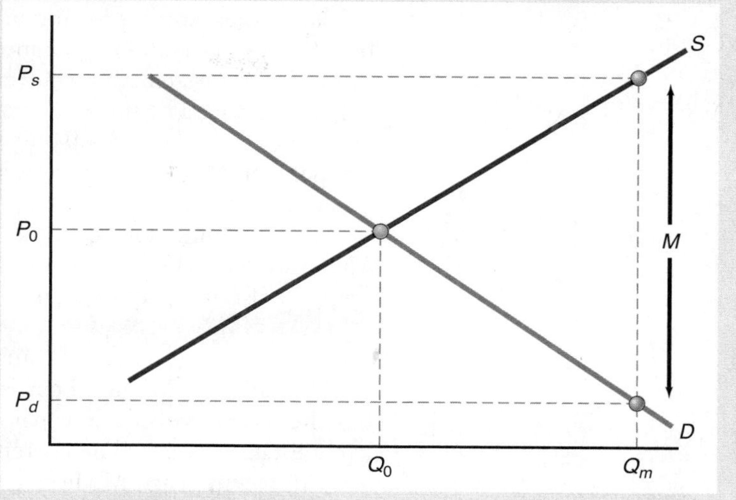

Second, government expenditures on Medicare have routinely turned out to be far in excess of the expenditures forecast at the time the program was put in place or was expanded. The reasons for this are easy to see. Bureaucratic planners often fail to recognize the incentive effects of government programs. On the demand side, they fail to account for the huge increase in consumption (from Q_0 to Q_m) that will result from a subsidy like Medicare. On the supply side, they fail to recognize that the larger number of services can only be extracted from suppliers at a higher price, P_s. Consequently, original projected spending on Medicare was an area like $Q_0 \times (P_0 - P_d)$, because original plans for the program only contemplated consumption of Q_0 and assumed that the subsidy would have to be only $P_0 - P_d$ per unit. In fact, consumption rises to Q_m, and the additional cost per unit of service rises to P_s, implying an increase in the per-unit subsidy to M. Hence, actual expenditures turn out to be the far larger number $Q_m \times M$. Every expansion of the program, including the 2004 broadening of Medicare to cover obesity as a new illness eligible for coverage and the extension of Medicare to cover patients' prescription drug expenses beginning in 2006, has followed the same pattern.

Third, total spending on medical services has soared, consuming far more income than initially expected. Originally, total spending on medical services was $P_0 \times Q_0$. In the presence of Medicare, spending rises to $P_s \times Q_m$.

In the past, why have government officials considerably underestimated taxpayers' actual expenses for health care programs such as Medicare?

POLICY EXAMPLE

The Great Underestimates of Government Health Care Expenses

When the federal government launched Medicare in 1965, officials estimated that its one-year inflation-adjusted cost in 1990 would turn out to be $12 billion, but the actual program cost in 1990 was $110 billion. When it initiated the Medicaid health-care-subsidy program for lower-income individuals in 1966, the government projected that its annual inflation-adjusted cost for 1990 would be about $7 billion, but that program's true expense in 1990 exceeded $45 billion. One reason for these underestimates was that as time passed, Congress expanded the number of people eligible for both programs. Another reason was that Congress assumed that creating the programs would not increase the quantity of health care demanded.

Of course, when the government offered per-unit subsidies that significantly pushed down the out-of-pocket price, people *did* raise their consumption. These increases in quantities of health care services consumed under Medicare and Medicaid dramatically raised the programs' actual expenses.

FOR CRITICAL THINKING

Why do you suppose that even though Medicare was supposed to be self-sustaining indefinitely, Medicare taxes will fail to cover program costs by 2024?

HEALTH CARE SUBSIDIES CONTINUE TO GROW Just how fast are Medicare subsidies growing? Medicare's cost has risen from 0.7 percent of U.S. national income in 1970 to more than 3.5 percent today, which amounts to nearly $550 billion per year. Because Medicare spending is growing much faster than total employer and employee contributions, future spending guarantees far outstrip the taxes to be collected in the future to pay for the system. (The current Medicare tax rate is 2.9 percent on all wages, with 1.45 percent paid by the employee and 1.45 percent paid by the employer. For certain income earned above $200,000 for individuals and $250,000 for married couples, a 3.8 percent Medicare tax rate applies.) Today, unfunded guarantees of Medicare spending in the future are estimated at more than $25 trillion (in today's dollars).

These amounts fail to reflect the costs of another federal health program called Medicaid. The Medicaid program is structured similarly to Medicare, in that the government also pays per-unit subsidies for health care to qualifying patients. Medicaid, however, provides subsidies only to people who qualify because they have lower incomes. At present, about 50 million people, or about one out of every six U.S. residents, qualify for Medicaid coverage. Medicaid is administered by state governments, but the federal government pays about 60 percent of the program's total cost from general tax revenues. The current cost of the program is more than $400 billion per year. In recent years, Medicaid spending has grown even faster than expenditures on Medicare, rising by more than 75 percent since 2000 alone.

Of course, in legislation enacted in 2010, the U.S. Congress further expanded by more than $100 billion per year the rate of growth of government health care spending, which already has been growing at an average pace of 8 percent per year.

WHAT IF... the federal government continues reducing the out-of-pocket prices that consumers must pay for health care services?

Persistent reductions in out-of-pocket prices of health care services would lead to higher quantities of services demanded by consumers. Providers of health care would be willing to supply these higher quantities only if they receive higher prices. Thus, to continue pushing downward the out-of-pocket price of health care services toward an explicit price of zero, the federal government would have to keep raising the per-unit subsidies that it pays health care providers. Multiplying the increased quantities of health care services consumed and provided times the higher per-unit subsidies would yield larger total subsidies that taxpayers would have to fund. Overall, the total expenses that society would incur for health care services would continue to climb.

Economic Issues of Public Education

In the United States, government involvement in health care is a relatively recent phenomenon. In contrast, state and local governments have assumed primary responsibility for public education for many years. Currently, these governments spend more than $900 billion on education—in excess of 6 percent of total U.S. national income. State and local sales, excise, property, and income taxes finance the bulk of these expenditures. In addition, each year the federal government provides tens of billions of dollars of support for public education through grants and other transfers to state and local governments.

THE NOW-FAMILIAR ECONOMICS OF PUBLIC EDUCATION State and local governments around the United States have developed a variety of complex mechanisms for funding public education. What all public education programs have in common, however, is the provision of educational services to primary, secondary, and college students at prices well below those that would otherwise prevail in the marketplace for these services.

So how do state and local governments accomplish this? The answer is that they operate public education programs that share some of the features of government-subsidized health care programs such as Medicare. Analogously to Figure 5-4 on page 111, public schools provide educational services at a price below the market price. They are willing to produce the quantity of educational services demanded at this below-market price as long as they receive a sufficiently high per-unit subsidy from state and local governments.

THE INCENTIVE PROBLEMS OF PUBLIC EDUCATION Since the 1960s, various measures of the performance of U.S. primary and secondary students have failed to increase even as public spending on education has risen. Some measures of student performance have even declined.

Many economists argue that the incentive effects that have naturally arisen with higher government subsidies for public education help to explain this lack of improvement in student performance. A higher per-pupil subsidy creates a difference between the relatively high per-unit costs of providing the number of educational services that parents and students are willing to purchase and lower valuations of those services. As a consequence, some schools have provided services, such as after-school babysitting and various social services, that have contributed relatively little to student learning.

A factor that complicates efforts to assess the effects of education subsidies is that the public schools often face little or no competition from unsubsidized providers of educational services. In addition, public schools rarely compete against each other. In most locales, therefore, parents who are unhappy with the quality of services provided at the subsidized price cannot transfer their child to a different public school.

Are higher school subsidies associated with improved learning outcomes?

YOU ARE THERE

To consider another setting in which government per-unit subsidies are important, read **The U.S. Government Ensures That an Airport Is "Convenient"** on page 116.

POLICY EXAMPLE

A Weak Relationship between Spending and Schooling Results

In a recent year, the five U.S. states with highest annual per-pupil spending were Alaska, New Jersey, New York, Vermont, and Washington, in which an average level of per-student expenditures was $16,106. This amount was more than twice as much as the average per-student expenditures of $7,409 in Arizona, Idaho, Oklahoma, Tennessee, and Utah, the five lowest-spending states. The differences in measurable outcomes were only minor, however.

For instance, in the five states with highest spending, an average of 25.2 percent of students failed to meet basic goals for math and reading. In the five states with lowest spending, this figure was only slightly higher at 30.6 percent. New York, the state with highest per-student expenditures, spent nearly three times as much per pupil as lowest-spending Utah, yet both states had just over 26 percent of students who failed to satisfy basic math and reading objectives. By virtually every measure of schooling outcomes, studies consistently find at best a weak relationship—and often find no relationship—between per-pupil expenditures and educational results.

FOR CRITICAL THINKING

Could the fact that the valuation of the last unit of services falls as the per-student subsidy rises help to explain why higher spending is not closely related to learning outcomes?

QUICK QUIZ

See page 121 for the answers. Review concepts from this section in MyEconLab.

Medicare subsidizes the consumption of medical care by the elderly, thus increasing the amount of such care consumed. People tend to purchase large amounts of __________-value, __________-cost services in publicly funded health care programs such as Medicare, because they do not directly bear the full cost of their decisions.

Basic economic analysis indicates that higher subsidies for public education have widened the differential between parents' and students' relatively __________ per-unit valuations of the educational services of public schools and the __________ costs that schools incur in providing those services.

Collective Decision Making: The Theory of Public Choice

Governments consist of individuals. No government actually thinks and acts. Instead, government actions are the result of decision making by individuals in their roles as elected representatives, appointed officials, and salaried bureaucrats. Therefore, to understand how government works, we must examine the incentives of the people in government as well as those who would like to be in government—avowed or would-be candidates for elective or appointed positions—and special-interest lobbyists attempting to get government to do something. At issue is the analysis of **collective decision making.**

Collective decision making
How voters, politicians, and other interested parties act and how these actions influence nonmarket decisions.

Theory of public choice
The study of collective decision making.

Collective decision making involves the actions of voters, politicians, political parties, interest groups, and many other groups and individuals. The analysis of collective decision making is usually called the **theory of public choice.** It has been given this name because it involves hypotheses about how choices are made in the public sector, as opposed to the private sector. The foundation of public-choice theory is the assumption that individuals will act within the political process to maximize their *individual* (not collective) well-being. In that sense, the theory is similar to our analysis of the market economy, in which we also assume that individuals act as though they are motivated by self-interest.

To understand public-choice theory, it is necessary to point out other similarities between the private market sector and the public, or government, sector. Then we will look at the differences.

Similarities in Market and Public-Sector Decision Making

In addition to the assumption of self-interest being the motivating force in both sectors, there are other similarities.

OPPORTUNITY COST Everything that is spent by all levels of government plus everything that is spent by the private sector must add up to the total income available at any point in time. Hence, every government action has an opportunity cost, just as in the market sector.

COMPETITION Although we typically think of competition as a private market phenomenon, it is also present in collective action. Given the scarcity constraint government faces, bureaucrats, appointed officials, and elected representatives will always be in competition for available government funds. Furthermore, the individuals within any government agency or institution will act as individuals do in the private sector: They will try to obtain higher wages, better working conditions, and higher job-level classifications. We assume that they will compete and act in their own interest, not society's.

SIMILARITY OF INDIVIDUALS Contrary to popular belief, the types of individuals working in the private sector and working in the public sector are not inherently different. The difference, as we shall see, is that the individuals in government face a different **incentive structure** than those in the private sector. For example, the costs and benefits of being efficient or inefficient differ in the private and public sectors.

Incentive structure
The system of rewards and punishments individuals face with respect to their own actions.

One approach to predicting government bureaucratic behavior is to ask what incentives bureaucrats face. Take the U.S. Postal Service (USPS) as an example. The bureaucrats running that government corporation are human beings with IQs not dissimilar to those possessed by workers in similar positions at Google or Apple. Yet the USPS does not function like either of these companies. The difference can be explained in terms of the incentives provided for managers in the two types of institutions. When the bureaucratic managers and workers at Google make incorrect decisions, work slowly, produce shoddy programs, and are generally "inefficient," the profitability of the company declines. The owners—millions of shareholders—express their displeasure by selling some of their shares of company stock. The market value, as tracked on the stock exchange, falls. This induces owners of shares of stock to pressure managers to pursue strategies more likely to boost revenues and reduce costs.

But what about the USPS? If a manager, a worker, or a bureaucrat in the USPS gives shoddy service, the organization's owners—the taxpayers—have no straightforward mechanism for expressing their dissatisfaction. Despite the postal service's status as a "government corporation," taxpayers as shareholders do not really own shares of stock in the organization that they can sell.

Thus, to understand purported inefficiency in the government bureaucracy, we need to examine incentives and institutional arrangements—not people and personalities.

Differences between Market and Collective Decision Making

There are probably more dissimilarities between the market sector and the public sector than there are similarities.

GOVERNMENT GOODS AND SERVICES AT ZERO PRICE The majority of goods that governments produce are furnished to the ultimate consumers without payment required. **Government,** or **political, goods** can be either private or public goods. The fact that they are furnished to the ultimate consumer free of charge does *not* mean that the cost to society of those goods is zero, however. It only means that the price *charged* is zero. The full opportunity cost to society is the value of the resources used in the production of goods produced and provided by the government.

Government, or **political, goods**
Goods (and services) provided by the public sector; they can be either private or public goods.

For example, none of us pays directly for each unit of consumption of defense or police protection. Rather, we pay for all these items indirectly through the taxes that support our governments—federal, state, and local. This special feature of government can be looked at in a different way. There is no longer a one-to-one relationship between consumption of government-provided goods and services and payment for these items. Indeed, most taxpayers will find that their tax bill is the same whether or not they consume government-provided goods.

USE OF FORCE All governments can resort to using force in their regulation of economic affairs. For example, governments can use *expropriation,* which means that if you refuse to pay your taxes, your bank account and other assets may be seized by the Internal Revenue Service. In fact, you have no choice in the matter of paying taxes to governments. Collectively, we decide the total size of government through the political process, but individually, we cannot determine how much service we pay for during any one year.

VOTING VERSUS SPENDING In the private market sector, a dollar voting system is in effect. This dollar voting system is not equivalent to the voting system in the public sector. There are at least three differences:

1. In a political system, one person gets one vote, whereas in the market system, each dollar a person spends counts separately.
2. The political system is run by **majority rule,** whereas the market system is run by **proportional rule.**
3. The spending of dollars can indicate intensity of want, whereas because of the all-or-nothing nature of political voting, a vote cannot.

Majority rule
A collective decision-making system in which group decisions are made on the basis of more than 50 percent of the vote. In other words, whatever more than half of the electorate votes for, the entire electorate has to accept.

Proportional rule
A decision-making system in which actions are based on the proportion of the "votes" cast and are in proportion to them. In a market system, if 10 percent of the "dollar votes" are cast for blue cars, 10 percent of automobile output will be blue cars.

Political outcomes often differ from economic outcomes. Remember that economic efficiency is a situation in which, given the prevailing distribution of income, consumers obtain the economic goods they want. There is no corresponding situation when political voting determines economic outcomes. Thus, a political voting process is unlikely to lead to the same decisions that a dollar voting process would yield in the marketplace.

Indeed, consider the dilemma every voter faces. Usually, a voter is not asked to decide on a single issue (although this happens). Rather, a voter is asked to choose among candidates who present a large number of issues and state a position on each of them. Just consider the average U.S. senator, who has to vote on several thousand different issues during a six-year term. When you vote for that senator, you are voting for a person who must make thousands of decisions during the next six years.

QUICK QUIZ See page 121 for the answers. Review concepts from this section in MyEconLab.

The theory of __________ __________ examines how voters, politicians, and other parties collectively reach decisions in the public sector of the economy.

As in private markets, __________ __________ and __________ have incentive effects that influence public-sector decision making. In contrast to private market situations, however, there is not a one-to-one relationship between consumption of a publicly provided good and the payment for that good.

YOU ARE THERE

The U.S. Government Ensures That an Airport Is "Convenient"

Phil Ridenour, director of Hagerstown Regional Airport, in Hagerstown, Maryland, surveys the surroundings: free parking, short security lines for departing passengers, and plenty of space for passengers at the baggage carousel. "The convenience of it all is just phenomenal compared to going to any major airport," Ridenour remarks. Indeed, a flight to Baltimore takes only 40 minutes in the air, compared with an 80-minute automobile drive via highways, and each passenger's out-of-pocket ticket price is less than $60.

Nonetheless, all of this convenience comes at considerable expense to U.S. taxpayers. Each time a passenger boards a nine-seat plane providing the airline service connecting Hagerstown to Baltimore, the cost to taxpayers is $191. This is the additional per-passenger payment required to induce Cape Air to provide its daily flights to and from Baltimore. Summing all of the subsidies that the federal government provides to keep the Hagerstown Regional Airport operating at its current pace requires an amount exceeding $1.2 million per year.

Critical Thinking Questions

1. What is the total subsidy paid by U.S. taxpayers each time a full Cape Air flight departs from Hagerstown for Baltimore?
2. Why do you suppose that 109 regional airports receiving federal support require about $175 million per year in total subsidies to provide current service flows?

ISSUES & APPLICATIONS

The Government-Sponsored U.S. Postal Service

CONCEPTS APPLIED

- Government-Sponsored Goods
- Monopoly
- Subsidies

Since 1971, the legal classification of the U.S. Postal Service (USPS) has been as a private enterprise. That is, the USPS officially is a nongovernmental business. *Economic* functions of the USPS remain government-sponsored, however.

Implicit Government Sponsorship via Regulatory Controls

The USPS operates a network of more than 31,000 post offices. The majority of these post offices do not generate revenues sufficiently high in relation to costs to justify keeping them in operation. If the USPS were truly a private firm, many of these post offices would be closed.

Until recently, what has enabled the USPS to keep these post offices operating in spite of their meager rates of profitability has been the receipt of an implicit subsidy in the form of protection from competition. The USPS is the only institution in the United States authorized to make regular deliveries of "non-urgent letters" to mailboxes of households, businesses, and government offices. Thus, the USPS faces no threat of being undersold by competitors in its primary business of delivering non-urgent mail.

Government Sponsorship Becomes Much More Explicit

In spite of these government protections of the USPS, the annual volume of mail handled by the USPS has fallen from 213 billion items per year in 2006 to about 165 billion items per year today. As a consequence, postage revenues at USPS have plummeted even as its labor expenses have remained nearly unchanged. Since 2007, the USPS has experienced average annual *losses* from its operations exceeding *$7 billion* per year.

What allows the USPS to continue operating without employee layoffs in spite of annual losses exceeding $120,000 per USPS worker per year? The answer is the sponsorship of U.S. taxpayers. The federal government continues lending funds to the USPS to enable it to keep providing the same level of services with an unchanged workforce. Few observers anticipate that the USPS will ever repay the loans, which likely will become explicit subsidies to this government-sponsored institution.

For Critical Thinking

1. Why would a non-government-sponsored firm have difficulty remaining in operation incurring $7 billion in losses per year?
2. Why might a government-sponsored firm such as the USPS be more willing than a non-government-sponsored firm to agree to non-layoff contracts for workers?

Web Resources

1. For a discussion of the deteriorating situation at the USPS, go to **www.econtoday.com/chap05**.
2. Take a look at a list of contemplated USPS post office closings—but no planned employee layoffs at **www.econtoday.com/chap05**.

MyEconLab

For more questions on this chapter's Issues & Applications, go to **MyEconLab**. In the Study Plan for this chapter, select Section N: News.

MyEconLab

Here is what you should know after reading this chapter. MyEconLab will help you identify what you know, and where to go when you need to practice.

WHAT YOU SHOULD KNOW		WHERE TO GO TO PRACTICE
How Market Failures Such as Externalities Might Justify Economic Functions of Government A market failure occurs when too many or too few resources are directed to a specific form of economic activity. One type of market failure is an externality, which is a spillover effect on third parties not directly involved in producing or purchasing a good or service. In the case of a negative externality, firms do not pay for the costs arising from spillover effects that their production of a good imposes on others, so they produce too much of the good in question. In the case of a positive externality, buyers fail to take into account the benefits that their consumption of a good yields to others, so they purchase too little of the good.	market failure, 101 externality, 101 third parties, 101 property rights, 102 effluent fee, 103 antitrust legislation, 106 monopoly, 106 **Key Figure** Figure 5-1, 102	• MyEconLab Study Plans 5.1, 5.2 • Animated Figure 5-1

MyEconLab *continued*

WHAT YOU SHOULD KNOW		WHERE TO GO TO PRACTICE
Private Goods versus Public Goods and the Free-Rider Problem Private goods are subject to the principle of rival consumption, meaning that one person's consumption of such a good reduces the amount available for another person to consume. In contrast, public goods can be consumed by many people simultaneously at no additional opportunity cost and with no reduction in quality or quantity. In addition, no individual can be excluded from the benefits of a public good even if that person fails to help pay for it.	private goods, 106 principle of rival consumption, 106 public goods, 106 free-rider problem, 107	• MyEconLab Study Plan 5.3
Political Functions of Government That Lead to Its Involvement in the Economy As a result of the political process, government may seek to promote the production and consumption of government-sponsored goods. The government may also seek to restrict the production and sale of goods that have been deemed socially undesirable, called government-inhibited goods. In addition, the political process may determine that income redistribution is socially desirable.	government-sponsored good, 108 government-inhibited good, 108 transfer payments, 108 transfers in kind, 108	• MyEconLab Study Plan 5.4
The Effect of Medicare on the Incentives to Consume Medical Services Medicare subsidizes the consumption of medical services. As a result, the quantity consumed is higher, as is the price sellers receive per unit of those services. Medicare also encourages people to consume medical services that are very low in per-unit value relative to the cost of providing them.	**Key Figures** Figure 5-2, 109 Figure 5-4, 111	• MyEconLab Study Plan 5.5 • Animated Figures 5-2, 5-4
Why Bigger Subsidies for Public Schools Do Not Necessarily Translate into Improved Student Performance When governments subsidize public schools, the last unit of educational services provided by public schools costs more than its valuation by parents and students. Thus, public schools provide services in excess of those best suited to promoting student learning.		• MyEconLab Study Plan 5.5
Central Elements of the Theory of Public Choice The theory of public choice applies to collective decision making, or the process through which voters and politicians interact to influence nonmarket choices. Certain aspects of public-sector decision making, such as scarcity and competition, are similar to those that affect private-sector choices. Others, however, such as legal coercion and majority-rule decision making, differ from those involved in the market system.	collective decision making, 114 theory of public choice, 114 incentive structure, 114 government, or political, goods, 115 majority rule, 115 proportional rule, 115	• MyEconLab Study Plan 5.6

Log in to MyEconLab, take a chapter test, and get a personalized Study Plan that tells you which concepts you understand and which ones you need to review. From there, MyEconLab will give you further practice, tutorials, animations, videos, and guided solutions. For more information, visit www.myeconlab.com

PROBLEMS

All problems are assignable in MyEconLab. *Answers to odd-numbered problems appear at the back of the book.*

5-1. Many people who do not smoke cigars are bothered by the odor of cigar smoke. If private contracting is impossible, will too many or too few cigars be produced and consumed? Taking *all* costs into account, is the market price of cigars too high or too low? (See page 102.)

5-2. Suppose that repeated application of a pesticide used on orange trees causes harmful contamination of groundwater. The pesticide is applied annually in almost all of the orange groves throughout the world. Most orange growers regard the pesticide as a key input in their production of oranges. (See page 102.)

a. Use a diagram of the market for the pesticide to illustrate the implications of a failure of orange producers' costs to reflect the social costs of groundwater contamination.

b. Use your diagram from part (a) to explain a government policy that might be effective in achieving the amount of orange production that fully reflects all social costs.

5-3. Now draw a diagram of the market for oranges. Explain how the government policy you discussed in part (b) of Problem 5-2 is likely to affect the market price and equilibrium quantity in the orange market. In what sense do consumers of oranges now "pay" for dealing with the spillover costs of pesticide production? (See page 102.)

5-4. Suppose that the U.S. government determines that cigarette smoking creates social costs not reflected in the current market price and equilibrium quantity of cigarettes. A study has recommended that the government can correct for the externality effect of cigarette consumption by paying farmers *not* to plant tobacco used to manufacture cigarettes. It also recommends raising the funds to make these payments by increasing taxes on cigarettes. Assuming that the government is correct that cigarette smoking creates external costs, evaluate whether the study's recommended policies might help correct this negative externality. (See page 102.)

5-5. A nation's government has determined that mass transit, such as bus lines, helps alleviate traffic congestion, thereby benefiting both individual auto commuters and companies that desire to move products and factors of production speedily along streets and highways. Nevertheless, even though several private bus lines are in service, the country's commuters are failing to take into account the social benefits of the use of mass transit. (See pages 102–103.)

a. Discuss, in the context of demand-supply analysis, the essential implications of commuters' failure to take into account the social benefits associated with bus ridership.

b. Explain a government policy that might be effective in achieving the socially efficient use of bus services.

5-6. Draw a diagram of this nation's market for automobiles, which are a substitute for buses. Explain how the government policy you discussed in part (b) of Problem 5-5 is likely to affect the market price and equilibrium quantity in the country's auto market. How are auto consumers affected by this policy to attain the spillover benefits of bus transit? (See pages 102–103.)

5-7. Consider a nation with a government that does not provide people with property rights for a number of items and that fails to enforce the property rights it does assign for remaining items. Would externalities be more or less common in this nation than in a country such as the United States? Explain. (See page 105.)

5-8. Many economists suggest that our nation's legal system is an example of a public good. Does the legal system satisfy the key properties of a public good? Explain your reasoning. (See page 106.)

5-9. Displayed in the diagram below are conditions in the market for residential Internet access in a U.S. state. The government of this state has determined that access to the Internet improves the learning skills of children, which it has concluded is an external benefit of Internet access. The government has also concluded that if these external benefits were to be taken into account, 3 million residences would have Internet access. Suppose that the state government's judgments about the

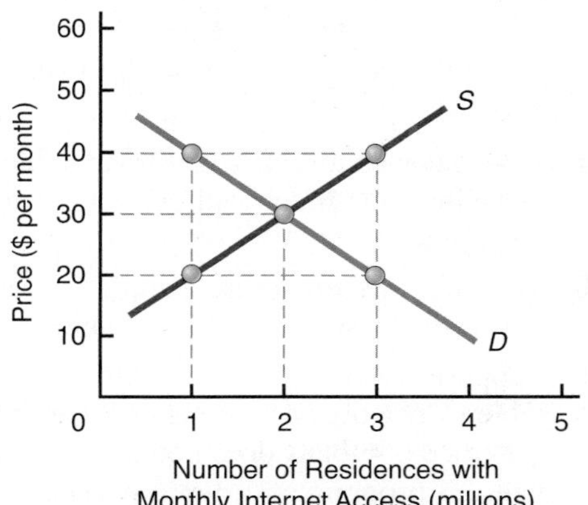

benefits of Internet access are correct and that it wishes to offer a per-unit subsidy just sufficient to increase total Internet access to 3 million residences. What per-unit subsidy should it offer? Use the diagram to explain how providing this subsidy would affect conditions in the state's market for residential Internet access. (See pages 102–103.)

5-10. The French government recently allocated the equivalent of more than $120 million in public funds to *Quaero* (Latin for "I search"), an Internet search engine analogous to Google or Yahoo. Does an Internet search engine satisfy the key characteristics of a public good? Why or why not? Based on your answer, is a publicly funded Internet search engine a public good or a government-sponsored good? (See page 106.)

5-11. A government offers to let a number of students at a public school transfer to a private school under two conditions: It will transmit to the private school the same per-pupil subsidy it provides the public school, and the private school will be required to admit the students at a below-market net tuition rate. Will the economic outcome be the same as the one that would have arisen if the government instead simply provided students with grants to cover the current market tuition rate at the private school? (Hint: Does it matter if schools receive payments directly from the government or from consumers? See pages 111–113.)

5-12. After a government implements a voucher program, granting funds that families can spend at schools of their choice, numerous students in public schools switch to private schools. Parents' and students' valuations of the services provided at both private and public schools adjust to equality with the true market price of educational services. Is anyone likely to lose out nonetheless? If so, who? (See page 113.)

5-13. Suppose that the current price of a tablet device is $300 and that people are buying 1 million drives per year. The government decides to begin subsidizing the purchase of new tablet devices. The government believes that the appropriate price is $260 per tablet, so the program offers to send people cash for the difference between $260 and whatever the people pay for each tablet they buy. (See page 111.)

a. If no consumers change their tablet-buying behavior, how much will this program cost the taxpayers?

b. Will the subsidy cause people to buy more, fewer, or the same number of tablets? Explain.

c. Suppose that people end up buying 1.5 million tablets once the program is in place. If the market price of tablets does not change, how much will this program cost the taxpayers?

d. Under the assumption that the program causes people to buy 1.5 million tablets and also causes the market price of tablets to rise to $320, how much will this program cost the taxpayers?

5-14. Scans of internal organs using magnetic resonance imaging (MRI) devices are often covered by subsidized health insurance programs such as Medicare. Consider the following table illustrating hypothetical quantities of individual MRI testing procedures demanded and supplied at various prices, and then answer the questions that follow. (See page 111.)

Price	Quantity Demanded	Quantity Supplied
$100	100,000	40,000
$300	90,000	60,000
$500	80,000	80,000
$700	70,000	100,000
$900	60,000	120,000

a. In the absence of a government-subsidized health plan, what is the equilibrium price of MRI tests? What is the amount of society's total spending on MRI tests?

b. Suppose that the government establishes a health plan guaranteeing that all qualified participants can purchase MRI tests at an effective price (that is, out-of-pocket cost) to the individual of $100 per test. How many MRI tests will people consume?

c. What is the per-unit price that induces producers to provide the number of MRI tests demanded at the government-guaranteed price of $100? What is society's total spending on MRI tests?

d. Under the government's coverage of MRI tests, what is the per-unit subsidy it provides? What is the total subsidy that the government pays to support MRI testing at its guaranteed price?

5-15. Suppose that, as part of an expansion of its State Care health system, a state government decides to offer a $50 subsidy to all people who, according to their physicians, should have their own blood pressure monitoring devices. Prior to this governmental decision, the market clearing price of blood pressure monitors in this state was $50, and the equilibrium quantity purchased was 20,000 per year. (See page 111.)

a. After the government expands its State Care plan, people in this state desire to purchase 40,000 devices each year. Manufacturers of blood pressure monitors are willing to provide 40,000 devices at a price of $60 per device. What out-of-pocket price does each consumer pay for a blood pressure monitor?

b. What is the dollar amount of the increase in total expenditures on blood pressure monitors in this state following the expansion in the State Care program?

c. Following the expansion of the State Care program, what *percentage* of total expenditures on blood pressure monitors is paid by the government? What percentage of total expenditures is paid by consumers of these devices?

5-16. A government agency is contemplating launching an effort to expand the scope of its activities. One rationale for doing so is that another government agency might make the same effort and, if successful, receive larger budget allocations in future years. Another rationale for expanding the agency's activities is that this will make the jobs of its workers more interesting, which may help the government agency attract better-qualified employees. Nevertheless, to broaden its legal mandate, the agency will have to convince more than half of the House of Representatives and the Senate to approve a formal proposal to expand its activities. In addition, to expand its activities, the agency must have the authority to force private companies it does not currently regulate to be officially licensed by agency personnel. Identify which aspects of this problem are similar to those faced by firms that operate in private markets and which aspects are specific to the public sector. (See pages 114–115.)

ECONOMICS ON THE NET

Putting Tax Dollars to Work In this application, you will learn about how the U.S. government allocates its expenditures. This will enable you to conduct an evaluation of the current functions of the federal government.

Title: Historical Tables: Budget of the United States Government

Navigation: Go to www.econtoday.com/chap05 to visit the home page of the U.S. Government Printing Office. Click on "Browse the FY Budget" for the applicable year, and then click on "PDF" next to *Historical Tables*.

Application After the document downloads, examine Section 3, Federal Government Outlays by Function, and in particular Table 3.1, Outlays by Superfunction and Function. Then answer the following questions.

1. What government functions have been capturing growing shares of government spending in recent years? Which of these do you believe are related to the problem of addressing externalities, providing public goods, or dealing with other market failures? Which appear to be related to political functions instead of economic functions?
2. Which government functions are receiving declining shares of total spending? Are any of these related to the problem of addressing externalities, providing public goods, or dealing with other market failures? Are any related to political functions instead of economic functions?

For Group Study and Analysis Assign groups to the following overall categories of government functions: national defense, health, income security, and Social Security. Have each group prepare a brief report concerning long-term and recent trends in government spending on its category. Each group should take a stand on whether specific spending on items in its category is likely to relate to resolving market failures, public funding of government-sponsored goods, regulating the sale of government-inhibited goods, and so on.

ANSWERS TO QUICK QUIZZES

p. 105: (i) costs . . . taxation . . . regulation; (ii) benefits . . . financing . . . subsidizing . . . regulation

p. 109: (i) externalities . . . legal system . . . competition . . . public . . . economywide stability; (ii) rival consumption; (iii) opportunity cost . . . charged; (iv) government-sponsored . . . government-inhibited . . . income

p. 113: (i) low . . . high; (ii) low . . . higher

p. 116: (i) public choice; (ii) opportunity cost . . . competition

6 Funding the Public Sector

During the past few years, federal government spending as a percentage of total national income rose to about 25 percent before declining slightly. At the same time, total federal revenues from taxes and other sources fell to approximately 15 percent of national income before recovering somewhat. To cover expenditures out of national income not directly funded by revenues, the federal government resorted to borrowing. As you will learn in this chapter, however, the *government budget constraint* faced by the federal government dictates that ultimately spending and revenues must balance. As a consequence, eventually federal spending as a percentage of national income will have to equalize with federal revenues as a percentage of national income, which you will also learn is a measure of the nation's average federal tax rate.

LEARNING OBJECTIVES

After reading this chapter, you should be able to:

- Distinguish between average tax rates and marginal tax rates
- Explain the structure of the U.S. income tax system
- Understand the key factors influencing the relationship between tax rates and the tax revenues governments collect
- Explain how the taxes governments levy on purchases of goods and services affect market prices and equilibrium quantities

MyEconLab helps you master each objective and study more efficiently. See end of chapter for details.

? DID YOU KNOW THAT... governments of more than a dozen states have sold bonds promising annual payments based on more than $100 billion in projected shares of revenues from a legal settlement with the tobacco industry? The state governments have sold these "tobacco bonds" to raise funds for financing their operations now, rather than waiting for the streams of payments to arrive in future years. Of course, many state governments also have been selling more traditional bonds offering annual payments they plan to cover with future taxation. State and local governments assess sales taxes, property taxes, income taxes, hotel occupancy taxes, and electricity, gasoline, water, and sewage taxes. At the federal level, there are income taxes, Social Security taxes, Medicare taxes, and so-called excise taxes. When a person dies, state and federal governments also collect estate taxes. Clearly, governments give considerable attention to their roles as tax collectors.

Paying for the Public Sector

There are three sources of funding available to governments. One source is explicit fees, called user *charges*, for government services. The second and main source of government funding is taxes. Nevertheless, sometimes federal, state, and local governments spend more than they collect in taxes. To do this, they must rely on a third source of financing, which is borrowing. A government cannot borrow unlimited amounts, however. After all, a government, like an individual or a firm, can convince others to lend it funds only if it can provide evidence that it will repay its debts. A government must ultimately rely on taxation and user charges, the sources of its own current and future revenues, to repay its debts.

Over the long run, therefore, taxes and user charges are any government's *fundamental* sources of revenues. The **government budget constraint** states that each dollar of public spending on goods, services, transfer payments, and repayments of borrowed funds during a given period must be provided by tax revenues and user charges collected by the government. This long-term constraint indicates that the total amount a government plans to spend and transfer today and into the future cannot exceed the total taxes and user charges that it currently earns and can reasonably anticipate collecting in future years. Taxation dwarfs user charges as a source of government resources, so let's begin by looking at taxation from a government's perspective.

How has the fact that states must satisfy government budget constraints impinged directly on the personal budgets of students at a number of state universities?

YOU ARE THERE

To consider a real-world application regarding government budget constraints, take a look at **How to Keep Social Security in Business** on page 134.

Government budget constraint
The limit on government spending and transfers imposed by the fact that every dollar the government spends, transfers, or uses to repay borrowed funds must ultimately be provided by the user charges and taxes it collects.

EXAMPLE

State University Tuition Rates Jump—Even at the Last Moment

Spending on public education is one of the larger components of most states' budgets. Dampened economic activity since 2008 has led to lower tax revenues throughout the fifty states. To continue operating within their government budget constraints, more than half of the states have cut their spending on higher education. State universities face their own budget constraints, and in response to reduced funding from state governments, they have raised tuition rates charged to enrolled students.

At a number of state universities, tuition rates have jumped as late as the time of final course registration. In a few instances, state universities have even raised tuition after completion of the first semester of the academic year, before the start of the second semester. Students affected by such last-minute tuition increases have first-hand experience with government budget constraints.

FOR CRITICAL THINKING

How does the fact that government budget constraints must be satisfied help explain why many states have taken back scholarships that they initially offered to university enrollees?

Systems of Taxation

In light of the government budget constraint, a major concern of any government is how to collect taxes. Jean-Baptiste Colbert, the seventeenth-century French finance minister, said the art of taxation was in "plucking the goose so as to obtain the largest amount of feathers with the least possible amount of hissing." In the United States, governments have designed a variety of methods of plucking the private-sector goose.

The Tax Base and the Tax Rate

Tax base
The value of goods, services, wealth, or incomes subject to taxation.

Tax rate
The proportion of a tax base that must be paid to a government as taxes.

To collect a tax, a government typically establishes a **tax base,** which is the value of goods, services, wealth, or incomes subject to taxation. Then it assesses a **tax rate,** which is the proportion of the tax base that must be paid to the government as taxes.

As we discuss shortly, for the federal government and many state governments, incomes are key tax bases. Therefore, to discuss tax rates and the structure of taxation systems in more detail, let's focus for now on income taxation.

Marginal and Average Tax Rates

Marginal tax rate
The change in the tax payment divided by the change in income, or the percentage of *additional* dollars that must be paid in taxes. The marginal tax rate is applied to the highest tax bracket of taxable income reached.

If somebody says, "I pay 28 percent in taxes," you cannot really tell what that person means unless you know whether he or she is referring to average taxes paid or the tax rate on the last dollars earned. The latter concept refers to the **marginal tax rate,** with the word *marginal* meaning "incremental."

The marginal tax rate is expressed as follows:

$$\text{Marginal tax rate} = \frac{\text{change in taxes due}}{\text{change in taxable income}}$$

Tax bracket
A specified interval of income to which a specific and unique marginal tax rate is applied.

Average tax rate
The total tax payment divided by total income. It is the proportion of total income paid in taxes.

It is important to understand that the marginal tax rate applies only to the income in the highest **tax bracket** reached, with a tax bracket defined as a specified range of taxable income to which a specific and unique marginal tax rate is applied.

The marginal tax rate is not the same thing as the **average tax rate,** which is defined as follows:

$$\text{Average tax rate} = \frac{\text{total taxes due}}{\text{total taxable income}}$$

Why are governments contemplating a change in the tax base for the gasoline taxes that currently ring up at the pumps?

POLICY EXAMPLE

Is It Time to Replace Gasoline Taxes with Mileage Taxes?

A main source of revenues used by federal, state, and local governments to finance road construction and repair is taxation of gasoline purchases. As more vehicles that partly or fully rely on battery power have hit the road, gasoline purchases have been declining at any given price of gasoline. Thus, the gasoline tax base has been shrinking, so gasoline tax collections are dropping.

Battery-powered vehicles continue to subject roadways to wear and tear, so governments somehow must still obtain funds to finance road maintenance. Recently, the Congressional Budget Office has proposed a *mileage* tax base. Under a mileage-based taxation system, governments would require vehicles to be equipped with special mileage meters. Government agencies would periodically tally the number of miles traveled by each vehicle, which would constitute a tax base. Then application of mileage tax rates to the new mileage tax base would determine the total mileage taxes owed by the vehicle's owner. In this way, governments could collect taxes on miles driven as well as on the gasoline that fuels the vehicle down the road.

FOR CRITICAL THINKING

Why would a mileage tax constitute "double taxation"?

Taxation Systems

No matter how governments raise revenues—from income taxes, sales taxes, or other taxes—all of those taxes fit into one of three types of taxation systems: proportional, progressive, or regressive, according to the relationship between the tax rate and income. To determine whether a tax system is proportional, progressive, or regressive, we simply ask, What is the relationship between the average tax rate and the marginal tax rate?

Proportional taxation
A tax system in which, regardless of an individual's income, the tax bill comprises exactly the same proportion.

PROPORTIONAL TAXATION **Proportional taxation** means that regardless of an individual's income, taxes comprise exactly the same proportion. In a proportional taxation system, the marginal tax rate is always equal to the average tax rate. If every dollar is taxed at 20 percent, then the average tax rate is 20 percent, and so is the marginal tax rate.

Under a proportional system of taxation, taxpayers at all income levels end up paying the same *percentage* of their income in taxes. With a proportional tax rate of 20 percent, an individual with an income of $10,000 pays $2,000 in taxes, while an individual making $100,000 pays $20,000. Thus, the identical 20 percent rate is levied on both taxpayers.

Go to www.econtoday.com/chap06 to learn from the National Center for Policy Analysis about what distinguishes recent flat tax proposals from a truly proportional income tax system. Click on "Flat Tax Proposals."

PROGRESSIVE TAXATION Under **progressive taxation,** as a person's taxable income increases, the percentage of income paid in taxes increases. In a progressive system, the marginal tax rate is above the average tax rate. If you are taxed 5 percent on the first $10,000 you earn, 10 percent on the next $10,000 you earn, and 30 percent on the last $10,000 you earn, you face a progressive income tax system. Your marginal tax rate is always above your average tax rate.

Progressive taxation
A tax system in which, as income increases, a higher percentage of the additional income is paid as taxes. The marginal tax rate exceeds the average tax rate as income rises.

What is the marginal income tax rate faced by the highest U.S. income earners?

POLICY EXAMPLE

Calculating the Top U.S. Marginal Tax Rate

Because the income tax systems of the federal government and of most state governments are progressive, the highest-income earners pay the highest overall income tax rates. The top federal income tax rate is at least 35 percent. In addition, the highest-income earners face the 2.9 percent Medicare payroll tax rate plus a "higher-earners surcharge" of 0.9 percent. Finally, the highest-income earners are hit with a 3.8 percent surcharge on investment and royalty earnings to fund the new national health care system. After taking into account allowed federal tax deductions based on state tax payments, the effective marginal state income tax rate for the average high earner is approximately 4 percent. Summing these rates yields a current top marginal income tax rate for U.S. high-income earners with investment and royalty earnings of about 46.2 percent. Thus, the highest-income earners can keep for their own use just over half of the last dollar they earn.

FOR CRITICAL THINKING

How does the fact that a number of cities and counties also have their own income taxes affect the top marginal tax rate for some high earners?

REGRESSIVE TAXATION With **regressive taxation,** a smaller percentage of taxable income is taken in taxes as taxable income increases. The marginal rate is *below* the average rate. As income increases, the marginal tax rate falls, and so does the average tax rate. The U.S. Social Security tax is regressive. Once the legislative maximum taxable wage base is reached, no further Social Security taxes are paid. Consider a simplified hypothetical example: Suppose that every dollar up to $100,000 is taxed at 10 percent. After $100,000 there is no Social Security tax. Someone making $200,000 still pays only $10,000 in Social Security taxes. That person's average Social Security tax is 5 percent. The person making $100,000, by contrast, effectively pays 10 percent. The person making $1 million faces an average Social Security tax rate of only 1 percent in our simplified example.

Regressive taxation
A tax system in which as more dollars are earned, the percentage of tax paid on them falls. The marginal tax rate is less than the average tax rate as income rises.

QUICK QUIZ See page 138 for the answers. Review concepts from this section in MyEconLab.

Governments collect taxes by applying a tax __________ to a tax __________, which refers to the value of goods, services, wealth, or incomes. Income tax rates are applied to tax brackets, which are ranges of income over which the tax rate is constant.

The __________ tax rate is the total tax payment divided by total income, and the __________ tax rate is the change in the tax payment divided by the change in income.

Tax systems can be __________, __________, or __________, depending on whether the marginal tax rate is the same as, greater than, or less than the average tax rate as income rises.

The Most Important Federal Taxes

What types of taxes do federal, state, and local governments collect? The two pie charts in Figure 6-1 on the following page show the percentages of receipts from various taxes obtained by the federal government and by state and local governments. For the federal government, key taxes are individual income taxes, corporate income taxes, Social

FIGURE 6-1

Sources of Government Tax Receipts

As panel (a) shows, about 92 percent of federal revenues comes from income and Social Security and other social insurance taxes. State government revenues, shown in panel (b), are spread more evenly across sources, with less emphasis on taxes based on individual income.

Source: Economic Report of the President, Economic Indicators

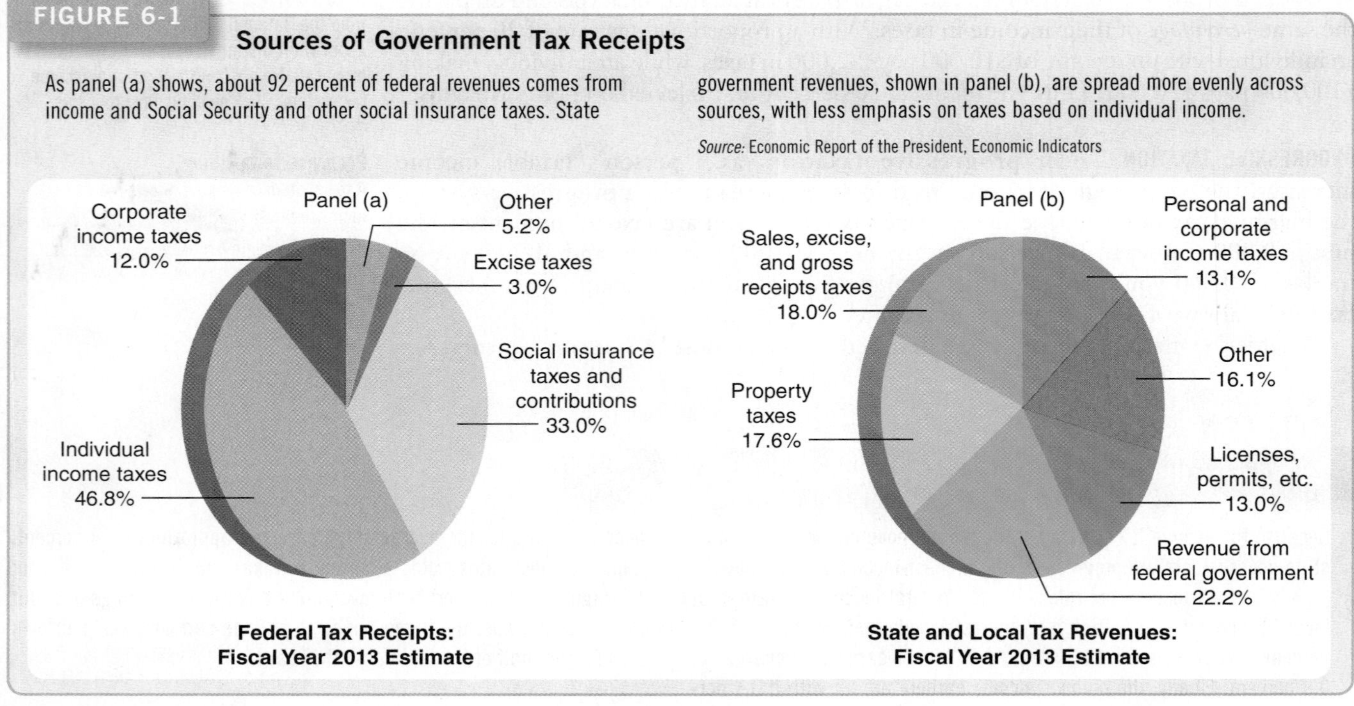

Security taxes, and excise taxes on items such as gasoline and alcoholic beverages. For state and local governments, sales taxes, property taxes, and personal and corporate income taxes are the main types of taxes.

The Federal Personal Income Tax

The most important tax in the U.S. economy is the federal personal income tax, which, as Figure 6-1 above indicates, accounts for almost 47 percent of all federal revenues. All U.S. citizens, resident aliens, and most others who earn income in the United States are required to pay federal income taxes on all taxable income, including income earned abroad.

The rates that are paid rise as income increases, as can be seen in Table 6-1 below. Marginal income tax rates at the federal level have ranged from as low as 1 percent after the 1913 passage of the Sixteenth Amendment, which made the individual income tax constitutional, to as high as 94 percent (reached in 1944). There were 14 separate tax brackets prior to the Tax Reform Act of 1986, which reduced the number to three (now six, as shown in Table 6-1).

TABLE 6-1

Federal Marginal Income Tax Rates

These rates applied in 2012.

Single Persons		Married Couples	
Marginal Tax Bracket	**Marginal Tax Rate**	**Marginal Tax Bracket**	**Marginal Tax Rate**
$0–$8,700	10%	$0–$17,400	10%
$8,701–$35,350	15%	$17,401–$70,700	15%
$35,351–$85,650	25%	$70,701–$142,700	25%
$85,651–$178,650	28%	$142,701–$217,450	28%
$178,651–$388,350	33%	$217,451–$388,350	33%
$388,351 and up	35%	$388,351 and up	35%

Source: U.S. Department of the Treasury.

What is the annual cost to U.S. taxpayers of determining how much they owe in income taxes?

POLICY EXAMPLE

Figuring Out How Much to Pay in Income Taxes Is Not Cheap

The Internal Revenue Service's Taxpayer Advocate Service has estimated that U.S. taxpayers spend nearly $200 billion per year to determine how much they owe in income taxes. In the process, taxpayers also devote 7.6 billion hours, or the equivalent of time that otherwise could have been spent in 3.8 million full-time jobs. The average hourly wage earned by a U.S. resident exceeds $16 per hour, so the opportunity cost of calculating U.S. income taxes is about $125 billion. Thus, the combined explicit and opportunity costs of complying with the U.S. income tax code amount to roughly $325 billion per year, which is about 20 percent of all federal income taxes collected.

FOR CRITICAL THINKING

What professions benefit from the nearly $200 billion per year spent on preparing tax returns?

The Treatment of Capital Gains

The difference between the purchase price and sale price of an asset, such as a share of stock or a plot of land, is called a **capital gain** if it is a profit and a **capital loss** if it is not. The federal government taxes capital gains, and as of 2013, there were several capital gains tax rates.

What appear to be capital gains are not always real gains. If you pay $100,000 for a financial asset in one year and sell it for 50 percent more 10 years later, your nominal capital gain is $50,000. But what if during those 10 years inflation has driven average asset prices up by 50 percent? Your *real* capital gain would be zero, but you would still have to pay taxes on that $50,000. To counter this problem, many economists have argued that capital gains should be indexed to the rate of inflation. This is exactly what is done with the marginal tax brackets in the federal income tax code. Tax brackets for the purposes of calculating marginal tax rates each year are expanded at the rate of inflation, that is, the rate at which the average of all prices is rising. So, if the rate of inflation is 10 percent, each tax bracket is moved up by 10 percent. The same concept could be applied to capital gains and financial assets. So far, Congress has refused to enact such a measure.

Capital gain
A positive difference between the purchase price and the sale price of an asset. If a share of stock is bought for $5 and then sold for $15, the capital gain is $10.

Capital loss
A negative difference between the purchase price and the sale price of an asset.

The Corporate Income Tax

Figure 6-1 on the facing page shows that corporate income taxes account for 12 percent of all federal taxes collected. They also make up about 2 percent of all state and local taxes collected. Corporations are generally taxed on the difference between their total revenues and their expenses. The federal corporate income tax structure is given in Table 6-2 below.

TABLE 6-2

Federal Corporate Income Tax Schedule

These corporate tax rates were in effect through 2013.

Corporate Taxable Income	Corporate Tax Rate
$0–$50,000	15%
$50,001–$75,000	25%
$75,001–$100,000	34%
$100,001–$335,000	39%
$335,001–$10,000,000	34%
$10,000,001–$15,000,000	35%
$15,000,001–$18,333,333	38%
$18,333,334 and up	35%

Source: Internal Revenue Service.

DOUBLE TAXATION Because individual stockholders must pay taxes on the dividends they receive, and those dividends are paid out of *after-tax* profits by the corporation, corporate profits are taxed twice. If you receive $1,000 in dividends, you have to declare them as income, and you must normally pay taxes on them. Before the corporation was able to pay you those dividends, it had to pay taxes on all its profits, including any that it put back into the company or did not distribute in the form of dividends. Eventually, the new investment made possible by those **retained earnings**—profits not given out to stockholders—along with borrowed funds will be reflected in the value of the stock in that company. When you sell your stock in that company, you will have to pay taxes on the difference between what you paid for the stock and what you sold it for. In both cases, dividends and retained earnings (corporate profits) are taxed twice. In 2003, Congress reduced the double taxation effect somewhat by enacting legislation that allowed most dividends to be taxed at lower rates than are applied to regular income through 2012.

Retained earnings
Earnings that a corporation saves, or retains, for investment in other productive activities; earnings that are not distributed to stockholders.

WHO REALLY PAYS THE CORPORATE INCOME TAX? Corporations can function only as long as consumers buy their products, employees make their goods, stockholders (owners) buy their shares, and bondholders buy their bonds. Corporations per se do not do anything. We must ask, then, who really pays the tax on corporate income? This is a question of **tax incidence.** (The question of tax incidence applies to all taxes, including sales taxes and Social Security taxes.) The incidence of corporate taxation is the subject of considerable debate. Some economists suggest that corporations pass their tax burdens on to consumers by charging higher prices.

Tax incidence
The distribution of tax burdens among various groups in society.

Other economists argue that it is the stockholders who bear most of the tax. Still others contend that employees pay at least part of the tax by receiving lower wages than they would otherwise. Because the debate is not yet settled, we will not hazard a guess here as to what the correct conclusion may be. Suffice it to say that you should be cautious when you advocate increasing corporation income taxes. *People,* whether owners, consumers, or workers, end up paying all of the increase—just as they pay all of any tax.

Social Security and Unemployment Taxes

Each year, taxes levied on payrolls account for an increasing percentage of federal tax receipts. These taxes, which are distinct from personal income taxes, are for Social Security, retirement, survivors' disability, and old-age medical benefits (Medicare). The Social Security tax is imposed on earnings up to roughly $110,100 at a rate of 6.2 percent on employers and 6.2 percent on employees. That is, the employer matches your "contribution" to Social Security. (The employer's contribution is really paid by the employees, at least in part, in the form of a reduced wage rate.) As Chapter 5 explained, a Medicare tax is imposed on all wage earnings at a combined rate of 2.9 percent. The 2010 federal health care law also added a 3.8 percent Medicare tax on certain income above $200,000.

Social Security taxes came into existence when the Federal Insurance Contributions Act (FICA) was passed in 1935. At that time, many more people paid into the Social Security program than the number who received benefits. Currently, however, older people drawing benefits make up a much larger share of the population. Consequently, in recent years, outflows of Social Security benefit payments have sometimes exceeded inflows of Social Security taxes. Various economists have advanced proposals to raise Social Security tax rates on younger workers or to reduce benefit payouts to older retirees and disabled individuals receiving Social Security payments. So far, however, the federal government has failed to address Social Security's deteriorating funding situation.

There is also a federal unemployment tax, which helps pay for unemployment insurance. This tax rate is 0.6 percent on the first $7,000 of annual wages of each employee who earns more than $1,500. Only the employer makes this tax payment. This tax covers the costs of the unemployment insurance system. In addition to this federal tax, some states with an unemployment system impose their own tax of up to about

3 percent, depending on the past record of the particular employer. An employer who frequently lays off workers typically will have a slightly higher state unemployment tax rate than an employer who never lays off workers.

QUICK QUIZ See page 138 for the answers. Review concepts from this section in MyEconLab.

The federal government raises most of its revenues through __________ taxes and social insurance taxes and contributions. State and local governments raise most of their tax revenues from __________ taxes, __________ taxes, and income taxes.

Because corporations must first pay an income tax on most earnings, the personal income tax shareholders pay on dividends received (or realized capital gains) constitutes __________ taxation.

Both employers and employees must pay __________ __________ taxes and contributions at rates of 6.2 percent on roughly the first $110,100 in wage earnings, and a 2.9 percent __________ tax rate is applied to all wage earnings. The federal government and some state governments also assess taxes to pay for __________ insurance systems.

Tax Rates and Tax Revenues

For most state and local governments, income taxes yield fewer revenues than taxes imposed on sales of goods and services. Figure 6-1 on page 126 shows that sales taxes, gross receipts taxes, and excise taxes generate almost one-fifth of the total funds available to state and local governments. Thus, from the perspective of many state and local governments, a fundamental issue is how to set tax rates on sales of goods and services to extract desired total tax payments.

Sales Taxes

Governments levy **sales taxes** on the prices that consumers pay to purchase each unit of a broad range of goods and services. Sellers collect sales taxes and transmit them to the government. Sales taxes are a form of **ad valorem taxation,** which means that the tax is applied "to the value" of the good. Thus, a government using a system of *ad valorem* taxation charges a tax rate equal to a fraction of the market price of each unit that a consumer buys. For instance, if the tax rate is 8 percent and the market price of an item is $100, then the amount of the tax on the item is $8.

Sales taxes
Taxes assessed on the prices paid on most goods and services.

***Ad valorem* taxation**
Assessing taxes by charging a tax rate equal to a fraction of the market price of each unit purchased.

A sales tax is therefore a proportional tax with respect to purchased items. The total amount of sales taxes a government collects equals the sales tax rate times the sales tax base, which is the market value of total purchases.

Static Tax Analysis

There are two approaches to evaluating how changes in tax rates affect government tax collections. **Static tax analysis** assumes that changes in the tax rate have no effect on the tax base. Thus, this approach implies that if a state government desires to increase its sales tax collections, it can simply raise the tax rate. Multiplying the higher tax rate by the tax base thereby produces higher tax revenues.

Static tax analysis
Economic evaluation of the effects of tax rate changes under the assumption that there is no effect on the tax base, meaning that there is an unambiguous positive relationship between tax rates and tax revenues.

Governments often rely on static tax analysis. Sometimes this yields unpleasant surprises. Consider, for instance, what happened in 1992 when Congress implemented a federal "luxury tax" on purchases of new pleasure boats priced at $100,000 or more. Applying the 10 percent luxury tax rate to the anticipated tax base—sales of new boats during previous years—produced a forecast of hundreds of millions of dollars in revenues from the luxury tax. What actually happened, however, was an 80 percent plunge in sales of new luxury boats. People postponed boat purchases or bought used boats instead. Consequently, the tax base all but disappeared, and the federal government collected only a few tens of millions of dollars in taxes on boat sales. Congress repealed the tax a year later.

Have recent efforts by several state governments to include cyberspace-generated sales in their tax bases paid off?

POLICY EXAMPLE

States Seek to Apply Sales Taxes to Internet Retailers' Sales

In recent years, U.S. states have collected too few taxes to fund their expenditures. State governments have responded by seeking new sources of tax revenues. Several states, such as Arkansas, Hawaii, North Carolina, and Rhode Island, have cast their sights on sales programs operated by Internet retailers such as Amazon and Overstock. Under these programs, sellers—called "affiliates"—post links on their own Web sites. When the affiliates' customers click on those links and purchase items, the affiliates receive referral fees from the Internet retailers. The states listed above have declared such affiliate programs to constitute the "physical presences" of Internet retailers. This means that Internet retailers would have to collect sales taxes on *all* of their companies' sales.

Each time that state governments have passed such sales tax laws, Internet retailers have responded by eliminating affiliate programs within those states. Thus, these efforts to expand sales tax bases to include Internet retailers have failed thus far.

FOR CRITICAL THINKING

What do you suppose has happened to state income taxes collected from Internet retailers' former affiliates in Arkansas, Hawaii, North Carolina, and Rhode Island?

Dynamic Tax Analysis

Dynamic tax analysis
Economic evaluation of tax rate changes that recognizes that the tax base eventually declines with ever-higher tax rates, so that tax revenues may eventually decline if the tax rate is raised sufficiently.

The problem with static tax analysis is that it ignores incentive effects created by new taxes or hikes in existing tax rates. According to **dynamic tax analysis,** a likely response to an increase in a tax rate is a *decrease* in the tax base. When a government pushes up its sales tax rate, for example, consumers have an incentive to cut back on their purchases of goods and services subjected to the higher rate, perhaps by buying them in a locale where there is a lower sales tax rate or perhaps no tax rate at all. As shown in Figure 6-2 below, the maximum sales tax rate varies considerably from state to state.

Consider someone who lives in a state bordering Oregon. In such a border state, the sales tax rate can be as high as 8 percent, so a resident of that state has a strong incentive to buy higher-priced goods and services in Oregon, where there is no sales tax. Someone who lives in a high-tax county in Alabama has an incentive to buy an item online from an out-of-state firm to avoid paying sales taxes. Such shifts in expenditures in response to higher relative tax rates will reduce a state's sales tax base and thereby result in lower sales tax collections than the levels predicted by static tax analysis.

FIGURE 6-2
States with the Highest and Lowest Sales Tax Rates

A number of states allow counties and cities to collect their own sales taxes in addition to state sales taxes. This figure shows the maximum sales tax rates for selected states, including county and municipal taxes. Delaware, Montana, New Hampshire, and Oregon have no sales taxes.

Source: U.S. Department of Commerce.

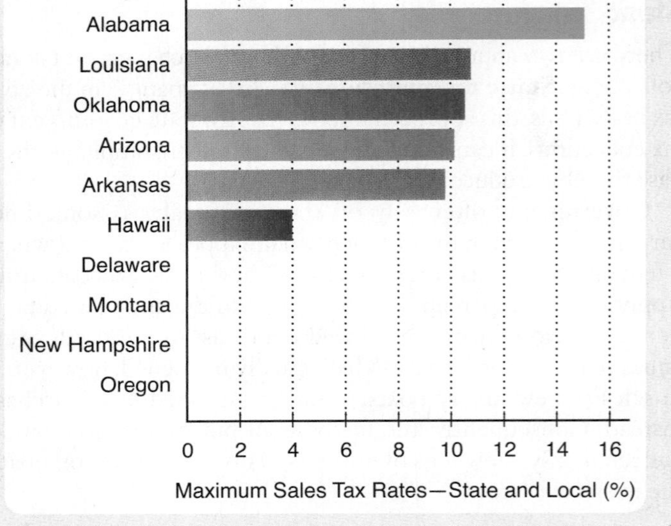

Dynamic tax analysis recognizes that increasing the tax rate could actually cause the government's total tax collections to *decline* if a sufficiently large number of consumers react to the higher sales tax rate by cutting back on purchases of goods and services included in the state's tax base. Some residents who live close to other states with lower sales tax rates might, for instance, drive across the state line to do more of their shopping. Other residents might place more orders with catalog companies or online firms located in other legal jurisdictions where their state's sales tax does not apply.

WHAT IF... the government seeks to collect higher taxes by increasing capital gains tax rates?

People who own assets the sale of which would generate capital gains subject to taxation have considerable discretion over when to sell assets and realize capital gains from such sales. When people learn about upcoming increases in tax rates that apply to capital gains, they can attempt to sell their assets immediately, before the higher tax rate goes into effect. Alternatively, they can indefinitely postpone sales of the assets in the hope that the tax rate will be cut in the future. Either response reduces capital gains subject to taxation when the higher tax rate becomes effective.

Indeed, the evidence for an inverse relationship between capital gains tax rates and realized capital gains is considerable. That is, when capital gains tax rates increase, taxable realized capital gains decline, and tax collections fail to rise as much as expected. Thus, as predicted by dynamic tax analysis, raising the tax rate causes an offsetting decline in the tax base, resulting in fewer tax collections than the government anticipates.

Maximizing Tax Revenues

Dynamic tax analysis indicates that whether a government's tax revenues ultimately rise or fall in response to a tax rate increase depends on exactly how much the tax base declines in response to the higher tax rate. On the one hand, the tax base may decline by a relatively small amount following an increase in the tax rate, or perhaps even imperceptibly, so that tax revenues rise. For instance, in the situation we imagine a government facing in Figure 6-3 below, a rise in the tax rate from 5 percent to 6 percent causes tax revenues to increase. Along this range, static tax analysis can provide a good approximation of the revenue effects of an increase in the tax rate. On the other hand, the tax base may decline so much that total tax revenues decrease. In Figure 6-3, for example, increasing the tax rate from 6 percent to 7 percent causes tax revenues to *decline*.

What is most likely is that when the tax rate is already relatively low, increasing the tax rate causes relatively small declines in the tax base. Within a range of relatively low sales tax rates, therefore, increasing the tax rate generates higher sales tax revenues, as illustrated along the upward-sloping portion of the curve depicted in Figure 6-3. If the government

FIGURE 6-3

Maximizing the Government's Sales Tax Revenues

Dynamic tax analysis predicts that ever-higher tax rates bring about declines in the tax base, so that at sufficiently high tax rates the government's tax revenues begin to fall off. This implies that there is a tax rate, 6 percent in this example, at which the government can collect the maximum possible revenues, T_{max}.

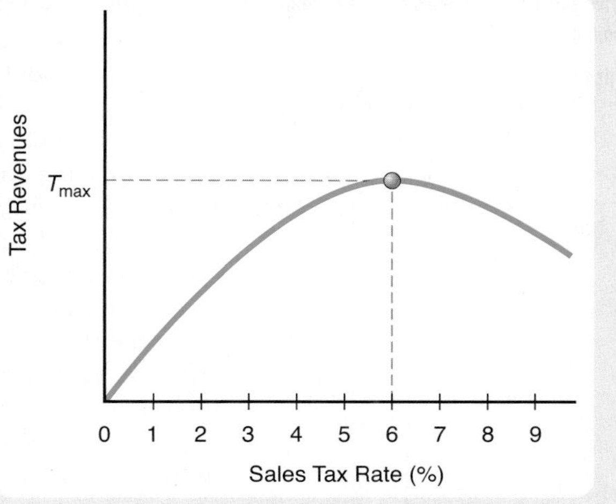

continues to push up the tax rate, however, people increasingly have an incentive to find ways to avoid purchasing taxable goods and services. Eventually, the tax base decreases sufficiently that the government's tax collections decline with ever-higher tax rates.

Consequently, governments that wish to maximize their tax revenues should not necessarily assess a high tax rate. In the situation illustrated in Figure 6-3, on the previous page, the government maximizes its tax revenues at T_{max} by establishing a sales tax rate of 6 percent. If the government were to raise the rate above 6 percent, it would induce a sufficient decline in the tax base that its tax collections would decline. If the government wishes to collect more than T_{max} in revenues to fund various government programs, it must somehow either expand its sales tax base or develop another tax.

QUICK QUIZ See page 138 for the answers. Review concepts from this section in MyEconLab.

The __________ view of the relationship between tax rates and tax revenues implies that higher tax rates always generate increased government tax collections.

According to __________ tax analysis, higher tax rates cause the tax base to decrease. Tax collections will rise less than predicted by __________ tax analysis.

Dynamic tax analysis indicates that there is a tax rate that maximizes the government's tax collections. Setting the tax rate any higher would cause the tax base to __________ sufficiently that the government's tax revenues will __________.

Taxation from the Point of View of Producers and Consumers

Governments collect taxes on product sales at the source. They require producers to charge these taxes when they sell their output. This means that taxes on sales of goods and services affect market prices and quantities. Let's consider why this is so.

Taxes and the Market Supply Curve

Imposing taxes on final sales of a good or service affects the position of the market supply curve. To see why, consider panel (a) of Figure 6-4 on the facing page, which shows a gasoline market supply curve S_1 in the absence of taxation. At a price of $3.35 per gallon, gasoline producers are willing and able to supply 180,000 gallons of gasoline per week. If the price increases to $3.45 per gallon, firms increase production to 200,000 gallons of gasoline per week.

Excise tax
A tax levied on purchases of a particular good or service.

Unit tax
A constant tax assessed on each unit of a good that consumers purchase.

Both federal and state governments assess **excise taxes**—taxes on sales of particular commodities—on sales of gasoline. They levy gasoline excise taxes as a **unit tax,** or a constant tax per unit sold. On average, combined federal and state excise taxes on gasoline are about $0.40 per gallon.

Let's suppose, therefore, that a gasoline producer must transmit a total of $0.40 per gallon to federal and state governments for each gallon sold. Producers must continue to receive a net amount of $3.35 per gallon to induce them to supply 180,000 gallons each week, so they must now receive $3.75 per gallon to supply that weekly quantity. Likewise, gasoline producers now will be willing to supply 200,000 gallons each week only if they receive $0.40 more per gallon, or a total amount of $3.85 per gallon.

As you can see, imposing the combined $0.40 per gallon excise taxes on gasoline shifts the supply curve vertically by exactly that amount to S_2 in panel (a). Thus, the effect of levying excise taxes on gasoline is to shift the supply curve vertically by the total per-unit taxes levied on gasoline sales. Hence, there is a decrease in supply. (In the case of an *ad valorem* sales tax, the supply curve would shift vertically by a proportionate amount equal to the tax rate.)

FIGURE 6-4

The Effects of Excise Taxes on the Market Supply and Equilibrium Price and Quantity of Gasoline

Panel (a) shows what happens if the government requires gasoline sellers to collect and transmit a \$0.40 unit excise tax on gasoline. To be willing to continue supplying a given quantity, sellers must receive a price that is \$0.40 higher for each gallon they sell, so the market supply curve shifts vertically by the amount of the tax. As illustrated in panel (b), this decrease in market supply causes a reduction in the equilibrium quantity of gasoline produced and purchased. It also causes a rise in the market clearing price, to \$3.75, so that consumers pay part of the tax. Sellers pay the rest in lower profits.

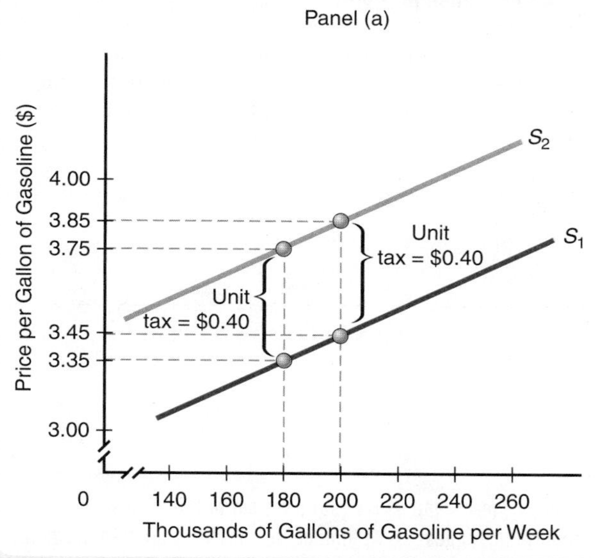

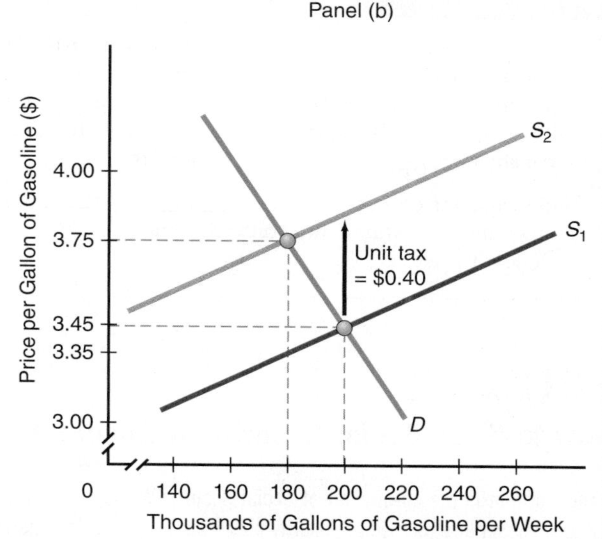

How Taxes Affect the Market Price and Equilibrium Quantity

Panel (b) of Figure 6-4 above shows how imposing \$0.40 per gallon in excise taxes affects the market price of gasoline and the equilibrium quantity of gasoline produced and sold. In the absence of excise taxes, the market supply curve S_1 crosses the demand curve D at a market price of \$3.45 per gallon. At this market price, the equilibrium quantity of gasoline is 200,000 gallons of gasoline per week.

The excise tax levy of \$0.40 per gallon shifts the supply curve to S_2. At the original \$3.45 per gallon price, there is now an excess quantity of gasoline demanded, so the market price of gasoline rises to \$3.75 per gallon. At this market price, the equilibrium quantity of gasoline produced and consumed each week is 180,000 gallons.

What factors determine how much the equilibrium quantity of a good or service declines in response to taxation? The answer to this question depends on how responsive quantities demanded and supplied are to changes in price.

Who Pays the Tax?

In our example, imposing excise taxes of \$0.40 per gallon of gasoline causes the market price to rise to \$3.75 per gallon from \$3.45 per gallon. Thus, the price that each consumer pays is \$0.30 per gallon higher. Consumers pay three-fourths of the excise tax levied on each gallon of gasoline produced and sold in our example.

Gasoline producers must pay the rest of the tax. Their profits decline by \$0.10 per gallon because costs have increased by \$0.40 per gallon while consumers pay \$0.30 more per gallon.

In the gasoline market, as in other markets for products subject to excise taxes and other taxes on sales, the shapes of the market demand and supply curves determine who pays most of a tax. The reason is that the shapes of these curves reflect the responsiveness to price changes of the quantity demanded by consumers and of the quantity supplied by producers.

In the example illustrated in Figure 6-4 on the previous page, the fact that consumers pay most of the excise taxes levied on gasoline reflects a relatively low responsiveness of quantity demanded by consumers to a change in the price of gasoline. Consumers pay most of the excise taxes on each gallon produced and sold because in this example the amount of gasoline they desire to purchase is relatively (but not completely) unresponsive to a change in the market price induced by excise taxes.

QUICK QUIZ See page 138 for the answers. Review concepts from this section in MyEconLab.

When the government levies a tax on sales of a particular product, firms must receive a higher price to continue supplying the same quantity as before, so the supply curve shifts __________. If the tax is a unit excise tax, the supply curve shifts __________ by the amount of the tax.

Imposing a tax on sales of an item __________ the equilibrium quantity produced and consumed and __________ the market price.

When a government assesses a unit excise tax, the market price of the good or service typically rises by an amount __________ than the per-unit tax. Hence, consumers pay a portion of the tax, and firms pay the remainder.

YOU ARE THERE

How to Keep Social Security in Business

Nancy Altman is the co-director of Social Security Works, a group dedicated to preserving the Social Security programs that provide benefits to the elderly and disabled. Altman's view is that these programs are "of crucial importance to every working American and his or her family." Nevertheless, the programs face eventual shortfalls of taxes in relation to promised benefits. Projections indicate that the government will be unable to fund promised benefits to the elderly sometime during the 2030s. The disability program will break down by the end of the 2010s.

Altman proposes two ways of preserving both Social Security programs. One is to combine the programs, so that tax dollars originally intended to fund only benefits for the elderly would begin covering disability benefits. Choosing this option would leave fewer tax funds to pay for elderly benefits and cause that program to fail even sooner. The other option Altman suggests is to finance the disability program by increasing the Social Security tax rate.

One other approach could keep the disability program in operation. This option, which Altman opposes, would be to reduce disability benefits.

Critical Thinking Questions

1. Could borrowing help to finance Social Security benefits indefinitely? Explain.
2. What will be the effects of Social Security shortfalls on the overall U.S. government budget constraint, which sums all programs' constraints?

ISSUES & APPLICATIONS

What Determines the U.S. Long-Run Average Tax Rate?

CONCEPTS APPLIED

- Tax Rate
- Average Tax Rate
- Government Budget Constraint

If we view the overall tax base as the income earned by all residents during a given year, then the average tax rate equals all tax payments divided by income. This average tax rate is the proportion of total national income paid in taxes.

FIGURE 6-5

The Overall Average Federal Tax Rate and Its Components and Federal Spending as a Percentage of National Income

The overall average tax rate exhibits short-term volatility mainly because of changes in marginal tax rates and tax collections of individual income taxes. Ultimately, this overall tax rate must equal the ratio of federal spending to national income, but currently the government is making up the difference via borrowing.

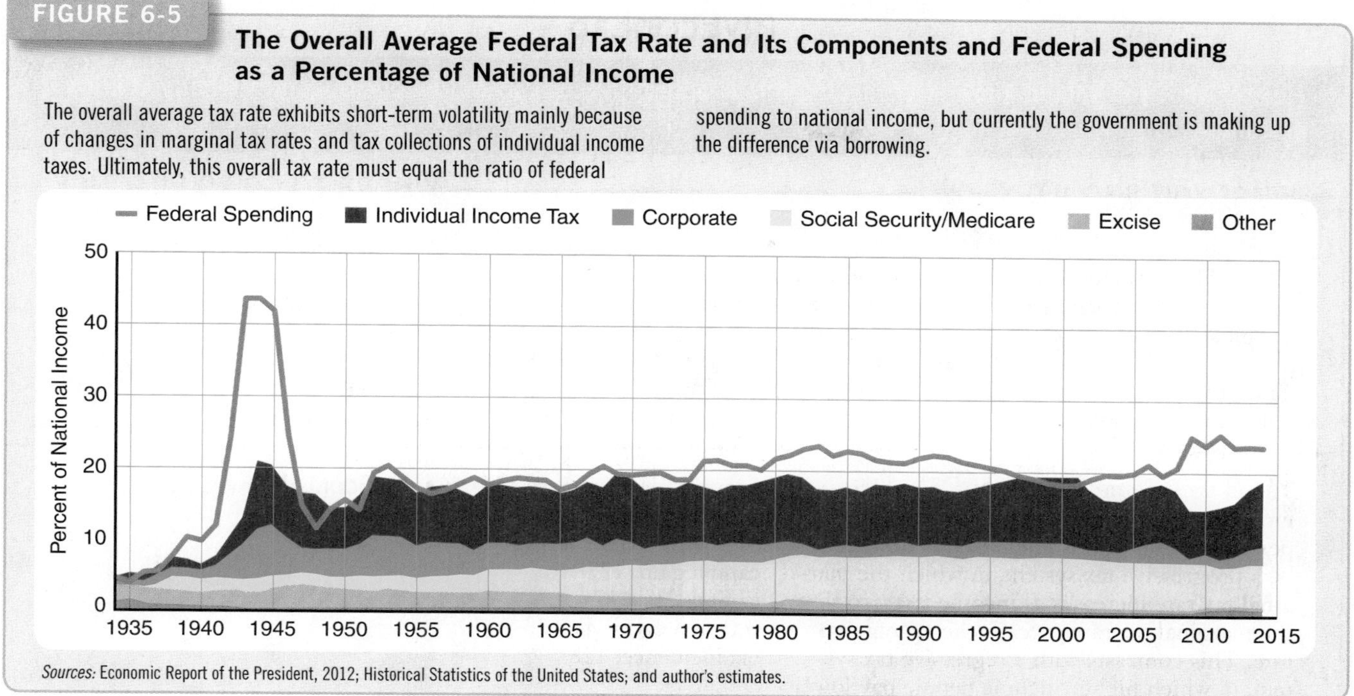

Sources: Economic Report of the President, 2012; Historical Statistics of the United States; and author's estimates.

The Overall Average U.S. Tax Rate and Its Components

Figure 6-5 above displays the average U.S. federal tax rate each year since 1934. Since the early 1950s, this overall average tax rate has ranged between 15 and 21 percent. The shaded regions show how this rate has been split among various forms of taxation.

The greater instability of the average individual income tax rate largely reflects two factors: changes in marginal income tax rates assessed by the federal government and variations in individual income subject to taxation. For instance, the gradual increase in the average individual income tax rate during the 1990s reflects higher marginal tax rates imposed in 1993. Drops in this average tax rate in the early 1980s and early 2000s help to account for declines in the average individual income rate during these intervals. Another key determinant, however, was declines in taxes collected during economic downturns. Since 2007, the significant dropoff in tax collections has been the primary reason for the fall in the average individual income tax rate.

The Role of the Government Budget Constraint

Recall that government spending ultimately must equal all revenues derived from taxes and fees. Thus, the average rate of federal spending out of national income eventually must be equalized with the overall average federal tax rate.

Plotted separately in the figure is federal spending as a percentage of national income. The current ratio of federal spending to national income of about 24 percent is well above the overall average tax rate of just over 15 percent. The federal government has had to make up the difference by borrowing, but it cannot do so indefinitely. If spending as a percentage of national income were to remain close to 24 percent, the overall average federal tax rate would have to rise to 24 percent as well. Ultimately, the average federal tax rate must adjust to equality with government spending's share of national income.

For Critical Thinking

1. If citizens were to decide that the overall average federal tax rate should not be greater than 18 percent, what must happen to the long-term rate of federal expenditures in relation to national income?
2. If citizens were to decide that in the long run, federal expenditures should be 28 percent of national income, what must be the required overall average federal tax rate?

Web Resources

1. Take a look at average federal tax rates for people in different income categories at **www.econtoday.com/chap06**.
2. Figure 6-5 displays only official "on-budget" federal spending as a percentage of national income. For a look at total—the sum of on-budget and unofficial "off-budget"—spending as a percentage of national income, go to **www.econtoday.com/chap06**.

MyEconLab

For more questions on this chapter's Issues & Applications, go to MyEconLab. In the Study Plan for this chapter, select Section N: News.

MyEconLab

Here is what you should know after reading this chapter. MyEconLab will help you identify what you know, and where to go when you need to practice.

WHAT YOU SHOULD KNOW		WHERE TO GO TO PRACTICE
Average Tax Rates versus Marginal Tax Rates The average tax rate is the ratio of total tax payments to total income. In contrast, the marginal tax rate is the change in tax payments induced by a change in total taxable income. Thus, the marginal tax rate applies to the last dollar that a person earns.	government budget constraint, 123 tax base, 124 tax rate, 124 marginal tax rate, 124 tax bracket, 124 average tax rate, 124	• MyEconLab Study Plans 6.1, 6.2
The U.S. Income Tax System The U.S. income tax system assesses taxes against both personal and business income. It is designed to be a progressive tax system, in which the marginal tax rate increases as income rises, so that the marginal tax rate exceeds the average tax rate. This contrasts with a regressive tax system, in which higher-income people pay lower marginal tax rates, resulting in a marginal tax rate that is less than the average tax rate. The marginal tax rate equals the average tax rate only under proportional taxation, in which the marginal tax rate does not vary with income.	proportional taxation, 124 progressive taxation, 125 regressive taxation, 125 capital gain, 127 capital loss, 127 retained earnings, 128 tax incidence, 128	• MyEconLab Study Plan 6.3
The Relationship between Tax Rates and Tax Revenues Static tax analysis assumes that the tax base does not respond significantly to an increase in the tax rate, so it seems to imply that a tax rate hike must always boost a government's total tax collections. Dynamic tax analysis reveals, however, that increases in tax rates cause the tax base to decline. Thus, there is a tax rate that maximizes the government's tax revenues. If the government pushes the tax rate higher, tax collections decline.	sales taxes, 129 *ad valorem* taxation, 129 static tax analysis, 129 dynamic tax analysis, 130 **Key Figure** Figure 6-3, 131	• MyEconLab Study Plan 6.4 • Animated Figure 6-3
How Taxes on Purchases of Goods and Services Affect Market Prices and Quantities When a government imposes a per-unit tax on a good or service, a seller is willing to supply any given quantity only if the seller receives a price that is higher by exactly the amount of the tax. Hence, the supply curve shifts vertically by the amount of the tax per unit. In a market with typically shaped demand and supply curves, this results in a fall in the equilibrium quantity and an increase in the market price. To the extent that the market price rises, consumers pay a portion of the tax on each unit they buy. Sellers pay the remainder in lower profits.	excise tax, 132 unit tax, 132 **Key Figure** Figure 6-4, 133	• MyEconLab Study Plan 6.5 • Animated Figure 6-4

Log in to MyEconLab, take a chapter test, and get a personalized Study Plan that tells you which concepts you understand and which ones you need to review. From there, MyEconLab will give you further practice, tutorials, animations, videos, and guided solutions. For more information, visit www.myeconlab.com

PROBLEMS

All problems are assignable in MyEconLab. *Answers to odd-numbered problems appear at the back of the book.*

6-1. A senior citizen gets a part-time job at a fast-food restaurant. She earns $8 per hour for each hour she works, and she works exactly 25 hours per week. Thus, her total pretax weekly income is $200. Her total income tax assessment each week is $40, but she has determined that she is assessed $3 in taxes for the final hour she works each week. (See page 124.)

a. What is this person's average tax rate each week?

b. What is the marginal tax rate for the last hour she works each week?

6-2. For purposes of assessing income taxes, there are three official income levels for workers in a small country: high, medium, and low. For the last hour on the job during a 40-hour workweek, a high-income worker pays a marginal income tax rate of 15 percent, a medium-income worker pays a marginal tax rate of 20 percent, and a low-income worker is assessed a 25 percent marginal income tax rate. Based only on this information, does this nation's income tax system appear to be progressive, proportional, or regressive? (See page 125.)

6-3. Consider the table below, in which each person's marginal tax rate is constant but differs from others' marginal tax rates, when answering the questions that follow. Show your work, and explain briefly. (See page 127.)

Christino		Jarius		Meg	
Income	**Taxes Paid**	**Income**	**Taxes Paid**	**Income**	**Taxes Paid**
$1,000	$200	$1,000	$200	$1,000	$200
$2,000	$300	$2,000	$400	$2,000	$500
$3,000	$400	$3,000	$600	$3,000	$800

a. What is Christino's marginal tax rate?

b. What is Jarius's marginal tax rate?

c. What is Meg's marginal tax rate?

6-4. Refer to the table in Problem 6-3 when answering the following questions. Show your work, and explain briefly. (See pages 124–125.)

a. Does Christino experience progressive, proportional, or regressive taxation?

b. Does Jarius experience progressive, proportional, or regressive taxation?

c. Does Meg experience progressive, proportional, or regressive taxation?

6-5. Suppose that a state has increased its sales tax rate every other year since 2005. Assume that the state collected all sales taxes that residents legally owed. The table below summarizes its experience. What were total taxable sales in this state during each year displayed in the table? (See page 129.)

Year	Sales Tax Rate	Sales Tax Collections
2005	0.03 (3 percent)	$9.0 million
2007	0.04 (4 percent)	$14.0 million
2009	0.05 (5 percent)	$20.0 million
2011	0.06 (6 percent)	$24.0 million
2013	0.07 (7 percent)	$29.4 million

6-6. The sales tax rate applied to all purchases within a state was 0.04 (4 percent) throughout 2012 but increased to 0.05 (5 percent) during all of 2013. The state government collected all taxes due, but its tax revenues were equal to $40 million each year. What happened to the sales tax base between 2012 and 2013? What could account for this result? (See pages 130–131.)

6-7. The British government recently imposed a unit excise tax of about $154 per ticket on airline tickets applying to flights to or from London airports. In answering the following questions, assume normally shaped demand and supply curves. (See page 133.)

a. Use an appropriate diagram to predict effects of the ticket tax on the market clearing price of London airline tickets and on the equilibrium number of flights into and out of London.

b. What do you predict is likely to happen to the equilibrium price of tickets for air flights into and out of cities that are in close proximity to London but are not subject to the new ticket tax? Explain your reasoning.

6-8. To raise funds aimed at providing more support for public schools, a state government has just imposed a unit excise tax equal to $4 for each monthly unit of wireless phone services sold by each company operating in the state. The following diagram depicts the positions of the demand and supply curves for wireless phone services *before* the unit excise tax was imposed. Use this diagram to determine the position of the new market supply curve now that the tax hike has gone into effect. (See pages 132–133.)

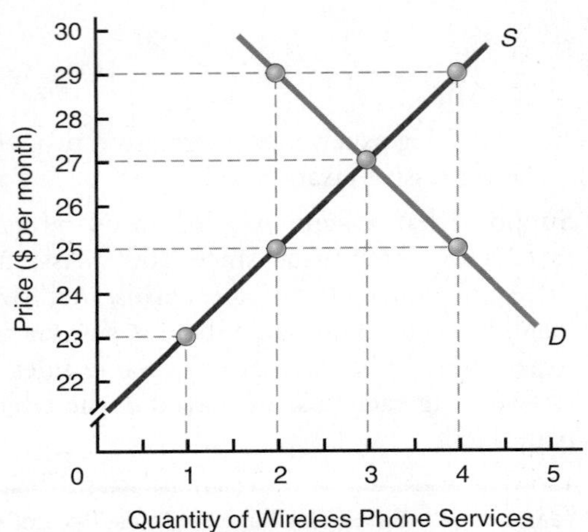

a. Does imposing the $4-per-month unit excise tax cause the market price of wireless phone services to rise by $4 per month? Why or why not?

b. What portion of the $4-per-month unit excise tax is paid by consumers? What portion is paid by providers of wireless phone services?

6-9. The following information applies to the market for a particular item in the *absence* of a unit excise tax (see pages 132–133):

Price ($ per unit)	Quantity Supplied	Quantity Demanded
4	50	200
5	75	175
6	100	150
7	125	125
8	150	100
9	175	75

a. According to the information in the table, in the *absence* of a unit excise tax, what is the market price? What is the equilibrium quantity?

b. Suppose that the government decides to subject producers of this item to a unit excise tax equal to $2 per unit sold. What is the new market price? What is the new equilibrium quantity?

c. What portion of the tax is paid by producers? What portion of the tax is paid by consumers?

ECONOMICS ON THE NET

Social Security Reform There are many proposals for reforming Social Security. The purpose of this exercise is to learn more about why changing Social Security is so often under discussion.

Title: Social Security Privatization

Navigation: Go to **www.econtoday.com/chap06** to learn about Social Security privatization. Under "Recent Social Security Publications," click on "*Social Security, Ponzi Schemes, and the Need for Reform.*"

Application For each of the three entries noted here, read the entry and answer the question.

1. According to this article, when will the system begin to experience difficulties? Why?
2. Why does this article contend that Social Security is similar to a "Ponzi scheme"?
3. Why does this article argue that simply adding personal accounts will not solve Social Security's problems?

For Group Study and Analysis Go to **www.econtoday.com/chap06** to read a proposal for Social Security reform. Accept or rebut the proposal, depending on the side to which you have been assigned. Be prepared to defend your reasons with more than just your feelings. At a minimum, be prepared to present arguments that are logical, if not entirely backed by facts.

ANSWERS TO QUICK QUIZZES

p. 125: (i) rate . . . base; (ii) average . . . marginal; (iii) proportional . . . progressive . . . regressive

p. 129: (i) income . . . sales . . . property; (ii) double; (iii) Social Security . . . Medicare . . . unemployment

p. 132: (i) static; (ii) dynamic . . . static; (iii) fall . . . decline

p. 134: (i) vertically . . . vertically; (ii) reduces . . . raises; (iii) less

The Macroeconomy: Unemployment, Inflation, and Deflation

7

LEARNING OBJECTIVES

After reading this chapter, you should be able to:

- Explain how the U.S. government calculates the official unemployment rate
- Discuss the types of unemployment
- Describe how price indexes are calculated and define the key types of price indexes
- Distinguish between nominal and real interest rates
- Evaluate who loses and who gains from inflation
- Understand key features of business fluctuations

MyEconLab helps you master each objective and study more efficiently. See end of chapter for details.

At one time, a person who qualified for *unemployment benefits*—monthly payments that are coordinated by a U.S. government insurance program financed by taxes on employers—was eligible to receive benefits for no longer than 26 weeks. Since 2009, however, Congress has used general taxpayer funds to extend the duration of unemployment benefits. Thus, most people who qualify for such benefits are eligible to receive them for as long as 99 weeks. A number of economists have suggested that this policy change has resulted in at least 600,000 and perhaps even more than 4 million additional jobless people at any given time. In this chapter, you will learn how economists define unemployment. In addition, you will study concepts that will help you understand how extending unemployment benefits may have contributed to higher measured unemployment.

DID YOU KNOW THAT... between 2008 and 2010, the number of people gainfully employed in the United States declined by nearly 9 million? Since then, more than 2 million of these people have found new jobs. Nevertheless, in excess of 6 million people who had jobs in 2008 were still not employed in 2013. Some of these people have given up looking for work, but most are classified by economists as *unemployed*—looking for positions, but so far unable to obtain jobs.

Trying to understand determinants of unemployment and of the overall performance of the national economy is a central objective of macroeconomics. This branch of economics seeks to explain and predict movements in the average level of prices, unemployment, and the total production of goods and services. This chapter introduces you to these key issues of macroeconomics.

Unemployment

Unemployment
The total number of adults (aged 16 years or older) who are willing and able to work and who are actively looking for work but have not found a job.

Unemployment is normally defined as the number of adults who are actively looking for work but do not have a job. Unemployment is costly in terms of lost output for the entire economy. One estimate indicates that at the end of the first decade of the twenty-first century, when the unemployment rate rose by more than 4 percentage points and firms were operating below 80 percent of their capacity, the amount of output that the economy lost due to idle resources was roughly 5 percent of the total production throughout the United States. (In other words, we were somewhere inside the production possibilities curve that we talked about in Chapter 2.)

That was the equivalent of more than an inflation-adjusted $700 billion of schools, houses, restaurant meals, cars, and movies that *could have been* produced. It is no wonder that policymakers closely watch the unemployment figures published by the Department of Labor's Bureau of Labor Statistics.

On a more personal level, the state of being unemployed often results in hardship and failed opportunities as well as a lack of self-respect. Psychological researchers believe that being fired creates at least as much stress as the death of a close friend. The numbers that we present about unemployment can never fully convey its true cost to the people of this or any other nation.

Historical Unemployment Rates

Labor force
Individuals aged 16 years or older who either have jobs or who are looking and available for jobs; the number of employed plus the number of unemployed.

The unemployment rate, defined as the proportion of the measured **labor force** that is unemployed, hit a low of 1.2 percent of the labor force at the end of World War II, after having reached 25 percent during the Great Depression in the 1930s. You can see in Figure 7-1 on the facing page what has happened to the unemployment rate in the United States since 1890. The highest level ever was reached in the Great Depression, but the unemployment rate was also high during the Panic of 1893.

Employment, Unemployment, and the Labor Force

Figure 7-2 on the facing page presents the population of individuals 16 years of age or older broken into three segments: (1) employed, (2) unemployed, and (3) not in the civilian labor force (a category that includes homemakers, full-time students, military personnel, persons in institutions, and retired persons). The employed and the unemployed, added together, make up the labor force. In 2013, the labor force amounted to 142.1 million + 12.4 million = 154.5 million people. To calculate the unemployment rate, we simply divide the number of unemployed by the number of people in the labor force and multiply by 100: 12.4 million/154.5 million × 100 = 8.0 percent.

MyEconLab Real-time data

FIGURE 7-1

More Than a Century of Unemployment

The U.S. unemployment rate dropped below 2 percent during World Wars I and II but exceeded 25 percent during the Great Depression. During the period following 2007, the unemployment rate rose to about 10 percent.

Source: U.S. Department of Labor, Bureau of Labor Statistics.

Unemployed as a Percentage of the Labor Force
Year
0
5
10
15
20
25
1890
1900
1910
1920
1930
1940
1950
1960
1970
1980
1990
2000
2010
2020
Panic of 1893
(Touched off by bankruptcy of Philadelphia and Reading Railroad)
Banking Panic of 1907
(Failure of Knickerbocker Trust)
World War I
Great Depression
World War II
Korean War
Vietnam War
Persian Gulf War
Dot.Com Meltdown
Financial Meltdown
Iraq War

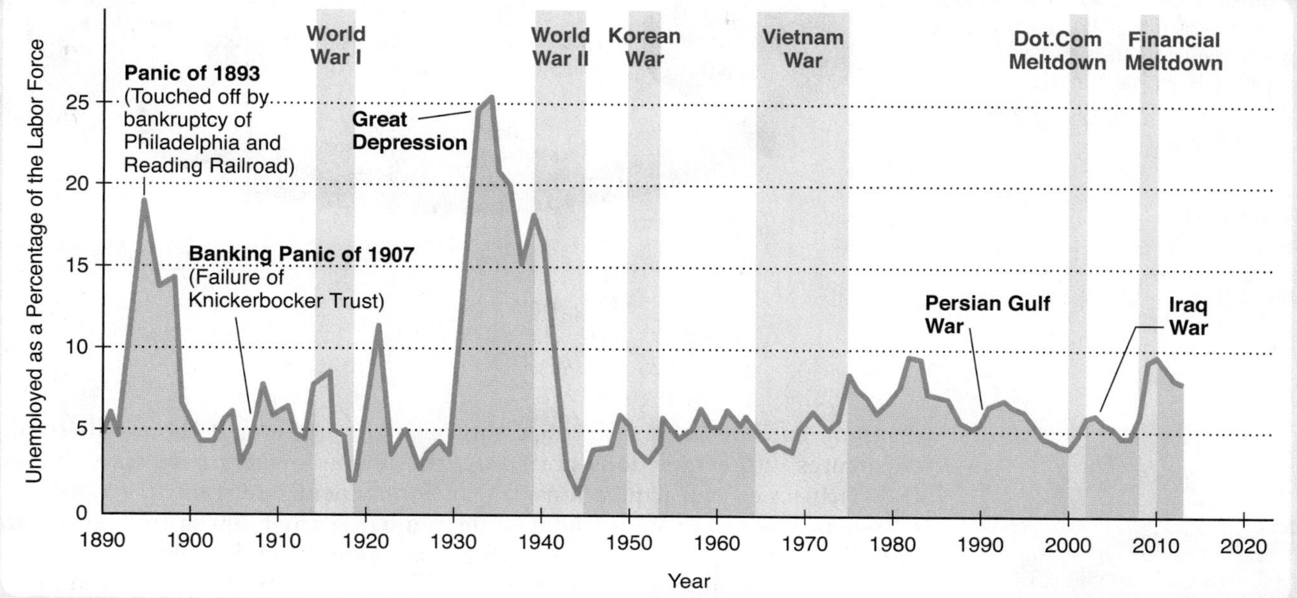

The Arithmetic Determination of Unemployment

Because there is a transition between employment and unemployment at any point in time—people are leaving jobs and others are finding jobs—there is a simple relationship between the employed and the unemployed, as can be seen in Figure 7-3 on the following page. Job departures are shown at the top of the

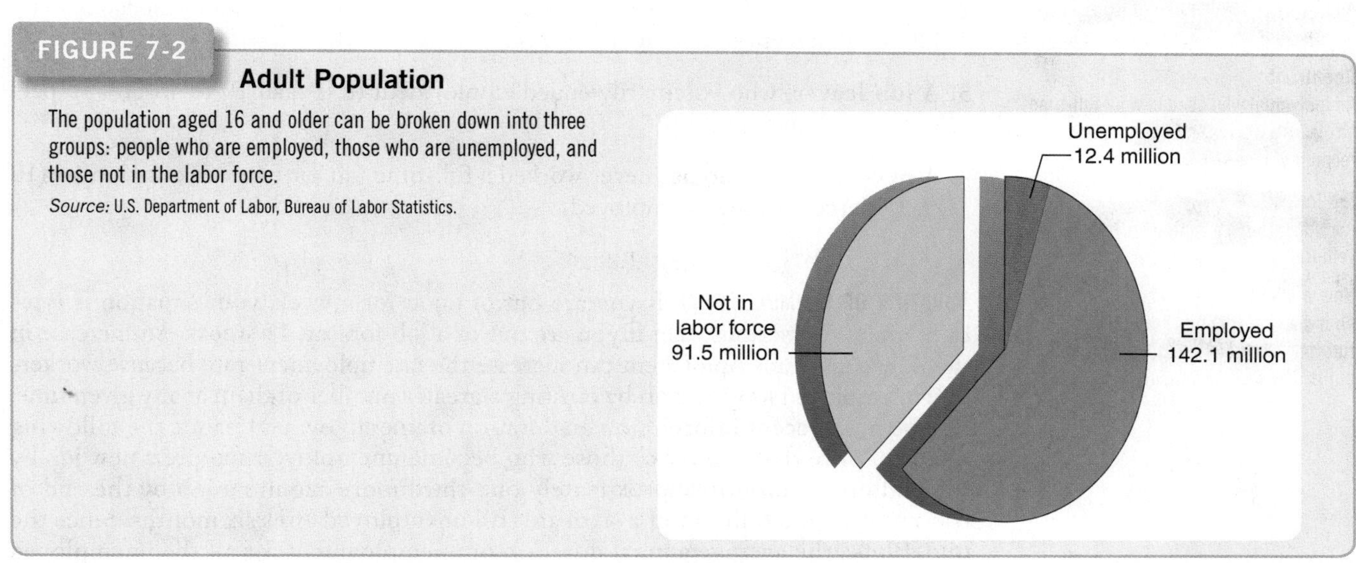

FIGURE 7-2

Adult Population

The population aged 16 and older can be broken down into three groups: people who are employed, those who are unemployed, and those not in the labor force.

Source: U.S. Department of Labor, Bureau of Labor Statistics.

Unemployed
12.4 million
Not in labor force
91.5 million
Employed
142.1 million

FIGURE 7-3

The Logic of the Unemployment Rate

Individuals who depart jobs but remain in the labor force are subtracted from the employed and added to the unemployed. When the unemployed acquire jobs, they are subtracted from the unemployed and added to the employed. In an unchanged labor force, if both flows are equal, the unemployment rate is stable. If more people depart jobs than acquire them, the unemployment rate increases, and vice versa.

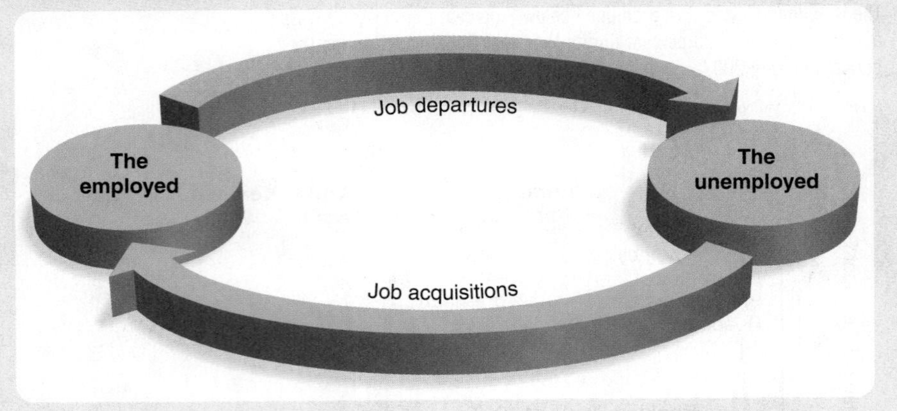

diagram, and job acquisitions are shown at the bottom. If the numbers of job departures and acquisitions are equal, the unemployment rate stays the same. If departures exceed acquisitions, the unemployment rate rises.

The number of unemployed is some number at any point in time. It is a **stock** of individuals who do not have a job but are actively looking for one. The same is true for the number of employed. The number of people departing jobs, whether voluntarily or involuntarily, is a **flow,** as is the number of people acquiring jobs.

Stock
The quantity of something, measured at a given point in time—for example, an inventory of goods or a bank account. Stocks are defined independently of time, although they are assessed at a point in time.

Flow
A quantity measured per unit of time; something that occurs over time, such as the income you make per week or per year or the number of individuals who are fired every month.

Job loser
An individual in the labor force whose employment was involuntarily terminated.

Reentrant
An individual who used to work full-time but left the labor force and has now reentered it looking for a job.

Job leaver
An individual in the labor force who quits voluntarily.

New entrant
An individual who has never held a full-time job lasting two weeks or longer but is now seeking employment.

CATEGORIES OF INDIVIDUALS WHO ARE WITHOUT WORK According to the Bureau of Labor Statistics, an unemployed individual will fall into any of four categories:

1. A **job loser,** whose employment was involuntarily terminated or who was laid off (40 to 60 percent of the unemployed)
2. A **reentrant,** who worked a full-time job before but has been out of the labor force (20 to 30 percent of the unemployed)
3. A **job leaver,** who voluntarily ended employment (less than 10 to around 15 percent of the unemployed)
4. A **new entrant,** who has never worked a full-time job for two weeks or longer (10 to 15 percent of the unemployed)

DURATION OF UNEMPLOYMENT If you are out of a job for a week, your situation is typically much less serious than if you are out of a job for, say, 14 weeks. An increase in the duration of unemployment can increase the unemployment rate because workers stay unemployed longer, thereby creating a greater number of them at any given time.

The most recent information on duration of unemployment paints the following picture: More than a third of those who become unemployed acquire a new job by the end of one month, approximately one-third more acquire a job by the end of two months, and only about a sixth are still unemployed after six months. Since the mid-1960s, the average annual duration of unemployment for all the unemployed has varied between 10 and 20 weeks. The overall average duration for the past 25 years has been at least 16 weeks.

When overall business activity goes into a downturn, the duration of unemployment tends to rise, thereby accounting for much of the increase in the estimated unemployment rate. In a sense, then, it is the increase in the *duration* of unemployment during a downturn in national economic activity that generates the bad news that concerns policymakers in Washington, D.C. Furthermore, the individuals who stay unemployed longer than six months are the ones who create pressure on Congress to "do something." What Congress does, typically, is extend and supplement unemployment benefits.

THE DISCOURAGED WORKER PHENOMENON Critics of the published unemployment rate calculated by the federal government believe that it fails to reflect the true numbers of **discouraged workers** and "hidden unemployed." Though there is no agreed-on method to measure discouraged workers, the Department of Labor defines them as people who have dropped out of the labor force and are no longer looking for a job because they believe that the job market has little to offer them. To what extent do we want to include in the measured labor force individuals who voluntarily choose not to look for work or those who take only a few minutes a day to scan the want ads and then decide that there are no jobs?

Discouraged workers
Individuals who have stopped looking for a job because they are convinced that they will not find a suitable one.

Some economists argue that people who work part-time but are willing to work full-time should be classified as "semihidden" unemployed. Estimates range as high as 6 million workers at any one time. Offsetting this factor, though, is *overemployment.* An individual working 50 or 60 hours a week is still counted as only one full-time worker. Some people hold two or three jobs but still are counted as just one employed person.

LABOR FORCE PARTICIPATION The way in which we define unemployment and membership in the labor force will affect the **labor force participation rate.** It is defined as the proportion of noninstitutionalized (i.e., not in prisons, mental institutions, etc.) working-age individuals who are employed or seeking employment.

Labor force participation rate
The percentage of noninstitutionalized working-age individuals who are employed or seeking employment.

The U.S. labor force participation rate has risen somewhat over time, from 60 percent in 1950 to almost 64 percent today. The gender composition of the U.S. labor force has changed considerably during this time. In 1950, more than 83 percent of men and fewer than 35 percent of women participated in the U.S. labor force. Today, fewer than 70 percent of men and nearly 60 percent of women are U.S. labor force participants.

What do you suppose accounts for a recent decline in the U.S. labor force participation rate?

EXAMPLE

Fewer Men Are at Work—or Even Looking for It

Since the beginning of 2008, the overall U.S. labor force participation rate has decreased by nearly 3 percentage points, to less than 64 percent. Three percentage points may not sound like very much. Nevertheless, this reduction in labor force participation represents the steepest decline within a few years' time to have taken place over the past several decades. The nearly 3-percentage-point decrease translates into a labor force reduction of more than 7 million people.

Male workers who have dropped out of the labor force account for the bulk of this reduction. During the 2008–2009 recession, the unemployment rates of both men and women shot up, but occupations dominated by male workers, such as construction and manufacturing, experienced the largest job losses. Consequently, the differential between male and female unemployment rates rose by nearly 3 percentage points. Many of the men who lost jobs did not find new positions, became discouraged workers, and departed from the labor force. Thus, the primary element accounting for the recent drop in U.S. labor force participation is the transformation, since 2008, of millions of male employees into discouraged workers.

FOR CRITICAL THINKING

What would happen to the overall U.S. labor force participation rate if the construction and manufacturing industries were to experience significant upswings?

QUICK QUIZ See page 160 for the answers. Review concepts from this section in MyEconLab.

__________ persons are adults who are willing and able to work and are actively looking for a job but have not found one. The unemployment rate is computed by dividing the number of unemployed by the total __________ __________, which is equal to those who are employed plus those who are unemployed.

The unemployed are classified as __________ __________, __________, __________ __________, and __________ __________ to the labor force. The flow of people departing jobs and people acquiring jobs determines the stock of the unemployed as well as the stock of the employed.

The duration of unemployment affects the unemployment rate. If the duration of unemployment increases, the measured unemployment rate will __________, even though the number of unemployed workers may remain the same.

Whereas overall labor force participation on net has risen only modestly since World War II, there has been a major increase in __________ labor force participation.

The Major Types of Unemployment

Unemployment has been categorized into four basic types: frictional, structural, cyclical, and seasonal.

Frictional Unemployment

Frictional unemployment
Unemployment due to the fact that workers must search for appropriate job offers. This activity takes time, and so they remain temporarily unemployed.

Of the more than 154 million people in the labor force, more than 50 million will either change jobs or take new jobs during the year. In the process, in excess of 22 million persons will report themselves unemployed at one time or another each year. This continuous flow of individuals from job to job and in and out of employment is called **frictional unemployment.** There will always be some frictional unemployment as resources are redirected in the economy, because job-hunting costs are never zero, and workers never have full information about available jobs. To eliminate frictional unemployment, we would have to prevent workers from leaving their present jobs until they had already lined up other jobs at which they would start working immediately. And we would have to guarantee first-time job seekers a job *before* they started looking.

Structural Unemployment

Structural unemployment
Unemployment of workers over lengthy intervals resulting from skill mismatches with position requirements of employers and from fewer jobs being offered by employers constrained by governmental business regulations and labor market policies.

Structural changes in our economy cause some workers to become unemployed for very long periods of time because they cannot find jobs that use their particular skills. This is called **structural unemployment.** Structural unemployment is not caused by general business fluctuations, although business fluctuations may affect it. And unlike frictional unemployment, structural unemployment is not related to the movement of workers from low-paying to high-paying jobs.

At one time, economists thought about structural unemployment only from the perspective of workers. The concept applied to workers who did not have the ability, training, and skills necessary to obtain available jobs. Today, it still encompasses these workers. In addition, however, economists increasingly look at structural unemployment from the viewpoint of employers, many of whom face government mandates requiring them to take such steps as providing funds for social insurance programs for their employees and announcing plant closings months or even years in advance.

There is now considerable evidence that government labor market policies influence how many job positions businesses wish to create, thereby affecting structural unemployment. In the United States, many businesses appear to have adjusted to these policies by hiring more "temporary workers" or establishing short-term contracts with "private consultants." Such measures may have increased the extent of U.S. structural unemployment in recent years.

How may a federal law be increasing structural unemployment?

POLICY EXAMPLE

Warning: WARN May Boost the Natural Unemployment Rate

In 1989, Congress passed the Worker Adjustment and Retraining Notification (WARN) Act. The law required firms to notify and provide special benefits to employees in advance of what the legislation defines as a "mass layoff" involving fifty or more full-time workers constituting at least one-third of a company's staff. The law rarely applied until the 2008–2009 recession. When their sales plummeted during that recession, a number of companies rapidly laid off large numbers of workers to cut costs in an attempt to remain in business. Job losers alleged violations of WARN and sought extra termination payments and benefits.

As economic activity recovered somewhat but remained dampened in the years following the recession, managers found out that WARN-related caseloads in the courts had tripled. Those managers worried that if they were to hire workers they might later have to lay off, WARN might apply. This concern discouraged managers from hiring back as many workers as they might have otherwise. As a consequence, unemployment remained high even as companies' prospects improved. Thus, the WARN law undoubtedly contributed to greater structural unemployment.

FOR CRITICAL THINKING

How has structural unemployment been affected by the actions of several state governments in requiring firms to grant longer paid "family leaves"?

Cyclical Unemployment

Cyclical unemployment is related to business fluctuations. It is defined as unemployment associated with changes in business conditions—primarily recessions and depressions. The way to lessen cyclical unemployment would be to reduce the intensity, duration, and frequency of downturns of business activity. Economic policymakers attempt, through their policies, to reduce cyclical unemployment by keeping business activity on an even keel.

Cyclical unemployment
Unemployment resulting from business recessions that occur when aggregate (total) demand is insufficient to create full employment.

YOU ARE THERE

To consider how difficulties in finding workers with required skills might contribute to unemployment, take a look at **Struggling to Hire with the Unemployment Rate above 9 Percent** on page 155.

Seasonal Unemployment

Seasonal unemployment comes and goes with seasons of the year in which the demand for particular jobs rises and falls. In northern states, construction workers can often work only during the warmer months. They are seasonally unemployed during the winter. Summer resort workers can usually get jobs in resorts only during the summer season. They, too, sometimes become seasonally unemployed during the winter. The opposite is sometimes true for ski resort workers.

The unemployment rate that the Bureau of Labor Statistics releases each month is "seasonally adjusted." This means that the reported unemployment rate has been adjusted to remove the effects of variations in seasonal unemployment. Thus, the unemployment rate that the media dutifully announce reflects only the sum of frictional unemployment, structural unemployment, and cyclical unemployment.

Seasonal unemployment
Unemployment resulting from the seasonal pattern of work in specific industries. It is usually due to seasonal fluctuations in demand or to changing weather conditions that render work difficult, if not impossible, as in the agriculture, construction, and tourist industries.

Full Employment and the Natural Rate of Unemployment

Does full employment mean that everybody has a job? Certainly not, for not everyone is looking for a job—full-time students and full-time homemakers, for example, are not. Is it always possible for everyone who is looking for a job to find one? No, because transaction costs (see Chapter 4) in the labor market are not zero. Transaction costs are those associated with any activity whose goal is to enter into, carry out, or terminate contracts. In the labor market, these costs involve time spent looking for a job, being interviewed, negotiating the terms of employment, and the like.

Full Employment

Full employment
An arbitrary level of unemployment that corresponds to "normal" friction in the labor market. In 1986, a 6.5 percent rate of unemployment was considered full employment. Today it is somewhat higher.

We will always have some frictional unemployment as individuals move in and out of the labor force, seek higher-paying jobs, and move to different parts of the country. **Full employment** is therefore a concept that implies some sort of balance or equilibrium in an ever-shifting labor market. Of course, this general notion of full employment must somehow be put into numbers so that economists and others can determine whether the economy has reached the full-employment point.

The Natural Rate of Unemployment

Natural rate of unemployment
The rate of unemployment that is estimated to prevail in long-run macroeconomic equilibrium, when all workers and employers have fully adjusted to any changes in the economy.

In trying to assess when a situation of balance has been attained in the labor market, economists estimate the **natural rate of unemployment,** the rate that is expected to prevail in the long run once all workers and employers have fully adjusted to any changes in the economy. If correctly estimated, the natural rate of unemployment should not include cyclical unemployment. When seasonally adjusted, the natural unemployment rate should include only frictional and structural unemployment.

A long-standing difficulty, however, has been a lack of agreement about how to estimate the natural unemployment rate. Until the late 2000s, most economists, including those with the president's Council of Economic Advisers and those at the Federal Reserve, had concluded that the natural unemployment rate was slightly above 5 percent.

Since the 2008–2009 recession, the actual unemployment rate has remained considerably above 5 percent. This fact suggests that perhaps the natural rate of unemployment has increased because of a rise in structural unemployment. Some economists propose that the collapse of the U.S. housing industry precipitated this rise. The housing meltdown, these economists suggest, left people possessing skills that were poorly matched to the requirements of jobs other than those in construction, housing finance, and real estate. In contrast, other economists contend that increases in the scope of government regulations and taxes have raised the costs confronted by firms when they contemplate hiring job applicants. Government policies, these economists argue, are to blame for a higher natural unemployment rate.

Of course, both explanations together could help to account for an upswing in structural unemployment. What has yet to be determined by economists is exactly how much higher than 5 percent the natural unemployment rate now may be. Some estimates indicate that it may be at least 7 percent.

WHAT IF... city governments passed more laws to benefit all employees?

Beginning in 2013, a new health care law went into effect that most businesses predict will raise their costs of providing health insurance coverage to employees. In addition, new federal laws and court interpretations of existing laws are increasing the number of days off that firms are obliged to grant employees who are parents of a new child. Many municipalities, such as Seattle, Washington, have even passed ordinances requiring companies to provide more paid "sick days" each year. These and many other laws reduce the incentive for companies to hire workers and thereby decrease employment. As a result, the proliferation of such laws drives up structural unemployment and boosts the natural rate of unemployment.

QUICK QUIZ

See page 160 for the answers. Review concepts from this section in MyEconLab.

__________ **unemployment** occurs because of transaction costs in the labor market. For example, workers do not have full information about vacancies and must search for jobs.

__________ **unemployment** occurs when there is a poor match of workers' skills and abilities with available jobs, perhaps because workers lack appropriate training or government labor rules reduce firms' willingness to hire.

The levels of frictional and structural unemployment are used in part to determine our (somewhat arbitrary) measurement of the __________ rate of unemployment.

Inflation and Deflation

During World War II, you could buy bread for 8 to 10 cents a loaf and have milk delivered fresh to your door for about 25 cents a half gallon. The average price of a new car was less than $700, and the average house cost less than $3,000. Today, bread, milk, cars, and houses all cost more—a lot more. Prices are about 15 times what they were in 1940. Clearly, this country has experienced quite a bit of *inflation* since then. We define **inflation** as an upward movement in the average level of prices. The opposite of inflation is **deflation,** defined as a downward movement in the average level of prices. Notice that these definitions depend on the *average* level of prices. This means that even during a period of inflation, some prices can be falling if other prices are rising at a faster rate. The prices of electronic equipment have dropped dramatically since the 1960s, even though there has been general inflation.

Inflation
A sustained increase in the average of all prices of goods and services in an economy.

Deflation
A sustained decrease in the average of all prices of goods and services in an economy.

Inflation and the Purchasing Power of Money

By definition, the value of a dollar does not stay constant when there is inflation. The value of money is usually talked about in terms of **purchasing power.** A dollar's purchasing power is the real goods and services that it can buy. Consequently, another way of defining inflation is as a decline in the purchasing power of money. The faster the rate of inflation, the greater the rate of decline in the purchasing power of money.

Purchasing power
The value of money for buying goods and services. If your money income stays the same but the price of one good that you are buying goes up, your effective purchasing power falls.

One way to think about inflation and the purchasing power of money is to discuss dollar values in terms of *nominal* versus *real* values. The nominal value of anything is simply its price expressed in today's dollars. In contrast, the real value of anything is its value expressed in purchasing power, which varies with the overall price level. Let's say that you received a $100 bill from your grandparents this year. One year from now, the nominal value of that bill will still be $100. The real value will depend on what the purchasing power of money is after one year's worth of inflation. Obviously, if there is inflation during the year, the real value of that $100 bill will have diminished. For example, if you keep the $100 bill in your pocket for a year during which the rate of inflation is 3 percent, at the end of the year you will have to come up with $3 more to buy the same amount of goods and services that the $100 bill can purchase today.

To discuss what has happened to prices here and in other countries, we have to know how to measure inflation.

Measuring the Rate of Inflation

How can we measure the rate of inflation? It is easy to determine how much the price of an individual commodity has risen: If last year a light bulb cost 50 cents, and this year it costs 75 cents, there has been a 50 percent rise in the price of that light bulb over a one-year period. We can express the change in the individual light bulb price in one of several ways: The price has gone up 25 cents. The price is one and a half (1.5) times as high. The price has risen by 50 percent. An *index number* of this price rise is simply the second way (1.5) multiplied by 100, meaning that the index today would stand at 150. We multiply by 100 to eliminate decimals because it is easier to think in terms of percentage changes using whole numbers. This is the standard convention adopted for convenience in dealing with index numbers or price levels.

Computing a Price Index

The measurement problem becomes more complicated when it involves a large number of goods, especially if some prices have risen faster than others and some have even fallen. What we have to do is pick a representative bundle, a so-called market basket, of goods and compare the cost of that market basket of goods over time. When we do this, we obtain a **price index,** which is defined as the cost of a market basket of goods today, expressed as a percentage of the cost of that identical market basket of goods in some starting year, known as the **base year.**

Price index
The cost of today's market basket of goods expressed as a percentage of the cost of the same market basket during a base year.

Base year
The year that is chosen as the point of reference for comparison of prices in other years.

$$\text{Price index} = \frac{\text{cost of market basket today}}{\text{cost of market basket in base year}} \times 100$$

TABLE 7-1

Calculating a Price Index for a Two-Good Market Basket

In this simplified example, there are only two goods—corn and digital devices. The quantities and base-year prices are given in columns 2 and 3. The 2005 cost of the market basket, calculated in column 4, comes to $1,400. The 2015 prices are given in column 5. The cost of the market basket in 2015, calculated in column 6, is $1,650. The price index for 2015 compared with 2005 is 117.86.

(1) Commodity	(2) Market Basket Quantity	(3) 2005 Price per Unit	(4) Cost of Market Basket in 2005	(5) 2015 Price per Unit	(6) Cost of Market Basket in 2015
Corn	100 bushels	$ 4	$ 400	$ 8	$ 800
Digital devices	2	500	1,000	425	850
Totals			**$1,400**		**$1,650**

$$\textbf{Price index} = \frac{\text{cost of market basket in 2015}}{\text{cost of market basket in base year 2005}} \times 100 = \frac{\$1{,}650}{\$1{,}400} \times 100 = 117.86$$

In the base year, the price index will always be 100, because the year in the numerator and in the denominator of the fraction is the same. Therefore, the fraction equals 1, and when we multiply it by 100, we get 100. A simple numerical example is given in Table 7-1 above. In the table, there are only two goods in the market basket—corn and digital devices. The *quantities* in the basket are the same in the base year, 2005, and the current year, 2015. Only the *prices* change. Such a *fixed-quantity* price index is the easiest to compute because the statistician need only look at prices of goods and services sold every year rather than observing how much of these goods and services consumers actually purchase each year.

Consumer Price Index (CPI)
A statistical measure of a weighted average of prices of a specified set of goods and services purchased by typical consumers in urban areas.

Producer Price Index (PPI)
A statistical measure of a weighted average of prices of goods and services that firms produce and sell.

GDP deflator
A price index measuring the changes in prices of all new goods and services produced in the economy.

Personal Consumption Expenditure (PCE) Index
A statistical measure of average prices that uses annually updated weights based on surveys of consumer spending.

REAL-WORLD PRICE INDEXES Government statisticians calculate a number of price indexes. The most often quoted are the **Consumer Price Index (CPI),** the **Producer Price Index (PPI),** the **GDP deflator,** and the **Personal Consumption Expenditure (PCE) Index.** The CPI attempts to measure changes only in the level of prices of goods and services purchased by consumers. The PPI attempts to show what has happened to the average price of goods and services produced and sold by a typical firm. (There are also *wholesale price indexes* that track the price level for commodities that firms purchase from other firms.) The GDP deflator is the most general indicator of inflation because it measures changes in the level of prices of all new goods and services produced in the economy. The PCE Index measures average prices using weights from surveys of consumer spending.

THE CPI The Bureau of Labor Statistics (BLS) has the task of identifying a market basket of goods and services of the typical consumer. Today, the BLS uses the time period 1982–1984 as its base of market prices. The BLS has indicated an intention to change the base to 1993–1995 but has yet to do so. It has, though, updated the expenditure weights for its market basket of goods to reflect consumer spending patterns in 2001–2002. All CPI numbers since February 1998 reflect these expenditure weights.

Economists have known for years that there are possible problems in the CPI's market basket. Specifically, the BLS has been unable to account for the way consumers substitute less expensive items for higher-priced items. The reason is that the CPI is a fixed-quantity price index, meaning that the BLS implicitly ignores changes in consumption patterns that occur between years in which it revises the index. Until recently, the BLS has also been unable to take quality changes into account as they occur. Now, though, it is subtracting from certain list prices estimated effects of qualitative improvements and adding to other list prices to account for deteriorations in quality. An additional flaw is that the CPI usually ignores successful new products until long after they have been introduced. Despite these flaws, the CPI is widely followed because its level is calculated and published monthly.

Within which group of products are prices rising with sufficient speed to account for a significant portion of China's annual rate of consumer price inflation?

INTERNATIONAL EXAMPLE

Why the Value of China's Consumer Price Index Is Rising

In China, food's weight in the CPI is slightly below 35 percent. Food prices have been rising so rapidly, though, that the overall rate of increase in food prices per year has been contributing to 75 percent of China's officially measured annual rate of CPI inflation. Consequently, during a recent 12-month period in which the nation's measured rate of CPI inflation was 6.4 percent, the rate of increase in food prices accounted for 4.8 percentage points of that annual rate of inflation.

FOR CRITICAL THINKING

Food's weight in the U.S. CPI is about 16 percent. If U.S. food prices rose as rapidly as Chinese food prices, would the U.S. CPI increase as much as the CPI in China? Explain.

THE PPI There are a number of Producer Price Indexes, including one for foodstuffs, another for intermediate goods (goods used in the production of other goods), and one for finished goods. Most of the producer prices included are in mining, manufacturing, and agriculture. The PPIs can be considered general-purpose indexes for nonretail markets.

Although in the long run the various PPIs and the CPI generally show the same rate of inflation, that is not the case in the short run. Most often the PPIs increase before the CPI because it takes time for producer price increases to show up in the prices that consumers pay for final products. Changes in the PPIs are watched closely as a hint that CPI inflation is going to increase or decrease.

THE GDP DEFLATOR The broadest price index reported in the United States is the GDP deflator, where GDP stands for gross domestic product, or annual total national income. Unlike the CPI and the PPIs, the GDP deflator is *not* based on a fixed market basket of goods and services. The basket is allowed to change with people's consumption and investment patterns. In this sense, the changes in the GDP deflator reflect both price changes and the public's market responses to those price changes. Why? Because new expenditure patterns are allowed to show up in the GDP deflator as people respond to changing prices.

Go to **www.econtoday.com/chap07** to obtain information about inflation and unemployment in other countries from the International Monetary Fund. Click on "World Economic Outlook Databases."

THE PCE INDEX Another price index that takes into account changing expenditure patterns is the Personal Consumption Expenditure (PCE) Index. The Bureau of Economic Analysis, an agency of the U.S. Department of Commerce, uses continuously updated annual surveys of consumer purchases to construct the weights for the PCE Index. Thus, an advantage of the PCE Index is that weights in the index are updated every year. The Federal Reserve has used the rate of change in the PCE Index as its primary inflation indicator because Fed officials believe that the updated weights in the PCE Index make it more accurate than the CPI as a measure of consumer price changes. Nevertheless, the CPI remains the most widely reported price index, and the U.S. government continues to use the CPI to adjust the value of Social Security benefits to account for inflation.

HISTORICAL CHANGES IN THE CPI Between World War II and the early 1980s, the Consumer Price Index showed a fairly dramatic trend upward. Figure 7-4 on the following page shows the annual rate of change in the CPI since 1860. Prior to World War II, there were numerous periods of deflation interspersed with periods of inflation. Persistent year-in and year-out inflation seems to be a post–World War II phenomenon, at least in this country. As far back as before the American Revolution, prices used to rise during war periods but then would fall back toward prewar levels afterward. This occurred after the Revolutionary War, the War of 1812, the Civil War, and to a lesser extent World War I. Consequently, the overall price level in 1940 wasn't much different from 150 years earlier.

MyEconLab Real-time data

FIGURE 7-4

Inflation and Deflation in U.S. History

For 80 years after the Civil War, the United States experienced alternating inflation and deflation. Here we show them as reflected by changes in the Consumer Price Index. Since World War II, the periods of inflation have not been followed by periods of deflation. Even during peacetime, the price index has continued to rise. The shaded areas represent wartime.

Source: U.S. Department of Labor, Bureau of Labor Statistics.

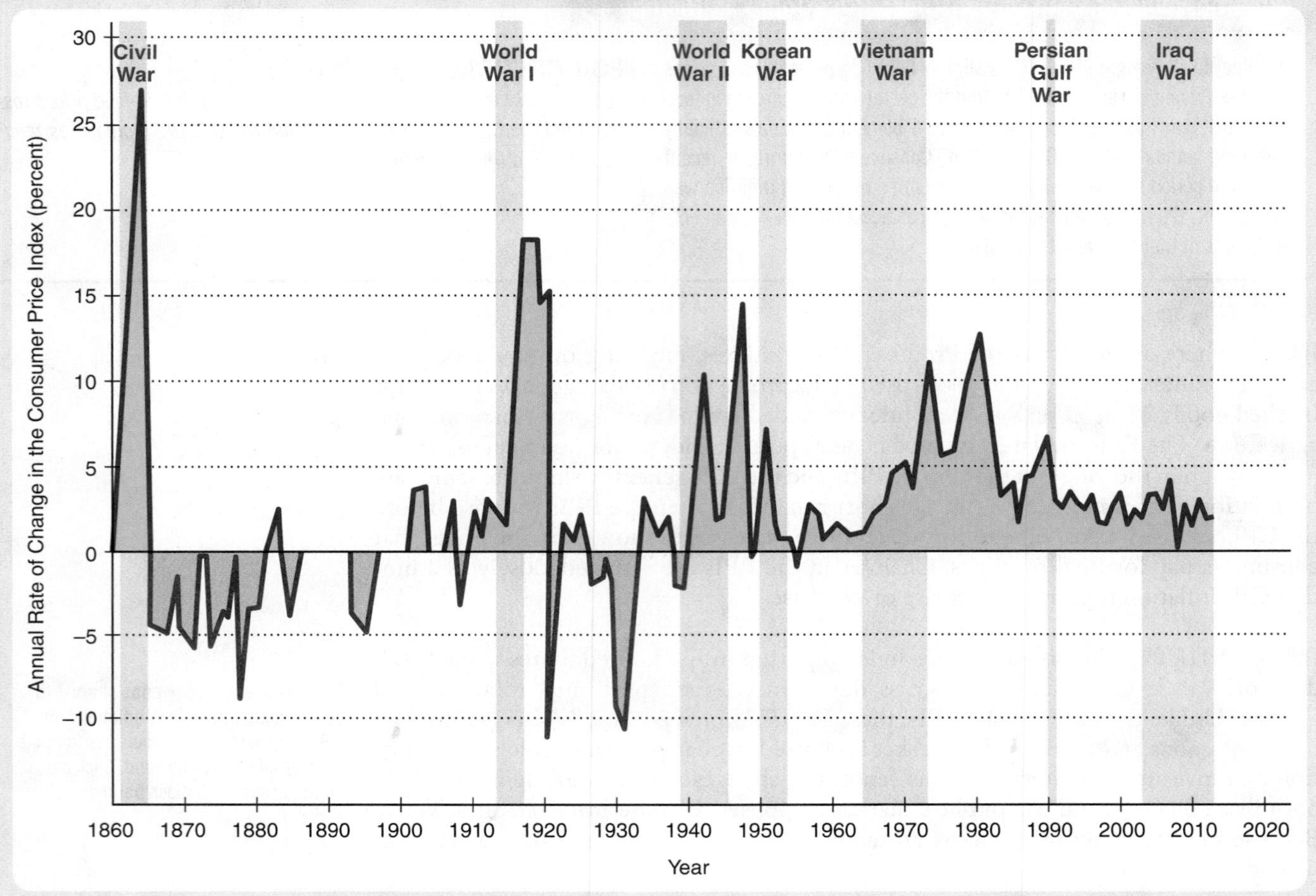

Why is Argentina's government imposing substantial fines on private firms that release their own independent estimates of the nation's inflation rate?

INTERNATIONAL POLICY EXAMPLE

Argentina Penalizes Inflation Estimates That Are "Too High"

Argentina's national statistics agency, Indec, releases official government measures of consumer price inflation. Many observers question the reliability of this agency's tabulations of price indexes and inflation rates. These observers give more credence to inflation estimates tabulated and released by private economic consulting firms in Argentina.

Recently, private firms such as Econviews, Finsoport, and GRA Consultoras have released estimates of annual inflation rates for Argentina that have been more than twice as high as Indec's. Argentina's government has accused these companies of engaging in activities that "lack scientific vigor" and that "undermine confidence in the nation's economy." The government has imposed fines exceeding $120,000 for publicly releasing inflation estimates that differ substantially from those of Indec. Today, most private companies in Argentina that independently tabulate price index and inflation data will provide them only to private customers at a price—and under the condition of confidentiality.

FOR CRITICAL THINKING

Argentina's government offers extra payments based on Indec's inflation tabulations to induce savers to buy its bonds. Could this explain its concern about competing private inflation estimates? Explain.

QUICK QUIZ See page 160 for the answers. Review concepts from this section in MyEconLab.

Once we pick a market basket of goods, we can construct a **price index** that compares the cost of that market basket today with the cost of the same market basket in a __________ year.

The __________ __________ Index is the most often used price index in the United States. The **Producer Price Index (PPI)** is also widely mentioned.

The __________ __________ measures what is happening to the average price level of *all* new, domestically produced final goods and services in our economy.

The __________ __________ __________ Index uses annually updated weights from consumer spending surveys to measure average prices faced by consumers.

Anticipated versus Unanticipated Inflation

To determine who is hurt by inflation and what the effects of inflation are in general, we have to distinguish between anticipated and unanticipated inflation. We will see that the effects on individuals and the economy are vastly different, depending on which type of inflation exists.

Anticipated inflation is the rate of inflation that most individuals believe will occur. If the rate of inflation this year turns out to be 5 percent, and that's about what most people thought it was going to be, we are in a situation of fully anticipated inflation.

Anticipated inflation
The inflation rate that we believe will occur. When it does occur, we are in a situation of fully anticipated inflation.

Unanticipated inflation is inflation that comes as a surprise to individuals in the economy. For example, if the inflation rate in a particular year turns out to be 10 percent when, on average, people thought it was going to be 3 percent, there was unanticipated inflation—inflation greater than anticipated.

Unanticipated inflation
Inflation at a rate that comes as a surprise, either higher or lower than the rate anticipated.

Some of the problems caused by inflation arise when it is unanticipated, because then many people are unable to protect themselves from its ravages. Keeping the distinction between anticipated and unanticipated inflation in mind, we can easily see the relationship between inflation and interest rates.

Inflation and Interest Rates

Let's start in a hypothetical world in which there is no inflation and anticipated inflation is zero. In that world, you may be able to borrow funds—to buy a house or a car, for example—at a **nominal rate of interest** of, say, 6 percent. If you borrow the funds to purchase a house or a car and your anticipation of inflation turns out to be accurate, neither you nor the lender will have been fooled. Each dollar you pay back in the years to come will be just as valuable in terms of purchasing power as the dollar that you borrowed.

Nominal rate of interest
The market rate of interest observed in contracts expressed in today's dollars.

What you ordinarily want to know when you borrow is the *real* rate of interest that you will have to pay. The **real rate of interest** is defined as the nominal rate of interest minus the anticipated rate of inflation. In effect, we can say that the nominal rate of interest is equal to the real rate of interest plus an *inflationary premium* to take account of anticipated inflation. That inflationary premium covers depreciation in the purchasing power of the dollars repaid by borrowers. (Whenever there are relatively high rates of anticipated inflation, we must add an additional factor to the inflationary premium—the product of the real rate of interest times the anticipated rate of inflation. Usually, this last term is omitted because the anticipated rate of inflation is not high enough to make much of a difference.)

Real rate of interest
The nominal rate of interest minus the anticipated rate of inflation.

Does Inflation Necessarily Hurt Everyone?

Most people think that inflation is bad. After all, inflation means higher prices, and when we have to pay higher prices, are we not necessarily worse off? The truth is that inflation affects different people differently. Its effects also depend on whether it is anticipated or unanticipated.

UNANTICIPATED INFLATION: CREDITORS LOSE AND DEBTORS GAIN In most situations, unanticipated inflation benefits borrowers because the nominal interest rate they are being charged does not fully compensate creditors for the inflation that actually occurred. In other words, the lender did not anticipate inflation correctly. Whenever inflation rates are underestimated for the life of a loan, creditors lose and debtors gain. Periods of considerable unanticipated (higher than anticipated) inflation occurred in the late 1960s and all of the 1970s. During those years, creditors lost and debtors gained.

PROTECTING AGAINST INFLATION Lenders attempt to protect themselves against inflation by raising nominal interest rates to reflect anticipated inflation. Adjustable-rate mortgages in fact do just that: The interest rate varies according to what happens to interest rates in the economy. Workers can protect themselves from inflation by obtaining **cost-of-living adjustments (COLAs),** which are automatic increases in wage rates to take account of increases in the price level.

Cost-of-living adjustments (COLAs)
Clauses in contracts that allow for increases in specified nominal values to take account of changes in the cost of living.

To the extent that you hold non-interest-bearing cash, you will lose because of inflation. If you have put $100 in a mattress and the inflation rate is 5 percent for the year, you will have lost 5 percent of the purchasing power of that $100. If you have your funds in a non-interest-bearing checking account, you will suffer the same fate. Individuals attempt to reduce the cost of holding cash by putting it into interest-bearing accounts, some of which pay nominal rates of interest that reflect anticipated inflation.

THE RESOURCE COST OF INFLATION Some economists believe that the main cost of inflation is the opportunity cost of resources used to protect against distortions that inflation introduces as firms attempt to plan for the long run. Individuals have to spend time and resources to figure out ways to adjust their behavior in case inflation is different from what it has been in the past. That may mean spending a longer time working out more complicated contracts for employment, for purchases of goods in the future, and for purchases of raw materials to be delivered later.

Inflation requires that price lists be changed. This is called the **repricing,** or **menu, cost of inflation.** The higher the rate of inflation, the higher the repricing cost of inflation, because prices must be changed more often within a given period of time.

Repricing, or menu, cost of inflation
The cost associated with recalculating prices and printing new price lists when there is inflation.

QUICK QUIZ See page 160 for the answers. Review concepts from this section in MyEconLab.

Whenever inflation is __________ than anticipated, creditors lose and debtors gain. Whenever the rate of inflation is __________ than anticipated, creditors gain and debtors lose.

Holders of cash lose during periods of inflation because the __________ __________ of their cash depreciates at the rate of inflation.

Households and businesses spend resources in attempting to protect themselves against the prospect of inflation, thus imposing a __________ cost on the economy.

Changing Inflation and Unemployment: Business Fluctuations

Some years unemployment goes up, and some years it goes down. Some years there is a lot of inflation, and other years there isn't. We have fluctuations in all aspects of our macroeconomy. The ups and downs in economywide economic activity are sometimes called **business fluctuations.** When business fluctuations are positive, they are called **expansions**—speedups in the pace of national economic activity. The opposite of an expansion is a **contraction,** which is a slowdown in the pace of national economic activity. The top of an expansion is usually called its *peak*, and the bottom of a contraction is usually called its *trough*. Business fluctuations used to be called *business cycles*, but that term no longer seems appropriate because *cycle* implies regular or automatic recurrence, and we have never had automatic recurrent fluctuations in general business and

Business fluctuations
The ups and downs in business activity throughout the economy.

Expansion
A business fluctuation in which the pace of national economic activity is speeding up.

Contraction
A business fluctuation during which the pace of national economic activity is slowing down.

FIGURE 7-5

The Idealized Course of Business Fluctuations

A hypothetical business cycle would go from peak to trough and back again in a regular cycle. Real-world business cycles are not as regular as this hypothetical cycle.

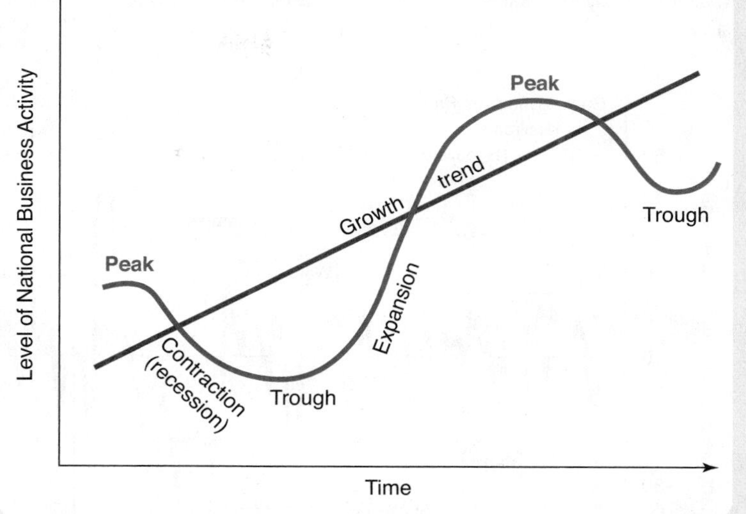

economic activity. What we have had are contractions and expansions that vary greatly in length. For example, the 10 post–World War II expansions have averaged 57 months, but three of those exceeded 90 months, and two lasted less than 25 months.

If the contractionary phase of business fluctuations becomes severe enough, we call it a **recession.** An extremely severe recession is called a **depression.** Typically, at the beginning of a recession, there is a marked increase in the rate of unemployment, and the duration of unemployment increases. In addition, people's incomes start to decline. In times of expansion, the opposite occurs.

Recession
A period of time during which the rate of growth of business activity is consistently less than its long-term trend or is negative.

Depression
An extremely severe recession.

In Figure 7-5 above, you see that typical business fluctuations occur around a growth trend in overall national business activity shown as a straight upward-sloping line. Starting out at a peak, the economy goes into a contraction (recession). Then an expansion starts that moves up to its peak, higher than the last one, and the sequence starts over again.

A Historical Picture of Business Activity in the United States

Figure 7-6 on the following page traces changes in U.S. business activity from 1880 to the present. Note that the long-term trend line is shown as horizontal, so all changes in business activity focus around that trend line. Major changes in business activity in the United States occurred during the Great Depression, World War II, and, most recently, the sharp recession of the late 2000s. Note that none of the actual business fluctuations in Figure 7-6, exactly mirror the idealized course of a business fluctuation shown in Figure 7-5 above.

Go to www.econtoday.com/chap07 to learn how economists at the National Bureau of Economic Research formally determine when a recession started.

Explaining Business Fluctuations: External Shocks

As you might imagine, because changes in national business activity affect everyone, economists for decades have attempted to understand and explain business fluctuations. For years, one of the most obvious explanations has been external events that tend to disrupt the economy. In many of the graphs in this chapter, you have seen that World War II was a critical point in this nation's economic history. A war is certainly an external shock—something that originates outside our economy.

In trying to help account for shocks to economic activity that may induce business fluctuations and thereby make fluctuations easier to predict, the U.S. Department of Commerce and private firms and organizations tabulate indexes (weighted averages) of

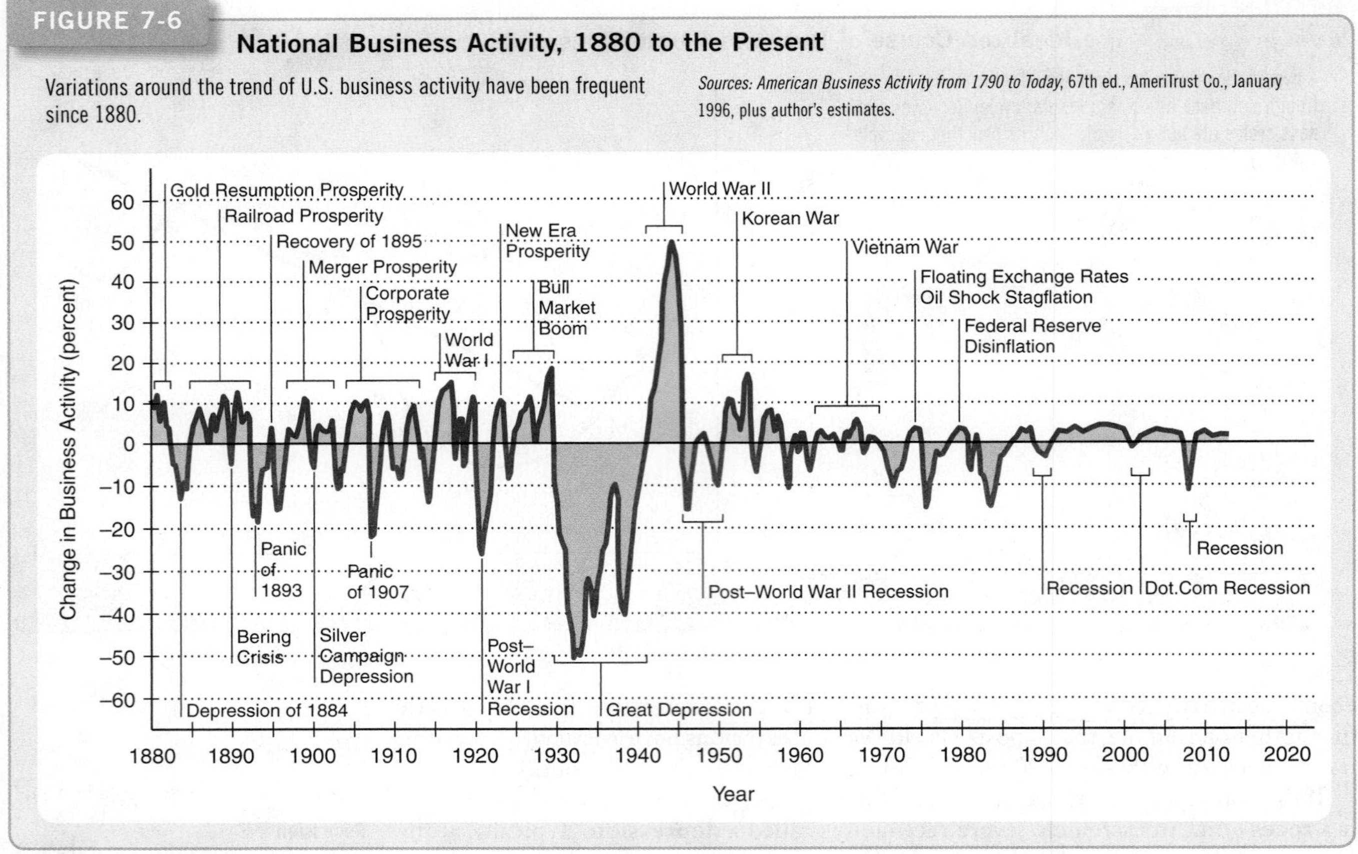

FIGURE 7-6

National Business Activity, 1880 to the Present

Variations around the trend of U.S. business activity have been frequent since 1880.

Sources: American Business Activity from 1790 to Today, 67th ed., AmeriTrust Co., January 1996, plus author's estimates.

Leading indicators
Events that have been found to occur before changes in business activity.`

leading indicators. These are events that economists have noticed typically occur *before* changes in business activity. For example, economic downturns often follow such events as a reduction in the average workweek, an increase in unemployment insurance claims, a decrease in the prices of raw materials, or a drop in the quantity of money in circulation.

What new measure are economists at the Bank of England thinking of adding to their list of leading economic indicators?

INTERNATIONAL POLICY EXAMPLE

Internet Search Activity as a Leading Indicator

Economists at the Bank of England are studying the volume of Internet searches as a leading indicator of economic activity. The economists have found that Web search activity possesses appealing leading-indicator properties. First, Internet search data are readily available on a daily basis. Second, nearly 60 percent of the United Kingdom's adult population now regularly engages in Web searches every day. Third, evidence is increasing that the volume of online searches is related to key measures of economic activity, such as transactions in housing and labor markets. Thus, the Bank of England is already employing data on Internet search volumes as leading indicators of activity in each of these sectors of the British economy. Its economists are experimenting with using these data as overall economic indicators.

FOR CRITICAL THINKING

Why are Bank of England economists seeking to determine whether the number of searches is closely related to purchases of goods and services from businesses?

To better understand the role of shocks in influencing business fluctuations, we need a theory of why national economic activity changes. The remainder of the macro chapters in this book develop the models that will help you understand the ups and downs of our business fluctuations.

QUICK QUIZ See page 160 for the answers. Review concepts from this section in MyEconLab.

The ups and downs in economywide business activity are called __________ __________, which consist of **expansions** and **contractions** in overall business activity.

The lowest point of a contraction is called the __________. The highest point of an expansion is called the __________.

A __________ is a downturn in business activity for some length of time.

One possible explanation for business fluctuations relates to __________ __________, such as wars, dramatic increases in the prices of raw materials, and earthquakes, floods, and droughts.

YOU ARE THERE

Struggling to Hire with the Unemployment Rate above 8 Percent

Jack Kelly, chief executive officer of Hamill Manufacturing, is looking for people to hire, as the company seeks to replace older skilled workers who are choosing to retire. Even though millions of U.S. residents are unemployed and seeking work, Kelly is having trouble filling a handful of open positions. Kelly has received many applications. So far, however, none of the applicants possesses the skills required to operate and repair computer-controlled metal-shaping equipment.

Key skills sought by Kelly are not far beyond those that students can learn in high school courses in trigonometry and science. Kelly's problem is that most students who take such courses in high school go on to college and never consider a career as a skilled manufacturing laborer earning as much as $80,000 per year. Among the non-college-bound high school graduates who might consider such a position, it is rare to find one who has learned enough math and science even to begin to know how to set up and direct the firm's machinery. Thus, although thousands of people are unemployed in the area near Hamill's manufacturing facilities, Kelly finds it difficult to fill positions that have been open for several months. Amid a sea of unemployment, Kelly cannot find anyone to hire.

Critical Thinking Questions

1. What type of unemployment issue is Kelly confronting?
2. Is Kelly's failure to hire contributing to higher natural unemployment? Explain.

ISSUES & APPLICATIONS

Have Unemployment Benefits Boosted Unemployment?

CONCEPTS APPLIED

- Unemployment Rate
- Cyclical Unemployment
- Structural Unemployment

Between June 2008 and February 2009, the U.S. unemployment rate rose sharply, from 5.6 percent to more than 8 percent. Although the recession officially ended in June 2009, the unemployment rate ultimately reached a peak of 10.1 percent in October 2009. Since then, the unemployment rate has stayed near 8 percent. Thus, the unemployment rate remained above its prior level by at least 2 percentage points for more than three years. Many economists conclude that structural unemployment has risen. One element contributing to this rise, they suggest, was a substantial increase in the length of time the government paid benefits to unemployed workers.

The Significant Extension of Unemployment Benefits

People who lose jobs and are unable to find new positions are eligible for government unemployment benefits. Traditionally, these benefits constitute a form of insurance. Employers have long contributed to a government fund from which benefit payments to unemployed workers can be drawn for intervals up to 26 weeks. Nevertheless, during business contractions, Congress commonly has dipped into taxpayer funds to extend the duration of unemployment benefits. Such extensions typically have lasted for periods of about 15 weeks.

During 2008 and 2009, however, Congress nearly *quadrupled* the duration of unemployment benefits, to 99 weeks. This lengthened stream of government benefits reduced the incentive to find new jobs. As a consequence, many people spent more time searching for jobs that they hoped might be "better" instead of seeking out work that might have been more readily obtainable. So, the unemployment-benefits extension to 99 weeks tended to drive up structural unemployment and increase the measured unemployment rate.

The Benefits Extension's Impact on Structural Unemployment

Economists at the Federal Reserve Bank of San Francisco have estimated that the increase in unemployment benefits was sufficient to boost the U.S. unemployment rate by about 0.4 percentage point. Robert Barro of Harvard University has estimated a much larger effect—in excess of 2.7 percentage points.

Most other estimates of the benefits extension's impact on structural unemployment are about midway between these two extremes. If these "midpoint estimates" are correct, then the government's action to extend the duration of unemployment benefits by a factor of nearly four raised the U.S. unemployment rate by approximately 1.5 percentage points.

For Critical Thinking

1. What else might have accounted for an increase in structural unemployment in recent years? (Hint: Take a look back at the definition of structural unemployment on page 144.)
2. Given that the recession officially ended in June 2009, why might some economists contend that very little of the persistently high unemployment is cyclical unemployment?

Web Resources

1. Learn how economists at the Federal Reserve Bank of San Francisco obtained their estimate of the impact of extended unemployment benefits on structural unemployment at **www.econtoday.com/chap07**.
2. Read about how Robert Barro arrived at his much larger estimate of the effect of extended unemployment benefits on structural unemployment at **www.econtoday.com/chap07**.

MyEconLab

For more questions on this chapter's Issues & Applications, go to MyEconLab. In the Study Plan for this chapter, select Section N: News.

MyEconLab

Here is what you should know after reading this chapter. MyEconLab will help you identify what you know, and where to go when you need to practice.

WHAT YOU SHOULD KNOW		WHERE TO GO TO PRACTICE
How the U.S. Government Calculates the Official Unemployment Rate The total number of workers who are officially unemployed consists of noninstitutionalized people aged 16 or older who are willing and able to work and who are actively looking for work but have not found a job. To calculate the unemployment rate, the government determines what percentage this quantity is of the labor force, which consists of all noninstitutionalized people aged 16 years or older who either have jobs or are available for and actively seeking employment.	unemployment, 140 labor force, 140 stock, 142 flow, 142 job loser, 142 reentrant, 142 job leaver, 142 new entrant, 142 discouraged workers, 143 labor force participation rate, 143 **Key Figure** Figure 7-3, 142	• MyEconLab Study Plan 7.1 • Animated Figure 7-3

MyEconLab *continued*

WHAT YOU SHOULD KNOW		WHERE TO GO TO PRACTICE
The Types of Unemployment Temporarily unemployed workers who are searching for appropriate job offers are frictionally unemployed. The structurally unemployed lack the skills currently required by prospective employers. People unemployed due to business contractions are cyclically unemployed. Seasonal patterns of occupations within specific industries generate seasonal unemployment.	frictional unemployment, 144 structural unemployment, 144 cyclical unemployment, 145 seasonal unemployment, 145 full employment, 146 natural rate of unemployment, 146	• MyEconLab Study Plans 7.2, 7.3
How Price Indexes Are Calculated and Key Price Indexes To calculate any price index, economists multiply 100 times the ratio of the cost of a market basket of goods and services in the current year to the cost of the same market basket in a base year. The Consumer Price Index (CPI) is computed using a weighted set of goods and services purchased by a typical consumer in urban areas. The Producer Price Index (PPI) is a weighted average of prices of goods sold by a typical firm. The GDP deflator measures changes in the overall level of prices of all goods produced during a given interval. The Personal Consumption Expenditure (PCE) Index is a measure of average prices using weights from surveys of consumer spending.	inflation, 146 deflation, 146 purchasing power, 147 price index, 147 base year, 147 Consumer Price Index (CPI), 148 Producer Price Index (PPI), 148 GDP deflator, 148 Personal Consumption Expenditure (PCE) Index, 148 **Key Figure** Figure 7-4, 150	• MyEconLab Study Plan 7.4 • Animated Figure 7-4
Nominal Interest Rate versus Real Interest Rate The nominal interest rate applies to contracts expressed in current dollars. The real interest rate is net of inflation anticipated to erode the value of nominal interest payments during the period that a loan is repaid. Hence, the real interest rate equals the nominal interest rate minus the expected inflation rate.	anticipated inflation, 151 unanticipated inflation, 151 nominal rate of interest, 151 real rate of interest, 151	• MyEconLab Study Plan 7.5
Losers and Gainers from Inflation Creditors lose as a result of unanticipated inflation, because the real value of the interest payments they receive will turn out to be lower than they had expected. Borrowers gain when unanticipated inflation occurs, because the real value of their interest and principal payments declines. Key costs of inflation include expenses of protecting against inflation, costs of altering business plans because of unexpected changes in prices, and menu costs of repricing goods and services.	cost-of-living adjustments (COLAs), 152 repricing, or menu, cost of inflation, 152	• MyEconLab Study Plan 7.5

MyEconLab *continued*

WHAT YOU SHOULD KNOW		WHERE TO GO TO PRACTICE
Key Features of Business Fluctuations Business fluctuations are increases and decreases in business activity. A positive fluctuation is an expansion, which is an upward movement in business activity from a trough, or low point, to a peak, or high point. A negative fluctuation is a contraction, which is a drop in the pace of business activity from a previous peak to a new trough.	business fluctuations, 152 expansion, 152 contraction, 152 recession, 153 depression, 153 leading indicators, 154 **Key Figure** Figure 7-6, 154	• MyEconLab Study Plan 7.6 • Animated Figure 7-6

Log in to MyEconLab, take a chapter test, and get a personalized Study Plan that tells you which concepts you understand and which ones you need to review. From there, MyEconLab will give you further practice, tutorials, animations, videos, and guided solutions. For more information, visit www.myeconlab.com

PROBLEMS

All problems are assignable in MyEconLab; *exercises that update with real-time data are marked with* ●. *Answers to odd-numbered problems appear at the back of the book.*

7-1. Suppose that you are given the following information (see page 140):

Total population	300.0 million
Adult, noninstitutionalized, nonmilitary population	200.0 million
Unemployment	7.5 million

a. If the labor force participation rate is 70 percent, what is the labor force?

b. How many workers are employed?

c. What is the unemployment rate?

7-2. Suppose that you are given the following information (see page 140):

Labor force	206.2 million
Adults in the military	1.5 million
Nonadult population	48.0 million
Employed adults	196.2 million
Institutionalized adults	3.5 million
Nonmilitary, noninstitutionalized adults not in labor force	40.8 million

a. What is the total population?

b. How many people are unemployed, and what is the unemployment rate?

c. What is the labor force participation rate?

7-3. Suppose that the U.S. nonmilitary, noninstitutionalized adult population is 224 million, the number employed is 156 million, and the number unemployed is 8 million. (See page 140.)

a. What is the unemployment rate?

b. Suppose that there is a difference of 60 million between the adult population and the combined total of people who are employed and unemployed. How do we classify these 60 million people? Based on these figures, what is the U.S. labor force participation rate?

7-4. During the course of a year, the labor force consists of the same 1,000 people. Employers have chosen not to hire 20 of these people in the face of government regulations making it too costly to employ them. Hence, they remain unemployed throughout the year. At the same time, every month during the year, 30 different people become unemployed, and 30 other different people who were unemployed find jobs. There is no seasonal employment. (See pages 142–144.)

a. What is the frictional unemployment rate?

b. What is the unemployment rate?

c. Suppose that a system of unemployment compensation is established. Each month, 30 new people (not including the 20 that employers have chosen not to employ) continue to become unemployed, but each monthly group of newly unemployed now takes two months to find a job. After this change, what is the frictional unemployment rate?

d. After the change discussed in part (c), what is the unemployment rate?

7-5. Suppose that a nation has a labor force of 100 people. In January, Amy, Barbara, Carine, and Denise are unemployed. In February, those four find jobs, but Evan, Francesco, George, and Horatio become unemployed. Suppose further that every month, the previous four who were unemployed find jobs and four different people become unemployed. Throughout the year, however, three people—Ito, Jack, and Kelley—continually remain unemployed because firms facing government regulations view them as too costly to employ. (See page 144.)

a. What is this nation's frictional unemployment rate?

b. What is its structural unemployment rate?

c. What is its unemployment rate?

7-6. In a country with a labor force of 200, a different group of 10 people becomes unemployed each month, but becomes employed once again a month later. No others outside these groups are unemployed. (See pages 142–144.)

a. What is this country's unemployment rate?

b. What is the average duration of unemployment?

c. Suppose that establishment of a system of unemployment compensation increases to two months the interval that it takes each group of job losers to become employed each month. Nevertheless, a different group of 10 people still becomes unemployed each month. Now what is the average duration of unemployment?

d. Following the change discussed in part (c), what is the country's unemployment rate?

7-7. A nation's frictional unemployment rate is 1 percent. Seasonal unemployment does not exist in this country. Its cyclical rate of unemployment is 3 percent, and its structural unemployment rate is 4 percent. What is this nation's overall rate of unemployment? (See pages 144–145.)

7-8. In 2012, the cost of a market basket of goods was $2,000. In 2014, the cost of the same market basket of goods was $2,100. Use the price index formula to calculate the price index for 2014 if 2012 is the base year. (See pages 147–148.)

7-9. Suppose that in 2013, a typical U.S. student attending a state-supported college bought 10 textbooks at a price of $100 per book and enrolled in 25 credit hours of coursework at a price of $360 per credit hour. In 2014, the typical student continued to purchase 10 textbooks and enroll in 25 credit hours, but the price of a textbook rose to $110 per book, and the tuition price increased to $400 per credit hour. The base year for computing a "student price index" using this information is 2013. What is the value of the student price index in 2013? In 2014? Show your work. (See pages 147–148.)

7-10. Between 2013 and 2014 in a particular nation, the value of the consumer price index—for which the base year is 2010—rose by 9.091 percent, to a value of 120 in 2014. What was the value of the price index in 2013? (See pages 147–148.)

7-11. Consider the following price indexes: 90 in 2013, 100 in 2014, 110 in 2015, 121 in 2016, and 150 in 2017. Answer the following questions. (See pages 147–148.)

a. Which year is likely the base year?

b. What is the inflation rate from 2014 to 2015?

c. What is the inflation rate from 2015 to 2016?

d. If the cost of a market basket in 2014 is $2,000, what is the cost of the same basket of goods and services in 2013? In 2017?

7-12. The real interest rate is 4 percent, and the nominal interest rate is 6 percent. What is the anticipated rate of inflation? (See page 151.)

7-13. Currently, the price index used to calculate the inflation rate is equal to 90. The general expectation throughout the economy is that next year its value will be 99. The current nominal interest rate is 12 percent. What is the real interest rate? (See page 151.)

7-14. At present, the nominal interest rate is 7 percent, and the expected inflation rate is 5 percent. The current year is the base year for the price index used to calculate inflation. (See page 151.)

a. What is the real interest rate?

b. What is the anticipated value of the price index next year?

7-15. Suppose that in 2017 there is a sudden, unanticipated burst of inflation. Consider the situations faced by the following individuals. Who gains and who loses? (See pages 151–152.)

a. A homeowner whose wages will keep pace with inflation in 2017 but whose monthly mortgage payments to a savings bank will remain fixed

b. An apartment landlord who has guaranteed to his tenants that their monthly rent payments during 2017 will be the same as they were during 2016

c. A banker who made an auto loan that the auto buyer will repay at a fixed rate of interest during 2017

d. A retired individual who earns a pension with fixed monthly payments from her past employer during 2017

7-16. Consider the diagram at the right. The line represents the economy's growth trend, and the curve represents the economy's actual course of business fluctuations. For each part below, provide the letter label from the portion of the curve that corresponds to the associated term. (See page 153.)

a. Contraction

b. Peak

c. Trough

d. Expansion

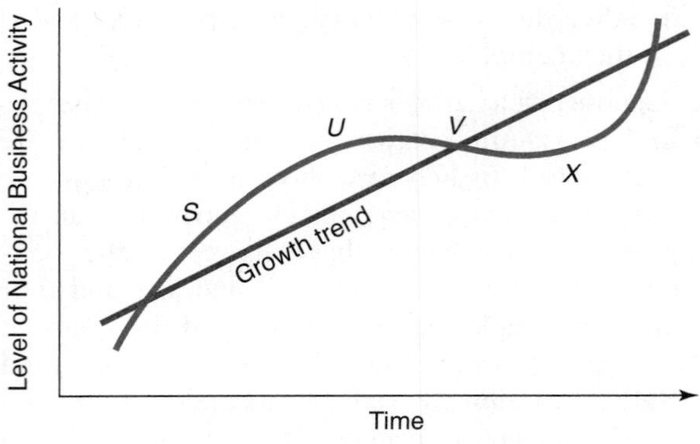

ECONOMICS ON THE NET

Looking at the Unemployment and Inflation Data This chapter reviewed key concepts relating to unemployment and inflation. In this application, you get a chance to examine U.S. unemployment and inflation data on your own.

Title: Bureau of Labor Statistics: Employment and Unemployment

Navigation: Use the link at **www.econtoday.com/chap07** to visit the "Employment" page of the Bureau of Labor Statistics (BLS). Click on "Top Picks" next to *Labor Force Statistics (Current Population Survey–CPS)*.

Application Perform the indicated operations, and answer the following questions.

1. Retrieve data for Civilian Labor Force Level, Employment Level, and Unemployment Level. Can you identify periods of sharp cyclical swings? Do they show up in data for the labor force, employment, or unemployment?
2. Are cyclical factors important?

For Group Study and Analysis Divide the class into groups, and assign a price index to each group. Ask each group to take a look at the index for All Years at the link to the BLS statistics on inflation at **www.econtoday.com/chap07**. Have each group identify periods during which their index accelerated or decelerated (or even fell). Do the indexes ever provide opposing implications about inflation and deflation?

ANSWERS TO QUICK QUIZZES

p. 143: (i) Unemployed . . . labor force; (ii) job losers . . . reentrants . . . job leavers . . . new entrants; (iii) increase; (iv) female

p. 146: (i) **Frictional;** (ii) **Structural;** (iii) natural

p. 151: (i) base; (ii) Consumer Price; (iii) GDP deflator; (iv) Personal Consumption Expenditure

p. 152: (i) greater . . . less; (ii) purchasing power; (iii) resource

p. 155: (i) business fluctuations; (ii) trough . . . peak; (iii) recession; (iv) external shocks

Measuring the Economy's Performance

8

LEARNING OBJECTIVES

After reading this chapter, you should be able to:

- Describe the circular flow of income and output
- Define gross domestic product (GDP)
- Understand the limitations of using GDP as a measure of national welfare
- Explain the expenditure approach to tabulating GDP
- Explain the income approach to computing GDP
- Distinguish between nominal GDP and real GDP

MyEconLab helps you master each objective and study more efficiently. See end of chapter for details.

Some commentators are already referring to the twenty-first century as the "Asian century." In contrast to the dampened economies of the United States and Europe, economic activity has been booming in China, Hong Kong, Singapore, South Korea, Taiwan, and other Asian countries. Some media reports are suggesting that China's economy will be "larger" than the U.S. economy by 2020. How might we go about trying to measure an economy's "size"? How could we then compare its "size" to the economy of another nation? The starting point for contemplating these questions is the market value of all final goods and services produced within a nation's borders during a given year. Economists refer to this quantity as *gross domestic product*, or *GDP*, which is a key concept covered in this chapter

DID YOU KNOW THAT... the flow of U.S. economic activity since June 2009, when the 2008–2009 recession officially ended, has been more dampened than during any other comparable postrecession period since the Great Depression of the 1930s? To measure the nation's overall economic performance over time, the government utilizes what has become known as **national income accounting.** How this measurement is done is the main focus of this chapter. But first we need to look at the flow of income within an economy, for it is the flow of goods and services from businesses to consumers and of payments from consumers to businesses, that constitutes economic activity.

National income accounting
A measurement system used to estimate national income and its components. One approach to measuring an economy's aggregate performance.

The Simple Circular Flow

The concept of a circular flow of income (ignoring taxes) involves two principles:

1. In every economic exchange, the seller receives exactly the same amount that the buyer spends.
2. Goods and services flow in one direction and money payments flow in the other.

In the simple economy shown in Figure 8-1 below, there are only businesses and households. It is assumed that businesses sell their *entire* output in the current period to households and that households spend their *entire* income in the current period on consumer products. Households receive their income by selling the use of whatever factors of production they own, such as labor services.

FIGURE 8-1
The Circular Flow of Income and Product

Businesses provide final goods and services to households (upper clockwise loop), who in turn pay for them (upper counterclockwise loop). Payments flow in a counterclockwise direction and can be thought of as a circular flow. The dollar value of output is identical to total income because profits are defined as being equal to total business receipts minus business outlays for wages, rents, and interest. Households provide factor services to businesses and receive income (lower loops).

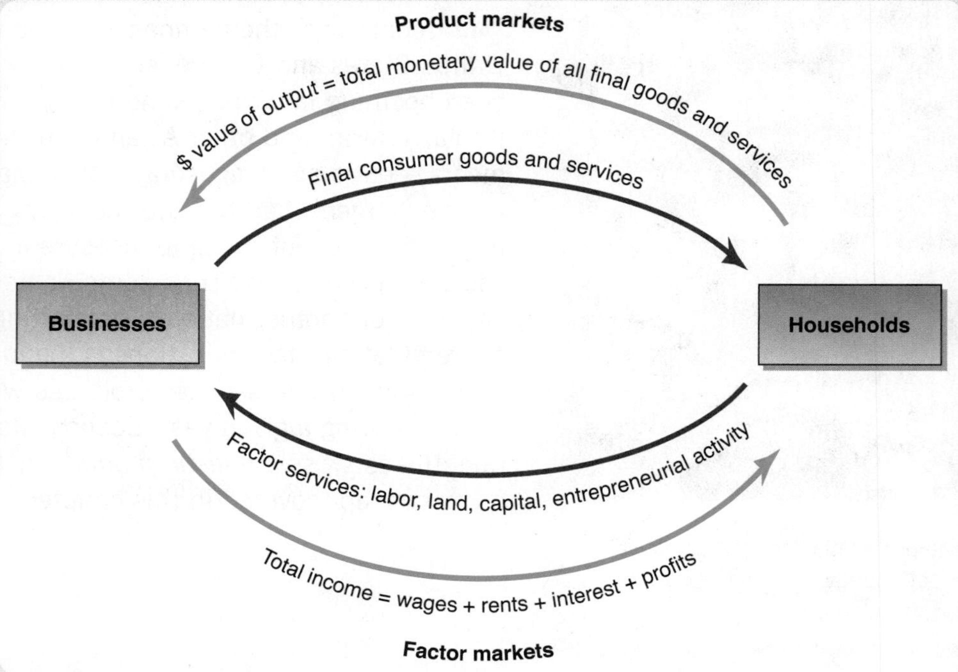

Profits Explained

We have indicated in Figure 8-1 on the facing page that profit is a cost of production. You might be under the impression that profits are not part of the cost of producing goods and services, but profits are indeed a part of this cost because entrepreneurs must be rewarded for providing their services or they won't provide them. Their reward, if any, is profit. The reward—the profit—is included in the cost of the factors of production. If there were no expectations of profit, entrepreneurs would not incur the risk associated with the organization of productive activities. That is why we consider profits a cost of doing business. Just as workers expect wages, entrepreneurs expect profits.

Total Income or Total Output

The arrow that goes from businesses to households at the bottom of Figure 8-1 is labeled "Total income." What would be a good definition of **total income?** If you answered "the total of all individuals' income," you would be right. But all income is actually a payment for something, whether it be wages paid for labor services, rent paid for the use of land, interest paid for the use of capital, or profits paid to entrepreneurs. It is the amount paid to the resource suppliers. Therefore, total income is also defined as the annual *cost* of producing the entire output of **final goods and services.**

Total income
The yearly amount earned by the nation's resources (factors of production). Total income therefore includes wages, rent, interest payments, and profits that are received by workers, landowners, capital owners, and entrepreneurs, respectively.

Final goods and services
Goods and services that are at their final stage of production and will not be transformed into yet other goods or services. For example, wheat ordinarily is not considered a final good because it is usually used to make a final good, bread.

The arrow going from households to businesses at the top of Figure 8-1 represents the dollar value of output in the economy. This is equal to the total monetary value of all final goods and services for this simple economy. In essence, it represents the total business receipts from the sale of all final goods and services produced by businesses and consumed by households. Business receipts are the opposite side of household expenditures. When households purchase goods and services, those payments become a *business receipt.* Every transaction, therefore, simultaneously involves an expenditure and a receipt.

PRODUCT MARKETS Transactions in which households buy goods take place in the product markets—that's where households are the buyers and businesses are the sellers of consumer goods. *Product market* transactions are represented in the upper loops in Figure 8-1 on the facing page. Note that consumer goods and services flow to household demanders, while money flows in the opposite direction to business suppliers.

FACTOR MARKETS *Factor market* transactions are represented by the lower loops in Figure 8-1. In the factor market, households are the sellers. They sell resources such as labor, land, capital, and entrepreneurial ability. Businesses are the buyers in factor markets. Business expenditures represent receipts or, more simply, income for households. Also, in the lower loops of Figure 8-1, factor services flow from households to businesses, while the payments for these services flow in the opposite direction from businesses to households. Observe also the flow of money (counterclockwise) from households to businesses and back again from businesses to households: It is an endless circular flow.

Why the Dollar Value of Total Output Must Equal Total Income

Total income represents the income received by households in payment for the production of goods and services. Why must total income be identical to the dollar value of total output? First, as Figure 8-1 shows, spending by one group is income to another. Second, it is a matter of simple accounting and the economic definition of profit as a cost of production. Profit is defined as what is *left over* from total business receipts after all other costs—wages, rents, interest—have been paid. If the dollar value of total output is $1,000 and the total of wages, rent, and interest for producing that output is $900, profit is $100. Profit is always the *residual* item that makes total income equal to the dollar value of total output.

QUICK QUIZ See page 186 for the answers. Review concepts from this section in MyEconLab.

In the circular flow model of income and output, households sell __________ services to businesses that pay for those services. The receipt of payments is total __________. Businesses sell goods and services to households that pay for them.

The dollar value of total output is equal to the total monetary value of all __________ goods and services produced.

The dollar value of final output must always equal total income. The variable that adjusts to make this so is known as __________.

National Income Accounting

We have already mentioned that policymakers require information about the state of the national economy. Economists use historical statistical records on the performance of the national economy for testing their theories about how the economy really works. Thus, national income accounting is important. Let's start with the most commonly presented statistic on the national economy.

Gross Domestic Product (GDP)

Gross domestic product (GDP)
The total market value of all final goods and services produced during a year by factors of production located within a nation's borders.

Gross domestic product (GDP) represents the total market value of the nation's annual final product, or output, produced by factors of production located within national borders. We therefore formally define GDP as the total market value of all final goods and services produced in an economy during a year. We are referring here to the value of a *flow of production.* A nation produces at a certain rate, just as you receive income at a certain rate. Your income flow might be at a rate of $20,000 per year or $100,000 per year. Suppose you are told that someone earns $5,000. Would you consider this a good salary? There is no way to answer that question unless you know whether the person is earning $5,000 per month or per week or per day. Thus, you have to specify a time period for all flows. Income received is a flow. You must contrast this with, for example, your total accumulated savings, which are a stock measured at a point in time, not over time. Implicit in just about everything we deal with in this chapter is a time period—usually one year. All the measures of domestic product and income are specified as *rates* measured in dollars per year.

Stress on Final Output

Intermediate goods
Goods used up entirely in the production of final goods.

GDP does not count **intermediate goods** (goods used up entirely in the production of final goods) because to do so would be to count them twice. For example, even though grain that a farmer produces may be that farmer's final product, it is not the final product for the nation. It is sold to make bread. Bread is the final product.

Value added
The dollar value of an industry's sales minus the value of intermediate goods (for example, raw materials and parts) used in production.

We can use a numerical example to clarify this point further. Our example will involve determining the value added at each stage of production. **Value added** is the dollar value contributed to a product at each stage of its production. In Table 8-1 on the facing page, we see the difference between total value of all sales and value added in the production of a donut. We also see that the sum of the values added is equal to the sale price to the final consumer. It is the 45 cents that is used to measure GDP, not the 97 cents. If we used the 97 cents, we would be double counting from stages 2 through 5, for each intermediate good would be counted at least twice—once when it was produced and again when the good it was used in making was sold. Such double counting would greatly exaggerate GDP.

TABLE 8-1

Sales Value and Value Added at Each Stage of Donut Production

(1) Stage of Production	(2) Dollar Value of Sales	(3) Value Added
Stage 1: Fertilizer and seed	$.03	$.03
Stage 2: Growing	.07	.04
Stage 3: Milling	.12	.05
Stage 4: Baking	.30	.18
Stage 5: Retailing	.45	.15
	Total dollar value of all sales $.97	Total value added $.45

Stage 1: A farmer purchases 3 cents worth of fertilizer and seed, which are used as factors of production in growing wheat.

Stage 2: The farmer grows the wheat, harvests it, and sells it to a miller for 7 cents. Thus, we see that the farmer has added 4 cents' worth of value. Those 4 cents represent income over and above expenses incurred by the farmer.

Stage 3: The miller purchases the wheat for 7 cents and adds 5 cents as the value added. That is, there is 5 cents for the miller as income. The miller sells the ground wheat flour to a donut-baking company.

Stage 4: The donut-baking company buys the flour for 12 cents and adds 18 cents as the value added. It then sells the donut to the final retailer.

Stage 5: The donut retailer sells donuts at 45 cents apiece, thus creating an additional value of 15 cents.

We see that the total value of the transactions involved in the production of one donut is 97 cents, but the total value added is 45 cents, which is exactly equal to the retail price. The total value added is equal to the sum of all income payments.

Exclusion of Financial Transactions, Transfer Payments, and Secondhand Goods

Remember that GDP is the measure of the dollar value of all final goods and services produced in one year. Many more transactions occur that have nothing to do with final goods and services produced. There are financial transactions, transfers of the ownership of preexisting goods, and other transactions that should not (and do not) get included in our measure of GDP.

Go to **www.econtoday.com/chap08** for the most up-to-date U.S. economic data at the Web site of the Bureau of Economic Analysis.

FINANCIAL TRANSACTIONS There are three general categories of purely financial transactions: (1) the buying and selling of securities, (2) government transfer payments, and (3) private transfer payments.

Securities When you purchase shares of existing stock in Apple, Inc., someone else has sold it to you. In essence, there was merely a *transfer* of ownership rights. You paid $100 to obtain the stock. Someone else received the $100 and gave up the stock. No producing activity was consummated at that time, unless a broker received a fee for performing the transaction, in which case only the fee is part of GDP. The $100 transaction is not included when we measure GDP.

Government Transfer Payments Transfer payments are payments for which no productive services are concurrently provided in exchange. The most obvious government transfer payments are Social Security benefits and unemployment compensation. The recipients add nothing to current production in return for such transfer payments (although they may have contributed in the past to be eligible to receive them). Government transfer payments are not included in GDP.

Private Transfer Payments Are you receiving funds from your parents in order to attend school? Has a wealthy relative ever given you a gift of cash? If so, you have been the recipient of a private transfer payment. This payment is merely a transfer of funds from one individual to another. As such, it does not constitute productive activity and is not included in GDP.

YOU ARE THERE

To consider how much difference it can make if economists broaden the measure of GDP in just a few ways, read on page 180 **Has the Economy Grown More Than Official GDP Data Suggest?**

TRANSFER OF SECONDHAND GOODS If I sell you my two-year-old laptop computer, no current production is involved. I transfer to you the ownership of a computer that was produced years ago. In exchange, you transfer to me $350. The original purchase price of the computer was included in GDP in the year I purchased it. To include the price again when I sell it to you would be counting the value of the computer a second time.

OTHER EXCLUDED TRANSACTIONS Many other transactions are not included in GDP for practical reasons:

- Household production—housecleaning, child care, and other tasks performed by people in their *own* households and for which they receive no payments through the marketplace
- Otherwise legal underground transactions—those that are legal but not reported and hence not taxed, such as paying housekeepers in cash that is not declared as income to the Internal Revenue Service
- Illegal underground activities—these include prostitution, illegal gambling, and the sale of illicit drugs

WHAT IF... market prices of housecleaning, child care, and lawn care services were valued for inclusion in GDP?

Even if the prices of household services determined in markets were used to try to place a dollar value on nonmarket household production, national income accountants still would not know annual *volumes* of such nonmarket services. Thus, to attempt to include the total value of nonmarket household production in GDP, the accountants would have to *estimate* the volumes of production performed outside markets. Then they would multiply these volumes times the market prices. The resulting new measure of GDP would be subject to likely estimation mistakes, in addition to the measurement errors that already occur. This would make GDP a less reliable measure of the overall value of final production of goods and services within U.S. borders each year.

Recognizing the Limitations of GDP

Like any statistical measure, gross domestic product is a concept that can be both well used and misused. Economists find it especially valuable as an overall indicator of a nation's economic performance. But it is important to realize that GDP has significant weaknesses. Because it includes only the value of goods and services traded in markets, it excludes *nonmarket* production, such as the household services of homemakers discussed earlier. This can cause some problems in comparing the GDP of an industrialized country with the GDP of a highly agrarian nation in which nonmarket production is relatively more important.

It also causes problems if nations have different definitions of legal versus illegal activities. For instance, a nation with legalized gambling will count the value of gambling services, which has a reported market value as a legal activity. But in a country where gambling is illegal, individuals who provide such services will not report the market value of gambling activities, and so they will not be counted in that country's GDP. This can complicate comparing GDP in the nation where gambling is legal with GDP in the country that prohibits gambling.

Furthermore, although GDP is often used as a benchmark measure for standard-of-living calculations, it is not necessarily a good measure of the well-being of a nation. No measured figure of total national annual income can take account of changes in the degree of labor market discrimination, declines or improvements in personal safety, or the quantity or quality of leisure time. Measured GDP also says little about our environmental quality of life.

As the now-defunct Soviet Union illustrated to the world, the large-scale production of such items as minerals, electricity, and irrigation for farming can have negative effects on the environment: deforestation from strip mining, air and soil pollution from particulate emissions or nuclear accidents at power plants, and erosion of the natural balance between water and salt in bodies of water such as the Aral Sea. Other nations, such as China and India, have also experienced greater pollution problems as their levels of GDP have increased. Hence, it is important to recognize the following point:

GDP is a measure of the value of production in terms of market prices and an indicator of economic activity. It is not a measure of a nation's overall welfare.

Nonetheless, GDP is a relatively accurate and useful measure of the economy's domestic economic activity, measured in current dollars. Understanding GDP is thus an important first step for analyzing changes in economic activity over time.

What new index of a country's broad economic performance has been developed by a large group of developed nations?

POLICY EXAMPLE

Developed Nations Look for a "Happier" Alternative to GDP

The thirty-four member nations of the Organization for Economic Cooperation and Development (OECD) are aiming to supplement or even replace GDP with a new gauge of a country's standard of living and well-being called "Your Better Life Index." This index is geared to measure determinants of human happiness levels. Toward this end, it tabulates a nation's "quality scores" in eleven areas: community, education, environment, governance, health, housing, income, jobs, life satisfaction, safety, and work-life balance. A nation's scores in each of these areas are based on various economic indicators and public opinion polls.

To determine how these scores should be combined to calculate a single value for each nation's Your Better Life Index, the OECD is conducting surveys of large groups of residents in each member country. Each nation's weights for the eleven sets of quality scores will differ, but the OECD plans to rate nations on the basis of their overall index values. The OECD's initial values for the Your Better Life Index yielded rankings in which Denmark, Canada, and Norway rate highest among OECD nations, with Hungary, Portugal, and Estonia rating lowest.

FOR CRITICAL THINKING

How would you determine each person's level of life satisfaction?

QUICK QUIZ

See page 186 for the answers. Review concepts from this section in MyEconLab.

_________ _________ _________ is the total market value of final goods and services produced in an economy during a one-year period by factors of production within the nation's borders. It represents the dollar value of the flow of final production over a one-year period.

To avoid double counting, we look only at final goods and services produced or, equivalently, at _________ _________.

In measuring GDP, we must _________ (1) purely financial transactions, such as the buying and selling of securities; (2) government transfer payments and private transfer payments; and (3) the transfer of secondhand goods.

Many other transactions are excluded from measured _________, among them household services rendered by homemakers, underground economy transactions, and illegal economic activities, even though many of these result in the production of final goods and services.

GDP is a useful measure for tracking changes in the _________ _________ of overall economic activity over time, but it is not a measure of the well-being of a nation's residents because it fails to account for nonmarket transactions, the amount and quality of leisure time, environmental or safety issues, labor market discrimination, and other factors that influence general welfare.

Two Main Methods of Measuring GDP

The definition of GDP is the total dollar value of all final goods and services produced during a year. How, exactly, do we go about actually computing this number?

The circular flow diagram presented in Figure 8-1 on page 162 gave us a shortcut method for calculating GDP. We can look at the *flow of expenditures*, which consists of consumption, investment, government purchases of goods and services, and net expenditures in the foreign sector (net exports). In this **expenditure approach** to measuring GDP, we add the dollar value of all final goods and services. We could also use the *flow of income*, looking at the income received by everybody producing goods and services. In this **income approach,** we add the income received by all factors of production.

Expenditure approach
Computing GDP by adding up the dollar value at current market prices of all final goods and services.

Income approach
Measuring GDP by adding up all components of national income, including wages, interest, rent, and profits.

Deriving GDP by the Expenditure Approach

To derive GDP using the expenditure approach, we must look at each of the separate components of expenditures and then add them together. These components are consumption expenditures, investment, government expenditures, and net exports.

CONSUMPTION EXPENDITURES How do we spend our income? As households or as individuals, we spend our income through consumption expenditure (C), which falls into three categories: **durable consumer goods, nondurable consumer goods,** and **services.** Durable goods are *arbitrarily* defined as items that last more than three years. They include automobiles, furniture, and household appliances. Nondurable goods are all the rest, such as food and gasoline. Services are intangible commodities: medical care, education, and the like.

Durable consumer goods
Consumer goods that have a life span of more than three years.

Nondurable consumer goods
Consumer goods that are used up within three years.

Services
Mental or physical labor or assistance purchased by consumers. Examples are the assistance of physicians, lawyers, dentists, repair personnel, housecleaners, educators, retailers, and wholesalers; items purchased or used by consumers that do not have physical characteristics.

Housing expenditures constitute a major proportion of anybody's annual expenditures. Rental payments on apartments are automatically included in consumption expenditure estimates. People who own their homes, however, do not make rental payments. Consequently, government statisticians estimate what is called the *implicit rental value* of existing owner-occupied homes. It is roughly equal to the amount of rent you would have to pay if you did not own the home but were renting it from someone else.

GROSS PRIVATE DOMESTIC INVESTMENT We now turn our attention to **gross private domestic investment** (I) undertaken by businesses. When economists refer to investment, they are referring to additions to productive capacity. **Investment** may be thought of as an activity that uses resources today in such a way that they allow for greater production in the future and hence greater consumption in the future. When a business buys new equipment or puts up a new factory, it is investing. It is increasing its capacity to produce in the future.

Gross private domestic investment
The creation of capital goods, such as factories and machines, that can yield production and hence consumption in the future. Also included in this definition are changes in business inventories and repairs made to machines or buildings.

Investment
Any use of today's resources to expand tomorrow's production or consumption.

In estimating gross private domestic investment, government statisticians also add consumer expenditures on *new* residential structures because new housing represents an addition to our future productive capacity in the sense that a new house can generate housing services in the future.

The layperson's notion of investment often relates to the purchase of stocks and bonds. For our purposes, such transactions simply represent the *transfer of ownership* of assets called stocks and bonds. Thus, you must keep in mind the fact that in economics, investment refers *only* to *additions* to productive capacity, not to transfers of assets.

Producer durables, or **capital goods**
Durable goods having an expected service life of more than three years that are used by businesses to produce other goods and services.

Fixed investment
Purchases by businesses of newly produced producer durables, or capital goods, such as production machinery and office equipment.

FIXED VERSUS INVENTORY INVESTMENT In our analysis, we will consider the basic components of investment. We have already mentioned the first one, which involves a firm's purchase of equipment or construction of a new factory. These are called **producer durables,** or **capital goods.** A producer durable, or a capital good, is simply a good that is purchased not to be consumed in its current form but to be used to make other goods and services. The purchase of equipment and factories—capital goods—is called **fixed investment.**

The other type of investment has to do with the change in inventories of raw materials and finished goods. Firms do not immediately sell off all their products to consumers. Some of this final product is usually held in inventory waiting to be sold. Firms hold inventories to meet future expected orders for their products. When a firm increases its inventories of finished products, it is engaging in **inventory investment.** Inventories consist of all finished goods on hand, goods in process, and raw materials.

Inventory investment
Changes in the stocks of finished goods and goods in process, as well as changes in the raw materials that businesses keep on hand. Whenever inventories are decreasing, inventory investment is negative. Whenever they are increasing, inventory investment is positive.

The reason that we can think of a change in inventories as being a type of investment is that an increase in such inventories provides for future increased consumption possibilities. When inventory investment is zero, the firm is neither adding to nor subtracting from the total stock of goods or raw materials on hand. Thus, if the firm keeps the same amount of inventories throughout the year, inventory *investment* has been zero.

GOVERNMENT EXPENDITURES In addition to personal consumption expenditures, there are government purchases of goods and services (G). The government buys goods and services from private firms and pays wages and salaries to government employees. Generally, we value goods and services at the prices at which they are sold. But many government goods and services are not sold in the market. Therefore, we cannot use their market value when computing GDP. The value of these goods is considered equal to their *cost*. For example, the value of a newly built road is considered equal to its construction cost and is included in the GDP for the year it was built.

What portion of official U.S. GDP comprises transactions not directly valued in terms of actual market prices?

EXAMPLE

Imputing Part of the Government's Contribution to GDP

A number of items included in U.S. GDP are not explicitly priced in markets. This is particularly true of a significant portion of the government's provision of goods such as public education, fire protection, and national defense. National income accountants have decided that government expenditures on these activities understate the values they would have if private firms provided them in private markets. Thus, the accountants "impute" dollar amounts to these items by valuing them in terms of prices determined in markets for privately produced education, fire protection, and security services.

In recent years, imputed values of such government-provided activities have constituted as much as 15 percent of GDP. As the share of GDP involving activities by federal, state, and local governments continues to rise, this percentage likely will increase as well.

FOR CRITICAL THINKING

If governmental payments for educational services exceed families' valuations of those services, does the imputing process overstate or understate public education's contribution to GDP?

NET EXPORTS (FOREIGN EXPENDITURES) To obtain an accurate representation of GDP, we must include the foreign sector. As U.S. residents, we purchase foreign goods called *imports.* The goods that foreign residents purchase from us are our *exports.* To determine the *net* expenditures from the foreign sector, we subtract the value of imports from the value of exports to get net exports (X) for a year:

$$\text{Net exports } (X) = \text{total exports} - \text{total imports}$$

To understand why we subtract imports rather than ignoring them altogether, recall that we want to estimate *domestic* output, so we have to subtract U.S. expenditures on the goods produced in other nations.

Presenting the Expenditure Approach

We have just defined the components of GDP using the expenditure approach. When we add them all together, we get a definition for GDP, which is as follows:

$$\text{GDP} = C + I + G + X$$

MyEconLab Real-time data

FIGURE 8-2

GDP and Its Components

Here we see a display of gross domestic product, personal consumption expenditures, government purchases, and gross private domestic investment plus net exports for the years since 1929. (Note that the scale of the vertical axis changes as we move up the axis.) During the Great Depression of the 1930s, gross private domestic investment *plus* net exports was negative because we were investing very little at that time. Since the late 1990s, the sum of gross private domestic investment and net exports has been highly variable.

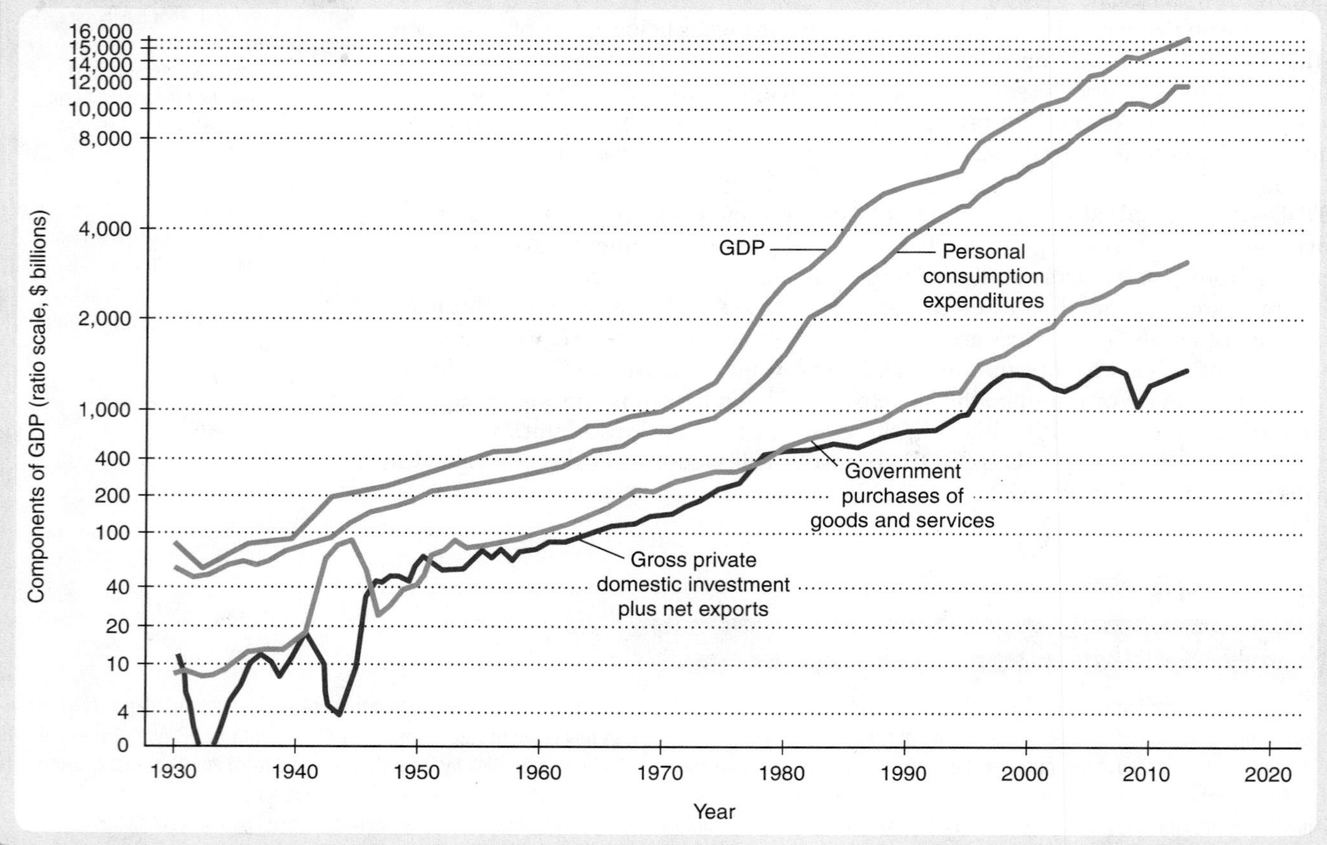

where

C = consumption expenditures
I = investment expenditures
G = government expenditures
X = net exports

THE HISTORICAL PICTURE To get an idea of the relationship among C, I, G, and X, look at Figure 8-2 above, which shows GDP, personal consumption expenditures, government purchases, and gross private domestic investment plus net exports since 1929. When we add up the expenditures of the household, business, government, and foreign sectors, we get GDP.

DEPRECIATION AND NET DOMESTIC PRODUCT We have used the terms *gross domestic product* and *gross private domestic investment* without really indicating what *gross* means. The dictionary defines it as "without deductions," the opposite of *net.* Deductions for what? you might ask. The deductions are for something we call **depreciation.** In the course of a year, machines and structures wear out or are used up in the production of domestic product. For example, houses deteriorate as they are occupied, and machines need repairs or they will fall apart and stop working. Most capital, or durable, goods depreciate.

Depreciation
Reduction in the value of capital goods over a one-year period due to physical wear and tear and also to obsolescence; also called *capital consumption allowance.*

Net domestic product (NDP)
GDP minus depreciation.

An estimate of the amount that capital goods have depreciated during the year is subtracted from gross domestic product to arrive at a figure called **net domestic product (NDP),** which we define as follows:

$$\text{NDP} = \text{GDP} - \text{depreciation}$$

Depreciation is also called **capital consumption allowance** because it is the amount of the capital stock that has been consumed over a one-year period. In essence, it equals the amount a business would have to put aside to repair and replace deteriorating machines. Because we know that

Capital consumption allowance
Another name for depreciation, the amount that businesses would have to put aside in order to take care of deteriorating machines and other equipment.

$$\text{GDP} = C + I + G + X$$

we know that the formula for NDP is

$$\text{NDP} = C + I + G + X - \text{depreciation}$$

Alternatively, because net $I = I -$ depreciation,

$$\text{NDP} = C + \text{net}\, I + G + X$$

Net investment measures *changes* in our capital stock over time and is positive nearly every year. Because depreciation does not vary greatly from year to year as a percentage of GDP, we get a similar picture of what is happening to our national economy by looking at either NDP or GDP data.

Net investment
Gross private domestic investment minus an estimate of the wear and tear on the existing capital stock. Net investment therefore measures the change in the capital stock over a one-year period.

Net investment is an important variable to observe over time nonetheless. If everything else remains the same in an economy, changes in net investment can have dramatic consequences for future economic growth (a topic we cover in more detail in Chapter 9). Positive net investment by definition expands the productive capacity of our economy.

This capacity expansion means that there is increased capital, which will generate even more income in the future. When net investment is zero, we are investing just enough to take account of depreciation. Our economy's productive capacity remains unchanged. Finally, when net investment is negative, we can expect negative economic growth prospects in the future. Negative net investment means that our productive capacity is actually declining—we are disinvesting. This actually occurred during the Great Depression.

QUICK QUIZ See page 186 for the answers. Review concepts from this section in MyEconLab.

The __________ approach to measuring GDP requires that we add up consumption expenditures, gross private investment, government purchases, and net exports. Consumption expenditures include consumer __________, consumer __________, and __________.

Gross private domestic investment *excludes* transfers of asset ownership. It includes only additions to the productive __________ of a nation, repairs on existing capital goods, and changes in business __________.

We value most government expenditures at their cost because we usually do not have __________ prices at which to value government goods and services.

To obtain **net domestic product (NDP),** we subtract from GDP the year's __________ of the existing capital stock.

Deriving GDP by the Income Approach

If you go back to the circular flow diagram in Figure 8-1 on page 162, you see that product markets are at the top of the diagram and factor markets are at the bottom. We can calculate the value of the circular flow of income and product by looking at expenditures—which we just did—or by looking at total factor payments. Factor payments are called income. We calculate **gross domestic income (GDI),** which we will see is identical to gross domestic product (GDP). Using the income approach, we have four categories of payments to individuals: wages, interest, rent, and profits.

Gross domestic income (GDI)
The sum of all income—wages, interest, rent, and profits—paid to the four factors of production.

1. *Wages.* The most important category is, of course, wages, including salaries and other forms of labor income, such as income in kind and incentive payments.

We also count Social Security taxes (both the employees' and the employers' contributions).

Go to www.econtoday.com/chap08 to examine recent trends in U.S. GDP and its components.

2. *Interest.* Here interest payments do not equal the sum of all payments for the use of funds in a year. Instead, interest is expressed in *net* rather than in gross terms. The interest component of total income is only net interest received by households plus net interest paid to us by foreign residents. Net interest received by households is the difference between the interest they receive (from savings accounts, certificates of deposit, and the like) and the interest they pay (to banks for home mortgages, credit cards, and other loans).

3. *Rent.* Rent is all income earned by individuals for the use of their real (nonmonetary) assets, such as farms, houses, and stores. As stated previously, we have to include here the implicit rental value of owner-occupied houses. Also included in this category are royalties received from copyrights, patents, and assets such as oil wells.

4. *Profits.* Our last category includes total gross corporate profits plus *proprietors' income.* Proprietors' income is income earned from the operation of unincorporated businesses, which include sole proprietorships, partnerships, and producers' cooperatives. It is unincorporated business profit.

Indirect business taxes
All business taxes except the tax on corporate profits. Indirect business taxes include sales and business property taxes.

All of the payments listed are *actual* factor payments made to owners of the factors of production. When we add them together, though, we do not yet have gross domestic income. We have to take account of two other components: **indirect business taxes,** such as sales and business property taxes, and depreciation, which we have already discussed.

INDIRECT BUSINESS TAXES Indirect taxes are the (nonincome) taxes paid by consumers when they buy goods and services. When you buy a book, you pay the price of the book plus any state and local sales tax. The business is actually acting as the government's agent in collecting the sales tax, which it in turn passes on to the government. Such taxes therefore represent a business expense and are included in gross domestic income.

DEPRECIATION Just as we had to deduct depreciation to get from GDP to NDP, so we must *add* depreciation to go from net domestic income to gross domestic income. Depreciation can be thought of as the portion of the current year's GDP that is used to replace physical capital consumed in the process of production. Because somebody has paid for the replacement, depreciation must be added as a component of gross domestic income.

Nonincome expense items
The total of indirect business taxes and depreciation.

The last two components of GDP—indirect business taxes and depreciation—are called **nonincome expense items.**

Figure 8-3 on the facing page shows a comparison between estimated gross domestic product and gross domestic income for 2013. Whether you decide to use the expenditure approach or the income approach, you will come out with the same number. There are sometimes statistical discrepancies, but they are usually relatively small.

QUICK QUIZ See page 186 for the answers. Review concepts from this section in MyEconLab.

To derive GDP using the income approach, we add up all factor payments, including __________, __________, __________, and __________.	To get an accurate measure of GDP using the income approach, we must also add __________ __________ __________ and __________ to those total factor payments.

FIGURE 8-3

Gross Domestic Product and Gross Domestic Income, 2013 (in billions of 2005 dollars per year)

By using the two different methods of computing the output of the economy, we come up with gross domestic product and gross domestic income, which are by definition equal. One approach focuses on expenditures, or the flow of product. The other approach concentrates on income, or the flow of costs.

Sources: U.S. Department of Commerce and author's estimates.

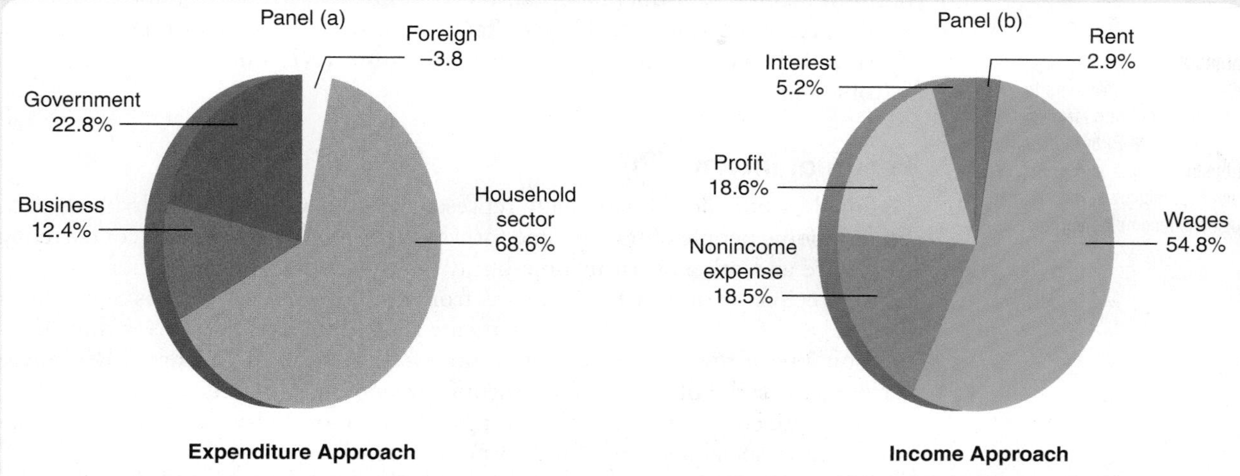

Expenditure Point of View—Product Flow		**Income Point of View—Cost Flow**	
Expenditure by Different Sectors:		**Domestic Income (at Factor Cost):**	
Household sector		*Wages*	
Personal consumption expenses	$11,211.5	All wages, salaries, and supplemental employee compensation	$8,955.8
Government sector			
Purchase of goods and services	3,726.6	*Rent*	
		All rental income of individuals plus implicit rent on owner-occupied dwellings	474.3
Business sector			
Gross private domestic investment (including depreciation)	2,033.3	*Interest* Net interest paid by business	849.0
Foreign sector			
Net exports of goods and services	−626.7	*Profit*	
		Proprietorial income	1,411.3
		Corporate profits before taxes deducted	1,621.9
		Nonincome expense items	
		Indirect business taxes	824.3
		Depreciation	2,111.6
		Statistical discrepancy	96.5
Gross domestic product	$16,344.7	Gross domestic income	$16,344.7

Other Components of National Income Accounting

Gross domestic income or product does not really tell us how much income people have access to for spending purposes. To get to those kinds of data, we must make some adjustments, which we now do.

National Income (NI)

We know that net domestic product (NDP) is the total market value of goods and services available to consume and to add to the capital stock. NDP, however, includes indirect business taxes and transfers, which should not count as part of income earned by U.S. factors of production, but does not include various business incomes that should. We therefore subtract from NDP indirect taxes and transfers and add other business income adjustments. Because U.S. residents earn income abroad and foreign residents earn income in the United States, we also add *net* U.S. income earned abroad. The result is what we define as **national income (NI)**—income earned by all U.S. factors of production.

National income (NI)
The total of all factor payments to resource owners. It can be obtained from net domestic product (NDP) by subtracting indirect business taxes and transfers and adding net U.S. income earned abroad and other business income adjustments.

Personal Income (PI)

National income does not actually represent what is available to individuals to spend because some people obtain income for which they have provided no concurrent good or service and others earn income but do not receive it. In the former category are mainly recipients of transfer payments from the government, such as Social Security, welfare, and food stamps. These payments represent shifts of funds within the economy by way of the government, with no goods or services concurrently rendered in exchange. For the other category, income earned but not received, the most obvious examples are corporate retained earnings that are plowed back into the business, contributions to social insurance, and corporate income taxes.

When transfer payments are added and when income earned but not received is subtracted, we end up with **personal income (PI)**—income *received* by the factors of production prior to the payment of personal income taxes.

Personal income (PI)
The amount of income that households actually receive before they pay personal income taxes.

Why are economists becoming increasingly concerned about trends in the sources of U.S. personal income?

EXAMPLE

Sources of U.S. Personal Income Exhibit Unsustainable Trends

During the years since early 2010, the share of personal income derived from private payrolls has dropped to the lowest levels in U.S. history. At the same time, the portion of personal income obtained from government-provided benefits, such as Social Security, food stamps, and unemployment insurance, has risen to the highest level ever. These trends are unsustainable because the government finances its benefit programs by taxing privately generated income sources. In the future, therefore, either the private-payroll share of personal income must increase, or the government-benefit portion must decrease.

FOR CRITICAL THINKING

How could a sustained upswing in economic activity in the private sector of the economy help to reverse both trends in the sources of personal income?

Disposable Personal Income (DPI)

Disposable personal income (DPI)
Personal income after personal income taxes have been paid.

Everybody knows that you do not get to take home all your salary. To obtain **disposable personal income (DPI),** we subtract all personal income taxes from personal income. This is the income that individuals have left for consumption and saving.

Deriving the Components of GDP

Table 8-2 on the facing page shows how to derive the various components of GDP. It explains how to go from gross domestic product to net domestic product to national income to personal income and then to disposable personal income. On the frontpapers of your book, you can see the historical record for GDP, NDP, NI, PI, and DPI for selected years since 1929.

TABLE 8-2

Going from GDP to Disposable Income, 2013

	Billions of Dollars
Gross domestic product (GDP)	16,344.7
Minus depreciation	−2,111.6
Net domestic product (NDP)	14,233.1
Minus indirect business taxes and transfers	−1,409.6
Plus other business income adjustments	1,521.5
Plus net U.S. income earned abroad	205.6
National income (NI)	14,550.6
Minus corporate taxes, Social Security contributions, corporate retained earnings	−2,220.3
Plus government transfer payments	1,752.5
Personal income (PI)	14,082.8
Minus personal income taxes	−1,569.2
Disposable personal income (DPI)	12,513.6

Sources: U.S. Department of Commerce and author's estimates.

We have completed our rundown of the different ways that GDP can be computed and of the different variants of national income and product. What we have not yet touched on is the difference between national income measured in this year's dollars and national income representing real goods and services.

QUICK QUIZ See page 186 for the answers. Review concepts from this section in MyEconLab.

To obtain __________ __________, we subtract indirect business taxes and transfers from net domestic product and add other business income adjustments and net U.S. income earned abroad.

To obtain __________ __________, we must add government transfer payments, such as Social Security benefits and food stamps. We must subtract income earned but not received by factor owners, such as corporate retained earnings, Social Security contributions, and corporate income taxes.

To obtain disposable personal income, we subtract all personal __________ __________ from personal income. Disposable personal income is income that individuals actually have for consumption or saving.

Distinguishing between Nominal and Real Values

So far, we have shown how to measure *nominal* income and product. When we say "nominal," we are referring to income and product expressed in the current "face value" of today's dollar. Given the existence of inflation or deflation in the economy, we must also be able to distinguish between the **nominal values** that we will be looking at and the **real values** underlying them. Nominal values are expressed in current dollars. Real income involves our command over goods and services—purchasing power—and therefore depends on money income and a set of prices. Thus, real income refers to nominal income corrected for changes in the weighted average of all prices. In other words, we must make an adjustment for changes in the price level.

Nominal values
The values of variables such as GDP and investment expressed in current dollars, also called *money values;* measurement in terms of the actual market prices at which goods and services are sold.

Real values
Measurement of economic values after adjustments have been made for changes in the average of prices between years.

Consider an example. Nominal income *per person* in 1960 was only about $2,800 per year. In 2013, nominal income per person was about $50,000. Were people really that badly off in 1960? No, for nominal income in 1960 is expressed in 1960 prices, not in the prices of today. In today's dollars, the per-person income of 1960 would be closer to $14,500, or about 30 percent of today's income per person. This is a meaningful comparison between income in 1960 and income today. Next we will show how we can translate nominal measures of income into real measures by using an appropriate price index, such as the Consumer Price Index or the GDP deflator discussed in Chapter 7.

Correcting GDP for Price Changes

If a tablet device costs $200 this year, 10 tablet devices will have a market value of $2,000. If next year they cost $250 each, the same 10 tablet devices will have a market value of $2,500. In this case, there is no increase in the total quantity of tablet devices, but the market value will have increased by one-fourth. Apply this to every single good and service produced and sold in the United States, and you realize that changes in GDP, measured in *current* dollars, may not be a very useful indication of economic activity.

If we are really interested in variations in the *real* output of the economy, we must correct GDP (and just about everything else we look at) for changes in the average of overall prices from year to year. Basically, we need to generate an index that approximates the average prices and then divide that estimate into the value of output in current dollars to adjust the value of output to what is called **constant dollars,** or dollars corrected for general price level changes. This price-corrected GDP is called *real GDP.*

Constant dollars
Dollars expressed in terms of real purchasing power, using a particular year as the base or standard of comparison, in contrast to current dollars.

How much has correcting for price changes caused real GDP to differ from nominal GDP during the past few years?

EXAMPLE

Correcting GDP for Price Index Changes, 2003–2013

Let's take a numerical example to see how we can adjust GDP for changes in the price index. We must pick an appropriate price index in order to adjust for these price level changes. We mentioned the Consumer Price Index, the Producer Price Index, and the GDP deflator in Chapter 7. Let's use the GDP deflator to adjust our figures. Table 8-3 on the facing page gives 11 years of GDP figures. Nominal GDP figures are shown in column 2. The price index (GDP deflator) is in column 3, with base year of 2005, when the GDP deflator equals 100. Column 4 shows real (inflation-adjusted) GDP in 2005 dollars.

The formula for real GDP is

$$\text{Real GDP} = \frac{\text{nominal GDP}}{\text{price index}} \times 100$$

The step-by-step derivation of real (constant-dollar) GDP is as follows: The base year is 2005, so the price index for that year must equal 100. In 2005, nominal GDP was $12,623.0 billion, and so was real GDP expressed in 2005 dollars. In 2006, the price index increased to 103.23108. Thus, to correct 2006's nominal GDP for inflation, we divide the price index, 103.23108, into the nominal GDP figure of $13,377.2 billion and then multiply it by 100. The rounded result is $12,958.5 billion, which is 2006 GDP expressed in terms of the purchasing power of dollars in 2005. What about a situation when the price index is lower than in 2005? Look at 2003. Here the price index shown in column 3 is only 94.13504. That means that in 2003, the average of all prices was just above 94 percent of prices in 2005. To obtain 2003 GDP expressed in terms of 2005 purchasing power, we divide nominal GDP, $11,142.2 billion, by 94.13504 and then multiply by 100. The rounded result is a larger number—$11,836.4 billion. Column 4 in Table 8-3 is a better measure of how the economy has performed than column 2, which shows nominal GDP changes.

FOR CRITICAL THINKING

Based on the information in Table 8-3, in what years was the economy in a recession? Explain briefly.

Plotting Nominal and Real GDP

Nominal GDP and real GDP since 1970 are plotted in Figure 8-4 on the facing page. There is quite a big gap between the two GDP figures, reflecting the amount of inflation that has occurred. Note that the choice of a base year is arbitrary. We have chosen 2005 as the base year in our example. This happens to be the base year that is currently used by the government for the GDP deflator.

MyEconLab Real-time data

TABLE 8-3

Correcting GDP for Price Index Changes

To correct GDP for price index changes, we first have to pick a price index (the GDP deflator) with a specific year as its base. In our example, the base year is 2005. The price index for that year is 100. To obtain 2005 constant-dollar GDP, we divide the price index into nominal GDP and multiply by 100. In other words, we divide column 3 into column 2 and multiply by 100. This gives us column 4, which (taking into account rounding of the deflator) is a measure of real GDP expressed in 2005 purchasing power.

(1) Year	(2) Nominal GDP (billions of dollars per year)	(3) Price Index (base year 2005 = 100)	(4) = [(2) ÷ (3)] × 100 Real GDP (billions of dollars per year, in constant 2005 dollars)
2003	11,142.2	94.13504	11,836.4
2004	11,853.3	96.78613	12,246.9
2005	12,623.0	100.00000	12,623.0
2006	13,377.2	103.23108	12,958.5
2007	14,028.7	106.22653	13,206.4
2008	14,291.5	108.58235	13,161.9
2009	13,939.0	109.72912	12,703.1
2010	14,526.5	110.99098	13,088.0
2011	15,094.0	113.36002	13,315.1
2012	15,706.9	115.51386	13,597.4
2013	16,344.7	117.93965	13,858.5

Sources: U.S. Department of Commerce, Bureau of Economic Analysis, and author's estimates.

Per Capita Real GDP

Looking at changes in real GDP as a measure of economic growth may be deceiving, particularly if the population size has changed significantly. If real GDP over a 10-year period went up 100 percent, you might jump to the conclusion that the real income of a typical person in the economy had increased by that amount. But what if during the

MyEconLab Real-time data

FIGURE 8-4

Nominal and Real GDP

Here we plot both nominal and real GDP. Real GDP is expressed in the purchasing power of 2005 dollars. The gap between the two represents price level changes.

Source: U.S. Department of Commerce.

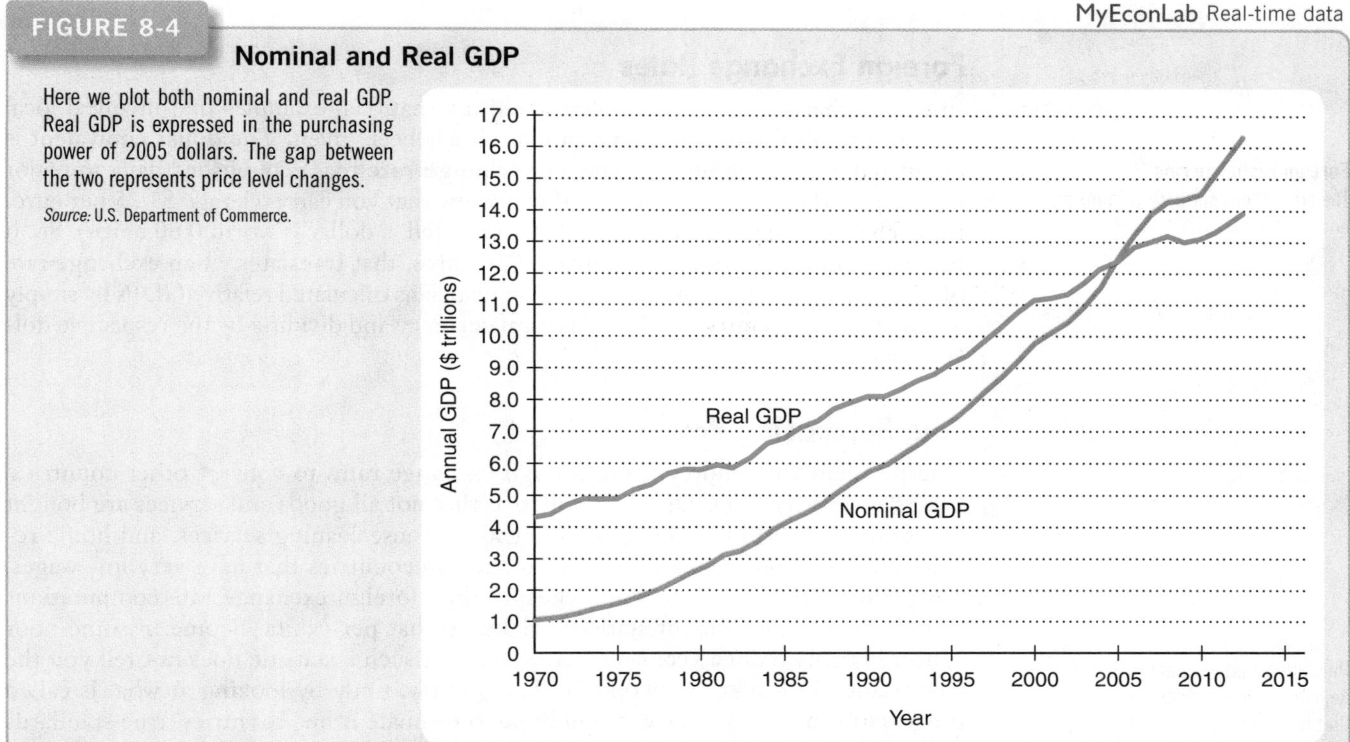

same period the population increased by 200 percent? Then what would you say? Certainly, the amount of real GDP per person, or *per capita real GDP*, would have fallen, even though *total* real GDP had risen. To account not only for price changes but also for population changes, we must first deflate GDP and then divide by the total population, doing this for each year. If we were to look at certain less developed countries, we would find that in many cases, even though real GDP has risen over the past several decades, per capita real GDP has remained constant or fallen because the population has grown just as rapidly or even more rapidly.

QUICK QUIZ See page 186 for the answers. Review concepts from this section in MyEconLab.

To correct **nominal GDP** for price changes, we first select a base year for our price index and assign it the number _________. Then we construct an index based on how a weighted average of prices has changed relative to that base year. For example, if in the next year a weighted average of the prices indicates that prices have increased by 10 percent, we would assign it the number _________. We then divide each year's price index, so constructed, into its respective nominal GDP figure (and multiply by 100).

We can divide the _________ into real GDP to obtain per capita real GDP.

Comparing GDP throughout the World

It is relatively easy to compare the standard of living of a family in Los Angeles with that of one living in Boston. Both families get paid in dollars and can buy the same goods and services at Wal-Mart, McDonald's, and Costco. It is not so easy, however, to make a similar comparison between a family living in the United States and one in, say, Indonesia. The first problem concerns currency comparisons. Indonesian residents get paid in rupiah, their national currency, and buy goods and services with those rupiah. How do we compare the average standard of living measured in rupiah with that measured in dollars?

Foreign Exchange Rates

Foreign exchange rate
The price of one currency in terms of another.

In earlier chapters, you have encountered international examples that involved local currencies, but the dollar equivalent has always been given. The dollar equivalent is calculated by looking up the **foreign exchange rate** that is published daily in major newspapers throughout the world. If you know that you can exchange $1.25 per euro, the exchange rate is 1.25 to 1 (or otherwise stated, a dollar is worth 0.80 euros). So, if French incomes per capita are, say, 33,936 euros, that translates, at an exchange rate of $1.25 per euro, to $42,420. For years, statisticians calculated relative GDPs by simply adding up each country's GDP in its local currency and dividing by the respective dollar exchange rate.

True Purchasing Power

Purchasing power parity
Adjustment in exchange rate conversions that takes into account differences in the true cost of living across countries.

The problem with simply using foreign exchange rates to convert other countries' GDPs and per capita GDPs into dollars is that not all goods and services are bought and sold in a world market. Restaurant food, housecleaning services, and home repairs do not get exchanged across countries. In countries that have very low wages, those kinds of services are much cheaper than foreign exchange rate computations would imply. Government statistics claiming that per capita income in some poor country is only $300 a year seem shocking. But such a statistic does not tell you the true standard of living of people in that country. Only by looking at what is called **purchasing power parity** can you hope to estimate other countries' true standards of living compared to ours.

Given that nations use different currencies, how can we compare nations' levels of real GDP per capita?

INTERNATIONAL EXAMPLE

Purchasing Power Parity Comparisons of World Incomes

A few years ago, the International Monetary Fund accepted the purchasing power parity approach as the correct one. It started presenting international statistics on each country's GDP relative to every other's based on purchasing power parity relative to the U.S. dollar. The results were surprising. As you can see from Table 8-4 below, China's per capita GDP is higher based on purchasing power parity than when measured at market foreign exchange rates.

FOR CRITICAL THINKING

What is the percentage increase in China's per capita GDP when one switches from foreign exchange rates to purchasing power parity?

TABLE 8-4

Comparing GDP Internationally

Country	Annual GDP Based on Purchasing Power Parity (billions of U.S. dollars)	Per Capita GDP Based on Purchasing Power Parity (U.S. dollars)	Per Capita GDP Based on Foreign Exchange Rates (U.S. dollars)
United States	15,094	48,450	48,450
United Kingdom	2,287	36,511	37,780
Germany	3,221	39,414	43,980
France	2,303	35,194	42,420
Japan	4,381	34,278	45,180
Italy	1,979	32,569	35,330
Russia	3,031	21,358	10,400
Brazil	2,305	11,719	10,720
China	11,347	8,442	4,930
Indonesia	1,131	4,668	2,940

Source: World Bank.

QUICK QUIZ See page 186 for the answers. Review concepts from this section in MyEconLab.

The foreign __________ __________ is the price of one currency in terms of another.

Statisticians often calculate relative GDP by adding up each country's GDP in its local currency and dividing by the dollar __________ __________.

Because not all goods and services are bought and sold in the world market, we must correct exchange rate conversions of other countries' GDP figures to take into account differences in the true __________ of __________ across countries.

YOU ARE THERE

Has the Economy Grown More Than Official GDP Data Suggest?

Economists Bart Hobijn and Charles Steindel of the Federal Reserve Bank of New York are studying how to adjust GDP to take into account three items that the official measure ignores: (1)"intangible investment," including spending on research into new processes or products that currently is not counted within GDP as business fixed investment; (2) real investment in capital goods undertaken by the government but potentially undercounted in official GDP tabulations; and (3) the shift from nonmarket home production not counted as GDP to market production because more women are entering the U.S. labor force.

Hobijn and Steindel find that adding the first two items tends to push up fixed investment measures and consequently increases their broadened GDP measure. Taking into account the third item tends to reduce this broadened measure, because it subtracts an imputed value of home production from the higher official market production of women who have joined the labor force. The net effect of taking all three items into account, Hobijn and Steindel conclude, is that the average official growth rate of inflation-adjusted (real) GDP is nearly 0.5 percentage point per year lower than the rate of growth of their altered GDP measure after adjusting for inflation. Consequently, they conclude that the official U.S. economic growth rate may be significantly understated.

Critical Thinking Questions

1. Why is intangible investment harder to measure than tangible investment?
2. What makes it difficult to assign a dollar value to nonmarket home production?

ISSUES & APPLICATIONS

Asia's "Economic Size" Depends on How It Is Measured

CONCEPTS APPLIED

- Real GDP
- Purchasing Power Parity
- Per Capita Real GDP

The media have reported on the growing economic clout of Asian nations. How large is the combined "economic size" of Asian nations in comparison with other nations, such as the United States? The answer depends on what measure we use when making comparisons between Asia and the world as a whole.

Asian Real GDP as a Percentage of Global Real GDP

Figure 8-5 on the facing page displays the combined real GDP of Asia as a percentage of the combined real GDP of the entire world. The figure displays this percentage according to two different measures. One measure uses prevailing exchange rates in currency markets to adjust all countries' real GDP levels to allow for comparisons. The other measure utilizes purchasing power parity adjustments.

Utilizing market exchange rates indicates that Asian real GDP's share of global real GDP generally rose steadily between 1980 and the mid-1990s from less than one-fifth to slightly more than one-fourth of global GDP. In contrast, purchasing power parity measures of real GDP indicate that Asia's measured share of the world economy has grown to more than 35 percent.

Asian versus Global Per Capita Real GDP

Another measure for comparing the relative "economic sizes" of Asia and the world is per capita real GDP. This measure also can be computed using either foreign exchange rates or purchasing power parities to allow for cross-country comparisons.

When per capita real GDP is computed using foreign exchange rates, Asian per capita real GDP is only 11 percent of global per capita real GDP. When the tabulation uses purchasing power parity adjustments, Asian per capita real GDP is 26 percent of global real GDP per capita. Thus, both measures indicate that although Asia's economic size has risen in relation to the world as a whole, Asia's per capita real GDP remains relatively low. Even though Asian real GDP is relatively high, so is Asia's population, which is why the region's per capita real GDP remains only a fraction of the global level.

FIGURE 8-5

Asia's Share of Global Real GDP

This figure displays two measures of real GDP in Asia as a percentage of worldwide real GDP. The measure that uses foreign exchange rates to adjust real GDP data to comparable amounts across countries indicates a rise in Asia's share until the mid-1990s and a leveling off since then. The measure based on purchasing power parity comparisons shows a larger and longer-lived rise in Asia's share of global real GDP.

Source: International Monetary Fund.

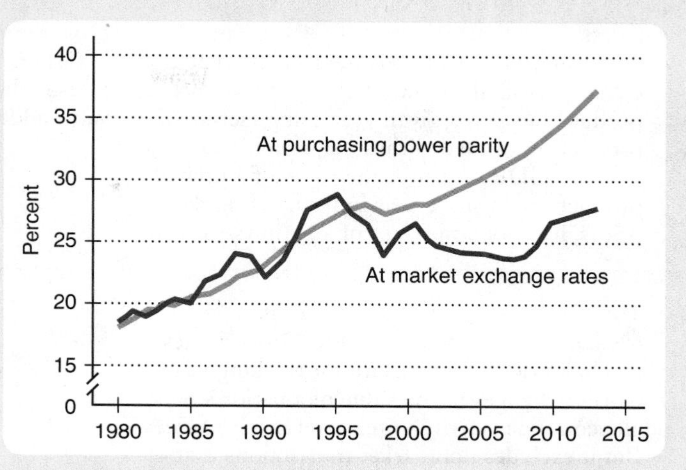

For Critical Thinking

1. Why is there such a difference in Asia's share of global real GDP, depending on whether the computation uses purchasing power parities or exchange rates?
2. Why is Asia's "economic size" so much smaller on a per capita basis than on an absolute basis?

Web Resources

1. For a recent analysis of the growth of Asia's share of global economic activity, go to **www.econtoday.com/chap08**.
2. To learn about a recent claim that China's economy is already "larger" than the U.S. economy, go to **www.econtoday.com/chap08**.

MyEconLab

For more questions on this chapter's Issues & Applications, go to MyEconLab. In the Study Plan for this chapter, select Section N: News.

MyEconLab

Here is what you should know after reading this chapter. MyEconLab will help you identify what you know, and where to go when you need to practice.

WHAT YOU SHOULD KNOW | **WHERE TO GO TO PRACTICE**

The Circular Flow of Income and Output The circular flow of income and output captures two principles: (1) In every transaction, the seller receives the same amount that the buyer spends; and (2) goods and services flow in one direction, and money payments flow in the other direction. Households ultimately purchase the nation's total output of final goods and services. They make these purchases using income—wages, rents, interest, and profits—earned from selling labor, land, capital, and entrepreneurial services, respectively. Hence, income equals the value of output.

national income accounting, 162
total income, 163
final goods and services, 163

Key Figure
Figure 8-1, 162

- MyEconLab Study Plan 8.1
- Animated Figure 8-1

MyEconLab *continued*

WHAT YOU SHOULD KNOW		WHERE TO GO TO PRACTICE
Gross Domestic Product (GDP) A nation's gross domestic product is the total market value of its final output of goods and services produced within a given year using factors of production located within the nation's borders. Because GDP measures the value of a flow of production during a year in terms of market prices, it is not a measure of a nation's wealth.	gross domestic product (GDP), 164 intermediate goods, 164 value added, 164	• MyEconLab Study Plan 8.2
The Limitations of Using GDP as a Measure of National Welfare Gross domestic product is a useful measure for tracking year-to-year changes in the value of a nation's overall economic activity in terms of market prices. But it excludes nonmarket transactions that may add to or detract from general welfare. It also fails to account for factors such as environmental quality and the amount and quality of leisure time.		• MyEconLab Study Plan 8.2
The Expenditure Approach to Tabulating GDP To calculate GDP using the expenditure approach, we sum consumption spending, investment expenditures, government spending, and net export expenditures. Thus, we add up the total amount spent on newly produced goods and services to obtain the dollar value of the output produced and purchased during the year.	expenditure approach, 167 income approach, 167 durable consumer goods, 168 nondurable consumer goods, 168 services, 168 gross private domestic investment, 168 investment, 168 producer durables, or capital goods, 168 fixed investment, 168 inventory investment, 169 depreciation, 170 net domestic product (NDP), 170 capital consumption allowance, 171 net investment, 171 **Key Figure** Figure 8-2, 170	• MyEconLab Study Plan 8.3 • Animated Figure 8-2
The Income Approach to Computing GDP To tabulate GDP using the income approach, we add total wages and salaries, rental income, interest income, profits, and nonincome expense items—indirect business taxes and depreciation—to obtain gross domestic income, which is equivalent to gross domestic product. Thus, the total value of all income earnings (equivalent to total factor costs) equals GDP.	gross domestic income (GDI), 171 indirect business taxes, 172 nonincome expense items, 172 national income (NI), 174 personal income (PI), 174 disposable personal income (DPI), 174	• MyEconLab Study Plans 8.3, 8.4

MyEconLab *continued*

WHAT YOU SHOULD KNOW		WHERE TO GO TO PRACTICE
Distinguishing between Nominal GDP and Real GDP Nominal GDP is the value of newly produced output during the current year measured at current market prices. Real GDP adjusts the value of current output into constant dollars by correcting for changes in the overall level of prices from year to year. To calculate real GDP, we divide nominal GDP by the price index (the GDP deflator) and multiply by 100.	nominal values, 175 real values, 175 constant dollars, 176 foreign exchange rate, 178 purchasing power parity, 178 **Key Figure** Figure 8-4, 177	• MyEconLab Study Plans 8.5, 8.6 • Animated Figure 8-4

Log in to MyEconLab, take a chapter test, and get a personalized Study Plan that tells you which concepts you understand and which ones you need to review. From there, MyEconLab will give you further practice, tutorials, animations, videos, and guided solutions. For more information, visit www.myeconlab.com

PROBLEMS

All problems are assignable in MyEconLab; *exercises that update with real-time data are marked with* [icon]. *Answers to odd-numbered problems appear at the back of the book.*

8-1. Explain in your own words why the flow of gross domestic product during a given interval must always be equivalent to the flow of gross domestic income within that same period. (See page 162.)

8-2. In the first stage of manufacturing each final unit of a product, a firm purchases a key input at a price of $4 per unit. The firm then pays a wage rate of $3 for the time that labor is exerted, combining an additional $2 of inputs for each final unit of output produced. The firm sells every unit of the product for $10. What is the contribution of each unit of output to GDP in the current year? (See page 165.)

8-3. Each year after a regular spring cleaning, Maria spruces up her home a little by retexturing and repainting the walls of one room in her house. In a given year, she spends $25 on magazines to get ideas about wall textures and paint shades, $45 on newly produced texturing materials and tools, $35 on new paintbrushes and other painting equipment, and $175 on newly produced paint. Normally, she preps the walls, a service that a professional wall-texturing specialist would charge $200 to do, and applies two coats of paint, a service that a painter would charge $350 to do, on her own. (See pages 164–166.)

a. When she purchases her usual set of materials and does all the work on her home by herself in a given spring, how much does Maria's annual spring texturing and painting activity contribute to GDP?

b. Suppose that Maria hurt her back this year and is recovering from surgery. Her surgeon has instructed her not to do any texturing work, but he has given her the go-ahead to paint a room as long as she is cautious. Thus, she buys all the equipment required to both texture and paint a room. She hires someone else to do the texturing work but does the painting herself. How much would her spring painting activity add to GDP?

c. As a follow-up to part (b), suppose that as soon as Maria bends down to dip her brush into the paint, she realizes that painting will be too hard on her back after all. She decides to hire someone else to do all the work using the materials she has already purchased. In this case, how much will her spring painting activity contribute to GDP?

8-4. Each year, Johan typically does all his own landscaping and yard work. He spends $200 per year on mulch for his flower beds, $225 per year on flowers and plants, $50 on fertilizer for his lawn, and $245 on gasoline and lawn mower maintenance. The lawn and garden store where he obtains his mulch and fertilizer charges other customers $500 for the service of spreading that much mulch in flower beds and $50 for the service of distributing fertilizer over a yard the size of Johan's. Paying a professional yard care service to mow his lawn would require an expenditure of $1,200 per year, but in that case Johan would not have to buy gasoline or maintain his own lawn mower. (See pages 164–166.)

a. In a normal year, how much does Johan's landscaping and yard work contribute to GDP?

b. Suppose that Johan has developed allergy problems this year and will have to reduce the amount of his yard work. He can wear a mask while running his lawn mower, so he will keep mowing his yard, but he will pay the lawn and garden center to spread mulch and distribute fertilizer. How much will all the work on Johan's yard contribute to GDP this year?

c. As a follow-up to part (b), at the end of the year, Johan realizes that his allergies are growing worse and that he will have to arrange for all his landscaping and yard work to be done by someone else next year. How much will he contribute to GDP next year?

8-5. Consider the following hypothetical data for the U.S. economy in 2016 (all amounts are in trillions of dollars; see pages 168–171).

Consumption	11.0
Indirect business taxes	.8
Depreciation	1.3
Government spending	2.8
Imports	2.7
Gross private domestic investment	3.0
Exports	2.5

a. Based on the data, what is GDP? NDP? NI?

b. Suppose that in 2017, exports fall to $2.3 trillion, imports rise to $2.85 trillion, and gross private domestic investment falls to $2.25 trillion. What will GDP be in 2017, assuming that other values do not change between 2016 and 2017?

8-6. Look back at Table 8-3 on page 177, which explains how to calculate real GDP in terms of 2005 constant dollars. Change the base year to 2003. Recalculate the price index, and then recalculate real GDP—that is, express column 4 of Table 8-3 in terms of 2003 dollars instead of 2005 dollars. (See page 177.)

8-7. Consider the following hypothetical data for the U.S. economy in 2016 (in trillions of dollars), and assume that there are no statistical discrepancies or other adjustments. (See pages 169–175.)

Profit	2.8
Indirect business taxes and transfers	.8
Rent	.7
Interest	.8
Wages	8.2
Depreciation	1.3
Consumption	11.0
Exports	1.5
Government transfer payments	2.0
Personal income taxes and nontax payments	1.7
Imports	1.7
Corporate taxes and retained earnings	.5
Social Security contributions	2.0
Government spending	1.8

a. What is gross domestic income? GDP?

b. What is gross private domestic investment?

c. What is personal income? Personal disposable income?

8-8. Which of the following are production activities that are included in GDP? Which are not? (See pages 164–166.)

a. Mr. King performs the service of painting his own house instead of paying someone else to do it.

b. Mr. King paints houses for a living.

c. Mrs. King earns income from parents by taking baby photos in her digital photography studio.

d. Mrs. King takes photos of planets and stars as part of her astronomy hobby.

e. E*Trade charges fees to process Internet orders for stock trades.

f. Mr. Ho spends $10,000 on shares of stock via an Internet trade order and pays a $10 brokerage fee.

g. Mrs. Ho receives a Social Security payment.

h. Ms. Hernandez makes a $300 payment for an Internet-based course on stock trading.

i. Mr. Langham sells a used laptop computer to his neighbor.

8-9. Explain what happens to contributions to GDP in each of the following situations. (See page 165.)

a. A woman who makes a living charging for investment advice on her Internet Web site marries one of her clients, to whom she now provides advice at no charge.

b. A man who had washed the windows of his own house every year decides to pay a private company to wash those windows this year.

c. A company that had been selling used firearms illegally finally gets around to obtaining an operating license and performing background checks as specified by law prior to each gun sale.

8-10. Explain what happens to the official measure of GDP in each of the following situations. (See page 165.)

a. Air quality improves significantly throughout the United States, but there are no effects on aggregate production or on market prices of final goods and services.

b. The U.S. government spends considerably less on antipollution efforts this year than it did in recent years.

c. The quality of cancer treatments increases, so patients undergo fewer treatments, which hospitals continue to provide at the same price per treatment as before.

8-11. Which of the following activities of a computer manufacturer during the current year are included in this year's measure of GDP? (See page 165.)

a. The manufacturer produces a chip in June, uses it as a component in a computer in August, and sells the computer to a customer in November.

b. A retail outlet of the firm sells a computer completely built during the current year.

c. A marketing arm of the company receives fee income during the current year when a buyer of one of its computers elects to use the computer manufacturer as her Internet service provider.

8-12. A number of economists contend that official measures of U.S. gross private investment expenditures are understated. Answer parts (a) and (b) below to determine just how understated these economists believe that officially measured investment spending may be. (See page 168.)

a. Household spending on education, such as college tuition expenditures, is counted as consumption spending. Some economists suggest that these expenditures, which amount to 6 percent of GDP, should be counted as investment spending instead. Based on this 6 percent estimate and the GDP computations detailed in Figure 8-3 on page 173, how many billions of dollars would shift from consumption to investment if this suggestion was adopted?

b. Some economists argue that intangible forms of investment—business research spending, educational expenses for employees, and the like—should be included in the official measure of gross private domestic investment. These expenditures, which amount to about 9 percent of GDP, currently are treated as business input expenses and are not included in GDP. Based on this 9 percent estimate and the GDP computations detailed in Figure 8-3 on page 173, how much higher would gross private domestic investment be if intangible investment expenditures were counted as investment spending?

c. Based on your answers to parts (a) and (b), what is the total amount that gross private domestic investment may be understated, according to economists who argue that household education spending and business intangible investments should be added? How much may GDP be understated?

8-13. Consider the table at the top of the next column for the economy of a nation whose residents produce five final goods. (See pages 175–176.)

	2013		2017	
Good	Price	Quantity	Price	Quantity
Shampoo	$ 2	15	$ 4	20
External hard drives	200	10	250	10
Books	40	5	50	4
Milk	3	10	4	3
Candy	1	40	2	20

Assuming a 2013 base year:

a. What is nominal GDP for 2013 and 2017?

b. What is real GDP for 2013 and 2017?

8-14. Consider the following table for the economy of a nation whose residents produce four final goods. (See pages 175–176.)

	2015		2016	
Good	Price	Quantity	Price	Quantity
Computers	$1,000	10	$800	15
Bananas	6	3,000	11	1,000
Televisions	100	500	150	300
Cookies	1	10,000	2	10,000

Assuming a 2016 base year:

a. What is nominal GDP for 2015 and 2016?

b. What is real GDP for 2015 and 2016?

8-15. In the table for Problem 8-14, if 2016 is the base year, what is the price index for 2015? (Round decimal fractions to the nearest tenth.)

8-16. Suppose that early in a year, a hurricane hits a town in Florida and destroys a substantial number of homes. A portion of this stock of housing, which had a market value of $100 million (not including the market value of the land), was uninsured. The owners of the residences spent a total of $5 million during the rest of the year to pay salvage companies to help them save remaining belongings. A small percentage of uninsured owners had sufficient resources to spend a total of $15 million during the year to pay construction companies to rebuild their homes. Some were able to devote their own time, the opportunity cost of which was valued at $3 million, to work on rebuilding their homes. The remaining people, however, chose to sell their land at its market value and abandon the remains of their houses. What was the combined effect of these transactions on GDP for this year? (Hint: Which transactions took place in the markets for *final* goods and services?) In what ways, if any, does the effect on GDP reflect a loss in welfare for these individuals? (See page 165.)

8-17. Suppose that in 2015, geologists discover large reserves of oil under the tundra in Alaska. These new reserves have a market value estimated at $50 billion at current oil prices. Oil companies spend $1 billion to hire workers and move and position equipment to begin exploratory pumping during that same year. In the process of loading some of the oil onto tankers at a port, one company accidentally spills some of the oil into a bay and by the end of the year pays $1 billion to other companies to clean it up. The oil spill kills thousands of birds, seals, and other wildlife. What was the combined effect of these events on GDP for this year? (Hint: Which transactions took place in the markets for *final* goods and services?) In what ways, if any, does the effect on GDP reflect a loss in national welfare? (See page 165.)

8-18. Consider the diagram below, and answer the following questions. (See page 177.)

a. What is the base year? Explain.

b. Has this country experienced inflation or deflation since the base year? How can you tell?

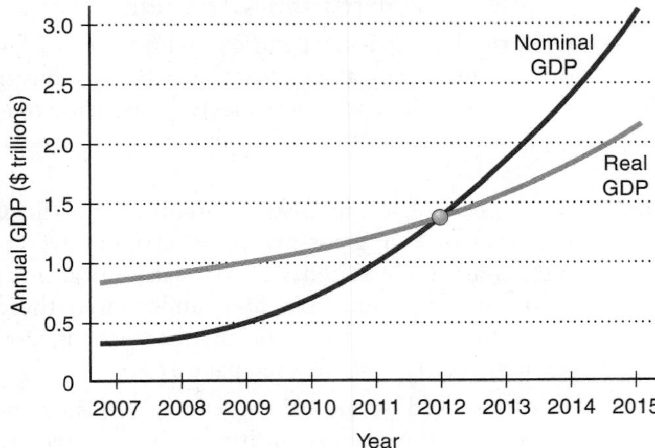

ECONOMICS ON THE NET

Tracking the Components of Gross Domestic Product

One way to keep tabs on the components of GDP is via the FRED database at the Web site of the Federal Reserve Bank of St. Louis.

Title: Gross Domestic Product and Components

Navigation: Use the link at **www.econtoday.com/chap08** to visit the home page of the Federal Reserve Bank of St. Louis. Click on *Gross Domestic Product (GDP) and Components.*

Application

1. Click on *GDP/GNP*, and then click a checkmark next to *GDP (Gross Domestic Product)*. Write down nominal GDP data for the past 10 quarters.

2. Back up to *GDPCA (Real Gross Domestic Product) Dollars.* Write down the amounts for the past 10 quarters. Use the formula on page XXX to calculate the price level for each quarter. Has the price level decreased or increased in recent quarters?

For Group Study and Analysis Divide the class into "consumption," "investment," "government sector," and "foreign sector" groups. Have each group evaluate the contribution of each category of spending to GDP and to its quarter-to-quarter volatility. Reconvene the class, and discuss the factors that appear to create the most variability in GDP.

ANSWERS TO QUICK QUIZZES

p. 164: (i) factor . . . income; (ii) final; (iii) profit

p. 167: (i) Gross domestic product; (ii) value added; (iii) exclude; (iv) GDP; (v) market value

p. 171: (i) expenditure . . . durables . . . nondurables . . . services; (ii) capacity . . . inventories; (iii) market; (iv) depreciation

p. 172: (i) wages . . . interest . . . rent . . . profits; (ii) indirect business taxes . . . depreciation

p. 175: (i) national income; (ii) personal income; (iii) income taxes

p. 178: (i) 100 . . . 110; (ii) population

p. 179: (i) exchange rate; (ii) exchange rate; (iii) cost . . . living

Global Economic Growth and Development

9

LEARNING OBJECTIVES

After reading this chapter, you should be able to:

- Define economic growth
- Recognize the importance of economic growth rates
- Explain why productivity increases are crucial for maintaining economic growth
- Describe the fundamental determinants of economic growth
- Understand the basis of new growth theory
- Discuss the fundamental factors that contribute to a nation's economic development

MyEconLab helps you master each objective and study more efficiently. See end of chapter for details.

From the late 1990s through most of the first decade of the 2000s, media reports bemoaned the sorry state of the U.S. private *saving rate,* or the annual flow of saving per year as a percentage of households' personal disposable income per year. U.S. residents were saving only a little over 2 percent of their annual personal disposable income, so few resources were available to finance the purchase of capital goods. This fact, observers worried, would tend to drag down U.S. economic growth. Since 2007, the average private saving rate has increased significantly, which has led some observers to become more optimistic about U.S. growth prospects. Nevertheless, others point to a sharp drop in the *overall* national saving rate, inclusive of *government* saving, as reason for even greater concern about the prospects for future U.S. economic growth. By the time you have completed this chapter, you will be able to evaluate these alternative perspectives about the U.S. saving rate and economic growth.

DID YOU KNOW THAT... since 2009, the U.S. birthrate has been at its lowest level in a century? This development is a striking turnabout from 2007, when more babies were born in the United States than in any prior year in the nation's history. In this chapter, you will learn why this lower U.S. birthrate would tend to boost the near-term measured rate of U.S. *economic growth,* other things being equal. You will also discover why a prolonged drop in the country's birthrate would have a theoretically ambiguous effect on the long-term economic growth rate.

How Do We Define Economic Growth?

Recall from Chapter 2 that we can show economic growth graphically as an outward shift of a production possibilities curve, as is seen in Figure 9-1 below. If there is economic growth between 2015 and 2037, the production possibilities curve will shift outward toward the red curve. The distance that it shifts represents the amount of economic growth, defined as the increase in the productive capacity of a nation. Although it is possible to come up with a measure of a nation's increased productive capacity, it would not be easy. Therefore, we turn to a more readily obtainable definition of economic growth.

Most people have a general idea of what economic growth means. When a nation grows economically, its citizens must be better off in at least some ways, usually in terms of their material well-being. Typically, though, we do not measure the well-being of any nation solely in terms of its total output of real goods and services or in terms of real GDP without making some adjustments. After all, India has a real GDP more than 15 times as large as that of Denmark. The population in India, though, is about 200 times greater than that of Denmark. Consequently, we view India as a relatively poor country and Denmark as a relatively rich country. Thus, when we measure economic growth, we must adjust for population growth. Our formal definition becomes this: **Economic growth** occurs when there are increases in *per capita* real GDP, measured by the rate of change in per capita real GDP per year. Figure 9-2 on page 190 presents the historical record of real GDP per person in the United States.

Economic growth
Increases in per capita real GDP measured by its rate of change per year.

Problems in Definition

Our definition of economic growth says nothing about the *distribution* of output and income. A nation might grow very rapidly in terms of increases in per capita real GDP, while its poor people remain poor or become even poorer. Therefore, in assessing the economic growth record of any nation, we must be careful to pinpoint which income groups have benefited the most from such growth. How much does economic growth differ across countries?

FIGURE 9-1
Economic Growth

If there is growth between 2015 and 2037, the production possibilities curve for the entire economy will shift outward from the blue line labeled 2015 to the red line labeled 2037. The distance that it shifts represents an increase in the productive capacity of the nation.

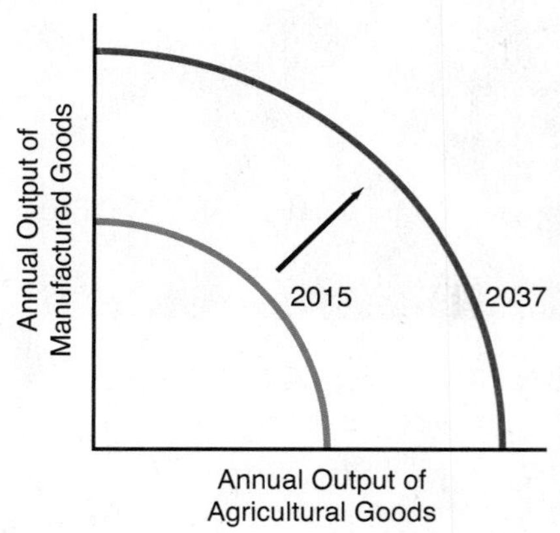

INTERNATIONAL EXAMPLE

Growth Rates around the World

Table 9-1 shows the average annual rate of growth of real GDP per person in selected countries since 1970. During this time period, the United States has been positioned about midway in the pack. Thus, even though we are one of the world's richest countries, our rate of economic growth has been in the middle range. The reason that U.S. per capita real GDP has remained higher than per capita real GDP in most other nations is that, despite the late-2000s downturn, U.S. growth has been sustained over many decades. This is something that most other countries have so far been unable to accomplish.

FOR CRITICAL THINKING

"The largest change is from zero to one." Does this statement have anything to do with relative growth rates in poorer versus richer countries?

TABLE 9-1

Per Capita Real GDP Growth Rates in Various Countries

Country	Average Annual Rate of Growth of Real GDP Per Capita, 1970–2013 (%)
Sweden	1.6
France	1.7
Germany	1.7
United States	1.8
Canada	1.9
Japan	2.0
Turkey	2.0
Brazil	2.3
India	3.3
Indonesia	4.3
Malaysia	4.8
China	7.1

Sources: World Bank, International Monetary Fund, and author's estimates.

Real standards of living can go up without any positive economic growth. This can occur if individuals are, on average, enjoying more leisure by working fewer hours but producing as much as they did before. For example, if per capita real GDP in the United States remained at $55,000 a year for a decade, we could not automatically jump to the conclusion that U.S. residents were, on average, no better off. What if, during that same 10-year period, average hours worked fell from 37 per week to 33 per week? That would mean that during the 10 years under study, individuals in the labor force were "earning" 4 more hours of leisure a week.

Go to www.econtoday.com/chap09 to get the latest figures and estimates on economic growth throughout the world.

Nothing so extreme as this example has occurred in this country, but something similar has. Average hours worked per week fell steadily until the 1960s, when they leveled off. That means that during much of the history of this country, the increase in per capita real GDP *understated* the growth in living standards that we were experiencing because we were enjoying more and more leisure as time passed.

Is Economic Growth Bad?

Some commentators on our current economic situation believe that the definition of economic growth ignores its negative effects. Some psychologists even contend that economic growth makes us worse off. They say that the more the economy grows, the more "needs" are created so that we feel worse off as we become richer. Our expectations are rising faster than reality, so we presumably always suffer from a sense of disappointment. Also, economists' measurement of economic growth does not take into account the spiritual and cultural aspects of the good life. As with all activities, both costs and benefits are associated with growth. You can see some of those listed in Table 9-2 on the bottom of the next page.

MyEconLab Real-time data

FIGURE 9-2

The Historical Record of U.S. Economic Growth

The graph traces per capita real GDP in the United States since 1900. Data are given in 2005 dollars.

Source: U.S. Department of Commerce.

Any measure of economic growth that we use will be imperfect. Nonetheless, the measures that we do have allow us to make comparisons across countries and over time and, if used judiciously, can enable us to gain important insights. Per capita real GDP, used so often, is not always an accurate measure of economic well-being, but it is a serviceable measure of productive activity.

The Importance of Growth Rates

Notice in Table 9-1 on the previous page that the growth rates in real per capita income for most countries differ very little—generally by only a few percentage points. You might want to know why such small differences in growth rates are important. What does it matter if we grow at 3 percent rather than at 4 percent per year? The answer is that in the long run, it matters a lot.

A small difference in the rate of economic growth does not matter very much for next year or the year after. For the more distant future, however, it makes considerable difference. The power of *compounding* is impressive. Let's see what happens with three different annual rates of growth: 3 percent, 4 percent, and 5 percent. We start with

TABLE 9-2

Costs and Benefits of Economic Growth

Benefits	Costs
Reduction in illiteracy	Environmental pollution
Reduction in poverty	Breakdown of the family
Improved health	Isolation and alienation
Longer lives	Urban congestion
Political stability	

TABLE 9-3

One Dollar Compounded Annually at Different Interest Rates

Here we show the value of a dollar at the end of a specified period during which it has been compounded annually at a specified interest rate. For example, if you took $1 today and invested it at 5 percent per year, it would yield $1.05 at the end of one year. At the end of 10 years, it would equal $1.63, and at the end of 50 years, it would equal $11.50.

	Interest Rate						
Number of Years	3%	4%	5%	6%	8%	10%	20%
1	1.03	1.04	1.05	1.06	1.08	1.10	1.20
2	1.06	1.08	1.10	1.12	1.17	1.21	1.44
3	1.09	1.12	1.16	1.19	1.26	1.33	1.73
4	1.13	1.17	1.22	1.26	1.36	1.46	2.07
5	1.16	1.22	1.28	1.34	1.47	1.61	2.49
6	1.19	1.27	1.34	1.41	1.59	1.77	2.99
7	1.23	1.32	1.41	1.50	1.71	1.94	3.58
8	1.27	1.37	1.48	1.59	1.85	2.14	4.30
9	1.30	1.42	1.55	1.68	2.00	2.35	5.16
10	1.34	1.48	1.63	1.79	2.16	2.59	6.19
20	1.81	2.19	2.65	3.20	4.66	6.72	38.30
30	2.43	3.24	4.32	5.74	10.00	17.40	237.00
40	3.26	4.80	7.04	10.30	21.70	45.30	1,470.00
50	4.38	7.11	11.50	18.40	46.90	117.00	9,100.00

$1 trillion per year of U.S. GDP at some time in the past. We then compound this $1 trillion, or allow it to grow at these three different growth rates. The difference is huge. In 50 years, $1 trillion per year becomes $4.38 trillion per year if compounded at 3 percent per year. Just one percentage point more in the growth rate, 4 percent, results in a real GDP of $7.11 trillion per year in 50 years, almost double the previous amount. Two percentage points' difference in the growth rate—5 percent per year—results in a real GDP of $11.5 trillion per year in 50 years, or nearly three times as much. Obviously, very small differences in annual growth rates result in great differences in cumulative economic growth. That is why nations are concerned if the growth rate falls even a little in absolute percentage terms.

Thus, when we talk about growth rates, we are talking about compounding. In Table 9-3 above, we show how $1 compounded annually grows at different interest rates. We see in the 3 percent column that $1 in 50 years grows to $4.38. We merely multiplied $1 trillion times 4.38 to get the growth figure in our earlier example. In the 5 percent column, $1 grows to $11.50 after 50 years. Again, we multiplied $1 trillion times 11.50 to get the growth figure for 5 percent in the preceding example.

How much of a difference in your future income would result from a 1-percentage-point drop in the long-term U.S. growth rate?

EXAMPLE

Gauging the Future Impact of a 1-Percentage-Point Growth Drop

Over nearly four decades, the rate of growth in U.S. per capita real GDP has averaged close to 2 percent. Since 2008, however, the average growth rate of the nation's per capita real GDP has remained below 1 percent. If this were to become the new long-term average rate of economic growth in a dampened U.S. economy, how much lower would per capita real GDP be in future years?

Gross domestic product represents both the value of production of goods and services per year and the income generated during that year. Thus, U.S. per capita real GDP is equal to the annual inflation-adjusted income earned by an average resident during a year. This means that a permanent drop in the rate of economic growth from 2 percent to 1 percent would translate into an 18 percent dampening in that resident's income after 20 years. After 50 years, the 1-percentage-point reduction in the growth rate would cause the resident's real income to be more than 60 percent less than it would have been at the higher growth rate.

FOR CRITICAL THINKING

Why does just a 1-percentage-point reduction in the rate of economic growth make such a significant difference if it persists for many years?

Rule of 70
A rule stating that the approximate number of years required for per capita real GDP to double is equal to 70 divided by the average rate of economic growth.

THE RULE OF 70 Table 9-3 on the preceding page indicates that how quickly the level of a nation's per capita real GDP increases depends on the rate of economic growth. A formula called the **rule of 70** provides a shorthand way to calculate approximately how long it will take a country to experience a significant increase in per capita real GDP. According to the rule of 70, the approximate number of years necessary for a nation's per capita real GDP to increase by 100 percent—that is, to *double*—is equal to 70 divided by the average rate of economic growth. Thus, at an annual growth rate of 10 percent, per capita real GDP should double in about 7 years.

As you can see in Table 9-3, at a 10 percent growth rate, in 7 years per capita real GDP would rise by a factor of 1.94, which is very close to 2, or very nearly the doubling predicted by the rule of 70. At an annual growth rate of 8 percent, the rule of 70 predicts that nearly 9 years will be required for a nation's per capita real GDP to double. Table 9-3 verifies that this prediction is correct. Indeed, the table shows that after 9 years an exact doubling will occur at a growth rate of 8 percent.

The rule of 70 implies that at lower rates of economic growth, much more time must pass before per capita real GDP will double. At a 3 percent growth rate, just over 23 (70 ÷ 3) years must pass before per capita real income doubles. At a rate of growth of only 1 percent per year, 70 (70 ÷ 1) years must pass. This means that if a nation's average rate of economic growth is 1 percent instead of 3 percent, 47 more years—about two generations—must pass for per capita real GDP to double. Clearly, the rule of 70 verifies that even very slight differences in economic growth rates are important.

QUICK QUIZ See page 209 for the answers. Review concepts from this section in MyEconLab.

Economic growth can be defined as the increase in __________ __________ real GDP, measured by its rate of change per year.

The __________ of economic growth are reductions in illiteracy, poverty, and illness and increases in life spans and political stability. The __________ of economic growth may include environmental pollution, alienation, and urban congestion.

Small percentage-point differences in growth rates lead to __________ differences in per capita real GDP over time. These differences can be seen by examining a compound interest table such as the one in Table 9-3 on page 191.

Productivity Increases: The Heart of Economic Growth

Let's say that you are required to type 10 term papers and homework assignments a year. You have a digital device, but you do not know how to touch-type. You end up spending an average of two hours per typing job. The next summer, you buy a touch-typing tutorial to use on your digital device and spend a few minutes a day improving your speed. The following term, you spend only one hour per typing assignment, thereby saving 10 hours a semester. You have become more productive. This concept of productivity summarizes your ability (and everyone else's) to produce the same output with fewer inputs. Thus, **labor productivity** is normally measured by dividing total real domestic output (real GDP) by the number of workers or the number of labor hours. By definition, labor productivity increases whenever average output produced per worker (or per hour worked) during a specified time period increases.

Labor productivity
Total real domestic output (real GDP) divided by the number of workers (output per worker).

Clearly, there is a relationship between economic growth and increases in labor productivity. If you divide all resources into just capital and labor, economic growth can be defined simply as the cumulative contribution to per capita GDP growth of three components: the rate of growth of capital, the rate of growth of labor, and the rate of growth of capital and labor productivity. If everything else remains constant, improvements in labor productivity ultimately lead to economic growth and higher living standards.

Go to www.econtoday.com/chap09 for information about the latest trends in U.S. labor productivity.

FIGURE 9-3

Factors Accounting for Economic Growth in Selected Regions

In the United States, South Asia, and Latin America, growth in labor resources is the main contributor to economic growth.

Source: International Monetary Fund.

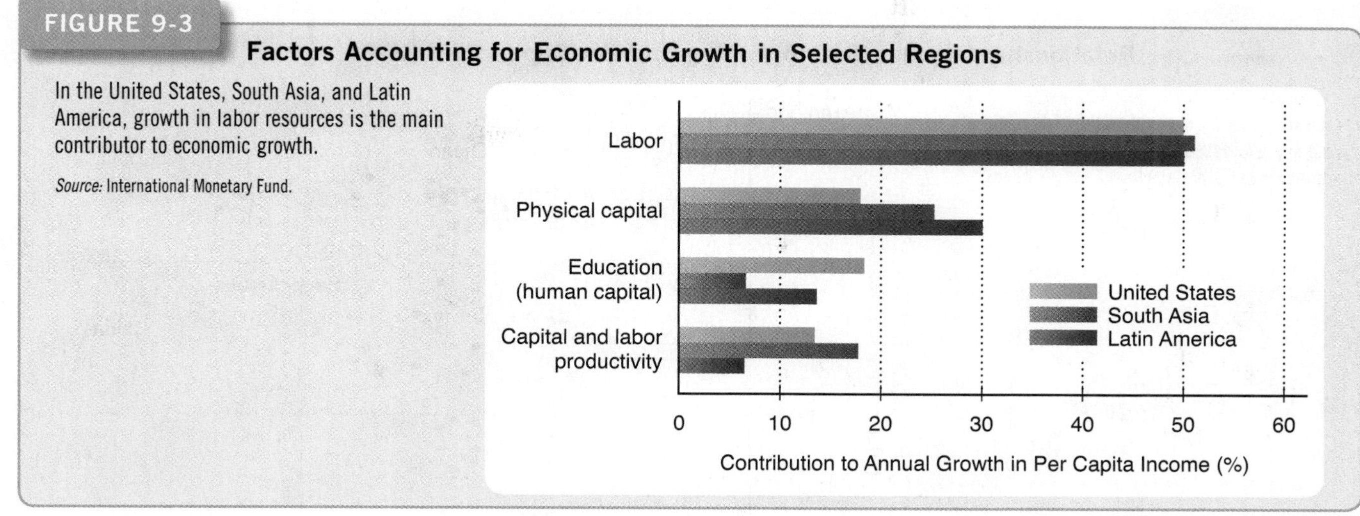

Figure 9-3 above displays estimates of the relative contributions of the growth of labor and capital and the growth of labor and capital productivity to economic growth in the United States, nations in South Asia, and Latin American countries. The growth of labor resources, through associated increases in labor force participation, has contributed to the expansion of output that has accounted for at least half of economic growth in all three regions. Total capital is the sum of physical capital, such as tools and machines, and human capital, which is the amount of knowledge acquired from research and education.

Figure 9-3 shows the separate contributions of the growth of these forms of capital, which together have accounted for roughly a third of the growth rate of per capita incomes in the United States, South Asia, and Latin America. In these three parts of the world, growth in overall capital and labor productivity has contributed the remaining 7 to 18 percent.

Saving: A Fundamental Determinant of Economic Growth

Economic growth does not occur in a vacuum. It is not some predetermined fate of a nation. Rather, economic growth depends on certain fundamental factors. One of the most important factors that affect the rate of economic growth and hence long-term living standards is the rate of saving.

A basic proposition in economics is that if you want more tomorrow, you have to consume less today.

To have more consumption in the future, you have to consume less today and save the difference between your income and your consumption.

On a national basis, this implies that higher saving rates eventually mean higher living standards in the long run, all other things held constant. Although the U.S. saving rate has recently increased, concern has been growing that we still are not saving enough. Saving is important for economic growth because without saving, we cannot have investment. If there is no investment in our capital stock, there would be much less economic growth.

The relationship between the rate of saving and per capita real GDP is shown in Figure 9-4 on the next page. Among the nations with the highest rates of saving are China, Germany, Japan, and Saudi Arabia.

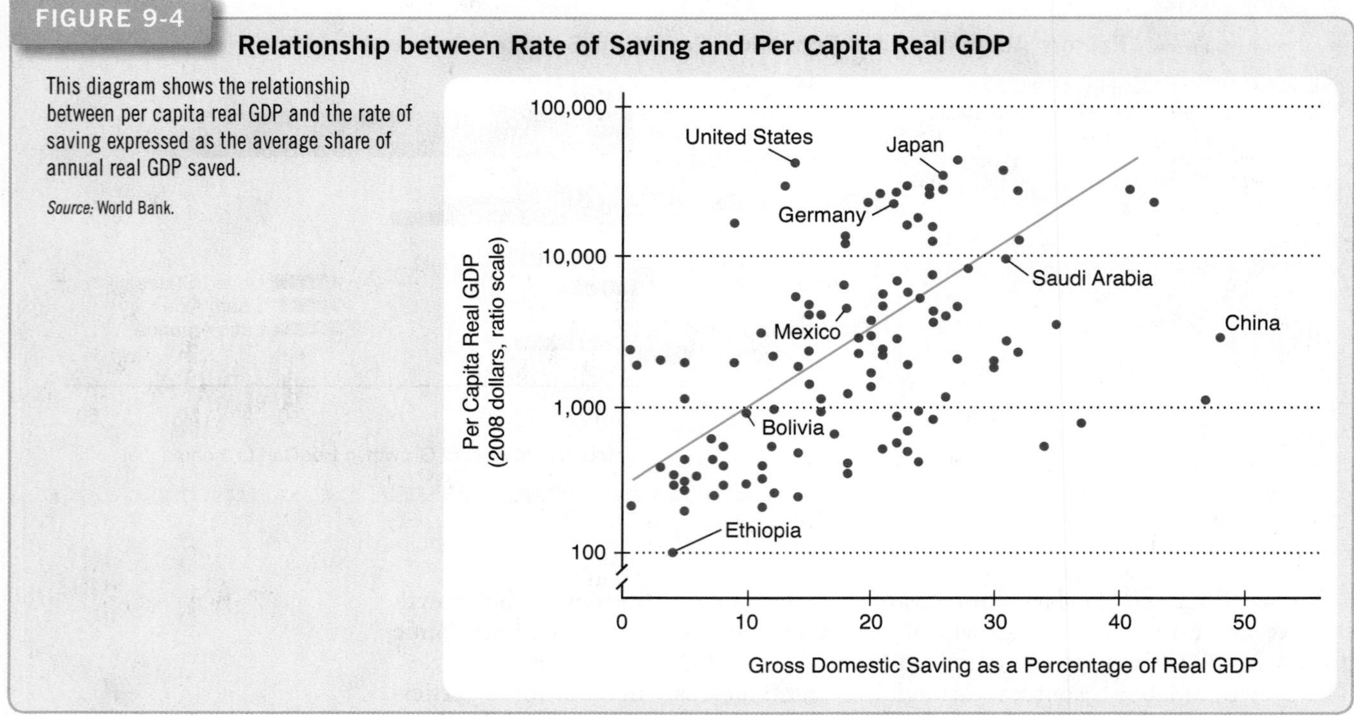

FIGURE 9-4

Relationship between Rate of Saving and Per Capita Real GDP

This diagram shows the relationship between per capita real GDP and the rate of saving expressed as the average share of annual real GDP saved.

Source: World Bank.

QUICK QUIZ See page 209 for the answers. Review concepts from this section in MyEconLab.

Economic growth is numerically equal to the rate of growth of __________ plus the rate of growth of __________ plus the rate of growth in the productivity of __________ and of __________. Improvements in labor productivity, all other things being equal, lead to greater economic growth and higher living standards.

One fundamental determinant of the rate of growth is the rate of __________. To have more consumption in the future, we have to __________ rather than consume. In general, countries that have had higher rates of __________ have had higher rates of growth in per capita real GDP.

New Growth Theory and the Determinants of Growth

New growth theory
A theory of economic growth that examines the factors that determine why technology, research, innovation, and the like are undertaken and how they interact.

A simple arithmetic definition of economic growth has already been given. The per capita growth rates of capital and labor plus the per capita growth rate of their productivity constitute the rate of economic growth. Economists have had good data on the growth of the physical capital stock in the United States as well as on the labor force. But when you add those two growth rates together, you still do not get the total economic growth rate in the United States. The difference has to be due to improvements in productivity. Economists typically labeled this "improvements in technology," and that was that. More recently, proponents of what is now called **new growth theory** argue that technology cannot simply be viewed as an outside factor without explanation. Technology must be understood in terms of what drives it. What are the forces that make productivity grow in the United States and elsewhere?

Growth in Technology

Consider some startling statistics about the growth in technology. Microprocessor speeds may increase from 4,000 megahertz to 10,000 megahertz by the year 2025. By that same year, the size of the thinnest circuit line within a transistor may decrease by 90 percent. The typical memory capacity (RAM) of digital devices will jump from 8 gigabytes, or more than 100 times the equivalent text in the Internal Revenue Code, to more than 400 gigabytes. Recent developments in phase-change memory technologies and in new techniques for storing bits of data on molecules and even individual atoms promise even greater expansions of digital memory capacities. Predictions are that computers may become as powerful as the human brain by 2030.

Technology: A Separate Factor of Production

We now recognize that technology must be viewed as a separate factor of production that is sensitive to rewards. Indeed, one of the major foundations of new growth theory is this:

When the rewards are greater, more technological advances will occur.

Let's consider several aspects of technology here, the first one being research and development.

Research and Development

A certain amount of technological advance results from research and development (R&D) activities that have as their goal the development of specific new materials, new products, and new machines. How much spending a nation devotes to R&D can have an impact on its long-term economic growth. Part of how much a nation spends depends on what businesses decide is worth spending. That in turn depends on their expected rewards from successful R&D. If your company develops a new way to produce computer memory chips, how much will it be rewarded? The answer depends on what you can charge others to use the new technique.

YOU ARE THERE

To learn about the economic implications of a change in how the U.S. legal system handles patents, take a look at **Implementing a New Patent Framework to Promote Innovation** on page 204.

PATENTS To protect new techniques developed through R&D, we have a system of **patents,** in which the federal government gives the patent holder the exclusive right to make, use, and sell an invention for a period of 20 years. One can argue that this special protection given to owners of patents increases expenditures on R&D and therefore adds to long-term economic growth. Figure 9-5 below shows

Patent
A government protection that gives an inventor the exclusive right to make, use, or sell an invention for a limited period of time (currently, 20 years).

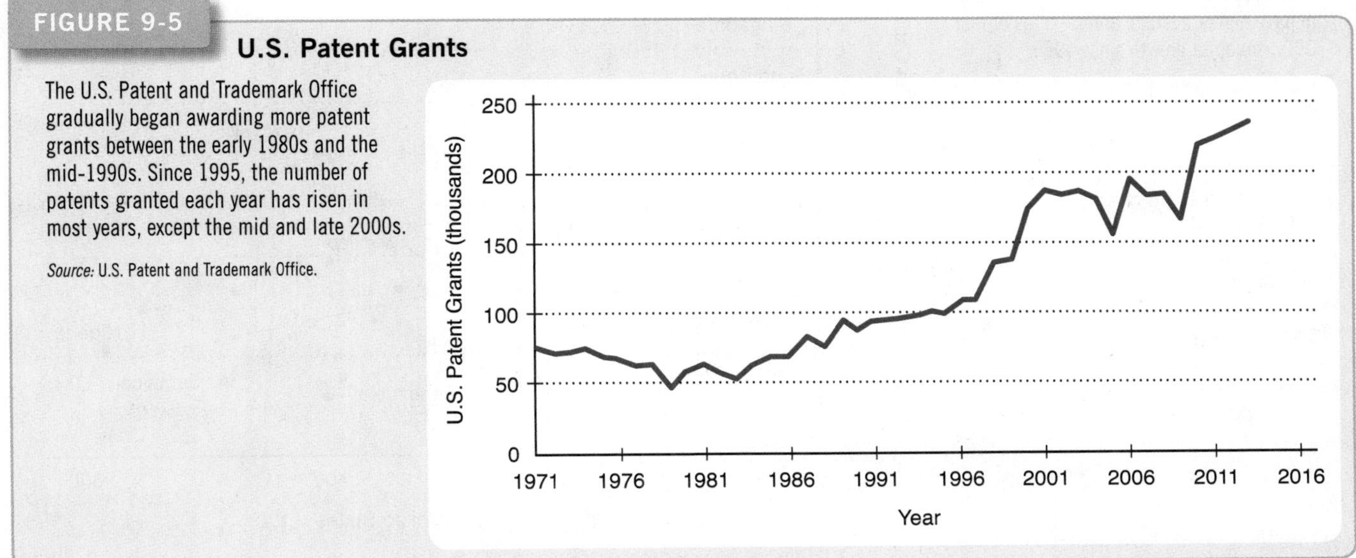

FIGURE 9-5
U.S. Patent Grants

The U.S. Patent and Trademark Office gradually began awarding more patent grants between the early 1980s and the mid-1990s. Since 1995, the number of patents granted each year has risen in most years, except the mid and late 2000s.

Source: U.S. Patent and Trademark Office.

that U.S. patent grants fell during the 1970s, increased steadily after 1982, surged following 1995, dropped in 2004 and 2005, and increased again after 2007.

POSITIVE EXTERNALITIES AND R&D As we discussed in Chapter 5, positive externalities are benefits from an activity that are enjoyed by someone besides the instigator of the activity. In the case of R&D spending, a certain amount of the benefits go to other companies that do not have to pay for them. In particular, according to economists David Coe of the International Monetary Fund and Elhanan Helpman of Harvard University, about a quarter of the global productivity gains of R&D investment in the top seven industrialized countries goes to other nations. For every 1 percent rise in the stock of R&D in the United States alone, for example, productivity in the rest of the world increases by about 0.25 percent.

One country's R&D expenditures benefit other countries because they are able to import capital goods—say, computers and telecommunications networks—from technologically advanced countries and then use them as inputs in making their own industries more efficient. In addition, countries that import high-tech goods are able to imitate the technology.

The Open Economy and Economic Growth

People who study economic growth today emphasize the importance of the openness of the economy. Free trade encourages a more rapid spread of technology and industrial ideas. Moreover, open economies may experience higher rates of economic growth because their own industries have access to a bigger market. When trade barriers are erected in the form of tariffs and the like, domestic industries become isolated from global technological progress. This occurred for many years in Communist countries and in most developing countries in Africa, Latin America, and elsewhere. Figure 9-6 below shows the relationship between economic growth and openness as measured by the level of tariff barriers.

Is China's rapid pace of economic growth threatened by a reduction in the nation's international openness?

FIGURE 9-6

The Relationship between Economic Growth and Tariff Barriers to International Trade

Nations with low tariff barriers are relatively open to international trade and have tended to have higher average annual rates of real GDP per capita growth since 1965.

Source: World Bank.

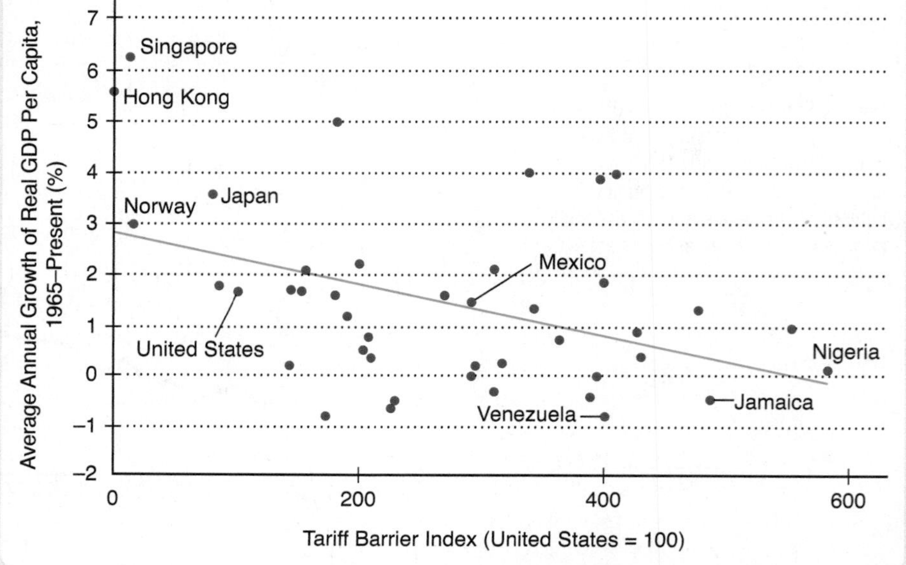

INTERNATIONAL POLICY EXAMPLE

China Rethinks Its Openness to Merchandise Trade

During the latter 1990s and 2000s, China's annual rate of economic growth often exceeded 8 percent. In recent years, however, its average growth rate has dropped slightly. Some observers suggest that this growth dip has resulted from an "indigenous (home-developed) innovation" policy implemented by the nation's government. This policy gives advantages to domestic sellers of a variety of goods, including computing and telecommunications devices and office equipment. The policy thus effectively discourages imports of these items.

China's government has extended special protections to financial services, such as property-casualty and life insurance, from foreign competition. The indigenous innovation policy therefore now includes imports of services as well as physical goods. Consequently, China has a less open economy, one not so likely to grow quite as rapidly as before.

FOR CRITICAL THINKING

Why might restrictions on imports of the latest digital devices particularly threaten China's rapid pace of economic growth?

Innovation and Knowledge

We tend to think of technological progress as, say, the invention of the transistor. But invention means little by itself. **Innovation** is required. Innovation involves the transformation of something new, such as an invention, into something that benefits the economy either by lowering production costs or by providing new goods and services. Indeed, the new growth theorists believe that real wealth creation comes from innovation and that invention is but a facet of innovation.

Innovation
Transforming an invention into something that is useful to humans.

Historically, technologies have moved relatively slowly from invention to innovation to widespread use. The dispersion of new technology remains for the most part slow and uncertain. The inventor of the transistor thought it might be used to make better hearing aids. At the time it was invented, the *New York Times*'s sole reference to it was in a small weekly column called "News of Radio." When the laser was invented, no one really knew what it could be used for. It was initially used to help in navigation, measurement, and chemical research. Today, it is used in the reproduction of music, printing, surgery, telecommunications, and optical data transmittal and storage. Tomorrow, who knows?

Typically, thousands of raw ideas emerge each year at a large firm's R&D laboratories. Only a few hundred of these ideas develop into formal proposals for new processes or products. Of these proposals, the business selects perhaps a few dozen that it deems suitable for further study to explore their feasibility. After careful scrutiny, the firm concludes that only a handful of these ideas are inventions worthy of being integrated into actual production processes or launched as novel products. The firm is fortunate if one or two ultimately become successful marketplace innovations.

How have efforts by physicists to hide objects from sight set off a search for innovations applying to a variety of markets?

EXAMPLE

The Quest for Invisibility Promises Waves of Innovation

Physicists have developed ways to make objects disappear by using fabrics called *metamaterials* to deflect electromagnetic—for instance, light and magnetic—waves and thereby create artificial blind spots. Originally, the idea behind such inventive activities was to make items invisible to the human eye, thereby rendering magicians' tricks using mirrors and sleight of hand obsolete. Once physicists realized that metamaterials could effectively cancel out electromagnetic waves, however, they began to concentrate on developing potentially marketable innovations.

One possible innovation is elimination of cell phone static by making buildings disappear to wireless signals. Another is the potential for dramatic improvements in magnetic resonance images (MRIs) used to diagnose physical ailments. Finally, deflection of electromagnetic waves offers promise in canceling out waves of water, such as tsunamis that otherwise might damage offshore oil platforms. Thus, the pursuit of invisibility may produce several innovations.

FOR CRITICAL THINKING

So far, does invisibility research appear to have yielded inventions or innovations? Explain.

The Importance of Ideas and Knowledge

Economist Paul Romer has added at least one other important factor that determines the rate of economic growth. He contends that production and manufacturing knowledge is just as important as the other determinants and perhaps even more so. He considers knowledge a factor of production that, like capital, has to be paid for by forgoing current consumption. Economies must therefore invest in knowledge just as they invest in machines. Because past investment in capital may make it more profitable to acquire more knowledge, there may be an investment-knowledge cycle in which investment spurs knowledge and knowledge spurs investment.

A once-and-for-all increase in a country's rate of investment may permanently raise that country's growth rate. (According to traditional theory, a once-and-for-all increase in the rate of saving and therefore in the rate of investment simply leads to a new steady-state standard of living, not one that continues to increase.)

Another way of looking at knowledge is that it is a store of ideas. According to Romer, ideas are what drive economic growth. In fact, we have become an idea economy. Consider Apple, Inc. A relatively small percentage of that company's labor force is involved in actually building products. Rather, a majority of Apple's employees are attempting to discover new ideas that can be translated into computer code that can then be turned into products. The major conclusion that Romer and other new growth theorists draw is this:

Economic growth can continue as long as we keep coming up with new ideas.

The Importance of Human Capital

Knowledge, ideas, and productivity are all tied together. One of the threads is the quality of the labor force. Increases in the productivity of the labor force are a function of increases in human capital, the fourth factor of production discussed in Chapter 2. Recall that human capital consists of the knowledge and skills that people in the workforce acquire through education, on-the-job training, and self-teaching. To increase your own human capital, you have to invest by forgoing income-earning activities while you attend school. Society also has to invest in the form of teachers and education.

According to the new growth theorists, human capital is becoming nearly as important as physical capital, particularly when trying to explain international differences in living standards. It is therefore not surprising that one of the most effective ways that developing countries can become developed is by investing in secondary schooling.

One can argue that policy changes that increase human capital will lead to more technological improvements. One of the reasons that concerned citizens, policymakers, and politicians are looking for a change in the U.S. schooling system is that our educational system seems to be falling behind those of other countries. This lag is greatest in science and mathematics—precisely the areas required for developing better technology.

How have periodic drains of human capital affected economic growth in Ireland?

INTERNATIONAL EXAMPLE

Ireland Experiences Yet Another Big "Brain Drain"

It is common to refer to an emigration of many of a nation's most skilled residents to other countries as a "brain drain." During the past two centuries, Ireland has experienced several brain drains. Most well known was the departure of about a million Irish residents in response to the great potato famine of the mid-nineteenth century. About a century later, an economic meltdown induced tens of thousands of Irish residents to move to Britain. A similar population shift took place in the late 1980s, when about 120,000 Irish residents left for England.

Following a major business downturn in Ireland in 2008, yet another emigration wave began. During the past couple of years, about 1,000 people per week have departed from Ireland's shores. Current forecasts suggest that this latest population shift away from Ireland eventually will total at least 150,000 people, including many of that nation's best-educated professionals. In response to this latest Irish brain drain, many economists have reduced substantially their estimates for Ireland's long-term rate of economic growth.

FOR CRITICAL THINKING

Can you think of any policy actions, short of explicit limits on emigration, that a nation's government might implement in an effort to slow or even halt a brain drain?

QUICK QUIZ See page 209 for the answers. Review concepts from this section in MyEconLab.

__________ __________ theory argues that the greater the rewards, the more rapid the pace of technology. And greater rewards spur research and development.

The openness of a nation's economy to international __________ seems to correlate with its rate of economic growth.

Invention and innovation are not the same thing. __________ are useless until __________ transforms them into goods and services that people find valuable.

According to __________ __________ theory, economic growth can continue as long as we keep coming up with new ideas.

Increases in __________ capital can lead to greater rates of economic growth. These come about by increased education, on-the-job training, and self-teaching.

Immigration, Property Rights, and Growth

New theories of economic growth have also shed light on two additional factors that play important roles in influencing a nation's rate of growth of per capita real GDP: immigration and property rights.

Population and Immigration as They Affect Economic Growth

There are several ways to view population growth as it affects economic growth. On the one hand, population growth can result in a larger labor force and increases in human capital, which contribute to economic growth. On the other hand, population growth can be seen as a drain on the economy because for any given amount of GDP, more population means lower per capita GDP. According to Harvard economist Michael Kremer, the first of these effects is historically more important. His conclusion is that population growth drives technological progress, which then increases economic growth. The theory is simple: If there are 50 percent more people in the United States, there will be 50 percent more geniuses. And with 50 percent more people, the rewards for creativity are commensurately greater. Otherwise stated, the larger the potential market, the greater the incentive to become ingenious.

A larger market also provides an incentive for well-trained people to immigrate, which undoubtedly helps explain why the United States attracts a disproportionate number of top scientists from around the globe.

Does immigration help spur economic growth? Yes, according to the late economist Julian Simon, who pointed out that "every time our system allows in one more immigrant, on average, the economic welfare of American citizens goes up. . . . Additional immigrants, both the legal and the illegal, raise the standard of living of U.S. natives and have little or no negative impact on any occupational or income class." He further argued that immigrants do not displace natives from jobs but rather create jobs through their purchases and by starting new businesses. Immigrants' earning and spending simply expand the economy.

Not all researchers agree with Simon, and few studies have tested the theories he and Kremer have advanced. This area is currently the focus of much research.

WHAT IF... the government halted inflows of immigrants possessing scientific training?

Economists have found that the influx of scientifically trained immigrants contributes to about one-third of the annual flow of new inventions that obtain U.S. patents. This means that if the already-constrained inflow of immigrants with academic backgrounds in math and science were halted, the number of inventions per year likely would drop to about two-thirds of its current number. Thus, further limits on immigration of foreign scientists would substantially reduce innovative activity in the United States.

Property Rights and Entrepreneurship

If you were in a country where bank accounts and businesses were periodically expropriated by the government, how willing would you be to leave your financial assets in a savings account or to invest in a business? Certainly, you would be less willing than if such actions never occurred. In general, the more securely private property rights (see page 102) are assigned, the more capital accumulation there will be. People will be willing to invest their savings in endeavors that will increase their wealth in future years. This requires that property rights in their wealth be sanctioned and enforced by the government. In fact, some economic historians have attempted to show that it was the development of well-defined private property rights and legal structures that allowed Western Europe to increase its growth rate after many centuries of stagnation. The ability and certainty with which they can reap the gains from investing also determine the extent to which business owners in other countries will invest capital in developing countries. The threat of loss of property rights that hangs over some developing nations undoubtedly stands in the way of foreign investments that would allow these nations to develop more rapidly.

The legal structure of a nation is closely tied to the degree with which its citizens use their own entrepreneurial skills. In Chapter 2, we identified entrepreneurship as the fifth factor of production. Entrepreneurs are the risk takers who seek out new ways to do things and create new products. To the extent that entrepreneurs are allowed to capture the rewards from their entrepreneurial activities, they will seek to engage in those activities. In countries where such rewards cannot be captured because of a lack of property rights, there will be less entrepreneurship. Typically, this results in fewer investments and a lower rate of growth. We shall examine the implications this has for policymakers in Chapter 18.

QUICK QUIZ See page 209 for the answers. Review concepts from this section in MyEconLab.

While some economists argue that population growth reduces __________ growth, others contend that the opposite is true. The latter economists consequently believe that immigration should be encouraged rather than discouraged.

Well-defined and protected __________ rights are important for fostering entrepreneurship. In the absence of well-defined __________ rights, individuals have less incentive to take risks, and economic growth rates suffer.

Economic Development

Development economics
The study of factors that contribute to the economic growth of a country.

How did developed countries travel paths of growth from extreme poverty to relative riches? That is the essential issue of **development economics,** which is the study of why some countries grow and develop and others do not and of policies that might help developing economies get richer. It is not enough simply to say that people in different countries are different and that is why some countries are rich and some countries are poor. Economists do not deny that different cultures have different work ethics, but they are unwilling to accept such a pat and fatalistic answer.

Look at any world map. About four-fifths of the countries you will see on the map are considered relatively poor. The goal of economists who study development is to help the more than 4 billion people today with low living standards join the more than 2 billion people who have at least moderately high living standards.

Putting World Poverty into Perspective

Most U.S. residents cannot even begin to understand the reality of poverty in the world today. At least one-half, if not two-thirds, of the world's population lives at subsistence level, with just enough to eat for survival. Indeed, the World Bank estimates that nearly 20 percent of the world's people live on less than $1.50 per day. The official poverty line in the United States is above the annual income of at least half the human beings on the planet. This is not to say that we should ignore domestic problems with the poor and homeless simply because they are living better than many people elsewhere in the world. Rather, it is necessary for us to maintain an appropriate perspective on what are considered problems for this country relative to what are considered problems elsewhere.

The Relationship between Population Growth and Economic Development

The world's population is growing at the rate of about 2 people a second. That amounts to 172,800 a day or 63.1 million a year. Today, there are more than 6.8 billion people on earth. By 2050, according to the United Nations, the world's population will be close to leveling off at around 9 billion. Panel (a) of Figure 9-7 on the following page shows population growth. Panel (b) emphasizes an implication of panel (a), which is that almost all the growth in population is occurring in developing nations. Many developed countries are expected to lose population over the next several decades.

Ever since the Reverend Thomas Robert Malthus wrote *An Essay on the Principle of Population* in 1798, excessive population growth has been a concern. Modern-day Malthusians are able to generate great enthusiasm for the concept that population growth is bad. Over and over, media pundits and a number of scientists tell us that rapid population growth threatens economic development and the quality of life.

MALTHUS WAS PROVED WRONG Malthus predicted that population would outstrip food supplies. This prediction has never been supported by the facts, according to economist Nicholas Eberstadt of the American Enterprise Institute for Public Policy Research. As the world's population has grown, so has the world's food stock, measured by calories per person. Furthermore, the price of food, corrected for inflation, has generally been falling for more than a century. That means that the amount of food has been expanding faster than the increase in demand caused by increased population.

GROWTH LEADS TO SMALLER FAMILIES Furthermore, economists have found that as nations become richer, average family size declines. Otherwise stated, the more economic development occurs, the slower the population growth rate becomes. This has certainly been true in Western Europe and in the former Soviet Union, where populations in some countries are actually declining. Predictions of birthrates in developing countries have often turned out to be overstated if those countries experience rapid economic growth. This was the case in Chile, Hong Kong, Mexico, and Taiwan.

Recent research on population and economic development has revealed that social and economic modernization has been accompanied by a decline in childbearing significant enough that it might be called a fertility revolution. Modernization reduces infant mortality, which in turn reduces the incentive for couples to have many children to make sure that a certain number survive to adulthood. Modernization also lowers the demand for children for a variety of reasons, not the least being that couples in more developed countries do not need to rely on their children to take care of them in old age.

The Stages of Development: Agriculture to Industry to Services

If we analyze the development of modern rich nations, we find that they went through three stages. First is the agricultural stage, when most of the population is involved in agriculture. Then comes the manufacturing stage, when much of the population becomes involved in the industrialized sector of the economy. And finally there is a shift toward services. That is exactly what happened in the United States: The so-called tertiary, or service, sector of the economy continues to grow, whereas the manufacturing sector (and its share of employment) is declining in relative importance.

FIGURE 9-7

Expected Growth in World Population by 2050

Panel (a) displays the percentages of the world's population residing in the various continents by 2050 and shows projected population growth for these continents and for selected nations. It indicates that Asia and Africa are expected to gain the most in population by the year 2050.

Panel (b) indicates that population will increase in developing countries before beginning to level off around 2050, whereas industrially advanced nations will grow very little in population in the first half of this century.

Source: United Nations.

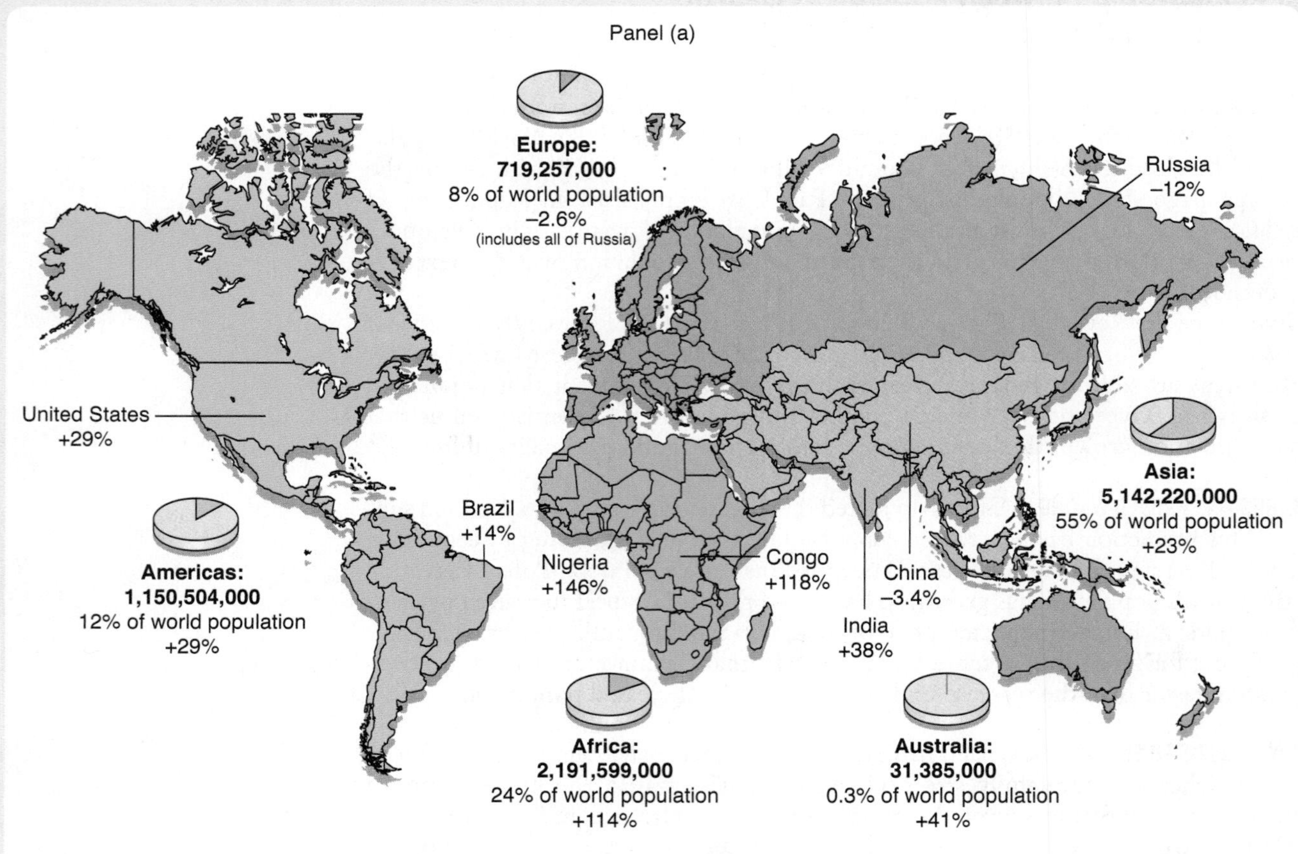

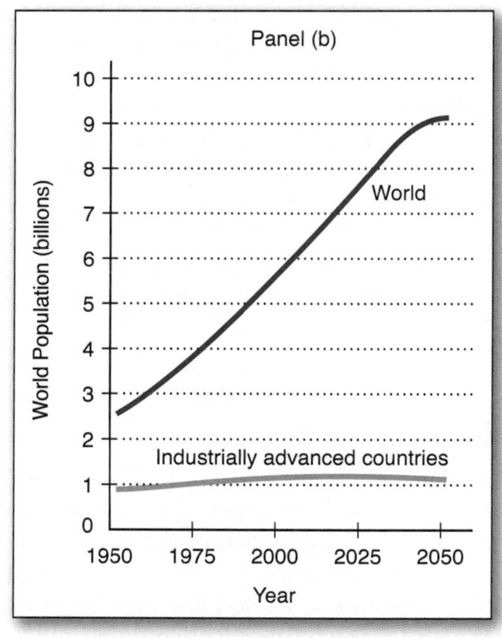

Of particular significance, however, is the requirement for early specialization in a nation's comparative advantage (see Chapter 2). The doctrine of comparative advantage is particularly appropriate for the developing countries of the world. If trading is allowed among nations, a country is best off if it produces what it has a comparative advantage in producing and imports the rest (for more details, see Chapter 32). This means that many developing countries should continue to specialize in agricultural production or in labor-intensive manufactured goods.

Keys to Economic Development

According to one theory of development, a country must have a large natural resource base in order to develop. This theory goes on to assert that much of the world is running out of natural resources, thereby limiting economic growth and development. Only the narrowest definition of a natural resource, however, could lead to such an opinion. In broader terms, a natural resource is something occurring in nature that we can use for our own purposes. As emphasized by new growth theory, natural resources therefore include human capital—education and experience. Also, natural resources change over time. Several hundred years ago, for example, they did not include hydroelectric power—no one knew that such a natural resource existed or how to bring it into existence.

Go to www.econtoday.com/chap09 to contemplate whether there may be a relationship between inequality and a nation's growth and to visit the home page of the World Bank's Thematic Group on Inequality, Poverty, and Socioeconomic Performance.

Natural resources by themselves are not a prerequisite for or a guarantee of economic development, as demonstrated by Japan's extensive development despite a lack of domestic oil resources and by Brazil's slow pace of development in spite of a vast array of natural resources. Resources must be transformed into something usable for either investment or consumption.

Economists have found that four factors seem to be highly related to the pace of economic development:

1. *Establishing a system of property rights.* As noted earlier, if you were in a country where bank accounts and businesses were periodically expropriated by the government, you would be reluctant to leave some of your wealth in a savings account or to invest in a business. Expropriation of private property rarely takes place in developed countries. It has occurred in numerous developing countries, however. For example, private property has been nationalized in Venezuela and in Cuba. Economists have found that other things being equal, the more secure private property rights are, the more private capital accumulation and economic growth there will be.

2. *Developing an educated population.* Both theoretically and empirically, we know that a more educated workforce aids economic development because it allows individuals to build on the ideas of others. Thus, developing countries can advance more rapidly if they increase investments in education. Or, stated in the negative, economic development is difficult to sustain if a nation allows a sizable portion of its population to remain uneducated. Education allows impoverished young people to acquire skills that enable them to avoid poverty as adults.

3. *Letting "creative destruction" run its course.* The twentieth-century Harvard economist Joseph Schumpeter championed the concept of "creative destruction," through which new businesses ultimately create new jobs and economic growth after first destroying old jobs, old companies, and old industries. Such change is painful and costly, but it is necessary for economic advancement. Nowhere is this more important than in developing countries, where the principle is often ignored. Many governments in developing nations have had a history of supporting current companies and industries by discouraging new technologies and new companies from entering the marketplace. The process of creative destruction has not been allowed to work its magic in these countries.

4. *Limiting protectionism.* Open economies experience faster economic development than economies closed to international trade. Trade encourages people and businesses to discover ways to specialize so that they can become more productive and earn higher incomes. Increased productivity and subsequent increases in economic growth are the results. Thus, having fewer trade barriers promotes faster economic development.

Go to www.econtoday.com/chap09 to link to a World Trade Organization explanation of how free trade promotes greater economic growth and higher employment.

QUICK QUIZ See page 209 for the answers. Review concepts from this section in MyEconLab.

Although many people believe that population growth hinders economic development, there is little evidence to support that notion. What is clear is that economic development tends to lead to a reduction in the rate of __________ growth.

Historically, there are three stages of economic development: the __________ stage, the __________ stage, and the __________-__________ stage, when a large part of the workforce is employed in providing services.

Although one theory of economic development holds that a sizable natural resource base is the key to a nation's development, this fails to account for the importance of the human element: The __________ __________ must be capable of using a country's natural resources.

Fundamental factors contributing to the pace of economic development are a well-defined system of __________ __________, training and __________, allowing new generations of companies and industries to __________ older generations, and promoting an open economy by allowing __________ __________.

YOU ARE THERE

Implementing a New Patent Framework to Promote Innovation

Senator Patrick Leahy looks on as President Barack Obama signs into law the America Invents Act, a law Leahy had authored with the aim of boosting the rate of U.S. innovation via an overhaul of the nation's patent system. Under the prior law governing patents, property rights to the returns from invention were determined on a "first-to-invent" basis. This meant that if two individuals or companies happened to invent similar products or processes at about the same time, they had to prove in court whose invention was first. Over the years, this requirement had touched off thousands of court fights among patent holders.

The legislation drawn up by Leahy and approved by Congress and the president has established a "first-to-file" rule for patents. Now the property rights associated with any invention are automatically assigned to the first individual or firm to apply for a patent for that invention. Leahy's expectation is that patent holders who once directed financial resources toward funding court battles now will use them to transform more inventions into market innovations. Speeding along the innovation process, Leahy anticipates, will help to fuel economic growth.

Critical Thinking Questions

1. Why are inventions alone insufficient to help boost economic growth?
2. What role do you think that markets perform in determining whether inventions of new products or processes translate into longer-lasting innovations?

ISSUES & APPLICATIONS

Does a Household Shift to Thrift Signal a Growth Recovery?

CONCEPTS APPLIED

- Saving Rate
- Economic Growth
- Investment

A nation's saving rate is fundamental to its economic growth. Higher saving today can be channeled to current investment in capital goods, which people can use to produce more goods and services for future consumption.

FIGURE 9-8

The U.S. Private Saving Rate since 1999

This figure shows that prior to 2009, the U.S. private saving rate was rarely higher than 4 percent and sometimes even dipped below 1 percent. Since 2009, however, the private saving rate has averaged above 3 percent.

Source: Bureau of Economic Analysis.

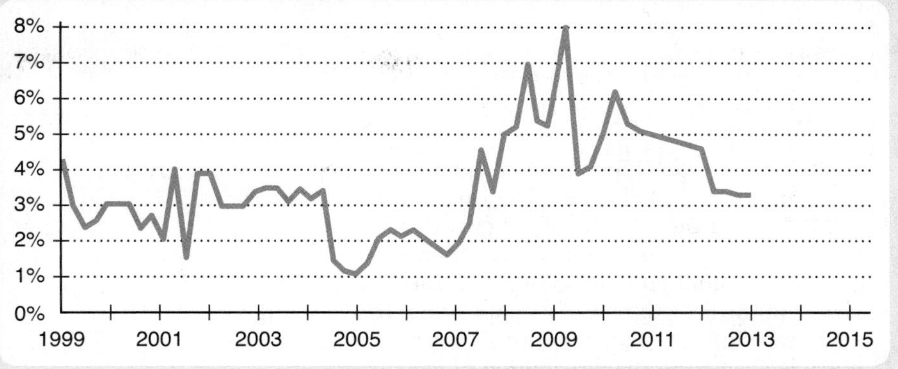

A Higher Private Saving Rate in the United States

Figure 9-8 above indicates that during the 2000s, the U.S. *private* saving rate—annual saving as a percentage of disposable personal income—averaged only about 2.5 percent per year. This low private saving rate helped to explain the dampened growth rate of about 1 percent during subsequent years.

Figure 9-8 shows that the private saving rate has averaged above 3 percent since 2009. This fact has generated greater optimism for some economists that U.S. economic growth might begin to recover.

A Still Low—Actually, Negative—*Overall* National Saving Rate

Bringing government actions into the story complicates the picture. Between 2000 and 2008, the government borrowed an average of $264 billion per year, so flows of public saving were *negative*. This implied an average public saving rate, relative to disposable personal income, of about −2.4 percent. Adding the private saving rate for 2000–2008 of +2.5 percent suggests that over this interval the national saving rate was about 0.1 percent. Overall, therefore, the national saving rate between 2000 and 2008 was nearly zero.

Since 2009, government borrowing has ballooned to about $1,300 billion per year, yielding a public saving rate, in relation to disposable personal income, equal to approximately –11 percent. Adding this negative public saving rate to the private saving rate of about 3 percent yields an overall national saving rate of –8 percent. The fact that the national saving rate in the United States has become highly *negative* since 2009 implies that U.S. economic growth prospects actually have diminished.

For Critical Thinking

1. Why does borrowing constitute negative saving?
2. Given that a negative flow of annual national saving implies that residents of the United States are net borrowers, who must be funding this borrowing each year?

Web Resources

1. For the latest data on U.S. private saving, go to **www.econtoday.com/chap09**.
2. To see when the overall U.S. national saving rate first became negative, go to **www.econtoday.com/chap09**.

MyEconLab

For more questions on this chapter's Issues & Applications, go to MyEconLab. In the Study Plan for this chapter, select Section N: News.

MyEconLab

Here is what you should know after reading this chapter. MyEconLab will help you identify what you know, and where to go when you need to practice.

WHAT YOU SHOULD KNOW		WHERE TO GO TO PRACTICE
Economic Growth The rate of economic growth is the annual rate of change in per capita real GDP. This measure of the rate of growth of a nation's economy takes into account both its growth in overall production of goods and services and the growth rate of its population. It is an average measure that does not account for possible changes in the distribution of income or various welfare costs or benefits.	economic growth, 188 **Key Figures** Figure 9-1, 188 Figure 9-2, 190	• MyEconLab Study Plan 9.1 • Animated Figures 9-1, 9-2
Why Economic Growth Rates Are Important Economic growth compounds over time. Thus, over long intervals, relatively small differences in the rate of economic growth can accumulate to produce large disparities in per capita incomes.	rule of 70, 192	• MyEconLab Study Plan 9.1
Why Productivity Increases Are Crucial for Maintaining Economic Growth Productivity growth is a fundamental factor influencing near-term changes in economic growth. Higher productivity growth unambiguously contributes to greater annual increases in a nation's per capita real GDP.	labor productivity, 192	• MyEconLab Study Plan 9.2
The Key Determinants of Economic Growth The fundamental factors contributing to economic growth are growth in a nation's pool of labor, growth of its capital stock, and growth in the productivity of its capital and labor. A key determinant of capital accumulation is a nation's saving rate. Higher saving rates contribute to greater investment and hence increased capital accumulation and economic growth.		• MyEconLab Study Plan 9.3
New Growth Theory This theory examines why individuals and businesses conduct research into inventing and developing new technologies and how this innovation process interacts with the rate of economic growth. A key implication of the theory is that ideas and knowledge are crucial elements of the growth process.	new growth theory, 194 patent, 195 innovation, 197 **Key Figures** Figure 9-5, 195 Figure 9-6, 196	• MyEconLab Study Plan 9.4 • Animated Figures 9-5, 9-6

MyEconLab *continued*

WHAT YOU SHOULD KNOW		WHERE TO GO TO PRACTICE
Fundamental Factors That Contribute to a Nation's Economic Development Key features shared by nations that attain higher levels of economic development are protection of property rights, significant opportunities for their residents to obtain training and education, policies that permit new companies and industries to replace older ones, and the avoidance of protectionist barriers that hinder international trade.	development economics, 200 **Key Figure** Figure 9-7, 202	• MyEconLab Study Plans 9.5, 9.6 • Animated Figure 9-7

Log in to MyEconLab, take a chapter test, and get a personalized Study Plan that tells you which concepts you understand and which ones you need to review. From there, MyEconLab will give you further practice, tutorials, animations, videos, and guided solutions. For more information, visit www.myeconlab.com

PROBLEMS

All problems are assignable in MyEconLab; *exercises that update with real-time data are marked with* [icon]. *Answers to odd-numbered problems appear at the back of the book.*

9-1. The graph below shows a production possibilities curve for 2016 and two potential production possibilities curves for 2017, denoted 2017_A and 2017_B. (See page 188.)

a. Which of the labeled points corresponds to maximum feasible 2016 production that is more likely to be associated with the curve denoted 2017_A?

b. Which of the labeled points corresponds to maximum feasible 2016 production that is more likely to be associated with the curve denoted 2017_B?

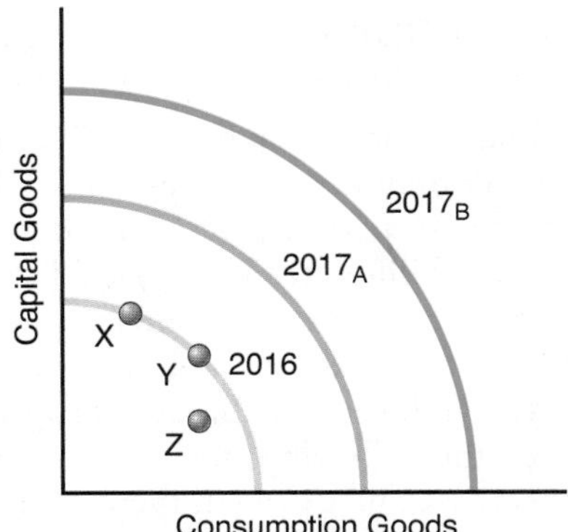

9-2. A nation's capital goods wear out over time, so a portion of its capital goods become unusable every year. Last year, its residents decided to produce no capital goods. It has experienced no growth in its population or in the amounts of other productive resources during the past year. In addition, the nation's technology and resource productivity have remained unchanged during the past year. Will the nation's economic growth rate for the current year be negative, zero, or positive? (See page 192.)

9-3. In the situation described in Problem 9-2, suppose that vocational training during the past year enable the people of this nation to repair all capital goods so that they continue to function as well as new. All other factors are unchanged, however. In light of this single change to the conditions faced in this nation, will the nation's economic growth rate for the current year be negative, zero, or positive? (See page 192.)

9-4. Consider the following data. What is the per capita real GDP in each of these countries? (See page 189.)

Country	Population (millions)	Real GDP ($ billions)
A	10	55
B	20	60
C	5	70

9-5. Suppose that during the next 10 years, real GDP triples and population doubles in each of the nations in Problem 9-4. What will per capita real GDP be in each country after 10 years have passed? (See pages 188–190.)

9-6. Consider the following table displaying annual growth rates for nations X, Y, and Z, each of which entered 2013 with real per capita GDP equal to $20,000 (see pages 188–190.)

	Annual Growth Rate (%)			
Country	**2013**	**2014**	**2015**	**2016**
X	7	1	3	4
Y	4	5	7	9
Z	5	5	3	2

a. Which nation most likely experienced a sizable earthquake in late 2013 that destroyed a significant portion of its stock of capital goods, but was followed by speedy investments in rebuilding the nation's capital stock? What is this nation's per capita real GDP at the end of 2016, rounded to the nearest dollar?

b. Which nation most likely adopted policies in 2013 that encouraged a gradual shift in production from capital goods to consumption goods? What is this nation's per capita real GDP at the end of 2016, rounded to the nearest dollar?

c. Which nation most likely adopted policies in 2013 that encouraged a quick shift in production from consumption goods to capital goods? What is this nation's per capita real GDP at the end of 2016, rounded to the nearest dollar?

9-7. Per capita real GDP grows at a rate of 3 percent in country F and at a rate of 6 percent in country G. Both begin with equal levels of per capita real GDP. Use Table 9-3 on page 191 to determine how much higher per capita real GDP will be in country G after 20 years. How much higher will real GDP be in country G after 40 years? (See page 191.)

9-8. Per capita real GDP in country L is three times as high as in country M. The economic growth rate in country M, however, is 8 percent, while country L's economy grows at a rate of 5 percent. Use Table 9-3 on page 191 to determine approximately how many years will pass before per capita real GDP in country M surpasses per capita real GDP in country L. (See page 191.)

9-9. Per capita real GDP in country S is only half as great as per capita real GDP in country T. Country T's rate of economic growth is 4 percent. The government of country S, however, enacts policies that achieve a growth rate of 20 percent. Use Table 9-3 on page 191 to determine how long country S must maintain this growth rate before its per capita real GDP surpasses that of country T. (See page 191.)

9-10. Since the early 1990s, the average rate of growth of per capita real GDP in Mozambique has been 3 percent per year, as compared with a growth rate of 8 percent in China. Refer to Table 9-3 on page 191. If a typical resident of each of these nations begins this year with a per capita real GDP of $3,000 per year, about how many more dollars' worth of real GDP per capita would the person in China be earning 10 years from now than the individual in Mozambique? (See page 191.)

9-11. On the basis of the information in Problem 9-10 and reference to Table 9-3 on page 191, about how many more dollars' worth of real GDP per capita would the person in China be earning 50 years from now than the individual in Mozambique? (See page 191.)

9-12. In 2014, a nation's population was 10 million. Its nominal GDP was $40 billion, and its price index was 100. In 2015, its population had increased to 12 million, its nominal GDP had risen to $57.6 billion, and its price index had increased to 120. What was this nation's economic growth rate during the year? (See page 191.)

9-13. Between the start of 2014 and the start of 2015, a country's economic growth rate was 4 percent. Its population did not change during the year, nor did its price level. What was the rate of increase of the country's nominal GDP during this one-year interval? (See page 191.)

9-14. In 2014, a nation's population was 10 million, its real GDP was $1.21 billion, and its GDP deflator had a value of 121. By 2015, its population had increased to 12 million, its real GDP had risen to $1.5 billion, and its GDP deflator had a value of 125. What was the percentage change in per capita real GDP between 2014 and 2015? (See page 191.)

9-15. A nation's per capita real GDP was $2,000 in 2013, and the nation's population was 5 million in that year. Between 2013 and 2014, the inflation rate in this country was 5 percent, and the nation's annual rate of economic growth was 10 percent. Its population remained unchanged. What was per capita real GDP in 2014? What was the *level* of real GDP in 2014? (See page 191.)

9-16. Brazil has a population of about 200 million, with about 145 million over the age of 15. Of these, an estimated 25 percent, or 35 million people, are functionally illiterate. The typical literate individual reads only about two nonacademic books per year, which is less than half the number read by the typical literate U.S. or European resident. Answer the following questions solely from the perspective of new growth theory (see page 194):

a. Discuss the implications of Brazil's literacy and reading rates for its growth prospects in light of the key tenets of new growth theory.

b. What types of policies might Brazil implement to improve its growth prospects? Explain.

ECONOMICS ON THE NET

Multifactor Productivity and Its Growth Growth in productivity is a key factor determining a nation's overall economic growth.

Title: Bureau of Labor Statistics: Multifactor Productivity Trends

Navigation: Use the link at **www.econtoday.com/chap09** to visit the multifactor productivity home page of the Bureau of Labor Statistics.

Application Read the summary, and answer the following questions.

1. What does multifactor productivity measure? Based on your reading of this chapter, how does multifactor productivity relate to the determination of economic growth?
2. Click on *Multifactor Productivity Trends in Manufacturing*. According to these data, which industries have exhibited the greatest productivity growth in recent years?

For Group Study and Analysis Divide the class into three groups to examine multifactor productivity data for the private business sector, the private nonfarm business sector, and the manufacturing sector. Have each group identify periods when multifactor productivity growth was particularly fast or slow. Then compare notes. Does it appear to make a big difference which sector one looks at when evaluating periods of greatest and least growth in multifactor productivity?

ANSWERS TO QUICK QUIZZES

p. 192: (i) per capita; (ii) benefits . . . costs; (iii) large

p. 194: (i) capital . . . labor . . . capital . . . labor; (ii) saving . . . save . . . saving

p. 199: (i) New growth; (ii) trade; (iii) Inventions . . . innovation; (iv) new growth; (v) human

p. 200: (i) economic; (ii) property . . . property

p. 204: (i) population; (ii) agricultural . . . manufacturing . . . service-sector; (iii) working population; (iv) property rights . . . education . . . replace . . . international trade

10 Real GDP and the Price Level in the Long Run

Economic growth has trended steadily downward during the past four decades in nations with northern borders that lie within the Arctic Circle, such as Canada, Russia, and the United States. Nevertheless, estimates indicate that if underutilized and untapped Arctic and near-Arctic resources were fully exploited, substantial long-term improvements in these nations' economic growth rates would occur. How could increased use of resources within Arctic regions, as well as in other areas, contribute to the aggregate production of goods and services? What would be additional economywide effects of increased resource exploitation, such as impacts on the average level of prices? In this chapter, you will contemplate the answers to these questions.

LEARNING OBJECTIVES

After reading this chapter, you should be able to:

- Understand the concept of long-run aggregate supply
- Describe the effect of economic growth on the long-run aggregate supply curve
- Explain why the aggregate demand curve slopes downward and list key factors that cause this curve to shift
- Discuss the meaning of long-run equilibrium for the economy as a whole
- Evaluate why economic growth can cause deflation
- Evaluate likely reasons for persistent inflation in recent decades

MyEconLab helps you master each objective and study more efficiently. See end of chapter for details.

DID YOU KNOW THAT... the Venezuelan president has used powers granted him by the nation's parliament to decree legislation, called the Fair Prices and Costs Law, that prevents increases in the prices of all goods and services? In this way, the Venezuelan government essentially sought to make illegal an increase in the overall level of prices, or *inflation.* In most nations, of course, governments rarely resort to such dramatic efforts to contain inflation. What causes inflation? In this chapter, you will find out the answer.

Output Growth and the Long-Run Aggregate Supply Curve

In Chapter 2, we showed the derivation of the production possibilities curve (PPC). At any point in time, the economy can be inside or on the PPC but never outside it. Along the PPC, a country's resources are fully employed in the production of goods and services, and the sum total of the inflation-adjusted value of all final goods and services produced is the nation's real GDP. Economists refer to the total of all planned production for the entire economy as the **aggregate supply** of real output.

Aggregate supply The total of all planned production for the economy.

The Long-Run Aggregate Supply Curve

Put yourself in a world in which nothing has been changing, year in and year out. The price level has not changed. Technology has not changed. The prices of inputs that firms must purchase have not changed. Labor productivity has not changed. All resources are fully employed, so the economy operates on its production possibilities curve, such as the one depicted in panel (a) of Figure 10-1 below. This is a world that is fully adjusted and in which people have all the information they are ever going to have about that world. The **long-run aggregate supply curve** (*LRAS*) in this world is some amount of real GDP—say, $15 trillion of real GDP—which is the value of the flow of production of final goods and services measured in **base-year dollars.**

We can represent long-run aggregate supply by a vertical line at $15 trillion of real GDP. This is what you see in panel (b) of the figure below. That curve, labeled *LRAS*, is a vertical line determined by technology and **endowments,** or resources that exist in our economy. It is the full-information and full-adjustment level of real output of goods and services. It is the level of real GDP that will continue being produced year after year, forever, if nothing changes.

Long-run aggregate supply curve A vertical line representing the real output of goods and services after full adjustment has occurred. It can also be viewed as representing the real GDP of the economy under conditions of full employment—the full-employment level of real GDP.

Base-year dollars The value of a current sum expressed in terms of prices in a base year.

Endowments The various resources in an economy, including both physical resources and such human resources as ingenuity and management skills.

FIGURE 10-1

The Production Possibilities Curve and the Economy's Long-Run Aggregate Supply Curve

At a point in time, a nation's base of resources and its technological capabilities define the position of its production possibilities curve (PPC), as shown in panel (a). This defines the real GDP that the nation can produce when resources are fully employed, which determines the position of the long-run aggregate supply curve (*LRAS*) displayed in panel (b). Because people have complete information and input prices adjust fully in the long run, the *LRAS* is vertical.

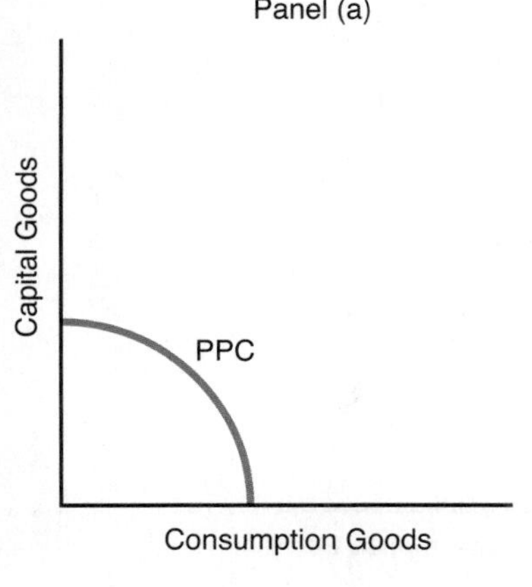

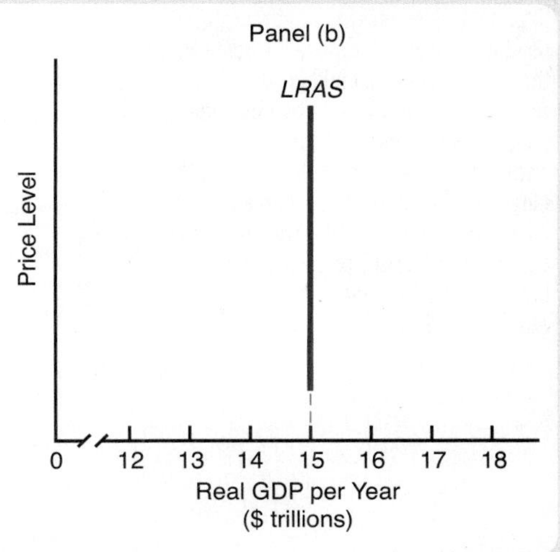

THE *LRAS* CURVE AND FULL-EMPLOYMENT REAL GDP Another way of viewing the *LRAS* is to think of it as the full-employment level of real GDP. When the economy reaches full employment along its production possibilities curve, no further adjustments will occur unless a change occurs in the other variables that we are assuming to be stable.

Some economists suggest that the *LRAS* occurs at the level of real GDP consistent with the natural rate of unemployment, the unemployment rate that occurs in an economy with full adjustment in the long run. As we discussed in Chapter 7, many economists like to think of the natural rate of unemployment as consisting of frictional and structural unemployment.

WHY THE *LRAS* CURVE IS VERTICAL To understand why the *LRAS* is vertical, think about the long run. To an economist examining the economy as a whole, the long run is a sufficiently long period that all factors of production and prices, including wages and other input prices, can change.

Go to www.econtoday.com/chap10 to find out how fast wages are adjusting. Under "Latest Numbers," click on "Employment Cost Index."

A change in the level of prices of goods and services has no effect on real GDP per year in the long run, because higher prices will be accompanied by comparable changes in input prices. Suppliers will therefore have no incentive to increase or decrease their production of goods and services. Remember that in the long run, everybody has full information, and there is full adjustment to price level changes. (Of course, this is not necessarily true in the short run, as we shall discuss in Chapter 11.)

Economic Growth and Long-Run Aggregate Supply

In Chapter 9, you learned about the determinants of growth in per capita real GDP: the annual growth rate of labor, the rate of year-to-year capital accumulation, and the rate of growth of the productivity of labor and capital. As time goes by, population gradually increases, and labor force participation rates may even rise. The capital stock typically grows as businesses add such capital equipment as new information-technology hardware. Furthermore, technology improves. Thus, the economy's production possibilities increase, and as a consequence, the production possibilities curve shifts outward, as shown in panel (a) of Figure 10-2 below.

The result is economic growth: Aggregate real GDP and per capita real GDP increase. This means that in a growing economy such as ours, the *LRAS* will shift outward to the right, as in panel (b) below. We have drawn the *LRAS* for the year 2015 to the right of our original *LRAS* of $14.3 trillion of real GDP. We assume that between

FIGURE 10-2

The Long-Run Aggregate Supply Curve and Shifts in It

In panel (a), we repeat a diagram that we used in Chapter 2, on page 37, to show the meaning of economic growth. Over time, the production possibilities curve shifts outward. In panel (b), we demonstrate the same principle by showing the long-run aggregate supply curve initially as a vertical line at $14.3 trillion of real GDP per year. As our productive abilities increase, the *LRAS* moves outward to $LRAS_{2015}$ at $15 trillion.

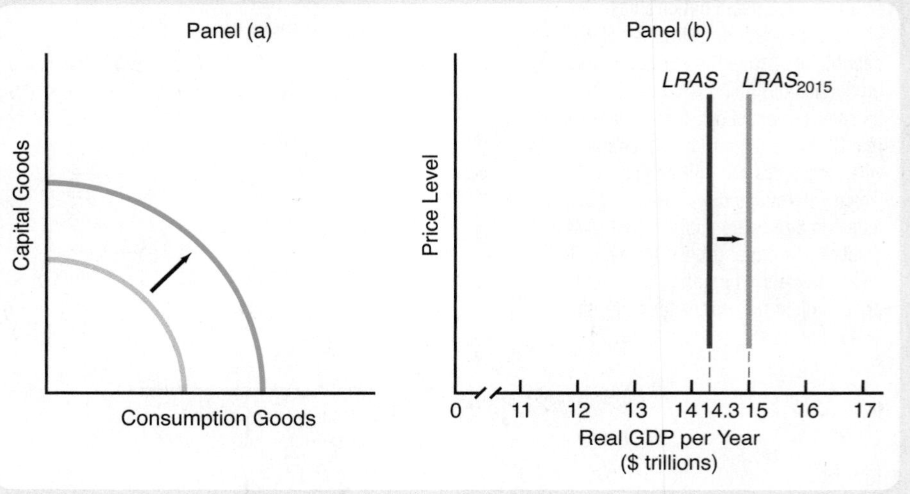

FIGURE 10-3

A Sample Long-Run Growth Path for Real GDP

Year-to-year shifts in the long-run aggregate supply curve yield a long-run trend path for real GDP growth. In this example, from 2015 onward, real GDP grows by a steady 3 percent per year.

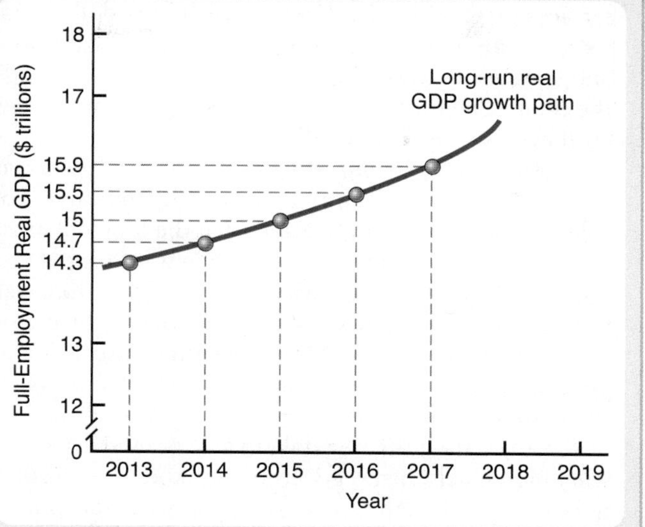

now and 2015, real GDP increases to $15 trillion, to give us the position of the $LRAS_{2015}$ curve. Thus, it is to the right of today's *LRAS* curve.

We may conclude that in a growing economy, the *LRAS* shifts ever farther to the right over time. If the *LRAS* happened to shift rightward at a constant pace, real GDP would increase at a steady annual rate. As shown in Figure 10-3, this means that real GDP would increase along a long-run, or *trend*, path that is an upward-sloping line. Thus, if the *LRAS* shifts rightward from $14.3 trillion to $15 trillion between now and 2015 and then increases at a steady 3 percent annual rate every year thereafter, in 2016 long-run real GDP will equal $15.5 trillion, in 2017 it will equal $15.9 trillion, and so on.

How much less is the U.S. long-run aggregate supply shifting to the right each year as a consequence of dampened economic growth?

YOU ARE THERE

To contemplate how a country's long-run trend path for real GDP could slope *downward*, take a look at **A Nation Confronts a Leftward-Shifting *LRAS* Curve** on page 223.

POLICY EXAMPLE

Shrinking Rightward Shifts in the U.S. *LRAS* Curve

Between 2000 and 2007, U.S. real GDP grew at an average annual rate of 2.6 percent. As a consequence, U.S. long-run aggregate supply increased by an average of nearly $300 billion per year. Since 2007, U.S. real GDP grew on average at a much slower pace of about 0.5 percent per year. During this interval, the nation's long-run aggregate supply rose by an average of less than $70 billion per year. Thus, the average annual amount by which the U.S. long-run aggregate supply curve is shifting rightward is now considerably reduced.

FOR CRITICAL THINKING

Is the U.S. production possibilities curve shifting outward more or less rapidly today than it was a decade ago? Explain your answer.

QUICK QUIZ

See page 228 for the answers. Review concepts from this section in MyEconLab.

The **long-run aggregate supply curve,** *LRAS,* is a __________ line determined by amounts of available resources such as labor and capital and by technology and resource productivity. The position of the *LRAS* gives the full-information and full-adjustment level of real GDP per year.

The __________ rate of unemployment occurs at the long-run level of real GDP per year given by the position of the *LRAS.*

If labor or capital increases from year to year or if the productivity of either of these resources rises from one year to the next, the *LRAS* shifts __________. In a growing economy, therefore, real GDP per year gradually __________ over time.

Total Expenditures and Aggregate Demand

In equilibrium, individuals, businesses, and governments purchase all the goods and services produced, valued in trillions of real dollars. As explained in Chapters 7 and 8, GDP is the dollar value of total expenditures on domestically produced final goods and services. Because all expenditures are made by individuals, firms, or governments, the total value of these expenditures must be what these market participants decide it shall be.

The decisions of individuals, managers of firms, and government officials determine the annual dollar value of total expenditures. You can certainly see this in your role as an individual. You decide what the total dollar amount of your expenditures will be in a year. You decide how much you want to spend and how much you want to save. Thus, if we want to know what determines the total value of GDP, the answer is clear: the spending decisions of individuals like you, firms, and local, state, and national governments. In an open economy, we must also include foreign individuals, firms, and governments (foreign residents, for short) that decide to spend their money income in the United States.

Simply stating that the dollar value of total expenditures in this country depends on what individuals, firms, governments, and foreign residents decide to do really doesn't tell us much, though. Two important issues remain:

1. What determines the total amount that individuals, firms, governments, and foreign residents want to spend?

2. What determines the equilibrium price level and the rate of inflation (or deflation)?

The *LRAS* tells us only about the economy's long-run real GDP. To answer these additional questions, we must consider another important concept. This is **aggregate demand,** which is the total of all *planned* real expenditures in the economy.

Aggregate demand
The total of all planned expenditures in the entire economy.

The Aggregate Demand Curve

Aggregate demand curve
A curve showing planned purchase rates for all final goods and services in the economy at various price levels, all other things held constant.

The **aggregate demand curve,** *AD*, gives the various quantities of all final commodities demanded at various price levels, all other things held constant. Recall the components of GDP that you studied in Chapter 8: consumption spending, investment expenditures, government purchases, and net foreign demand for domestic production. They are all components of aggregate demand. Throughout this chapter and the next, whenever you see the aggregate demand curve, realize that it is a shorthand way of talking about the components of GDP that are measured by government statisticians when they calculate total economic activity each year. In Chapter 12, you will look more closely at the relationship between these components and, in particular, at how consumption spending depends on income.

The aggregate demand curve gives the total amount, measured in base-year dollars, of *real* domestic final goods and services that will be purchased at each price level—everything produced for final use by households, businesses, the government, and foreign (non-U.S.) residents. It includes iPads, socks, shoes, medical and legal services, digital devices, and millions of other goods and services that people buy each year.

A graphical representation of the aggregate demand curve is seen in Figure 10-4 on the facing page. On the horizontal axis, real GDP is measured. For our measure of the price level, we use the GDP price deflator on the vertical axis. The aggregate demand curve is labeled *AD.* If the GDP deflator is 110, aggregate quantity demanded is $15 trillion per year (point *A*). At the price level 115, it is $14 trillion per year (point *B*). At the price level 120, it is $13 trillion per year (point *C*). The higher the price level, the lower the total real amount of final goods and services demanded in the economy, everything else remaining constant, as shown by the arrow along *AD* in Figure 10-4. Conversely, the lower the price level, the higher the total real GDP demanded by the economy, everything else staying constant.

FIGURE 10-4

The Aggregate Demand Curve

The aggregate demand curve, *AD*, slopes downward. If the price level is 110, we will be at point *A* with $15 trillion of real GDP demanded per year. As the price level increases to 115 and to 120, we move up the aggregate demand curve to points *B* and *C*.

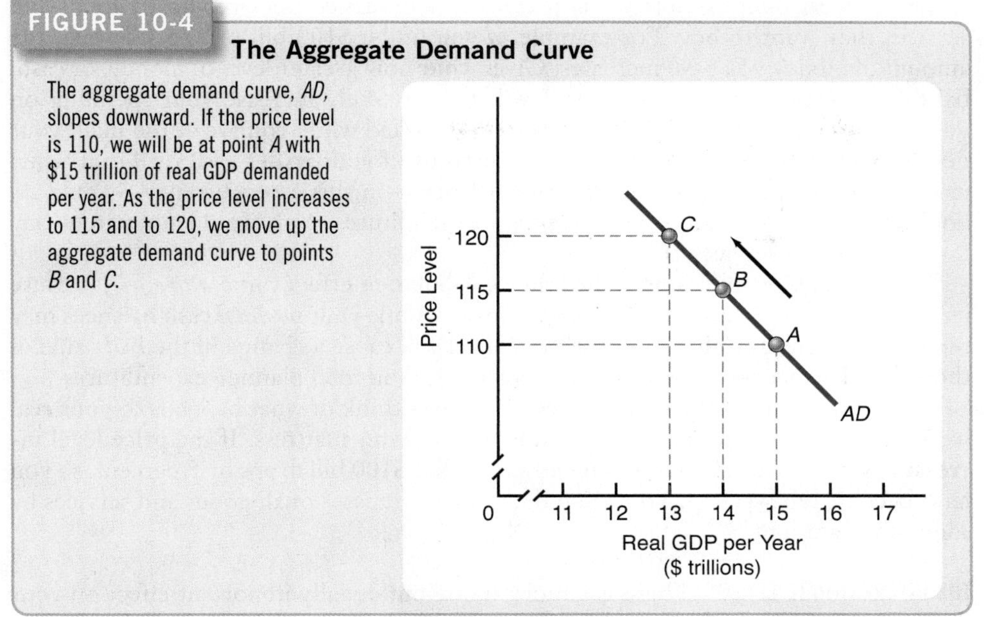

Let's take the year 2013. Estimates based on U.S. Department of Commerce preliminary statistics reveal the following information:

- Nominal GDP was estimated to be $16,344.7 billion.
- The price level as measured by the GDP deflator was about 117.9 (base year is 2005, for which the index equals 100).
- Real GDP was approximately $13,858.5 billion in 2005 dollars.

What can we say about 2013? Given the dollar cost of buying goods and services and all of the other factors that go into spending decisions by individuals, firms, governments, and foreign residents, the total amount of planned spending on final goods and services by firms, individuals, governments, and foreign residents was $13,858.5 billion in 2013 (in terms of 2005 dollars).

What Happens When the Price Level Rises?

What if the price level in the economy rose to 160 tomorrow? What would happen to the amount of real goods and services that individuals, firms, governments, and foreigners wish to purchase in the United States? We know from Chapter 3 that when the price of one good or service rises, the quantity of it demanded will fall. But here we are talking about the *price level*—the average price of *all* goods and services in the economy.

The answer is still that the total quantities of real goods and services demanded would fall, but the reasons are different. When the price of one good or service goes up, the consumer substitutes other goods and services. For the entire economy, when the price level goes up, the consumer doesn't simply substitute one good for another, for now we are dealing with the demand for *all* goods and services in the nation. There are *economywide* reasons that cause the aggregate demand curve to slope downward. They involve at least three distinct forces: the *real-balance effect*, the *interest rate effect*, and the *open economy effect*.

THE REAL-BALANCE EFFECT A rise in the price level will have an effect on spending. Individuals, firms, governments, and foreign residents carry out transactions using money, a portion of which consists of currency and coins that you have in your pocket (or stashed away) right now. Because people use money to purchase goods and services, the amount of money that people have influences the amount of goods and services they want to buy. For example, if you find a $100 bill on the sidewalk, the amount of money you have increases. Given your now greater level of money, or cash, balances—currency in this case—you will almost surely increase your spending on goods and services. Similarly, if your pocket is picked while you are at the mall, your desired spending would be affected. For instance, if your wallet had $150 in it when it was stolen, the reduction in your cash balances—in this case, currency—would no doubt cause you to reduce your planned expenditures. You would ultimately buy fewer goods and services.

Real-balance effect
The change in expenditures resulting from a change in the real value of money balances when the price level changes, all other things held constant; also called the *wealth effect*.

This response is sometimes called the **real-balance effect** (or *wealth effect*) because it relates to the real value of your cash balances. While your *nominal* cash balances may remain the same, any change in the price level will cause a change in the *real* value of those cash balances—hence the real-balance effect on total planned expenditures.

When you think of the real-balance effect, just think of what happens to your real wealth if you have, say, a $100 bill hidden under your mattress. If the price level increases by 5 percent, the purchasing power of that $100 bill drops by 5 percent, so you have become less wealthy. You will reduce your purchases of all goods and services by some small amount.

THE INTEREST RATE EFFECT There is a more subtle but equally important effect on your desire to spend. A higher price level leaves people with too few money balances. Hence, they try to borrow more (or lend less) to replenish their real money holdings. This drives up interest rates. Higher interest rates raise borrowing costs for consumers and businesses. They will borrow less and consequently spend less. The fact that a higher price level pushes up interest rates and thereby reduces borrowing and spending is known as the **interest rate effect.**

Interest rate effect
One of the reasons that the aggregate demand curve slopes downward: Higher price levels increase the interest rate, which in turn causes businesses and consumers to reduce desired spending due to the higher cost of borrowing.

Higher interest rates make it more costly for people to finance purchases of houses and cars. Higher interest rates also make it less profitable for firms to install new equipment and to erect new office buildings. Whether we are talking about individuals or firms, a rise in the price level will cause higher interest rates, which in turn reduce the amount of goods and services that people are willing to purchase. Therefore, an increase in the price level will tend to reduce total planned expenditures. (The opposite occurs if the price level declines.)

THE OPEN ECONOMY EFFECT: THE SUBSTITUTION OF FOREIGN GOODS Recall from Chapter 8 that GDP includes net exports—the difference between exports and imports. In an open economy, we buy imports from other countries and ultimately pay for them through the foreign exchange market. The same is true for foreign residents who purchase our goods (exports). Given any set of exchange rates between the U.S. dollar and other currencies, an increase in the price level in the United States makes U.S. goods more expensive relative to foreign goods. Foreign residents have downward-sloping demand curves for U.S. goods. When the relative price of U.S. goods goes up, foreign residents buy fewer U.S. goods and more of their own. At home, relatively cheaper prices for foreign goods cause U.S. residents to want to buy more foreign goods instead of domestically produced goods. Thus, when the domestic price level rises, the result is a fall in exports and a rise in imports. That means that a price level increase tends to reduce net exports, thereby reducing the amount of real goods and services purchased in the United States. This is known as the **open economy effect.**

Open economy effect
One of the reasons that the aggregate demand curve slopes downward: Higher price levels result in foreign residents desiring to buy fewer U.S.-made goods, while U.S. residents now desire more foreign-made goods, thereby reducing net exports. This is equivalent to a reduction in the amount of real goods and services purchased in the United States.

What Happens When the Price Level Falls?

What about the reverse? Suppose now that the GDP deflator falls to 100 from an initial level of 120. You should be able to trace the three effects on desired purchases of goods and services. Specifically, how do the real-balance, interest rate, and open economy effects cause people to want to buy more? You should come to the conclusion that the lower the price level, the greater the total planned spending on goods and services.

The aggregate demand curve, *AD*, shows the quantity of aggregate output that will be demanded at alternative price levels. It is downward sloping, just like the demand curve for individual goods. The higher the price level, the lower the real amount of total planned expenditures, and vice versa.

Demand for All Goods and Services versus Demand for a Single Good or Service

Even though the aggregate demand curve, *AD*, in Figure 10-4 on page 215 looks similar to the one for individual demand, *D*, for a single good or service that you encountered in Chapters 3 and 4, the two are not the same. When we derive the aggregate demand curve, we are looking at the entire economic system. The aggregate demand curve, *AD*, differs from an individual demand curve, *D*, because we are looking at total planned expenditures on *all* goods and services when we construct *AD*.

Shifts in the Aggregate Demand Curve

In Chapter 3, you learned that any time a nonprice determinant of demand changes, the demand curve will shift inward to the left or outward to the right. The same analysis holds for the aggregate demand curve, except we are now talking about the non-price-level determinants of aggregate demand. So, when we ask the question, "What determines the position of the aggregate demand curve?" the fundamental proposition is as follows:

> ***Any non-price-level change that increases aggregate spending (on domestic goods) shifts* AD *to the right. Any non-price-level change that decreases aggregate spending (on domestic goods) shifts* AD *to the left.***

The list of potential determinants of the position of the aggregate demand curve is long. Some of the most important "curve shifters" for aggregate demand are presented in Table 10-1 below.

TABLE 10-1

Determinants of Aggregate Demand

Aggregate demand consists of the demand for domestically produced consumption goods, investment goods, government purchases, and net exports. Consequently, any change in total planned spending on any one of these components of real GDP will cause a change in aggregate demand. Some possibilities are listed here.

Changes That Cause an Increase in Aggregate Demand	Changes That Cause a Decrease in Aggregate Demand
An increase in the amount of money in circulation	A decrease in the amount of money in circulation
Increased security about jobs and future income	Decreased security about jobs and future income
Improvements in economic conditions in other countries	Declines in economic conditions in other countries
A reduction in real interest rates (nominal interest rates corrected for inflation) not due to price level changes	A rise in real interest rates (nominal interest rates corrected for inflation) not due to price level changes
Tax decreases	Tax increases
A drop in the foreign exchange value of the dollar	A rise in the foreign exchange value of the dollar

How can economists track the extent to which changes in security about jobs and future incomes affect aggregate demand?

POLICY EXAMPLE

The Consumer Confidence Index and Aggregate Demand

An independent economic research organization called The Conference Board tracks an indicator of U.S. consumer sentiment called the Consumer Confidence Index (CCI). The CCI is intended to measure the degree of security that U.S. households have about their future employment and income status, as revealed by a range of data on their spending and saving activities.

Because consumer spending typically accounts for at least two-thirds of total U.S. planned expenditures, variations in the CCI normally indicate changes in U.S. aggregate demand. For instance, during a 6-month interval between late 2007 and early 2008, the CCI lost nearly half of its value. Then U.S. aggregate demand, which had been rising at about $300 billion per year during the 5 years preceding 2008, suddenly *decreased* by more than $300 billion between 2008 and 2009. Thus, a significant reduction in household security about the future, as revealed by the CCI, is associated with a leftward shift in the aggregate demand curve.

FOR CRITICAL THINKING

What would be the predicted effect on the position of the aggregate demand curve of a substantial increase in the Consumer Confidence Index?

QUICK QUIZ

See page 228 for the answers. Review concepts from this section in MyEconLab.

Aggregate demand is the total of all planned __________ in the economy, and **aggregate supply** is the total of all planned __________ in the economy. The aggregate demand curve shows the various quantities of total planned __________ on final goods and services at various price levels; it is downward sloping.

There are three reasons why the aggregate demand curve is downward sloping. They are the __________-__________ effect, the __________ __________ effect, and the __________ __________ effect.

The __________-__________ effect occurs because price level changes alter the real value of cash balances, thereby causing people to desire to spend more or less, depending on whether the price level decreases or increases.

The __________ __________ effect is caused by interest rate changes that mimic price level changes. At higher interest rates, people seek to buy __________ houses and cars, and at lower interest rates, they seek to buy __________.

The **open economy effect** occurs because of a shift away from expenditures on __________ goods and a shift toward expenditures on __________ goods when the domestic price level increases.

Long-Run Equilibrium and the Price Level

As noted in Chapter 3, equilibrium occurs where the demand and supply curves intersect. The same is true for the economy as a whole, as shown in Figure 10-5 on the facing page: The equilibrium price level occurs at the point where the aggregate demand curve *(AD)* crosses the long-run aggregate supply curve *(LRAS)*. At this equilibrium price level of 120, the total of all planned real expenditures for the entire economy is equal to actual real GDP produced by firms after all adjustments have taken place. Thus, the equilibrium depicted in Figure 10-5 is the economy's *long-run equilibrium.*

The Long-Run Equilibrium Price Level

Note in Figure 10-5 that if the price level were to increase to 140, actual real GDP would exceed total planned real expenditures. Inventories of unsold goods would begin to accumulate, and firms would stand ready to offer more services than people wish to purchase. As a result, the price level would tend to fall.

In contrast, if the price level were 100, then total planned real expenditures by individuals, businesses, and the government would exceed actual real GDP. Inventories of unsold goods would begin to be depleted. The price level would rise toward 120, and higher prices would encourage firms to expand production and replenish inventories of goods available for sale.

FIGURE 10-5

Long-Run Economywide Equilibrium

For the economy as a whole, long-run equilibrium occurs at the price level where the aggregate demand curve crosses the long-run aggregate supply curve. At this long-run equilibrium price level, which is 120 in the diagram, total planned real expenditures equal real GDP at full employment, which in our example is a real GDP of $15 trillion.

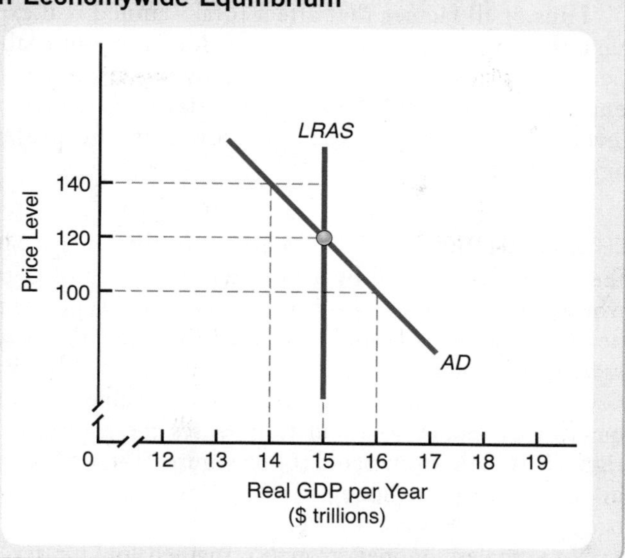

The Effects of Economic Growth on the Price Level

We now have a basic theory of how real GDP and the price level are determined in the long run when all of a nation's resources can change over time and all input prices can adjust fully to changes in the overall level of prices of goods and services that firms produce. Let's begin by evaluating the effects of economic growth on the nation's price level.

ECONOMIC GROWTH AND SECULAR DEFLATION Take a look at panel (a) of Figure 10-6 below, which shows what happens, other things being equal, when the *LRAS* shifts rightward over time. If the economy were to grow steadily during, say, a 10-year interval, the long-run aggregate supply schedule would shift to the right, from $LRAS_1$ to $LRAS_2$.

FIGURE 10-6

Secular Deflation versus Long-Run Price Stability in a Growing Economy

Panel (a) illustrates what happens when economic growth occurs without a corresponding increase in aggregate demand. The result is a decline in the price level over time, known as *secular deflation.* Panel (b) shows that, in principle, secular deflation can be eliminated if the aggregate demand curve shifts rightward at the same pace that the long-run aggregate supply curve shifts to the right.

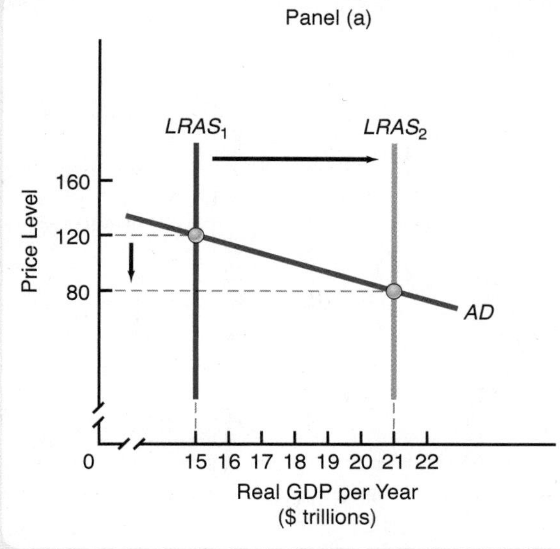

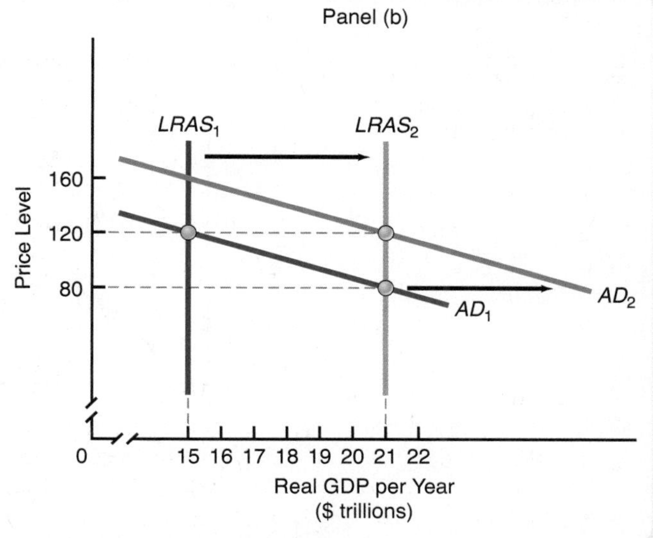

In panel (a), this results in a downward movement along the aggregate demand schedule. The equilibrium price level falls, from 120 to 80.

Thus, if all factors that affect total planned real expenditures are unchanged, so that the aggregate demand curve does not noticeably move during the 10-year period of real GDP growth, the growing economy in the example would experience deflation. This is known as **secular deflation,** or a persistently declining price level resulting from economic growth in the presence of relatively unchanged aggregate demand.

Secular deflation
A persistent decline in prices resulting from economic growth in the presence of stable aggregate demand.

SECULAR DEFLATION IN THE UNITED STATES In the United States, between 1872 and 1894, the price of bricks fell by 50 percent, the price of sugar by 67 percent, the price of wheat by 69 percent, the price of nails by 70 percent, and the price of copper by nearly 75 percent. Founders of a late-nineteenth-century political movement called *populism* offered a proposal for ending deflation: They wanted the government to issue new money backed by silver. As noted in Table 10-1 on page 217, an increase in the quantity of money in circulation causes the aggregate demand curve to shift to the right. It is clear from panel (b) of Figure 10-6 on the previous page that the increase in the quantity of money would indeed have pushed the price level back upward, because the *AD* curve would shift from AD_1 to AD_2.

Go to www.econtoday.com/chap10 to learn about how the price level has changed during recent years. Then click on "Gross Domestic Product and Components" (for GDP deflators) or "Consumer Price Indexes."

Nevertheless, money growth remained low for several more years. Not until the early twentieth century would the United States put an end to secular deflation, namely, by creating a new monetary system.

Causes of Inflation

Of course, so far during your lifetime, deflation has not been a problem in the United States. Instead, what you have experienced is inflation. Figure 10-7 below shows annual U.S. inflation rates for the past few decades. Clearly, inflation rates have been variable. The other obvious fact, however, is that inflation rates have been consistently *positive.* The price level in the United States has *risen* almost every year. For today's United States, secular deflation has not been a big political issue. If anything, it is secular *inflation* that has plagued the nation.

MyEconLab Real-time data

FIGURE 10-7

Inflation Rates in the United States

Annual U.S. inflation rates rose considerably during the 1970s but declined to lower levels after the 1980s. The inflation rate has declined significantly in recent years after creeping upward during the early and middle 2000s.

Sources: Economic Report of the President; Economic Indicators, various issues.

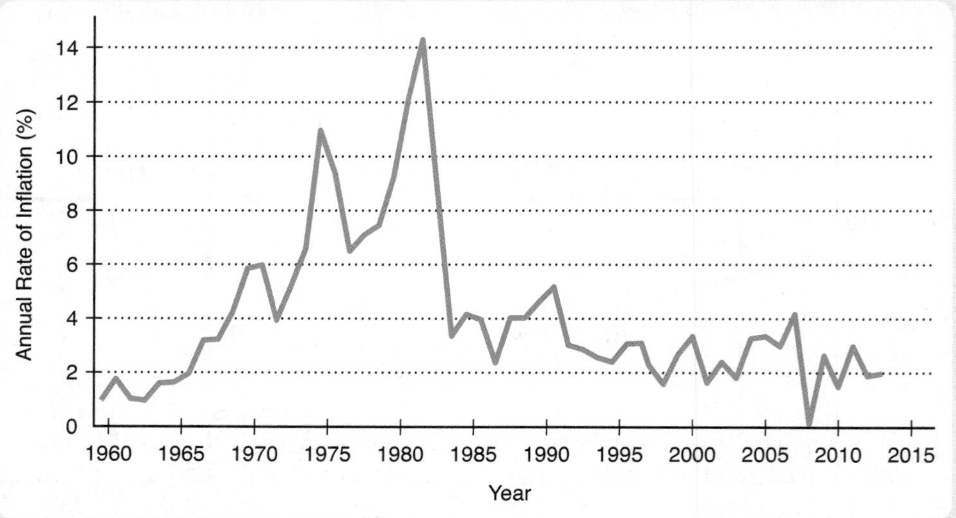

FIGURE 10-8

Explaining Persistent Inflation

As shown in panel (a), it is possible for a decline in long-run aggregate supply to cause a rise in the price level. Long-run aggregate supply *increases* in a growing economy, however, so this cannot explain the observation of persistent U.S. inflation. Panel (b) provides the actual explanation of persistent inflation in the United States and most other nations today, which is that increases in aggregate demand push up the long-run equilibrium price level. Thus, it is possible to explain persistent inflation if the aggregate demand curve shifts rightward at a faster pace than the long-run aggregate supply curve.

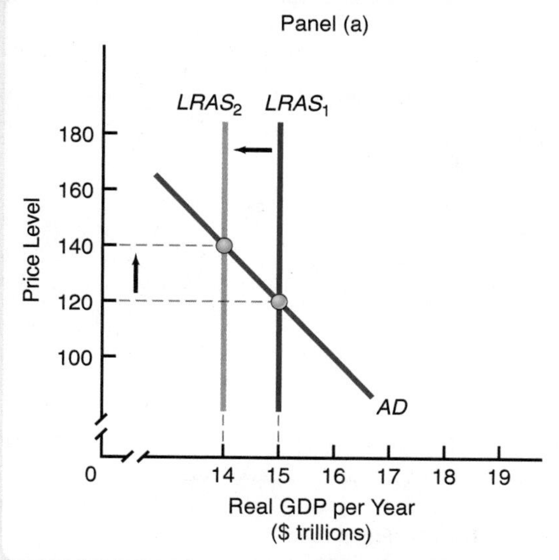

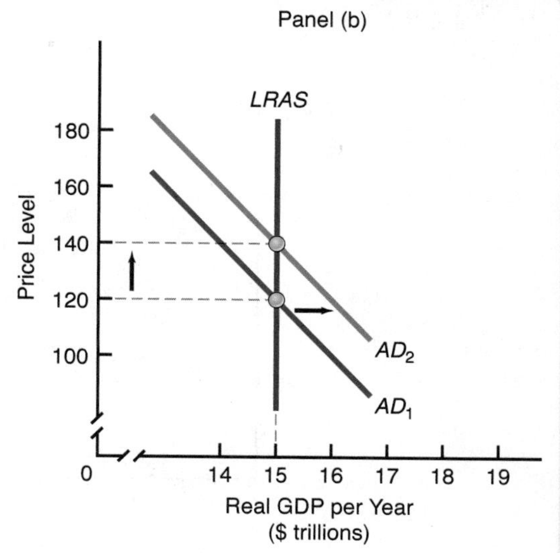

Supply-Side Inflation?

What causes such persistent inflation? The model of aggregate demand and long-run aggregate supply provides two possible explanations for inflation. One potential rationale is depicted in panel (a) of Figure 10-8 above. This panel shows a rise in the price level caused by a *decline in long-run aggregate supply*. Hence, one possible reason for persistent inflation would be continual reductions in economywide production.

A leftward shift in the aggregate supply schedule could be caused by several factors, such as reductions in labor force participation, higher marginal tax rates on wages, or the provision of government benefits that give households incentives *not* to supply labor services to firms. Tax rates and government benefits have increased during recent decades, but so has the U.S. population. The significant overall rise in real GDP that has taken place during the past few decades tells us that population growth and productivity gains undoubtedly have dominated other factors. In fact, the aggregate supply schedule has actually shifted *rightward*, not leftward, over time. Consequently, this supply-side explanation for persistent inflation *cannot* be the correct explanation.

Demand-Side Inflation

This leaves only one other explanation for the persistent inflation that the United States has experienced in recent decades. This explanation is depicted in panel (b) of Figure 10-8 above. If aggregate demand increases for a given level of long-run aggregate supply, the price level must increase. The reason is that at an initial price level such as 120, people desire to purchase more goods and services than firms are willing and able to produce, given currently available resources and technology. As a result, the rise in aggregate demand leads only to a general rise in the price level, such as the increase to a value of 140, depicted in the figure.

MyEconLab Real-time data

FIGURE 10-9

Real GDP and the Price Level in the United States, 1970 to the Present

This figure shows the points where aggregate demand and aggregate supply have intersected each year from 1970 to the present. The United States has experienced economic growth over this period, but not without inflation.

Sources: Economic Report of the President; Economic Indicators, various issues; author's estimates.

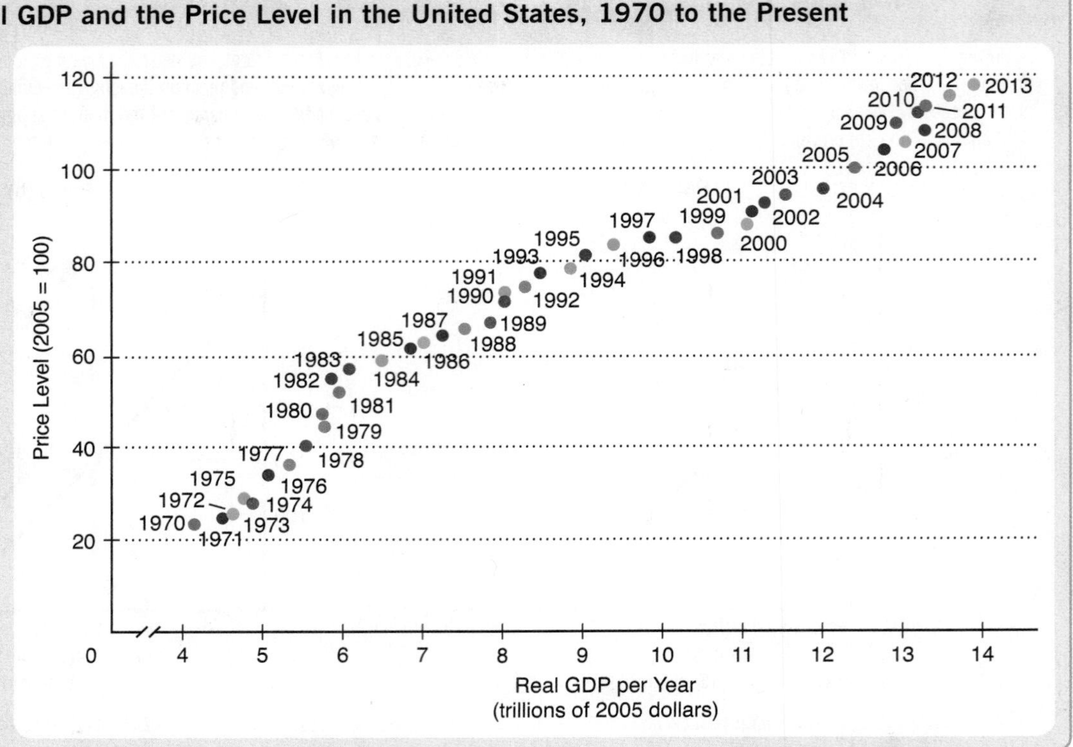

WHAT IF... there was a sustained increase in the amount of money in circulation intended to generate a rise in the nation's real GDP per year?

A sustained increase in the quantity of money in circulation would cause persistent rightward shifts in the aggregate demand curve. Because the long-run aggregate supply curve is vertical at the annual real output level after full adjustment has taken place, increases in aggregate demand cannot influence the equilibrium level of *real* GDP per year. What a sustained increase in the amount of money in circulation *can* do is bring about persistently higher values of the equilibrium price level. Thus, this monetary policy action would generate only sustained inflation and would fail in its objective to raise long-run annual real GDP.

From a long-run perspective, we are left with only one possibility: Persistent inflation in a growing economy is possible only if the aggregate demand curve shifts rightward over time at a faster pace than the rightward progression of the long-run aggregate supply curve. Thus, in contrast to the experience of people who lived in the latter portion of the nineteenth century, when aggregate demand grew too slowly relative to aggregate supply to maintain price stability, your grandparents, parents, and you have lived in times when aggregate demand has grown too *speedily*. The result has been a continual upward drift in the price level, or long-term inflation.

Figure 10-9 above shows that U.S. real GDP has grown in most years since 1970. Nevertheless, this growth has been accompanied by a higher price level every single year.

Has aggregate supply growth dropped below growth in aggregate demand?

EXAMPLE

Will Slowed Growth of Potential U.S. Real GDP Fuel Inflation?

To measure the pace of growth of long-run aggregate supply, economists estimate the rate of growth of *potential real GDP*, which is a measure of how fast the long-run aggregate supply curve shifts outward. Most economists conclude that U.S. potential real GDP growth rose from about 3.5 percent in the 1940s to above 4 percent in the 1960s.

Between the 1970s and 1990s, however, this growth rate dropped to nearly 3 percent. During the 2000s, it fell even further, to between 2 and 2.5 percent. By the early 2010s, potential real GDP growth was between 1 and 1.5 percent. Thus, the position of the U.S. long-run aggregate supply curve now is shifting rightward at the slowest pace in more than 80 years. If aggregate demand continues growing at the same average pace as in years past, the U.S. inflation rate necessarily will tend to rise.

FOR CRITICAL THINKING

Could the lower growth of long-run aggregate supply in the 2000s help account for why the average inflation rate was higher in the 2000s than in the 1990s? Explain.

QUICK QUIZ See page 228 for the answers. Review concepts from this section in MyEconLab.

When the economy is in long-run equilibrium, the price level adjusts to equate total planned real __________ by individuals, businesses, the government, and foreign (non-U.S.) residents with total planned __________ by firms.

Economic growth causes the long-run aggregate supply schedule to shift __________ over time. If the position of the aggregate demand curve does not change, the long-run equilibrium price level tends to __________, and there is **secular deflation.**

Because the U.S. economy has grown in recent decades, the persistent inflation during those years has been caused by the aggregate demand curve shifting __________ at a faster pace than the long-run aggregate supply curve.

YOU ARE THERE

A Nation Confronts a Leftward-Shifting *LRAS* Curve

Goncalo Pascoal, chief economist at Millennium BCP, the largest bank in Portugal, sees little to cheer about when he examines the nation's economic performance. In the years since 2007, Portugal's real GDP has been *shrinking* at an average pace of 1 percent per year. Thus, the nation's long-run aggregate supply curve has been exhibiting a sustained leftward shift.

Pascoal does not have to look far for the causes of this shrinkage. In cities such as Felgueiras, once a thriving center of shoe production, empty factories with mostly broken windows line the streets. Throughout the nation, many textile and clothing facilities lie vacant. Over the years, these and other Portuguese manufacturing resources began wearing out. Instead of preventing obsolescence from reducing the nation's stock of productive capital goods, the countries' residents directed many available resources to consumption goods. Eventually, the country's overall capital stock began to shrink. Now, Pascoal realizes, so much of the nation's capital stock is depleted and unusable that the flow of production of goods and services has declined with each passing year. This is why real GDP is steadily dropping, yielding leftward shifts in Portugal's long-run aggregate supply curve.

Critical Thinking Questions

1. In what direction is Portugal's production possibilities curve shifting over time?
2. What type of inflation might Portugal experience during the coming years?

ISSUES & APPLICATIONS

Will Arctic Assets Unfreeze Long-Run Aggregate Supply?

CONCEPTS APPLIED

- Aggregate Supply
- Long-Run Aggregate Supply Curve
- Endowments

Some economists have begun factoring into their long-run aggregate supply evaluations the underutilized and untapped resource endowments near and within the Arctic Circle. Bringing those resources into broader use, these economists suggest, could do much to generate speedier rightward shifts of the long-run aggregate supply curves of the United States and other northern nations.

Lands with Unexploited Resource Endowments

The Arctic, the global region north of 66.33 degrees latitude, contains only slightly more than 4 percent of the earth's surface area. Nevertheless, nearby regions stretching southward to 45 degrees latitude encompass another 11 percent of the earth's surface and an additional 25 percent of its land mass. Wide swaths of these lands contain significant endowments of as-yet unexploited resources, including minerals, oil, and natural gas.

Three key explanations can be offered for the meager utilization of Arctic and near-Arctic resources. First, the region is not particularly hospitable to people, who must adapt to long summer days and winter nights and to lengthy periods of extreme cold. Second, large tracts of land are covered with thick permafrost and with heavy sheets of ice, or glaciers. Third, much of the land near and within the Arctic is publicly owned. Governments have fewer incentives than private individuals and businesses to extract productive resources from these lands. Indeed, failure to place Arctic and near-Arctic resources in private hands has done more to consign them to an economic deep freeze than the cold air above them.

Could Unfreezing Arctic Endowments Heat Up Aggregate Supply Growth?

The volume of untapped Arctic oil is thought to be sufficiently large to provide the *entire world's* requirements for about half a year, and today's technology could fuel *global* natural gas requirements for an estimated 2 years. If all estimated Arctic oil could be extracted, it would last the world at least 3 years, and all of the region's likely natural gas reserves would be enough for about 25 years. Mineral endowments are less certain, but most geologists suspect that unexploited Arctic and near-Arctic lands contain vast amounts of metal ores.

Of course, making most Arctic resources accessible to private producers would *gradually* add to annual flows of resources that residents of northern nations such as the United States could use to produce goods and services. Estimates indicate that drawing on these endowments would boost annual U.S. real GDP growth by an appreciable fraction of a percentage point. Thus, reducing government ownership of these underutilized and untapped endowments would contribute to higher economic growth.

For Critical Thinking

1. Why do you suppose that firms in Arctic nations are already developing specialized tanker ships and platforms for use in privately accessible Arctic areas?
2. What are possible opportunity costs of opening Arctic lands to private extraction of as-yet unavailable resource endowments?

Web Resources

1. For a summary of current data about likely Arctic oil and natural gas endowments, go to **www.econtoday.com/chap10**.
2. To learn about economic issues faced in extracting metal ores in the Arctic, go to **www.econtoday.com/chap10**.

> **MyEconLab**
>
> For more questions on this chapter's Issues & Applications, go to **MyEconLab**. In the Study Plan for this chapter, select Section N: News.

MyEconLab

Here is what you should know after reading this chapter. MyEconLab will help you identify what you know, and where to go when you need to practice.

WHAT YOU SHOULD KNOW		WHERE TO GO TO PRACTICE
Long-Run Aggregate Supply The long-run aggregate supply curve is vertical at the amount of real GDP that firms plan to produce when they have full information and when complete adjustment of input prices to any changes in output prices has taken place.	aggregate supply, 211 long-run aggregate supply curve, 211 base-year dollars, 211 endowments, 211 **Key Figure** Figure 10-1, 211	• MyEconLab Study Plan 10.1 • Animated Figure 10-1

MyEconLab *continued*

WHAT YOU SHOULD KNOW		WHERE TO GO TO PRACTICE
Economic Growth and the Long-Run Aggregate Supply Curve The production possibilities curve shifts rightward when the economy grows, and so does the nation's long-run aggregate supply curve. In a growing economy, the changes in full-employment real GDP defined by the shifting long-run aggregate supply curve define the nation's long-run, or trend, growth path.	**Key Figures** Figure 10-2, 212 Figure 10-3, 213	• MyEconLab Study Plan 10.1 • Animated Figures 10-2, 10-3
Why the Aggregate Demand Curve Slopes Downward and Factors That Cause It to Shift The real-balance effect occurs when a rise in the price level reduces the real value of cash balances, which induces people to cut back on planned spending. Higher interest rates typically accompany increases in the price level, and this interest rate effect induces people to cut back on borrowing and spending. Finally, a rise in the price level at home causes domestic goods to be more expensive relative to foreign goods, so there is a fall in exports and a rise in imports, both of which cause domestic planned expenditures to fall. These three factors together account for the downward slope of the aggregate demand curve, which shifts if there is any other change in total planned real expenditures at any given price level.	aggregate demand, 214 aggregate demand curve, 214 real-balance effect, 216 interest rate effect, 216 open economy effect, 216 **Key Figure** Figure 10-4, 215	• MyEconLab Study Plans 10.2, 10.3 • Animated Figure 10-4
Long-Run Equilibrium for the Economy In a long-run economywide equilibrium, the price level adjusts until total planned real expenditures equal actual real GDP. Thus, the long-run equilibrium price level is determined at the point where the aggregate demand curve intersects the long-run aggregate supply curve.	**Key Figure** Figure 10-5, 219	• MyEconLab Study Plan 10.4 • Animated Figure 10-5
Why Economic Growth Can Cause Deflation If the aggregate demand curve is stationary during a period of economic growth, the long-run aggregate supply curve shifts rightward along the aggregate demand curve. The long-run equilibrium price level falls, so there is secular deflation.	secular deflation, 220 **Key Figure** Figure 10-6, 219	• MyEconLab Study Plan 10.4 • Animated Figure 10-6
Likely Reasons for Recent Persistent Inflation Inflation can result from a fall in long-run aggregate supply, but in a growing economy, long-run aggregate supply generally rises. Thus, a much more likely cause of persistent inflation is a pace of aggregate demand growth that exceeds the pace at which long-run aggregate supply increases.	**Key Figures** Figure 10-7, 220 Figure 10-8, 221	• MyEconLab Study Plan 10.5 • Animated Figures 10-7, 10-8

Log in to MyEconLab, take a chapter test, and get a personalized Study Plan that tells you which concepts you understand and which ones you need to review. From there, MyEconLab will give you further practice, tutorials, animations, videos, and guided solutions. For more information, visit www.myeconlab.com

PROBLEMS

All problems are assignable in MyEconLab. *Answers to odd-numbered problems appear at the back of the book.*

10-1. Many economists view the natural rate of unemployment as the level observed when real GDP is given by the position of the long-run aggregate supply curve. How can there be positive unemployment in this situation? (See page 211.)

10-2. Suppose that the long-run aggregate supply curve is positioned at a real GDP level of $15 trillion in base-year dollars, and the long-run equilibrium price level (in index number form) is 115. What is the full-employment level of *nominal* GDP? (See page 219.)

10-3. Continuing from Problem 10-2, suppose that the full-employment level of *nominal* GDP in the following year rises to $17.7 trillion. The long-run equilibrium price level, however, remains unchanged. By how much (in real dollars) has the long-run aggregate supply curve shifted to the right in the following year? By how much, if any, has the aggregate demand curve shifted to the right? (Hint: The equilibrium price level can stay the same only if *LRAS* and *AD* shift rightward by the same amount (See page 219.)

10-4. Suppose that the position of a nation's long-run aggregate supply curve has not changed, but its long-run equilibrium price level has increased. Which of the following factors might account for this event? (See page 219.)

a. A rise in the value of the domestic currency relative to other world currencies

b. An increase in the quantity of money in circulation

c. An increase in the labor force participation rate

d. A decrease in taxes

e. A rise in real incomes of countries that are key trading partners of this nation

f. Increased long-run economic growth

10-5. Identify the combined shifts in long-run aggregate supply and aggregate demand that could explain the following simultaneous occurrences. (See page 219).

a. An increase in equilibrium real GDP and an increase in the equilibrium price level

b. A decrease in equilibrium real GDP with no change in the equilibrium price level

c. An increase in equilibrium real GDP with no change in the equilibrium price level

d. A decrease in equilibrium real GDP and a decrease in the equilibrium price level

10-6. Suppose that during the past 3 years, equilibrium real GDP in a country rose steadily, from $450 billion to $500 billion, but even though the position of its aggregate demand curve remained unchanged, its equilibrium price level steadily declined, from 110 to 103. What could have accounted for these outcomes, and what is the term for the change in the price level experienced by this country? (See page 219.)

10-7. Suppose that during a given year, the quantity of U.S. real GDP that can be produced in the long run rises from $14.9 trillion to $15.0 trillion, measured in base-year dollars. During the year, no change occurs in the various factors that influence aggregate demand. What will happen to the U.S. long-run equilibrium price level during this particular year? (See page 219.)

10-8. Assume that the position of a nation's aggregate demand curve has not changed, but the long-run equilibrium price level has declined. Other things being equal, which of the following factors might account for this event? (See page 219.)

a. An increase in labor productivity

b. A decrease in the capital stock

c. A decrease in the quantity of money in circulation

d. The discovery of new mineral resources used to produce various goods

e. A technological improvement

10-9. Suppose that there is a sudden rise in the price level. What will happen to economywide planned spending on purchases of goods and services? Why? (See page 215.)

10-10. Assume that the economy is in long-run equilibrium with complete information and that input prices adjust rapidly to changes in the prices of goods and services. If there is a rise in the price level induced by an increase in aggregate demand, what happens to real GDP? (See page 219.)

10-11. Consider the diagram below when answering the questions that follow. (See page 219.)

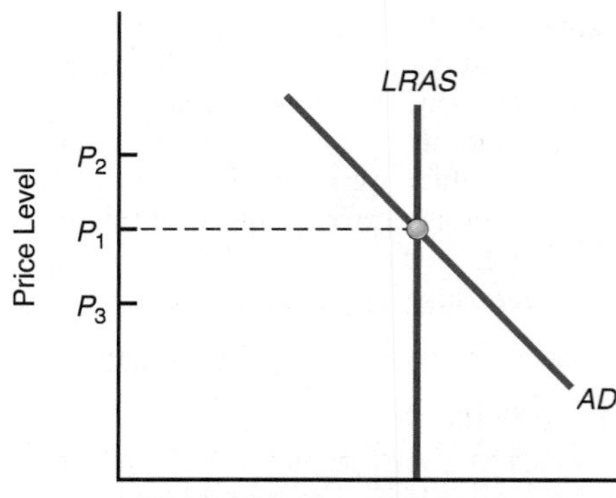

a. Suppose that the current price level is P_2. Explain why the price level will decline toward P_1.

b. Suppose that the current price level is P_3. Explain why the price level will rise toward P_1.

10-12. Explain whether each of the following events would cause a movement along or a shift in the position of the *LRAS* curve, other things being equal. In each case, explain the direction of the movement along the curve or shift in its position. (See page 212.)

a. Last year, businesses invested in new capital equipment, so this year the nation's capital stock is higher than it was last year.

b. There has been an 8 percent increase in the quantity of money in circulation that has shifted the *AD* curve.

c. A hurricane of unprecedented strength has damaged oil rigs, factories, and ports all along the nation's coast.

d. Inflation has occurred during the past year as a result of rightward shifts of the *AD* curve.

10-13. Explain whether each of the following events would cause a movement along or a shift in the position of the *AD* curve, other things being equal. In each case, explain the direction of the movement along the curve or shift in its position. (See page 217.)

a. Deflation has occurred during the past year.

b. Real GDP levels of all the nation's major trading partners have declined.

c. There has been a decline in the foreign exchange value of the nation's currency.

d. The price level has increased this year.

10-14. This year, a nation's long-run equilibrium real GDP and price level both increased. Which of the following combinations of factors might simultaneously account for *both* occurrences? (See page 219.)

a. An isolated earthquake at the beginning of the year destroyed part of the nation's capital stock, and the nation's government significantly reduced its purchases of goods and services.

b. There was a technological improvement at the end of the previous year, and the quantity of money in circulation rose significantly during the year.

c. Labor productivity increased throughout the year, and consumers significantly increased their total planned purchases of goods and services.

d. The capital stock increased somewhat during the year, and the quantity of money in circulation declined considerably.

10-15. Explain how, if at all, each of the following events would affect equilibrium real GDP and the long-run equilibrium price level. (See page 219.)

a. A reduction in the quantity of money in circulation

b. An income tax rebate (the return of previously paid taxes) from the government to households, which they can apply only to purchases of goods and services

c. A technological improvement

d. A decrease in the value of the home currency in terms of the currencies of other nations

10-16. For each question, suppose that the economy *begins* at the long-run equilibrium point *A* in the diagram below. Identify which of the other points on the diagram—points *B*, *C*, *D*, or *E*—could represent a *new* long-run equilibrium after the described events take place and move the economy away from point *A*. (See page 219.)

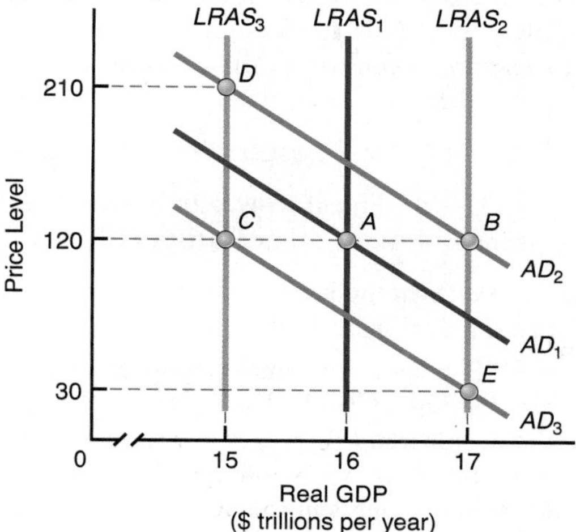

a. Significant productivity improvements occur, and the quantity of money in circulation increases.

b. No new capital investment takes place, and a fraction of the existing capital stock depreciates and becomes unusable. At the same time, the government imposes a large tax increase on the nation's households.

c. More efficient techniques for producing goods and services are adopted throughout the economy at the same time that the government reduces its spending on goods and services.

10-17. In Ciudad Barrios, El Salvador, the latest payments from relatives working in the United States have finally arrived. When the credit unions open for business, up to 150 people are already waiting in line. After receiving the funds their relatives have transmitted to these institutions, customers go off to outdoor markets to stock up on food or clothing or to appliance stores to purchase new stereos or televisions. Similar scenes occur throughout the developing world, as each year migrants working in higher-income, developed nations send around $200 billion of their earnings back to their relatives in less developed nations.

Evidence indicates that the relatives, such as those in Ciudad Barrios, typically spend nearly all of the funds on current consumption. (See page 219.)

a. Based on the information supplied, are developing countries' income inflows transmitted by migrant workers primarily affecting their economies' long-run aggregate supply curves or aggregate demand curves?

b. How are equilibrium price levels in nations that are recipients of large inflows of funds from migrants likely to be affected? Explain your reasoning.

ECONOMICS ON THE NET

Wages, Productivity, and Aggregate Supply How much firms pay their employees and the productivity of those employees influence firms' total planned production, so changes in these factors affect the position of the aggregate supply curve. This application gives you the opportunity to examine recent trends in measures of the overall wages and productivity of workers.

Title: Bureau of Labor Statistics: Economy at a Glance

Navigation: Use the link at **www.econtoday.com/chap10** to visit the Bureau of Labor Statistics (BLS) Web site.

Application Perform the indicated operations, and answer the following questions.

1. In the "Pay and Benefits" popup menu, click on *Employment Costs*. Choose *Employment Cost Index*. What are the recent trends in wages and salaries and in benefits? In the long run, how should these trends be related to movements in the overall price level?
2. Back up to the home page, and in the "Productivity" popup menu, click on *Labor Productivity and Costs* and then on *PDF* next to "LPC News Releases: Productivity and Costs." How has labor productivity behaved recently? What does this imply for the long-run aggregate supply curve?
3. Back up to the home page, and now in the "Employment" popup menu, click on *National Employment* and then on *PDF* next to "Current CES Economic News Release: Employment Situation Summary." Does it appear that the U.S. economy is currently in a long-run growth equilibrium?

For Group Study and Analysis

1. Divide the class into aggregate demand and long-run aggregate supply groups. Have each group search the Internet for data on factors that influence its assigned curve. For which factors do data appear to be most readily available? For which factors are data more sparse or more subject to measurement problems?
2. The BLS home page displays a map of the United States. Assign regions of the nation to different groups, and have each group develop a short report about current and future prospects for economic growth within its assigned region. What similarities exist across regions? What regional differences are there?

ANSWERS TO QUICK QUIZZES

p. 213: (i) vertical; (ii) natural; (iii) rightward . . . increases

p. 218: (i) expenditures . . . production . . . spending; (ii) real-balance . . . interest rate . . . open economy; (iii) real-balance; (iv) interest rate . . . fewer . . . more; (v) domestic . . . foreign

p. 223: (i) expenditures . . . production; (ii) rightward . . . decline; (iii) rightward

Classical and Keynesian Macro Analyses

11

LEARNING OBJECTIVES

After reading this chapter, you should be able to:

- Discuss the central assumptions of the classical model
- Describe the short-run determination of equilibrium real GDP and the price level in the classical model
- Explain circumstances under which the short-run aggregate supply curve may be either horizontal or upward sloping
- Understand what factors cause shifts in the short-run and long-run aggregate supply curves
- Evaluate the effects of aggregate demand and supply shocks on equilibrium real GDP in the short run
- Determine the causes of short-run variations in the inflation rate

MyEconLab helps you master each objective and study more efficiently. See end of chapter for details.

Many Wall Street observers refer to it as the "fear index." Its true name is the *VIX index*, and it has become the most commonly used gauge of volatility in U.S. financial markets. Prior to and during the severe 2008–2009 recession, the VIX index increased substantially, reflecting significant variability of the value of financial claims traded in financial markets as well as volatility in real interest rates. How can major disturbances in financial markets sometimes translate into reductions in real GDP and even decreases in the price level? To understand the answer, you must learn about determination of the equilibrium price level in the short run, which is a fundamental topic of this chapter.

? DID YOU KNOW THAT... the price of a bottle containing 6.5 ounces of Coca-Cola remained unchanged at 5 cents from 1886 to 1959? The prices of many other goods and services changed at least slightly during that 73-year period, and since then the prices of most items, including Coca-Cola, have generally moved in an upward direction. Nevertheless, prices of final goods and services have not always adjusted immediately in response to changes in aggregate demand. Consequently, one approach to understanding the determination of real GDP and the price level emphasizes *incomplete* adjustment in the prices of many goods and services. The simplest version of this approach was first developed by a twentieth-century economist named John Maynard Keynes (pronounced like *canes*). It assumes that in the short run, prices of most goods and services are nearly as rigid as the price of Coca-Cola from 1886 to 1959. Although the modern version of the Keynesian approach allows for greater flexibility of prices in the short run, incomplete price adjustment still remains a key feature of the modern Keynesian approach.

The Keynesian approach does not retain the long-run assumption, which you encountered in Chapter 10, of fully adjusting prices. Economists who preceded Keynes employed this assumption in creating an approach to understanding variations in real GDP and the price level that Keynes called the *classical model.* Like Keynes, we shall begin our study of variations in real GDP and the price level by considering the earlier, classical approach.

The Classical Model

The classical model, which traces its origins to the 1770s, was the first systematic attempt to explain the determinants of the price level and the national levels of real GDP, employment, consumption, saving, and investment. Classical economists—Adam Smith, J. B. Say, David Ricardo, John Stuart Mill, Thomas Malthus, A. C. Pigou, and others—wrote from the 1770s to the 1930s. They assumed, among other things, that all wages and prices were flexible and that competitive markets existed throughout the economy.

Say's Law

Every time you produce something for which you receive income, you generate the income necessary to make expenditures on other goods and services. That means that an economy producing $15 trillion of real GDP, measured in base-year dollars (the value of current goods and services expressed in terms of prices in a base year), simultaneously produces the income with which these goods and services can be purchased. As an accounting identity, *actual* aggregate output always equals *actual* aggregate income. Classical economists took this accounting identity one step further by arguing that total national supply creates its own national demand. They asserted what has become known as **Say's law:**

Say's law
A dictum of economist J. B. Say that supply creates its own demand. Producing goods and services generates the means and the willingness to purchase other goods and services.

> ***Supply creates its own demand. Hence, it follows that* desired *expenditures will equal* actual *expenditures.***

THE IMPLICATION OF SAY'S LAW What does Say's law really mean? It states that the very process of producing specific goods (supply) is proof that other goods are desired (demand). People produce more goods than they want for their own use only if they seek to trade them for other goods. Someone offers to supply something only because he or she has a demand for something else.

The implication of this, according to Say, is that no general glut, or overproduction, is possible in a market economy. From this reasoning, it seems to follow that full employment of labor and other resources would be the normal state of affairs in such an economy.

Say acknowledged that an oversupply of some goods might occur in particular markets. He argued that such surpluses would simply cause prices to fall, thereby decreasing production as the economy adjusted. The opposite would occur in markets in which shortages temporarily appeared.

FIGURE 11-1

Say's Law and the Circular Flow

Here we show the circular flow of income and output. The very act of supplying a certain level of goods and services necessarily equals the level of goods and services demanded, in Say's simplified world.

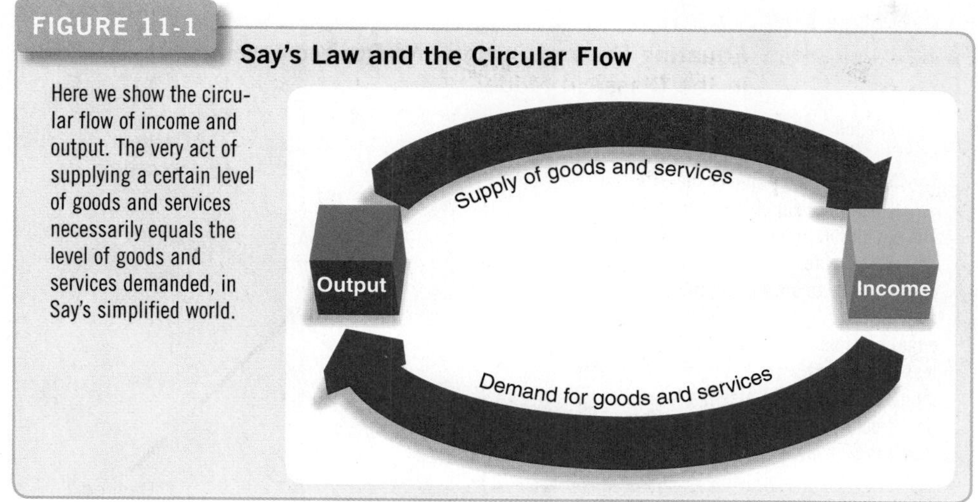

SAY'S LAW IN A MODERN ECONOMY All this seems reasonable enough in a simple barter economy in which households produce most of the goods they want and trade for the rest. This is shown in Figure 11-1 above, where there is a simple circular flow. But what about a more sophisticated economy in which people work for others and money is used instead of barter? Can these complications create the possibility of unemployment? And does the fact that laborers receive money income, some of which can be saved, lead to unemployment? No, said the classical economists to these last two questions. They based their reasoning on a number of key assumptions.

Assumptions of the Classical Model

The classical model makes four major assumptions:

1. *Pure competition exists.* No single buyer or seller of a commodity or an input can affect its price.

2. *Wages and prices are flexible.* The assumption of pure competition leads to the notion that prices, wages and interest rates are free to move to whatever level supply and demand dictate (as the economy adjusts). Although no *individual* buyer can set a price, the community of buyers or sellers can cause prices to rise or to fall to an equilibrium level.

3. *People are motivated by self-interest.* Businesses want to maximize their profits, and households want to maximize their economic well-being.

4. *People cannot be fooled by money illusion.* Buyers and sellers react to changes in relative prices. That is to say, they do not suffer from **money illusion.** For example, workers will not be fooled into thinking that doubling their wages makes them better off if the price level has also doubled during the same time period.

Money illusion
Reacting to changes in money prices rather than relative prices. If a worker whose wages double when the price level also doubles thinks he or she is better off, that worker is suffering from money illusion.

The classical economists concluded, after taking account of the four major assumptions, that the role of government in the economy should be minimal. They assumed that pure competition prevails, all prices and wages are flexible, and people are self-interested and do not experience money illusion. If so, they argued, then any problems in the macroeconomy will be temporary. The market will correct itself.

Equilibrium in the Credit Market

When income is saved, it is not reflected in product demand. It is a type of *leakage* from the circular flow of income and output because saving withdraws funds from the income stream. Therefore, total planned consumption spending *can* fall short of total current real GDP. In such a situation, it appears that supply does not necessarily create its own demand.

FIGURE 11-2

Equating Desired Saving and Desired Investment in the Classical Model

The schedule showing planned investment is labeled "Desired investment." The desired saving curve is shown as an upward-sloping supply curve of saving. The equilibrating force here is, of course, the interest rate. At higher interest rates, people desire to save more. But at higher interest rates, businesses wish to engage in less investment because it is less profitable to invest. In this model, at an interest rate of 5 percent, planned investment just equals planned saving, which is $2 trillion per year.

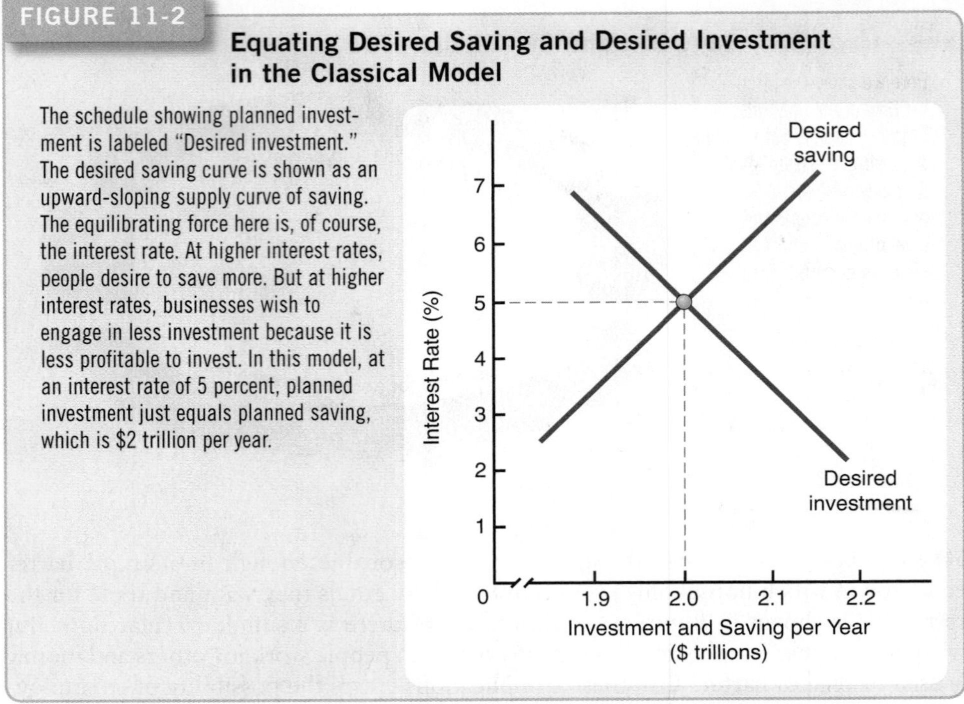

THE RELATIONSHIP BETWEEN SAVING AND INVESTMENT The classical economists did not believe that the complicating factor of saving in the circular flow model of income and output was a problem. They contended that each dollar saved would be invested by businesses so that the leakage of saving would be matched by the injection of business investment. *Investment* here refers only to additions to the nation's capital stock. The classical economists believed that businesses as a group would intend to invest as much as households wanted to save.

Go to www.econtoday.com/chap11 to link to Federal Reserve data on U.S. interest rates.

THE EQUILIBRIUM INTEREST RATE Equilibrium between the saving plans of consumers and the investment plans of businesses comes about, in the classical model, through the working of the credit market. In the credit market, the *price* of credit is the interest rate. At equilibrium, the price of credit—the interest rate—ensures that the amount of credit demanded equals the amount of credit supplied. Planned investment just equals planned saving, so there is no reason to be concerned about the leakage of saving. This fact is illustrated graphically in Figure 11-2 above.

In the figure, the vertical axis measures the rate of interest in percentage terms, and the horizontal axis measures flows of desired saving and desired investment per unit time period. The desired saving curve is really a supply curve of saving. It shows that people wish to save more at higher interest rates than at lower interest rates.

In contrast, the higher the rate of interest, the less profitable it is to invest and the lower is the level of desired investment. Thus, the desired investment curve slopes downward. In this simplified model, the equilibrium rate of interest is 5 percent, and the equilibrium quantity of saving and investment is $2 trillion per year.

Equilibrium in the Labor Market

Go to www.econtoday.com/chap11 to find out the latest U.S. saving rate from the Bureau of Economic Analysis. Select "Personal saving as a percentage of disposable personal income."

Now consider the labor market. If an excess quantity of labor is supplied at a particular wage level, the wage level must be above equilibrium. By accepting lower wages, unemployed workers will quickly be put back to work. We show equilibrium in the labor market in Figure 11-3 on the facing page.

FIGURE 11-3

Equilibrium in the Labor Market

The demand for labor is downward sloping. At higher wage rates, firms will employ fewer workers. The supply of labor is upward sloping. At higher wage rates, more workers will work longer, and more people will be willing to work. The equilibrium wage rate is $18 with an equilibrium employment per year of 160 million workers.

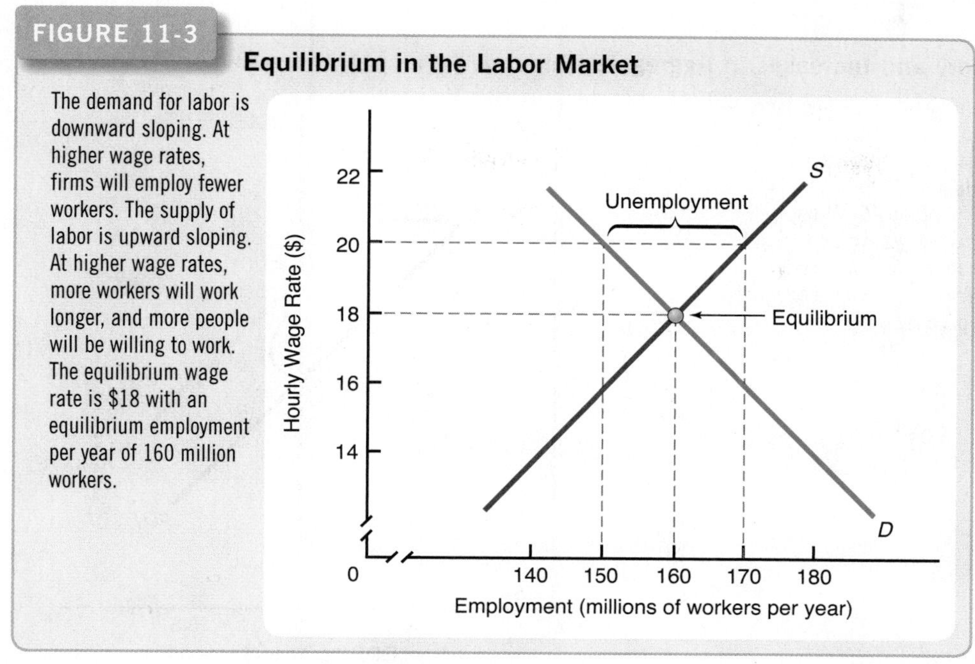

Assume that equilibrium exists at $18 per hour and 160 million workers employed. If the wage rate were $20 per hour, there would be unemployment—170 million workers would want to work, but businesses would want to hire only 150 million. In the classical model, this unemployment is eliminated rather rapidly by wage rates dropping back to $18 per hour, as seen in Figure 11-3 above.

THE RELATIONSHIP BETWEEN EMPLOYMENT AND REAL GDP Employment is not to be regarded simply as some isolated figure that government statisticians estimate. Rather, the level of employment in an economy determines its real GDP (output), other things held constant. A hypothetical relationship between input (number of employees) and the value of output (real GDP per year) is shown in Table 11-1 below. The row that has 160 million workers per year as the labor input is highlighted. That might be considered a hypothetical level of full employment, and it is related to a rate of real GDP, in base-year dollars, of $15 trillion per year.

Classical Theory, Vertical Aggregate Supply, and the Price Level

In the classical model, unemployment greater than the natural unemployment rate is impossible. Say's law, coupled with flexible interest rates, prices, and wages, would always tend to keep workers fully employed so that the aggregate supply curve, as

TABLE 11-1

The Relationship between Employment and Real GDP

Other things being equal, an increase in the quantity of labor input increases real GDP. In this example, if 160 million workers are employed, real GDP is $15 trillion in base-year dollars.

Labor Input per Year (millions of workers)	Real GDP per Year ($ trillions)
150	12
154	13
158	14
160	15
164	16
166	17

FIGURE 11-4

Classical Theory and Increases in Aggregate Demand

The classical theorists believed that Say's law and flexible interest rates, prices, and wages would always lead to full employment at real GDP of $15 trillion, in base-year dollars, along the vertical aggregate supply curve, *LRAS*. With aggregate demand AD_1, the price level is 120. An increase in aggregate demand shifts AD_1 to AD_2. At price level 120, the quantity of real GDP demanded per year would be $15.5 trillion at point *A* on AD_2. But $15.5 trillion in real GDP per year is greater than real GDP at full employment. Prices rise, and the economy quickly moves from E_1 to E_2, at the higher price level of 130.

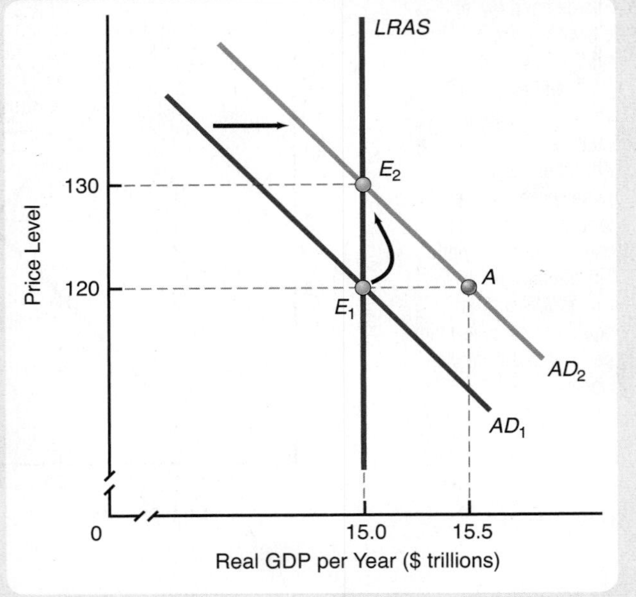

shown in Figure 11-4 above, is vertical at the real GDP of $15 trillion, in base-year dollars. We have labeled the supply curve *LRAS*, which is the long-run aggregate supply curve introduced in Chapter 10. It was defined there as the real GDP that would be produced in an economy with full information and full adjustment of wages and prices year in and year out. *LRAS* therefore corresponds to the long-run rate of unemployment.

In the classical model, this happens to be the *only* aggregate supply curve. The classical economists made little distinction between the long run and the short run. Prices adjust so fast that the economy is essentially always on or quickly moving toward *LRAS*. Furthermore, because the labor market adjusts rapidly, real GDP is always at, or soon to be at, full employment. Full employment does not mean zero unemployment because there is always some frictional and structural unemployment (discussed in Chapter 7), which yields the natural rate of unemployment.

EFFECT OF AN INCREASE IN AGGREGATE DEMAND IN THE CLASSICAL MODEL In this model, any change in aggregate demand will quickly cause a change in the price level. Consider starting at E_1, at price level 120, in Figure 11-4. If aggregate demand shifts to AD_2, the economy will tend toward point *A*, but because this is beyond full-employment real GDP, prices will rise, and the economy will find itself back on the vertical *LRAS* at point E_2 at a higher price level, 130. The price level will increase as a result of the increase in *AD* because employers will end up bidding up wages for workers, as well as bidding up the prices of other inputs.

The level of real GDP per year clearly does not depend on the level of aggregate demand. Hence, we say that in the classical model, the equilibrium level of real GDP per year is completely *supply determined.* Changes in aggregate demand affect only the price level, not real GDP.

EFFECT OF A DECREASE IN AGGREGATE DEMAND IN THE CLASSICAL MODEL The effect of a decrease in aggregate demand in the classical model is the converse of the analysis just presented for an increase in aggregate demand. You can simply reverse AD_2 and AD_1 in Figure 11-4 above. To help you see how this analysis works, consider the flowchart in Figure 11-5 on the facing page.

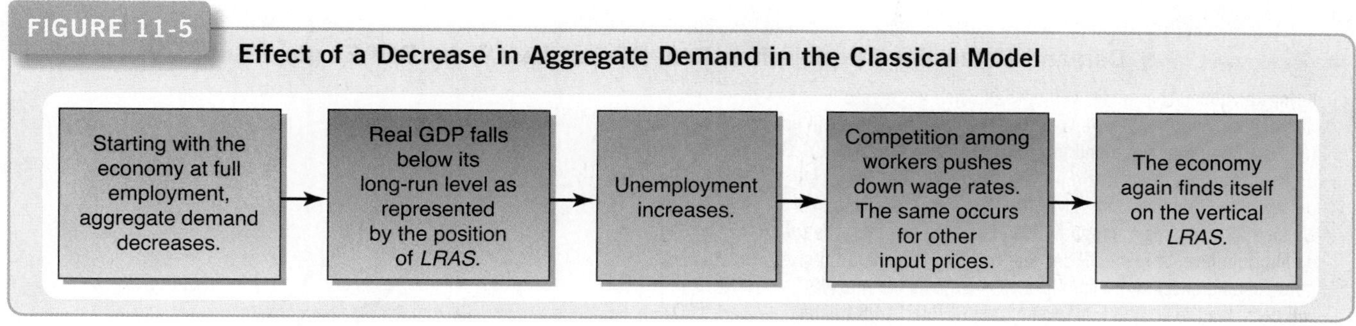

FIGURE 11-5 **Effect of a Decrease in Aggregate Demand in the Classical Model**

QUICK QUIZ See page 249 for the answers. Review concepts from this section in MyEconLab.

Say's law states that __________ creates its own __________ and therefore *desired* expenditures will equal *actual* expenditures.

The classical model assumes that (1) __________ __________ exists, (2) __________ and __________ are completely flexible, (3) individuals are motivated by __________-__________, and (4) they cannot be fooled by __________ __________.

When saving is introduced into the model, equilibrium occurs in the credit market through changes in the interest rate such that desired __________ equals desired __________ at the equilibrium rate of interest.

In the labor market, full employment occurs at a __________ __________ at which quantity demanded equals quantity supplied. That particular level of employment is associated with the full-employment level of real GDP per year.

In the classical model, because *LRAS* is __________, the equilibrium level of real GDP is supply determined. Any changes in aggregate demand simply change the __________ __________.

Keynesian Economics and the Keynesian Short-Run Aggregate Supply Curve

The classical economists' world was one of fully utilized resources. There would be no unused capacity and no unemployment. But then in the 1930s, Europe and the United States entered a period of economic decline that seemingly could not be explained by the classical model. John Maynard Keynes developed an explanation that has since become known as the Keynesian model. Keynes and his followers argued that prices, especially the price of labor (wages), were inflexible downward due to the existence of unions and long-term contracts between businesses and workers. That meant that prices were "sticky." Keynes contended that in such a world, which has large amounts of excess capacity and unemployment, an increase in aggregate demand will not raise the price level, and a decrease in aggregate demand will not cause firms to lower prices.

Demand-Determined Real GDP

This situation is depicted in Figure 11-6 on the next page. For simplicity, Figure 11-6 does not show the point where the economy reaches capacity, and that is why the *short-run aggregate supply curve* (to be discussed later) never starts to slope upward and is simply the horizontal line labeled *SRAS.* Moreover, we don't show *LRAS* in Figure 11-6 either. It would be a vertical line at the level of real GDP per year that is consistent with full employment. If we start out in equilibrium with aggregate demand at AD_1, the equilibrium level of real GDP per year, measured in base-year dollars, is \$15 trillion at point E_1, and the equilibrium price level is 120. If there is a rise in aggregate demand, so that the aggregate demand curve shifts outward to the right to AD_2, the equilibrium price level at point E_2 will not change. Only the equilibrium level of real GDP per year will increase, to \$15.5 trillion. Conversely, if there is a fall in aggregate demand that shifts the aggregate demand curve to AD_3, the equilibrium price level will again remain at 120 at point E_3, but the equilibrium level of real GDP per year will fall to \$14.5 trillion.

FIGURE 11-6

Demand-Determined Equilibrium Real GDP at Less Than Full Employment

Keynes assumed that prices will not fall when aggregate demand falls and that there is excess capacity, so prices will not rise when aggregate demand increases. Thus, the short-run aggregate supply curve is simply a horizontal line at the given price level, 120, represented by *SRAS*. An aggregate demand shock that increases aggregate demand to AD_2 will increase the equilibrium level of real GDP per year to $15.5 trillion. An aggregate demand shock that decreases aggregate demand to AD_3 will decrease the equilibrium level of real GDP to $14.5 trillion. The equilibrium price level will not change.

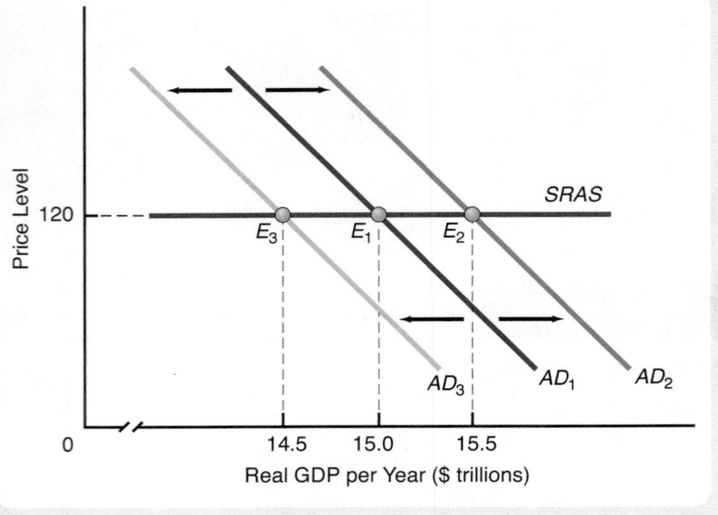

Under such circumstances, the equilibrium level of real GDP per year is completely *demand determined.*

The Keynesian Short-Run Aggregate Supply Curve

Keynesian short-run aggregate supply curve
The horizontal portion of the aggregate supply curve in which there is excessive unemployment and unused capacity in the economy.

The horizontal short-run aggregate supply curve represented in Figure 11-6 above is often called the **Keynesian short-run aggregate supply curve.** According to Keynes, unions and long-term contracts are real-world factors that explain the inflexibility of *nominal* wage rates. Such stickiness of wages makes *involuntary* unemployment of labor a distinct possibility, because leftward movements along the Keynesian short-run aggregate supply curve reduce real production and, hence, employment. The classical assumption of everlasting full employment no longer holds.

Have U.S. nominal wages remained too high to reduce unemployment?

EXAMPLE

Have Inflation-Adjusted U.S. Wages Been "Too High"?

Unemployment occurs when a surplus exists in the labor market—that is, when the quantity of labor supplied by workers at the current inflation-adjusted, or *real*, wage rate exceeds the quantity of labor that firms demand at that real wage rate. Other things being equal, a labor surplus will begin to disappear only if the inflation-adjusted wage rate drops toward that market clearing wage rate.

Since 2008, inflation-adjusted wages in the United States have declined by about 0.2 percent per year. Many economists contend that this low rate of decrease explains why unemployment has declined only from 14.3 million at the end of 2008 to just about 12.5 million today. Because the U.S. inflation rate has remained very low, they argue, nominal wages would have to drop at a faster pace to push down the labor market surplus more rapidly and thereby bring about a quicker decline in U.S. unemployment. Thus, they conclude that nominal wages have been too inflexible to reduce the nation's unemployment level significantly.

FOR CRITICAL THINKING

In principle, if nominal wages were to remain "too high," could a sustained increase in the inflation rate significantly reduce labor unemployment? Explain.

Data from the 1930s offer evidence of a nearly horizontal aggregate supply curve. Between 1934 and 1940, the GDP deflator stayed in a range from about 8.3 to less than 9.0, implying that the price level changed by no more than 8 percent. Yet the level of real GDP measured in 2005 dollars varied between nearly $0.7 trillion and close to $1.1 trillion, or by more than 50 percent. Thus, between 1934 and 1940, the U.S. short-run aggregate supply curve was almost flat.

FIGURE 11-7

Real GDP Determination with Fixed versus Flexible Prices

In panel (a), the price level index is fixed at 120. An increase in aggregate demand from AD_1 to AD_2 moves the equilibrium level of real GDP from $15 trillion per year to $16 trillion per year in base-year dollars. In panel (b), *SRAS* is upward sloping. The same shift in aggregate demand yields an equilibrium level of real GDP of only $15.5 trillion per year and a higher price level index at 130.

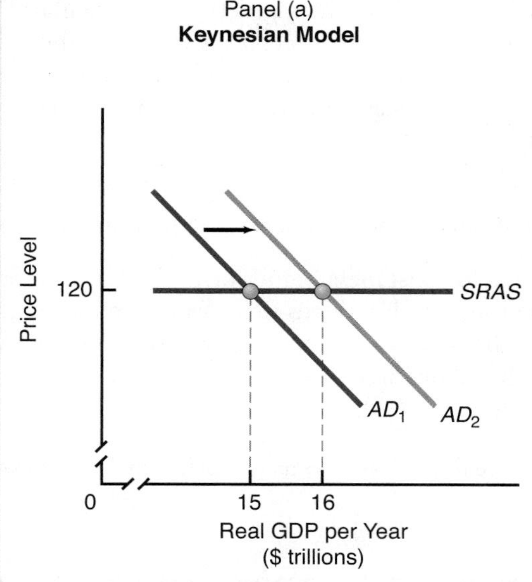

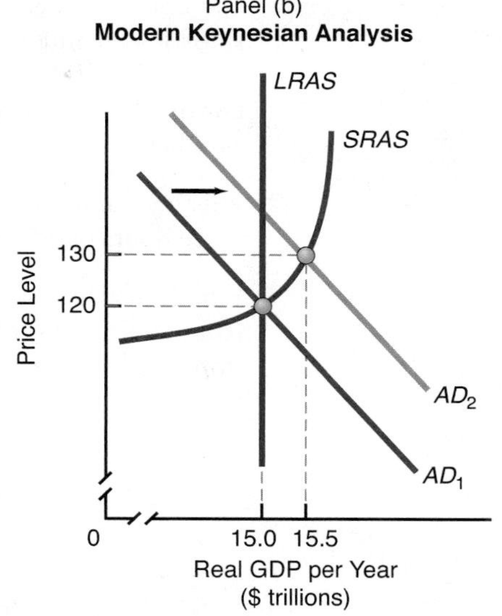

Output Determination Using Aggregate Demand and Aggregate Supply: Fixed versus Changing Price Levels in the Short Run

The underlying assumption of the simplified Keynesian model is that the relevant range of the short-run aggregate supply schedule (*SRAS*) is horizontal, as depicted in panel (a) of Figure 11-7 above. There you see that short-run aggregate supply is fixed at price level 120. If aggregate demand is AD_1, then the equilibrium level of real GDP, in base-year dollars, is $15 trillion per year. If aggregate demand increases to AD_2, then the equilibrium level of real GDP increases to $16 trillion per year.

As discussed in Chapter 10, the price level has drifted upward during recent decades. Hence, prices are not totally sticky. Modern Keynesian analysis recognizes that *some*—but not complete—price adjustment takes place in the short run. Panel (b) of Figure 11-7 above displays a more general **short-run aggregate supply curve** (*SRAS*). This curve represents the relationship between the price level and real GDP with incomplete price adjustment and in the absence of complete information in the short run. Allowing for partial price adjustment implies that *SRAS* slopes upward, and its slope is steeper after it crosses long-run aggregate supply, *LRAS*. This is because higher and higher prices are required to induce firms to raise their production of goods and services to levels that temporarily exceed full-employment real GDP.

Short-run aggregate supply curve The relationship between total planned economywide production and the price level in the short run, all other things held constant. If prices adjust incompletely in the short run, the curve is positively sloped.

With partial price adjustment in the short run, if aggregate demand is AD_1, then the equilibrium level of real GDP in panel (b) is also $15 trillion per year, at a price level of 120, too. An increase in aggregate demand to AD_2 such as occurred in panel (a) produces a different short-run equilibrium, however. Equilibrium real GDP increases to $15.5 trillion per year, which is less than in panel (a) because an increase in the price level to 130 causes planned purchases of goods and services to decline.

In the modern Keynesian short run, when the price level rises partially, real GDP can be expanded beyond the level consistent with its long-run growth path, discussed in Chapter 10, for a variety of reasons:

1. In the short run, most labor contracts implicitly or explicitly call for flexibility in hours of work at the given wage rate. Therefore, firms can use existing workers more intensively in a variety of ways: They can get workers to work harder, to work more hours per day, and to work more days per week. Workers can also be switched from *uncounted* production, such as maintenance, to *counted* production, which generates counted production of goods and services. The distinction between counted and uncounted is what is measured in the marketplace, particularly by government statisticians and accountants. If a worker cleans a machine, there is no measured output. But if that worker is put on the production line and helps increase the number of units produced each day, measured output will go up. That worker's production has then been counted.

2. Existing capital equipment can be used more intensively. Machines can be worked more hours per day. Some can be made to operate faster. Maintenance can be delayed.

3. Finally, if wage rates are held constant, a higher price level leads to increased profits from additional production, which induces firms to hire more workers. The duration of unemployment falls, and thus the unemployment rate falls. And people who were previously not in the labor force (homemakers and younger or older workers) can be induced to enter it.

All these adjustments cause real GDP to rise as the price level increases.

Shifts in the Aggregate Supply Curve

Just as non-price-level factors can cause a shift in the aggregate demand curve, there are non-price-level factors that can cause a shift in the aggregate supply curve. The analysis here is more complicated than the analysis for the non-price-level determinants for aggregate demand, for here we are dealing with both the short run and the long run—*SRAS* and *LRAS*. Still, anything other than the price level that affects the production of final goods and services will shift aggregate supply curves.

Shifts in Both Short- and Long-Run Aggregate Supply

There is a core class of events that cause a shift in both the short-run aggregate supply curve and the long-run aggregate supply curve. These include any change in our endowments of the factors of production. Any change in factors of production—labor, capital, or technology—that influence economic growth will shift *SRAS* and *LRAS*. Look at Figure 11-8 on the facing page. Initially, the two curves are $SRAS_1$ and $LRAS_1$. Now consider a situation in which large amounts of irreplaceable resources are lost *permanently* in a major oil spill and fire. This shifts $LRAS_1$ to $LRAS_2$ at $14.5 trillion of real GDP, measured in base-year dollars. $SRAS_1$ also shifts leftward horizontally to $SRAS_2$.

Shifts in *SRAS* Only

Some events, particularly those that are short-lived, will temporarily shift *SRAS* but not *LRAS*. One of the most obvious is a change in production input prices, particularly those caused by external events that are not expected to last forever. Consider a major hurricane that temporarily shuts down a significant portion of U.S. oil production. Oil is an important input in many production activities. The resulting drop in oil production would cause at least a temporary increase in the price of this input. In this case, the long-run aggregate supply curve would remain at $LRAS_1$ in Figure 11-8.

The short-run aggregate supply curve *alone* would shift from $SRAS_1$ to $SRAS_2$, reflecting the increase in input prices—the higher price of oil. This is because the rise in the costs of production at each level of real GDP per year would require a higher price level to cover those increased costs.

FIGURE 11-8

Shifts in Long-Run and Short-Run Aggregate Supply

Initially, the two aggregate supply curves are $SRAS_1$ and $LRAS_1$. An event that permanently reduces reserves of a key productive resource such as oil shifts $LRAS_1$ to $LRAS_2$ at $14.5 trillion of real GDP, in base-year dollars, and also shifts $SRAS_1$ horizontally leftward to $SRAS_2$. If, instead, a temporary increase in an input price occurred, $LRAS_1$ would remain unchanged, and only the short-run aggregate supply curve would shift, from $SRAS_1$ to $SRAS_2$.

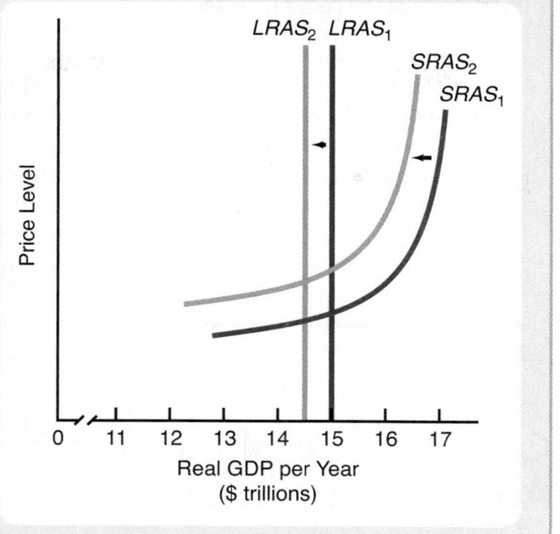

How can a single insect species generate an aggregate supply shock?

INTERNATIONAL EXAMPLE

Australia's Short-Run Aggregate Supply Hit by a Locust Plague

Recently, Australia has experienced its worst plague of locusts in half of a century. The 3-inch-long insects, ferocious eaters that forage in massive swarms, have ravaged large portions of the nation's crops. Included among the damaged crops are cereal grains, such as rice, wheat, and barley, which are important inputs for many food products. Also heavily damaged by the insects are feed crops that are key inputs in livestock production. The resulting decreases in market supplies of these fundamental inputs have pushed up a wide array of input prices. The result has been a decrease in short-run aggregate supply. Thus, the plague of locusts has shifted Australia's short-run aggregate supply curve leftward.

FOR CRITICAL THINKING

Why would a plague of locusts, which rarely lasts more than two or three crop seasons, fail to generate a leftward shift of the long-run aggregate supply curve?

We summarize the possible determinants of aggregate supply in Table 11-2 on the next page. These determinants will cause a shift in the short-run or the long-run aggregate supply curve or both, depending on whether they are temporary or permanent.

QUICK QUIZ

See page 249 for the answers. Review concepts from this section in MyEconLab.

If we assume that the economy is operating on a horizontal short-run aggregate supply curve, the equilibrium level of real GDP per year is completely __________ determined.

The horizontal short-run aggregate supply curve has been called the **Keynesian short-run aggregate supply curve** because Keynes believed that many prices, especially wages, would not be __________ even when aggregate demand decreased.

In modern Keynesian theory, the **short-run aggregate supply curve, *SRAS***, shows the relationship between the price level and real GDP without full adjustment or full information. It is upward sloping because it allows for only __________ price adjustment in the short run.

Real GDP can be expanded in the short run because firms can use existing workers and capital equipment more __________. Also, in the short run, when input prices are fixed, a higher price level means __________ profits, which induce firms to hire more workers.

Any change in factors influencing long-run output, such as labor, capital, or technology, will shift both *SRAS* and *LRAS*. A temporary change in input prices, however, will shift only __________.

Table 11-2

Determinants of Aggregate Supply

The determinants listed here can affect short-run or long-run aggregate supply (or both), depending on whether they are temporary or permanent.

Changes That Cause an Increase in Aggregate Supply	Changes That Cause a Decrease in Aggregate Supply
Discoveries of new raw materials	Depletion of raw materials
Increased competition	Decreased competition
A reduction in international trade barriers	An increase in international trade barriers
Fewer regulatory impediments to business	More regulatory impediments to business
An increase in the supply of labor	A decrease in labor supplied
Increased training and education	Decreased training and education
A decrease in marginal tax rates	An increase in marginal tax rates
A reduction in input prices	An increase in input prices

Consequences of Changes in Aggregate Demand

We now have a basic model to apply when evaluating short-run adjustments of the equilibrium price level and equilibrium real GDP when there are shocks to the economy. Whenever there is a shift in the aggregate demand or short-run aggregate supply curves, the short-run equilibrium price level or real GDP level (or both) may change. These shifts are called **aggregate demand shocks** on the demand side and **aggregate supply shocks** on the supply side.

Aggregate demand shock
Any event that causes the aggregate demand curve to shift inward or outward.

Aggregate supply shock
Any event that causes the aggregate supply curve to shift inward or outward.

When Aggregate Demand Falls While Aggregate Supply Is Stable

Now we can show what happens in the short run when aggregate supply remains stable but aggregate demand falls. The short-run outcome will be a rise in the unemployment rate. In Figure 11-9 below, you see that with AD_1, both long-run and short-run

FIGURE 11-9

The Short-Run Effects of Stable Aggregate Supply and a Decrease in Aggregate Demand: The Recessionary Gap

If the economy is at equilibrium at E_1, with price level 120 and real GDP per year of \$15 trillion, a shift inward of the aggregate demand curve to AD_2 will lead to a new short-run equilibrium at E_2. The equilibrium price level will fall to 115, and the short-run equilibrium level of real GDP per year will fall to \$14.8 trillion. There will be a recessionary gap of \$200 billion.

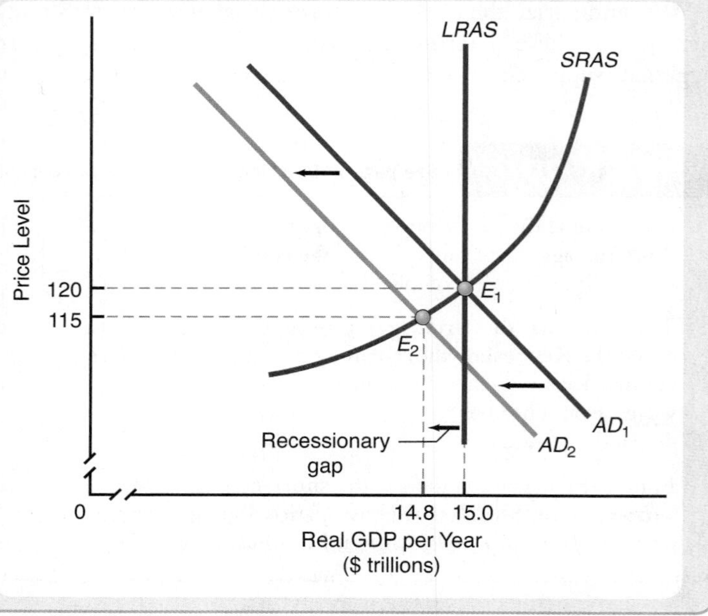

FIGURE 11-10

The Effects of Stable Aggregate Supply with an Increase in Aggregate Demand: The Inflationary Gap

The economy is at equilibrium at E_1. An increase in aggregate demand to AD_2 leads to a new short-run equilibrium at E_2, with the price level rising from 120 to 125 and equilibrium real GDP per year rising from $15 trillion to $15.2 trillion. The difference, $200 billion, is called the inflationary gap.

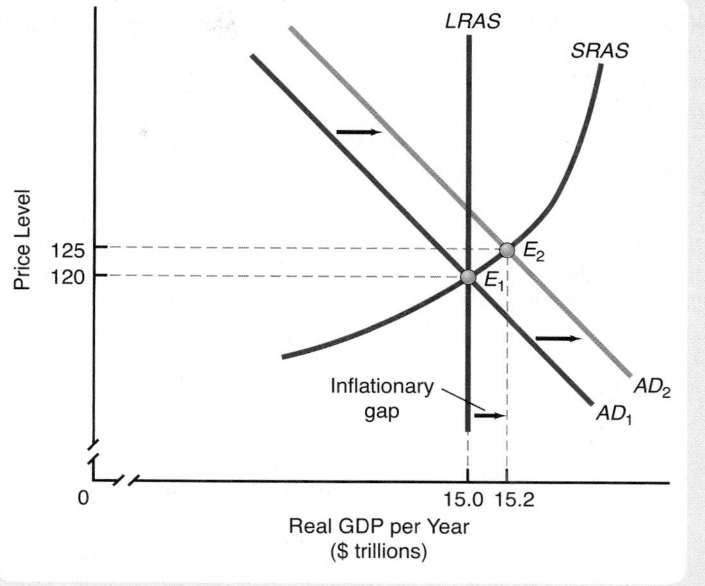

equilibrium are at $15 trillion (in base-year dollars) of real GDP per year (because *SRAS* and *LRAS* also intersect AD_1 at that level of real GDP). The long-run equilibrium price level is 120. A reduction in aggregate demand shifts the aggregate demand curve to AD_2. The new intersection with *SRAS* is at $14.8 trillion per year, which is less than the long-run equilibrium level of real GDP. The difference between $15 trillion and $14.8 trillion is called a **recessionary gap,** defined as the difference between the short-run equilibrium level of real GDP and real GDP if the economy were operating at full employment on its *LRAS.*

Recessionary gap
The gap that exists whenever equilibrium real GDP per year is less than full-employment real GDP as shown by the position of the long-run aggregate supply curve.

In effect, at E_2, the economy is in short-run equilibrium at less than full employment. With too many unemployed inputs, input prices will begin to fall. Eventually, *SRAS* will have to shift vertically downward.

Short-Run Effects When Aggregate Demand Increases

We can reverse the situation and have aggregate demand increase to AD_2, as is shown in Figure 11-10 above. The initial equilibrium conditions are exactly the same as in Figure 11-9 on the facing page. The move to AD_2 increases the short-run equilibrium from E_1 to E_2 such that the economy is operating at $15.2 trillion of real GDP per year, which exceeds *LRAS.* This is a condition of an overheated economy, typically called an **inflationary gap.**

Inflationary gap
The gap that exists whenever equilibrium real GDP per year is greater than full-employment real GDP as shown by the position of the long-run aggregate supply curve.

At E_2 in Figure 11-10, the economy is at a short-run equilibrium that is beyond full employment. In the short run, more can be squeezed out of the economy than occurs in the long-run, full-information, full-adjustment situation. Firms will be operating beyond long-run capacity. Inputs will be working too hard. Input prices will begin to rise. That will eventually cause *SRAS* to shift vertically upward.

YOU ARE THERE

To contemplate cost-push and demand-pull inflation from the perspective of a business manager, take a look at **Worried about Shocks to Aggregate Supply—and Demand** on page 244.

Explaining Short-Run Variations in Inflation

In Chapter 10, we noted that in a growing economy, the explanation for persistent inflation is that aggregate demand increases over time at a faster pace than the full-employment level of real GDP. Short-run variations in inflation, however, can arise as a result of both demand *and* supply factors.

Demand-Pull versus Cost-Push Inflation

Demand-pull inflation
Inflation caused by increases in aggregate demand not matched by increases in aggregate supply.

Cost-push inflation
Inflation caused by decreases in short-run aggregate supply.

Figure 11-10 on the previous page presents a demand-side theory explaining a short-run jump in prices, sometimes called *demand-pull inflation*. Whenever the general level of prices rises in the short run because of increases in aggregate demand, we say that the economy is experiencing **demand-pull inflation**—inflation caused by increases in aggregate demand.

An alternative explanation for increases in the price level comes from the supply side. Look at Figure 11-11 below. The initial equilibrium conditions are the same as in Figure 11-10. Now, however, there is a leftward shift in the short-run aggregate supply curve, from $SRAS_1$ to $SRAS_2$. Equilibrium shifts from E_1 to E_2. The price level increases from 120 to 125, while the equilibrium level of real GDP per year decreases from \$15 trillion to \$14.8 trillion. Persistent decreases in aggregate supply causes what is called **cost-push inflation.**

As the example of cost-push inflation shows, if the economy is initially in equilibrium on its *LRAS*, a decrease in *SRAS* will lead to a rise in the price level. Thus, any abrupt change in one of the factors that determine aggregate supply will alter the equilibrium level of real GDP per year and the equilibrium price level. If the economy is for some reason operating to the left of its *LRAS*, an increase in *SRAS* will lead to a simultaneous *increase* in the equilibrium level of real GDP per year and a *decrease* in the price level. You should be able to show this in a graph similar to Figure 11-11.

Aggregate Demand and Supply in an Open Economy

In many of the international examples in the early chapters of this book, we had to translate foreign currencies into dollars when the open economy was discussed. We used the exchange rate, or the dollar price of other currencies. In Chapter 10, you also learned that the open economy effect was one of the reasons why the aggregate demand curve slopes downward. When the domestic price level rises, U.S. residents want to buy cheaper-priced foreign goods. The opposite occurs when the U.S. domestic price level falls. Currently, the foreign sector of the U.S. economy constitutes more than 15 percent of all economic activities.

FIGURE 11-11
Cost-Push Inflation

If aggregate demand remains stable but $SRAS_1$ shifts to $SRAS_2$, equilibrium changes from E_1 to E_2. The price level rises from 120 to 125. If there are continual decreases in aggregate supply of this nature, the situation is called cost-push inflation.

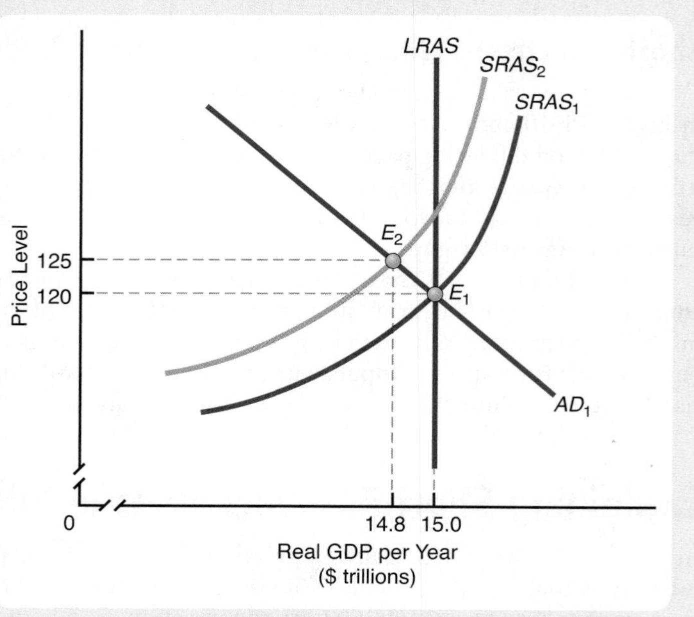

HOW A STRONGER DOLLAR AFFECTS AGGREGATE SUPPLY Assume that the dollar becomes stronger in international foreign exchange markets. If last year the dollar could buy 50 *rupees*, the Indian currency, but this year it buys 60 rupees, the dollar has become stronger. To the extent that U.S. companies import physical inputs and labor services from India, a stronger dollar can lead to lower input prices.

For instance, if a U.S. firm purchases 5 million rupees' worth of labor services per year from an Indian company, then before the strengthening of the dollar, that company paid $100,000 per year for those labor services. After the dollar's strengthening, however, the U.S. firm's Indian-labor-input expense drops to $83,333. This U.S. firm's cost reduction generated by the dollar's strengthening, as well as similar reductions in foreign-input expenses at other U.S. firms, will induce those firms to produce more final goods and services per year at any given price level.

Go to **www.econtoday.com/chap11** for Federal Reserve Bank of New York data showing how the dollar's value is changing relative to other currencies.

Thus, a general strengthening of the dollar against the rupee and other world currencies will lead the short-run aggregate supply curve to shift outward to the right, as shown in panel (a) of Figure 11-12 below. In that simplified model, equilibrium real GDP would rise, and the price level would decline. Employment would also tend to increase.

HOW A STRONGER DOLLAR AFFECTS AGGREGATE DEMAND A stronger dollar has another effect that we must consider. Foreign residents will find that U.S.-made goods are now more expensive, expressed in their own currency. Suppose that as a result of the dollar's strengthening, the dollar, which previously could buy 0.80 euro, can now buy 0.85 euro. Before the dollar strengthened, a U.S.-produced $10 downloadable music album cost a French resident 8.00 euros at the exchange rate of 0.80 euro per $1. After the dollar strengthens and the exchange rate changes to 0.85 euro per $1, that same $10 digital album will cost 8.50 euros. Conversely, U.S. residents will find that the stronger dollar makes imported goods less expensive. The result for U.S. residents is fewer exports and more imports, or lower net exports (exports minus imports). If net exports fall,

FIGURE 11-12

The Two Effects of a Stronger Dollar

When the dollar increases in value in the international currency market, there are two effects. The first is lower prices for imported inputs, causing a shift in the short-run aggregate supply schedule outward and to the right, from $SRAS_1$ to $SRAS_2$ in panel (a). Equilibrium tends to move from E_1 to E_2 at a lower price level and a higher equilibrium real GDP per year. Second, a stronger dollar can also affect the aggregate demand curve because it will lead to lower net exports and cause AD_1 to shift inward to AD_2 in panel (b). Due to this effect, equilibrium will move from E_1 to E_2 at a lower price level and a lower equilibrium real GDP per year. On balance, the combined effects of the decrease in aggregate demand and increase in aggregate supply will be to push down the price level, but real GDP may rise or fall.

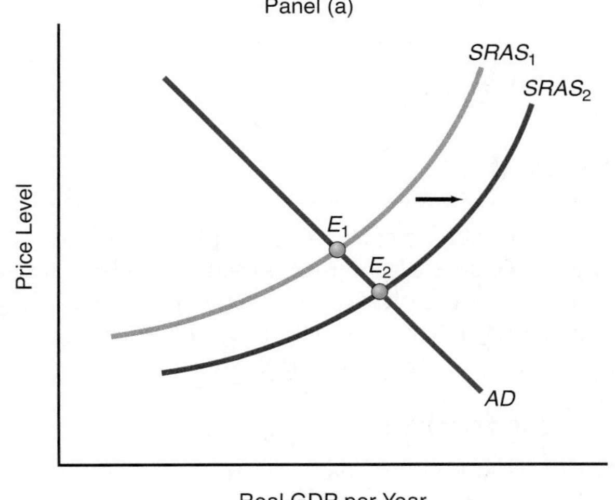

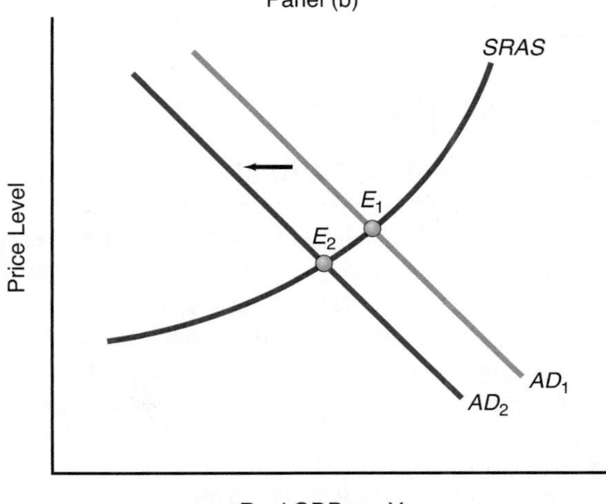

employment in export industries will fall: This is represented in panel (b) of Figure 11-12 on the previous page. After the dollar becomes stronger, the aggregate demand curve shifts inward from AD_1 to AD_2. The result is a tendency for equilibrium real GDP and the price level to fall and for unemployment to increase.

THE NET EFFECTS ON INFLATION AND REAL GDP We have learned, then, that a stronger dollar *simultaneously* leads to an increase in *SRAS* and a decrease in *AD*. In such situations, the equilibrium price level definitely falls. A stronger dollar contributes to deflation.

The effect of a stronger dollar on real GDP depends on which curve—*AD* or *SRAS*—shifts more. If the aggregate demand curve shifts more than the short-run aggregate supply curve, equilibrium real GDP will decline. Conversely, if the aggregate supply curve shifts more than the aggregate demand curve, equilibrium real GDP will rise.

You should be able to redo this entire analysis for a weaker dollar.

WHAT IF... a nation's government tries to head off a recession by pushing down the exchange value of the country's currency?

On the one hand, reducing the exchange value of the currency would make the nation's export goods less expensive in foreign currencies, thereby boosting foreign spending on home exports and, hence, domestic aggregate demand. On the other hand, the fall in the foreign value of the nation's currency would cause home-currency prices of inputs that home firms import from abroad to increase. This would induce the country's firms to cut back on production of final goods and services at any given price level. The result would be a reduction in aggregate supply, which would reinforce any economic downturn already under way. On net, therefore, pushing down the exchange value of the home currency might not necessarily help to head off an economic downturn.

QUICK QUIZ

See page 249 for the answers. Review concepts from this section in MyEconLab.

__________-run equilibrium occurs at the intersection of the aggregate demand curve, *AD*, and the short-run aggregate supply curve, *SRAS*. __________-run equilibrium occurs at the intersection of *AD* and the long-run aggregate supply curve, *LRAS*. Any unanticipated shifts in aggregate demand or supply are called aggregate demand __________ or aggregate supply __________.

When aggregate demand decreases while aggregate supply is stable, a __________ gap can occur, defined as the difference between how much the economy could be producing if it were operating on its *LRAS* and the equilibrium level of real GDP. An increase in aggregate demand leads to an __________ gap.

With stable aggregate supply, an abrupt outward shift in *AD* may lead to what is called __________-__________ inflation. With stable aggregate demand, an abrupt shift inward in *SRAS* may lead to what is called __________-__________ inflation.

A __________ dollar will reduce the cost of imported inputs, thereby causing *SRAS* to shift outward to the right. At the same time, a __________ dollar will also lead to lower net exports, causing the aggregate demand curve to shift inward. The equilibrium price level definitely falls, but the net effect on equilibrium real GDP depends on which shift is larger.

YOU ARE THERE

Worried about Shocks to Aggregate Supply—and Demand

Vincent Hartnett, Jr., president of Penske Logistics, is confused. Federal Reserve officials have been expressing concerns about a perceived threat of "deflation." In Hartnett's view, cost-push sources of *inflationary* pressures abound. Hartnett has watched his firm's health care costs jump, including a 9 percent increase within the past year. Fuel costs continue to escalate, and market wages required to retain workers have risen. In response to these cost increases, his firm and others throughout the nation are producing fewer goods and services at any given price level. The implication, at least as far as Hartnett can discern, is that inflation is likely to increase, and he continues to see a steady upward creep in the annual U.S. inflation rate in monthly government reports.

The fact that Fed officials keep fretting about a potential decline in the price level has made Hartnett concerned that the Fed may unexpectedly increase the quantity of money in circulation to try to raise aggregate demand. Such an action, Hartnett worries, would essentially produce an aggregate demand shock that would lead to a higher rate of inflation.

Critical Thinking Questions

1. How would "cost-push pressures" that Hartnett perceives raise the price level?
2. Why would an unexpected increase in the quantity of money generate inflation?

ISSUES & APPLICATIONS

Gauging Financial Sources of Aggregate Demand Shocks

CONCEPTS APPLIED

- Aggregate Demand Shock
- Short-Run Aggregate Supply Curve
- Recessionary Gap

During a period spanning about 2 weeks in the summer of 2011, the average value of shares of corporate ownership traded in the U.S. stock market dropped by more than 15 percent. About $2 trillion of household wealth effectively ceased to exist. In response, total planned expenditures began to decline at any given price level. Financial-market shocks generated a negative aggregate demand shock.

Tracking Financial Shocks: The VIX Index

To gauge the size of financial shocks, many observers use a measure of financial-market volatility called the *VIX index*. This measure, displayed in Figure 11-13 below for the period since 1990, is intended to indicate variability that people interacting in financial markets anticipate in the near future.

As you can see, significant jumps in the VIX index can occur because of unusual events, such as the Persian Gulf War, the September 11, 2001 ("9/11") terrorist attacks, and the Iraq War. Usually, however, large changes in the VIX index result from shocks that occur solely within financial markets.

FIGURE 11-13 **The VIX Index of Financial-Market Volatility since 1990**

MyEconLab Real-time data

The VIX index measure of anticipated financial volatility has exhibited substantial jumps during wars and in response to major events affecting U.S. financial markets.

Source: U.S. Department of Commerce.

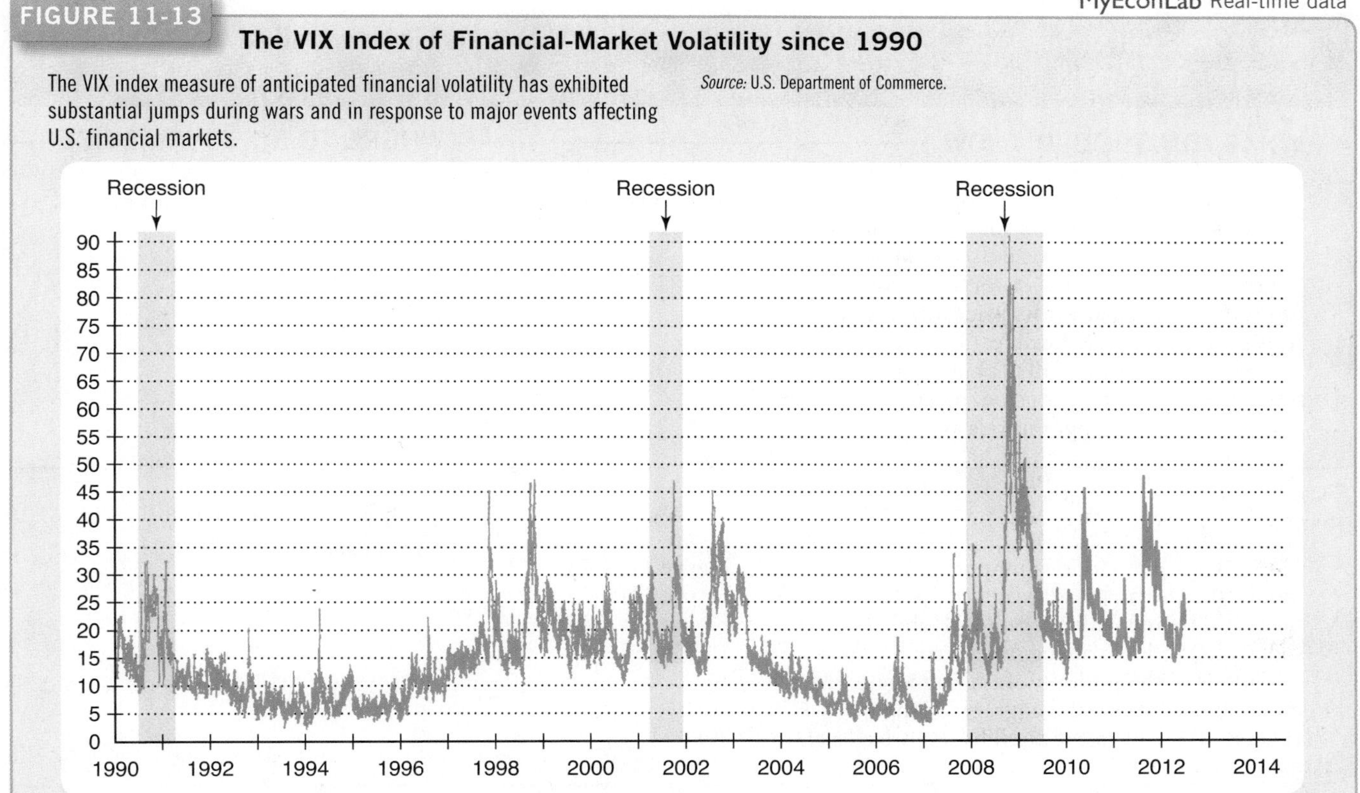

Examples include a default by a major financial firm called Long-Term Capital Management in 1998, substantial accounting scandals in 2002, and the massive credit crisis and associated financial panic in 2008. In addition, jumps in the VIX index in 2010 and 2011 were caused by worries about the inability of the Greek government to honor its debts and then broader concerns about debts of other European governments as well as the U.S. government. During this latter situation in the summer of 2011, U.S. residents briefly lost almost $2 trillion of financial wealth, and real interest rates began to rise, resulting in a temporary decrease in aggregate demand.

From Financial Shocks to Aggregate Demand Shocks

Also shown in Figure 11-13 on the previous page are shaded intervals of U.S. recessions.The most recent recession is clearly related to a substantial increase in the VIX index. Indeed, the VIX index began rising prior to the onset of the 2008–2009 recession and reached its highest peak in the midst of the business downturn.

In the case of this recent recession, financial shocks were so great that a significant, prolonged reduction in aggregate demand occurred. This decrease in aggregate demand generated a upward movement along the short-run aggregate supply curve, a recessionary gap, and a significant decline in U.S. real GDP.

For Critical Thinking

1. Why do you suppose that the U.S. price level decreased over a 12-month interval during the 2008–2009 recession?
2. On the basis of Figure 11-13, are jumps in the VIX index always associated with reductions in aggregate demand that induce recessions?

Web Resources

1. Learn about the VIX index at **www.econtoday.com/chap11**.
2. For a discussion of the rise in the VIX index as stock share prices declined and real interest rates rose in the summer of 2011, go to **www.econtoday.com/chap11**.

MyEconLab

For more questions on this chapter's Issues & Applications, go to MyEconLab. In the Study Plan for this chapter, select Section N: News.

MyEconLab

Here is what you should know after reading this chapter. MyEconLab will help you identify what you know, and where to go when you need to practice.

WHAT YOU SHOULD KNOW		WHERE TO GO TO PRACTICE
Central Assumptions of the Classical Model The classical model makes four key assumptions: (1) pure competition prevails, so no individual buyer or seller of a good or service or of a factor of production can affect its price, (2) wages and prices are completely flexible, (3) people are motivated by self-interest, and (4) buyers and sellers do not experience money illusion, meaning that they respond only to changes in relative prices.	Say's law, 230 money illusion, 231	• MyEconLab Study Plan 11.1
Short-Run Determination of Equilibrium Real GDP and the Price Level in the Classical Model Under the four assumptions of the classical model, the short-run aggregate supply curve is vertical at full-employment real GDP and thus corresponds to the long-run aggregate supply curve. Variations in the position of the aggregate demand curve along the classical aggregate supply curve generate changes in the equilibrium price level.	**Key Figures** Figure 11-2, 232 Figure 11-3, 233 Figure 11-4, 234 Figure 11-5, 235	• MyEconLab Study Plan 11.1 • Animated Figures 11-2, 11-3, 11-4, 11-5

MyEconLab *continued*

WHAT YOU SHOULD KNOW		WHERE TO GO TO PRACTICE
Circumstances under Which the Short-Run Aggregate Supply Curve May Be Horizontal or Upward Sloping If product prices and wages and other input prices are "sticky," the short-run aggregate supply schedule can be horizontal over much of its range. This is the Keynesian short-run aggregate supply curve. More generally, however, to the extent that there is incomplete adjustment of prices in the short run, the short-run aggregate supply curve slopes upward.	Keynesian short-run aggregate supply curve, 236 short-run aggregate supply curve, 237 **Key Figures** Figure 11-6, 236 Figure 11-7, 237	• MyEconLab Study Plans 11.2, 11.3 • Animated Figures 11-6, 11-7
Factors That Induce Shifts in the Short-Run and Long-Run Aggregate Supply Curves Both the long-run aggregate supply curve and the short-run aggregate supply curve shift in response to changes in the availability of labor or capital or to changes in technology and productivity. A widespread temporary change in the prices of factors of production, however, can cause a shift in the short-run aggregate supply curve without affecting the long-run aggregate supply curve.	**Key Table** Table 11-2, 240 **Key Figure** Figure 11-8, 239	• MyEconLab Study Plan 11.4 • Animated Figure 11-8
Effects of Aggregate Demand and Supply Shocks on Equilibrium Real GDP in the Short Run An aggregate demand shock that causes the aggregate demand curve to shift leftward pushes equilibrium real GDP below the level of full-employment real GDP in the short run, so there is a recessionary gap. An aggregate demand shock that induces a rightward shift in the aggregate demand curve results in an inflationary gap, in which short-run equilibrium real GDP exceeds full-employment real GDP.	aggregate demand shock, 240 aggregate supply shock, 240 recessionary gap, 241 inflationary gap, 241 **Key Figures** Figure 11-9, 240 Figure 11-10, 241	• MyEconLab Study Plan 11.5 • Animated Figures 11-9, 11-10
Causes of Short-Run Variations in the Inflation Rate Demand-pull inflation occurs when the aggregate demand curve shifts rightward along an upward-sloping short-run aggregate supply curve. Cost-push inflation occurs when the short-run aggregate supply curve shifts leftward along the aggregate demand curve. A strengthening of the dollar shifts the short-run aggregate supply curve rightward and the aggregate demand curve leftward, which causes inflation but has uncertain effects on real GDP.	demand-pull inflation, 242 cost-push inflation, 242 **Key Figure** Figure 11-11, 242	• MyEconLab Study Plan 11.6 • Animated Figure 11-11

Log in to MyEconLab, take a chapter test, and get a personalized Study Plan that tells you which concepts you understand and which ones you need to review. From there, MyEconLab will give you further practice, tutorials, animations, videos, and guided solutions. For more information, visit www.myeconlab.com

PROBLEMS

All problems are assignable in MyEconLab. *Answers to odd-numbered problems appear at the back of the book.*

11-1. Consider a country whose economic structure matches the assumptions of the classical model. After reading a recent best-seller documenting a growing population of low-income elderly people who were ill prepared for retirement, most residents of this country decide to increase their saving at any given interest rate. Explain whether or how this could affect the following (see page 232):

a. The current equilibrium interest rate

b. Current equilibrium real GDP

c. Current equilibrium employment

d. Current equilibrium investment

e. Future equilibrium real GDP (see Chapter 9)

11-2. Consider a country with an economic structure consistent with the assumptions of the classical model. Suppose that businesses in this nation suddenly anticipate higher future profitability from investments they undertake today. Explain whether or how this could affect the following (see page 232):

a. The current equilibrium interest rate

b. Current equilibrium real GDP

c. Current equilibrium employment

d. Current equilibrium saving

e. Future equilibrium real GDP (see Chapter 9)

11-3. "There is *absolutely no distinction* between the classical model and the model of long-run equilibrium discussed in Chapter 10." Is this statement true or false? Support your answer. (See page 234.)

11-4. Suppose that the Keynesian short-run aggregate supply curve is applicable for a nation's economy. Use appropriate diagrams to assist in answering the following questions (see page 236):

a. What are two factors that can cause the nation's real GDP to increase in the short run?

b. What are two factors that can cause the nation's real GDP to increase in the long run?

11-5. What determines how much real GDP responds to changes in the price level along the short-run aggregate supply curve? (See page 236.)

11-6. Suppose that there is a temporary, but significant, increase in oil prices in an economy with an upward-sloping *SRAS* curve. If policymakers wish to prevent the equilibrium price level from changing in response to the oil price increase, should they increase or decrease the quantity of money in circulation? Why? (See page 242.)

11-7. As in Problem 11-6, suppose that there is a temporary, but significant, increase in oil prices in an economy with an upward-sloping *SRAS* curve. In this case, however, suppose that policymakers wish to prevent equilibrium real GDP from changing in response to the oil price increase. Should they increase or decrease the quantity of money in circulation? Why? (See page 240.)

11-8. Based on your answers to Problems 11-6 and 11-7, can policymakers stabilize *both* the price level *and* real GDP simultaneously in response to a short-lived but sudden rise in oil prices? Explain briefly. (See pages 240–242.)

11-9. Between early 2005 and late 2007, total planned expenditures by U.S. households substantially increased in response to an increase in the quantity of money in circulation. Explain, from a short-run Keynesian perspective, the predicted effects of this event on the equilibrium U.S. price level and equilibrium U.S. real GDP. Be sure to discuss the spending gap that the Keynesian model indicates would result in the short run. (See page 241.)

11-10. Between early 2008 and the beginning of 2009, a gradual stock-market downturn and plummeting home prices generated a substantial reduction in U.S. household wealth that induced most U.S. residents to reduce their planned real spending at any given price level. Explain, from a short-run Keynesian perspective, the predicted effects of this event on the equilibrium U.S. price level and equilibrium U.S. real GDP. Be sure to discuss the spending gap that the Keynesian model indicates would result in the short run. (See page 240.)

11-11. For each question that follows, suppose that the economy *begins* at point *A*. Identify which of the other points on the diagram—point *B*, *C*, *D*, or *E*—could represent a *new* short-run equilibrium after the described events take place and move the economy away from point *A*. Briefly explain your answers. (See pages 240–242.)

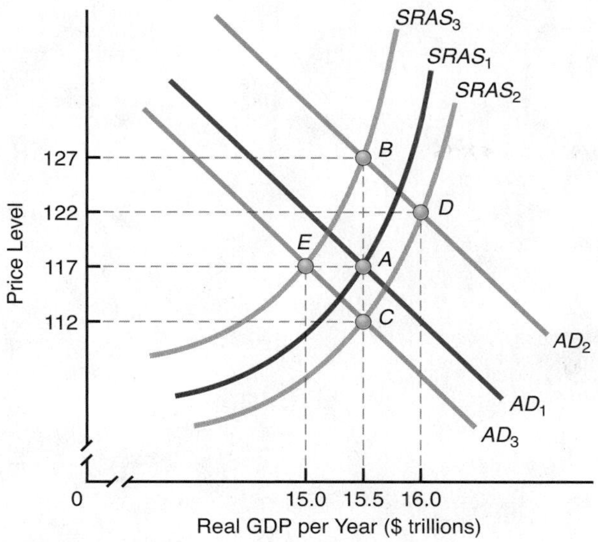

a. Most workers in this nation's economy are union members, and unions have successfully negotiated large wage boosts. At the same time, economic conditions suddenly worsen abroad, reducing real GDP and disposable income in other nations of the world.

b. A major hurricane has caused short-term halts in production at many firms and created major bottlenecks in the distribution of goods and services that had been produced prior to the storm. At the same time, the nation's central bank has significantly pushed up the rate of growth of the nation's money supply.

c. A strengthening of the value of this nation's currency in terms of other countries' currencies affects both the *SRAS* curve and the *AD* curve.

11-12. Consider an open economy in which the aggregate supply curve slopes upward in the short run. Firms in this nation do not import raw materials or any other productive inputs from abroad, but foreign residents purchase many of the nation's goods and services. What is the most likely short-run effect on this nation's economy if there is a significant downturn in economic activity in other nations around the world? (See page 243.)

ECONOMICS ON THE NET

Money, the Price Level, and Real GDP The classical and Keynesian theories have differing predictions about how changes in the money supply should affect the price level and real GDP. Here you get to look at data on growth in the money supply, the price level, and real GDP.

Title: Federal Reserve Bank of St. Louis Monetary Trends

Navigation: Use the link at **www.econtoday.com/chap11** to visit the Federal Reserve Bank of St. Louis. Click on *Gross Domestic Product and M2*.

Application Read the article; then answer these questions.

1. Classical theory indicates that, *ceteris paribus*, changes in the price level should be closely related to changes in aggregate demand induced by variations in the quantity of money. Click on *Gross Domestic Product and M2*, and take a look at the charts labeled "Gross Domestic Product Price Index" and "M2." (M2 is a measure of the quantity of money in circulation.) Are annual percentage changes in these variables closely related?
2. Keynesian theory predicts that, *ceteris paribus*, changes in GDP and the quantity of money should be directly related. Take a look at the charts labeled "Real Gross Domestic Product" and "M2." Are annual percentage changes in these variables closely related?

For Group Study and Analysis Both classical and Keynesian theories of relationships among real GDP, the price level, and the quantity of money hinge on specific assumptions. Have class groups search through the FRED database (accessible at **www.econtoday.com/chap11**) to evaluate factors that provide support for either theory's predictions. Which approach appears to receive greater support from recent data? Does this necessarily imply that this is the "true theory"? Why or why not?

ANSWERS TO QUICK QUIZZES

p. 235: (i) supply . . . demand; (ii) pure competition . . . wages . . . prices . . . self-interest . . . money illusion; (iii) saving . . . investment; (iv) wage rate; (v) vertical . . . price level

p. 239: (i) demand; (ii) reduced; (iii) partial; (iv) intensively . . . higher; (v) *SRAS*

p. 244: (i) Short . . . Long . . . shocks . . . shocks; (ii) recessionary . . . inflationary; (iii) demand-pull . . . cost-push; (iv) stronger . . . stronger

12 Consumption, Real GDP, and the Multiplier

Since the early 2000s, *planned real investment spending*—intended inflation-adjusted expenditures on new buildings and equipment and changes in business inventories—has increased in most of the world's nations. As a percentage of global real GDP, however, planned real investment spending in the world's developed countries, including the United States, has declined. In contrast, planned real investment spending as a percentage of global real GDP has been rising in *emerging-economy nations*—that is, countries with economies that are transitioning from a less developed to a developed status.How do changes in planned real investment spending affect a country's equilibrium annual flow of real GDP? In this chapter, you will learn the answer.

LEARNING OBJECTIVES

After reading this chapter, you should be able to:

- Distinguish between saving and savings and explain how saving and consumption are related
- Explain the key determinants of consumption and saving in the Keynesian model
- Identify the primary determinants of planned investment
- Describe how equilibrium real GDP is established in the Keynesian model
- Evaluate why autonomous changes in total planned expenditures have a multiplier effect on equilibrium real GDP
- Understand the relationship between total planned expenditures and the aggregate demand curve

MyEconLab helps you master each objective and study more efficiently. See end of chapter for details.

DID YOU KNOW THAT... the share of real GDP allocated to real consumption spending by households is about 60 percent in Germany, 66 percent in the United Kingdom, and 70 percent in the United States, but less than 41 percent in China? In all of the world's nations, inflation-adjusted consumption spending on domestically produced final goods and services is a significant component of real GDP. In this chapter, you will learn how an understanding of households' real consumption spending can assist in evaluating fluctuations in any country's real GDP.

Some Simplifying Assumptions in a Keynesian Model

Continuing in the Keynesian tradition, we will assume that the short-run aggregate supply curve within the current range of real GDP is horizontal. That is, we assume that it is similar to Figure 11-6 on page 236. Thus, the equilibrium level of real GDP is demand determined. This is why Keynes wished to examine the elements of desired aggregate expenditures. Because of the Keynesian assumption of inflexible prices, inflation is not a concern in this analysis. Hence, real values are identical to nominal values.

To simplify the income determination model that follows, a number of assumptions are made:

1. Businesses pay no indirect taxes (for example, sales taxes).
2. Businesses distribute all of their profits to shareholders.
3. There is no depreciation (capital consumption allowance), so gross private domestic investment equals net investment.
4. The economy is closed—that is, there is no foreign trade.

Given all these simplifying assumptions, **real disposable income**, or after-tax real income, will be equal to real GDP minus net taxes—taxes paid less transfer payments received.

Real disposable income
Real GDP minus net taxes, or after-tax real income.

Another Look at Definitions and Relationships

You can do only two things with a dollar of disposable income: Consume it or save it. If you consume it, it is gone forever. If you save the entire dollar, however, you will be able to consume it (and perhaps more if it earns interest) at some future time. That is the distinction between **consumption** and **saving.** Consumption is the act of using income for the purchase of consumption goods. **Consumption goods** are goods purchased by households for immediate satisfaction. (These also include services.) Consumption goods are such things as food and movies. By definition, whatever you do not consume you save and can consume at some time in the future.

Consumption
Spending on new goods and services to be used up out of a household's current income. Whatever is not consumed is saved. Consumption includes such things as buying food and going to a concert.

Saving
The act of not consuming all of one's current income. Whatever is not consumed out of spendable income is, by definition, saved. *Saving* is an action measured over time (a flow), whereas *savings* are a stock, an accumulation resulting from the act of saving in the past.

Consumption goods
Goods bought by households to use up, such as food and movies.

STOCKS AND FLOWS: THE DIFFERENCE BETWEEN SAVING AND SAVINGS It is important to distinguish between *saving* and *savings*. *Saving* is an action that occurs at a particular rate—for example, $40 per week or $2,080 per year. This rate is a flow. It is expressed per unit of time, usually a year. Implicitly, then, when we talk about saving, we talk about a *flow*, or rate, of saving. *Savings*, by contrast, are a *stock* concept, measured at a certain point or instant in time. Your current *savings* are the result of past *saving*. You may currently have *savings* of $8,000 that are the result of four years' *saving* at a rate of $2,000 per year. Consumption is also a flow concept. You consume from after-tax income at a certain rate per week, per month, or per year.

RELATING INCOME TO SAVING AND CONSUMPTION A dollar of take-home income can be allocated either to consumption or to saving. Realizing this, we can see the relationship among saving, consumption, and disposable income from the following expression:

$$\text{Consumption} + \text{saving} \equiv \text{disposable income}$$

This is called an *accounting identity*, meaning that it has to hold true at every moment in time. (To indicate that the relationship is always true, we use the ≡ symbol.)

From this relationship, we can derive the following definition of saving:

$$\text{Saving} \equiv \text{disposable income} - \text{consumption}$$

Hence, saving is the amount of disposable income that is not spent to purchase consumption goods.

Investment
Spending on items such as machines and buildings, which can be used to produce goods and services in the future. (It also includes changes in business inventories.) The investment part of real GDP is the portion that will be used in the process of producing goods *in the future.*

Capital goods
Producer durables; nonconsumable goods that firms use to make other goods.

Investment

Investment is also a flow concept. As noted in Chapter 8, *investment* as used in economics differs from the common use of the term. In common speech, it is often used to describe putting funds into the stock market or real estate. In economic analysis, investment is defined to include expenditures on new machines and buildings—**capital goods**—that are expected to yield a future stream of income. This is called *fixed investment.* We also include changes in business inventories in our definition. This we call *inventory investment.*

QUICK QUIZ See page 277 for the answers. Review concepts from this section in MyEconLab.

If we assume that we are operating on a __________ short-run aggregate supply curve, the equilibrium level of real GDP per year is completely demand determined.

__________ is a flow, something that occurs over time. It equals disposable income minus consumption.

__________ are a stock. They are the accumulation resulting from saving.

__________ is also a flow. It includes expenditures on new machines, buildings, and equipment and changes in business inventories.

Determinants of Planned Consumption and Planned Saving

In the classical model discussed in Chapter 11 on pages 230–235, the supply of saving was determined by the rate of interest. Specifically, the higher the rate of interest, the more people wanted to save and consequently the less people wanted to consume.

In contrast, according to Keynes, the interest rate is *not* the most important determinant of an individual's real saving and consumption decisions. In his view, the flow of income, not the interest rate, is the main determinant of consumption and saving.

How Income Flows Can Influence Consumption and Saving

When a person decides how much to consume and save today, Keynes reasoned, that individual must take into account both current and anticipated future incomes. After all, a higher income this year enables an individual *both* to purchase more final goods and services *and* to increase the flow of saving during the current year. Furthermore, a person's anticipation about the *future* flow of income likely influences how much of *current* income is allocated to consumption and how much to saving.

The Life-Cycle Theory of Consumption

The most realistic and detailed theory of consumption, often called the **life-cycle theory of consumption,** considers how a person varies consumption and saving as income ebbs and flows during the course of an entire life span. This theory predicts that when an individual anticipates a higher income in the future, the individual will tend to consume more and save less in the current period than would have been the case otherwise. In contrast, when a person expects the flow of income to drop in the future, the individual responds in the present by allocating less of current income to consumption and more to saving.

Life-cycle theory of consumption
A theory in which a person bases decisions about current consumption and saving on both current income and anticipated future income.

The Permanent Income Hypothesis

In a related theory, called the **permanent income hypothesis,** the income level that matters for a person's decision about current consumption and saving is *permanent income*, or expected average lifetime income. The permanent income hypothesis suggests that people increase their flow of consumption only if their anticipated average lifetime income rises. Thus, if a person's flow of income temporarily rises without an increase in average lifetime income, the individual responds by saving the extra income and leaving consumption unchanged.

Permanent income hypothesis
A theory of consumption in which an individual determines current consumption based on anticipated average lifetime income.

The Keynesian Theory of Consumption and Saving

Keynes recognized that expectations about future income could affect current consumption and saving decisions. For purposes of developing a basic theory of consumption and saving, however, Keynes focused solely on the relationship between current income and current consumption and saving. Thus:

> ***Keynes argued that real consumption and saving decisions depend primarily on a household's current real disposable income.***

YOU ARE THERE

To consider a real-world application of the basic consumption and saving functions, read **Evaluating the Effects of Declining Real Disposable Income** on page 271.

The relationship between planned real consumption expenditures of households and their current level of real disposable income has been called the **consumption function.** It shows how much all households plan to consume per year at each level of real disposable income per year. Columns (1) and (2) of Table 12-1 on the following page illustrate a consumption function for a hypothetical household.

Consumption function
The relationship between amount consumed and disposable income. A consumption function tells us how much people plan to consume at various levels of disposable income.

We see from Table 12-1 that as real disposable income rises, planned consumption also rises, but by a smaller amount, as Keynes suggested. Planned saving also increases with disposable income. Notice, however, that below an income of \$60,000, the planned saving of this hypothetical household is actually negative. The further that income drops below that level, the more the household engages in **dissaving,** either by going into debt or by using up some of its existing wealth.

Dissaving
Negative saving; a situation in which spending exceeds income. Dissaving can occur when a household is able to borrow or use up existing assets.

Graphing the Numbers

We now graph the consumption and saving relationships presented in Table 12-1. In the upper part of Figure 12-1 on page 255, the vertical axis measures the level of planned real consumption per year, and the horizontal axis measures the level of real disposable income per year. In the lower part of the figure, the horizontal axis is again real disposable income per year, but now the vertical axis is planned real saving per year. All of these are on a dollars-per-year basis, which emphasizes the point that we are measuring flows, not stocks.

CONSUMPTION AND SAVING FUNCTIONS As you can see, we have taken income-consumption and income-saving combinations *A* through *K* and plotted them. In the upper part of

TABLE 12-1

Real Consumption and Saving Schedules: A Hypothetical Case

Column 1 presents real disposable income from zero up to $120,000 per year. Column 2 indicates planned real consumption per year. Column 3 presents planned real saving per year. At levels of real disposable income below $60,000, planned real saving is negative. In column 4, we see the average propensity to consume, which is merely planned consumption divided by disposable income. Column 5 lists average propensity to save, which is planned saving divided by disposable income. Column 6 is the marginal propensity to consume, which shows the proportion of *additional* income that will be consumed. Finally, column 7 shows the proportion of *additional* income that will be saved, or the marginal propensity to save. (Δ represents "change in.")

Combination	(1) Real Disposable Income per Year (Y_d)	(2) Planned Real Consumption per Year (C)	(3) Planned Real Saving per Year ($S \equiv Y_d - C$) (1) − (2)	(4) Average Propensity to Consume ($APC \equiv C/Y_d$) (2) ÷ (1)	(5) Average Propensity to Save ($APS \equiv S/Y_d$) (3) ÷ (1)	(6) Marginal Propensity to Consume ($MPC \equiv \Delta C/\Delta Y_d$)	(7) Marginal Propensity to Save ($MPS \equiv \Delta S/\Delta Y_d$)
A	$ 0	$ 12,000	$−12,000	–	–	–	–
B	12,000	21,600	−9,600	1.8	−0.8	0.8	0.2
C	24,000	31,200	−7,200	1.3	−0.3	0.8	0.2
D	36,000	40,800	−4,800	1.133	−0.133	0.8	0.2
E	48,000	50,400	−2,400	1.05	−0.05	0.8	0.2
F	60,000	60,000	0	1.0	0.0	0.8	0.2
G	72,000	69,600	2,400	0.967	0.033	0.8	0.2
H	84,000	79,200	4,800	0.943	0.057	0.8	0.2
I	96,000	88,800	7,200	0.925	0.075	0.8	0.2
J	108,000	98,400	9,600	0.911	0.089	0.8	0.2
K	120,000	108,000	12,000	0.9	0.1	0.8	0.2

Figure 12-1 on the facing page, the result is called the *consumption function.* In the lower part, the result is called the *saving function.*

Mathematically, the saving function is the *complement* of the consumption function because consumption plus saving always equals disposable income. What is not consumed is, by definition, saved. The difference between actual disposable income and the planned rate of consumption per year *must* be the planned rate of saving per year.

45-degree reference line
The line along which planned real expenditures equal real GDP per year.

THE 45-DEGREE REFERENCE LINE How can we find the rate of saving or dissaving in the upper part of Figure 12-1? We begin by drawing a line that is equidistant from both the horizontal and the vertical axes. This line is 45 degrees from either axis and is often called the **45-degree reference line.** At every point on the 45-degree reference line, a vertical line drawn to the income axis is the same distance from the origin as a horizontal line drawn to the consumption axis. Thus, at point *F*, where the consumption function intersects the 45-degree line, real disposable income equals planned real consumption.

Point *F* is sometimes called the *break-even income point* because there is neither positive nor negative real saving. This can be seen in the lower part of Figure 12-1 as well. The planned annual rate of real saving at a real disposable income level of $60,000 is indeed zero.

Dissaving and Autonomous Consumption

To the left of point *F* in either part of Figure 12-1, this hypothetical family engages in dissaving, either by going into debt or by consuming existing assets. The rate of real saving or dissaving in the upper part of the figure can be found by measuring the

FIGURE 12-1

The Consumption and Saving Functions

If we plot the combinations of real disposable income and planned real consumption from columns 1 and 2 in Table 12-1 on the facing page, we get the consumption function.

At every point on the 45-degree line, a vertical line drawn to the income axis is the same distance from the origin as a horizontal line drawn to the consumption axis. Where the consumption function crosses the 45-degree line at *F*, we know that planned real consumption equals real disposable income and there is zero saving. The vertical distance between the 45-degree line and the consumption function measures the rate of real saving or dissaving at any given income level.

If we plot the relationship between column 1 (real disposable income) and column 3 (planned real saving) from Table 12-1 on the facing page, we arrive at the saving function shown in the lower part of this diagram. It is the complement of the consumption function presented above it.

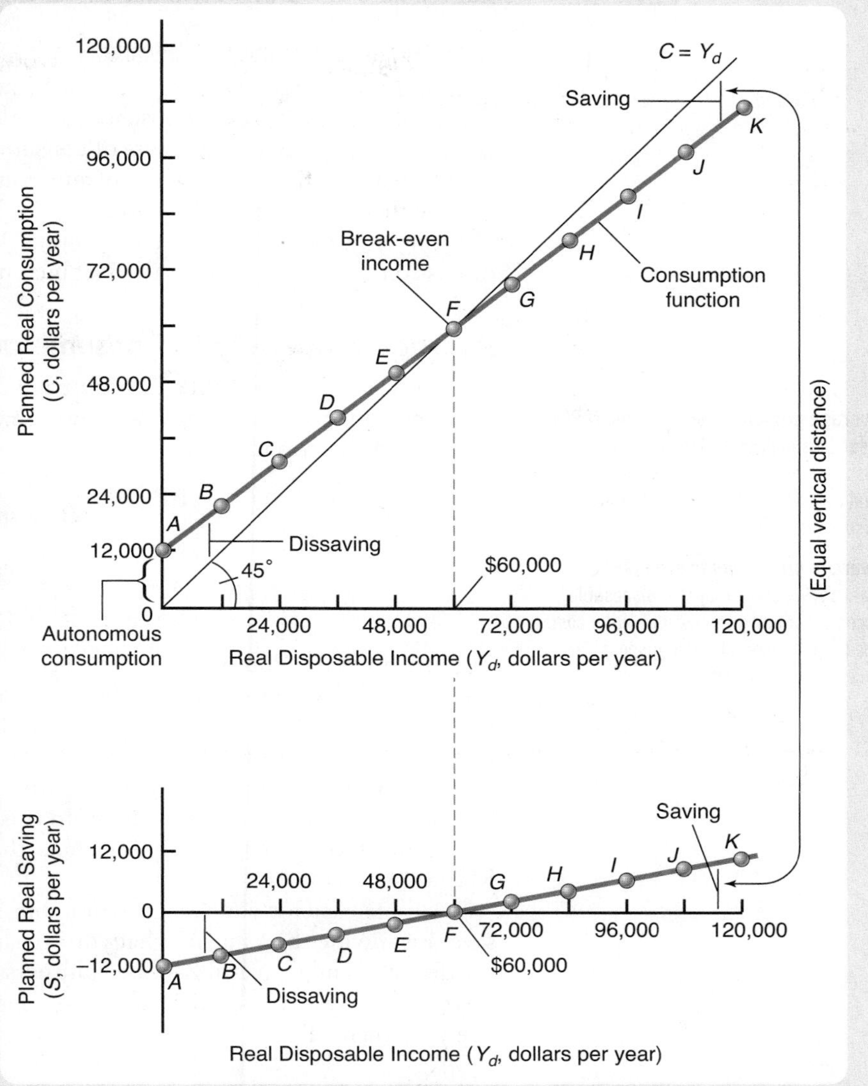

vertical distance between the 45-degree line and the consumption function. This simply tells us that if our hypothetical household sees its real disposable income fall to less than $60,000, it will not limit its consumption to this amount. It will instead go into debt or consume existing assets in some way to compensate for part of the lost income.

AUTONOMOUS CONSUMPTION Now look at the point on the diagram where real disposable income is zero but planned consumption is $12,000. This amount of real planned consumption, which does not depend at all on actual real disposable income, is called **autonomous consumption.** The autonomous consumption of $12,000 is *independent* of disposable income. That means that no matter how low the level of real income of our hypothetical household falls, the household will always attempt to consume at least $12,000 per year. (We are, of course, assuming here that the household's real disposable income does not equal zero year in and year out. There is certainly a limit to how long our hypothetical household could finance autonomous consumption without any income.)

Autonomous consumption
The part of consumption that is independent of (does not depend on) the level of disposable income. Changes in autonomous consumption shift the consumption function.

The $12,000 of yearly consumption is determined by things other than the level of income. We don't need to specify what determines autonomous consumption. We merely state that it exists and that in our example it is $12,000 per year.

THE MEANING OF AUTONOMOUS SPENDING Just remember that the word *autonomous* means "existing independently." In our model, autonomous consumption exists independently of the hypothetical household's level of real disposable income. (Later we will review some of the determinants of consumption other than real disposable income.)

There are many possible types of autonomous expenditures. Hypothetically, we can assume that investment is autonomous—independent of income. We can assume that government expenditures are autonomous. We will do just that at various times in our discussions to simplify our analysis of income determination.

Average Propensity to Consume and to Save

Average propensity to consume (APC) Real consumption divided by real disposable income. For any given level of real income, the proportion of total real disposable income that is consumed.

Average propensity to save (APS) Real saving divided by real disposable income. For any given level of real income, the proportion of total real disposable income that is saved.

Let's now go back to Table 12-1 on page 254, and this time let's look at columns 4 and 5: **average propensity to consume (APC)** and **average propensity to save (APS).** They are defined as follows:

$$\text{APC} \equiv \frac{\text{real consumption}}{\text{real disposable income}}$$

$$\text{APS} \equiv \frac{\text{real saving}}{\text{real disposable income}}$$

Notice from column 4 in Table 12-1 that for this hypothetical household, the average propensity to consume decreases as real disposable income increases. This decrease simply means that the fraction of the household's real disposable income going to consumption falls as income rises. Column 5 shows that the average propensity to save, which at first is negative, finally hits zero at an income level of $60,000 and then becomes positive. In this example, the APS reaches a value of 0.1 at income level $120,000. This means that the household saves 10 percent of a $120,000 income.

It's quite easy for you to figure out your own average propensity to consume or to save. Just divide the value of what you consumed by your total real disposable income for the year, and the result will be your personal APC at your current level of income. Also, divide your real saving during the year by your real disposable income to calculate your own APS.

Marginal Propensity to Consume and to Save

Marginal propensity to consume (MPC) The ratio of the change in consumption to the change in disposable income. A marginal propensity to consume of 0.8 tells us that an additional $100 in take-home pay will lead to an additional $80 consumed.

Marginal propensity to save (MPS) The ratio of the change in saving to the change in disposable income. A marginal propensity to save of 0.2 indicates that out of an additional $100 in take-home pay, $20 will be saved. Whatever is not saved is consumed. The marginal propensity to save plus the marginal propensity to consume must always equal 1, by definition.

Now we go to the last two columns in Table 12-1 on page 254: **marginal propensity to consume (MPC)** and **marginal propensity to save (MPS).** The term *marginal* refers to a small incremental or decremental change (represented by the Greek letter delta, Δ, in Table 12-1). The marginal propensity to consume, then, is defined as

$$\text{MPC} \equiv \frac{\text{change in real consumption}}{\text{change in real disposable income}}$$

The marginal propensity to save is defined similarly as

$$\text{MPS} \equiv \frac{\text{change in real saving}}{\text{change in real disposable income}}$$

MARGINAL VERSUS AVERAGE PROPENSITIES What do MPC and MPS tell you? They tell you what percentage of a given increase or decrease in real income will go toward consumption and saving, respectively. The emphasis here is on the word *change*.

The marginal propensity to consume indicates how much you will change your planned real consumption if there is a change in your actual real disposable income.

If your marginal propensity to consume is 0.8, that does *not* mean that you consume 80 percent of *all* disposable income. The percentage of your total real disposable income that you consume is given by the average propensity to consume, or APC. As Table 12-1 on page 254 indicates, the APC is not equal to 0.8 anywhere in its column. Instead, an MPC of 0.8 means that you will consume 80 percent of any *increase* in your disposable income. Hence, the MPC cannot be less than zero or greater than one. It follows that households increase their planned real consumption by between 0 and 100 percent of any increase in real disposable income that they receive.

DISTINGUISHING THE MPC FROM THE APC Consider a simple example in which we show the difference between the average propensity to consume and the marginal propensity to consume. Assume that your consumption behavior is exactly the same as our hypothetical household's behavior depicted in Table 12-1. You have an annual real disposable income of $108,000. Your planned consumption rate, then, from column 2 of Table 12-1 is $98,400. So your average propensity to consume is $98,400/$108,000 = 0.911. Now suppose that at the end of the year, your boss gives you an after-tax bonus of $12,000.

What would you do with that additional $12,000 in real disposable income? According to the table, you would consume $9,600 of it and save $2,400. In that case, your *marginal* propensity to consume would be $9,600/$12,000 = 0.8 and your marginal propensity to save would be $2,400/$12,000 = 0.2. What would happen to your *average* propensity to consume? To find out, we add $9,600 to $98,400 of planned consumption, which gives us a new consumption rate of $108,000. The average propensity to consume is then $108,000 divided by the new higher salary of $120,000. Your APC drops from 0.911 to 0.9.

In contrast, your MPC remains, in our simplified example, 0.8 all the time. Look at column 6 in Table 12-1. The MPC is 0.8 at every level of income. (Therefore, the MPS is always equal to 0.2 at every level of income.) The constancy of MPC reflects the assumption that the amount that you are willing to consume out of additional income will remain the same in percentage terms no matter what level of real disposable income is your starting point.

Some Relationships

Consumption plus saving must equal income. Both your total real disposable income and the change in total real disposable income are either consumed or saved. The sums of the proportions of either measure that are consumed and saved must equal 1, or 100 percent. This allows us to make the following statements:

$$\text{APC} + \text{APS} \equiv 1\ (= 100 \text{ percent of total income})$$

$$\text{MPC} + \text{MPS} \equiv 1\ (= 100 \text{ percent of the } \textit{change} \text{ in income})$$

The average propensities as well as the marginal propensities to consume and save must total 1, or 100 percent. Check the two statements by adding the figures in columns 4 and 5 for each level of real disposable income in Table 12-1 on page 254. Do the same for columns 6 and 7.

Causes of Shifts in the Consumption Function

A change in any other relevant economic variable besides real disposable income will cause the consumption function to shift. The number of such nonincome determinants of the position of the consumption function is almost unlimited. Real household **net wealth** is one determinant of the position of the consumption function. An increase in the real net wealth of the average household will cause the consumption function to shift upward. A decrease in real net wealth will cause it to shift downward. So far we have been talking about the consumption function of an individual or a household. Now let's move on to the national economy.

Net wealth
The stock of assets owned by a person, household, firm, or nation (net of any debts owed). For a household, net wealth can consist of a house, cars, personal belongings, stocks, bonds, bank accounts, and cash (minus any debts owed).

Why did real consumption expenditures of U.S. households decline between 2008 and 2009 and then fail to bounce back quickly in subsequent years?

EXAMPLE

Lower Household Wealth and Subdued Growth in Consumption

Between 2007 and 2009, two key components of real household wealth—inflation-adjusted wealth in housing and in corporate stocks—declined substantially. During that interval, aggregate real wealth in housing dropped by about 25 percent, and at one point real household wealth held in stocks fell by more than 50 percent. These wealth reductions shifted the U.S. consumption function downward. Real disposable income also fell. Consequently, there was also a leftward movement along the now lower consumption function that contributed to a further drop in real household consumption between 2008 and 2009.

Inflation-adjusted household disposable income has increased each year since 2009. Nevertheless, real housing wealth held by households has declined by another 10 percentage points. Inflation-adjusted household wealth in corporate stocks has recovered considerably but has remained between 10 percent and 20 percent lower than the peak it had reached in 2008. As a result, the U.S. consumption function has remained at a lower position than in 2007, which has dampened growth in real consumption spending during the following years.

FOR CRITICAL THINKING

Why do both *movements along and any shifts in the consumption function ultimately* jointly *determine observed changes in desired total real consumption spending?*

QUICK QUIZ

See page 277 for the answers. Review concepts from this section in MyEconLab.

The **consumption function** shows the relationship between planned rates of real consumption and real __________ __________ per year. The saving function is the complement of the consumption function because real saving plus real __________ must equal real disposable income.

The __________ propensity to consume is equal to real consumption divided by real disposable income. The __________ propensity to save is equal to real saving divided by real disposable income.

The __________ propensity to consume is equal to the change in planned real consumption divided by the change in real disposable income. The __________ propensity to save is equal to the change in planned real saving divided by the change in real disposable income.

Any change in real disposable income will cause the planned rate of consumption to change. This is represented by a __________ __________ the consumption function. Any change in a nonincome determinant of consumption will cause a __________ __________ the consumption function.

Determinants of Investment

Investment, you will remember, consists of expenditures on new buildings and equipment and changes in business inventories. Historically, real gross private domestic investment in the United States has been extremely volatile over the years, relative to real consumption. If we were to look at net private domestic investment (investment after depreciation has been deducted), we would see that in the depths of the Great Depression and at the peak of the World War II effort, the figure was negative. In other words, we were eating away at our capital stock—we weren't even maintaining it by fully replacing depreciated equipment.

If we compare real investment expenditures historically with real consumption expenditures, we find that the latter are less variable over time than the former. Why is this so? One possible reason is that the real investment decisions of businesses are based on highly variable, subjective estimates of how the economic future looks.

The Planned Investment Function

Consider that at all times, businesses perceive an array of investment opportunities. These investment opportunities have rates of return ranging from zero to very high, with the number (or dollar value) of all such projects increasing if the rate of return rises.

FIGURE 12-2

Planned Real Investment

As shown in the hypothetical planned investment schedule in panel (a), the rate of planned real investment is inversely related to the rate of interest. If we plot the data pairs from panel (a), we obtain the investment function, *I*, in panel (b). It is negatively sloped.

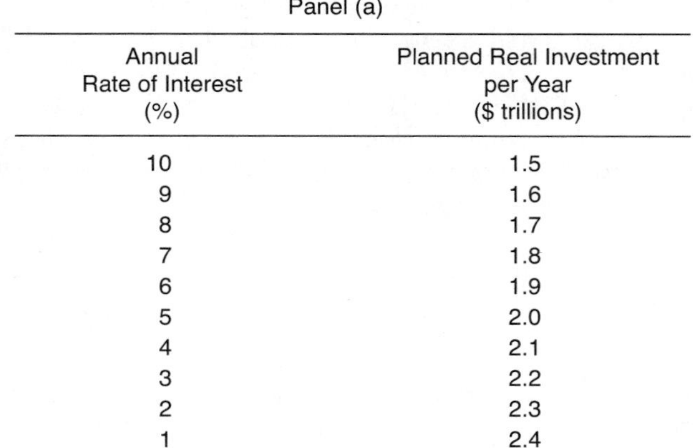

Panel (a)

Annual Rate of Interest (%)	Planned Real Investment per Year ($ trillions)
10	1.5
9	1.6
8	1.7
7	1.8
6	1.9
5	2.0
4	2.1
3	2.2
2	2.3
1	2.4

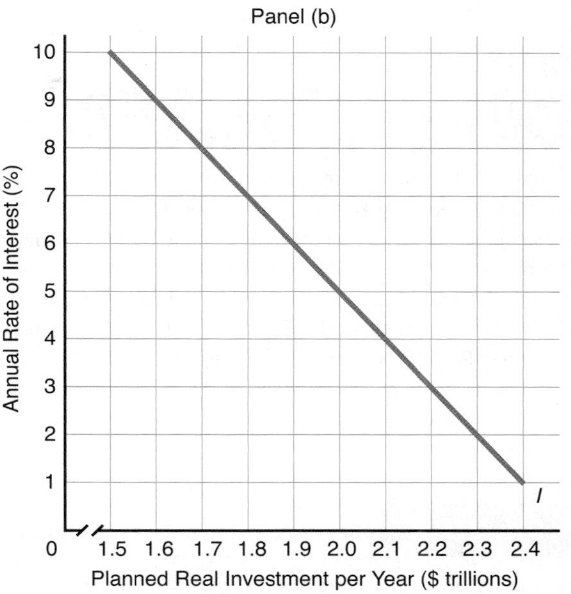

Because a project is profitable only if its rate of return exceeds the opportunity cost of the investment—the rate of interest—it follows that as the interest rate falls, planned investment spending increases, and vice versa. Even if firms use retained earnings (internal financing) to fund an investment, the lower the market rate of interest, the smaller the *opportunity cost* of using those retained earnings.

Thus, it does not matter in our analysis whether the firm must seek financing from external sources or can obtain such financing by using retained earnings. Whatever the method of financing, as the interest rate falls, more investment opportunities will be profitable, and planned investment will be higher.

It should be no surprise, therefore, that the investment function is represented as an inverse relationship between the rate of interest and the value of planned real investment. In Figure 12-2 above, a hypothetical investment schedule is given in panel (a) and plotted in panel (b). We see from this schedule that if, for example, the rate of interest is 5 percent, the dollar value of planned investment will be $2 trillion per year. Notice that planned investment is also given on a per-year basis, showing that it represents a flow, not a stock. (The stock counterpart of investment is the stock of capital in the economy measured in inflation-adjusted dollars at a point in time.)

What Causes the Investment Function to Shift?

Because planned real investment is assumed to be a function of the rate of interest, any non-interest-rate variable that changes can have the potential of shifting the investment function. One of those variables is the expectations of businesses. If higher profits are expected, more machines and bigger plants will be planned for the future. More investment will be undertaken because of the expectation of higher profits. In this case, the investment function, *I*, in panel (b) of Figure 12-2, would shift outward to the right, meaning that more investment would be desired at all rates of interest.

Any change in productive technology can potentially shift the investment function. A positive change in productive technology would stimulate demand for additional

Go to economic data provided by the Federal Reserve Bank of St. Louis via the link at www.econtoday.com/chap12 to see how U.S. real private investment has varied in recent years.

capital goods and shift I outward to the right. Changes in business taxes can also shift the investment schedule. If they increase, we predict a leftward shift in the planned investment function because higher taxes imply a lower (after-tax) rate of return.

How has a technological change in the display of films led to a significant upswing in investment spending by movie-theater chains?

EXAMPLE

Adding a Third Dimension Requires New Investment Spending

Of the approximately 40,000 movie screens in the United States, fewer than 8,000 utilize the digital technology required for projection of three-dimensional (3D) movies. Converting a typical multiscreen theater from a projection system using celluloid film reels to a system with digital screens and projectors requires an expenditure of about $70,000. Major movie-theater chains such as AMC Entertainment, Inc., Cinemark Holdings, Inc., and Regal Entertainment Group are in the midst of investing in new projection systems for more than 1,000 theaters. Hence, putting the latest 3D movie-projection technology into place is requiring an aggregate investment expenditure of about $70 million.

FOR CRITICAL THINKING

Will the movie-theater chains' total investment in 3D projection systems generate a movement along or a shift in the planned investment function for the United States?

QUICK QUIZ

See page 277 for the answers. Review concepts from this section in MyEconLab.

The planned investment schedule shows the relationship between real investment and the __________ __________; it slopes __________.

The non-interest-rate determinants of planned investment are __________, innovation and technological changes, and __________ __________.

Any change in the non-interest-rate determinants of planned investment will cause a __________ __________ the planned investment function so that at each and every rate of interest a different amount of planned investment will be made.

Determining Equilibrium Real GDP

We are interested in determining the equilibrium level of real GDP per year. But when we examined the consumption function earlier in this chapter, it related planned real consumption expenditures to the level of real disposable income per year. We have already shown where adjustments must be made to GDP in order to get real disposable income (see Table 8-2 on page 175). Real disposable income turns out to be less than real GDP because real net taxes (real taxes minus real government transfer payments) are usually about 14 to 21 percent of GDP. A representative average is about 18 percent, so disposable income, on average, has in recent years been around 82 percent of GDP.

Consumption as a Function of Real GDP

To simplify our model, assume that real disposable income, Y_d, differs from real GDP by the same absolute amount every year. Therefore, we can relatively easily substitute real GDP for real disposable income in the consumption function.

We can now plot any consumption function on a diagram in which the horizontal axis is no longer real disposable income but rather real GDP, as in Figure 12-3 on the facing page. Notice that there is an autonomous part of real consumption that is so labeled. The difference between this graph and the graphs presented earlier in this chapter is the change in the horizontal axis from real disposable income to real GDP per year. For the rest of this chapter, assume that the MPC out of real GDP equals 0.8, so that 20 percent of changes in real disposable income is saved. Of an additional after-tax $100 earned, an additional $80 will be consumed.

FIGURE 12-3
Consumption as a Function of Real GDP

This consumption function shows the rate of planned expenditures for each level of real GDP per year. Autonomous consumption is $0.2 trillion. Along the 45-degree reference line, planned real consumption expenditures per year, *C*, are identical to real GDP per year, *Y*. The consumption curve intersects the 45-degree reference line at a value of $1 trillion per year in base-year dollars (the value of current GDP expressed in prices in a base year).

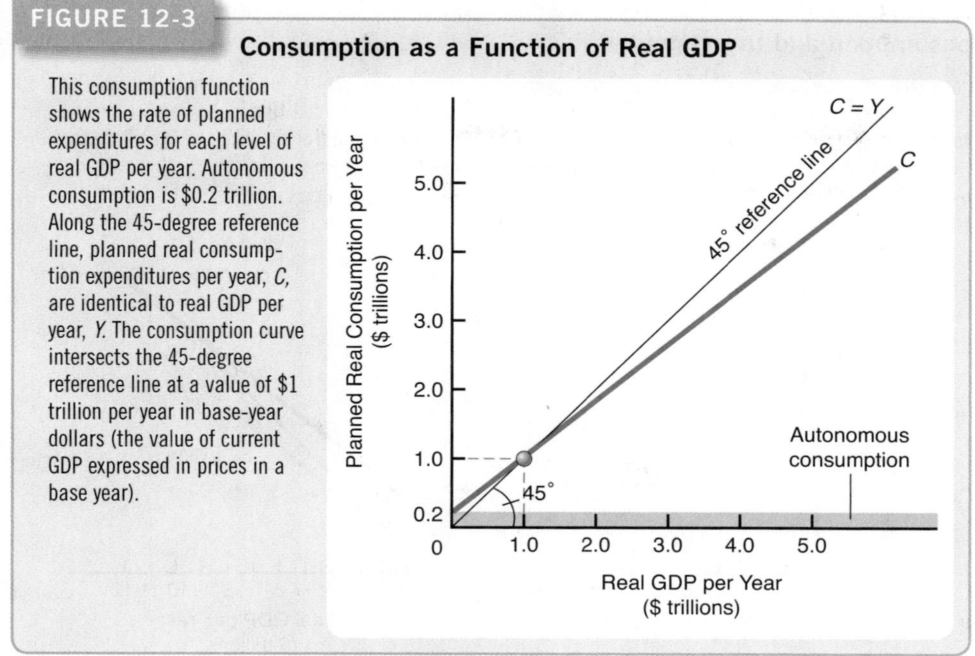

The 45-Degree Reference Line

As in the earlier graphs, Figure 12-3 above shows a 45-degree reference line. The 45-degree line bisects the quadrant into two equal spaces. Thus, along the 45-degree reference line, planned real consumption expenditures, *C*, equal real GDP per year, *Y*. One can see, then, that at any point where the consumption function intersects the 45-degree reference line, planned real consumption expenditures will be exactly equal to real GDP per year, or $C = Y$. Note that in this graph, because we are looking only at planned real consumption on the vertical axis, the 45-degree reference line is where planned real consumption, *C*, is always equal to real GDP per year, *Y*. Later, when we add real investment, government spending, and net exports to the graph, *all* planned real expenditures will be labeled along the vertical axis. In any event, real consumption and real GDP are equal at $1 trillion per year. That is where the consumption curve, *C*, intersects the 45-degree reference line. At that GDP level, all real GDP is consumed.

Adding the Investment Function

Another component of private aggregate demand is, of course, real investment spending, *I*. We have already looked at the planned investment function, which related real investment, which includes changes in inventories of final products, to the rate of interest.

PLANNED INVESTMENT AND THE INTEREST RATE In panel (a) of Figure 12-4 on the following page, you see that at an interest rate of 5 percent, the rate of real investment is $2 trillion per year. The $2 trillion of real investment per year is *autonomous* with respect to real GDP—that is, it is independent of real GDP.

In other words, given that we have a determinant investment level of $2 trillion at a 5 percent rate of interest, we can treat this level of real investment as constant, regardless of the level of GDP. This is shown in panel (b) of Figure 12-4. The vertical distance of real investment spending is $2 trillion. Businesses plan on investing a particular amount—$2 trillion per year—and will do so no matter what the level of real GDP.

COMBINING PLANNED INVESTMENT AND CONSUMPTION How do we add this amount of real investment spending to our consumption function? We simply add a line above the *C*

FIGURE 12-4

Combining Consumption and Investment

In panel (a), we show that at an interest rate of 5 percent, real investment is equal to \$2 trillion per year. In panel (b), investment is a constant \$2 trillion per year. When we add this amount to the consumption line, we obtain in panel (c) the $C + I$ line, which is vertically higher than the C line by exactly \$2 trillion. Real GDP is equal to $C + I$ at \$11 trillion per year where total planned real expenditures, $C + I$, are equal to actual real GDP, for this is where the $C + I$ line intersects the 45-degree reference line, on which $C + I$ is equal to Y at every point. (For simplicity, we ignore the fact that the dependence of saving on income can influence investment.)

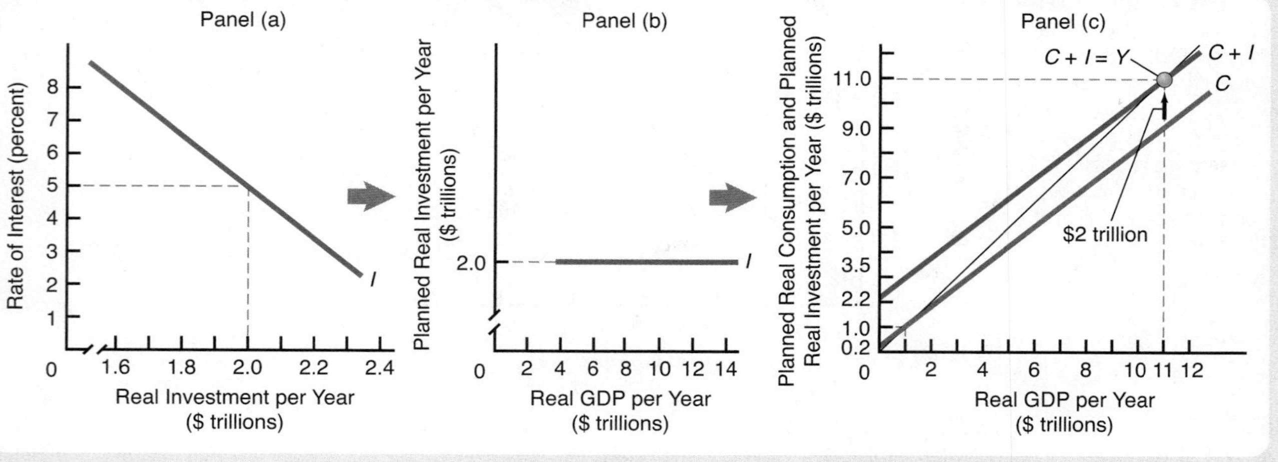

line that we drew in Figure 12-3 on the previous page that is higher by the vertical distance equal to \$2 trillion of autonomous real investment spending. This is shown by the arrow in panel (c) of Figure 12-4 above.

Our new line, now labeled $C + I$, is called the *consumption plus investment line.* In our simple economy without real government expenditures and net exports, the $C + I$ curve represents total planned real expenditures as they relate to different levels of real GDP per year. Because the 45-degree reference line shows all the points where planned real expenditures (now $C + I$) equal real GDP, we label it $C + I = Y$. Thus, in equilibrium, the sum of consumption spending (C) and investment spending (I) equals real GDP (Y), which is \$11 trillion per year. Equilibrium occurs when total planned real expenditures equal real GDP (given that any amount of production of goods and services in this model in the short run can occur without a change in the price level).

Saving and Investment: Planned versus Actual

Figure 12-5 on the facing page shows the planned investment curve as a horizontal line at \$2 trillion per year in base-year dollars. Real investment is completely autonomous in this simplified model—it does not depend on real GDP.

The planned saving curve is represented by S. Because in our model whatever is not consumed is, by definition, saved, the planned saving schedule is the complement of the planned consumption schedule, represented by the C line in Figure 12-3 on the previous page. For better exposition, we look at only a part of the saving and investment schedules—annual levels of real GDP between \$9 trillion and \$13 trillion.

Why does equilibrium have to occur at the intersection of the planned saving and planned investment schedules? If we are at E in Figure 12-5, planned saving equals planned investment. All anticipations are validated by reality. There is no tendency for businesses to alter the rate of production or the level of employment because they are neither increasing nor decreasing their inventories in an unplanned way.

UNPLANNED CHANGES IN BUSINESS INVENTORIES If real GDP is \$13 trillion instead of \$11 trillion, planned investment, as usual, is \$2 trillion per year. It is exceeded, however, by planned saving, which is \$2.4 trillion per year. The additional \$0.4 trillion

FIGURE 12-5

Planned and Actual Rates of Saving and Investment

Only at the equilibrium level of real GDP of $11 trillion per year will planned saving equal actual saving, planned investment equal actual investment, and hence planned saving equal planned investment.

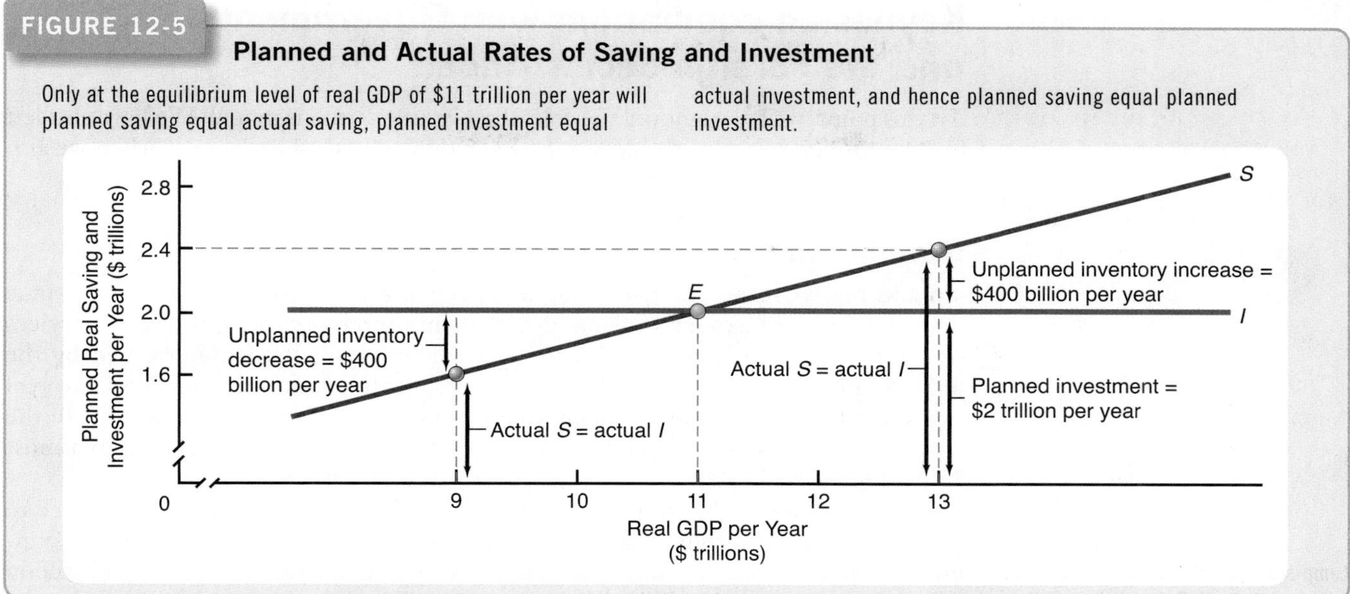

($400 billion) in saving by households over and above planned investment represents less consumption spending and will translate into unsold goods that accumulate as unplanned business inventory investment. Thus, consumers will *actually* purchase fewer goods and services than businesses had *anticipated.* This will leave firms with unsold products, and their inventories will begin to rise above the levels they had planned.

Unplanned business inventories will now rise at the rate of $400 billion per year, or $2.4 trillion in actual investment (including inventories) minus $2 trillion in planned investment by firms that had not anticipated an inventory buildup. But this situation cannot continue for long. Businesses will respond to the unplanned increase in inventories by cutting back production of goods and services and reducing employment, and we will move toward a lower level of real GDP.

Naturally, the adjustment process works in reverse if real GDP is less than the equilibrium level. For instance, if real GDP is $9 trillion per year, an unintended inventory decrease of $0.4 trillion ultimately brings about an increase in real GDP toward the equilibrium level of $11 trillion.

Every time the saving rate planned by households differs from the investment rate planned by businesses, there will be a shrinkage or an expansion in the circular flow of income and output (introduced in Chapter 8) in the form of unplanned inventory changes. Real GDP and employment will change until unplanned inventory changes are again zero—that is, until we have attained the equilibrium level of real GDP.

QUICK QUIZ

See page 277 for the answers. Review concepts from this section in MyEconLab.

We assume that the consumption function has an __________ part that is independent of the level of real GDP per year. It is labeled "__________ consumption."

For simplicity, we assume that real investment is __________ with respect to real GDP and therefore unaffected by the level of real GDP per year.

The __________ level of real GDP can be found where planned saving equals planned investment.

Whenever planned saving exceeds planned investment, there will be unplanned inventory __________, and real GDP will fall as producers cut production of goods and services. Whenever planned saving is less than planned investment, there will be unplanned inventory __________, and real GDP will rise as producers increase production of goods and services.

Keynesian Equilibrium with Government and the Foreign Sector Added

To this point, we have ignored the role of government in our model. We have also left out the foreign sector of the economy. Let's think about what happens when we also consider these as elements of the model.

Government

To add real government spending, G, to our macroeconomic model, we assume that the level of resource-using government purchases of goods and services (federal, state, and local), *not* including transfer payments, is determined by the political process. In other words, G will be considered autonomous, just like real investment (and a certain relatively small component of real consumption). In the United States, resource-using federal government expenditures account for almost 25 percent of real GDP.

The other side of the coin, of course, is that there are real taxes, which are used to pay for much of government spending. We will simplify our model greatly by assuming that there is a constant **lump-sum tax** of \$2.3 trillion a year to finance \$2.3 trillion of government spending. This lump-sum tax will reduce disposable income by the same amount. We show this below in Table 12-2 (column 2) below, where we give the numbers for a complete model.

Lump-sum tax
A tax that does not depend on income. An example is a \$1,000 tax that every household must pay, irrespective of its economic situation.

The Foreign Sector

For years, the media have focused attention on the nation's foreign trade deficit. We have been buying merchandise and services from foreign residents—real imports—the value of which exceeds the value of the real exports we have been selling to them. The difference between real exports and real imports is *real net exports*, which we will label X in our graphs. The level of real exports depends on

TABLE 12-2

The Determination of Equilibrium Real GDP with Government and Net Exports Added
Figures are trillions of dollars.

(1) Real GDP	(2) Real Taxes	(3) Real Disposable Income	(4) Planned Real Consumption	(5) Planned Real Saving	(6) Planned Real Investment	(7) Real Government Spending	(8) Real Net Exports (exports minus imports)	(9) Total Planned Real Expenditures (4) + (6) + (7) + (8)	(10) Unplanned Inventory Changes	(11) Direction of Change in Real GDP
9.0	2.3	6.7	6.7	0.0	2.0	2.3	−0.8	10.2	−1.2	Increase
10.0	2.3	7.7	7.5	0.2	2.0	2.3	−0.8	11.0	−1.0	Increase
11.0	2.3	8.7	8.3	0.4	2.0	2.3	−0.8	11.8	−0.8	Increase
12.0	2.3	9.7	9.1	0.6	2.0	2.3	−0.8	12.6	−0.6	Increase
13.0	2.3	10.7	9.9	0.8	2.0	2.3	−0.8	13.4	−0.4	Increase
14.0	2.3	11.7	10.7	1.0	2.0	2.3	−0.8	14.2	−0.2	Increase
15.0	2.3	12.7	11.5	1.2	2.0	2.3	−0.8	15.0	0	Neither (equilibrium)
16.0	2.3	13.7	12.3	1.4	2.0	2.3	−0.8	15.8	+0.2	Decrease
17.0	2.3	14.7	13.1	1.6	2.0	2.3	−0.8	16.6	+0.4	Decrease

international economic conditions, especially in the countries that buy our products. Real imports depend on economic conditions here at home. For simplicity, assume that real imports exceed real exports (real net exports, X, is negative) and furthermore that the level of real net exports is autonomous—independent of real national income. Assume a level of X of –\$0.8 trillion per year, as shown in column 8 of Table 12-2 on the facing page.

Determining the Equilibrium Level of GDP per Year

We are now in a position to determine the equilibrium level of real GDP per year under the continuing assumptions that the price level is unchanging; that investment, government, and the foreign sector are autonomous; and that planned consumption expenditures are determined by the level of real GDP. As can be seen in Table 12-2, total planned real expenditures of \$15 trillion per year equal real GDP of \$15 trillion per year, and this is where we reach equilibrium.

Remember that equilibrium *always* occurs when total planned real expenditures equal real GDP. Now look at Figure 12-6 below, which shows the equilibrium level of real GDP. There are two curves, one showing the consumption function, which is the exact duplicate of the one shown in Figure 12-3 on page 261, and the other being the $C + I + G + X$ curve, which intersects the 45-degree reference line (representing equilibrium) at \$15 trillion per year.

Whenever total planned real expenditures differ from real GDP, there are unplanned inventory changes. When total planned real expenditures are greater than real GDP, inventory levels drop in an unplanned manner. To get inventories back up, firms seek to expand their production of goods and services, which increases real GDP. Real GDP rises toward its equilibrium level. Whenever total planned real expenditures are less than real GDP, the opposite occurs. There are unplanned inventory increases, causing firms to cut back on their production of goods and services in an effort to push inventories back down to planned levels. The result is a drop in real GDP toward the equilibrium level.

FIGURE 12-6

The Equilibrium Level of Real GDP

The consumption function, with no government and thus no taxes, is shown as C. When we add autonomous investment, government spending, and net exports, we obtain $C + I + G + X$. We move from E_1 to E_2. Equilibrium real GDP is \$15 trillion per year.

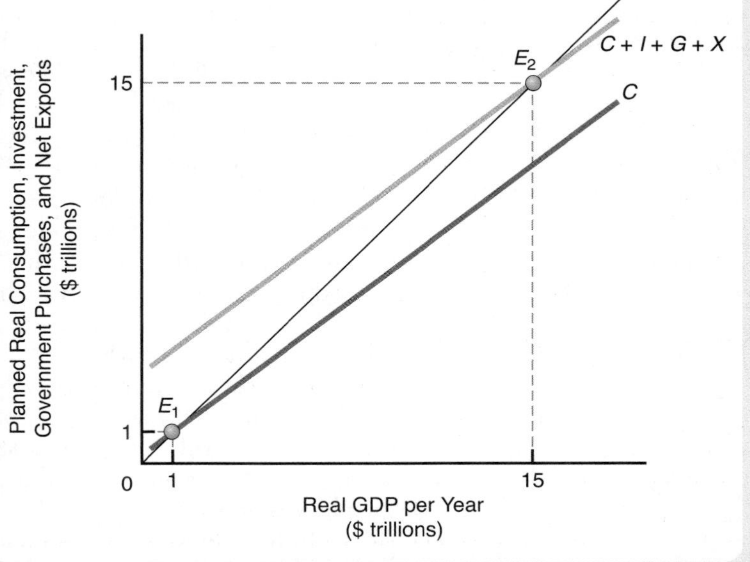

QUICK QUIZ See page 277 for the answers. Review concepts from this section in MyEconLab.

When we add autonomous investment, *I*, and autonomous government spending, *G*, to the consumption function, we obtain the $C + I + G$ curve, which represents total __________ __________ for a closed economy. In an open economy, we add the foreign sector, which consists of exports minus imports, or net exports, *X*. Total planned expenditures are thus represented by the $C + I + G + X$ curve.

Equilibrium real GDP can be found by locating the intersection of the total planned real expenditures curve with the __________-__________ reference line. At that level of real GDP per year, planned real consumption plus planned real investment plus real government expenditures plus real net exports will equal real GDP.

Whenever total planned real expenditures exceed real GDP, there will be unplanned __________ in inventories. Production of goods and services will increase, and a higher level of equilibrium real GDP will prevail. Whenever total planned real expenditures are less than real GDP, there will be unplanned __________ in inventories. Production of goods and services will decrease, and equilibrium real GDP will decrease.

The Multiplier

Look again at panel (c) of Figure 12-4 on page 262. Assume for the moment that the only real expenditures included in real GDP are real consumption expenditures. Where would the equilibrium level of real GDP be in this case? It would be where the consumption function (*C*) intersects the 45-degree reference line, which is at $1 trillion per year. Now we add the autonomous amount of planned real investment, $2 trillion, and then determine what the new equilibrium level of real GDP will be. It turns out to be $11 trillion per year. Adding $2 trillion per year of investment spending increased equilibrium real GDP by *five* times that amount, or by $10 trillion per year.

The Multiplier Effect

Multiplier
The ratio of the change in the equilibrium level of real GDP to the change in autonomous real expenditures. The number by which a change in autonomous real investment or autonomous real consumption, for example, is multiplied to get the change in equilibrium real GDP.

What is operating here is the multiplier effect of changes in autonomous spending. The **multiplier** is the number by which a permanent change in autonomous real investment or autonomous real consumption is multiplied to get the change in the equilibrium level of real GDP. Any permanent increases in autonomous real investment or in any autonomous component of consumption will cause an even larger increase in real GDP. Any permanent decreases in autonomous real spending will cause even larger decreases in real GDP per year. To understand why this multiple expansion (or contraction) in equilibrium real GDP occurs, let's look at a simple numerical example.

We'll use the same figures we used for the marginal propensity to consume and to save. MPC will equal 0.8, or $\frac{4}{5}$, and MPS will equal 0.2, or $\frac{1}{5}$. Now let's run an experiment and say that businesses decide to increase planned real investment permanently by $100 billion a year. We see in Table 12-3 on the facing page that during what we'll call the first round in column 1, investment is increased by $100 billion. This also means an increase in real GDP of $100 billion, because the spending by one group represents income for another, shown in column 2. Column 3 gives the resultant increase in consumption by households that received this additional $100 billion in income. This rise in consumption spending is found by multiplying the MPC by the increase in real GDP. Because the MPC equals 0.8, real consumption expenditures during the first round will increase by $80 billion.

But that's not the end of the story. This additional household consumption is also spending, and it will provide $80 billion of additional income for other individuals. Thus, during the second round, we see an increase in real GDP of $80 billion. Now, out of this increased real GDP, what will be the resultant increase in consumption expenditures? It will be 0.8 times $80 billion, or $64 billion. We continue these induced expenditure rounds and find that an initial increase in autonomous investment expenditures of $100 billion will eventually cause the equilibrium level of real GDP to increase by $500 billion. A permanent $100 billion increase in autonomous real investment spending has induced an additional $400 billion increase in real consumption

TABLE 12-3

The Multiplier Process

We trace the effects of a *permanent* \$100 billion increase in autonomous real investment spending on real GDP per year. If we assume a marginal propensity to consume of 0.8, such an increase will eventually elicit a \$500 billion increase in equilibrium real GDP per year.

Assumption: MPC = 0.8, or $\frac{4}{5}$

(1) Round	(2) Annual Increase in Real GDP (\$ billions)	(3) Annual Increase in Planned Real Consumption (\$ billions)	(4) Annual Increase in Planned Real Saving (\$ billions)
1 (\$100 billion per year increase in I)	100.00	80.000	20.000
2	80.00	64.000	16.000
3	64.00	51.200	12.800
4	51.20	40.960	10.240
5	40.96	32.768	8.192
.	.	.	.
.	.	.	.
.	.	.	.
All later rounds	163.84	131.072	32.768
Totals ($C + I + X$)	500.00	400.000	100.000

spending, for a total increase in real GDP of \$500 billion. In other words, equilibrium real GDP will change by an amount equal to five times the change in real investment.

The Multiplier Formula

It turns out that the autonomous spending multiplier is equal to 1 divided by the marginal propensity to save. In our example, the MPC was 0.8, or $\frac{4}{5}$. Therefore, because MPC + MPS = 1, the MPS was equal to 0.2, or $\frac{1}{5}$. When we divide 1 by $\frac{1}{5}$, we get 5. That was our multiplier. A \$100 billion increase in real planned investment led to a \$500 billion increase in the equilibrium level of real GDP. Our multiplier will always be the following:

$$\text{Multiplier} \equiv \frac{1}{1 - \text{MPC}} \equiv \frac{1}{\text{MPS}}$$

You can always figure out the multiplier if you know either the MPC or the MPS. Let's consider an example. If MPS = 0.25 or $\frac{1}{4}$,

$$\text{Multiplier} = \frac{1}{\frac{1}{4}} = 4$$

Because MPC + MPS = 1, it follows that MPS = 1 − MPC. Hence, we can always figure out the multiplier if we are given the marginal propensity to consume. In this example, if the marginal propensity to consume is given as 0.75 or $\frac{3}{4}$,

$$\text{Multiplier} = \frac{1}{1 - \frac{3}{4}} = \frac{1}{\frac{1}{4}} = 4$$

By taking a few numerical examples, you can demonstrate to yourself an important property of the multiplier:

The smaller the marginal propensity to save, the larger the multiplier.

Otherwise stated:

The larger the marginal propensity to consume, the larger the multiplier.

Demonstrate this to yourself by computing the multiplier when the marginal propensity to save equals $\frac{3}{4}$, $\frac{1}{2}$, and $\frac{1}{4}$. What happens to the multiplier as the MPS gets smaller?

When you have the multiplier, the following formula will then give you the change in equilibrium real GDP due to a permanent change in autonomous spending:

$$\text{Change in equilibrium real GDP} = \text{multiplier} \times \text{change in autonomous spending}$$

The multiplier, as noted earlier, works for a permanent increase or a permanent decrease in autonomous spending per year. In our earlier example, if the autonomous component of real consumption had fallen permanently by $100 billion, the reduction in equilibrium real GDP would have been $500 billion per year.

Significance of the Multiplier

Depending on the size of the multiplier, it is possible that a relatively small change in planned investment or in autonomous consumption can trigger a much larger change in equilibrium real GDP per year. In essence, the multiplier magnifies the fluctuations in yearly equilibrium real GDP initiated by changes in autonomous spending.

As was just noted, the larger the marginal propensity to consume, the larger the multiplier. If the marginal propensity to consume is $\frac{1}{2}$, the multiplier is 2. In that case, a $1 billion decrease in (autonomous) real investment will elicit a $2 billion decrease in equilibrium real GDP per year. Conversely, if the marginal propensity to consume is $\frac{9}{10}$, the multiplier will be 10. That same $1 billion decrease in planned real investment expenditures with a multiplier of 10 will lead to a $10 billion decrease in equilibrium real GDP per year.

WHAT IF... the government seeks a larger multiplier effect by funding private spending on certain items rather than buying those items directly?

Whether the government gives private firms or households funds to purchase particular goods or purchases those same goods itself, the resulting increase in total autonomous expenditures is the same. The overall theoretical multiplier effect on equilibrium real GDP would be the same as well. Hence, providing a grant of public funds for private purchase of the same items the government alternatively would have bought with the same funds will not enlarge the overall theoretical multiplier effect.

How a Change in Real Autonomous Spending Affects Real GDP When the Price Level Can Change

So far, our examination of how changes in real autonomous spending affect equilibrium real GDP has considered a situation in which the price level remains unchanged. Thus, our analysis has only indicated how much the aggregate demand curve shifts in response to a change in investment, government spending, net exports, or lump-sum taxes.

Of course, when we take into account the aggregate supply curve, we must also consider responses of the equilibrium price level to a multiplier-induced change in aggregate demand. We do so in Figure 12-7 on the facing page. The intersection of AD_1 and *SRAS* is at a price level of 120 with equilibrium real GDP of $15 trillion per year. An increase in autonomous spending shifts the aggregate demand curve outward to the right to AD_2. If the price level remained at 120, the short-run equilibrium level of real GDP would increase to $15.5 trillion per year because, for the $100 billion increase in autonomous spending, the multiplier would be 5, as it was in Table 12-3 on the previous page.

FIGURE 12-7

Effect of a Rise in Autonomous Spending on Equilibrium Real GDP

A \$100 billion increase in autonomous spending (investment, government, or net exports) moves AD_1 to AD_2. If the price index increases from 120 to 125, equilibrium real GDP goes up only to, say, \$15.3 trillion per year instead of \$15.5 trillion per year.

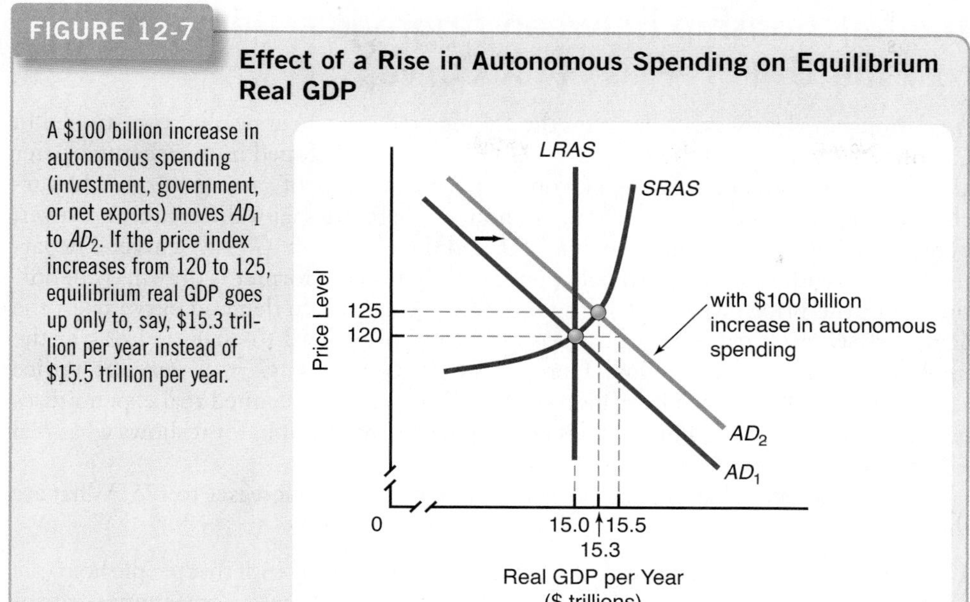

The price level does not stay fixed, however, because ordinarily the *SRAS* curve is positively sloped. In this diagram, the new short-run equilibrium level of real GDP is hypothetically \$15.3 trillion. The ultimate effect on real GDP is smaller than the multiplier effect on nominal income because part of the additional income is used to pay higher prices. Not all is spent on additional goods and services, as is the case when the price level is fixed.

If the economy is at an equilibrium level of real GDP that is greater than *LRAS*, the implications for the eventual effect on real GDP are even more severe. Look again at Figure 12-7 above. The *SRAS* curve starts to slope upward more dramatically after \$15 trillion of real GDP per year. Therefore, any increase in aggregate demand will lead to a proportionally greater increase in the price level and a smaller increase in equilibrium real GDP per year. The ultimate effect on real GDP of any increase in autonomous spending will be relatively small because most of the changes will be in the price level. Moreover, any increase in the short-run equilibrium level of real GDP will tend to be temporary because the economy is temporarily above *LRAS*—the strain on its productive capacity will raise the price level.

How much is the initial multiplier effect of a rise in real autonomous spending on real GDP in China offset by the resulting short-run adjustment in China's price level?

INTERNATIONAL EXAMPLE

The Effect of Higher Autonomous Spending on China's Real GDP

Most estimates indicate that the marginal propensity to consume in China is approximately 0.50. If we ignore a rise in the price level generated by a boost in aggregate demand that results from an increase in real autonomous spending, the value of the multiplier would be about 2. [This is so because $1/(1 - \text{MPC}) = 1/(1 - 0.5) = 1/0.5 = 2$.] Economists at the Hong Kong Monetary Authority have estimated, though, that the short-run effect of an initial rise in real autonomous spending on China's real GDP is actually much smaller—about 1.1. Therefore, once the effect on real GDP of an upward price level adjustment is taken into account, the estimated result from a one-unit increase in real autonomous expenditures is only a 1.1-unit increase in China's annual real GDP.

FOR CRITICAL THINKING

By about how much would China's equilibrium real GDP change if the nation's net export spending declined by 1 trillion yuan (the Chinese currency unit)?

The Relationship between Aggregate Demand and the $C + I + G + X$ Curve

A relationship clearly exists between the aggregate demand curves that you studied in Chapters 10 and 11 and the $C + I + G + X$ curve developed in this chapter. After all, aggregate demand consists of consumption, investment, and government purchases, plus the foreign sector of our economy. There is a major difference, however, between the aggregate demand curve, *AD*, and the $C + I + G + X$ curve: The latter is drawn with the price level held constant, whereas the former is drawn, by definition, with the price level changing. To derive the aggregate demand curve from the $C + I + G + X$ curve, we must now allow the price level to change. Look at the upper part of Figure 12-8 below. Here we see the $C + I + G + X$ curve at a price level equal to 100, and at $15 trillion of real GDP per year, planned real expenditures exactly equal real GDP. This gives us point *A* in the lower graph, for it shows what real GDP would be at a price level of 100.

Now let's assume that in the upper graph, the price level increases to 125. What are the effects?

1. A higher price level can decrease the purchasing power of any cash that people hold (the real-balance effect). This is a decrease in real wealth, and it causes consumption expenditures, *C*, to fall, thereby putting downward pressure on the $C + I + G + X$ curve.

FIGURE 12-8

The Relationship between *AD* and the $C + I + G + X$ Curve

In the upper graph, the $C + I + G + X$ curve at a price level equal to 100 intersects the 45-degree reference line at E_1, or $15 trillion of real GDP per year. That gives us point *A* (price level = 100; real GDP = $15 trillion) in the lower graph. When the price level increases to 125, the $C + I + G + X$ curve shifts downward, and the new level of real GDP at which planned real expenditures equal real GDP is at E_2 at $13 trillion per year. This gives us point *B* in the lower graph. Connecting points *A* and *B*, we obtain the aggregate demand curve.

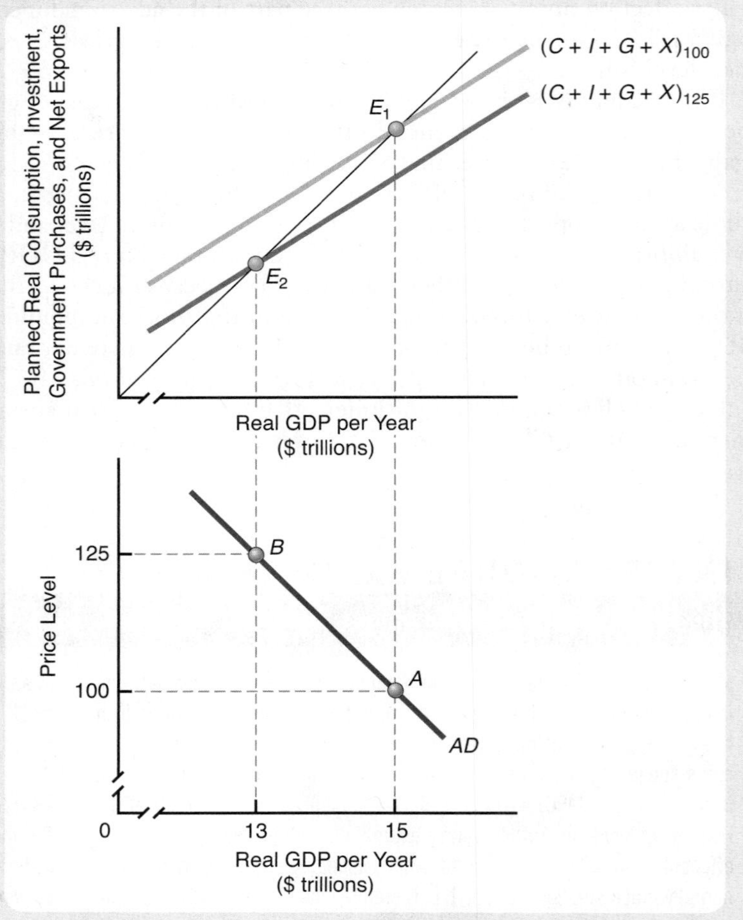

2. Because individuals attempt to borrow more to replenish their real cash balances, interest rates will rise, which will make it more costly for people to buy houses and cars (the interest rate effect). Higher interest rates also make it less profitable to install new equipment and to erect new buildings. Therefore, the rise in the price level indirectly causes a reduction in total planned spending on goods and services.

3. In an open economy, our higher price level causes foreign spending on our goods to fall (the open economy effect). Simultaneously, it increases our demand for others' goods. If the foreign exchange price of the dollar stays constant for a while, there will be an increase in imports and a decrease in exports, thereby reducing the size of X, again putting downward pressure on the $C + I + G + X$ curve.

The result is that a new $C + I + G + X$ curve at a price level equal to 125 generates an equilibrium at E_2 at \$13 trillion of real GDP per year. This gives us point B in the lower part of Figure 12-8 on the facing page. When we connect points A and B, we obtain the aggregate demand curve, AD.

QUICK QUIZ See page 277 for the answers. Review concepts from this section in MyEconLab.

Any change in autonomous spending shifts the expenditure curve and causes a __________ effect on equilibrium real GDP per year.

The **multiplier** is equal to 1 divided by the __________ propensity to __________.

The smaller the marginal propensity to __________, the larger the **multiplier.** Otherwise stated, the larger the marginal propensity to __________, the larger the **multiplier**.

The $C + I + G + X$ curve is drawn with the price level held constant, whereas the AD curve allows the price level to __________. Each different price level generates a new $C + I + G + X$ curve.

YOU ARE THERE

Evaluating the Effects of Declining Real Disposable Income

Mark Vitner, an economist with Wells Fargo Bank, examines the latest monthly economic data. U.S. real disposable personal income fell by 0.3 percent during the month, the first such decline since the 2008–2009 economic downturn. Vitner notes that other data display patterns consistent with the theory of consumption and saving. Because households consume and save out of real disposable income, real consumption spending and real saving both dipped during the month.

Vitner returns a call to a financial news reporter seeking his comments on the implications of these declines. "Everything that we see in these numbers tells us that household budgets are extremely tight and getting tighter," he states. "Consumers are having to pull out all the stops in order to try to maintain their standard of living." This dreary assessment is the best that Vitner can offer. After all, a key measure of households' living standards is real consumption spending, which in turn derives from real disposable income. If real disposable income continues to fall, persistent downward pressure will be exerted on real consumption spending—and, hence, on estimated standards of living—of U.S. households.

Critical Thinking Questions

1. Is Vitner contemplating a shift of or movement along the consumption function?
2. Did a shift of or movement along the *saving* function occur?

ISSUES & APPLICATIONS

A Global Reversal in Planned Investment Spending

CONCEPTS APPLIED

- Planned Investment Spending
- Multiplier
- Planned Investment Function

In years past, countries that experienced the largest upward shifts in their planned investment functions over time were developed countries, including European nations, Japan, and the United States. Recently, however, relatively larger upward shifts in planned investment functions have occurred among *emerging-economy nations*, such as China, India, South Korea, and Singapore.

Groups of Nations Trading Places in Planned Investment

Figure 12-9 below displays real investment spending as a percentage of global real GDP since the mid-1990s for developed versus emerging nations. The figure shows that in recent years, *decreases* in planned investment expenditures as a percentage of global real GDP have occurred in highly developed countries. In contrast, planned investment spending as a percentage of global real GDP has been *rising* for nations with emerging economies.

Global real GDP has increased every year except for a brief dip during 2009. Consequently, planned real investment has risen in all nations in most years. What Figure 12-9 depicts, therefore, is a shift toward relatively greater increases in planned investment in emerging nations compared with developed countries.

Higher Real Investment Yields Faster-Growing Real GDP

Within any nation's economy, variations in planned real investment spending operate through the multiplier to bring about changes in equilibrium real GDP. Thus, a country that experiences a larger upward shift in its planned investment function than another nation will, if both countries' multipliers have close to the same values, observe a greater increase in its equilibrium real GDP.

FIGURE 12-9

Real Investment Spending as a Percentage of Global Real GDP in Two Groups of Nations since 1995

Since the early 2000s, developed countries have experienced a decrease in planned investment expenditures as a percentage of global real GDP, whereas nations with emerging economies have observed an increase in planned investment spending as a percentage of global real GDP.

Sources: International Monetary Fund; author's estimates.

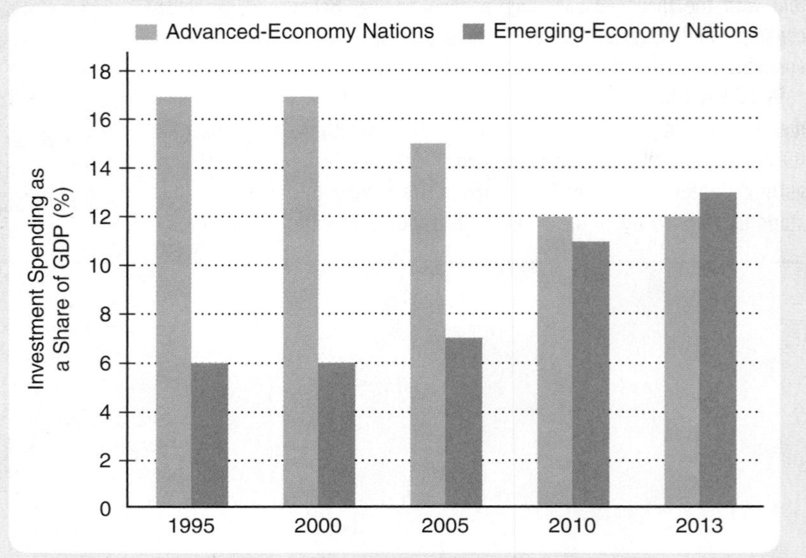

This relatively larger increase in investment spending helps to explain why countries such as China, India, South Korea, and Singapore are *emerging* from a status of less developed toward eventual classification among developed nations. Relatively higher planned real investment expenditures in these nations are, through multiplier effects, boosting real GDP per year. Thus, flows of real GDP are expanding faster in these emerging-economy countries than in developed ones.

For Critical Thinking

1. If interest rates, or opportunity costs of investment, happened to be the same in both developed countries and emerging-economy nations, what could account for faster upward shifts in the latter group's planned investment functions?
2. Are stocks of productive capital currently growing at a faster pace in developed countries or in emerging-economy nations? Explain.

Web Resources

1. To track real investment spending as a percentage of real GDP in recent years for individual nations, go to www.econtoday.com/chap12.
2. For links to economic data for both developed countries and emerging-economy nations, go to www.econtoday.com/chap12.

MyEconLab

For more questions on this chapter's Issues & Applications, go to MyEconLab. In the Study Plan for this chapter, select Section N: News.

MyEconLab

Here is what you should know after reading this chapter. MyEconLab will help you identify what you know, and where to go when you need to practice.

WHAT YOU SHOULD KNOW		WHERE TO GO TO PRACTICE
The Difference between Saving and Savings and the Relationship between Saving and Consumption Saving is a flow over time, whereas savings are a stock of resources at a point in time. Thus, the portion of your disposable income that you do not consume during a week, a month, or a year is an addition to your stock of savings. By definition, saving during a year plus consumption during that year must equal total disposable (after-tax) income earned that year.	real disposable income, 251 consumption, 251 saving, 251 consumption goods, 251 investment, 252 capital goods, 252	• MyEconLab Study Plan 12.1
Key Determinants of Consumption and Saving in the Keynesian Model In the Keynesian model, as real disposable income increases, so do real consumption expenditures. The portion of consumption unrelated to disposable income is autonomous consumption. The ratio of saving to disposable income is the average propensity to save (APS), and the ratio of consumption to disposable income is the average propensity to consume (APC). A change in saving divided by the corresponding change in disposable income is the marginal propensity to save (MPS), and a change in consumption divided by the corresponding change in disposable income is the marginal propensity to consume (MPC).	life-cycle theory of consumption, 253 permanent income hypothesis, 253 consumption function, 253 dissaving, 253 45-degree reference line, 254 autonomous consumption, 255 average propensity to consume (APC), 256 average propensity to save (APS), 256 marginal propensity to consume (MPC), 256 marginal propensity to save (MPS), 256 net wealth, 257	• MyEconLab Study Plan 12.2 • Animated Figure 12-1

(continued)

MyEconLab *continued*

WHAT YOU SHOULD KNOW		WHERE TO GO TO PRACTICE
	Key Figure Figure 12-1, 255	
Key Determinants of Planned Investment Planned investment varies inversely with the interest rate, so the investment schedule slopes downward. Changes in business expectations, productive technology, or business taxes cause the investment schedule to shift.		• MyEconLab Study Plan 12.3
How Equilibrium Real GDP Is Established in the Keynesian Model In equilibrium, total planned real consumption, investment, government, and net export expenditures equal real GDP, so $C + I + G + X = Y$. This occurs at the point where the $C + I + G + X$ curve crosses the 45-degree reference line. In a world without government spending and taxes, equilibrium also occurs when planned saving is equal to planned investment, and there is no tendency for business inventories to expand or contract.	lump-sum tax, 264 Key Figures Figure 12-5, 263 Figure 12-6, 265	• MyEconLab Study Plans 12.4, 12.5 • Animated Figures 12-5, 12-6
Why Autonomous Changes in Total Planned Real Expenditures Have a Multiplier Effect on Equilibrium Real GDP Any increase in autonomous expenditures causes a direct rise in real GDP. The resulting increase in disposable income in turn stimulates increased consumption by an amount equal to the marginal propensity to consume multiplied by the rise in disposable income that results. As consumption increases, so does real GDP, which induces a further increase in consumption spending. The ultimate expansion of real GDP is equal to the multiplier, $1/(1 - \text{MPC})$, or $1/\text{MPS}$, times the increase in autonomous expenditures.	multiplier, 266 Key Table Table 12-3, 267	• MyEconLab Study Plans 12.6, 12.7 • Animated Table 12-3
The Relationship between Total Planned Expenditures and the Aggregate Demand Curve An increase in the price level induces households and businesses to cut back on spending. Thus, the $C + I + G + X$ curve shifts downward following a rise in the price level, so that equilibrium real GDP falls. This yields the downward-sloping aggregate demand curve.	Key Figures Figure 12-7, 269 Figure 12-8, 270	• MyEconLab Study Plan 12.8 • Animated Figures 12-7, 12-8

Log in to MyEconLab, take a chapter test, and get a personalized Study Plan that tells you which concepts you understand and which ones you need to review. From there, MyEconLab will give you further practice, tutorials, animations, videos, and guided solutions. For more information, visit www.myeconlab.com

PROBLEMS

All problems are assignable in MyEconLab. *Answers to odd-numbered problems appear at the back of the book.*

12-1. Classify each of the following as either a stock or a flow. (See page 251.)

a. Myung Park earns $850 per week.

b. Time Warner purchases $100 million in new telecomunications equipment this month.

c. Sally Schmidt has $1,000 in a savings account at a credit union.

d. XYZ, Inc., produces 200 units of output per week.

e. Giorgio Giannelli owns three private jets.

f. Apple's production declines by 750 digital devices per month.

g. Russia owes $25 billion to the International Monetary Fund.

12-2. Consider the table below when answering the following questions. For this hypothetical economy, the marginal propensity to save is constant at all levels of real GDP, and investment spending is autonomous. There is no government. (See pages 253–263.)

Real GDP	Consumption	Saving	Investment
$ 2,000	$2,200	$____	$400
4,000	4,000	____	____
6,000	____	____	____
8,000	____	____	____
10,000	____	____	____
12,000	____	____	____

a. Complete the table. What is the marginal propensity to save? What is the marginal propensity to consume?

b. Draw a graph of the consumption function. Then add the investment function to obtain $C + I$.

c. Under the graph of $C + I$, draw another graph showing the saving and investment curves. Note that the $C + I$ curve crosses the 45-degree reference line in the upper graph at the same level of real GDP where the saving and investment curves cross in the lower graph. (If not, redraw your graphs.) What is this level of real GDP?

d. What is the numerical value of the multiplier?

e. What is equilibrium real GDP without investment? What is the multiplier effect from the inclusion of investment?

f. What is the average propensity to consume at equilibrium real GDP?

g. If autonomous investment declines from $400 to $200, what happens to equilibrium real GDP?

12-3. Consider the table below when answering the following questions. For this economy, the marginal propensity to consume is constant at all levels of real GDP, and investment spending is autonomous. Equilibrium real GDP is equal to $8,000. There is no government. (See pages 253–263.)

Real GDP	Consumption	Saving	Investment
$ 2,000	$ 2,000	____	____
4,000	3,600	____	____
6,000	5,200	____	____
8,000	6,800	____	____
10,000	8,400	____	____
12,000	10,000	____	____

a. Complete the table. What is the marginal propensity to consume? What is the marginal propensity to save?

b. Draw a graph of the consumption function. Then add the investment function to obtain $C + I$.

c. Under the graph of $C + I$, draw another graph showing the saving and investment curves. Does the $C + I$ curve cross the 45-degree reference line in the upper graph at the same level of real GDP where the saving and investment curves cross in the lower graph, at the equilibrium real GDP of $8,000? (If not, redraw your graphs.)

d. What is the average propensity to save at equilibrium real GDP?

e. If autonomous consumption were to rise by $100, what would happen to equilibrium real GDP?

12-4. Calculate the multiplier for the following cases. (See page 267.)

a. MPS = 0.25

b. MPC = $\frac{5}{6}$

c. MPS = 0.125

d. MPC = $\frac{6}{7}$

12-5. Given each of the following values for the multiplier, calculate both the MPC and the MPS. (See page 267.)

a. 20

b. 10

c. 8

d. 5

12-6. The marginal propensity to consume is equal to 0.80. An increase in household wealth causes autonomous consumption to rise by $10 billion. By how much will equilibrium real GDP increase at the current price level, other things being equal? (See page 267.)

12-7. Assume that the multiplier in a country is equal to 4 and that autonomous real consumption spending is $1 trillion. If current real GDP is $15 trillion, what is the current value of real consumption spending? (See page 267.)

12-8. The multiplier in a country is equal to 5, and households pay no taxes. At the current equilibrium real GDP of $14 trillion, total real consumption spending by households is $12 trillion. What is real autonomous consumption in this country? (See page 267.)

12-9. At an initial point on the aggregate demand curve, the price level is 125, and real GDP is $15 trillion. When the price level falls to a value of 120, total autonomous expenditures increase by $250 billion. The marginal propensity to consume is 0.75. What is the level of real GDP at the new point on the aggregate demand curve? (See pages 270–271.)

12-10. At an initial point on the aggregate demand curve, the price level is 100, and real GDP is $15 trillion. After the price level rises to 110, however, there is an upward movement along the aggregate demand curve, and real GDP declines to $14 trillion. If total planned spending declined by $200 billion in response to the increase in the price level, what is the marginal propensity to consume in this economy? (See pages 270–271.)

12-11. In an economy in which the multiplier has a value of 3, the price level has decreased from 115 to 110. As a consequence, there has been a movement along the aggregate demand curve from $15 trillion in real GDP to $15.9 trillion in real GDP. (See pages 270–271.)

a. What is the marginal propensity to save?

b. What was the amount of the change in planned expenditures generated by the decline in the price level?

12-12. Consider the diagram below, which applies to a nation with no government spending, taxes, and net exports. Use the information in the diagram to answer the following questions, and explain your answers. (See pages 253–263.)

a. What is the marginal propensity to save?

b. What is the present level of planned investment spending for the present period?

c. What is the equilibrium level of real GDP for the present period?

d. What is the equilibrium level of saving for the present period?

e. If planned investment spending for the present period increases by $25 billion, what will be the resulting *change* in equilibrium real GDP? What will be the new equilibrium level of real GDP if other things, including the price level, remain unchanged?

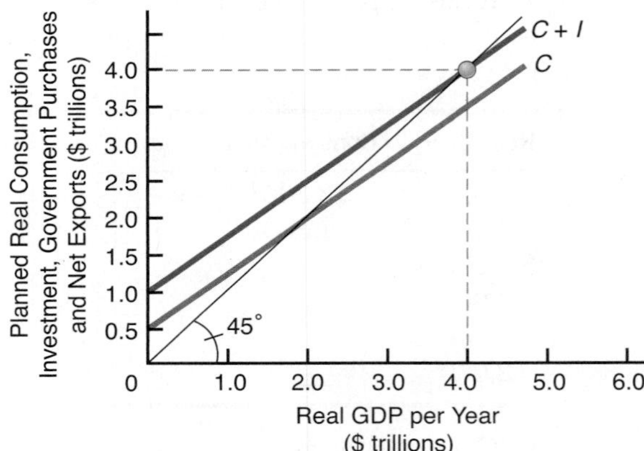

ECONOMICS ON THE NET

The Relationship between Consumption and Real GDP? According to the basic consumption function we considered in this chapter, consumption rises at a fixed rate when both disposable income and real GDP increase. Your task here is to evaluate how reasonable this assumption is and to determine the relative extent to which variations in consumption appear to be related to variations in real GDP.

Title: Gross Domestic Product and Components

Navigation: Use the link at **www.econtoday.com/chap12** to visit the Federal Reserve Bank of St. Louis's Web page on *National Income and Product Accounts.* Then click on *Personal Income and Outlays.*

Application

1. Scan down the list, and click on *Real Personal Consumption Expenditures.* Then click on "Download Data." Write down consumption expenditures for the past eight quarters. Now back up to *National Income and Product*

Accounts, click on *Gross GDP/GNP* and then *Real Gross Domestic Product, 1 Decimal*, click on "Download Data," and write down GDP for the past eight quarters. Use these data to calculate implied values for the marginal propensity to consume, assuming that taxes do not vary with income. Is there any problem with this assumption?

2. Back up to *National Income and Product Accounts*. Select "Price Indexes & Deflators." Now click on *Gross Domestic Product: Implicit Price Deflator*. Scan through the data since the mid-1960s. In what years did the largest variations in GDP take place? What component or components of GDP appear to have accounted for these large movements?

For Group Study and Analysis Assign groups to use the FRED database to try to determine the best measure of aggregate U.S. disposable income for the past eight quarters. Reconvene as a class, and discuss each group's approach to this issue.

ANSWERS TO QUICK QUIZZES

p. 252: (i) horizontal; (ii) Saving . . . Savings; (iii) Investment

p. 258: (i) disposable income . . . consumption; (ii) average . . . average; (iii) marginal . . . marginal; (iv) movement along . . . shift in

p. 260: (i) interest rate . . . downward; (ii) expectations . . . business taxes; (iii) shift in

p. 263: (i) autonomous . . . autonomous; (ii) autonomous; (iii) equilibrium; (iv) increases . . . decreases

p. 266: (i) planned expenditures; (ii) 45-degree; (iii) decreases . . . increases

p. 271: (i) multiplier; (ii) marginal . . . save; (iii) save . . . consume; (iv) change

APPENDIX C

The Keynesian Model and the Multiplier

We can see the multiplier effect more clearly if we look at Figure C-1 below, in which we see only a small section of the graphs that we used in Chapter 12. We start with equilibrium real GDP of \$14.5 trillion per year. This equilibrium occurs with total planned real expenditures represented by $C + I + G + X$. The $C + I + G + X$ curve intersects the 45-degree reference line at \$14.5 trillion per year. Now we increase real investment, I, by \$100 billion. This increase in investment shifts the entire $C + I + G + X$ curve vertically to $C + I' + G + X$. The vertical shift represents that \$100 billion increase in autonomous investment. With the higher level of planned expenditures per year, we are no longer in equilibrium at E. Inventories are falling. Production of goods and services will increase as firms try to replenish their inventories.

Eventually, real GDP will catch up with total planned expenditures. The new equilibrium level of real GDP is established at E' at the intersection of the new $C + I' + G + X$ curve and the 45-degree reference line, along which $C + I + G + X = Y$ (total planned expenditures equal real GDP). The new equilibrium level of real GDP is \$15 trillion per year. Thus, the increase in equilibrium real GDP is equal to five times the permanent increase in planned investment spending.

FIGURE C-1

Graphing the Multiplier

We can translate Table 12-3 on page 267 into graphic form by looking at each successive round of additional spending induced by an autonomous increase in planned investment of \$100 billion. The total planned expenditures curve shifts from $C + I + G + X$, with its associated equilibrium level of real GDP of \$14.5 trillion, to a new curve labeled $C + I' + G + X$. The new equilibrium level of real GDP is \$15 trillion. Equilibrium is again established.

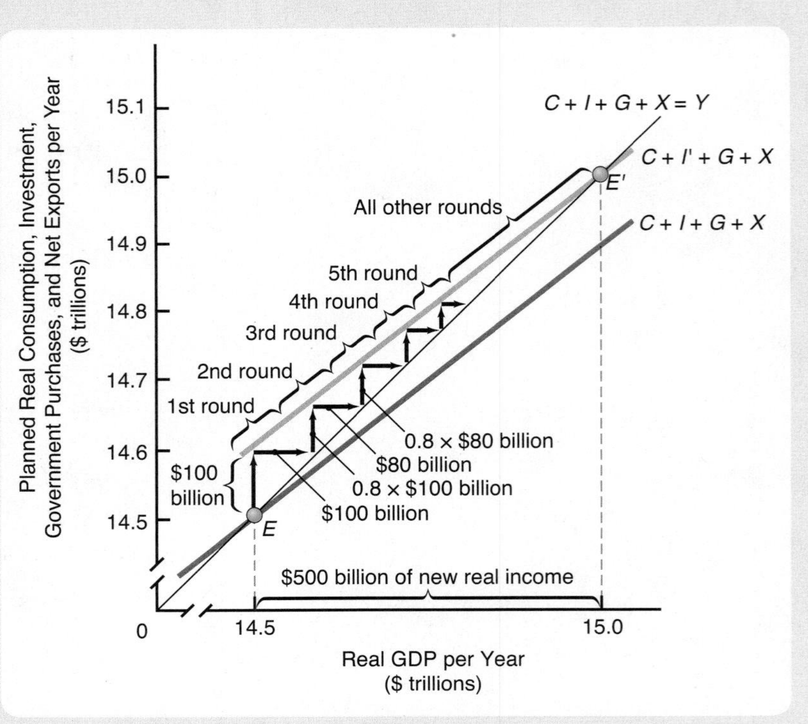

Fiscal Policy

13

LEARNING OBJECTIVES

After reading this chapter, you should be able to:

- Use traditional Keynesian analysis to evaluate the effects of discretionary fiscal policies
- Discuss ways in which indirect crowding out and direct expenditure offsets can reduce the effectiveness of fiscal policy actions
- Explain why the Ricardian equivalence theorem calls into question the usefulness of tax changes
- List and define fiscal policy time lags and explain why they complicate efforts to engage in fiscal "fine-tuning"
- Describe how certain aspects of fiscal policy function as automatic stabilizers for the economy

MyEconLab helps you master each objective and study more efficiently. See end of chapter for details.

In the midst of the sharp economic downturn of 2008–2009, Congress passed the American Recovery and Reinvestment Act (ARRA). The ARRA was meant to stimulate total planned expenditures via hundreds of billions of dollars of additional government spending. Hence, the media have tended to refer to the law as the "Stimulus Act." A large portion of the federal funds authorized by the ARRA went to state governments for spending at local levels. In fact, however, most estimates indicate that states used no more than 5 percent of the total ARRA funds they received to purchase final goods and services. What did the U.S. government hope to accomplish by adding hundreds of billions in additional spending to its budget? Why were so few of the funds distributed to state governments actually spent on goods and services? You will find out in this chapter.

DID YOU KNOW THAT... the U.S. government's American Recovery and Reinvestment Act of 2009 entailed a greater overall expenditure of funds than the eight-year-long Iraqi conflict? Military and other U.S. government spending related to the war effort in Iraq totaled $709 billion, or about 4.7 percent of the value of a typical year's output of goods and services. The 2009 "Stimulus Act," which was intended to boost economic activity and reduce the unemployment rate, authorized $862 billion in spending, or about 5.7 percent of the value of annual U.S. production. In this chapter, you will learn how variations in government spending and taxation affect both real GDP and the price level.

Discretionary Fiscal Policy

Fiscal policy
The discretionary changing of government expenditures or taxes to achieve national economic goals, such as high employment with price stability.

The making of deliberate, discretionary changes in federal government expenditures or taxes (or both) to achieve certain national economic goals is the realm of **fiscal policy.** Some national goals are high employment (low unemployment), price stability, and economic growth. Fiscal policy can be thought of as a deliberate attempt to cause the economy to move to full employment and price stability more quickly than it otherwise might.

Fiscal policy has typically been associated with the economic theories of John Maynard Keynes and what is now called *traditional* Keynesian analysis. Recall from Chapter 11 that Keynes's explanation of the Great Depression was that there was insufficient aggregate demand. Because he believed that wages and prices were "sticky downward," he argued that the classical economists' picture of an economy moving automatically and quickly toward full employment was inaccurate. To Keynes and his followers, government had to step in to increase aggregate demand. Expansionary fiscal policy initiated by the federal government was the preferred way to ward off recessions and depressions.

Changes in Government Spending

In Chapter 11, we looked at the recessionary gap and the inflationary gap (see Figures 11-9 and 11-10 on pages 242 and 243). The recessionary gap was defined as the amount by which the current level of real GDP falls short of the economy's *potential* production if it were operating on its *LRAS* curve. The inflationary gap was defined as the amount by which the short-run equilibrium level of real GDP exceeds the long-run equilibrium level as given by *LRAS*. Let us examine fiscal policy first in the context of a recessionary gap.

WHEN THERE IS A RECESSIONARY GAP The government, along with firms, individuals, and foreign residents, is one of the spending entities in the economy. When the government spends more, all other things held constant, the dollar value of total spending initially must rise. Look at panel (a) of Figure 13-1 on the facing page. We begin by assuming that some negative shock in the near past has left the economy at point E_1, which is a short-run equilibrium in which AD_1 intersects *SRAS* at $14.5 trillion of real GDP per year. There is a recessionary gap of $500 billion of real GDP per year—the difference between *LRAS* (the economy's long-run potential) and the short-run equilibrium level of real GDP per year.

When the government decides to spend more (expansionary fiscal policy), the aggregate demand curve shifts to the right to AD_2. Here we assume that the government knows exactly how much more to spend so that AD_2 intersects *SRAS* at $15 trillion, or at *LRAS*. Because of the upward-sloping *SRAS*, the price level rises from 120 to 130 as real GDP goes to $15 trillion per year.

Did U.S. government purchases of old cars induce enough private spending on new vehicles to contribute to higher real GDP?

FIGURE 13-1

Expansionary and Contractionary Fiscal Policy: Changes in Government Spending

If there is a recessionary gap and short-run equilibrium is at E_1, in panel (a), fiscal policy can presumably increase aggregate demand to AD_2. The new equilibrium is at E_2 at higher real GDP per year and a higher price level. In panel (b), the economy is at short-run equilibrium at E_1, which is at a higher real GDP than the *LRAS*. To reduce this inflationary gap, fiscal policy can be used to decrease aggregate demand from AD_1 to AD_2. Eventually, equilibrium will fall to E_2, which is on the *LRAS*.

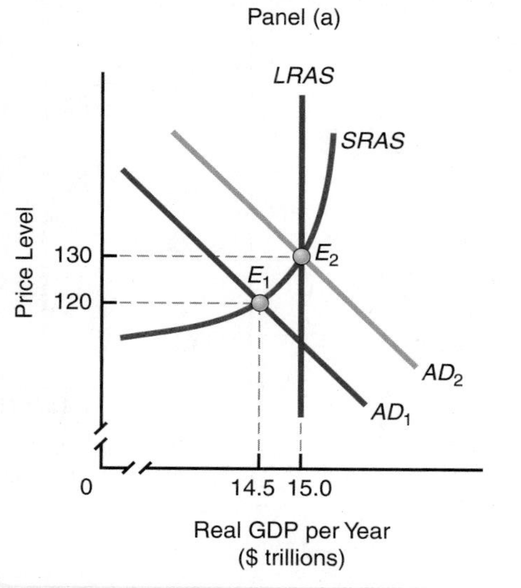

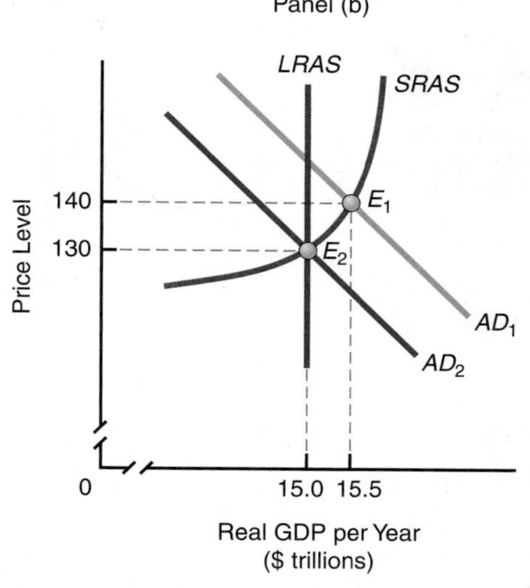

POLICY EXAMPLE

Net Real GDP Effect of "Cash-for-Clunkers" Spending: Zero

In 2009, the U.S. government offered \$3,500 to \$4,500 to people who surrendered used cars and bought new vehicles. Policymakers who promoted this "Cash-for-Clunkers" program at a \$2.8 billion expense for taxpayers argued that it had two desirable effects. One was the removal of high-pollution vehicles from roads. The other was that consumers bought 450,000 new vehicles, which generated \$12.6 billion in private expenditures that otherwise would not have taken place.

Adam Copeland and James Kahn, economists at the Federal Reserve Bank of Kansas City, have determined that many people delayed buying new vehicles until the Cash-for-Clunkers subsidies were available. Even more people bought vehicles earlier than originally planned. This meant that consumers responded to the program by shifting the *timing* of purchases of new vehicles they *already* intended to buy. Copeland and Kahn concluded that the real GDP impact of the program was zero. Hence, it was not a particularly effective fiscal policy program.

FOR CRITICAL THINKING

Why might any *temporary government subsidy program mainly end up affecting the* timing *of spending instead of actually boosting overall planned expenditures?*

WHEN THERE IS AN INFLATIONARY GAP The entire process shown above in panel (a) of Figure 13-1 can be reversed, as shown in panel (b). There, we assume that a recent shock has left the economy at point E_1, at which an inflationary gap exists at the intersection of *SRAS* and AD_1. Real GDP cannot be sustained at \$15.5 trillion indefinitely, because this exceeds long-run aggregate supply, which in real terms is \$15 trillion. If the government recognizes this and reduces its spending (pursues a contractionary fiscal policy), this action reduces aggregate demand from AD_1 to AD_2. Equilibrium will fall to E_2 on the *LRAS*, where real GDP per year is \$15 trillion. The price level will fall from 140 to 130.

Changes in Taxes

The spending decisions of firms, individuals, and other countries' residents depend on the taxes levied on them. Individuals in their role as consumers look to their disposable (after-tax) income when determining their desired rates of consumption. Firms look at their after-tax

FIGURE 13-2

Expansionary and Contractionary Fiscal Policy: Changes in Taxes

In panel (a), the economy is initially at E_1, where real GDP is less than long-run equilibrium real GDP. Expansionary fiscal policy via a tax reduction can move aggregate demand to AD_2 so that the new equilibrium is at E_2 at a higher price level. Real GDP is now consistent with *LRAS,* which eliminates the recessionary gap. In panel (b), with an inflationary gap (in this case of $500 billion), taxes are increased. AD_1 moves to AD_2. The economy moves from E_1 to E_2, and real GDP is now at $15 trillion per year, the long-run equilibrium level.

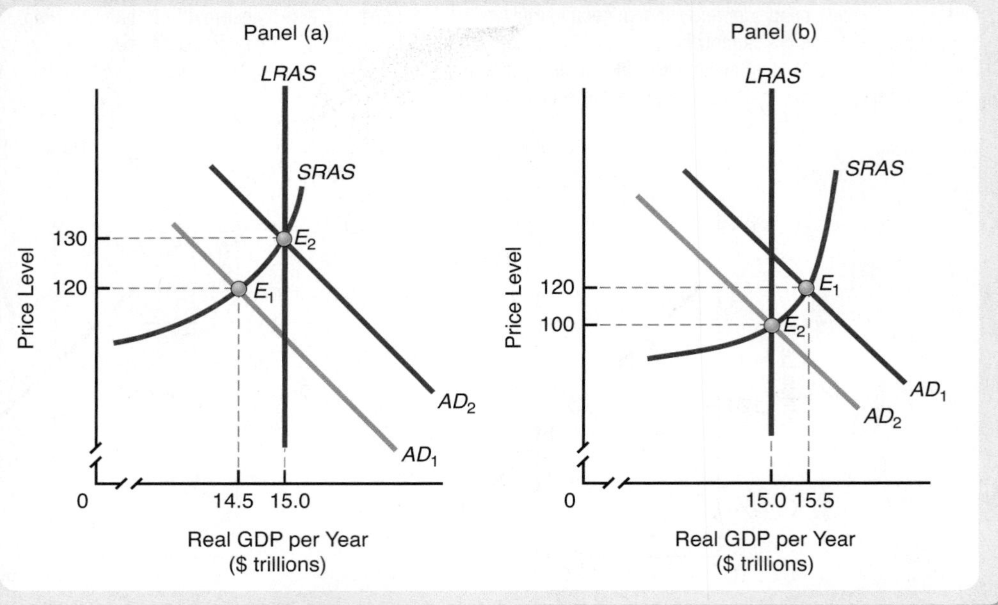

profits when deciding on the levels of investment per year to undertake. Foreign residents look at the tax-inclusive cost of goods when deciding whether to buy in the United States or elsewhere. Therefore, holding all other things constant, an increase in taxes causes a reduction in aggregate demand because it reduces consumption, investment, or net exports.

WHEN THE CURRENT SHORT-RUN EQUILIBRIUM IS TO THE LEFT OF *LRAS* Look at panel (a) in Figure 13-2. AD_1 intersects *SRAS* at E_1, with real GDP at $14.5 trillion, less than the *LRAS* of $15 trillion. In this situation, a decrease in taxes shifts the aggregate demand curve outward to the right. At AD_2, equilibrium is established at E_2, with the price level at 130 and equilibrium real GDP at $15 trillion per year.

WHEN THE CURRENT SHORT-RUN EQUILIBRIUM IS TO THE RIGHT OF *LRAS* Assume that aggregate demand is AD_1 in panel (b) of Figure 13-2 above. It intersects *SRAS* at E_1, which yields real GDP greater than *LRAS.* In this situation, an increase in taxes shifts the aggregate demand curve inward to the left. For argument's sake, assume that it intersects *SRAS* at E_2, or exactly where *LRAS* intersects AD_2. In this situation, the level of real GDP falls from $15.5 trillion per year to $15 trillion per year. The price level falls from 120 to 100.

QUICK QUIZ See page 296 for the answers. Review concepts from this section in MyEconLab.

Fiscal policy is defined as making discretionary changes in government __________ or __________ to achieve such national goals as high employment or reduced inflation.

To address a situation in which there is a __________ gap and the economy is operating at less than long-run aggregate supply (*LRAS*), the government can __________ its spending. This policy action shifts the aggregate demand curve to the right, causing the equilibrium level of real GDP per year to increase.

To address a situation in which there is an __________ gap, the government can __________ its spending and cause the aggregate demand curve to shift to the left, which reduces the equilibrium level of real GDP per year.

Changes in taxes can have similar effects on the equilibrium rate of real GDP and the price level. If there is an inflationary gap, an __________ in taxes can lead to a decrease in the equilibrium level of real GDP per year. In contrast, if there is a recessionary gap, a __________ in taxes can increase equilibrium real GDP per year.

Possible Offsets to Fiscal Policy

Fiscal policy does not operate in a vacuum. Important questions must be answered: If government spending rises by, say, $300 billion, how is the spending financed, and by whom? If taxes are increased, what does the government do with the taxes? What will happen if individuals anticipate higher *future* taxes because the government is spending more today without raising current taxes? These questions involve *offsets* to the effects of current fiscal policy. We consider them in detail here.

Indirect Crowding Out

Let's take the first example of fiscal policy in this chapter—an increase in government expenditures. If government expenditures rise and taxes are held constant, something has to give. Our government does not simply take goods and services when it wants them. It has to pay for them. When it pays for them and does not simultaneously collect the same amount in taxes, it must borrow. That means that an increase in government spending without raising taxes creates additional government borrowing from the private sector (or from other countries' residents).

INDUCED INTEREST RATE CHANGES If the government attempts to borrow in excess of $1 trillion more per year from the private sector, as it has since 2009, it will have to offer a higher interest rate to lure the additional funds from savers. This is the interest rate effect of expansionary fiscal policy financed by borrowing from the public. Consequently, when the federal government finances increased spending by additional borrowing, it will push interest rates up. When interest rates go up, firms' borrowing costs rise, which induces them to cut back on planned investment spending. Borrowing costs also increase for households, who reduce planned expenditures on cars and homes.

Thus, a rise in government spending, holding taxes constant (that is, deficit spending), tends to crowd out private spending, dampening the positive effect of increased government spending on aggregate demand. This is called the **crowding-out effect.** In the extreme case, the crowding out may be complete, with the increased government spending having no net effect on aggregate demand. The final result is simply more government spending and less private investment and consumption. Figure 13-3 below shows how the crowding-out effect occurs.

Crowding-out effect
The tendency of expansionary fiscal policy to cause a decrease in planned investment or planned consumption in the private sector. This decrease normally results from the rise in interest rates.

THE FIRM'S INVESTMENT DECISION To understand the crowding-out effect better, consider a firm that is contemplating borrowing $100,000 to expand its business. Suppose that the interest rate is 5 percent. The interest payments on the debt will be 5 percent times $100,000, or $5,000 per year ($417 per month). A rise in the interest rate to 8 percent will push the payments to 8 percent of $100,000, or $8,000 per year ($667 per month). The extra $250 per month in interest expenses will discourage some firms from making the investment. Consumers face similar decisions when they purchase

FIGURE 13-3
The Crowding-Out Effect, Step by Step

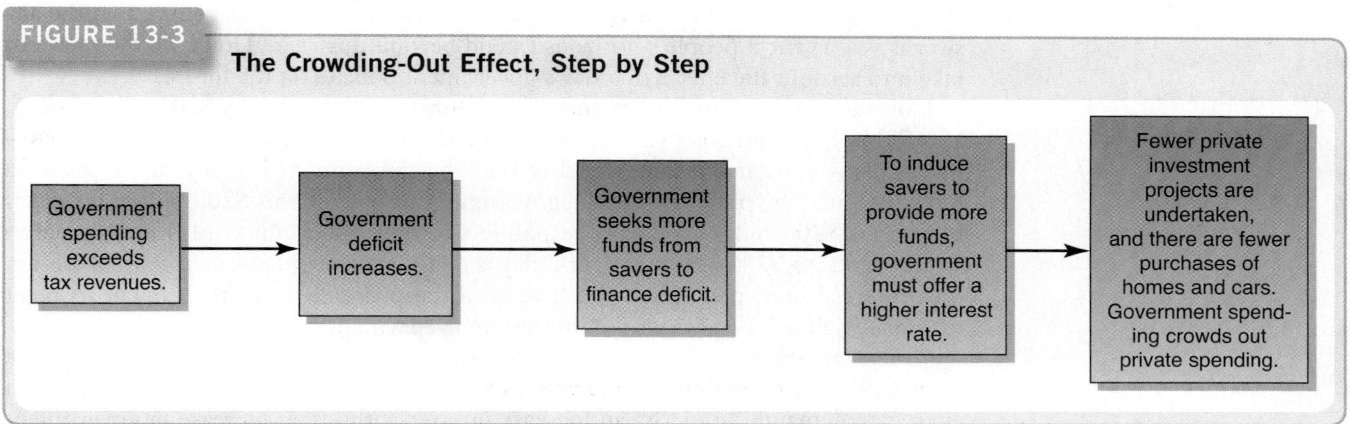

FIGURE 13-4

The Crowding-Out Effect

Expansionary fiscal policy that causes deficit financing initially shifts AD_1 to AD_2. Equilibrium initially moves toward E_2. But expansionary fiscal policy pushes up interest rates, thereby reducing interest-sensitive spending. This effect causes the aggregate demand curve to shift inward to AD_3, and the new short-run equilibrium is at E_3.

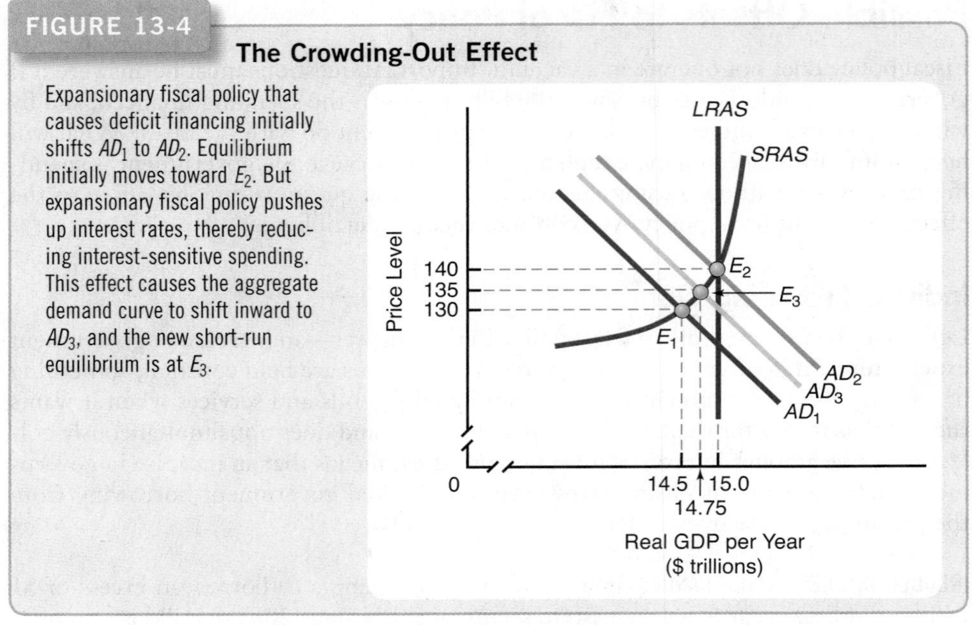

houses and cars. An increase in the interest rate causes their monthly payments to go up, thereby discouraging some of them from purchasing cars and houses.

GRAPHICAL ANALYSIS You see in Figure 13-4 above that the economy is in a situation in which, at point E_1, equilibrium real GDP is below the long-run level consistent with the position of the *LRAS* curve. But suppose that government expansionary fiscal policy in the form of increased government spending (without increasing current taxes) attempts to shift aggregate demand from AD_1 to AD_2. In the absence of the crowding-out effect, real GDP would increase to $15 trillion per year, and the price level would rise to 140 (point E_2). With the (partial) crowding-out effect, however, as investment and consumption decline, partly offsetting the rise in government spending, the aggregate demand curve shifts inward to the left to AD_3.

The new short-run equilibrium is now at E_3, with real GDP of $14.75 trillion per year at a price level of 135. In other words, crowding out dilutes the effect of expansionary fiscal policy, and a recessionary gap remains.

Planning for the Future: The Ricardian Equivalence Theorem

Economists have often implicitly assumed that people look at changes in taxes or changes in government spending only in the present. What if people actually think about the size of *future* tax payments? Does this have an effect on how they react to an increase in government spending with no current tax increases? Some economists believe that the answer is yes. What if people's horizons extend beyond this year? Don't we then have to take into account the effects of today's government policies on the future?

Consider an example. The government wants to reduce taxes by $200 billion today, as it did in 2008 and 2009 via tax "rebate" programs. Assume that government spending remains constant. Assume further that the government initially has a balanced budget. Thus, the only way for the government to pay for this $200 billion tax cut is to borrow $200 billion today. The public will owe $200 billion plus interest later. Realizing that a $200 billion tax cut today is mathematically equivalent to $200 billion plus interest later, people may wish to save the proceeds from the tax cut to meet future tax liabilities—payment of interest and repayment of debt.

Consequently, a tax cut may not affect total planned expenditures. A reduction in taxes without a reduction in government spending may therefore have no impact on aggregate demand. Similarly, an increase in taxes without an increase in government spending may not have a large (negative) impact on aggregate demand.

Suppose that a decrease in taxes shifts the aggregate demand curve from AD_1 to AD_2 in Figure 13-4 on the facing page. If consumers partly compensate for a higher future tax liability by saving more, the aggregate demand curve shifts leftward, to a position such as AD_3. In the extreme case in which individuals fully take into account their increased tax liabilities, the aggregate demand curve shifts all the way back to AD_1, so that there is no effect on the economy. This is known as the **Ricardian equivalence theorem,** after the nineteenth-century economist David Ricardo, who first developed the argument publicly.

Ricardian equivalence theorem
The proposition that an increase in the government budget deficit has no effect on aggregate demand.

According to the Ricardian equivalence theorem, it does not matter how government expenditures are financed—by taxes or by borrowing. Is the theorem correct? Research indicates that Ricardian equivalence effects likely exist but has not provided much compelling evidence about their magnitudes.

Restrained Consumption Effects of Temporary Tax Changes

Recall from Chapter 12 (page 253) that a person's consumption and saving decisions realistically depend on *both* current income *and* anticipated future income. On the basis of this fact, the theory of consumption known as the *permanent income hypothesis* proposes that an individual's current flow of consumption depends on the individual's permanent, or anticipated lifetime, income.

Sometimes, the government seeks to provide a short-term "stimulus" to economic activity through temporary tax cuts that last no longer than a year or two or by rebating lump-sum amounts back to taxpayers. According to the permanent income hypothesis, such short-term tax policies at best have minimal effects on total consumption spending. The reason is that *temporary* tax cuts or one-time tax rebates fail to raise the recipients' *permanent* incomes. Even after receiving such a temporary tax cut or rebate, therefore, people usually do not respond with significant changes in their consumption. Instead of spending the tax cut or rebate, they typically save most of the funds or use the funds to make payments on outstanding debts.

Thus, temporary tax cuts or rebates tend to have restrained effects on aggregate consumption, as the U.S. government has discovered when it has provided temporary tax rebates. For instance, one-time federal tax rebates totaling at least $200 billion in 2008 and again in 2009 boosted real disposable income temporarily in each year but had no perceptible effects on flows of real consumption spending.

Direct Expenditure Offsets

Government has a distinct comparative advantage over the private sector in certain activities such as diplomacy and national defense. Otherwise stated, certain resource-using activities in which the government engages do not compete with the private sector. In contrast, some of what government does, such as public education, competes directly with the private sector. When government competes with the private sector, **direct expenditure offsets** to fiscal policy may occur. For example, if the government starts providing milk at no charge to students who are already purchasing milk, there is a direct expenditure offset. Direct household spending on milk decreases, but government spending on milk increases.

Direct expenditure offsets
Actions on the part of the private sector in spending income that offset government fiscal policy actions. Any increase in government spending in an area that competes with the private sector will have some direct expenditure offset.

Normally, the impact of an increase in government spending on aggregate demand is analyzed by implicitly assuming that government spending is *not* a substitute for private spending. This is clearly the case for a cruise missile. Whenever government spending is a substitute for private spending, however, a rise in government spending causes a direct reduction in private spending to offset it.

THE EXTREME CASE In the extreme case, the direct expenditure offset is dollar for dollar, so we merely end up with a relabeling of spending from private to public. Assume that you have decided to spend $100 on groceries. Upon your arrival at the checkout counter, you find a U.S. Department of Agriculture official. She announces that she will pay for your groceries—but only the ones in the cart. Here increased government spending is $100. You leave the store in bliss. But just as you are deciding how to spend the $100, an Internal Revenue Service agent appears. He announces that as a result of the current budgetary crisis, your taxes are going to rise by $100. You have to pay on the spot. Increases in taxes have now been $100. We have a balanced-budget increase in government spending. In this scenario, *total* spending does not change. We simply end up with higher government spending, which directly offsets exactly an equal reduction in consumption. Aggregate demand and GDP are unchanged. Otherwise stated, if there is a full direct expenditure offset, the government spending multiplier is zero.

THE LESS EXTREME CASE Much government spending has a private-sector substitute. When government expenditures increase, private spending tends to decline somewhat (but generally not dollar for dollar), thereby mitigating the upward impact on total aggregate demand. To the extent that there are some direct expenditure offsets to expansionary fiscal policy, predicted changes in aggregate demand will be lessened. Consequently, real GDP and the price level will be less affected.

WHAT IF... the federal government seeks to boost real GDP by funding health care expenditures that people had already planned to undertake on their own?

In recent years, the U.S. government has shifted a larger share of discretionary expenditures toward construction of more public hospitals and clinics. A number of politicians have suggested that such federal health care spending adds to total planned expenditures in today's dampened economy. In many instances, however, private health care companies had originally planned to expand their facilities in response to an increasing demand for health care by an aging U.S. population. When the federal government funded construction of competing hospitals and clinics, the private firms' intended capital investments were no longer economically viable. Thus, public health care facilities were built, and private facilities were not constructed after all. Direct fiscal offsets occurred, and, on net, total planned expenditures did not change.

The Supply-Side Effects of Changes in Taxes

We have talked about changing taxes and changing government spending, the traditional tools of fiscal policy. Let's now consider the possibility of changing *marginal* tax rates.

ALTERING MARGINAL TAX RATES Recall from Chapter 6 that the marginal tax rate is the rate applied to the last, or highest, bracket of taxable income. In our federal tax system, higher marginal tax rates are applied as income rises. In that sense, the United States has a progressive federal individual income tax system. Expansionary fiscal policy could involve reducing marginal tax rates. Advocates of such changes argue that lower tax rates will lead to an increase in productivity. They contend that individuals will work harder and longer, save more, and invest more and that increased productivity will lead to more economic growth, which will lead to higher real GDP. The government, by applying lower marginal tax rates, will not necessarily lose tax revenues, for the lower marginal tax rates will be applied to a growing tax base because of economic growth—after all, tax revenues are the product of a tax rate times a tax base.

The relationship between tax rates and tax revenues, which you may recall from the discussion of sales taxes in Chapter 6, is sometimes called the *Laffer curve*, named after economist Arthur Laffer, who explained the relationship to some journalists and politicians in 1974. It is reproduced in Figure 13-5 on the facing page. On the vertical axis are tax revenues, and on the horizontal axis is the marginal tax rate. As you can see, total tax revenues initially rise but then eventually fall as the tax rate continues to increase after reaching some unspecified tax-revenue-maximizing rate at the top of the curve.

SUPPLY-SIDE ECONOMICS People who support the notion that reducing tax rates does not necessarily lead to reduced tax revenues are called supply-side economists. **Supply-side economics** involves changing the tax structure to create incentives to increase productivity. Due to a shift in the aggregate supply curve to the right, there can be greater real GDP without upward pressure on the price level.

Supply-side economics
The suggestion that creating incentives for individuals and firms to increase productivity will cause the aggregate supply curve to shift outward.

Consider the supply-side effects of changes in marginal tax rates on labor. An increase in tax rates reduces the opportunity cost of leisure, thereby inducing individuals to reduce their work effort and to consume more leisure. But an increase in tax rates

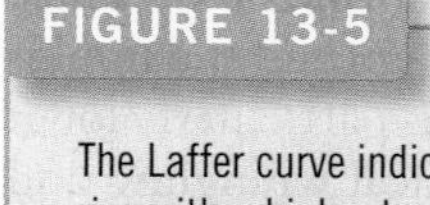

FIGURE 13-5

Laffer Curve

The Laffer curve indicates that tax revenues initially rise with a higher tax rate. Eventually, however, tax revenues decline as the tax rate increases.

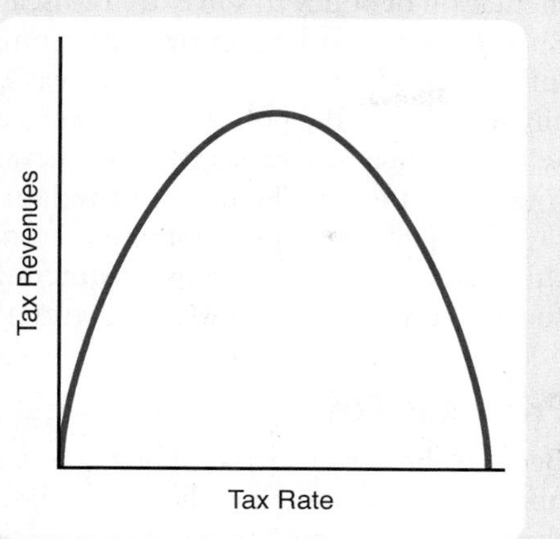

will also reduce spendable income, thereby shifting the demand curve for leisure inward to the left, which tends to increase work effort. The outcome of these two effects on the choice of leisure (and thus work) depends on which of them is stronger. Supply-side economists argue that the first effect often dominates: Increases in marginal tax rates cause people to work less, and decreases in marginal tax rates induce workers to work more.

QUICK QUIZ See page 296 for the answers. Review concepts from this section in MyEconLab.

Indirect crowding out occurs because of an interest rate effect in which the government's efforts to finance its deficit spending cause interest rates to __________, thereby crowding out private investment and spending, particularly on cars and houses. This is called the **crowding-out effect.**

__________ __________ __________ occur when government spending competes with the private sector and is increased. A direct crowding-out effect may occur.

The __________ __________ theorem holds that an increase in the government budget deficit has no effect on aggregate demand because individuals anticipate that their future taxes will increase and therefore save more today to pay for them.

Changes in marginal tax rates may cause __________-__________ effects if a reduction in marginal tax rates induces enough additional work, saving, and investing. Government tax receipts can actually increase. This is called __________-__________ economics.

Discretionary Fiscal Policy in Practice: Coping with Time Lags

We can discuss fiscal policy in a relatively precise way. We draw graphs with aggregate demand and supply curves to show what we are doing. We could in principle estimate the offsets that we just discussed. Even if we were able to measure all of these offsets exactly, however, would-be fiscal policymakers still face a problem: The conduct of fiscal policy involves a variety of time lags.

Policy Time Lags

Policymakers must take time lags into account. Not only is it difficult to measure economic variables, but it also takes time to collect and assimilate such data. Consequently, policymakers must contend with the **recognition time lag,** the months that may elapse before national economic problems can be identified.

Recognition time lag
The time required to gather information about the current state of the economy.

Action time lag
The time between recognizing an economic problem and implementing policy to solve it. The action time lag is quite long for fiscal policy, which requires congressional approval.

Effect time lag
The time that elapses between the implementation of a policy and the results of that policy.

After an economic problem is recognized, a solution must be formulated. Thus, there will be an **action time lag** between the recognition of a problem and the implementation of policy to solve it. For fiscal policy, the action time lag is particularly long. Such policy must be approved by Congress and is subject to political wrangling and infighting. The action time lag can easily last a year or two. Then it takes time to actually implement the policy. After Congress enacts fiscal policy legislation, it takes time to decide such matters as who gets new federal construction contracts.

Finally, there is the **effect time lag:** After fiscal policy is enacted, it takes time for the policy to affect the economy. To demonstrate the effects, economists need only shift curves on a chalkboard, a whiteboard, or a piece of paper, but in the real world, such effects take quite a while to work their way through the economy.

Problems Posed by Time Lags

Because the various fiscal policy time lags are long, a policy designed to combat a significant recession such as the recession of the late 2000s might not produce results until the economy is already out of that recession and perhaps experiencing inflation, in which case the fiscal policy action would worsen the situation. Or a fiscal policy designed to eliminate inflation might not produce effects until the economy is in a recession. In that case, too, fiscal policy would make the economic problem worse rather than better.

Furthermore, because fiscal policy time lags tend to be *variable* (each lasting anywhere from one to three years), policymakers have a difficult time fine-tuning the economy. Clearly, fiscal policy is more guesswork than science.

YOU ARE THERE

To consider a specific example of how time lags can slow the economic effects of fiscal policy, take a look at **Why a Federal Stimulus Project Took Time to Provide Stimulus** on page 291.

Automatic Stabilizers

Automatic, or built-in, stabilizers
Special provisions of certain federal programs that cause changes in desired aggregate expenditures without the action of Congress and the president. Examples are the federal progressive tax system and unemployment compensation.

Not all changes in taxes (or in tax rates) or in government spending (including government transfers) constitute discretionary fiscal policy. There are several types of automatic (or nondiscretionary) fiscal policies. Such policies do not require new legislation on the part of Congress. Specific automatic fiscal policies—called **automatic,** or **built-in, stabilizers**—include the tax system itself, unemployment compensation, and income transfer payments.

The Tax System as an Automatic Stabilizer

You know that if you work less, you are paid less, and therefore you pay fewer taxes. The amount of taxes that our government collects falls automatically during a recession. Basically, as observed in the U.S. economy during the severe recession of the late 2000s, incomes and profits fall when business activity slows down, and the government's tax revenues drop, too. Some economists consider this an automatic tax cut, which therefore may stimulate aggregate demand. It thereby may reduce the extent of any negative economic fluctuation.

The progressive nature of the federal personal and corporate income tax systems magnifies any automatic stabilization effect that might exist. If your hours of work are reduced because of a recession, you still pay some federal personal income taxes. But because of our progressive system, you may drop into a lower tax bracket, thereby paying a lower marginal tax rate. As a result, your disposable income falls by a smaller percentage than your before-tax income falls.

Unemployment Compensation and Income Transfer Payments

Like our tax system, unemployment compensation payments stabilize aggregate demand. Throughout the course of business fluctuations, unemployment compensation reduces *changes* in people's disposable income. When business activity drops, most laid-off workers automatically become eligible for unemployment compensation from their state governments. Their disposable income therefore remains positive, although at a lower level than when they were employed. During boom periods, there is less

FIGURE 13-6

Automatic Stabilizers

Here we assume that as real GDP rises, tax revenues rise and government transfers fall, other things remaining constant. Thus, as the economy expands from Y_f to Y_1, a budget surplus automatically arises. As the economy contracts from Y_f to Y_2, a budget deficit automatically arises. Such automatic changes tend to drive the economy back toward its full-employment real GDP.

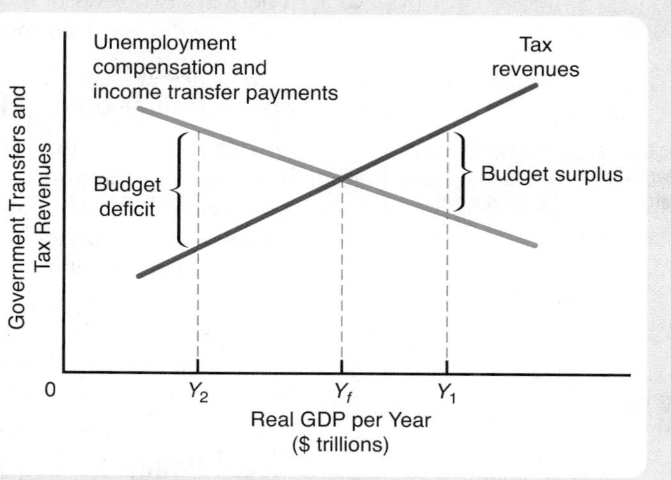

unemployment, and consequently fewer unemployment payments are made to the labor force. Less purchasing power is being added to the economy because fewer unemployment checks are paid out. In contrast, during recessions the opposite is true.

Income transfer payments act similarly as an automatic stabilizer. When a recession occurs, more people become eligible for income transfer payments, such as Supplemental Security Income and Temporary Assistance to Needy Families. Therefore, those people do not experience as dramatic a drop in disposable income as they otherwise would have.

Stabilizing Impact

The key stabilizing impact of our tax system, unemployment compensation, and income transfer payments is their ability to mitigate changes in disposable income, consumption, and the equilibrium level of real GDP. If disposable income is prevented from falling as much as it otherwise would during a recession, the downturn will be moderated. In contrast, if disposable income is prevented from rising as rapidly as it otherwise would during a boom, the boom is less likely to get out of hand. The progressive income tax and unemployment compensation thus provide automatic stabilization to the economy. We present the argument graphically in Figure 13-6 above.

Does the current state of the business cycle influence the effects of fiscal policy actions on real GDP?

POLICY EXAMPLE

Do Fiscal Policy Effects Vary as Real GDP Rises or Falls?

Alan Auerbach and Yuriy Gorodnichenko of the University of California at Berkeley have recently estimated the impacts of discretionary fiscal policy actions on U.S. real GDP. They found that increases in government *non*-defense spending have similar effects on real GDP during either business contractions or expansions. The effects are relatively small, with each $1 increase in *non*-defense expenditures estimated to boost real GDP by not much more than $1.10.

In contrast, Auerbach and Gorodnichenko's estimates indicate that changes in government *defense* spending consistently have larger ultimate real GDP effects during recessions than during business expansions. During a recession, each $1 increase in defense spending boosts real GDP by more than $3.50, whereas during an expansion, the resulting increase in real GDP is less than $1.20. Thus, if the effect lag associated with a rise in defense spending is the same during either a recession or an expansion, the "bang for the buck" from an increase in defense spending per unit of time is much greater during a recession.

FOR CRITICAL THINKING

Why might boosting defense *spending have a larger impact on real GDP than increasing* non*-defense spending? (Hint: Which form of spending is least likely to be subject to direct fiscal offsets?)*

What Do We Really Know about Fiscal Policy?

There are two ways of looking at fiscal policy. One prevails during normal times and the other during abnormal times.

Fiscal Policy during Normal Times

Go to **www.econtoday.com/chap13** to learn about expanding spending and budget deficits of the U.S. government.

During normal times (without "excessive" unemployment, inflation, or unusual problems in the national economy), we know that due to the recognition time lag and the modest size of any fiscal policy action that Congress will actually take, discretionary fiscal policy is probably not very effective. Congress ends up doing too little too late to help in a minor recession. Moreover, fiscal policy that generates repeated tax changes (as has happened) creates uncertainty, which may do more harm than good. To the extent that fiscal policy has any effect during normal times, it probably achieves this by way of automatic stabilizers rather than by way of discretionary policy.

Fiscal Policy during Abnormal Times

During abnormal times, fiscal policy may be effective. Consider some classic examples: the Great Depression and war periods.

THE GREAT DEPRESSION When there is a catastrophic drop in real GDP, as there was during the Great Depression, fiscal policy may be able to stimulate aggregate demand. Because so many people have few assets left and thus are income-constrained during such periods, government spending is a way to get income into their hands—income that they are likely to spend immediately.

WARTIME Wars are in fact reserved for governments. War expenditures are not good substitutes for private expenditures—they have little or no direct expenditure offsets. Consequently, war spending as part of expansionary fiscal policy usually has noteworthy effects, such as occurred while we were waging World War II, when real GDP increased dramatically (though much of the output of new goods and services was expended for military uses).

The "Soothing" Effect of Keynesian Fiscal Policy

One view of traditional Keynesian fiscal policy does not call for it to be used on a regular basis but nevertheless sees it as potentially useful. As you have learned in this chapter, many problems are associated with attempting to use fiscal policy. But if we should encounter a severe downturn, fiscal policy is available. Knowing this may reassure consumers and investors. Thus, the availability of fiscal policy may induce more buoyant and stable expectations of the future, thereby smoothing investment spending.

QUICK QUIZ See page 296 for the answers. Review concepts from this section in MyEconLab.

Time lags of various sorts reduce the effectiveness of fiscal policy. These include the __________ time lag, the __________ time lag, and the __________ time lag.

Two __________, or built-in, stabilizers are the progressive income tax and unemployment compensation.

Built-in stabilizers automatically tend to __________ changes in disposable income resulting from changes in overall business activity.

Although discretionary fiscal policy may not necessarily be a useful policy tool in normal times because of time lags, it may work well during __________ times, such as depressions and wartimes. In addition, the existence of fiscal policy may have a soothing effect on consumers and investors.

YOU ARE THERE

Why a Federal Stimulus Project Took Time to Provide Stimulus

Shenetta Coleman directs the Detroit agency charged with spending the city's share of $5 billion that the American Recovery and Reinvestment Act (ARRA) authorized to fund insulation of private homes. Hoping to help stimulate the struggling local economy, Coleman immediately placed a want ad for contractors to install insulation in drafty Detroit homes. Soon, 46 firms responded. When Coleman wanted to start home weatherizing projects, however, she learned that she had not met the federal government's requirements for placing her ad. The ad failed to specify wages that firms would have to pay their employees, rules governing other labor standards, legally permissible forms for contract bids, and special rules for preserving historic homes.

Thus, Coleman had to start the process all over again. Two years after her initial efforts to speed government spending on weatherizing Detroit homes, only about half of the houses she had targeted had new insulation. Thus, her efforts "stimulated" the Detroit economy at a much slower pace than she had anticipated when the ARRA funds first became available.

Critical Thinking Questions

1. What policy time lag did Detroit experience in implementing the ARRA?
2. Did another policy time lag likely follow the above lag? Explain.

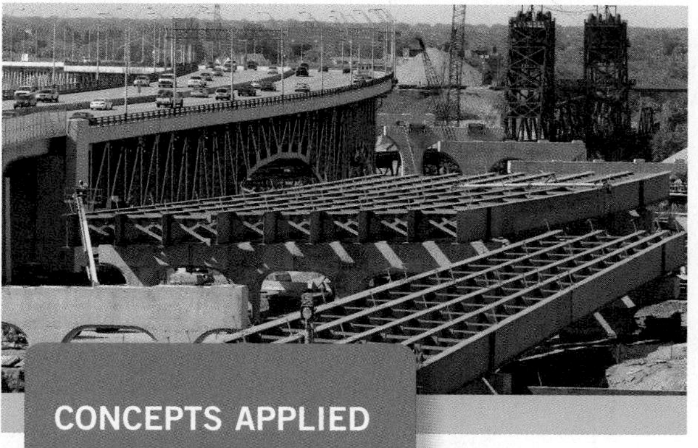

ISSUES & APPLICATIONS

How Federal "Stimulus" Was Swallowed Up by States

CONCEPTS APPLIED

- Fiscal Policy
- Direct Expenditure Offsets
- Effect Time Lag

Although the federal government directly spent some funds authorized by the American Recovery and Reinvestment Act (ARRA) of 2009, it turned many of those funds over to state governments to spend locally. The bulk of these funds contributed very little to raising the flow of total expenditures, however.

Paying Off State Debts Instead of Boosting Expenditures

Figure 13-7 on the following page displays two sets of data. One is the cumulative quantity of grants of discretionary funds transmitted from the federal government to state governments since late 2008. The other is the net amount of borrowing by state governments.

As grants of federal funds to state governments accumulated after 2008, the net borrowing of state governments declined. Many state governments were heavily in debt at the end of 2008, with borrowings in excess of $160 billion. For these states, the receipt of discretionary federal grants beginning in 2009 was a godsend, because it allowed them to start paying off a number of existing debts.

Debt Repayments Are Not Immediate Flows of Spending

The funds intended by the federal government to enter the nation's flow of income and expenditures did not reach that flow. States sent them to creditors.

Rather than direct the federal funds to *additional* spending, therefore, the state governments used the bulk of ARRA federal grants to pay off part of debts generated by spending projects completed in prior years. Most estimates indicate that of the federal "stimulus" funds given to state governments, less than 5 percent were directed toward *new* spending within the nation's flow of income and expenditures. Thus, a 95 percent direct fiscal offset resulted. Instead of providing an immediate boost in state infrastructure spending on roads, bridges, and the like, nearly all of the federal funds transmitted to state governments for spending instead were saved.

FIGURE 13-7

Federal Funds Transmittals to State Governments and Net Borrowings of State Governments since 2008

As discretionary funds transfers from the federal government to state governments increased from 2008 onward, the net amount of state government borrowing declined.

Source: U.S. Department of Commerce.

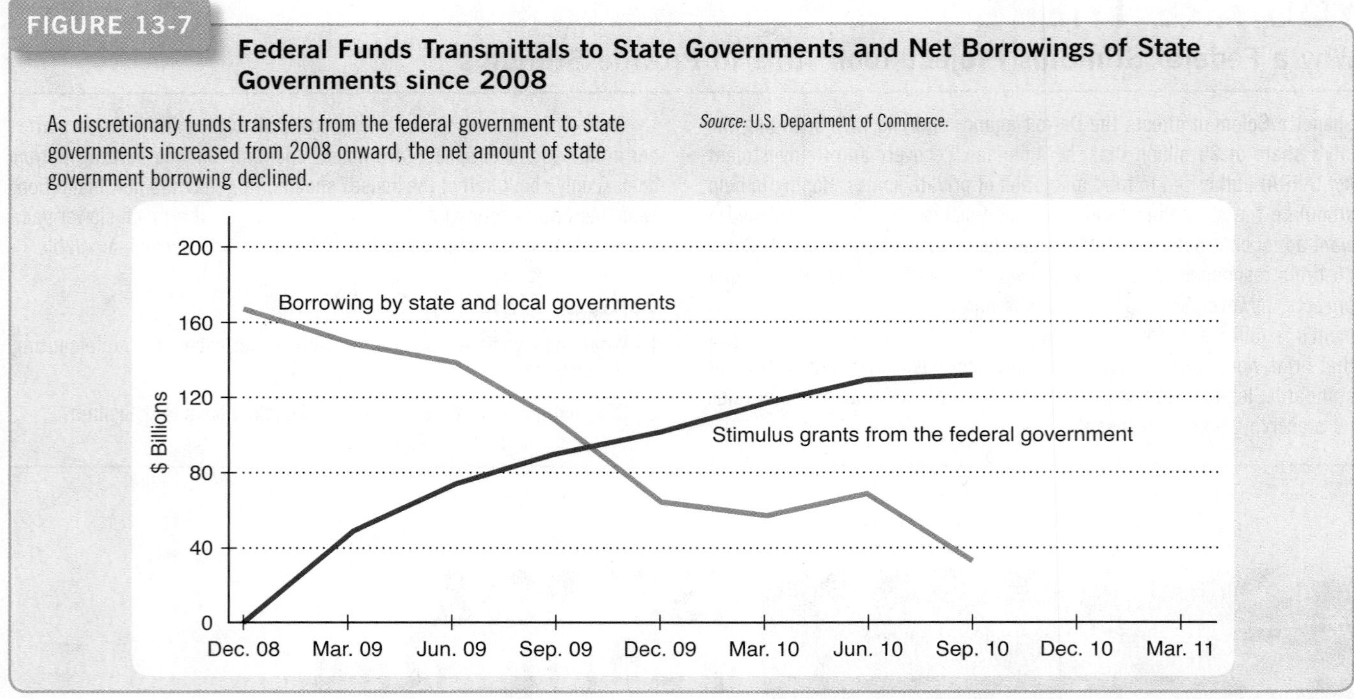

For Critical Thinking

1. Why might federal spending on roads, waterways, or national security be less subject to direct expenditure offsets than spending on health care or education?
2. What might account for the fact that estimates of effect time lags for fiscal policy often differ considerably across different types of government expenditures?

Web Resources

1. Take a look at the U.S. government's official Web site for tracking the use of ARRA funds at **www.econtoday.com/chap13**.
2. For further discussion of why directing so many federal ARRA funds to the states failed to produce very much fiscal stimulus to the U.S. economy, go to **www.econtoday.com/chap13**.

MyEconLab

For more questions on this chapter's Issues & Applications, go to MyEconLab. In the Study Plan for this chapter, select Section N: News.

MyEconLab

Here is what you should know after reading this chapter. MyEconLab will help you identify what you know, and where to go when you need to practice.

WHAT YOU SHOULD KNOW		WHERE TO GO TO PRACTICE
The Effects of Discretionary Fiscal Policies Using Traditional Keynesian Analysis In short-run Keynesian analysis, an increase in government spending or tax decrease shifts the aggregate demand curve outward and thereby closes a recessionary gap in which current real GDP is less than the long-run level of real GDP. Likewise, a reduction in government spending or a tax increase shifts the aggregate demand curve inward and closes an inflationary gap in which current real GDP exceeds the long-run level of real GDP.	fiscal policy, 280 **Key Figures** Figure 13-1, 281 Figure 13-2, 282	• MyEconLab Study Plan 13.1 • Animated Figures 13-1, 13-2

MyEconLab *continued*

WHAT YOU SHOULD KNOW		WHERE TO GO TO PRACTICE
How Indirect Crowding Out and Direct Expenditure Offsets Can Reduce the Effectiveness of Fiscal Policy Actions Indirect crowding out occurs when the government must borrow from the private sector because government spending exceeds tax revenues. To obtain the necessary funds, the government must offer a higher interest rate, thereby driving up market interest rates. This reduces, or crowds out, interest-sensitive private spending. Increased government spending may also substitute directly for private expenditures and thereby offset the increase in total planned expenditures that the government had intended to bring about.	crowding-out effect, 283 direct expenditure offsets, 285 supply-side economics, 286 **Key Figures** Figure 13-3, 283 Figure 13-4, 284 Figure 13-5, 287	• MyEconLab Study Plan 13.2 • Animated Figures 13-3, 13-4, 13-5
The Ricardian Equivalence Theorem This proposition states that when the government cuts taxes and borrows to finance the tax reduction, people realize that in the future the government will have to raise taxes to repay the loan. This induces them to save the proceeds of the tax cut to meet their future tax liabilities. Thus, a tax cut fails to induce an increase in aggregate consumption spending and consequently has no effect on total planned expenditures and aggregate demand.	Ricardian equivalence theorem, 285 **Key Figure** Figure 13-4, 284	• MyEconLab Study Plan 13.2 • Animated Figure 13-4
Fiscal Policy Time Lags and the Effectiveness of Fiscal "Fine-Tuning" Efforts to use fiscal policy to bring about changes in aggregate demand are complicated by policy time lags. One of these is the recognition time lag, which is the time required to collect information about the economy's current situation. Another is the action time lag, the period between recognition of a problem and implementation of a policy intended to address it. Finally, there is the effect time lag, which is the interval between the implementation of a policy and its having an effect on the economy.	recognition time lag, 287 action time lag, 288 effect time lag, 288	• MyEconLab Study Plan 13.3
Automatic Stabilizers Income taxes diminish automatically when economic activity drops, and unemployment compensation and income transfer payments increase. Thus, when there is a decline in real GDP, the automatic reduction in income tax collections and increases in unemployment compensation and income transfer payments tend to minimize the reduction in total planned expenditures that would otherwise have resulted.	automatic, or built-in, stabilizers, 288 **Key Figure** Figure 13-6, 289	• MyEconLab Study Plans 13.4, 13.5 • Animated Figure 13-6

Log in to MyEconLab, take a chapter test, and get a personalized Study Plan that tells you which concepts you understand and which ones you need to review. From there, MyEconLab will give you further practice, tutorials, animations, videos, and guided solutions. For more information, visit www.myeconlab.com

PROBLEMS

All problems are assignable in MyEconLab. *Answers to odd-numbered problems appear at the back of the book.*

13-1. Suppose that Congress and the president decide that the nation's economic performance is weakening and that the government should "do something" about the situation. They make no tax changes but do enact new laws increasing government spending on a variety of programs. (See page 281.)

a. Prior to the congressional and presidential action, careful studies by government economists indicated that the direct multiplier effect of a rise in government expenditures on equilibrium real GDP per year is equal to 3. In the 12 months since the increase in government spending, however, it has become clear that the actual ultimate effect on real GDP will be less than half of that amount. What factors might account for this?

b. Another year and a half elapses following passage of the government spending boost. The government has undertaken no additional policy actions, nor have there been any other events of significance. Nevertheless, by the end of the second year, real GDP has returned to its original level, and the price level has increased sharply. Provide a possible explanation for this outcome.

13-2. Suppose that Congress enacts a significant tax cut with the expectation that this action will stimulate aggregate demand and push up real GDP in the short run. In fact, however, neither real GDP nor the price level changes significantly as a result of the tax cut. What might account for this outcome? (See pages 284–285)

13-3. Explain how time lags in discretionary fiscal policy making could thwart the efforts of Congress and the president to stabilize real GDP in the face of an economic downturn. Is it possible that these time lags could actually cause discretionary fiscal policy to *destabilize* real GDP?

13-4. Determine whether each of the following is an example of a situation in which a direct expenditure offset to fiscal policy occurs. (See page 285.)

a. In an effort to help rejuvenate the nation's railroad system, a new government agency buys unused track, locomotives, and passenger and freight cars, many of which private companies would otherwise have purchased and put into regular use.

b. The government increases its expenditures without raising taxes. To cover the resulting budget deficit, it borrows more funds from the private sector, thereby pushing up the market interest rate and discouraging private planned investment spending.

c. The government finances the construction of a classical music museum that otherwise would never have received private funding.

13-5. Determine whether each of the following is an example of a situation in which there is indirect crowding out resulting from an expansionary fiscal policy action. (See pages 283–284.)

a. The government provides a subsidy to help keep an existing firm operating, even though a group of investors otherwise would have provided a cash infusion that would have kept the company in business.

b. The government reduces its taxes without decreasing its expenditures. To cover the resulting budget deficit, it borrows more funds from the private sector, thereby pushing up the market interest rate and discouraging private planned investment spending.

c. Government expenditures fund construction of a high-rise office building on a plot of land where a private company otherwise would have constructed an essentially identical building.

13-6. The U.S. government is in the midst of spending more than $1 billion on seven buildings containing more than 100,000 square feet of space to be used for study of infectious diseases. Prior to the government's decision to construct these buildings, a few universities had been planning to build essentially the same facilities using privately obtained funds. After construction on the government buildings began, however, the universities dropped their plans. Evaluate whether the government's $1 billion expenditure is actually likely to push U.S. real GDP above the level it would have reached in the absence of the government's construction spree. (See page 285.)

13-7. Determine whether each of the following is an example of a discretionary fiscal policy action. (See page 285.)

a. A recession occurs, and government-funded unemployment compensation is paid to laid-off workers.

b. Congress votes to fund a new jobs program designed to put unemployed workers to work.

c. The Federal Reserve decides to reduce the quantity of money in circulation in an effort to slow inflation.

d. Under powers authorized by an act of Congress, the president decides to authorize an emergency release of funds for spending programs intended to head off economic crises.

13-8. Determine whether each of the following is an example of an automatic fiscal stabilizer. (See pages 288–289.)

a. A federal agency must extend loans to businesses whenever an economic downturn begins.

b. As the economy heats up, the resulting increase in equilibrium real GDP per year immediately results in higher income tax payments, which dampen consumption spending somewhat.

c. As the economy starts to recover from a severe recession and more people go back to work, government-funded unemployment compensation payments begin to decline.

d. To stem an overheated economy, the president, using special powers granted by Congress, authorizes emergency impoundment of funds that Congress had previously authorized for spending on government programs.

13-9. Consider the diagram below, in which the current short-run equilibrium is at point *A*, and answer the questions that follow. (See pages 281–282.)

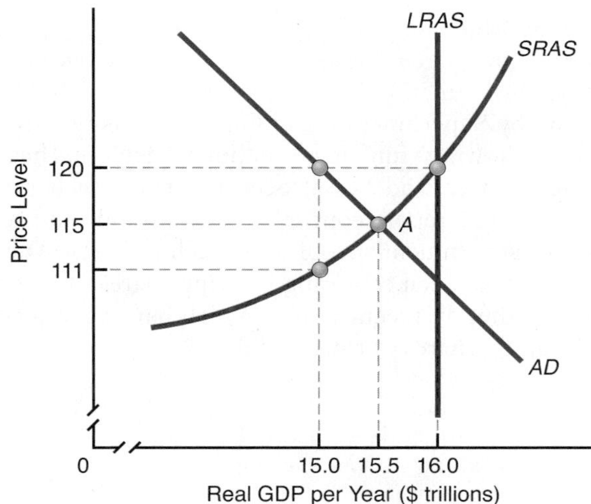

a. What type of gap exists at point *A*?

b. If the marginal propensity to save equals 0.20, what change in government spending financed by borrowing from the private sector could eliminate the gap identified in part (a)? Explain.

13-10. Consider the diagram in the next column, in which the current short-run equilibrium is at point *A*, and answer the questions that follow. (See pages 281–282.)

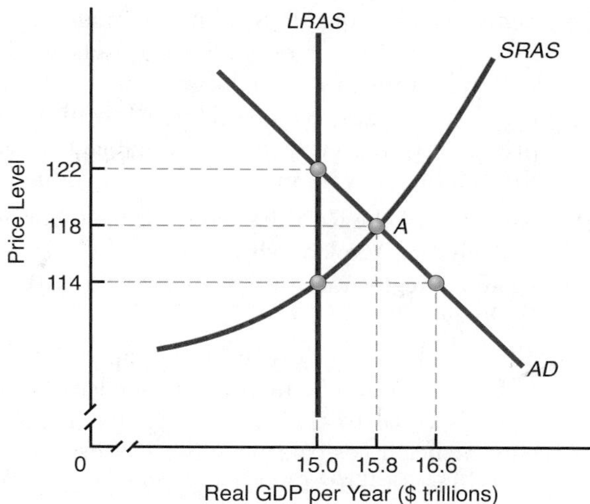

a. What type of gap exists at point *A*?

b. If the marginal propensity to consume equals 0.75, what change in government spending financed by borrowing from the private sector could eliminate the gap identified in part (a)? Explain.

13-11. Currently, a government's budget is balanced. The marginal propensity to consume is 0.80. The government has determined that each additional $10 billion it borrows to finance a budget deficit pushes up the market interest rate by 0.1 percentage point. It has also determined that every 0.1-percentage-point change in the market interest rate generates a change in planned investment expenditures equal to $2 billion. Finally, the government knows that to close a recessionary gap and take into account the resulting change in the price level, it must generate a net rightward shift in the aggregate demand curve equal to $200 billion. Assuming that there are no direct expenditure offsets to fiscal policy, how much should the government increase its expenditures? (See pages 283–284. Hint: How much private investment spending will each $10 billion increase in government spending crowd out?)

13-12. A government is currently operating with an annual budget deficit of $40 billion. The government has determined that every $10 billion reduction in the amount it borrows each year would reduce the market interest rate by 0.1 percentage point. Furthermore, it has determined that every 0.1-percentage-point change in the market interest rate generates a change in planned investment expenditures in the opposite direction equal to $5 billion. The marginal propensity to consume is 0.75. Finally, the government knows that to eliminate an inflationary gap and take into account the resulting change in the price level, it must generate a net leftward shift in the aggregate demand curve equal to $40 billion. Assuming that there are no direct expenditure offsets to fiscal policy, how much should the government increase taxes? (See pages 283–284. Hint: How much new private investment spending is induced by each $10 billion decrease in government spending?)

13-13. Assume that the Ricardian equivalence theorem is not relevant. Explain why an income-tax-rate cut should affect short-run equilibrium real GDP. (See pages 286–287.)

13-14. Suppose that Congress enacts a lump-sum tax cut of $750 billion. The marginal propensity to consume is equal to 0.75. Assuming that Ricardian equivalence holds true, what is the effect on equilibrium real GDP? On saving? (See page XXX.)

13-15. In May and June of 2008, the federal government issued one-time tax rebates—checks returning a small portion of taxes previously paid—to millions of U.S residents, and U.S. real disposable income temporarily jumped by nearly $500 billion. Household real consumption spending did not increase in response to the short-lived increase in real disposable income. Explain how the logic of the permanent income hypothesis might help to account for this apparent non-relationship between real consumption and real disposable income in the late spring of 2008. (See page 285.)

13-16. It is late 2017, and the U.S. economy is showing signs of slipping into a potentially deep recession. Government policymakers are searching for income-tax-policy changes that will bring about a significant and lasting boost to real consumption spending. According to the logic of the permanent income hypothesis, should the proposed income-tax-policy changes involve tax increases or tax reductions, and should the policy changes be short-lived or long-lasting? (See page 285.)

ECONOMICS ON THE NET

Federal Government Spending and Taxation A quick way to keep up with the federal government's spending and taxation is by examining federal budget data at the White House Internet address.

Title: Historical Tables: Budget of the United States Government

Navigation: Use the link at **www.econtoday.com/chap13** to visit the Office of Management and Budget. Select the most recent budget. Then click on *Historical Tables.*

Application After the document downloads, perform the indicated operations and answer the questions.

1. Go to section 2, "Composition of Federal Government Receipts." Take a look at Table 2.2, "Percentage Composition of Receipts by Source." Before World War II, what was the key source of revenues of the federal government? What has been the key revenue source since World War II?

2. Now scan down the document to Table 2.3, "Receipts by Source as Percentages of GDP." Have any government revenue sources declined as a percentage of GDP? Which ones have noticeably risen in recent years?

For Group Study and Analysis Split into four groups, and have each group examine section 3, "Federal Government Outlays by Function," and in particular Table 3-1, "Outlays by Superfunction and Function." Assign groups to the following functions: national defense, health, income security, and Social Security. Have each group prepare a brief report concerning recent and long-term trends in government spending on each function. Which functions have been capturing growing shares of government spending in recent years? Which have been receiving declining shares of total spending?

ANSWERS TO QUICK QUIZZES

p. 282: (i) expenditures . . . taxes; (ii) recessionary . . . increase; (iii) inflationary . . . decrease; (iv) increase . . . decrease

p. 287: (i) increase; (ii) Direct expenditure offsets; (iii) Ricardian equivalence; (iv) supply-side . . . supply-side

p. 290: (i) recognition . . . action . . . effect; (ii) automatic; (iii) moderate; (iv) abnormal

APPENDIX D

Fiscal Policy: A Keynesian Perspective

The traditional Keynesian approach to fiscal policy differs in three ways from that presented in Chapter 13. First, it emphasizes the underpinnings of the components of aggregate demand. Second, it assumes that government expenditures are not substitutes for private expenditures and that current taxes are the only taxes taken into account by consumers and firms. Third, the traditional Keynesian approach focuses on the short run and so assumes that as a first approximation, the price level is constant.

Changes in Government Spending

Figure D-1 below measures real GDP along the horizontal axis and total planned real expenditures (aggregate demand) along the vertical axis. The components of aggregate demand are real consumption (C), investment (I), government spending (G), and net exports (X). The height of the schedule labeled $C + I + G + X$ shows total planned real expenditures (aggregate demand) as a function of real GDP. This schedule slopes upward because consumption depends positively on real GDP. Everywhere along the 45-degree reference line, planned real spending equals real GDP.

At the point Y^*, where the $C + I + G + X$ line intersects the 45-degree line, planned real spending is consistent with real GDP per year. At any income less than Y^*, spending exceeds real GDP, and so real GDP and thus real spending will tend to rise. At any level of real GDP greater than Y^*, planned spending is less than real GDP, and so real GDP and thus spending will tend to decline. Given the determinants of C, I, G, and X, total real spending (aggregate demand) will be Y^*.

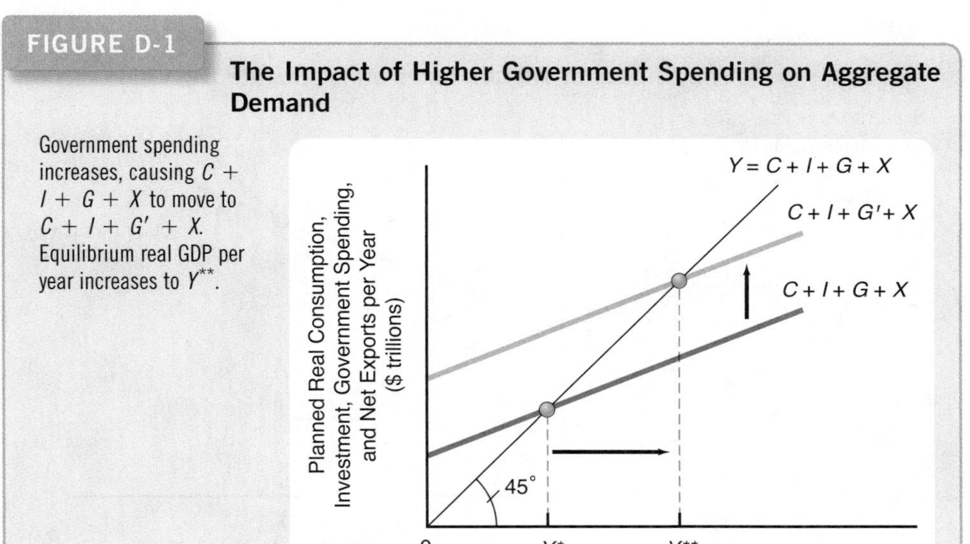

FIGURE D-1

The Impact of Higher Government Spending on Aggregate Demand

Government spending increases, causing $C + I + G + X$ to move to $C + I + G' + X$. Equilibrium real GDP per year increases to Y^{**}.

The Keynesian approach assumes that changes in government spending cause no direct offsets in either consumption or investment spending because G is not a substitute for C, I, or X. Hence, a rise in government spending from G to G' causes the $C + I + G + X$ line to shift upward by the full amount of the rise in government spending, yielding the line $C + I + G' + X$. The rise in real government spending causes real GDP to rise, which in turn causes consumption spending to rise, which further increases real GDP. Ultimately, aggregate demand rises to the level Y^{**}, where spending again equals real GDP. A key conclusion of the traditional Keynesian analysis is that total spending rises by *more* than the original rise in government spending because consumption spending depends positively on real GDP.

Changes in Taxes

According to the Keynesian approach, changes in current taxes affect aggregate demand by changing the amount of real disposable (after-tax) income available to consumers. A rise in taxes reduces disposable income and thus reduces real consumption; conversely, a tax cut raises disposable income and thus causes a rise in consumption spending. The effects of a tax increase are shown in Figure D-2 below. Higher taxes cause consumption spending to decline from C to C', causing total spending to shift downward to $C' + I + G + X$. In general, the decline in consumption will be less than the increase in taxes because people will also reduce their saving to help pay the higher taxes.

The Balanced-Budget Multiplier

One interesting implication of the Keynesian approach concerns the impact of a balanced-budget change in government real spending. Suppose that the government increases spending by $1 billion and pays for it by raising current taxes by $1 billion. Such a policy is called a *balanced-budget increase in real spending*. Because the higher spending tends to push aggregate demand *up* by *more* than $1 billion while the higher taxes tend to push aggregate demand *down* by *less* than $1 billion, a most remarkable thing happens: A balanced-budget increase in G causes total spending to rise by *exactly* the amount of the rise in G—in this case, $1 billion. We say that the *balanced-budget multiplier* is equal to 1. Similarly, a balanced-budget reduction in government spending will cause total spending to fall by exactly the amount of the government spending cut.

FIGURE D-2

The Impact of Higher Taxes on Aggregate Demand

Higher taxes cause consumption to fall to C'. Equilibrium real GDP per year decreases to Y''.

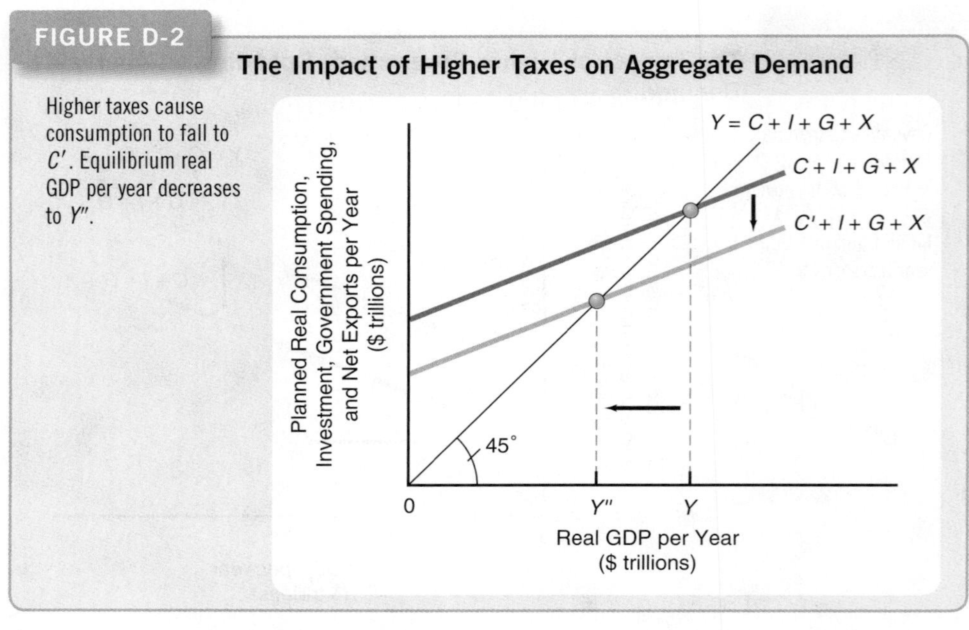

The Fixed Price Level Assumption

The final key feature of the traditional Keynesian approach is that it typically assumes that as a first approximation, the price level is fixed. Recall that nominal GDP equals the price level multiplied by real GDP. If the price level is fixed, an increase in government spending that causes nominal GDP to rise will show up exclusively as a rise in *real* GDP. This will in turn be accompanied by a decline in the unemployment rate because the additional real GDP can be produced only if additional factors of production, such as labor, are utilized.

PROBLEMS

All problems are assignable in MyEconLab. *Answers to odd-numbered problems appear at the back of the book.*

D-1. Assume that equilibrium real GDP is \$15.2 trillion and full-employment equilibrium (*FE*) is \$15.55 trillion. The marginal propensity to save is $\frac{1}{7}$. Answer the questions using the data in the following graph. (See pages 297–298.)

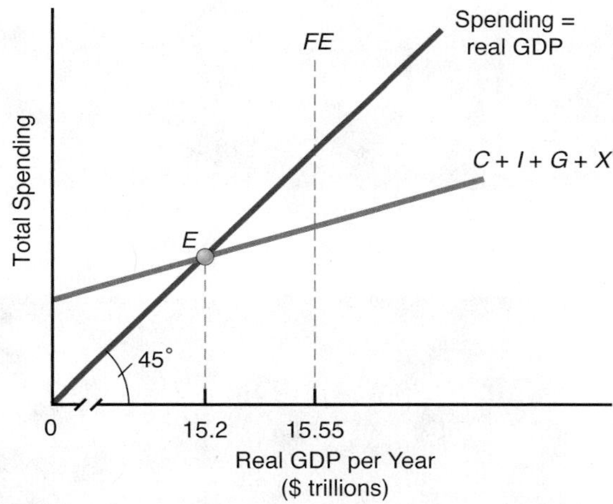

a. What is the marginal propensity to consume?

b. By how much must new investment or government spending increase to bring the economy up to full employment?

c. By how much must government cut personal taxes to stimulate the economy to the full-employment equilibrium?

D-2. Assume that MPC $= \frac{4}{5}$ when answering the following questions. (See pages 297–298.)

a. If government expenditures rise by \$2 billion, by how much will the aggregate expenditure curve shift upward? By how much will equilibrium real GDP per year change?

b. If taxes increase by \$2 billion, by how much will the aggregate expenditure curve shift downward? By how much will equilibrium real GDP per year change?

D-3. Assume that MPC $= \frac{4}{5}$ when answering the following questions (See pages 297–298.)

a. If government expenditures rise by \$1 billion, by how much will the aggregate expenditure curve shift upward?

b. If taxes rise by \$1 billion, by how much will the aggregate expenditure curve shift downward?

c. If both taxes and government expenditures rise by \$1 billion, by how much will the aggregate expenditure curve shift? What will happen to the equilibrium level of real GDP?

d. How does your response to the second question in part (c) change if MPC $= \frac{3}{4}$? If MPC $= \frac{1}{2}$?

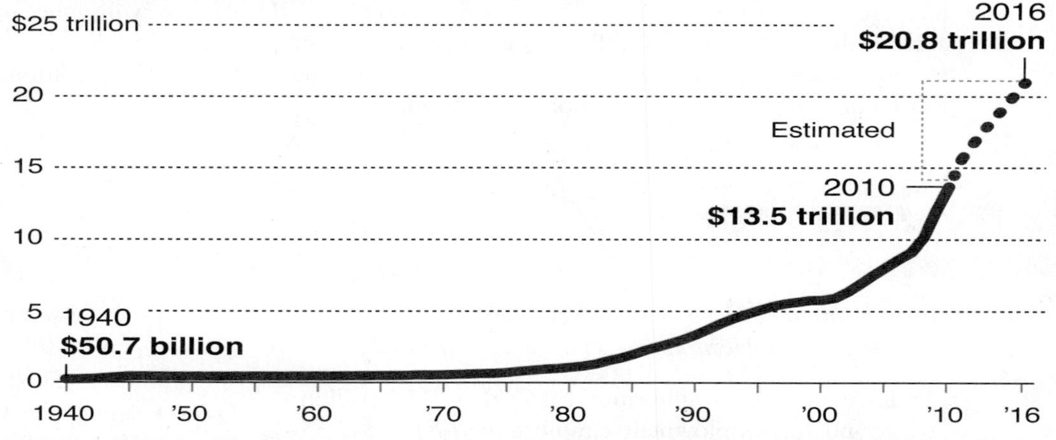

14 Deficit Spending and the Public Debt

In recent years, the federal government's total expenditures—the sum of discretionary spending and nondiscretionary expenditures on programs such as Social Security and Medicare—have been considerably greater than receipts. Indeed, total federal spending is now so high that discretionary spending eats up nearly all of the borrowed funds. Every discretionary federal spending program, including those for developing green technologies or finding cures for cancer and other diseases, has been financed almost fully with borrowed funds. Because its nondiscretionary discretionary spending has exceeded its tax revenues, the federal government has had to borrow more than $1 trillion per year to pay for its discretionary expenditures. In this chapter, you will contemplate the economic implications of this federal borrowing.

LEARNING OBJECTIVES

After reading this chapter, you should be able to:

- Explain how federal government budget deficits occur
- Define the public debt and understand alternative measures of the public debt
- Evaluate circumstances under which the public debt could be a burden to future generations
- Analyze the macroeconomic effects of government budget deficits
- Describe possible ways to reduce the government budget deficit

MyEconLab helps you master each objective and study more efficiently. See end of chapter for details.

DID YOU KNOW THAT... even though the government projected for two decades that 2020 would be the year in which tax collections to fund the Social Security program would fall below beneficiary payments, the actual year was 2011? The federal government is making up the difference by allocating a portion of regular government spending to payments to Social Security beneficiaries. Nevertheless, the federal government's tax revenues are already insufficient to cover all of its other expenditures—that is, the rest of the government's budget also is in deficit. Consequently, the federal government is borrowing from domestic and foreign residents, firms, and governments to finance a portion of the Social Security program's payments. Some elderly and disabled U.S. residents are receiving Social Security benefits from funds that the federal government has borrowed and must repay in future years.

Every year since 2001, the U.S. government has spent more than it collected in taxes. The government anticipates that it will continue to spend more than it receives indefinitely. Should you be worried about this? The answer, as you will see in this chapter, is both yes and no. First, let's examine what the government does when it spends more than it receives.

Public Deficits and Debts: Flows versus Stocks

A **government budget deficit** exists if the government spends more than it receives in taxes during a given period of time. The government has to finance this shortfall somehow. Barring any resort to money creation (the subject matter of Chapters 15 and 16), the U.S. Treasury sells IOUs on behalf of the U.S. government, in the form of securities that are normally called bonds. In effect, the federal government asks U.S. and foreign households, businesses, and governments to lend funds to the government to cover its deficit. For example, if the federal government spends $1 trillion more than it receives in revenues, the Treasury will obtain that $1 trillion by selling $1 trillion of new Treasury bonds. Those who buy the Treasury bonds (lend funds to the U.S. government) will receive interest payments over the life of the bond plus eventual repayment of the entire amount lent. In return, the U.S. Treasury receives immediate purchasing power. In the process, it also adds to its indebtedness to bondholders.

Government budget deficit
An excess of government spending over government revenues during a given period of time.

Distinguishing between Deficits and Debts

You have already learned about flows. GDP, for instance, is a flow because it is a dollar measure of the total amount of final goods and services produced within a given period of time, such as a year.

The federal deficit is also a flow. Suppose that the current federal deficit is $1.5 trillion. Consequently, the federal government is currently spending at a rate of $1.5 trillion *per year* more than it is collecting in taxes and other revenues.

Of course, governments do not always spend more each year than the revenues they receive. If a government spends an amount exactly equal to the revenues it collects during a given period, then during this interval the government operates with a **balanced budget.** If a government spends less than the revenues it receives during a given period, then during this interval it experiences a **government budget surplus.**

Balanced budget
A situation in which the government's spending is exactly equal to the total taxes and other revenues it collects during a given period of time.

Government budget surplus
An excess of government revenues over government spending during a given period of time.

The Public Debt

You have also learned about stocks, which are measured at a point in time. Stocks change between points in time as a result of flows. The amount of unemployment, for example, is a stock. It is the total number of people looking for work but unable to find it at a given point in time. Suppose that the stock of unemployed workers at the beginning of the month is 12.8 million and that at the end of the month the stock of unemployed workers has increased to 13.0 million. This means that during the month, assuming an unchanged labor force, there was a net flow of 0.2 million individuals away from the state of being employed into the state of being out of work but seeking employment.

Public debt
The total value of all outstanding federal government securities.

Likewise, the total accumulated **public debt** is a stock measured at a given point in time, and it changes from one time to another as a result of government budget deficits or surpluses. For instance, on December 31, 2011, one measure of the public debt was about $10.1 trillion. During 2012, the federal government operated at a deficit of about $1.3 trillion. As a consequence, on December 31, 2012, this measure of the public debt had increased to about $11.4 trillion.

Government Finance: Spending More Than Tax Collections

Go to www.econtoday.com/chap14 to learn more about the activities of the Congressional Budget Office, which reports to the legislative branch of the U.S. government about the current state of the federal government's spending and receipts.

Following four consecutive years—1998 through 2001—of official budget surpluses, the federal government began to experience budget deficits once more beginning in 2002. Since then, government spending has increased considerably, and tax revenues have failed to keep pace. Consequently, the federal government has operated with a deficit. Indeed, since 2009 the federal budget deficit has widened dramatically—to inflation-adjusted levels not seen since World War II.

The Historical Record of Federal Budget Deficits

Figure 14-1 below charts inflation-adjusted expenditures and revenues of the federal government since 1940. The *real* annual budget deficit is the arithmetic difference between real expenditures and real revenues during years in which the government's spending has exceeded its revenues. As you can see, this nation has experienced numerous years of federal budget deficits. Indeed, the annual budget surpluses of 1998 through 2001 were somewhat out of the ordinary. The 1998 budget surplus was the first since 1968, when the government briefly operated with a surplus. Before the 1998–2001 budget surpluses, the U.S. government had not experienced back-to-back annual surpluses since the 1950s.

FIGURE 14-1

MyEconLab Real-time data

Federal Budget Deficits and Surpluses since 1940

Federal budget deficits (expenditures in excess of receipts, in red) have been much more common than federal budget surpluses (receipts in excess of expenditures, in green).
Source: Office of Management and Budget.

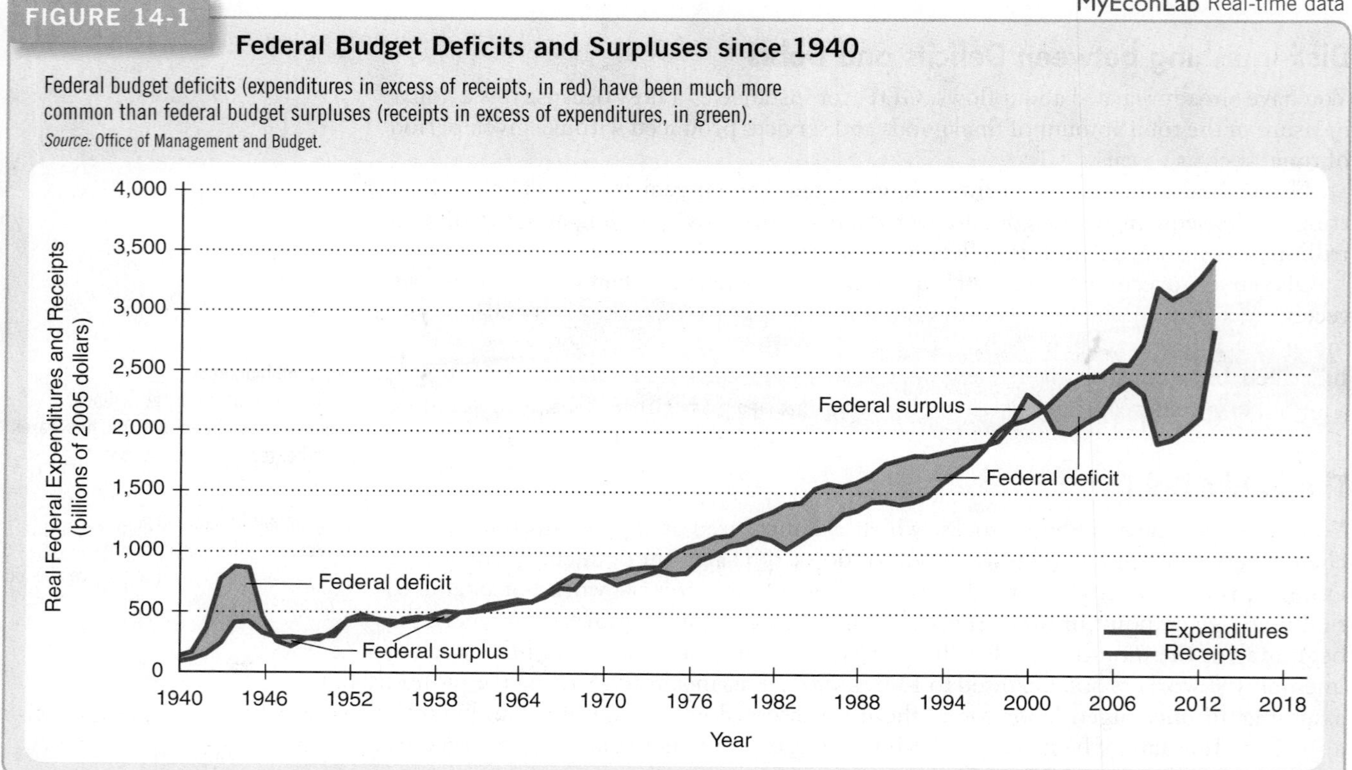

MyEconLab Real-time data

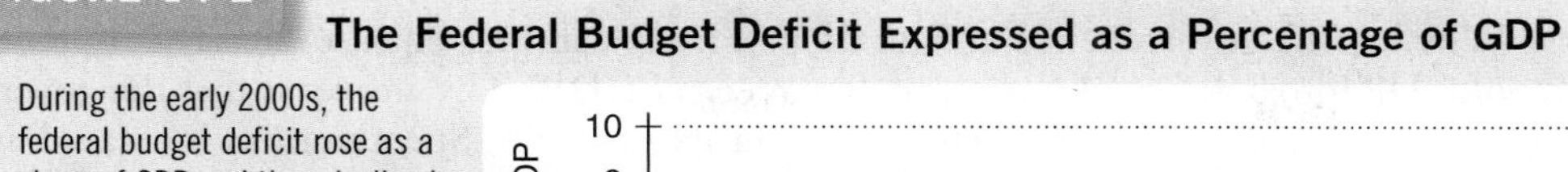

FIGURE 14-2

The Federal Budget Deficit Expressed as a Percentage of GDP

During the early 2000s, the federal budget deficit rose as a share of GDP and then declined somewhat until 2007. Since then, it has increased dramatically. (Note that the negative values for the 1998–2001 period designate budget surpluses as a percentage of GDP during those years.)

Sources: Economic Report of the President; Economic Indicators, various issues.

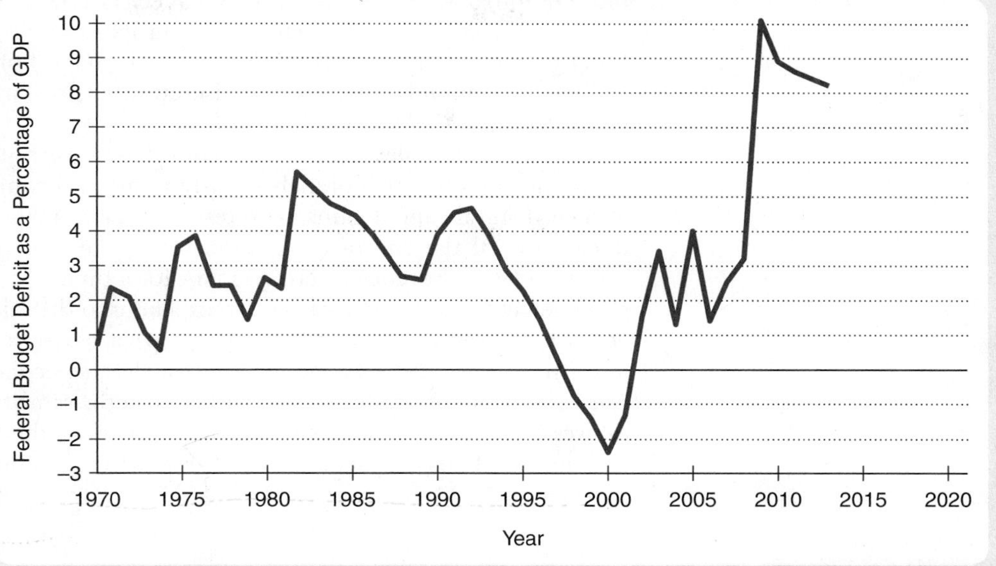

Indeed, since 1940 the U.S. government has operated with an annual budget surplus for a total of only 13 years. In all other years, it has collected insufficient taxes and other revenues to fund its spending. Every year this has occurred, the federal government has borrowed to finance its additional expenditures.

Even though Figure 14-1 on the facing page accounts for inflation, it does not give a clear picture of the size of the federal government's deficits or surpluses in relation to overall economic activity in the United States. Figure 14-2 above provides a clearer view of the size of government deficits or surpluses relative to the size of the U.S. economy by expressing them as percentages of GDP. As you can see, the federal budget deficit rose to nearly 6 percent of GDP in the early 1980s. It then fell back, increased once again during the late 1980s and early 1990s, and then declined steadily into the budget surplus years of 1998–2001. Since 2001, the government budget deficit has increased to nearly 4 percent of GDP, dropped back below 3 percent of GDP, and then risen rapidly, to more than 8 percent of GDP.

Why do you suppose some nations complain that the U.S. government performs "cosmetic surgery" on its reports about public deficits and debts?

INTERNATIONAL EXAMPLE

Cosmetic Enhancement of the U.S. Deficits and Debts?

The official U.S. government deficit and net public debt may be huge, but the reality is even worse. Most other countries' reports combine figures for *all* governments—that is, national, state or provincial, and municipal governments. U.S. reports, in contrast, typically provide only data on the *federal* government's annual budget deficit and net public debt. The U.S. federal government's budget deficit per year as a percentage of the nation's annual GDP is close to 8.2 percent.

If U.S. statistical reports were altered to include state and municipal budget deficits, about 2 more percentage points would be added. Thus, the resulting *aggregate* national government budget deficit, inclusive of *all* government entities in the United States, would rise as a percentage of U.S. annual GDP to more than 10.2 percent. In addition, if the net public indebtedness of U.S. states and municipalities were included, the aggregate net debt of all U.S. government entities would rise from more than 77 percent of GDP per year to about 80 percent of GDP per year.

FOR CRITICAL THINKING

Why might differences in the reporting of national debt and deficit levels complicate governments' abilities to finance these debts and deficits?

The Resurgence of Federal Government Deficits

Why has the government's budget slipped from a surplus equal to nearly 2.5 percent of GDP into a deficit of more than 8 percent of GDP? The answer is that the government has been spending much more than its revenues. Spending has increased at a faster pace since the early 2000s—particularly in light of the ongoing bailout of financial institutions and a sharp rise in discretionary fiscal expenditures—than during any other decade since World War II.

The more complex answer also considers government revenues. In 2001, Congress and the executive branch slightly reduced income tax rates, and in 2003 they also cut federal capital gains tax rates and estate tax tates. Because tax rates were reduced toward the end of a recession when real income growth was relatively low, government tax revenues were stagnant for a time.

When economic activity began to expand into the middle of the first decade of this century, tax revenues started rising at a pace closer to the rapid rate of growth of government spending. Then, later in that decade, economic activity dropped significantly. Thus, annual tax collections declined at the same time that annual federal expenditures increased. As long as this situation persists, the U.S. government will operate with massive budget deficits such as those observed in the late 2000s and early 2010s.

QUICK QUIZ See page 318 for the answers. Review concepts from this section in MyEconLab.

Whenever the federal government spends more than it receives during a given year, it operates with a __________ __________. If federal government spending exactly equals government revenues, then the government experiences a __________ __________. If the federal government collects more revenues than it spends, then it operates with a __________ __________.

The federal budget deficit is a flow, whereas accumulated budget deficits represent a __________, called the **public debt.**

The federal budget deficit expressed as a percentage of GDP rose to around 6 percent in the early 1980s. Between 1998 and 2001, the federal government experienced a budget __________, but since then its budget has once more been in __________. Currently, the budget __________ is more than 8 of GDP.

Evaluating the Rising Public Debt

Gross public debt
All federal government debt irrespective of who owns it.

Net public debt
Gross public debt minus all government interagency borrowing.

All federal public debt, taken together, is called the **gross public debt.** We arrive at the **net public debt** when we subtract from the gross public debt the portion that is held by government agencies (in essence, what the federal government owes to itself). For instance, if the Social Security Administration holds U.S. Treasury bonds, the U.S. Treasury makes debt payments to another agency of the government. On net, therefore, the U.S. government owes these payments to itself.

The net public debt increases whenever the federal government experiences a budget deficit. That is, the net public debt increases when government outlays are greater than total government receipts.

Accumulation of the Net Public Debt

Table 14-1 on the facing page displays, for various years since 1940, real values, in base-year 2005 dollars, of the federal budget deficit, the total and per capita net public debt (the amount owed on the net public debt by a typical individual), and the net interest cost of the public debt in total and as a percentage of GDP. It shows that the level of the real net public debt and the real net public debt per capita grew following the early 1980s and rose again very dramatically after 2007. Thus, the real, inflation-adjusted amount that a typical individual owes to holders of the net public debt has varied considerably over time.

TABLE 14-1

The Federal Deficit, Our Public Debt, and the Interest We Pay on It

The inflation-adjusted net public debt in column 3 is defined as total federal debt *excluding* all loans between federal government agencies. Per capita net public debt shown in column 4 is obtained by dividing the net public debt by the population.

(1) Year	(2) Federal Budget Deficit (billions of 2005 dollars)	(3) Net Public Debt (billions of 2005 dollars)	(4) Per Capita Net Public Debt (2005 dollars)	(5) Net Interest Costs (billions of 2005 dollars)	(6) Net Interest as a Percentage of GDP
1940	8.9	97.3	736.2	2.1	0.9
1945	492.9	2,150.7	15,372.8	28.3	1.45
1950	21.1	1,490.7	9,788.0	32.7	1.68
1955	18.0	1,360.8	8,202.8	29.4	1.23
1960	1.6	1,253.5	6,937.0	36.5	1.37
1965	7.9	1,287.7	6,627.5	42.3	1.26
1970	11.5	1,169.1	5,700.1	59.1	1.47
1975	134.1	1,180.0	5,463.1	69.3	1.52
1980	154.3	1,482.6	6,564.3	109.7	1.92
1985	344.1	2,430.0	10,247.4	209.7	3.22
1990	306.5	3,337.4	13,349.4	243.1	3.23
1995	201.2	4,421.6	16,585.2	284.7	3.24
2000	−267.1	3,853.1	13,644.1	252.0	2.34
2005	318.3	4,592.2	15,480.8	184.0	1.38
2010	1,165.3	8,125.1	29,814.3	176.8	1.35
2011	1,146.4	8,934.5	29,902.1	202.9	1.52
2012	1,189.5	10,379.5	33,309.6	201.5	1.63
2013	1,194.2	11,304.0	36,026.6	221.6	1.52

Sources: U.S. Department of the Treasury; Office of Management and Budget. *Note:* Data for 2013 are estimates.

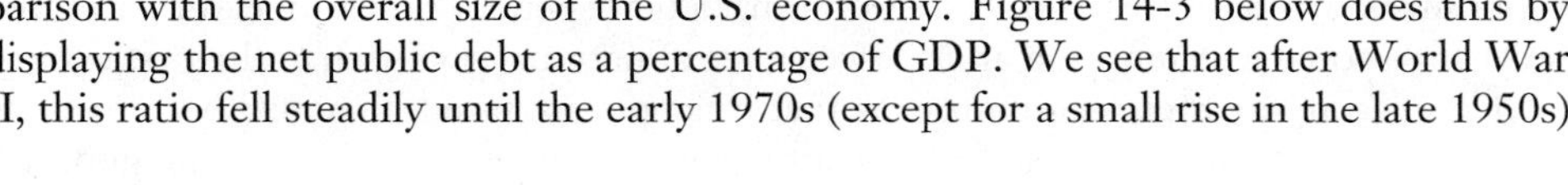
The net public debt levels reported in Table 14-1 do not provide a basis of comparison with the overall size of the U.S. economy. Figure 14-3 below does this by displaying the net public debt as a percentage of GDP. We see that after World War II, this ratio fell steadily until the early 1970s (except for a small rise in the late 1950s)

MyEconLab Real-time data

FIGURE 14-3

The Official Net U.S. Public Debt as a Percentage of GDP

During World War II, the officially reported net public debt grew dramatically. After the war, it fell until the 1970s, started rising in the 1980s, and then declined once more in the 1990s. Recently, it has increased significantly.

Source: U.S. Department of the Treasury.

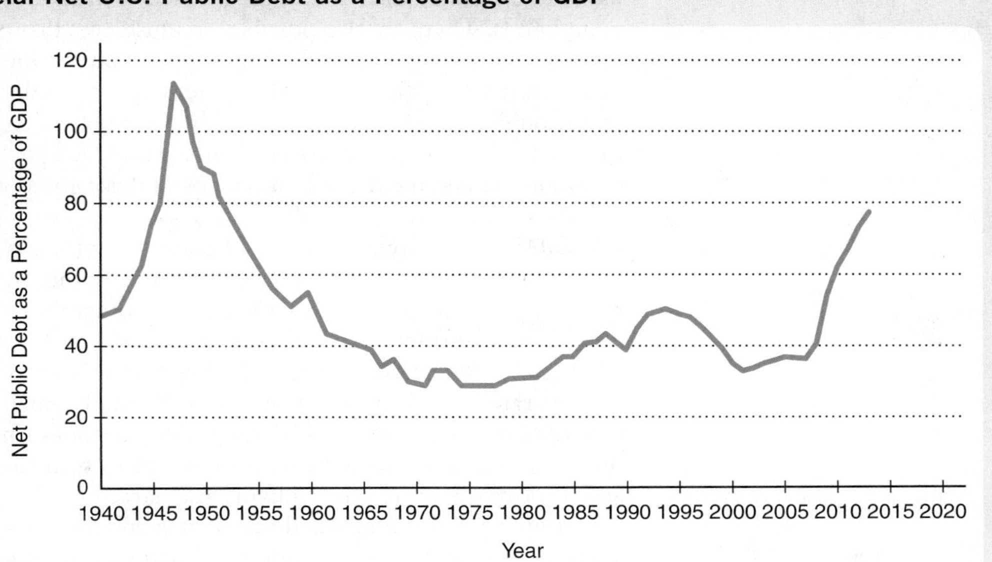

and then leveled off until the 1980s. After that, the ratio of the net public debt to GDP more or less continued to rise to around 50 percent of GDP, before dropping slightly in the late 1990s. The ratio has been rising once again since 2001 and has jumped dramatically since 2007.

Annual Interest Payments on the Public Debt

Columns 5 and 6 of Table 14-1 show an important consequence of the net public debt. This is the interest that the government must pay to those who hold the bonds it has issued to finance past budget deficits. Those interest payments started rising dramatically around 1975 and then declined into the middle of the first decade of this century. Deficits have recently been higher. Interest payments expressed as a percentage of GDP will rise in the years to come.

If U.S. residents were the sole owners of the government's debts, the interest payments on the net public debt would go only to U.S. residents. In this situation, we would owe the debt to ourselves, with most people being taxed so that the government could pay interest to others (or to ourselves). During the 1970s, however, the share of the net public debt owned by foreign individuals, businesses, and governments started to rise, reaching 20 percent in 1978. From there it declined until the late 1980s, when it began to rise rapidly. Today, foreign residents, businesses, and governments hold more than 50 percent of the net public debt. Thus, we do not owe the debt just to ourselves.

Burdens of the Public Debt

Do current budget deficits and the accumulating public debt create social burdens? One perspective on this question considers possible burdens on future generations. Another focuses on transfers from U.S. residents to residents of other nations.

HOW TODAY'S BUDGET DEFICITS MIGHT BURDEN FUTURE GENERATIONS If the federal government wishes to purchase goods and services valued at $300 billion, it can finance this expenditure either by raising taxes by $300 billion or by selling $300 billion in bonds. Many economists maintain that the second option, deficit spending, would lead to a higher level of national consumption and a lower level of national saving than the first option.

The reason, say these economists, is that if people are taxed, they will have to forgo private consumption now as society substitutes government goods for private goods. If the government does not raise taxes but instead sells bonds to finance the $300 billion in expenditures, the public's disposable income remains the same. Members of the public have merely shifted their allocations of assets to include $300 billion in additional government bonds. There are two possible circumstances that could cause people to treat government borrowing differently than they treat taxes. One is that people will fail to realize that their liabilities (in the form of higher future taxes due to increased interest payments on the public debt) have *also* increased by $300 billion. Another is that people will believe that they can consume the governmentally provided goods without forgoing any private consumption because the bill for the government goods will be paid by *future* taxpayers.

THE CROWDING-OUT EFFECT But if full employment exists, and society raises its present consumption by adding consumption of government-provided goods to the original quantity of privately provided goods, then something must be *crowded out*. In a closed economy, investment expenditures on capital goods must decline. As you learned in Chapter 13, the mechanism by which investment is crowded out is an increase in the interest rate. Deficit spending increases the total demand for credit but leaves the total supply of credit unaltered. The rise in interest rates causes a reduction in the growth of investment and capital formation, which in turn slows the growth of productivity and improvement in society's living standard.

This perspective suggests that deficit spending can impose a burden on future generations in two ways. First, unless the deficit spending is allocated to purchases that lead to long-term increases in real GDP, future generations will have to be taxed at a higher rate. That is, only by imposing higher taxes on future generations will the government be able to retire the higher public debt resulting from the present generation's consumption of governmentally provided goods. Second, the increased level of spending by the present generation crowds out investment and reduces the growth of capital goods, leaving future generations with a smaller capital stock and thereby reducing their wealth.

PAYING OFF THE PUBLIC DEBT IN THE FUTURE Suppose that after several more years of running substantial deficits financed by selling bonds to U.S. residents, the public debt becomes so large that each adult person's implicit share of the net public debt liability is $60,000. Suppose further that the government chooses (or is forced) to pay off the debt at that time. Will that generation be burdened with our government's overspending? Assume that all of the debt is owed to ourselves.

To learn about the agency that manages the public debt, go to **www.econtoday.com/chap14**.

It is true that every adult will have to come up with $60,000 in taxes to pay off the debt, but then the government will use these funds to pay off the bondholders. Sometimes the bondholders and taxpayers will be the same people. Thus, *some* people will be burdened because they owe $60,000 and own less than $60,000 in government bonds. Others, however, will receive more than $60,000 for the bonds they own. Nevertheless, as a generation within society, they could—if all government debt were issued within the nation's borders—pay and receive about the same amount of funds.

Of course, there could be a burden on some low-income adults who will find it difficult or impossible to obtain $60,000 to pay off the tax liability. Still, nothing says that taxes to pay off the debt must be assessed equally. Indeed, it seems likely that a special tax would be levied, based on the ability to pay.

OUR DEBT TO FOREIGN RESIDENTS So far we have been assuming that we owe all of the public debt to ourselves. But, as we saw earlier, that is not the case. What about the more than 50 percent owned by foreign residents?

It is true that if foreign residents buy U.S. government bonds, we do not owe that debt to ourselves. Thus, when debts held by foreign residents come due, future U.S. residents will be taxed to repay these debts plus accumulated interest. Portions of the incomes of future U.S. residents will then be transferred abroad. In this way, a potential burden on future generations may result.

But this transfer of income from U.S. residents to residents of other nations will not necessarily be a burden. It is important to realize that if the rate of return on projects that the government funds by operating with deficits exceeds the interest rate paid to foreign residents, both foreign residents and future U.S. residents will be better off. If funds obtained by selling bonds to foreign residents are expended on wasteful projects, however, a burden will be placed on future generations.

We can apply the same reasoning to the problem of current investment and capital creation being crowded out by current deficits. If deficits lead to slower growth rates, future generations will be poorer. But if the government expenditures are really investments, and if the rate of return on such public investments exceeds the interest rate paid on the bonds, both present and future generations will be economically better off.

QUICK QUIZ See page 318 for the answers. Review concepts from this section in MyEconLab.

When we subtract the funds that government agencies borrow from each other from the __________ public debt, we obtain the __________ public debt.

The public debt may impose a burden on __________ generations if they have to be taxed at higher rates to pay for the __________ generation's increased consumption of governmentally provided goods. In addition, there may be a burden if the debt leads to crowding out of current investment, resulting in __________ capital formation and hence a __________ economic growth rate.

If foreign residents hold a significant part of our public debt, then we no longer "owe it to ourselves." If the rate of return on the borrowed funds is __________ than the interest to be paid to foreign residents, future generations can be made better off by government borrowing. Future generations will be worse off, however, if the opposite is true.

MyEconLab Real-time data

FIGURE 14-4

The Related U.S. Deficits

The United States exported more than it imported until the mid-1970s. Then it started experiencing large trade deficits, as shown in this diagram. The federal budget has been in deficit most years since the 1960s. The question is, has the federal budget deficit created the trade deficit?

Sources: Economic Report of the President; Economic Indicators, various issues; author's estimates.

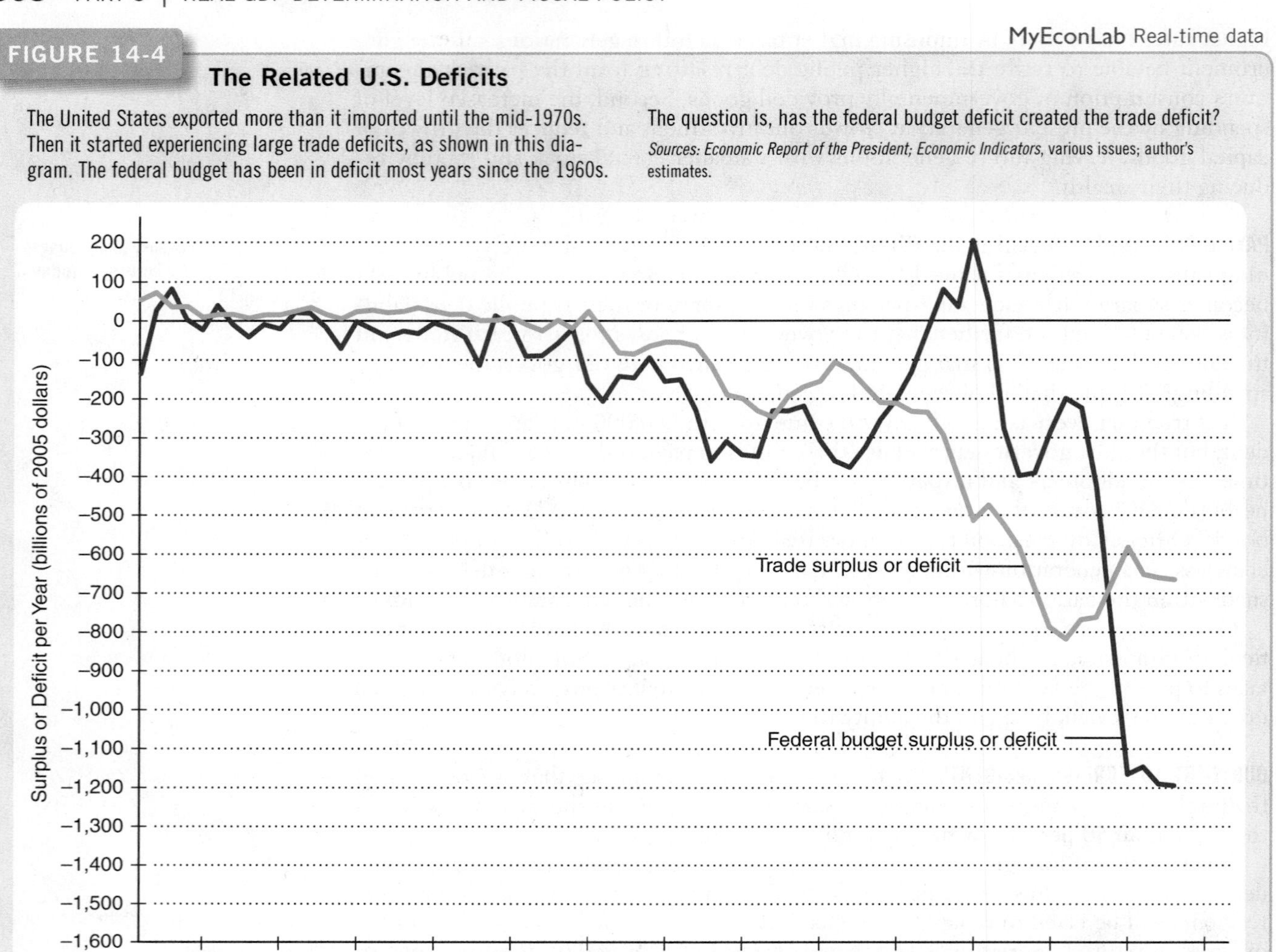

Federal Budget Deficits in an Open Economy

Many economists believe that it is no accident that foreign residents hold such a large portion of the U.S. public debt. Their reasoning suggests that a U.S. trade deficit—a situation in which the value of U.S. imports of goods and services exceeds the value of its exports—will often accompany a government budget deficit.

Trade Deficits and Government Budget Deficits

Figure 14-4 above shows U.S. trade deficits and surpluses compared with federal budget deficits and surpluses. In the mid-1970s, imports of goods and services began to consistently exceed exports of those items on an annual basis in the United States. At the same time, the federal budget deficit rose dramatically. Both deficits increased once again in the early 2000s. Then, during the economic turmoil of the late 2000s, the budget deficit exploded while the trade deficit shrank somewhat.

Overall, however, it appears that larger trade deficits tend to accompany larger government budget deficits.

Why the Two Deficits Tend to Be Related

Intuitively, there is a reason why we would expect federal budget deficits to be associated with trade deficits. You might call this the unpleasant arithmetic of trade and budget deficits.

Suppose that, initially, the government's budget is balanced; government expenditures are matched by an equal amount of tax collections and other government revenues. Now assume that the federal government begins to operate with a budget deficit. It increases its spending, collects fewer taxes, or both. Assume further that domestic consumption and domestic investment do not decrease relative to GDP. Where, then, do the funds come from to finance the government's budget deficit? A portion of these funds must come from abroad. That is to say, dollar holders abroad ultimately will purchase newly created government bonds.

Of course, foreign dollar holders will choose to hold the new U.S. government bonds only if there is an economic inducement to do so, such as an increase in U.S. interest rates. Given that private domestic spending and other factors are unchanged, interest rates will indeed rise whenever there is an increase in deficits financed by increased borrowing.

When foreign dollar holders purchase the new U.S. government bonds, they will have fewer dollars to spend on U.S. items, including U.S. export goods. Hence, when our nation's government operates with a budget deficit, we should expect to see foreign dollar holders spending more on U.S. government bonds and less on U.S.-produced goods and services. As a consequence of the U.S. government deficit, therefore, we should generally anticipate a decline in U.S. exports relative to U.S. imports, or a higher U.S. trade deficit.

Growing U.S. Government Deficits: Implications for U.S. Economic Performance

We have seen that one consequence of higher U.S. government budget deficits tends to be higher international trade deficits. Higher budget deficits, such as the much higher deficits of recent years (especially during the recession of the late 2000s), are also likely to have broader consequences for the economy.

For more information about the role of the Office of Management and Budget in the government's budgeting process, go to **www.econtoday.com/chap14**.

The Macroeconomic Consequences of Budget Deficits

When evaluating additional macroeconomic effects of government deficits, two important points must be kept well in mind. First, given the level of government expenditures, the main alternative to the deficit is higher taxes. Therefore, the effects of a deficit should be compared to the effects of higher taxes, not to zero. Second, it is important to distinguish between the effects of deficits when full employment exists and the effects when substantial unemployment exists.

SHORT-RUN MACROECONOMIC EFFECTS OF HIGHER BUDGET DEFICITS How do increased government budget deficits affect the economy in the short run? The answer depends on the initial state of the economy. Recall from Chapter 13 that higher government spending and lower taxes that generate budget deficits typically add to total planned expenditures, even after taking into account direct and indirect expenditure offsets. When there is a recessionary gap, the increase in aggregate demand can eliminate the recessionary gap and push the economy toward its full-employment real GDP level. In the presence of a short-run recessionary gap, therefore, government deficit spending can influence both real GDP and employment.

If the economy is at the full-employment level of real GDP, however, increased total planned expenditures and higher aggregate demand generated by a larger government budget deficit create an inflationary gap. Although greater deficit spending temporarily raises equilibrium real GDP above the full-employment level, the price level also increases.

LONG-RUN MACROECONOMIC EFFECTS OF HIGHER BUDGET DEFICITS In a long-run macroeconomic equilibrium, the economy has fully adjusted to changes in all factors. These factors include changes in government spending and taxes and, consequently, the government budget deficit. Although increasing the government budget deficit raises aggregate demand, in the long run equilibrium real GDP remains at its full-employment level. Further increases in the government deficit via higher government expenditures or tax cuts can only be inflationary. They have no effect on equilibrium real GDP, which remains at the full-employment level in the long run.

The fact that long-run equilibrium real GDP is unaffected in the face of increased government deficits has an important implication:

> ***In the long run, higher government budget deficits have no effect on equilibrium real GDP per year. Ultimately, therefore, government spending in excess of government receipts simply redistributes a larger share of real GDP per year to government-provided goods and services.***

Thus, if the government operates with higher deficits over an extended period, the ultimate result is a shrinkage in the share of privately provided goods and services. By continually spending more than it collects in taxes and other revenue sources, the government takes up a larger portion of economic activity.

QUICK QUIZ See page 318 for the answers. Review concepts from this section in MyEconLab.

To obtain the dollars required to purchase newly issued U.S. government bonds, foreign residents must sell __________ goods and services in the United States than U.S. residents sell abroad. Thus, U.S. imports must __________ U.S. exports. For this reason, the federal budget deficit and the international trade __________ tend to be related.

Higher government deficits arise from increased government spending or tax cuts, which raise aggregate demand. Thus, larger government budget deficits can raise real GDP in a __________ gap situation. If the economy is already at the full-employment level of real GDP, however, higher government deficits can only temporarily push equilibrium real GDP __________ the full-employment level.

In the long run, higher government budget deficits cause the equilibrium price level to rise but fail to raise equilibrium real GDP above the full-employment level. Thus, the long-run effect of increased government deficits is simply a redistribution of real GDP per year from __________ provided goods and services to __________-provided goods and services.

How Could the Government Reduce All of Its Red Ink?

There have been many suggestions about how to reduce the government deficit. One way to reduce the deficit is to increase tax collections.

YOU ARE THERE

To consider some "easy" cuts that the government could make to its budget deficit, read **A Long List of Ways to Cut the Federal Budget Deficit** on page 313.

INCREASING TAXES FOR EVERYONE From an arithmetic point of view, a federal budget deficit can be wiped out by simply increasing the amount of taxes collected. Let's see what this would require. Projections for 2013 are instructive. The Office of Management and Budget estimated the 2013 federal budget deficit at about \$1 trillion. To have prevented this deficit from occurring by raising taxes, in 2013 the government would have had to collect more than \$8,000 in additional taxes from *every worker* in the United States. Needless to say, reality is such that we will never see annual federal budget deficits wiped out by simple tax increases.

WHAT IF... the government imposed a one-time tax to pay off all of the net public debt?

The net public debt is nearly \$13 trillion and rising, while nominal GDP exceeds \$15 trillion. If the government confiscated about three-fourths of all income generated by production in a single year, it could repay the outstanding net public debt. To avoid creating more debt during that year, however, the government also would have to seize almost \$3 trillion to fund its continued spending. Thus, to eliminate the net public debt within a single year, the government would have to confiscate at least 100 percent of all income generated during that year. In theory, this could be done, but only at the expense of impoverishing the nation's residents for 12 months.

TAXING THE RICH Some people suggest that the way to eliminate the deficit is to raise taxes on the rich. What does it mean to tax the rich more? If you talk about taxing "millionaires," you are referring to those who pay taxes on more than $1 million in income per year. There are fewer than 100,000 of them. Even if you were to double the taxes they now pay, the reduction in the deficit would be relatively trivial. Changing marginal tax rates at the upper end will produce similarly unimpressive results. The Internal Revenue Service (IRS) has determined that an increase in the top marginal tax rate from 35 percent to 45 percent would raise, at best, only about $35 billion in additional taxes. (This assumes that people do not figure out a way to avoid the higher tax rate.) Extra revenues of $35 billion per year represent only about 3 percent of the estimated 2013 federal budget deficit.

The reality is that the data do not support the notion that tax increases can completely *eliminate* deficits. Although eliminating a deficit in this way is possible arithmetically, politically just the opposite has occurred. When more tax revenues have been collected, Congress has usually responded by increasing government spending.

Could taxing more of the incomes of people earning in excess of $1 million per year eliminate the federal government's current annual deficit?

POLICY EXAMPLE

Could a 100 Percent Tax on "Millionaires" Eliminate the Deficit?

Some have claimed that raising income tax rates for "millionaires and billionaires" could eliminate the federal deficit. To contemplate this suggestion, consider Figure 14-5 below, and imagine a 100 percent income tax rate on all people earning more than $1 million per year.

The last bar displayed in the figure indicates that in a typical year, the sum of *all* incomes earned by these high-income individuals is less than $1 trillion. Since 2008, however, the average federal deficit has exceeded $1 trillion per year. Thus, even if the federal government were to *confiscate* each year *all* of the earnings of people with incomes exceeding $1 million per year—thereby ending their incentives to earn incomes—this action could not cover the government's annual deficit.

FOR CRITICAL THINKING

Why do you think that most economists suggest that ending deficits without cutting spending would require the government to raise tax rates on middle-income earners?

FIGURE 14-5

Distribution of Total Taxable Income Based on Annual Taxpayer Earnings

This figure shows that the largest amount of total annual taxable income—more than $1.3 trillion per year—goes to people who earn between $100,000 and $200,000 per year. The total income received by individuals who earn more than $1 million per year—indicated by the last bar on the right-hand side of the figure—typically is less than $1 trillion.

Source: Internal Revenue Service.

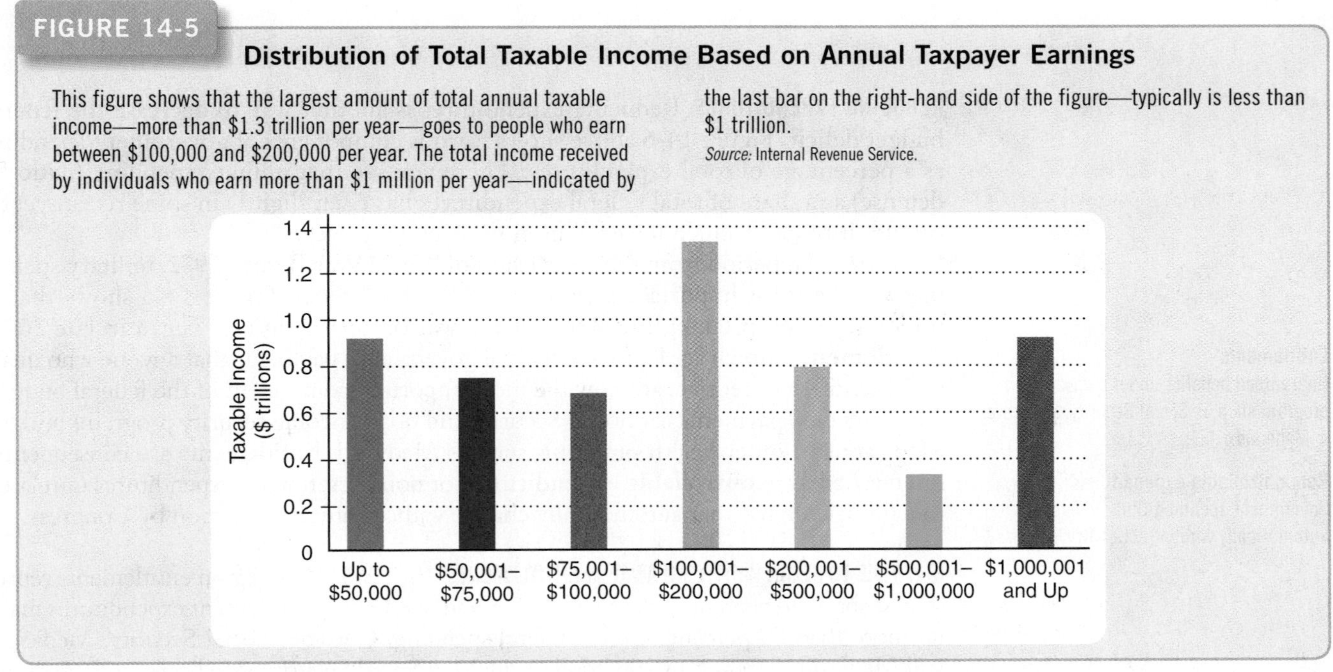

FIGURE 14-6

Components of Federal Expenditures as Percentages of Total Federal Spending

Although military spending as a percentage of total federal spending has risen and fallen with changing national defense concerns, national defense expenditures as a percentage of total spending have generally trended downward since the mid-1950s. Social Security and other income security programs and Medicare and other health programs now account for larger shares of total federal spending than any other programs.

Source: Office of Management and Budget.

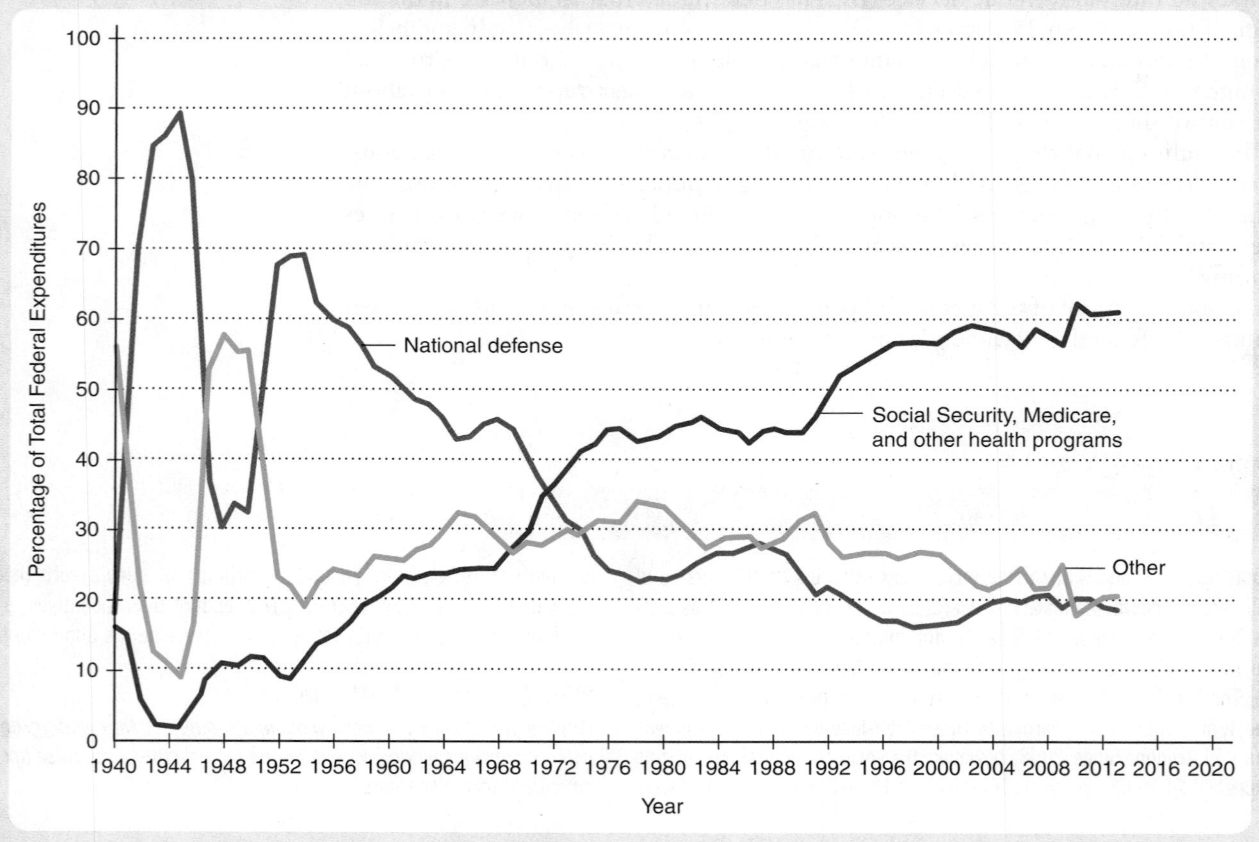

REDUCING EXPENDITURES Reducing expenditures is another way to decrease the federal budget deficit. Figure 14-6 above shows various components of government spending as a percentage of total expenditures. There you see that military spending (national defense) as a share of total federal expenditures has risen slightly in some recent years, though it remains much lower than in most previous years.

During the period from the conclusion of World War II until 1972, military spending was the most important aspect of the federal budget. Figure 14-6 shows that it no longer is, even taking into account the war on terrorism that began in late 2001. **Entitlements,** which are legislated federal government payments that anyone who qualifies is entitled to receive, are now the most important component of the federal budget. These include payments for Social Security and other income security programs and for Medicare and other health programs such as Medicaid. Entitlements are consequently often called **noncontrollable expenditures,** or nondiscretionary expenditures unrelated to national defense that automatically change without any direct action by Congress.

Entitlements
Guaranteed benefits under a government program such as Social Security, Medicare, or Medicaid.

Noncontrollable expenditures
Government spending that changes automatically without action by Congress.

IS IT TIME TO BEGIN WHITTLING AWAY AT ENTITLEMENTS? In 1960, spending on entitlements represented about 20 percent of the total federal budget. Today, entitlement expenditures make up more than 60 percent of total federal spending. Consider Social Security, Medicare, and Medicaid. In constant 2005 dollars, in 2013 Social Security, Medicare, and Medicaid represented about $2,200 billion of estimated federal expenditures. (This calculation excludes military and international payments and interest on the government debt.)

Entitlement payments for Social Security, Medicare, and Medicaid now exceed all other domestic spending. Entitlements are growing faster than any other part of the federal government budget. During the past two decades, real spending on entitlements (adjusted for inflation) grew between 7 and 8 percent per year, while the economy grew less than 3 percent per year. Social Security payments are growing in real terms at about 6 percent per year, but Medicare and Medicaid are growing at double-digit rates. The passage of Medicare prescription drug benefits in 2003 and the new federal health care legislation in 2010 simply added to the already rapid growth of these health care entitlements.

Many people believe that entitlement programs are "necessary" federal expenditures. Interest on the public debt must be paid, but Congress can change just about every other federal expenditure labeled "necessary." The federal budget deficit is not expected to drop in the near future because entitlement programs are not likely to be reduced. Governments have trouble cutting government benefit programs once they are established. One must conclude that containing federal budget deficits is likely to prove a difficult task.

By how much does an accurate accounting of entitlement promises by the U.S. government increase its measured indebtedness?

POLICY EXAMPLE

Federal Indebtedness Is *Much* Higher Than the Net Public Debt

The U.S. government's *official* net public debt has been ballooning in recent years, but its *actual* indebtedness has increased even more rapidly. Every year, Congress borrows and spends more than contributions to Social Security payments made to these beneficiaries. Thus, instead of saving these funds to finance payments to future Social Security beneficiaries, every year Congress uses the funds for other purposes. Congress likewise has promised Medicare and Medicaid benefits to future beneficiaries but has not set aside funds to pay for those benefits.

Laurence Kotlikoff of Boston University has calculated the current dollar value of all amounts the U.S. government has promised to provide to future Social Security, Medicare, and Medicaid recipients. Kotlikoff estimates that the total value of these currently *unfunded* promises amounts to more than $200 trillion. This amount, which is twelve times greater than a typical year's entire flow of national income, is almost *sixteen times* larger than the official value of today's net public debt.

FOR CRITICAL THINKING

How could the federal government try to reduce its entitlement indebtedness?

QUICK QUIZ

See page 318 for the answers. Review concepts from this section in MyEconLab.

One way to reduce federal budget __________ is to increase taxes. Proposals to reduce deficits by raising taxes on the highest-income individuals will not appreciably reduce budget deficits, however.

Another way to decrease federal budget __________ is to cut back on government spending, particularly on __________, defined as benefits guaranteed under government programs such as Social Security and Medicare.

YOU ARE THERE

A Long List of Ways to Cut the Federal Budget Deficit

Gene Dodaro, head of the Government Accountability Office (GAO), issues a report listing separately funded programs with "duplicative" objectives. Among these are:

- 100 programs related to highway and rail transportation
- 82 programs to improve teacher quality
- 80 programs to help low-income people with transportation
- 80 programs to promote economic development
- 57 programs to help U.S. residents become more financially literate
- 52 programs to promote entrepreneurship
- 47 programs to assist with job training

Eliminating the duplicative programs, Dodaro and the GAO report, would permit the federal government to cut about $200 billion per year from its annual deficit.

After reporting to Congress, Dodaro returns to his office. He and others at the GAO have accomplished their task. But only Congress can make budget cuts.

Critical Thinking Questions

1. By what percentage could a $1 trillion annual deficit be reduced if Congress were to enact the spending cuts identified by Dodaro and the GAO?
2. How much less would be added to the net public debt every year if duplicative programs were eliminated?

Rising deficit threatens U.S. credit rating

Standard & Poor's warned that it could downgrade the United States' sterling debt rating if the White House and Congress fail to reach a deal to control the massive federal deficit, which is feeding the nation's debt. Here is a look at growth of the debt in recent decades.

Annual gross national debt in trillions of dollars

$25 trillion
20
15
10
5
1940 **$50.7 billion**
2010 **$13.5 trillion**
Estimated
2016 **$20.8 trillion**
'90 '00 '10 '16

ISSUES & APPLICATIONS

Borrowing Total Discretionary Spending—And More

CONCEPTS APPLIED

- Government Budget Deficit
- Entitlements
- Noncontrollable Expenditures

Since 2008, higher federal budget deficits have had three causes: lower tax revenues, higher discretionary spending, and greater entitlement expenditures. Tax revenues have dropped so much that in some recent years, the government has borrowed to fund *all* discretionary spending.

The Share of Tax Revenues Going to Discretionary Spending

Figure 14-6 on page 312 shows that the share of total federal spending on entitlements has increased during the past 20 years. How has this trend affected the government's ability to fund its *discretionary* spending? Figure 14-7 below displays the percentage of tax revenues available to apply toward discretionary spending—that is, after paying for entitlement expenditures—since the early 1990s. During the late 1990s, this percentage rose above 100 percent, meaning that the federal government officially operated with surpluses and paid down some of its outstanding debts.

After the late 1990s, however, the percentage of tax revenues available to cover discretionary spending after paying entitlements steadily declined. Since the late 2000s, this percentage has dropped substantially.

FIGURE 14-7

The Percentage of Federal Tax Receipts Available for Federal Discretionary Spending

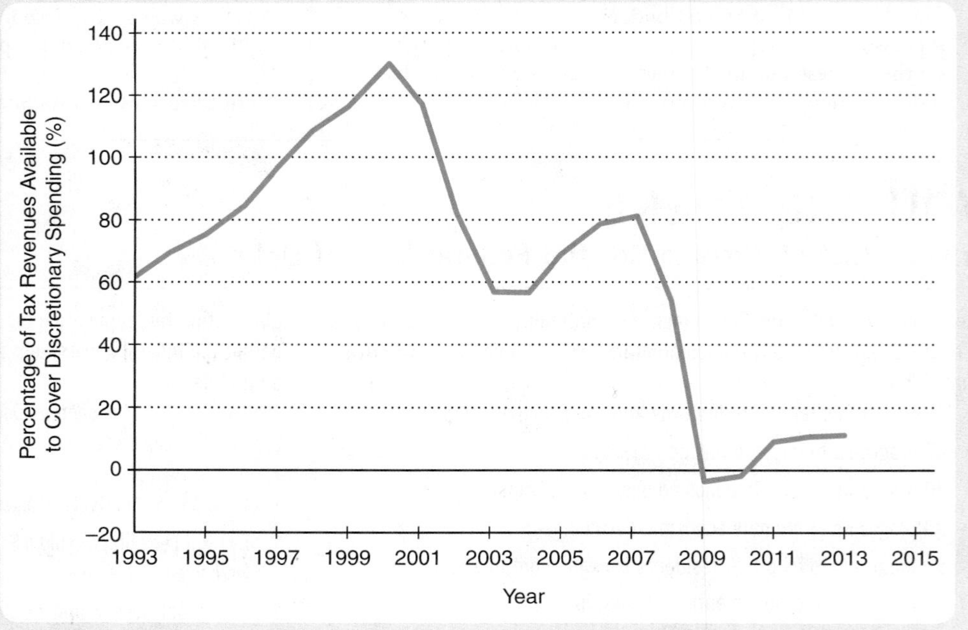

The share of federal tax revenues available for discretionary spending after paying for entitlement expenditures declined after the late 1990s and has fallen considerably since the mid-2000s. Indeed, during some recent years the percentage of federal tax receipts allocated to discretionary spending has even dropped to or below zero. Within these intervals, the federal government has had to borrow funds to finance all of its discretionary spending plus part of its noncontrollable expenditures on entitlements.

Source: Congressional Budget Office.

Indeed, during periods in which the percentage of tax revenues available to allocate to discretionary spending has been zero or negative, the federal government's tax revenues have been insufficient to pay for *any* of its discretionary spending. During these intervals, *all* discretionary spending has been financed with borrowed funds.

Borrowing in Part to Cover Entitlement Spending

When the share of federal tax revenues allocated to discretionary spending is below zero, the government borrows *more* than the amount of its discretionary spending. During these intervals, the government borrows funds to help pay some of its noncontrollable expenditures on entitlements as well as to cover its discretionary spending.

For Critical Thinking

1. What would be true of entitlement spending if the percentage of taxes allocated to discretionary spending rose to 100 percent and the federal budget was balanced? (Hint: Under a balanced budget, tax revenues equal the sum of discretionary and nondiscretionary expenditures.)
2. How would entitlement spending be funded if tax revenues just covered discretionary spending and there was a government budget deficit?

Web Resources

1. To review recent trends in federal discretionary and entitlement expenditures, go to **www.econtoday.com/chap14**.
2. For projections of federal entitlement expenditures for the first half of this century, go to **www.econtoday.com/chap14**.

MyEconLab

For more questions on this chapter's Issues & Applications, go to **MyEconLab**. In the Study Plan for this chapter, select Section N: News.

MyEconLab

Here is what you should know after reading this chapter. MyEconLab will help you identify what you know, and where to go when you need to practice.

WHAT YOU SHOULD KNOW		WHERE TO GO TO PRACTICE
Federal Government Budget Deficits A budget deficit occurs whenever the flow of government expenditures exceeds the flow of government revenues during a period of time. If government expenditures are less than government revenues during a given interval, a budget surplus occurs. The government operates with a balanced budget during a specific period if its expenditures equal its revenues. The deficit recently has risen to more than 8 percent of GDP.	government budget deficit, 301 balanced budget, 301 government budget surplus, 301 public debt, 302 **Key Figures** Figure 14-1, 302 Figure 14-2, 303	• MyEconLab Study Plans 14.1, 14.2 • Animated Figures 14-1, 14-2
The Public Debt The federal budget deficit is a flow, whereas accumulated budget deficits are a stock, called the public debt. The gross public debt is the stock of total government bonds, and the net public debt is the difference between the gross public debt and the amount of government agencies' holdings of government bonds. In recent years, the net public debt as a share of GDP has exceeded 70 percent of GDP.	gross public debt, 304 net public debt, 304 **Key Figure** Figure 14-3, 305	• MyEconLab Study Plan 14.3 • Figure 14-3

MyEconLab *continued*

WHAT YOU SHOULD KNOW		WHERE TO GO TO PRACTICE
How the Public Debt Might Prove a Burden to Future Generations People taxed at a higher rate must forgo private consumption as society substitutes government goods for private goods. Any current crowding out of investment as a consequence of additional debt accumulation can reduce capital formation and future economic growth. Furthermore, if capital invested by foreign residents who purchase some of the U.S. public debt has not been productively used, future generations will be worse off.	**Key Figure** Figure 14-4, 308	• MyEconLab Study Plans 14.3, 14.4 • Animated Figure 14-4
The Macroeconomic Effects of Government Budget Deficits Higher government deficits contribute to a rise in total planned expenditures and aggregate demand. If there is a short-run recessionary gap, higher government deficits can thereby push equilibrium real GDP toward the full-employment level. If the economy is already at the full-employment level of real GDP, however, then a higher deficit creates a short-run inflationary gap.		• MyEconLab Study Plan 14.5
Possible Ways to Reduce the Government Budget Deficit Suggested ways to reduce the deficit are to increase taxes, particularly on the rich, and to reduce expenditures, particularly on entitlements, defined as guaranteed benefits under government programs such as Social Security and Medicare.	entitlements, 312 noncontrollable expenditures, 312 **Key Figure** Figure 14-6, 312	• MyEconLab Study Plan 14.5 • Animated Figure 14-6

Log in to MyEconLab, take a chapter test, and get a personalized Study Plan that tells you which concepts you understand and which ones you need to review. From there, MyEconLab will give you further practice, tutorials, animations, videos, and guided solutions. For more information, visit www.myeconlab.com

PROBLEMS

All problems are assignable in MyEconLab; exercises that update with real-time data are marked with [real-time data icon]. *Answers to odd-numbered problems appear at the back of the book.*

14-1. In 2015, government spending is \$4.3 trillion, and taxes collected are \$3.9 trillion. What is the federal government deficit in that year? (See page 302.)

14-2. Suppose that the Office of Management and Budget provides the estimates of federal budget receipts, federal budget spending, and GDP at the right, all expressed in billions of dollars. Calculate the implied estimates of the federal budget deficit as a percentage of GDP for each year. (See pages 302–303.)

Year	Federal Budget Receipts	Federal Budget Spending	GDP
2015	3,829.8	4,382.6	15,573.2
2016	3,892.4	4,441.6	16,316.0
2017	3,964.2	4,529.3	16,852.1
2018	4,013.5	4,600.1	17,454.4

14-3. It may be argued that the effects of a higher public debt are the same as the effects of a higher deficit. Why? (See pages 302–304.)

14-4. What happens to the net public debt if the federal government operates next year with the following (see page 302):

a. A budget deficit?

b. A balanced budget?

c. A budget surplus?

14-5. What is the relationship between the gross public debt and the net public debt? (See page 304.)

14-6. Explain how each of the following will affect the net public debt, other things being equal. (See page 302.)

a. Previously, the government operated with a balanced budget, but recently there has been a sudden increase in federal tax collections.

b. The government had been operating with a very small annual budget deficit until three hurricanes hit the Atlantic Coast, and now government spending has risen substantially.

c. The Government National Mortgage Association, a federal government agency that purchases certain types of home mortgages, buys U.S. Treasury bonds from another government agency.

14-7. Explain in your own words why there is likely to be a relationship between federal budget deficits and U.S. international trade deficits. (See page 308.)

14-8. Suppose that the share of U.S. GDP going to domestic consumption remains constant. Initially, the federal government was operating with a balanced budget, but this year it has increased its spending well above its collections of taxes and other sources of revenues. To fund its deficit spending, the government has issued bonds. So far, very few foreign residents have shown any interest in purchasing the bonds. (See page 306.)

a. What must happen to induce foreign residents to buy the bonds?

b. If foreign residents desire to purchase the bonds, what is the most important source of dollars to buy them?

14-9. Suppose that the economy is experiencing the short-run equilibrium position depicted at point *A* in the diagram near the top of the next column. Then the government raises its spending and thereby runs a budget deficit in an effort to boost equilibrium real GDP to its long-run equilibrium level of $15 trillion (in base-year dollars). Explain the effects of an increase in the government deficit on equilibrium real GDP and the equilibrium price level. In addition, given that many taxes and government benefits vary with real GDP, discuss what change we might expect to see in the budget deficit as a result of the effects on equilibrium real GDP. (See pages 309–310.)

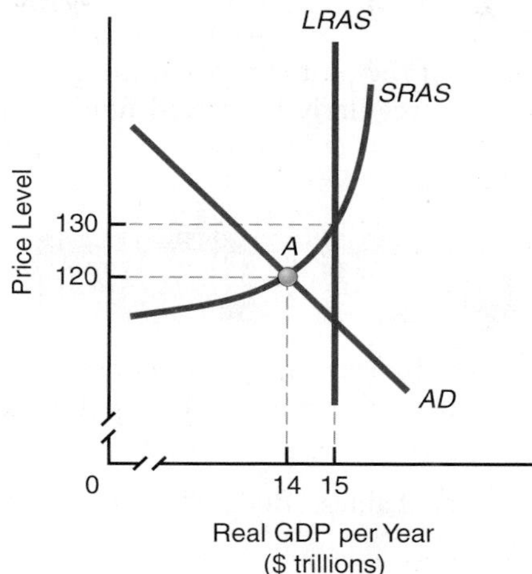

14-10. Suppose that the economy is experiencing the short-run equilibrium position depicted at point *B* in the diagram below. Explain the short-run effects of an increase in the government deficit on equilibrium real GDP and the equilibrium price level. What will be the long-run effects? (See pages 309–310.)

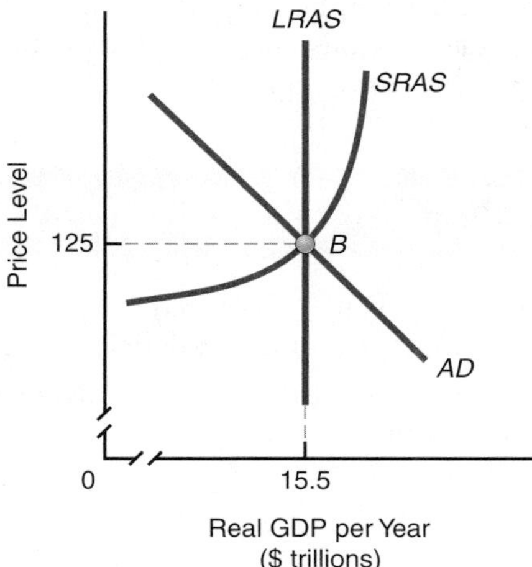

14-11. To eliminate the deficit (and halt the growth of the net public debt), a politician suggests that "we should tax the rich." The politician makes a simple arithmetic calculation in which he applies a higher tax rate to the total income reported by "the rich" in a previous year. He says that the government could thereby solve the deficit problem by taxing "the rich." What is the major fallacy in such a claim? (See page 311.)

14-12. Refer back to Problem 14-11. If the politician defines "the rich" as people with annual taxable incomes exceeding $1 million per year, what is another difficulty with the politician's reasoning, given that "the rich" rarely earn a combined taxable income exceeding $1 trillion, yet the federal deficit has regularly exceeded $1 trillion in recent years? (See page 311.)

14-13. In each of the past few years, the federal government has regularly borrowed funds to pay for at least one-third of expenditures that tax revenues were insufficient to cover. More than 60 percent of all federal expenditures now go for entitlement spending. What does this fact imply about how the government is paying for most of its discretionary expenditures? (See page 314.)

ECONOMICS ON THE NET

The Public Debt By examining the federal government's budget data, its current estimates of the public debt can be determined.

Title: Historical Tables: Budget of the United States Government

Navigation: Use the link at **www.econtoday.com/chap14** to visit the Office of Management and Budget. Select the most recent budget. Then select *Historical Tables*.

Application After the document downloads, perform each of the indicated operations and answer the following questions.

1. In the Table of Contents in the left-hand margin of the Historical Tables, click on Table 7.1, "Federal Debt at the End of the Year, 1940–2015." In light of the discussion in this chapter, which column shows the net public debt? What is the conceptual difference between the gross public debt and the net public debt? Last year, what was the dollar difference between these two amounts?
2. Table 7.1 includes estimates of the gross and net public debt over the next several years. Suppose that these estimates turn out to be accurate. Calculate how much the net public debt would increase on average each year. What are possible ways that the government could prevent these predicted increases from occurring?

For Group Study and Analysis Divide into two groups, and have each group take one side in answering the question, "Is the public debt a burden or a blessing?" Have each group develop rationales for supporting its position. Then reconvene the entire class, and discuss the relative merits of the alternative positions and rationales.

ANSWERS TO QUICK QUIZZES

p. 304: (i) budget deficit . . . balanced budget . . . budget surplus; (ii) stock; (iii) surplus . . . deficit . . . deficit

p. 307: (i) gross . . . net; (ii) future . . . current . . . less . . . lower; (iii) higher

p. 310: (i) more . . . exceed . . . deficit; (ii) recessionary . . . above; (iii) privately . . . government

p. 313: (i) deficits; (ii) deficits . . . entitlements

Money, Banking, and Central Banking

15

LEARNING OBJECTIVES

After reading this chapter, you should be able to:

- Define the fundamental functions of money and identify key properties that any good that functions as money must possess
- Explain official definitions of the quantity of money in circulation
- Understand why financial intermediaries such as banks exist
- Describe the basic structure and functions of the Federal Reserve System
- Determine the maximum potential extent that the money supply will change following a Federal Reserve monetary policy action
- Explain the essential features of federal deposit insurance

MyEconLab helps you master each objective and study more efficiently. See end of chapter for details.

During the early 2000s, bank managers across the United States sought to boost total deposits at their institutions, both by inducing existing customers to increase their deposits and by attracting new depositors. In the early 2010s, their efforts paid off: Total deposits at U.S. banks had increased by about 10 percent. Since then, however, banks generally have reversed course. Most banks have halted their efforts to gain more deposits, and a few even have begun actively discouraging increases in funds held on deposit with their institutions. What accounts for this abrupt change in course on the part of U.S. banks? In this chapter, you will find out.

DID YOU KNOW THAT... since 2009, U.S. consumers' use of currency and coins to make payments has, for the first time since the 1970s, increased relative to other means of making payments? In other words, consumers now are buying more items with cash. As a consequence, the public's desired holdings of currency and coins have risen even as they have boosted their holdings of funds on deposit with banks. The Federal Reserve includes currency and coins and deposits in its measure of the quantity of money in circulation. Thus, this increase in the public's holdings of cash and deposits has translated into substantial recent growth in these measures of the quantity of money.

Traditionally, the primary task of the Federal Reserve System has been to regulate the quantity of money in circulation in the U.S. economy—that is, to conduct *monetary policy.* Money has been important to society for thousands of years. In the fourth century BC, Aristotle claimed that everything had to "be accessed in money, for this enables men always to exchange their services, and so makes society possible." Money is indeed a part of our everyday existence. Nevertheless, we have to be careful when we talk about money. Often we hear a person say, "I wish I had more money," instead of "I wish I had more wealth," thereby confusing the concepts of money and wealth. Economists use the term **money** to mean anything that people generally accept in exchange for goods and services. Table 15-1 below provides a list of some items that various civilizations have used as money. The best way to understand how these items served this purpose is to examine the functions of money.

Money
Any medium that is universally accepted in an economy both by sellers of goods and services as payment for those goods and services and by creditors as payment for debts.

The Functions of Money

Money traditionally has four functions. The one that most people are familiar with is money's function as a *medium of exchange*. Money also serves as a *unit of accounting*, a *store of value* or *purchasing power*, and a *standard of deferred payment*. Anything that serves these four functions is money. Anything that could serve these four functions could be considered money.

Money as a Medium of Exchange

Medium of exchange
Any item that sellers will accept as payment.

Barter
The direct exchange of goods and services for other goods and services without the use of money.

When we say that money serves as a **medium of exchange,** we mean that sellers will accept it as payment in market transactions. Without some generally accepted medium of exchange, we would have to resort to *barter*. In fact, before money was used, transactions took place by means of barter. **Barter** is simply a direct exchange of goods for goods. In a barter economy, the shoemaker who wants to obtain a dozen water glasses must seek out a glassmaker who at exactly the same time is interested in obtaining a pair of shoes. For this to occur, there has to be a high likelihood of a *double coincidence of wants* for each specific item to be exchanged. If there isn't, the shoemaker

TABLE 15-1

Types of Money

This is a partial list of items that have been used as money. Native Americans used *wampum*, beads made from shells. Fijians used whale teeth. The early colonists in North America used tobacco. And cigarettes were used in post–World War II Germany and in Poland during the breakdown of Communist rule in the late 1980s.

Boar tusk	Goats	Rice
Boats	Gold	Round stones with centers removed
Cigarettes	Horses	Rum
Copper	Iron	Salt
Corn	Molasses	Silver
Cows	Polished beads (wampum)	Tobacco
Feathers	Pots	Tortoise shells
Glass	Red woodpecker scalps	Whale teeth

Source: Adapted from MONEY, BANKING, and FINANCIAL MARKETS, Third Edition, by Roger Miller and David VanHoose. Copyright © 2007 by Cengage Learning, Inc..

must go through several trades in order to obtain the desired dozen glasses—perhaps first trading shoes for jewelry, then jewelry for some pots and pans, and then the pots and pans for the desired glasses.

Money facilitates exchange by reducing the transaction costs associated with means-of-payment uncertainty. That is, the existence of money means that individuals no longer have to hold a diverse collection of goods as an exchange inventory. As a medium of exchange, money allows individuals to specialize in producing those goods for which they have a comparative advantage and to receive money payments for their labor. Money payments can then be exchanged for the fruits of other people's labor. The use of money as a medium of exchange permits more specialization and the inherent economic efficiencies that come with it (and hence greater economic growth).

Money as a Unit of Accounting

A **unit of accounting** is a way of placing a specific price on economic goods and services. It is the common denominator, the commonly recognized measure of value. The dollar is the unit of accounting in the United States. It is the yardstick that allows individuals easily to compare the relative value of goods and services. Accountants at the U.S. Department of Commerce use dollar prices to measure national income and domestic product, a business uses dollar prices to calculate profits and losses, and a typical household budgets regularly anticipated expenses using dollar prices as its unit of accounting.

Unit of accounting
A measure by which prices are expressed; the common denominator of the price system; a central property of money.

Another way of describing money as a unit of accounting is to say that it serves as a *standard of value* that allows people to compare the relative worth of various goods and services. This allows for comparison shopping, for example.

Money as a Store of Value

One of the most important functions of money is that it serves as a **store of value** or purchasing power. The money you have today can be set aside to purchase things later on. If you have $1,000 in your checking account, you can choose to spend it today on goods and services, spend it tomorrow, or spend it a month from now. In this way, money provides a way to transfer value (wealth) into the future.

Store of value
The ability to hold value over time; a necessary property of money.

Money as a Standard of Deferred Payment

The fourth function of the monetary unit is as a **standard of deferred payment.** This function involves the use of money both as a medium of exchange and as a unit of accounting. Debts are typically stated in terms of a unit of accounting, and they are paid with a monetary medium of exchange. That is to say, a debt is specified in a dollar amount and paid in currency (or by debit card or check). A corporate bond, for example, has a face value—the dollar value stated on it, which is to be paid upon maturity. The periodic interest payments on that corporate bond are specified and paid in dollars, and when the bond comes due (at maturity), the corporation pays the face value in dollars to the holder of the bond.

Standard of deferred payment
A property of an item that makes it desirable for use as a means of settling debts maturing in the future; an essential property of money.

Properties of Money

Money is an asset—something of value—that accounts for part of personal wealth. Wealth in the form of money can be exchanged for other assets, goods, or services. Although money is not the only form of wealth that can be exchanged for goods and services, it is the most widely and readily accepted one.

Money—The Most Liquid Asset

Money's attribute as the most readily tradable asset is called **liquidity.** We say that an asset is *liquid* when it can easily be acquired or disposed of without high transaction costs and with relative certainty as to its value. Money is by definition the most

Liquidity
The degree to which an asset can be acquired or disposed of without much danger of any intervening loss in *nominal* value and with small transaction costs. Money is the most liquid asset.

FIGURE 15-1

Degrees of Liquidity

The most liquid asset is cash. Liquidity decreases as you move from right to left.

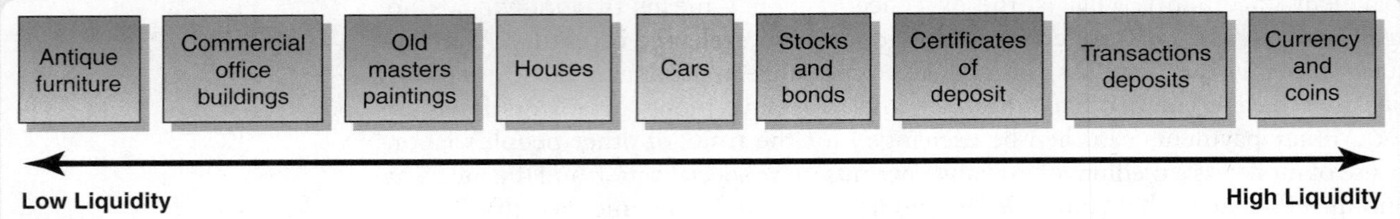

liquid asset. People can easily convert money to other asset forms. Therefore, most individuals hold at least a part of their wealth in the form of the most liquid of assets, money. You can see how assets rank in liquidity relative to one another in Figure 15-1 above.

When we hold money, however, we incur a cost for this advantage of liquidity. Because cash in your pocket and many checking or debit account balances do not earn interest, that cost is the interest yield that could have been obtained had the asset been held in another form—for example, in the form of stocks and bonds.

The cost of holding money (its opportunity cost) is measured by the alternative interest yield obtainable by holding some other asset.

Monetary Standards, or What Backs Money

In the past, many different monetary standards have existed. For example, commodity money, which is a physical good that may be valued for other uses it provides, has been used (see Table 15-1 on page 320). The main forms of commodity money were gold and silver. Today, though, most people throughout the world accept coins, paper currency, and balances held on deposit as **transactions deposits** (debitable and checkable accounts with banks and other financial institutions) in exchange for items sold, including labor services.

Transactions deposits
Checkable and debitable account balances in commercial banks and other types of financial institutions, such as credit unions and savings banks. Any accounts in financial institutions from which you can easily transmit debit-card and check payments without many restrictions.

Fiduciary monetary system
A system in which money is issued by the government and its value is based uniquely on the public's faith that the currency represents command over goods and services and will be accepted in payment for debts.

But these forms of money raise a question: Why are we willing to accept as payment something that has no intrinsic value? After all, you could not sell checks or debit cards to very many producers for use as a raw material in manufacturing. The reason is that payments in the modern world arise from a **fiduciary monetary system.** This concept refers to the fact that the value of the payments rests on the public's confidence that such payments can be exchanged for goods and services. *Fiduciary* comes from the Latin *fiducia*, which means "trust" or "confidence." In our fiduciary monetary system, there is no legal requirement for money, in the form of currency or transactions deposits, to be convertible to a fixed quantity of gold, silver, or some other precious commodity. The bills are just pieces of paper. Coins have a value stamped on them that today is usually greater than the market value of the metal in them. Nevertheless, currency and transactions deposits are money because of their acceptability and predictability of value.

ACCEPTABILITY Transactions deposits and currency are money because they are accepted in exchange for goods and services. They are accepted because people have confidence that these items can later be exchanged for other goods and services. This confidence is based on the knowledge that such exchanges have occurred in the past without problems.

PREDICTABILITY OF VALUE Money retains its usefulness even if its purchasing power is declining year in and year out, as during periods of inflation, if it still retains the characteristic of predictability of value. If you anticipate that the inflation rate is going to be around 3 percent during the next year, you know that any dollar you receive a year from now will have a purchasing power equal to 3 percent less than that same dollar today. Thus, you will not necessarily refuse to accept money in exchange simply because you know that its value will decline by the rate of inflation during the next year.

YOU ARE THERE

To learn about how private currencies are circulating widely in Brazil, read **Why a Currency Displaying a Giant Rodent Circulates in Brazil** on page 340.

QUICK QUIZ See page 345 for the. Review concepts from this section in MyEconLab.

Money is defined by its functions, which are as a __________ of __________, __________ of __________, __________ of __________, and __________ of __________ __________.

Money is a highly __________ asset because it can be disposed of with low transaction costs and with relative certainty as to its value.

Modern nations have __________ monetary systems—national currencies are not convertible into a fixed quantity of a commodity such as gold or silver.

Money is accepted in exchange for goods and services because people have confidence that it can later be exchanged for other goods and services. In addition, money has __________ value.

Defining Money

Money is important. Changes in the total **money supply**—the amount of money in circulation—and changes in the rate at which the money supply increases or decreases affect important economic variables, such as the rate of inflation, interest rates, and (at least in the short run) employment and the level of real GDP. Economists have struggled to reach agreement about how to define and measure money, however. There are two basic approaches: the **transactions approach,** which stresses the role of money as a medium of exchange, and the **liquidity approach,** which stresses the role of money as a temporary store of value.

Money supply
The amount of money in circulation.

Transactions approach
A method of measuring the money supply by looking at money as a medium of exchange.

Liquidity approach
A method of measuring the money supply by looking at money as a temporary store of value.

The Transactions Approach to Measuring Money: M1

Using the transactions approach to measuring money, the money supply consists of currency, transactions deposits, and traveler's checks not issued by banks. One key designation of the money supply, including currency, transactions deposits, and traveler's checks not issued by banks, is **M1.** The various elements of M1 for a typical year are presented in panel (a) of Figure 15-2 on the following page.

M1
The money supply, measured as the total value of currency plus transactions deposits plus traveler's checks not issued by banks.

CURRENCY The largest component of U.S. currency is paper bills called Federal Reserve notes, which are designed and printed by the U.S. Bureau of Engraving and Printing. U.S. currency also consists of coins minted by the U.S. Treasury. Federal Reserve banks (to be discussed shortly) issue paper notes and coins throughout the U.S. banking system.

TRANSACTIONS DEPOSITS Individuals transfer ownership of deposits in financial institutions by using debit cards and checks. Hence, debitable and checkable transactions deposits are normally acceptable as a medium of exchange. The **depository institutions** that offer transactions deposits are numerous and include commercial banks and almost all **thrift institutions**—savings banks, savings and loan associations (S&Ls), and credit unions.

Depository institutions
Financial institutions that accept deposits from savers and lend funds from those deposits out at interest.

Thrift institutions
Financial institutions that receive most of their funds from the savings of the public. They include savings banks, savings and loan associations, and credit unions.

TRAVELER'S CHECKS **Traveler's checks** are paid for by the purchaser at the time of transfer. The total quantity of traveler's checks outstanding issued by institutions other than banks is part of the M1 money supply. American Express and other institutions issue traveler's checks.

Traveler's checks
Financial instruments obtained from a bank or a nonbanking organization and signed during purchase that can be used in payment upon a second signature by the purchaser.

MyEconLab Real-time data

FIGURE 15-2

Composition of the U.S. M1 and M2 Money Supply, 2013

Panel (a) shows estimates of the M1 money supply, of which the largest component (over 52 percent) is transactions deposits. M2 consists of M1 plus three other components, the most important of which is savings deposits at all depository institutions.

Sources: Federal Reserve Bulletin; Economic Indicators, various issues; author's estimates.

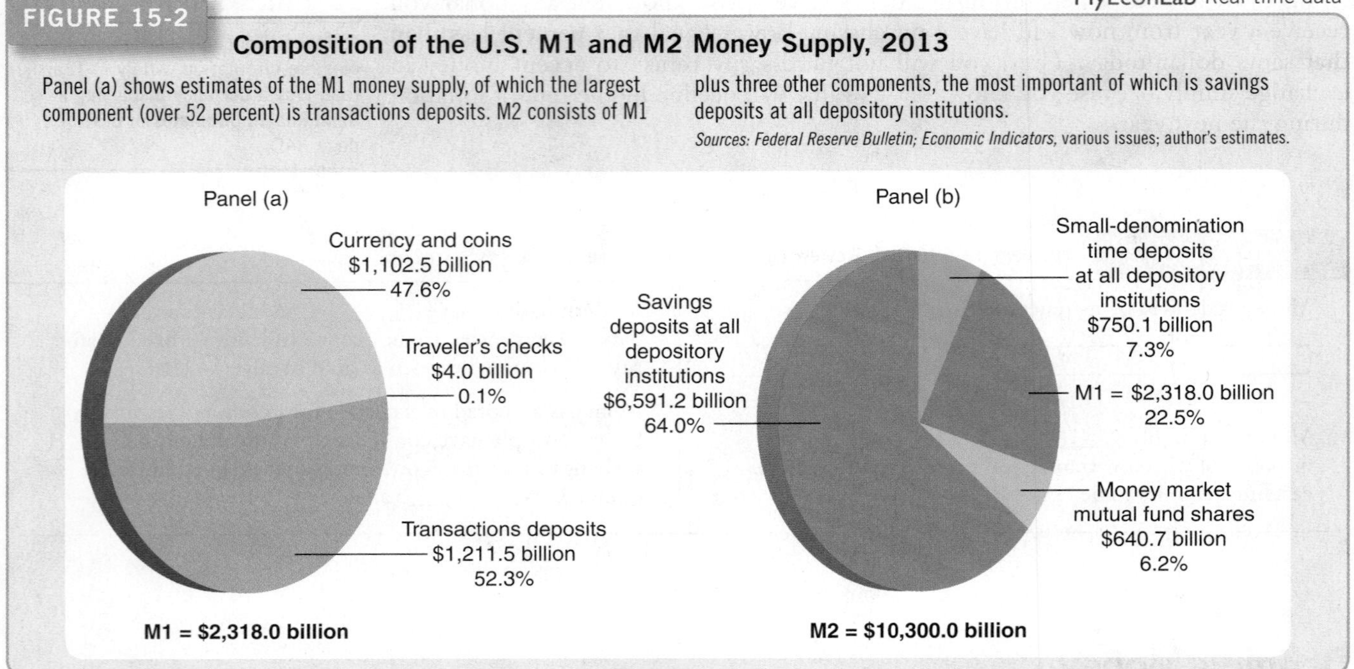

The Liquidity Approach to Measuring Money: M2

The liquidity approach to defining and measuring the U.S. money supply views money as a temporary store of value and so includes all of M1 *plus* several other highly liquid assets. Panel (b) of Figure 15-2 above shows the components of **M2**—money as a temporary store of value. These components include the following:

M2
M1 plus (1) savings deposits at all depository institutions, (2) small-denomination time deposits, and (3) balances in retail money market mutual funds.

1. ***Savings deposits.*** Total *savings deposits*—deposits with no set maturities—are the largest component of the M2 money supply.
2. ***Small-denomination time deposits.*** With a *time deposit,* the funds must be left in a financial institution for a given period before they can be withdrawn without penalty. To be included in the M2 definition of the money supply, time deposits must be less than $100,000—hence, the designation *small-denomination time deposits.*
3. ***Money market mutual fund balances.*** Many individuals keep part of their assets in the form of shares in *money market mutual funds*—highly liquid funds that investment companies obtain from the public. All money market mutual fund balances except those held by large institutions (which typically use them more like large time deposits) are included in M2 because they are very liquid.

When all of these assets are added together, the result is M2, as shown in panel (b) of Figure 15-2.

For Federal Reserve data concerning the latest trends in the monetary aggregates, go to www.econtoday.com/chap15 and click on "Money Stock Measures—H.6" under Money Stock and Reserve Balances.

OTHER MONEY SUPPLY DEFINITIONS Economists and other researchers have come up with additional definitions of money. Some businesspeople and policymakers prefer a monetary aggregate known as *MZM.* The MZM aggregate is the so-called money-at-zero-maturity money stock. Obtaining MZM entails adding to M1 those deposits without set maturities, such as savings deposits, that are included in M2. MZM includes *all* money market funds but excludes all deposits with fixed maturities, such as small-denomination time deposits.

QUICK QUIZ See page 345 for the answers. Review concepts from this section in MyEconLab.

The **money supply** can be defined in a variety of ways, depending on whether we use the transactions approach or the liquidity approach. Using the __________ approach, the money supply consists of currency, **transactions deposits,** and traveler's checks. This is called __________.

__________ deposits are any deposits in financial institutions from which the deposit owner can transfer funds using a debit card or checks.

When we add savings deposits, small-denomination time deposits, and retail money market mutual fund balances to __________, we obtain the measure known as __________.

Financial Intermediation and Banks

Most nations, including the United States, have a banking system that encompasses two types of institutions. One type consists of privately owned profit-seeking institutions, such as commercial banks and thrift institutions. The other type of institution is a **central bank,** which typically serves as a banker's bank and as a bank for the national treasury or finance ministry.

Central bank
A banker's bank, usually an official institution that also serves as a bank for a nation's government treasury. Central banks normally regulate commercial banks.

Direct versus Indirect Financing

When individuals choose to hold some of their savings in new bonds issued by a corporation, their purchases of the bonds are in effect direct loans to the business. This is an example of *direct finance*, in which people lend funds directly to a business. Business financing is not always direct. Individuals might choose instead to hold a time deposit at a bank. The bank may then lend to the same company. In this way, the same people can provide *indirect finance* to a business. The bank makes this possible by *intermediating* the financing of the company.

Financial Intermediation

Banks and other financial institutions are all in the same business—transferring funds from savers to investors. This process is known as **financial intermediation,** and its participants, such as banks and savings institutions, are **financial intermediaries.** The process of financial intermediation is illustrated in Figure 15-3 on the following page.

Financial intermediation
The process by which financial institutions accept savings from businesses, households, and governments and lend the savings to other businesses, households, and governments.

Financial intermediaries
Institutions that transfer funds between ultimate lenders (savers) and ultimate borrowers.

ASYMMETRIC INFORMATION, ADVERSE SELECTION, AND MORAL HAZARD Why might people wish to direct their funds through a bank instead of lending them directly to a business? One important reason is **asymmetric information**—the fact that the business may have better knowledge of its own current and future prospects than potential lenders do. For instance, the business may know that it intends to use borrowed funds for projects with a high risk of failure that would make repaying the loan difficult.

This potential for borrowers to use the borrowed funds in high-risk projects is known as **adverse selection.** Alternatively, a business that had intended to undertake low-risk projects may change management after receiving a loan, and the new managers may use the borrowed funds in riskier ways. The possibility that a borrower might engage in behavior that increases risk after borrowing funds is called **moral hazard.**

To minimize the possibility that a business might fail to repay a loan, people thinking about lending funds directly to the business must study the business carefully before making the loan, and they must continue to monitor its performance afterward. Alternatively, they can choose to avoid the trouble by holding deposits with financial intermediaries, which then specialize in evaluating the creditworthiness of business borrowers and in keeping tabs on their progress until loans are repaid. Thus, adverse selection and moral hazard both help explain why people use financial intermediaries.

Asymmetric information
Information possessed by one party in a financial transaction but not by the other party.

Adverse selection
The tendency for high-risk projects and clients to be overrepresented among borrowers.

Moral hazard
The possibility that a borrower might engage in riskier behavior after a loan has been obtained.

FIGURE 15-3

The Process of Financial Intermediation

The process of financial intermediation is depicted here. Note that ultimate lenders and ultimate borrowers are the same economic units—households, businesses, and governments—but not necessarily the same individuals. Whereas individual households can be net lenders or borrowers, households as an economic unit typically are net lenders. Specific businesses or governments similarly can be net lenders or borrowers. As economic units, both are net borrowers.

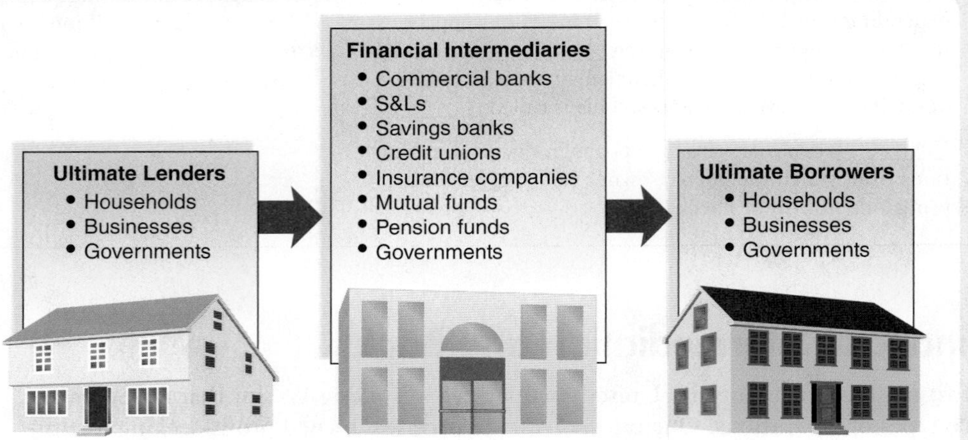

LARGER SCALE AND LOWER MANAGEMENT COSTS Another important reason that financial intermediaries exist is that they make it possible for many people to pool their funds, thereby increasing the size, or *scale*, of the total amount of savings managed by an intermediary. This centralization of management reduces costs and risks below the levels savers would incur if all were to manage their savings alone.

Pension fund companies, which are institutions that specialize in managing funds that individuals save for retirement, owe their existence largely to their abilities to provide such cost savings to individual savers. Likewise, *investment companies*, which are institutions that manage portfolios of financial instruments called mutual funds on behalf of shareholders, also exist largely because of cost savings from their greater scale of operations. In addition, *government-sponsored financial institutions*, such as the Federal National Mortgage Association, seek to reduce overall lending costs by pooling large volumes of funds from investors in order to buy groups of mortgage loans.

Liabilities
Amounts owed; the legal claims against a business or household by nonowners.

FINANCIAL INSTITUTION LIABILITIES AND ASSETS Every financial intermediary has its own sources of funds, which are **liabilities** of that institution. When you place $100 in your

TABLE 15-2

Financial Intermediaries and Their Assets and Liabilities

Financial Intermediary	Assets	Liabilities
Commercial banks, savings and loan associations, savings banks, and credit unions	Car loans and other consumer debt, business loans, government securities, home mortgages	Transactions deposits, savings deposits, various other time deposits
Insurance companies	Mortgages, stocks, bonds, real estate	Insurance contracts, annuities, pension plans
Pension and retirement funds	Stocks, bonds, mortgages, time deposits	Pension plans
Money market mutual funds	Short-term credit instruments such as large-denomination certificates of deposit, Treasury bills, and high-grade commercial paper	Fund shares with limited checking privileges
Government-sponsored financial institutions	Home mortgages	Mortgage-backed securities issued to investors

transactions deposit at a bank, the bank creates a liability—it owes you $100—in exchange for the funds deposited. A commercial bank gets its funds from transactions and savings accounts, and an insurance company gets its funds from insurance policy premiums.

Each financial intermediary has a different primary use of its **assets.** For example, a credit union usually makes small consumer loans, whereas a savings bank makes mainly mortgage loans. Table 15-2 on the bottom of the facing page lists the assets and liabilities of typical financial intermediaries. Be aware, though, that the distinctions between different types of financial institutions are becoming more and more blurred. As laws and regulations change, there will be less need to make any distinction. All may ultimately be treated simply as financial intermediaries.

Assets
Amounts owned; all items to which a business or household holds legal claim.

How are online firms pooling funds to assist small-business entrepreneurs in obtaining loans when banks have rejected their requests?

EXAMPLE

Going Online for Credit When Bank Loans Dry Up

Today, a growing number of entrepreneurs who fail to receive loans from banks instead obtain credit from Internet-based companies such as Lending Club and Prosper Marketplace. These firms provide online forums for entrepreneurs to post detailed business plans along with the specific amounts of credit desired to try to achieve success. Individual savers can assess these plans and, if they wish, commit some of their own funds to help fund entrepreneurs' projects.

In exchange for service fees, the online firms pool these individual funding commitments into larger loan packages. For example, if an entrepreneur requests $15,000 in credit and 150 savers provide an average amount of $100 each, the online company collects the savers' funds and extends a loan to the entrepreneur. In this way, firms such as Lending Club and Prosper Marketplace act as financial intermediaries.

FOR CRITICAL THINKING

Why do you suppose that default rates on loans arranged by online firms tend to be substantially higher than default rates on bank loans?

Transmitting Payments via Debit-Card Transactions

Since 2006, the dollar volume of payments transmitted using debit cards has exceeded the value of checking transactions. To see how a debit-card transaction clears, take a look at Figure 15-4 on the next page. Suppose that Bank of America has provided a debit card to a college student named Jill Jones, who in turn uses the card to purchase $200 worth of clothing from Macy's, which has an account at Citibank. The debit-card transaction generates an electronic record, which the debit-card system transmits to Citibank.

The debit-card system also automatically uses the electronic record to determine the bank that issued the debit card used to purchase the clothing. It transmits this information to Bank of America. Then Bank of America verifies that Jill Jones is an account holder, deducts $200 from her transactions deposit account, and transmits these funds electronically, via the debit-card system, to Citibank. Finally, Citibank credits $200 to Macy's transactions deposit account, and payment for the clothing purchase is complete.

How can food-cart and farmers' market vendors accept debit cards today?

EXAMPLE

Vendors Use Smartphones to Process Debit-Card Purchases

A company called Square makes it possible for small retailers on the move, such as mobile food-cart and farmers' market vendors, to accept card payments. Square distributes plastic card-reading devices at no charge to owners of such businesses. The retailers can attach them to smartphones and thereby transform the devices into payment terminals. After a payment card is swiped through the device, the smartphone transmits payment information for Square to process, at a fee, to complete a purchase. In this way, Square enables sellers to move wherever buyers are located while broadening the means of payment that sellers can accept.

FOR CRITICAL THINKING

In what sense is a payment order sent using a smartphone economically indistinguishable from a payment order made via a check?

FIGURE 15-4

How a Debit-Card Transaction Clears

A college student named Jill Jones uses a debit card issued by Bank of America to purchase clothing valued at $200 from Macy's, which has an account with Citibank. The debit-card transaction creates an electronic record that is transmitted to Citibank. The debit-card system forwards this record to Bank of America, which deducts $200 from Jill Jones's transactions deposit account. Then the debit-card system transmits the $200 payment to Citibank, which credits the $200 to Macy's account.

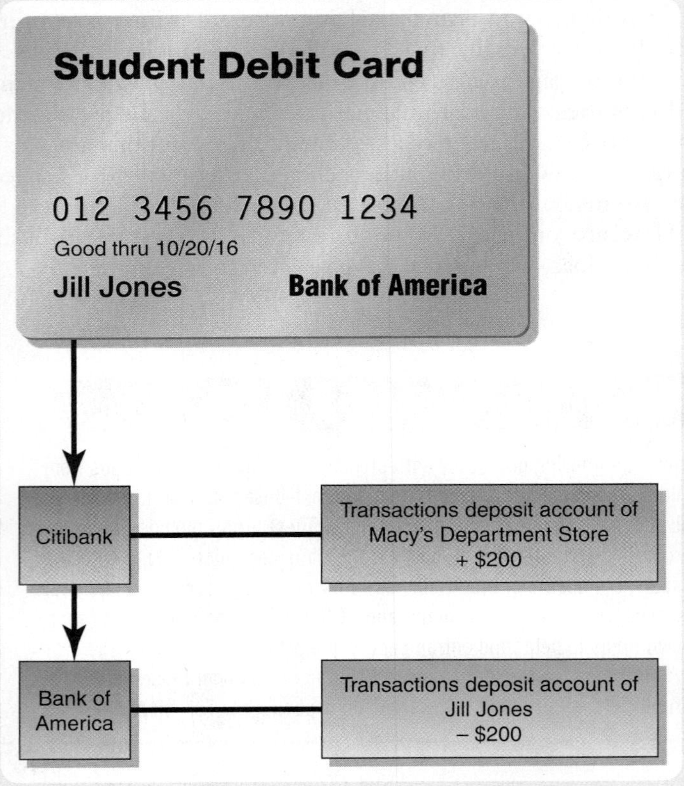

QUICK QUIZ See page 345 for the answers. Review concepts from this section in MyEconLab.

__________ intermediaries, including depository institutions such as commercial banks and savings institutions, insurance companies, mutual funds, and pension funds, transfer funds from ultimate lenders (savers) to ultimate borrowers.

Financial intermediaries specialize in tackling problems of __________ information. They address the __________ __________ problem by carefully reviewing the creditworthiness of loan applicants, and they deal with the __________ __________ problem by monitoring borrowers after they receive loans. Many financial intermediaries also take advantage of cost reductions arising from the centralized management of funds pooled from the savings of many individuals.

The Federal Reserve System: The U.S. Central Bank

The Federal Reserve System, which serves as the nation's central bank, is one of the key banking institutions in the United States. It is partly a creature of government and partly privately directed.

The Federal Reserve System

The Fed
The Federal Reserve System; the central bank of the United States.

The Federal Reserve System, also known simply as **the Fed,** is the most important regulatory agency in the U.S. monetary system and is usually considered the monetary authority. The Fed was established by the Federal Reserve Act, signed on December 13, 1913, by President Woodrow Wilson.

FIGURE 15-5

Organization of the Federal Reserve System

The 12 Federal Reserve district banks are headed by 12 separate presidents. The main authority of the Fed resides with the Board of Governors of the Federal Reserve System, whose seven members are appointed for 14-year terms by the president of the United States and confirmed by the Senate. Open market operations are carried out through the Federal Open Market Committee (FOMC), consisting of the seven members of the Board of Governors plus five presidents of the district banks (always including the president of the New York bank, with the others rotating).

Source: Board of Governors of the Federal Reserve System, *The Federal Reserve System: Purposes and Functions*, 7th ed. (Washington, D.C., 1984), p. 5.

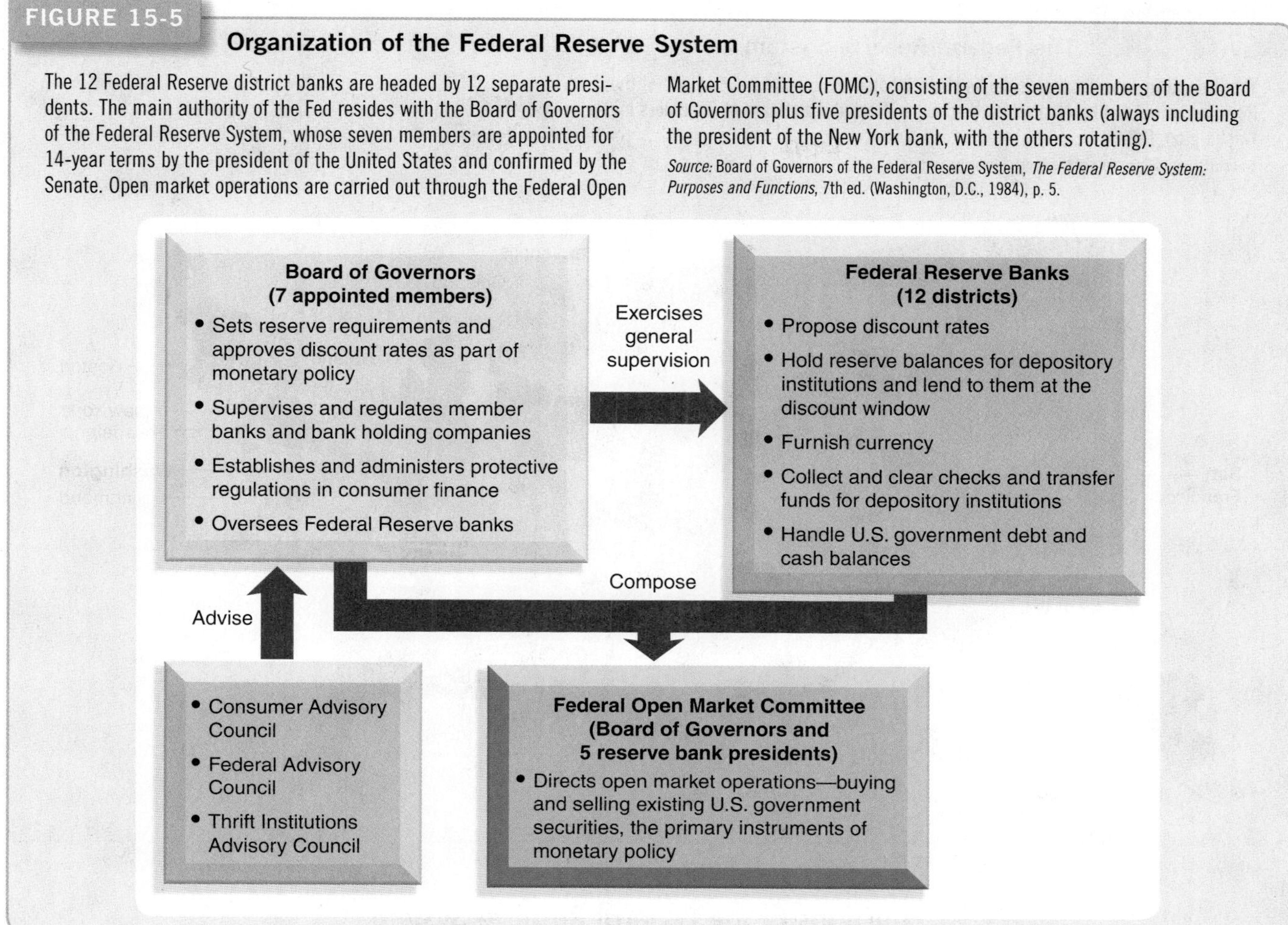

ORGANIZATION OF THE FEDERAL RESERVE SYSTEM Figure 15-5 above shows how the Federal Reserve System is organized. It is managed by the Board of Governors, composed of seven full-time members appointed by the U.S. president with the approval of the Senate. The chair of the Board of Governors is the leading official of the Board of Governors and of the Federal Reserve System. Since 2006, Ben Bernanke has held this position.

The 12 Federal Reserve district banks have a total of 25 branches. The boundaries of the 12 Federal Reserve districts and the cities in which Federal Reserve banks are located are shown in Figure 15-6 on the following page. The Federal Open Market Committee (FOMC) determines the future growth of the money supply and other important variables. This committee is composed of the members of the Board of Governors, the president of the New York Federal Reserve Bank, and presidents of four other Federal Reserve banks, rotated periodically. The chair of the Board of Governors also chairs the FOMC.

DEPOSITORY INSTITUTIONS Depository institutions—all financial institutions that accept deposits—comprise our monetary system consisting of nearly 6,500 commercial banks, 1,100 savings and loan associations and savings banks, and about 8,000 credit unions. All depository institutions may purchase services from the Federal Reserve System on an equal basis. Also, almost all depository institutions are required to keep a certain percentage of their deposits in reserve at the Federal Reserve district banks or as vault cash. This percentage depends on the bank's volume of business.

FIGURE 15-6

The Federal Reserve System

The Federal Reserve System is divided into 12 districts, each served by one of the Federal Reserve district banks, located in the cities indicated. The Board of Governors meets in Washington, D.C.

Source: Board of Governors of the Federal Reserve System.

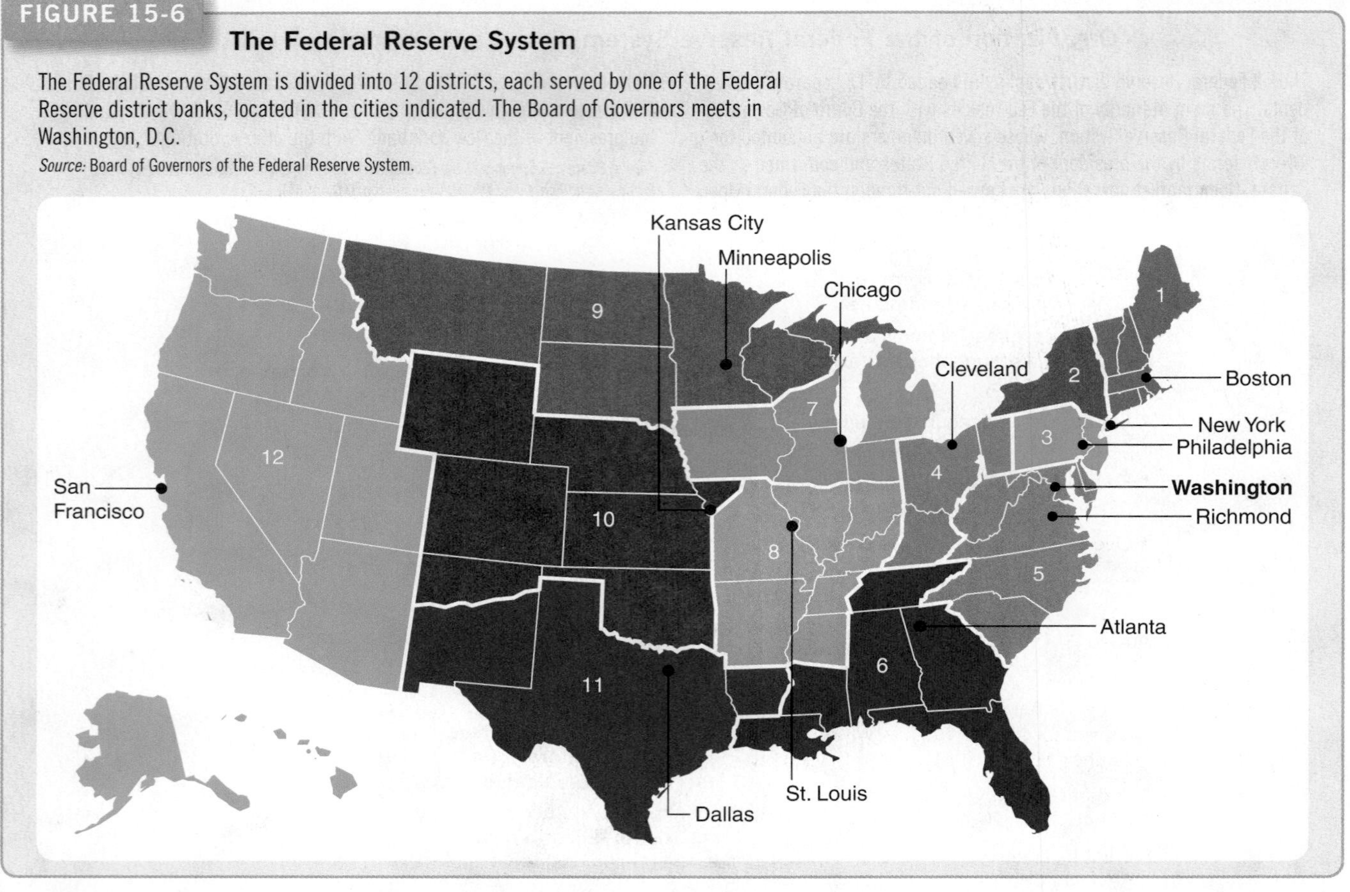

Functions of the Federal Reserve System

The Federal Reserve performs several functions:

1. ***The Fed supplies the economy with fiduciary currency.*** The Federal Reserve banks supply the economy with paper currency called Federal Reserve notes. Even though all Federal Reserve notes are printed at the Bureau of Engraving and Printing in Washington, D.C., each note is assigned a code indicating which of the 12 Federal Reserve banks first introduced the note into circulation. Moreover, each of these notes is an obligation (liability) of the Federal Reserve System, *not* the U.S. Treasury.

2. ***The Fed holds depository institutions' reserves and provides payment-clearing systems.*** The 12 Federal Reserve district banks hold the reserves (other than vault cash) of depository institutions. Depository institutions are required by law to keep a certain percentage of their transactions deposits as reserves. Even if they weren't required to do so by law, they would still wish to keep some reserves on which they can draw funds as needed for expected and unexpected transactions. The Federal Reserve System also operates systems for transmitting and clearing payments among depository institutions' reserve accounts. Federal Reserve banks all offer check-clearing services and electronic payments transfer services to commercial banks, savings institutions, and credit unions.

3. ***The Fed acts as the government's fiscal agent.*** The Federal Reserve is the primary banker and fiscal agent for the federal government. Consequently, the U.S. Treasury has a transactions account with the Federal Reserve, which helps the government collect certain tax revenues and aids in the purchase and sale of government securities.

4. ***The Fed supervises depository institutions.*** The Fed (along with the Comptroller of the Currency, the Federal Deposit Insurance Corporation, the Office of Thrift

Supervision in the Treasury Department, and the National Credit Union Administration) is a supervisor and regulator of depository institutions.

5. ***The Fed conducts monetary policy.*** Perhaps the Fed's most important task is to regulate the nation's money supply. To understand how the Fed manages the money supply, we must examine more closely its reserve-holding function and the way in which depository institutions aid in expansion and contraction of the money supply. We will do this later in this chapter.

6. ***The Fed intervenes in foreign currency markets.*** Sometimes the Fed attempts to keep the value of the dollar from changing. It does this by buying and selling U.S. dollars in foreign exchange markets. You will read more about this important topic in Chapter 33.

7. ***The Fed acts as the "lender of last resort."*** From time to time, an individual bank that is otherwise in good financial condition may be temporarily low on cash and other liquid assets. Such an institution is said to be illiquid. A key justification for the formation of the Federal Reserve System was that the Fed would stand ready to prevent temporarily illiquid banks from failing by serving as the financial system's **lender of last resort.** In this capacity, the Fed stands ready to lend to any temporarily illiquid but otherwise financially healthy banking institution. In this way, the Fed seeks to prevent illiquidity at a few banks from leading to a general loss of depositors' confidence in the overall soundness of the banking system.

Lender of last resort
The Federal Reserve's role as an institution that is willing and able to lend to a temporarily illiquid bank that is otherwise in good financial condition to prevent the bank's illiquid position from leading to a general loss of confidence in that bank or in others.

What institutions, to the surprise of many U.S. residents, were among the largest recipients of Fed lender-of-last-resort loans at the height of the financial panic of the late 2000s?

POLICY EXAMPLE

The Fed Becomes a Lender of Last Resort for Foreign Banks

During the financial meltdown that stretched across several months in the late 2000s, the Federal Reserve extended more than $3 trillion in emergency loans to financial institutions that it judged to be illiquid but otherwise financially healthy. What the Fed did not reveal until years later, however, was that emergency loans totaling hundreds of billions of dollars went to private financial institutions based outside the United States. The Fed also extended more than $600 billion in additional credit to a number of central banks around the globe. Thus, in the midst of the financial panic of 2008 and 2009, the Fed became a key lender of last resort for many financial institutions located outside the United States.

FOR CRITICAL THINKING

How do you suppose the fact that foreign banks owed substantial funds to U.S. banks influenced the Federal Reserve's decision to lend to these institutions?

QUICK QUIZ

See page 345 for the answers. Review concepts from this section in MyEconLab.

The central bank in the United States is the __________ __________ __________, which was established on December 13, 1913.

There are 12 Federal Reserve district banks, with 25 branches. The Federal Reserve System is managed by the __________ of __________ in Washington, D.C. The Fed interacts with almost all depository institutions in the United States, most of which must keep a certain percentage of their transactions deposits on reserve with the Fed. The Fed serves as the chief regulatory agency for all depository institutions that have Federal Reserve System membership.

The functions of the Federal Reserve System are to supply fiduciary __________, provide payment-clearing services, hold depository institution __________, act as the government's fiscal agent, supervise depository institutions, regulate the supply of money, intervene in foreign currency markets, and act as the __________ of __________ __________.

Fractional Reserve Banking, the Federal Reserve, and the Money Supply

As early as 1000 B.C., uncoined gold and silver were being used as money in Mesopotamia. Goldsmiths weighed and assessed the purity of those metals. Later they started issuing paper notes indicating that the bearers held gold or silver of given weights and purity on deposit with the goldsmith. These notes could be transferred in exchange for goods and became the first paper currency. The gold and silver on deposit with the goldsmiths were the first bank deposits. Eventually, goldsmiths realized that inflows of gold and silver for deposit always exceeded the average amount of gold and silver withdrawn at any given time—often by a predictable ratio.

These goldsmiths started making loans by issuing to borrowers paper notes that exceeded in value the amount of gold and silver the goldsmiths actually kept on hand. They charged interest on these loans. This constituted the earliest form of what is now called **fractional reserve banking.** We know that goldsmiths operated this way in Delphi, Didyma, and Olympia in Greece as early as the seventh century B.C. In Athens, fractional reserve banking was well developed by the sixth century B.C.

Fractional reserve banking
A system in which depository institutions hold reserves that are less than the amount of total deposits.

Depository Institution Reserves

In a fractional reserve banking system, banks do not keep sufficient funds on hand to cover 100 percent of their depositors' accounts. And the funds held by depository institutions in the United States are not kept in gold and silver, as they were with the early goldsmiths. Instead, the funds are held as **reserves** in the form of cash in banks' vaults and deposits that banks hold on deposit with Federal Reserve district banks.

The fraction of deposits that banks hold as reserves is called the **reserve ratio.** There are two determinants of the size of this ratio. One is the quantity of reserves that the Federal Reserve requires banks to hold, which are called *required reserves*. The other determinant of the reserve ratio is whatever additional amount of reserves that banks voluntarily hold, known as *excess reserves*.

To show the relationship between reserves and deposits at an individual bank, let's examine the **balance sheet,** or statement of assets owned and liabilities (amounts owed to others), for a particular depository institution. Balance Sheet 15-1 below displays a balance sheet for a depository institution called Typical Bank. Liabilities for this institution consist solely of $1 million in transactions deposits. Assets consist of $100,000 in reserves and $900,000 in loans to customers. Total assets of $1 million equal total liabilities of $1 million. Because Typical Bank has $100,000 of reserves and $1 million of transactions deposits, its reserve ratio is 10 percent. Thus, Typical Bank is part of a system of fractional reserve banking, in which it holds only 10 percent of its deposits as reserves.

Reserves
In the U.S. Federal Reserve System, deposits held by Federal Reserve district banks for depository institutions, plus depository institutions' vault cash.

Reserve ratio
The fraction of transactions deposits that banks hold as reserves.

Balance sheet
A statement of the assets and liabilities of any business entity, including financial institutions and the Federal Reserve System. Assets are what is owned; liabilities are what is owed.

BALANCE SHEET 15-1

Typical Bank

Assets		Liabilities	
Reserves	$100,000	Transactions deposits	$1,000,000
Loans	$900,000		
Total	$1,000,000	Total	$1,000,000

Fractional Reserve Banking and Money Expansion

Under fractional reserve banking, the Federal Reserve can add to the quantity of money in circulation by bringing about an expansion of deposits within the banking system. To understand how the Fed can create money within the banking system, we must look at how depository institutions respond to Fed actions that increase reserves in the entire system.

Let's consider the effect of a Fed **open market operation,** which is a Fed purchase or sale of existing U.S. government securities in the open market—the private secondary market in which people exchange securities that have not yet matured. Assume that the Fed engaged in an *open market purchase* by buying a $100,000 U.S. government security from a bond dealer. The Fed does this by electronically transferring $100,000 to the bond dealer's transactions deposit account at Bank 1. Thus, as shown in Balance Sheet 15-2 below, Bank 1's transactions deposit liabilities increase by $100,000.

Open market operations
The purchase and sale of existing U.S. government securities (such as bonds) in the open private market by the Federal Reserve System.

Let's suppose that the reserve ratio for Bank 1 and all other depository institutions is 10 percent. As shown in Balance Sheet 15-2, therefore, Bank 1 responds to this $100,000 increase in transactions deposits by adding 10 percent of this amount, or $10,000, to its reserves. The bank allocates the remaining $90,000 of additional deposits to new loans, so its loans increase by $90,000.

BALANCE SHEET 15-2

Bank 1

Assets		Liabilities	
Reserves	+$10,000	Transactions deposits	+$100,000
Loans	+$90,000		
Total	+$100,000	Total	+$100,000

EFFECT ON THE MONEY SUPPLY At this point, the Fed's purchase of a $100,000 U.S. government security from a bond dealer has increased the money supply immediately by $100,000. This occurs because transactions deposits held by the public—bond dealers are part of the public—are part of the money supply. Hence, the addition of $100,000 to deposits with Bank 1, with no corresponding deposit reduction elsewhere in the banking system, raises the money supply by $100,000. (If another member of the public, instead of the Fed, had purchased the bond, that person's transactions deposit would have been reduced by $100,000, so there would have been no change in the money supply.)

The process of money creation does not stop here. The borrower who receives the $90,000 loan from Bank 1 will spend these funds, which will then be deposited in other banks. In this instance, suppose that the $90,000 spent by Bank 1's borrower is deposited in a transactions deposit account at Bank 2. At this bank, as shown in Balance Sheet 15-3 below, transactions deposits and hence the money supply increase by $90,000. Bank 2 adds 10 percent of these deposits, or $9,000, to its reserves. It uses the remaining $81,000 of new deposits to add $81,000 to its loans.

BALANCE SHEET 15-3

Bank 2

Assets		Liabilities	
Reserves	+$9,000	Transactions deposits	+$90,000
Loans	+$81,000		
Total	+$90,000	Total	+$90,000

CONTINUATION OF THE DEPOSIT CREATION PROCESS Look at Bank 3's account in Balance Sheet 15-4 on the following page. Assume that the borrower receiving the $81,000 loan from Bank 2 spends these funds, which then are deposited in an account at Bank 3.

Transactions deposits and the money supply increase by $81,000. Reserves of Bank 3 rise by 10 percent of this amount, or $8,100. Bank 3 uses the rest of the newly deposited funds, or $72,900, to increase its loans.

BALANCE SHEET 15-4

Bank 3

Assets		Liabilities	
Reserves	+$8,100	Transactions deposits	+$81,000
Loans	+$72,900		
Total	+$81,000	Total	+$81,000

This process continues to Banks 4, 5, 6, and so forth. Each bank obtains smaller and smaller increases in deposits because banks hold 10 percent of new deposits as reserves. Thus, each succeeding depository institution makes correspondingly smaller loans. Table 15-3 below shows new deposits, reserves, and loans for the remaining depository institutions.

EFFECT ON TOTAL DEPOSITS AND THE MONEY SUPPLY In this example, deposits and the money supply increased initially by the $100,000 that the Fed paid the bond dealer in exchange for a U.S. government security. Deposits and the money supply were further increased by a $90,000 deposit in Bank 2, and they were again increased by an $81,000 deposit in Bank 3. Eventually, total deposits and the money supply increase by $1 million, as shown in Table 15-3. This $1 million expansion of deposits and the money supply consists of the original $100,000 created by the Fed, plus an extra $900,000 generated by deposit-creating bank loans. The deposit creation process is portrayed graphically in Figure 15-7 on the facing page.

You should be able to work through the foregoing example to show the reverse process when there is a *decrease* in reserves because the Fed engages in an *open market sale* by selling a $100,000 U.S. government security. The result is a multiple contraction of deposits and, therefore, of the total money supply in circulation.

The Money Multiplier

In the example just given, a $100,000 increase in reserves generated by the Fed's purchase of a security yielded a $1 million increase in transactions deposits and, hence, the money supply. Thus, deposits and the money supply increased by a multiple of

TABLE 15-3

Maximum Money Creation with 10 Percent Reserve Ratio

This table shows the maximum new loans that banks can make, given the Fed's electronic transfer of $100,000 to a transactions deposit account at Bank 1. The reserve ratio is 10 percent.

Bank	New Deposits	New Reserves	Maximum New Loans
1	$100,000 (from Fed)	$10,000	$90,000
2	90,000	9,000	81,000
3	81,000	8,100	72,900
4	72,900	7,290	65,610
.	.	.	.
.	.	.	.
.	.	.	.
All other banks	656,100	65,610	590,490
Totals	$1,000,000	$100,000	$900,000

FIGURE 15-7

The Multiple Expansion in the Money Supply Due to $100,000 in New Reserves When the Reserve Ratio Is 10 Percent

The banks are all aligned in decreasing order of new deposits created. Bank 1 receives the $100,000 in new reserves and lends out $90,000. Bank 2 receives the $90,000 and lends out $81,000. The process continues through Banks 3 to 19 and then the rest of the banking system. Ultimately, assuming no leakages into currency, the $100,000 of new reserves results in an increase in the money supply of $1 million, or 10 times the new reserves, because the reserve ratio is 10 percent.

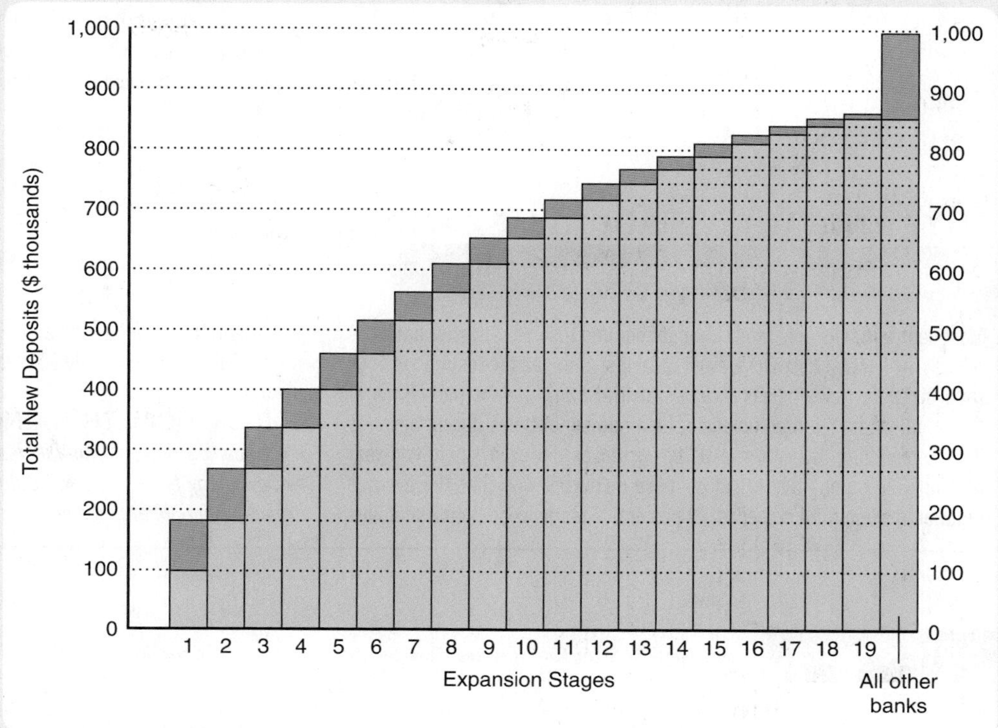

10 times the initial $100,000 increase in overall reserves. Conversely, a $100,000 decrease in reserves generated by a Fed sale of a security will yield a decrease in total deposits of $1 million—that is, a multiple of 10 times the initial $100,000 decrease in overall reserves.

We can now make a generalization about the extent to which the total money supply will change when the banking system's reserves are increased or decreased. The **money multiplier** gives the change in the money supply due to a change in reserves. In our example, the value of the money multiplier is 10.

Money multiplier
A number that, when multiplied by a change in reserves in the banking system, yields the resulting change in the money supply.

POTENTIAL VERSUS ACTUAL MONEY MULTIPLIERS If we assume, as in our example, that all loan proceeds are deposited with banks, we obtain the **potential money multiplier**—the *maximum* possible value of the money multiplier:

Potential money multiplier
The reciprocal of the reserve ratio, assuming no leakages into currency. It is equal to 1 divided by the reserve ratio.

$$\text{Potential money multiplier} = \frac{1}{\text{reserve ratio}}$$

That is, the potential money multiplier is equal to 1 divided by the fraction of transactions deposits that banks hold as reserves. In our example, the reserve ratio was 10 percent, or 0.10 expressed as a decimal fraction. Thus, in the example the value of the potential money multiplier was equal to 1 divided by 0.10, which equals 10.

What happens if the entire amount of a loan from a depository institution is not redeposited? When borrowers want to hold a portion of their loans as currency outside the banking system, these funds cannot be held by banks as reserves from which to make loans. The greater the amount of cash leakage, the smaller the *actual* money multiplier. Typically, borrowers do hold a portion of loan proceeds as currency, so the actual money multiplier usually is smaller than the potential money multiplier.

REAL-WORLD MONEY MULTIPLIERS The potential money multiplier is rarely attained for the banking system as a whole. Furthermore, each definition of the money supply, M1 or M2, will yield a different actual money multiplier.

In most years, the actual M1 multiplier has been in a range between 1.5 and 2.0. The actual M2 multiplier showed an upward trend until recently, rising from 6.5 in the 1960s to over 12 in the mid-2000s. Since then, however, it has dropped to about 6.

What was the ultimate effect of a steady stream of increases in the required reserve ratio for China's banking system?

INTERNATIONAL POLICY EXAMPLE

Seeking to Slash the Money Multiplier in China

Most central banks only rarely change required reserve ratios for bank deposits. The Federal Reserve, for instance, last changed the required reserve ratio in 1990. Nevertheless, China's central bank, the People's Bank of China, raised its required reserve ratio a number of times during the early 2010s, including more than a dozen increases during a single two-year interval. The cumulative effect of these increases was that the average required reserve ratio exceeded 20 percent—nearly twice its initial value. As a result, the potential and actual money multipliers for China's banking system fell to approximately 50 percent of their original levels.

FOR CRITICAL THINKING

If the People's Bank of China increases bank reserves by 100 billion yuan, by how many fewer yuan will China's quantity of money now potentially expand? (Hint: What is the new money multiplier?)

QUICK QUIZ

See page 345 for the answers. Review concepts from this section in MyEconLab.

__________ of depository institutions consist of their vault cash and deposits that they hold with __________ __________ district banks.

The fraction of transactions deposit liabilities that depository institutions hold as reserves is the __________ __________.

The __________ __________ __________ is equal to 1 divided by the reserve ratio.

Federal Deposit Insurance

As you have seen, fractional reserve banking enables the Federal Reserve to use an open market purchase (or sale) of U.S. government bonds to generate an expansion (or contraction) of deposits. The change in the money supply is a multiple of the open market purchase (or sale). Another effect of fractional reserve banking is to make depository institutions somewhat fragile. After all, the institutions have only a fraction of reserves on hand to honor their depositors' requests for withdrawals.

If many depositors simultaneously rush to their bank to withdraw all of their transactions and time deposits—a phenomenon called a **bank run**—the bank would be unable to satisfy their requests. The result would be the failure of that depository institution. Widespread bank runs could lead to the failure of many institutions.

Bank run
Attempt by many of a bank's depositors to convert transactions and time deposits into currency out of fear that the bank's liabilities may exceed its assets.

Seeking to Limit Bank Failures with Deposit Insurance

When businesses fail, they create hardships for creditors, owners, and customers. But when a depository institution fails, an even greater hardship results, because many individuals and businesses depend on the safety and security of banks. As Figure 15-8 on the facing page shows, during the 1920s an average of about 600 banks failed each year. In the early 1930s, during the Great Depression, that average soared to nearly 3,000 failures each year.

FIGURE 15-8

Bank Failures

A tremendous number of banks failed prior to the creation of federal deposit insurance in 1933. Thereafter, bank failures were few until the mid-1980s. Annual failure rates jumped again in the early and late 2000s.

Source: Federal Deposit Insurance Corporation.

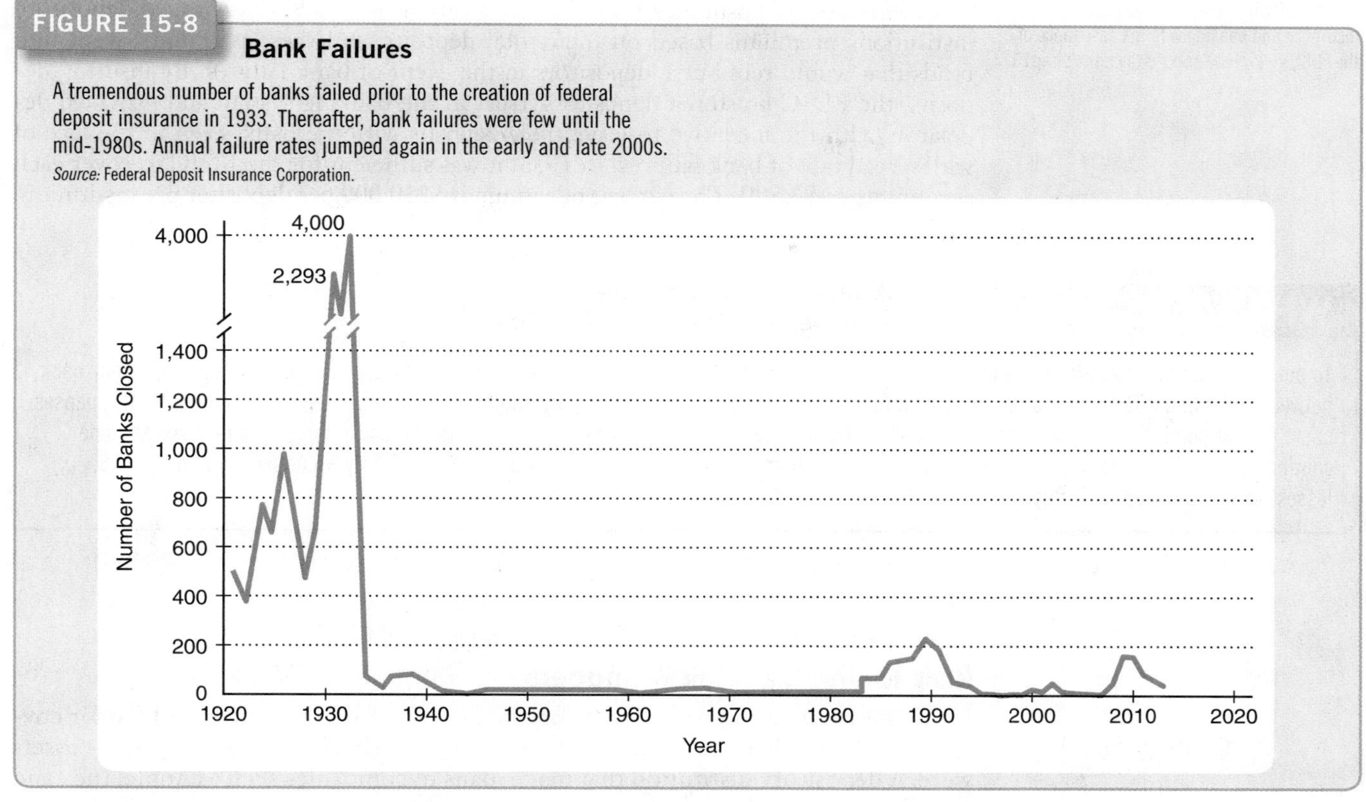

In 1933, at the height of these bank failures, the **Federal Deposit Insurance Corporation (FDIC)** was founded to insure the funds of depositors and remove the reason for ruinous runs on banks. In 1934, federal deposit insurance was extended to deposits in savings and loan associations and mutual savings banks, and in 1971 it was offered for deposits in credit unions.

Federal Deposit Insurance Corporation (FDIC)
A government agency that insures the deposits held in banks and most other depository institutions. All U.S. banks are insured this way.

As can be seen in Figure 15-8 above, bank failure rates dropped dramatically after passage of the early federal legislation. The long period from 1935 until the 1980s was relatively quiet. From World War II to 1984, fewer than nine banks failed per year. From 1995 until 2008, failures again averaged about nine per year. Since 2009, however, more than 400 banks have failed, and hundreds more are still in danger of failing. We will examine the reasons for this shortly. But first we need to understand how deposit insurance works.

The Rationale for Deposit Insurance

Consider the following scenario. A bank begins to look shaky. Its assets do not seem sufficient to cover its liabilities. If the bank has no deposit insurance, depositors in this bank (and any banks associated with it) will all want to withdraw their funds from the bank at the same time. Their concern is that this shaky bank will not have enough assets to return their deposits to them in the form of currency.

Indeed, this is what happens in a bank failure when insurance doesn't exist. Just as when a regular business fails, the creditors of the bank may not all get paid, or if they do, they will get paid less than 100 percent of what they are owed. Depositors are creditors of a bank because their funds are on loan to the bank. As explained earlier, however, banks do not hold 100 percent of their depositors' funds as cash. Instead, banks lend out most of their deposit funds to borrowers. Consequently, all depositors cannot withdraw all their funds simultaneously. Hence, the intent of the legislation enacted in the 1930s was to assure depositors that they could have their deposits converted into cash when they wished, no matter how serious the financial situation of the bank.

To keep up with the latest issues in deposit insurance and banking with the assistance of the FDIC, go to www.econtoday.com/chap15.

Federal deposit insurance provided this assurance. The FDIC charged depository institutions premiums based on their total deposits, and these premiums went into funds that would reimburse depositors in the event of bank failures. By insuring deposits, the FDIC bolstered depositors' trust in the banking system and provided depositors with the incentive to leave their deposits with the bank, even in the face of widespread talk of bank failures. In 1933, it was sufficient for the FDIC to cover each account up to $2,500. The current maximum is $250,000 per depositor per institution.

WHAT IF... the costs of bank failures exceeded the funds on hand at the Federal Deposit Insurance Corporation?

To put this issue into context, so many costly bank failures occurred between 2008 and 2010 that the FDIC's reserve fund did run out of cash. At that point, the FDIC borrowed from the U.S. Treasury to continue paying the costs of protecting banks' depositors from losses. The FDIC raised more deposit insurance premiums from banks. Ultimately, the FDIC raised sufficient premiums to pay back the Treasury and to replenish its reserve fund gradually. If expenses of bank failures were to rise above the FDIC's reserves at some future date, the FDIC undoubtedly would borrow from the U.S. Treasury once again.

How Deposit Insurance Causes Increased Risk Taking by Bank Managers

Until the 1990s, all insured depository institutions paid the same small fee for coverage. The fee that they paid was completely unrelated to how risky their assets were. A depository institution that made loans to companies such as Apple, Inc., and Google, Inc. paid the same deposit insurance premium as another depository institution that made loans (at higher interest rates) to the governments of developing countries that were teetering on the brink of financial collapse.

Although deposit insurance premiums for a while were adjusted somewhat in response to the riskiness of a depository institution's assets, they never reflected all of the relative risk. Indeed, between the late 1990s and the late 2000s, very few depository institutions paid *any* deposit insurance premiums. This lack of correlation between risk and premiums can be considered a fundamental flaw in the deposit insurance scheme. Because bank managers do not have to pay higher insurance premiums when they make riskier loans, they have an incentive to invest in more assets of higher yield, and therefore necessarily higher risk, than they would if there were no deposit insurance.

ARTIFICIALLY LOW INSURANCE PREMIUMS The problem with the insurance scheme is that the premium rate is artificially low. Depository institution managers are able to obtain deposits at less than full cost (because depositors will accept a lower interest payment on insured deposits). Consequently, managers can increase their profits by using insured deposits to purchase higher-yield, higher-risk assets. The gains to risk taking accrue to the managers and stockholders of the depository institutions. The losses go to the deposit insurer (and, as we will see, ultimately to taxpayers).

A REGULATORY SOLUTION To combat these flaws in the financial industry and in the deposit insurance system, a vast regulatory apparatus oversees depository institutions. The FDIC and other federal deposit insurance agencies possess regulatory powers to offset the risk-taking temptations to depository institution managers.

These regulatory powers include the ability to require higher capital investment, to regulate, examine, and supervise bank affairs, and to enforce regulatory decisions. Higher capital requirements were imposed in the early 1990s and then adjusted somewhat beginning in 2000, but the recent jump in bank failures reveals that basic flaws remain.

Deposit Insurance, Adverse Selection, and Moral Hazard

As a deposit insurer, the FDIC effectively acts as a government-run insurance company. This means that the FDIC's operations expose the federal government to the same kinds of asymmetric information problems that other financial intermediaries face.

ADVERSE SELECTION IN DEPOSIT INSURANCE One of these problems is *adverse selection*, which is often a problem when insurance is involved because people or firms that are relatively poor risks are sometimes able to disguise that fact from insurers. It is instructive to examine the way this works with the deposit insurance provided by the FDIC. Deposit insurance shields depositors from the potential adverse effects of risky decisions and so makes depositors willing to accept riskier investment strategies by their banks. Clearly, protection of depositors from risks encourages more high-flying, risk-loving entrepreneurs to become managers of banks.

Moreover, because depositors have so little incentive to monitor the activities of insured banks, it is also likely that the insurance actually encourages outright crooks—embezzlers and con artists—to enter the industry. The consequences for the FDIC—and for taxpayers—are larger losses.

MORAL HAZARD IN DEPOSIT INSURANCE Moral hazard is also an important phenomenon in the presence of insurance contracts, such as the deposit insurance provided by the FDIC. Insured depositors know that they will not suffer losses if their bank fails. Hence, they have little incentive to monitor their bank's investment activities or to punish their bank by withdrawing their funds if the bank assumes too much risk. This means that insured banks have incentives to take on more risks than they otherwise would.

Can Deposit Insurance Be Reformed?

Since 2005, Congress has sought to reform federal deposit insurance. These efforts are still under way.

A REFORM EFFORT THAT CAME TOO LATE The Federal Deposit Insurance Reform Act of 2005 aimed to reform federal deposit insurance. On the one hand, this legislation expanded deposit insurance coverage and potentially added to the system's moral hazard problems. It increased deposit insurance coverage for Individual Retirement Accounts (IRAs) offered by depository institutions from $100,000 to $250,000 and authorized the FDIC to periodically adjust the insurance limit on all deposits to reflect inflation.

On the other hand, the act provided the FDIC with improved tools for addressing moral hazard risks. The law changed a rule that had prevented the FDIC from charging deposit insurance premiums if total insurance funds exceeded 1.25 percent of all insured deposits. This limit had enabled practically all U.S. depository institutions to avoid paying deposit insurance premiums for about a decade. Now the FDIC can adjust deposit insurance premiums at any time.

A NEW STRUCTURAL REFORM IN PROGRESS During the banking troubles of the late 2000s, Congress sought to increase the public's confidence in depository institutions by extending coverage to virtually all liabilities in the banking system. Although this move succeeded in boosting trust in banks, it also expanded the scope of deposit insurance. To reflect this fact, in late 2010 the FDIC altered the structure for deposit insurance premiums. The FDIC now assesses premium rates on banks' total liabilities—that is, the banks' deposits plus their borrowings from other sources.

The FDIC also raised its premium rates. Because the base for assessing premiums and the premium rates are both higher, the FDIC is now collecting premiums and adding to its reserve fund at a faster pace. Nevertheless, most economists agree that, on net, the FDIC's exposure to moral hazard risks has increased considerably in recent years.

QUICK QUIZ See page 345 for the answers. Review concepts from this section in MyEconLab.

To limit the fallout from systemwide failures and bank runs, Congress created the __________ __________ __________ __________ in 1933. Since the advent of federal deposit insurance, there have been no true bank runs at federally insured banks.

Federal insurance of bank deposits insulates depositors from risks, so depositors are __________ concerned about riskier investment strategies by depository institutions. Thus, bank managers have an incentive to invest in __________ assets to make __________ rates of return.

On the one hand, the Federal Deposit Insurance Reform Act of 2005 expanded the __________ hazard risks associated with deposit insurance by increasing limits for insured retirement deposits and indexing limits for other deposits to inflation. On the other hand, the law granted the FDIC greater discretion to assess risk-based deposit insurance __________ intended to restrain __________ hazard risks.

YOU ARE THERE

Why a Currency Displaying a Giant Rodent Circulates in Brazil

What induces firms in Silva Jardim, Brazil, to accept a private regional money called the *capivari*—named for the capybara, a pig-sized rodent common in a local river—in payment for goods and services? Roseanne Augusto, the manager of a hardware store, offers a simple answer: "It brings customers through the door."

The *capivari* that Augusto accepts at her store is one of 63 circulating private currencies in Brazil. Each currency's value is based on Brazil's official currency, the *real* (with multiple units called *reais*). In Silva Jardim, a local bank holds, on deposit, an amount of *reais* equal to the number of *capivaris* placed into circulation. Merchants such as Augusto's retail establishment offer price discounts to customers who pay with the private *capivaris* instead of the official *reais*. Consequently, people who use the *capivari* add "discount coupon" to the currency's function as a medium of exchange. Indeed, for Silva Jardim consumers, this discount is the only advantage of the *capivari* over the government's *real*. For sellers, Augusto's statement above sums up the key advantage: Consumers are willing to use the currency to buy enough items to raise sales by more than the discounts offered by the sellers when they accept the currency.

Critical Thinking Questions

1. If price tags in Augusto's retail store display prices in terms of *capivaris,* what function does the currency fulfill?
2. When Silva Jardim residents set *capivari* notes aside today for possible use a few weeks from now, what function does the currency fulfill?

ISSUES & APPLICATIONS

Bankers Are Not Sure That They Want More Deposits

CONCEPTS APPLIED

- Balance Sheet
- Net Worth
- Fractional Reserve Banking

Between the early 1960s and late 2000s, bankers sought to raise and lend out more deposit funds. Today, however, a number of banks have stopped trying to attract more deposits. A few are even actively discouraging deposits by charging customers fees if they deposit "too many" funds. Why have bankers' views about the desirability of increased deposits shifted so dramatically in recent years?

Low Returns on Lending

One key reason that banks have soured on deposits is that earnings they can anticipate from lending deposit funds are now very low. In today's dampened U.S. economy, many fewer households and firms are seeking credit than in years past. As a consequence, banks have been competing with one another for a dwindling set of borrowers, and they have bid market interest rates on bank loans downward.

Thus, existing deposits are now yielding lower returns for banks. This fact gives them less incentive to seek out more deposits from current or new customers.

Higher Deposit Insurance Premiums

Even as banks' returns from lending deposit funds have dropped, the costs they must pay for deposits have increased. Since 2006, the premium rate that banks must pay the Federal Deposit Insurance Corporation has jumped from close to zero to more than $0.30 per $100 of insured deposits—the highest rate since the FDIC's establishment in 1933.

The net result? Some banks have begun actively discouraging customers from substantially increasing their deposits. Recently, for instance, the Bank of New York Mellon began *charging* large depositors for the privilege of holding federally insured deposits. The bank now charges an annual interest fee of 0.13 percent to customers with deposit accounts of $50 million or more. Unless market loan rates rise and deposit insurance premiums fall, it appears likely that other banks will follow suit. Some banking experts speculate that eventually banks might begin charging interest fees to customers with small deposits.

For Critical Thinking

1. Why do you suppose that the market clearing interest rates on bank savings and time deposits have fallen as the interest rates on bank loans have dropped?
2. If interest rates earned by banks on their assets fell close to zero, why might all bank customers have to pay interest fees on deposits they hold with banks?

Web Resources

1. To take a look at the latest statistics on the status and performance of U.S. commercial banks, go to **www.econtoday.com/chap15**.
2. For a look at historical U.S. commercial banking data, go to **www.econtoday.com/chap15**.

MyEconLab

For more questions on this chapter's Issues & Applications, go to MyEconLab. In the Study Plan for this chapter, select Section N: News.

MyEconLab

Here is what you should know after reading this chapter. **MyEconLab** will help you identify what you know, and where to go when you need to practice.

WHAT YOU SHOULD KNOW		WHERE TO GO TO PRACTICE
The Key Functions and Properties of Money Money is a medium of exchange that people use to make payments for goods, services, and financial assets. It is also a unit of accounting for quoting prices in terms of money values. In addition, money is a store of value, so people can hold money for future use in exchange. Finally, money is a standard of deferred payment, enabling lenders to make loans and buyers to repay those loans with money. A good will function as money only if people are widely willing to accept the good in exchange for other goods and services. People will use money only if its value is relatively predictable.	money, 320 medium of exchange, 320 barter, 320 unit of accounting, 321 store of value, 321 standard of deferred payment, 321 liquidity, 321 transactions deposits, 322 fiduciary monetary system, 322 **Key Figure** Figure 15-1, 322	• MyEconLab Study Plans 15.1, 15.2 • Animated Figure 15-1

MyEconLab *continued*

WHAT YOU SHOULD KNOW		WHERE TO GO TO PRACTICE
Official Definitions of the Quantity of Money in Circulation The narrow definition of the quantity of money in circulation, called M1, includes only currency, transactions deposits, and traveler's checks. A broader definition, called M2, is equal to M1 plus savings deposits, small-denomination time deposits, and noninstitutional holdings of money market mutual fund balances.	money supply, 323 transactions approach, 323 liquidity approach, 323 M1, 323 depository institutions, 323 thrift institutions, 323 traveler's checks, 323 M2, 324	• MyEconLab Study Plan 15.3
Why Financial Intermediaries Such as Banks Exist Financial intermediaries help reduce problems stemming from the existence of asymmetric information. Adverse selection arises when uncreditworthy individuals and firms seek loans, Moral hazard problems exist when an individual or business that has been granted credit begins to engage in riskier practices. Financial intermediaries may also permit savers to benefit from economies of scale, which is the ability to reduce the costs and risks of managing funds by pooling funds and spreading costs and risks across many savers.	central bank, 325 financial intermediation, 325 financial intermediaries, 325 asymmetric information, 325 adverse selection, 325 moral hazard, 325 liabilities, 326 assets, 327 **Key Figures** Figure 15-3, 326 Figure 15-4, 328	• MyEconLab Study Plan 15.4 • Animated Figures 15.3, 15.4
The Basic Structure and Functions of the Federal Reserve System The Federal Reserve System consists of 12 district banks overseen by the Board of Governors. The Fed's main functions are supplying fiduciary currency, holding banks' reserves and clearing payments, acting as the goverment's fiscal agent, supervising banks, regulating the money supply, intervening in foreign exchange markets, and acting as a lender of last resort.	The Fed, 328 lender of last resort, 331 **Key Figure** Figure 15-6, 330	• MyEconLab Study Plan 15.5 • Animated Figure 15-6
The Maximum Potential Change in the Money Supply Following a Federal Reserve Monetary Policy Action When a bond dealer deposits funds received from the Fed in payment for a security following a Fed open market purchase, there is an increase in the total deposits in the banking system. The money supply increases by the amount of the initial deposit. The bank receiving this deposit can lend out funds in excess of those it holds as reserves, which will generate a rise in deposits at another bank. The maximum potential change in deposits throughout the banking system equals the amount of reserves injected (or withdrawn) by the Fed times the potential money multiplier, which is 1 divided by the reserve ratio.	fractional reserve banking, 332 reserves, 332 reserve ratio, 332 balance sheet, 332 open market operations, 333 money multiplier, 335 potential money multiplier, 335 **Key Table** Table 15-3, 334 **Key Figure** Figure 15-7, 335	• MyEconLab Study Plan 15.6 • Animated Table 15-3 • Animated Figure 15-7

MyEconLab

WHAT YOU SHOULD KNOW		WHERE TO GO TO PRACTICE
Features of Federal Deposit Insurance The Federal Deposit Insurance Corporation (FDIC) charges some depository institutions premiums and places these funds in accounts for use in reimbursing failed banks' depositors.	bank run, 336 Federal Deposit Insurance Corporation (FDIC), 337	• MyEconLab Study Plan 15.7

Log in to MyEconLab, take a chapter test, and get a personalized Study Plan that tells you which concepts you understand and which ones you need to review. From there, MyEconLab will give you further practice, tutorials, animations, videos, and guided solutions. For more information, visit www.myeconlab.com

PROBLEMS

All problems are assignable in MyEconLab; *exercises that update with real-time data are marked with* . *Answers to odd-numbered problems appear at the back of the book.*

15-1. Until 1946, residents of the island of Yap used large doughnut-shaped stones as financial assets. Although prices of goods and services were not quoted in terms of the stones, the stones were often used in exchange for particularly large purchases, such as livestock. To make the transaction, several individuals would insert a large stick through a stone's center and carry it to its new owner. A stone was difficult for any one person to steal, so an owner typically would lean it against the side of his or her home as a sign to others of accumulated purchasing power that would hold value for later use in exchange. Loans would often be repaid using the stones. In what ways did these stones function as money? (See pages 320–322.)

15-2. During the late 1970s, prices quoted in terms of the Israeli currency, the shekel, rose so fast that grocery stores listed their prices in terms of the U.S. dollar and provided customers with dollar-shekel conversion tables that they updated daily. Although people continued to buy goods and services and make loans using shekels, many Israeli citizens converted shekels to dollars to avoid a reduction in their wealth due to inflation. In what way did the U.S. dollar function as money in Israel during this period? (See pages 320–322.)

15-3. During the 1945–1946 Hungarian hyperinflation, when the rate of inflation reached 41.9 *quadrillion* percent per month, the Hungarian government discovered that the real value of its tax receipts was falling dramatically. To keep real tax revenues more stable, it created a good called a "tax pengö," in which all bank deposits were denominated for purposes of taxation. Nevertheless, payments for goods and services were made only in terms of the regular Hungarian currency, whose value tended to fall rapidly even though the value of a tax pengö remained stable. Prices were also quoted only in terms of the regular currency. Lenders, however, began denominating loan payments in terms of tax pengös. In what ways did the tax pengö function as money in Hungary in 1945 and 1946? (See pages 320–322.)

15-4. Considering the following data (expressed in billions of U.S. dollars), calculate M1 and M2. (See pages 323–324.)

Currency	1,050
Savings deposits	5,500
Small-denomination time deposits	1,000
Traveler's checks outside banks and thrifts	10
Total money market mutual funds	800
Institution-only money market mutual funds	1,800
Transactions deposits	1,140

15-5. Considering the following data (expressed in billions of U.S. dollars), calculate M1 and M2. (See pages 323–324.)

Transactions deposits	1,025
Savings deposits	3,300
Small-denomination time deposits	1,450
Money market deposit accounts	1,950
Noninstitution money market mutual funds	1,900
Traveler's checks outside banks and thrifts	25
Currency	1,050
Institution-only money market mutual funds	1,250

15-6. Identify whether each of the following amounts is counted in M1 only, M2 only, both M1 and M2, or neither. (See pages 323–324.)

a. $50 billion in U.S. Treasury bills

b. $15 billion in small-denomination time deposits

c. $5 billion in traveler's checks not issued by a bank

d. $20 billion in money market deposit accounts

15-7. Identify whether each of the following items is counted in M1 only, M2 only, both M1 and M2, or neither. (See pages 323–324.)

a. A $1,000 balance in a transactions deposit at a mutual savings bank

b. A $100,000 time deposit in a New York bank

c. A $10,000 time deposit an elderly widow holds at her credit union

d. A $50 traveler's check not issued by a bank

e. A $50,000 savings deposit

15-8. Match each of the rationales for financial intermediation listed below with at least one of the following financial intermediaries: insurance company, pension fund, savings bank. Explain your choices. (See pages 325–326.)

a. Adverse selection

b. Moral hazard

c. Lower management costs generated by larger scale

15-9. Identify whether each of the following events poses an adverse selection problem or a moral hazard problem in financial markets. (See pages 325–326.)

a. A manager of a savings and loan association responds to reports of a likely increase in federal deposit insurance coverage. She directs loan officers to extend mortgage loans to less creditworthy borrowers.

b. A loan applicant does not mention that a legal judgment in his divorce case will require him to make alimony payments to his ex-wife.

c. An individual who was recently approved for a loan to start a new business decides to use some of the funds to take a Hawaiian vacation.

15-10. In what sense is currency a liability of the Federal Reserve System? (See page 330.)

15-11. In what respects is the Fed like a private banking institution? In what respects is it more like a government agency? (See pages 328–331.)

15-12. Take a look at the map of the locations of the Federal Reserve districts and their headquarters in Figure 15-6 on page 330. Today, the U.S. population is centered just west of the Mississippi River—that is, about half of the population is either to the west or the east of a line running roughly just west of this river. Can you reconcile the current locations of Fed districts and banks with this fact? Why do you suppose the Fed has its current geographic structure? (See page 330.)

15-13. Draw an empty bank balance sheet, with the heading "Assets" on the left and the heading "Liabilities" on the right. Then place the following items on the proper side of the balance sheet (see page 332):

a. Loans to a private company

b. Borrowings from a Federal Reserve district bank

c. Deposits with a Federal Reserve district bank

d. U.S. Treasury bills

e. Vault cash

f. Transactions deposits

15-14. Draw an empty bank balance sheet, with the heading "Assets" on the left and the heading "Liabilities" on the right. Then place the following items on the proper side of the balance sheet. (see page 332.)

a. Borrowings from another bank in the interbank loans market

b. Deposits this bank holds in an account with another private bank

c. U.S. Treasury bonds

d. Small-denomination time deposits

e. Mortgage loans to household customers

f. Money market deposit accounts

15-15. The reserve ratio is 11 percent. What is the value of the potential money multiplier? (See page 335.)

15-16. The Federal Reserve purchases $1 million in U.S. Treasury bonds from a bond dealer, and the dealer's bank credits the dealer's account. The reserve ratio is 15 percent. Assuming that no currency leakage occurs, how much will the bank lend to its customers following the Fed's purchase? (See pages 333–334.)

15-17. Suppose that the value of the potential money multiplier is equal to 4. What is the reserve ratio? (See page 335.)

15-18. Consider a world in which there is no currency and depository institutions issue only transactions deposits. The reserve ratio is 20 percent. The central bank sells $1 billion in government securities. What ultimately happens to the money supply? (See page 335.)

15-19. Assume a 1 percent reserve ratio and no currency leakages. What is the potential money multiplier? How will total deposits in the banking system ultimately change if the Federal Reserve purchases $5 million in U.S. government securities? (See page 335.)

ECONOMICS ON THE NET

What's Happened to the Money Supply? Deposits at banks and other financial institutions make up a portion of the U.S. money supply. This exercise gives you the chance to see how changes in these deposits influence the Fed's measures of money.

Title: FRED (Federal Reserve Economic Data)

Navigation: Go to **www.econtoday.com/chap15** to visit the Web page of the Federal Reserve Bank of St. Louis.

Application

1. Select the data series for *Demand Deposits at Commercial Banks (Bil. of $; M)*, either seasonally adjusted or not. Scan through the data. Do you notice any recent trend? (Hint: Compare the growth in the figures before 1993 with their growth after 1993.) In addition, take a look at the data series for currency and for other transactions deposits. Do you observe similar recent trends in these series?
2. Back up, and click on *M1 Money Stock (Bil. of $; M)*, again either seasonally adjusted or not. Does it show any change in pattern beginning around 1993?

For Group Study and Analysis FRED contains considerable financial data series. Assign individual members or groups of the class the task of examining data on assets included in M1, M2, and MZM. Have each student or group look for big swings in the data. Then ask the groups to report to the class as a whole. When did clear changes occur in various categories of the monetary aggregates? Were there times when people appeared to shift funds from one aggregate to another? Are there any other noticeable patterns that may have had something to do with economic events during various periods?

ANSWERS TO QUICK QUIZZES

p. 323: (i) medium of exchange . . . unit of accounting . . . store of value . . . standard of deferred payment; (ii) liquid; (iii) fiduciary; (iv) predictable

p. 325: (i) transactions . . . M1; (ii) Transactions; (iii) M1 . . . M2

p. 328: (i) Financial; (ii) asymmetric . . . adverse selection . . . moral hazard

p. 331: (i) Federal Reserve System; (ii) Board . . . Governors; (iii) currency . . . reserves . . . lender of last resort

p. 336: (i) Reserves . . . Federal Reserve; (ii) reserve ratio; (iii) potential money multiplier

p. 340: (i) Federal Deposit Insurance Corporation; (ii) less . . . riskier . . . higher; (iii) moral . . . premiums . . . moral

16 Domestic and International Dimensions of Monetary Policy

Since 2008, the Fed has provided a number of "credit programs" through which it transmitted funds directly to individual financial institutions. In addition, the Fed bought bad debts from selected institutions, and it even purchased securities issued by nonfinancial firms, such as General Electric and McDonald's. The fundamental aims of this new Fed *credit policy* included making banks and firms more liquid and preventing insolvencies of selected institutions. Another objective was to keep borrowing costs low for all households and firms in order to stimulate borrowing that would fuel increases in total planned expenditures and aggregate demand. At various times between 2008 and 2010, though, the Fed failed to make sure that its monetary policy actions supported this latter credit policy goal. To understand how this policy breakdown occurred, you first must learn about the implementation of monetary policy, a key topic of this chapter.

LEARNING OBJECTIVES

After reading this chapter, you should be able to:

- Identify the key factors that influence the quantity of money that people desire to hold
- Describe how Federal Reserve monetary policy actions influence market interest rates
- Evaluate how expansionary and contractionary monetary policy actions affect equilibrium real GDP and the price level in the short run
- Understand the equation of exchange and its importance in the quantity theory of money and prices
- Explain how the Federal Reserve has implemented credit policy since 2008

MyEconLab helps you master each objective and study more efficiently. See end of chapter for details.

DID YOU KNOW THAT... during a couple of brief intervals within the past few years, Apple had more cash on hand than did the U.S. Treasury? For instance, at one point, the U.S. Treasury held just over $73 billion in accounts from which federal government checks could be written, whereas Apple's accounts contained more than $76 billion. Of course, one reason for this situation has been that the federal government's tax collections have been lower than in prior years, leading to reduced Treasury cash balances. In addition, Apple has maintained unusually large stockpiles of funds in checkable accounts. Indeed, total cash balances across all U.S. nonfinancial companies have recently totaled in excess of $1.8 trillion, or about 7 percent of all businesses' assets, which is the highest percentage since the early 1960s.

Most economists agree that a major reason U.S. companies are holding so much cash is that the rate of interest—the opportunity cost of holding money instead of an interest-bearing asset—has been very low. In this chapter, you will learn about determinants of how much money people desire to hold—that is, about their *demand for money.*

The Demand for Money

In the previous chapter, we saw how the Federal Reserve's open market operations can increase or decrease the money supply. Our focus was on the effects of the Fed's actions on the banking system. In this chapter, we widen our discussion to see how Fed monetary policy actions have an impact on the broader economy by influencing market interest rates. First, though, you must understand the factors that determine how much money people desire to hold—in other words, you must understand the demand for money.

All of us engage in a flow of transactions. We buy and sell things all of our lives. But because we use money—dollars—as our medium of exchange, all *flows* of nonbarter transactions involve a *stock* of money. We can restate this as follows:

To use money, one must hold money.

Given that everybody must hold money, we can now talk about the *demand* to hold it. People do not demand to hold money just to look at pictures of past leaders. They hold it to be able to use it to buy goods and services.

The Demand for Money: What People Wish to Hold

People have certain motivations that cause them to want to hold **money balances.** Individuals and firms could try to do without non-interest-bearing money balances. But life is inconvenient without a ready supply of money balances. Thus, the public has a demand for money, motivated by several factors.

Money balances
Synonymous with money, money stock, money holdings.

THE TRANSACTIONS DEMAND The main reason people hold money is that money can be used to purchase goods and services. People are paid at specific intervals (once a week, once a month, and the like), but they wish to make purchases more or less continuously. To free themselves from having to buy goods and services only on payday, people find it beneficial to hold money. The benefit they receive is convenience: They willingly forgo interest earnings in order to avoid the inconvenience of cashing in nonmoney assets such as bonds every time they wish to make a purchase. Thus, people hold money to make regular, *expected* expenditures under the **transactions demand.** As nominal GDP (see page 176 in Chapter 8) rises, people will want to hold more money because they will be making more transactions.

Transactions demand
Holding money as a medium of exchange to make payments. The level varies directly with nominal GDP.

THE PRECAUTIONARY DEMAND The transactions demand involves money held to make *expected* expenditures. People also hold money for the **precautionary demand** to make *unexpected* purchases or to meet emergencies. When people hold money for the precautionary demand, they incur a cost in forgone interest earnings that they balance against the benefit of having cash on hand. The higher the rate of interest, the lower the precautionary money balances people wish to hold.

Precautionary demand
Holding money to meet unplanned expenditures and emergencies.

THE ASSET DEMAND Remember that one of the functions of money is to serve as a store of value. People can hold money balances as a store of value, or they can hold bonds or stocks or other interest-earning assets. The desire to hold money as a store of value leads to the **asset demand** for money. People choose to hold money rather than other assets for two reasons: its liquidity and the lack of risk.

Asset demand
Holding money as a store of value instead of other assets such as corporate bonds and stocks.

The disadvantage of holding money balances as an asset, of course, is the interest earnings forgone. Each individual or business decides how much money to hold as an asset by looking at the opportunity cost of holding money. The higher the interest rate—which is the opportunity cost of holding money—the lower the money balances people will want to hold as assets. Conversely, the lower the interest rate offered on alternative assets, the higher the money balances people will want to hold as assets.

The Demand for Money Curve

Assume for simplicity's sake that the amount of money demanded for transactions purposes is proportionate to income. That leaves the precautionary and asset demands for money, both determined by the opportunity cost of holding money. If we assume that the interest rate represents the cost of holding money balances, we can graph the relationship between the interest rate and the quantity of money demanded.

In Figure 16-1 below, the demand for money curve shows a familiar downward slope. The horizontal axis measures the quantity of money demanded, and the vertical axis is the interest rate. The rate of interest is the cost of holding money. At a higher interest rate, a lower quantity of money is demanded, and vice versa.

To see this, imagine two scenarios. In the first one, you can earn 20 percent a year if you put your funds into purchases of U.S. government securities. In the other scenario, you can earn 1 percent if you put your funds into purchases of U.S. government securities. If you have $1,000 average cash balances in a non-interest-bearing checking account, in the first scenario over a one-year period, your opportunity cost would be 20 percent of $1,000, or $200. In the second scenario, the opportunity cost that you would incur would be 1 percent of $1,000, or $10. Under which scenario would you hold more funds in your checking account instead of securities?

QUICK QUIZ See page 369 for the answers. Review concepts from this section in MyEconLab.

To use money, people must hold money. Therefore, they have a __________ for money balances.

The determinants of the demand for money balances are the __________ demand, the __________ demand, and the __________ demand.

Holding money carries an __________ cost—the interest income forgone. Hence, the demand for money curve showing the relationship between the quantity of money balances demanded and the interest rate slopes __________.

FIGURE 16-1

The Demand for Money Curve

If we use the interest rate as a proxy for the opportunity cost of holding money balances, the demand for money curve, M_d, is downward sloping, similar to other demand curves

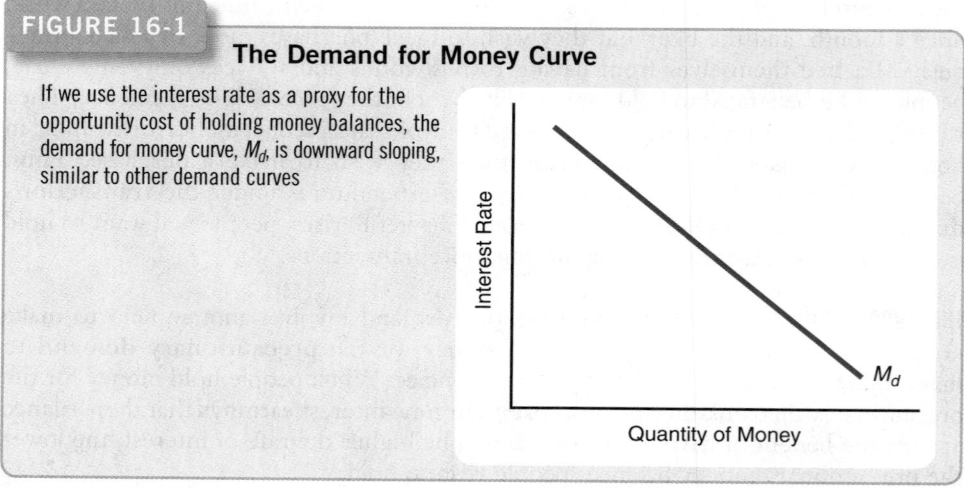

How the Fed Influences Interest Rates

When the Fed takes actions that alter the rate of growth of the money supply, it is seeking to influence investment, consumption, and total aggregate expenditures. In taking these monetary policy actions, the Fed in principle has four tools at its disposal: open market operations, changes in the reserve ratio, changes in the interest rates paid on reserves, and discount rate changes. The first two tools were introduced in Chapter 15. The discount rate and interest rates paid on reserves will be discussed later in this chapter. Let's consider the effects of open market operations, the tool that the Fed regularly employs on a day-to-day basis.

Open Market Operations

As we saw in the previous chapter, the Fed changes the amount of reserves in the banking system by its purchases and sales of government bonds issued by the U.S. Treasury. To understand how these actions by the Fed influence the market interest rate, we start out in an equilibrium in which all individuals, including the holders of bonds, are satisfied with the current situation. There is some equilibrium level of interest rate (and bond prices). Now, if the Fed wants to conduct open market operations, it must somehow induce individuals, businesses, and foreign residents to hold more or fewer U.S. Treasury bonds. The inducement must take the form of making people better off. So, if the Fed wants to buy bonds, it will have to offer to buy them at a higher price than exists in the marketplace. If the Fed wants to sell bonds, it will have to offer them at a lower price than exists in the marketplace. Thus, an open market operation must cause a change in the price of bonds.

Go to **www.econtoday.com/chap16** to learn about the Federal Reserve's current policy regarding open market operations. Scan down the page, and select the "Minutes" for the most recent date.

GRAPHING THE SALE OF BONDS The Fed sells some of the bonds it has on hand. This is shown in panel (a) of Figure 16-2 below. Notice that the supply of bonds in the private market is shown here as a vertical line with respect to price. The demand for bonds is downward sloping. If the Fed offers more bonds it owns for sale, the supply curve shifts from S_1 to S_2. People will not be willing to buy the extra bonds at the initial equilibrium bond price, P_1. They will be satisfied holding the additional bonds at the new equilibrium price, P_2.

THE FED'S PURCHASE OF BONDS The opposite occurs when the Fed purchases bonds. You can view this purchase of bonds as a reduction in the stock of bonds available for

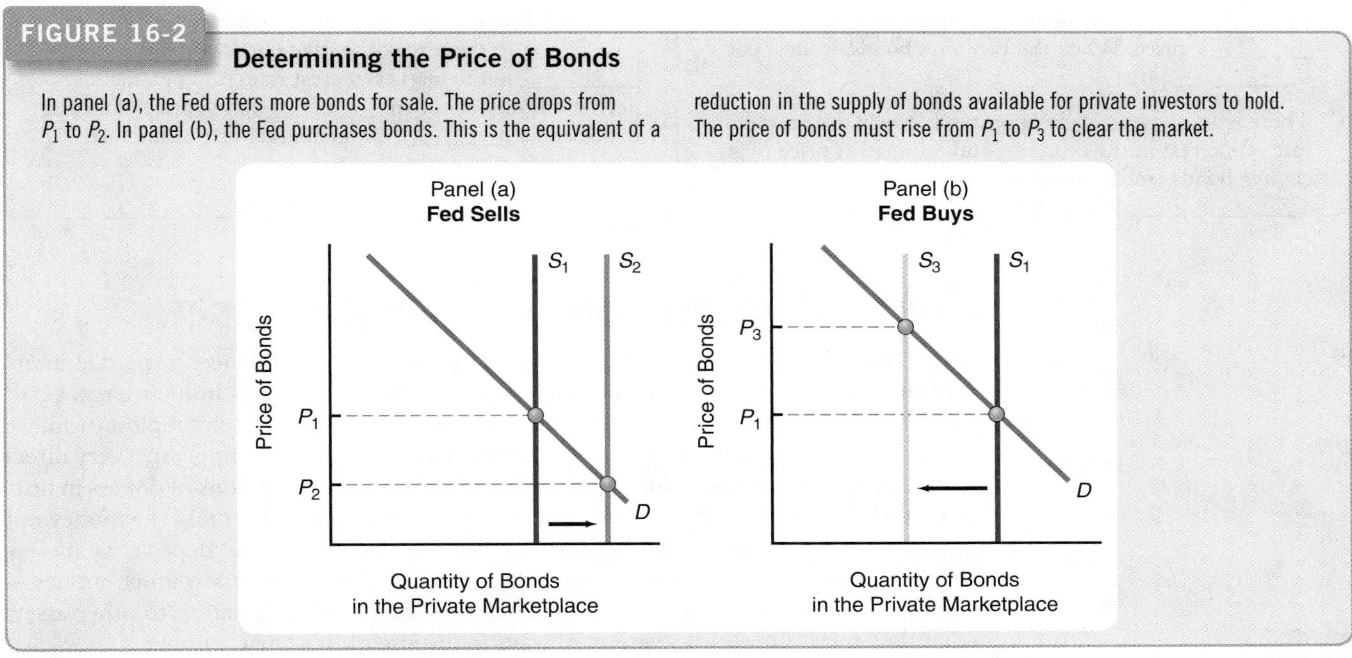

FIGURE 16-2
Determining the Price of Bonds

In panel (a), the Fed offers more bonds for sale. The price drops from P_1 to P_2. In panel (b), the Fed purchases bonds. This is the equivalent of a reduction in the supply of bonds available for private investors to hold. The price of bonds must rise from P_1 to P_3 to clear the market.

private investors to hold. In panel (b) of Figure 16-2 on the previous page, the original supply curve is S_1. The new supply curve of outstanding bonds will end up being S_3 because of the Fed's purchases of bonds. To get people to give up these bonds, the Fed must offer them a more attractive price. The price will rise from to P_1 to P_3.

Relationship between the Price of Existing Bonds and the Rate of Interest

The price of existing bonds and the rate of interest are inversely related. Assume that the average yield on bonds is 5 percent. You decide to purchase a bond. A local corporation agrees to sell you a bond that will pay you $50 a year forever. What is the price you are willing to pay for the bond? It is $1,000. Why? Because $50 divided by $1,000 equals 5 percent, which is as good as the best return you can earn elsewhere. You purchase the bond. The next year something happens in the economy, and you can now obtain bonds that have effective yields of 10 percent. (In other words, the prevailing interest rate in the economy is now 10 percent.) What will happen to the market price of the existing bond that you own, the one you purchased the year before? It will fall.

If you try to sell the bond for $1,000, you will discover that no investors will buy it from you. Why should they when they can obtain the same $50-a-year yield from someone else by paying only $500? Indeed, unless you offer your bond for sale at a price that is no higher than $500, no buyers will be forthcoming. Hence, an increase in the prevailing interest rate in the economy has caused the market value of your existing bond to fall.

The important point to be understood is this:

The market price of* existing *bonds (and all fixed-income assets) is inversely related to the rate of interest prevailing in the economy.

As a consequence of the inverse relationship between the price of existing bonds and the interest rate, the Fed is able to influence the interest rate by engaging in open market operations. A Fed open market sale that reduces the equilibrium price of bonds brings about an increase in the interest rate. A Fed open market purchase that boosts the equilibrium price of bonds generates a decrease in the interest rate.

QUICK QUIZ See page 369 for the answers. Review concepts from this section in MyEconLab.

When the Fed sells bonds, it must offer them at a __________ price. When the Fed buys bonds, it must pay a __________ price.

There is an __________ relationship between the prevailing rate of interest in the economy and the market price of *existing* bonds (and all fixed-income assets).

A Federal Reserve open market sale generates a __________ in the price of *existing* bonds and an __________ in the market interest rate. An open market purchase brings about an __________ in the price of *existing* bonds and a __________ in the market rate of interest.

Effects of an Increase in the Money Supply

Now that we've seen how the Fed's monetary policy actions influence the market interest rate, we can ask a broader question: How does monetary policy influence real GDP and the price level? To understand how monetary policy works in its simplest form, we are going to run an experiment in which you increase the money supply in a very direct way. Assume that the government has given you hundreds of millions of dollars in just-printed bills. You then fly around the country in a helicopter, dropping the money out of the window. People pick it up and put it in their pockets. Some deposit the money in their transactions deposit accounts. As a result, they now have too much money—not in the sense that they want to throw it away but rather in relation to other assets that they own. There are a variety of ways to dispose of this "new" money.

Direct Effect

The simplest thing that people can do when they have excess money balances is to go out and spend them on goods and services. Here they have a direct impact on aggregate demand. Aggregate demand rises because with an increase in the money supply, at any given price level people now want to purchase more output of real goods and services.

Indirect Effect

Not everybody will necessarily spend the newfound money on goods and services. Some people may wish to deposit a portion or all of those excess money balances in banks. The recipient banks now discover that they have higher reserves than they wish to hold. As you learned in Chapter 15, one thing that banks can do to get higher-interest-earning assets is to lend out the excess reserves. But banks cannot induce people to borrow more funds than they were borrowing before unless the banks lower the interest rate that they charge on loans. This lower interest rate encourages people to take out those loans. Businesses will therefore engage in new investment with the funds loaned. Individuals will engage in more consumption of durable goods such as housing, autos, and home entertainment centers. Either way, the increased loans generate a rise in aggregate demand. More people will be involved in more spending—even those who did not pick up any of the money that was originally dropped out of your helicopter.

What happens if the market interest rate on bonds falls close to zero, as has occurred in recent years? In that case, monetary policy traditionally must rely on the direct effect of a change in bank reserves and, through the money multiplier effect, the quantity of money in circulation. Monetary policy cannot depend on the indirect effect of an interest rate that is already at zero. A policy action in which the Federal Reserve conducts open market purchases to increase bank reserves without seeking to alter the interest rate, which is already zero, is called **quantitative easing.**

Quantitative easing
Federal Reserve open market purchases intended to generate an increase in bank reserves at a nearly zero interest rate.

Graphing the Effects of an Expansionary Monetary Policy

To consider the effects of an expansionary monetary policy on real GDP and the price level, look at Figure 16-3 below. We start out in a situation in which the economy is operating at less than full employment. You see a recessionary gap in the figure, which is

FIGURE 16-3
Expansionary Monetary Policy with Underutilized Resources

If we start out with equilibrium at E_1, expansionary monetary policy will shift AD_1 to AD_2. The new equilibrium will be at E_2.

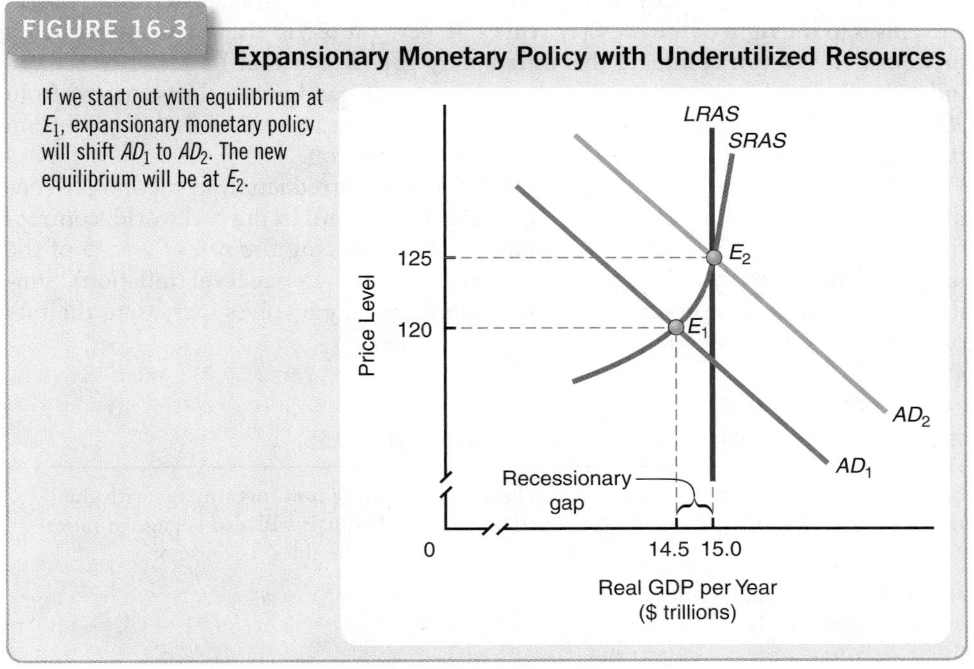

FIGURE 16-4

Contractionary Monetary Policy with Overutilized Resources

If we begin at short-run equilibrium at point E_1, contractionary monetary policy will shift the aggregate demand curve from AD_1 to AD_2. The new equilibrium will be at point E_2.

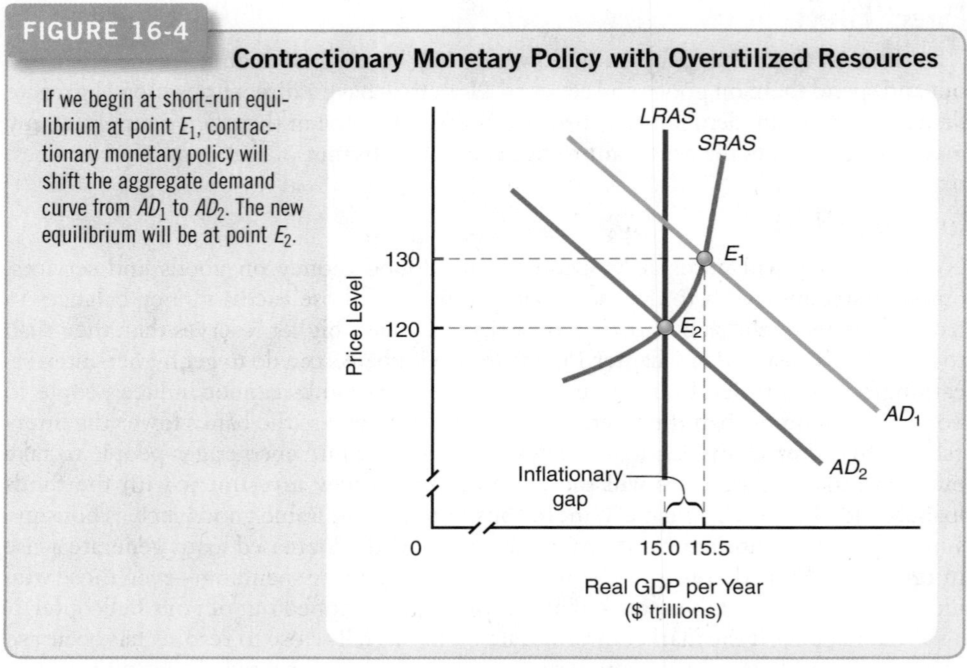

measured as the horizontal difference between the long-run aggregate supply curve, *LRAS*, and the current equilibrium. Short-run equilibrium is at E_1, with a price level of 120 and real GDP of $14.5 trillion. The *LRAS* curve is at $15 trillion. Assume now that the Fed increases the money supply. Because of the direct and indirect effects of this increase in the money supply, aggregate demand shifts outward to the right to AD_2. The new equilibrium is at an output rate of $15 trillion of real GDP per year and a price level of 125. Here expansionary monetary policy can move the economy toward its *LRAS* curve sooner than otherwise.

Graphing the Effects of Contractionary Monetary Policy

Assume that there is an inflationary gap as shown in Figure 16-4 above. There you see that the short-run aggregate supply curve, *SRAS*, intersects aggregate demand, AD_1, at E_1. This is to the right of the *LRAS* of real GDP per year of $15 trillion. Contractionary monetary policy can eliminate this inflationary gap. Because of both the direct and indirect effects of monetary policy, the aggregate demand curve shifts inward from AD_1 to AD_2. Equilibrium is now at E_2, which is at a lower price level, 120. Equilibrium real GDP has now fallen from $15.5 trillion to $15 trillion.

Note that contractionary monetary policy involves a reduction in the money supply, with a consequent decline in the price level (deflation). In the real world, contractionary monetary policy more commonly involves reducing the *rate of growth* of the money supply, thereby reducing the rate of increase in the price level (inflation). Similarly, real-world expansionary monetary policy typically involves increasing the rate of growth of the money supply.

QUICK QUIZ See page 369 for the answers. Review concepts from this section in MyEconLab.

The __________ effect of an increase in the money supply arises because people desire to spend more on real goods and services when they have excess money balances.

The __________ effect of an increase in the money supply works through a __________ in the interest rate, which encourages businesses to make new investments with the funds loaned to them. Individuals will also engage in more consumption (on consumer durables) because of __________ interest rates.

Open Economy Transmission of Monetary Policy

So far we have discussed monetary policy in a closed economy. When we move to an open economy, with international trade and the international purchases and sales of all assets including dollars and other currencies, monetary policy becomes more complex. Consider first the effect of monetary policy on exports.

Go to www.econtoday.com/chap16 for links to central banks around the globe, provided by the Bank for International Settlements.

The Net Export Effect of Contractionary Monetary Policy

To see how a change in monetary policy can affect net exports, suppose that the Federal Reserve implements a contractionary policy that boosts the market interest rate. The higher U.S. interest rate, in turn, tends to attract foreign investment in U.S. financial assets, such as U.S. government securities.

If more residents of foreign countries decide that they want to purchase U.S. government securities or other U.S. assets, they first have to obtain U.S. dollars. As a consequence, the demand for dollars goes up in foreign exchange markets. The international price of the dollar therefore rises. This is called an *appreciation* of the dollar, and it tends to reduce net exports because it makes our exports more expensive in terms of foreign currency and imports cheaper in terms of dollars. Foreign residents demand fewer of our goods and services, and we demand more of theirs.

This reasoning implies that when contractionary monetary policy increases the U.S. interest rate at the current price level, there will be a negative net export effect because foreign residents will want more U.S. financial instruments. Hence, they will demand additional dollars, thereby causing the international price of the dollar to rise. This makes our exports more expensive for the rest of the world, which then demands a smaller quantity of our exports. It also means that foreign goods and services are less expensive in the United States, so we therefore demand more imports. We come up with this conclusion:

> ***Contractionary monetary policy causes interest rates to rise. Such a* rise *will induce international inflows of funds, thereby raising the international value of the dollar and making U.S. goods less attractive abroad. The net export effect of contractionary monetary policy will be in the same direction as the monetary policy effect, thereby amplifying the effect of such policy.***

The Net Export Effect of Expansionary Monetary Policy

Now assume that the economy is experiencing a recession and the Federal Reserve wants to pursue an expansionary monetary policy. In so doing, it will cause interest rates to fall in the short run, as discussed earlier. Declining interest rates will cause funds to flow out of the United States. The demand for dollars will decrease, and their international price will go down. Foreign goods will now look more expensive to U.S. residents, and imports will fall. Foreign residents will desire more of our exports, and exports will rise. The result will be an increase in net exports. Again, the international consequences reinforce the domestic consequences of monetary policy, in this case by stimulating the economy.

On a broader level, the Fed's ability to control the rate of growth of the money supply may be hampered as U.S. money markets become less isolated. With the push of a computer button, billions of dollars can change hands halfway around the world. If the Fed reduces the growth of the money supply, individuals and firms in the United States can obtain dollars from other sources. People in the United States who want more liquidity can obtain their dollars from foreign residents. Indeed, as world markets become increasingly integrated, U.S. residents, who can already hold U.S. bank accounts denominated in foreign currencies, more regularly conduct transactions using other nations' currencies.

QUICK QUIZ See page 369 for the answers. Review concepts from this section in MyEconLab.

Monetary policy in an open economy has repercussions for net ________.

If contractionary monetary policy raises U.S. interest rates, there is a ________ net export effect because foreign residents will demand ________ U.S. financial instruments, thereby demanding ________ dollars and hence causing the international price of the dollar to rise.

This makes our exports more expensive for the rest of the world.

When expansionary monetary policy causes interest rates to fall, foreign residents will want ________ U.S. financial instruments. The resulting ________ in the demand for dollars will reduce the dollar's value in foreign exchange markets, leading to an ________ in net exports.

Monetary Policy and Inflation

Most media discussions of inflation focus on the short run. The price index can fluctuate in the short run because of events such as oil price shocks, labor union strikes, or discoveries of large amounts of new natural resources. In the long run, however, empirical studies show that excessive growth in the money supply results in inflation.

If the supply of money rises relative to the demand for money, people have more money balances than desired. They adjust their mix of assets to reduce money balances in favor of other items. This ultimately causes their spending on goods and services to increase. The result is a rise in the price level, or inflation.

The Equation of Exchange and the Quantity Theory

Equation of exchange
The formula indicating that the number of monetary units (M_s) times the number of times each unit is spent on final goods and services (V) is identical to the price level (P) times real GDP (Y).

Income velocity of money (V)
The number of times per year a dollar is spent on final goods and services; identically equal to nominal GDP divided by the money supply.

A simple way to show the relationship between changes in the quantity of money in circulation and the price level is through the **equation of exchange**, developed by Irving Fisher (note that ≡ refers to an identity or truism):

$$M_s V \equiv PY$$

where M_s = actual money balances held by the nonbanking public
V = **income velocity of money,** which is the number of times, on average per year, each monetary unit is spent on final goods and services
P = price level or price index
Y = real GDP per year

Consider a numerical example involving the entire economy. Assume that in this economy, the total money supply, Ms, is \$10 trillion; real GDP, Y, is \$15 trillion (in base-year dollars); and the price level, P, is 1.3333 (133.33 in index number terms). Using the equation of exchange,

$$\begin{aligned} M_s V &\equiv PY \\ \$10 \text{ trillion} \times V &\equiv 1.3333 \times \$15 \text{ trillion} \\ \$10 \text{ trillion} \times V &\equiv \$20 \text{ trillion} \\ V &\equiv 2.0 \end{aligned}$$

Thus, each dollar is spent an average of 2 times per year.

THE EQUATION OF EXCHANGE AS AN IDENTITY The equation of exchange must always be true—it is an *accounting identity*. The equation of exchange states that the total amount of funds spent on final output, $M_s V$, is equal to the total amount of funds *received* for final output, PY. Thus, a given flow of funds can be viewed from either the buyers' side or the producers' side. The value of goods purchased is equal to the value of goods sold.

If Y represents real GDP and P is the price level, PY equals the dollar value of national output of goods and services or *nominal* GDP. Thus,

$$M_s V \equiv PY \equiv \text{nominal GDP}$$

THE QUANTITY THEORY OF MONEY AND PRICES If we now make some assumptions about different variables in the equation of exchange, we come up with the simplified theory of

FIGURE 16-5

The Relationship between Money Supply Growth Rates and Rates of Inflation

If we plot rates of inflation and rates of monetary growth for different countries, we come up with a scatter diagram that reveals an obvious direct relationship. If you were to draw a line through the "average" of the points in this figure, it would be upward sloping, showing that an increase in the rate of growth of the money supply leads to an increase in the rate of inflation.

Sources: International Monetary Fund and national central banks. Data are for latest available periods.

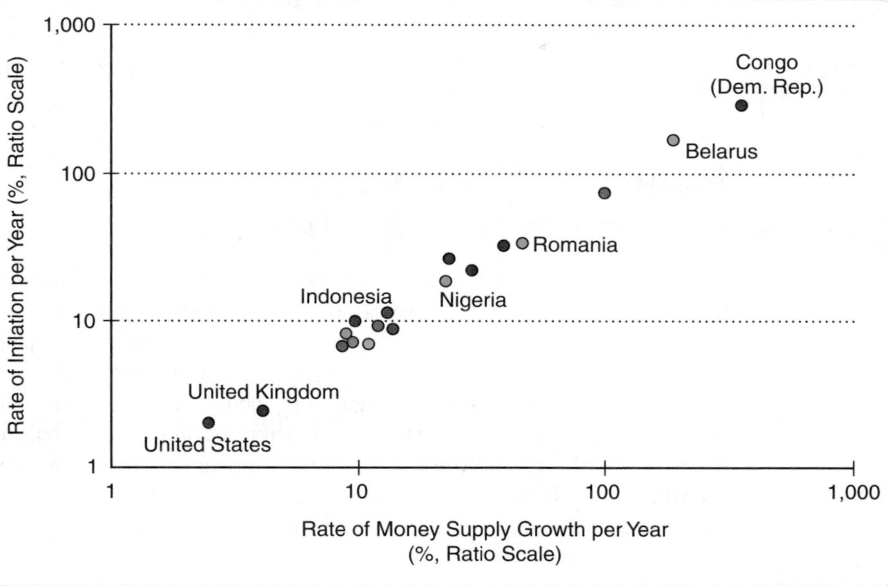

why the price level changes, called the **quantity theory of money and prices.** If we assume that the velocity of money, V, is constant and that real GDP, Y, is also constant, the simple equation of exchange tells us that a change in the money supply can lead only to an equiproportional change in the price level. Continue with our numerical example. Y is \$15 trillion. V equals 2.0. If the money supply increases by 20 percent, to \$12 trillion, the only thing that can happen is that the price level, P, has to go up from 1.3333 to 1.6. In other words, the price level must also increase by 20 percent. Otherwise the equation is no longer in balance. An increase in the money supply of 20 percent results in a rise in the price level (inflation) of 20 percent.

Quantity theory of money and prices The hypothesis that changes in the money supply lead to equiproportional changes in the price level.

YOU ARE THERE

To contemplate how the quantity theory of money and prices operates in a multiplayer online game, take a look at **Applying the Quantity Theory of Money and Prices to a Universe of Star Systems** on page 363.

EMPIRICAL VERIFICATION There is considerable evidence of the empirical validity of the relationship between monetary growth and high rates of inflation. Figure 16-5 above tracks the correspondence between money supply growth and the rates of inflation in various countries around the world.

Why did Iran recently decide to make each unit of its money 10,000 times smaller?

INTERNATIONAL POLICY EXAMPLE

Iran Removes Four Zeros from Each Unit of Its Currency

In recent years, the annual inflation rate reported by Iran's government has ranged from about 15 percent to just over 20 percent. These high inflation rates followed on the heels of double-digit-percentage rates of growth in the quantity of *rials*—Iran's currency—in circulation. So many rials circulated and the average price level rose so high that the currency note most widely used in trade was the 100,000-rial note (worth less than \$10).

To save Iranian residents the complication of keeping careful track of the extra zeros in their currency notes and posted prices, the Central Bank of the Iranian Republic took the step of dividing the value of every unit of its currency by 10,000. To implement this change, the central bank announced the formal removal of four zeros from every currency note. It also gradually introduced into circulation a new currency, called the *parsi,* defined as equal to 10,000 rials, and began gradually removing rials from circulation.

FOR CRITICAL THINKING

Even after the new parsi notes replace the old rial notes, will the inflation rate change if the rate of growth of Iran's money supply stays the same?

QUICK QUIZ See page 369 for the answers. Review concepts from this section in MyEconLab.

The __________ of __________ states that the expenditures by some people will equal income receipts by others, or $M_sV \equiv PY$ (money supply times velocity equals nominal GDP).

Viewed as an accounting identity, the equation of exchange is always __________, because the amount of funds __________ on final output of goods and services must equal the total amount of funds __________ for final output.

The quantity theory of money and prices states that a change in the __________ __________ will bring about a proportional change in the __________ __________.

Monetary Policy in Action: The Transmission Mechanism

Earlier in this chapter, we talked about the direct and indirect effects of monetary policy. The direct effect is simply that an increase in the money supply causes people to have excess money balances. To get rid of these excess money balances, people increase their expenditures. The indirect effect, depicted in Figure 16-6 below, as the interest-rate-based money transmission mechanism, occurs because some people have decided to purchase interest-bearing assets with their excess money balances. This causes the price of such assets—bonds—to go up. Because of the inverse relationship between the price of existing bonds and the interest rate, the interest rate in the economy falls. This lower interest rate induces people and businesses to spend more than they otherwise would have spent.

An Interest-Rate-Based Transmission Mechanism

The indirect, interest-rate-based transmission mechanism can be seen explicitly in Figure 16-7 on the facing page. In panel (a), you see that an increase in the money supply reduces the interest rate. The economywide demand curve for money is labeled M_d in panel (a). At first, the money supply is at M_s, a vertical line determined by the Federal Reserve. The equilibrium interest rate is r_1. This occurs where the money supply curve intersects the money demand curve.

Now assume that the Fed increases the money supply, say, via open market operations. This will shift the money supply curve outward to the right to M_s'. People find themselves with too much cash (liquidity). They buy bonds. When they buy bonds, they bid up the prices of bonds, thereby lowering the interest rate. The interest rate falls to r_2, where the new money supply curve M_s' intersects the money demand curve M_d. This reduction in the interest rate from r_1 to r_2 has an effect on planned investment, as can be seen in panel (b). Planned investment per year increases from I_1 to I_2. An increase in investment will increase aggregate demand, as shown in panel (c). Aggregate demand increases from AD_1 to AD_2. Equilibrium in the economy increases from real GDP per year of $14.5 trillion, which is not on the *LRAS*, to equilibrium real GDP per year of $15 trillion, which is on the *LRAS*.

FIGURE 16-6

The Interest-Rate-Based Money Transmission Mechanism

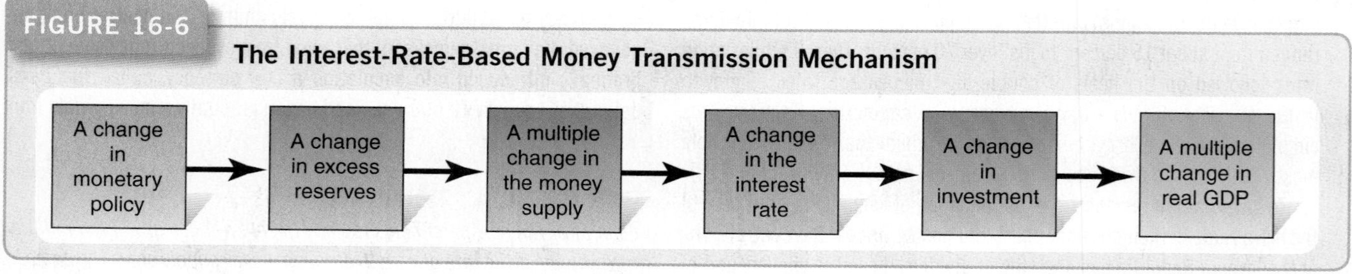

FIGURE 16-7

Adding Monetary Policy to the Aggregate Demand–Aggregate Supply Model

In panel (a), we show a demand for money function, M_d. It slopes downward to show that at lower rates of interest, a larger quantity of money will be demanded. The money supply is given initially as M_s, so the equilibrium rate of interest will be r_1. At this rate of interest, we see from the planned investment schedule given in panel (b) that the quantity of planned investment demanded per year will be I_1. After the shift in the money supply to M_s', the resulting increase in investment from I_1 to I_2 shifts the aggregate demand curve in panel (c) outward from AD_1 to AD_2. Equilibrium moves from E_1 to E_2, at real GDP of $15 trillion per year.

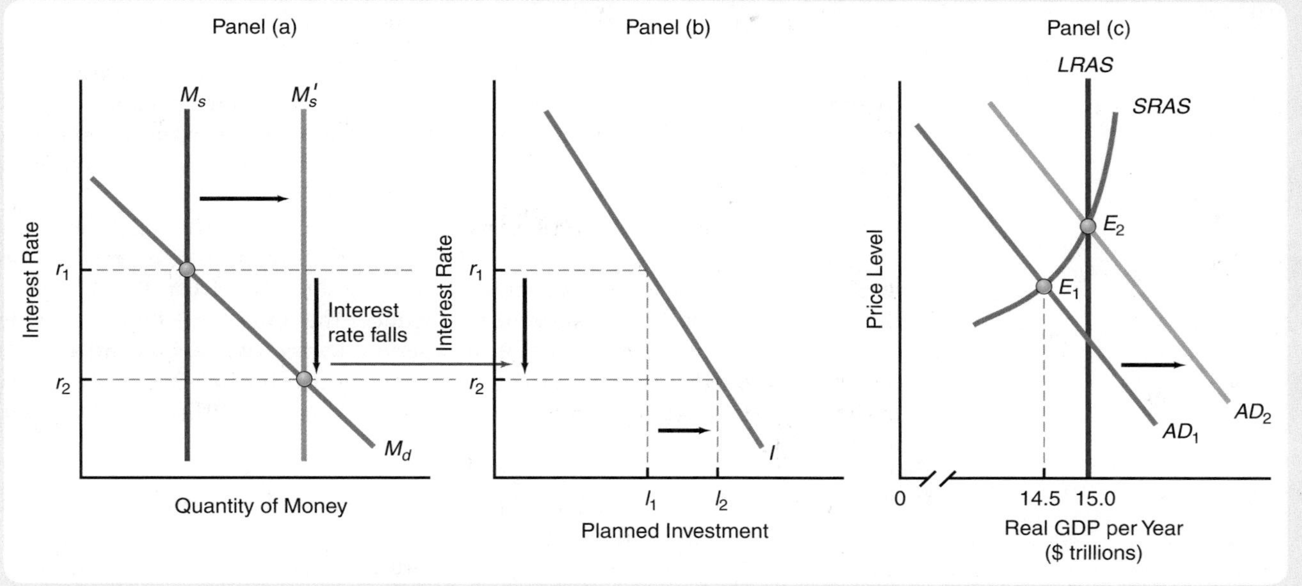

Targeting the Federal Funds Rate

As we have seen, the Fed can influence interest rates only by actively entering the market for federal government securities (usually Treasury bills). So, if the Fed wants to raise "the" interest rate, it essentially must engage in contractionary open market operations. That is to say, it must sell more Treasury securities than it buys, thereby reducing total reserves in the banking system and, hence, the money supply. This tends to boost the rate of interest. Conversely, when the Fed wants to decrease "the" rate of interest, it engages in expansionary open market operations, thereby increasing reserves and the money supply. But what interest rate is the Fed attempting to change?

In reality, more than one interest rate matters for Fed policymaking. Three interest rates are particularly relevant.

1. ***The Federal Funds Rate.*** In normal times, depository institutions wishing to borrow funds rarely seek to borrow directly from the Fed. In years past, this was because the Fed would not lend them all they wanted to borrow. Instead, the Fed encouraged banks to obtain funds in the **federal funds market** when they wanted to expand their reserves. The federal funds market is an interbank market in reserves where one bank borrows the excess reserves—resources held voluntarily over and above required reserves—of another. The generic term *federal funds market* refers to the borrowing or lending of reserve funds that are usually repaid within the same 24-hour period.

   Depository institutions that borrow in the federal funds market pay an interest rate called the **federal funds rate.** Because the federal funds rate is a ready measure of the cost that banks must incur to raise funds, the Federal Reserve often uses it as a yardstick by which to measure the effects of its policies. Consequently, the federal funds rate is closely watched as an indicator of the Fed's intentions.

Federal funds market
A private market (made up mostly of banks) in which banks can borrow reserves from other banks that want to lend them. Federal funds are usually lent for overnight use.

Federal funds rate
The interest rate that depository institutions pay to borrow reserves in the interbank federal funds market.

Discount rate
The interest rate that the Federal Reserve charges for reserves that it lends to depository institutions. It is sometimes referred to as the *rediscount rate* or, in Canada and England, as the *bank rate*.

2. ***The Discount Rate.*** When the Fed does lend reserves directly to depository institutions, the rate of interest that it charges is called the **discount rate.** When depository institutions borrow reserves from the Fed at this rate, they are said to be borrowing through the Fed's "discount window." Borrowing from the Fed increases reserves and thereby expands the money supply, other things being equal.

   Since 2003, the differential between the discount rate and the federal funds rate has ranged from 0.25 percentage point to 1.0 percentage point. An increase in this differential reduces depository institutions' incentive to borrow from the Fed and thereby generates a reduction in discount window borrowings.

3. ***The Interest Rate on Reserves.*** In October 2008, Congress granted the Fed authority to pay interest on both required reserves and excess reserves of depository institutions. Initially, the Fed paid different rates of interest on required and excess reserves, but since late 2008 the Fed has paid the same interest rate on both categories of reserves.

   Varying the interest rate on reserves alters the incentives that banks face when deciding whether to hold any additional reserves they obtain as excess reserves or to lend those reserves out to other banks in the federal funds market. If the Fed raises the interest rate on reserves and thereby reduces the differential between the federal funds rate and the interest rate on reserves, banks have less incentive to lend reserves in the federal funds market. Thus, it is not surprising that excess reserves in the U.S. banking system now amount to more than $1.5 trillion, as discussed in more detail later in this chapter.

ESTABLISHING THE FED POLICY STRATEGY The policy decisions that determine open market operations by which the Fed pursues its announced objective for the federal funds rate are made by the Federal Open Market Committee (FOMC). Every six to eight weeks, the voting members of the FOMC—the seven Fed board governors and five regional bank presidents—determine the Fed's general strategy of open market operations.

FOMC Directive
A document that summarizes the Federal Open Market Committee's general policy strategy, establishes near-term objectives for the federal funds rate, and specifies target ranges for money supply growth.

The FOMC outlines its strategy in a document called the **FOMC Directive.** This document lays out the FOMC's general economic objectives, establishes short-term federal funds rate objectives, and specifies target ranges for money supply growth. After each meeting, the FOMC issues a brief statement to the media, which then publish stories about the Fed's action or inaction and what it is likely to mean for the economy. Typically, these stories have headlines such as "Fed Cuts Key Interest Rate," "Fed Acts to Push Up Interest Rates," or "Fed Decides to Leave Interest Rates Alone."

Trading Desk
An office at the Federal Reserve Bank of New York charged with implementing monetary policy strategies developed by the Federal Open Market Committee.

THE TRADING DESK The FOMC leaves the task of implementing the Directive to officials who manage an office at the Federal Reserve Bank of New York known as the **Trading Desk.** The media spend little time considering how the Fed's Trading Desk conducts its activities, taking for granted that the Fed can implement the policy action that it has announced to the public. The Trading Desk's open market operations typically are confined within a one-hour interval each weekday morning.

The Taylor Rule

Taylor rule
An equation that specifies a federal funds rate target based on an estimated long-run real interest rate, the current deviation of the actual inflation rate from the Federal Reserve's inflation objective, and the gap between actual real GDP per year and a measure of potential real GDP per year.

In 1990, John Taylor of Stanford University suggested a relatively simple equation that the Fed might use for the purpose of selecting a federal funds rate target. This equation would direct the Fed to set the federal funds rate target based on an estimated long-run real interest rate (see page 151 in Chapter 7), the current deviation of the actual inflation rate from the Fed's inflation objective, and the proportionate gap between actual real GDP per year and a measure of potential real GDP per year. Taylor and other economists have applied his equation, which has become known as the **Taylor rule,** to actual Fed policy choices. They have concluded that the Taylor rule's recommendations for federal funds rate target values come close to the actual targets the Fed has selected over time.

MyEconLab Real-time data

FIGURE 16-8

Actual Federal Funds Rates and Values Predicted by a Taylor Rule

This figure displays both the actual path of the federal funds rate since 2002 and the target paths specified by a Taylor-rule equation for a Federal Reserve annual inflation objective of 0 percent.

Source: Federal Reserve Bank of St. Louis; *Monetary Trends*, various issues.

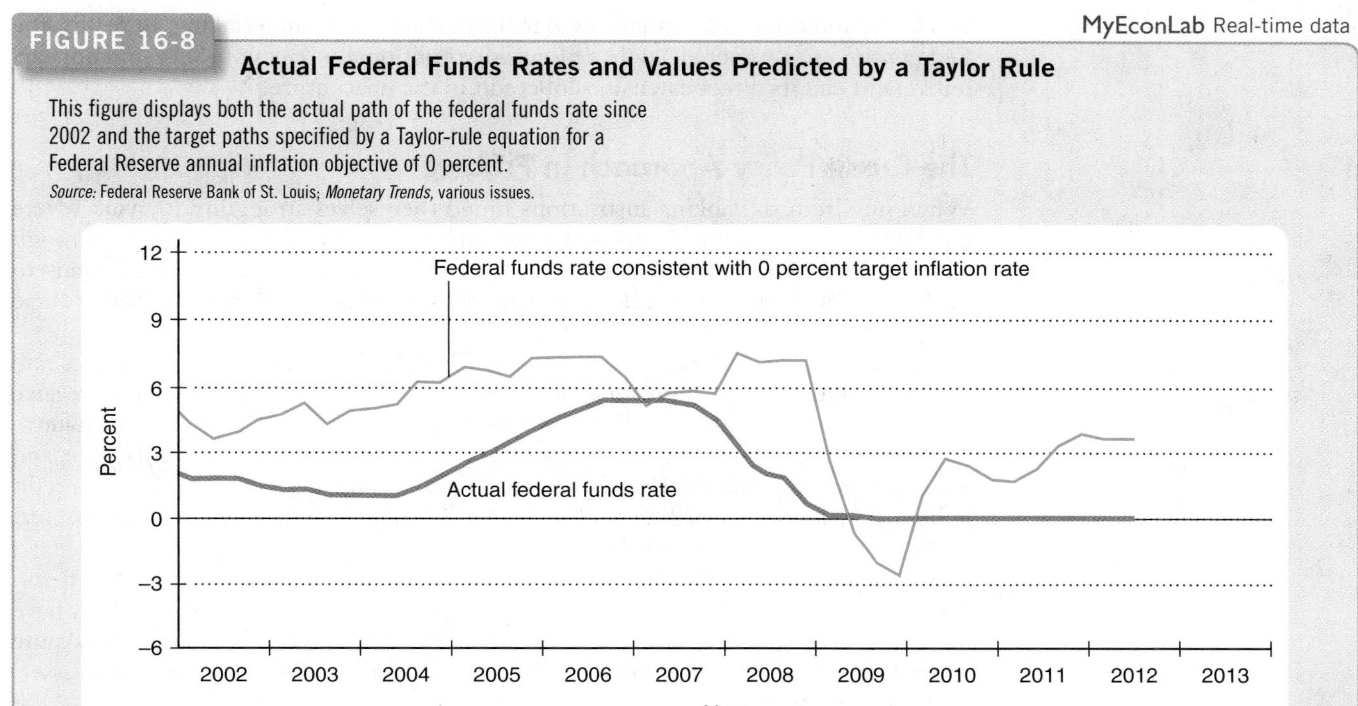

PLOTTING THE TAYLOR RULE ON A GRAPH The Federal Reserve Bank of St. Louis now regularly tracks target levels for the federal funds rate predicted by a basic Taylor-rule equation. Figure 16-8 above displays paths of both the actual federal funds rate (the orange line) and the Taylor-rule recommendation if the Fed's inflation objective (the green line) is 0 percent inflation.

ASSESSING THE STANCE OF FED POLICY WITH THE TAYLOR RULE Suppose that the actual federal funds rate is *below* the rate implied by a 0 percent inflation goal. In this situation, the Taylor rule implies that the Fed's policymaking is expansionary. As a consequence, the actual inflation rate will rise above 0 percent. Thus, during the 2003–2005 interval, the actual federal funds rate was well below the level consistent with a 0 percent inflation rate. This implies that Fed policymaking was very expansionary during this period, sufficiently so as to be expected to yield a long-run inflation rate substantially in excess of 0 percent per year. The Taylor-rule graph implies that in late 2006, the Fed's policy stance became much more contractionary, with the actual federal funds rate above the level consistent with 0 percent inflation. Then, the graph suggests, Fed policymaking became expansionary once more beginning in late 2007.

Until the early 2000s, the actual federal funds rate remained relatively close to the Taylor-rule predictions over time. Since 2003, the Fed has failed to set its federal funds rate target in a manner consistent with the Taylor rule.

Credit Policy at Today's Fed

Federal Reserve policymakers continue to announce and to try to achieve a target value for the federal funds rate. Since the financial meltdown of the late 2000s, however, the Fed has pursued a new approach to policymaking, called **credit policy,** under which it directly extends credit to specific banks, other financial intermediaries, and even nonfinancial companies. When Fed officials initiated this new policy approach in

Credit policy
Federal Reserve policymaking involving direct lending to financial and nonfinancial firms.

2008, they indicated their intention to make it a temporary undertaking. In reality, the Fed continues to use credit policy alongside traditional monetary policy and appears unlikely to end its direct extensions of credit in the near future.

The Credit Policy Approach in Practice

When hundreds of banking institutions found themselves struggling to avoid severe illiquidity and bankruptcy in 2008, the Fed introduced a number of programs through which it provided credit directly to these institutions. The Fed auctioned funds to banking institutions and also bought many debt securities held by a number of these institutions.

In addition, the Fed purchased some of the debts of auto finance companies and then later allowed the companies to obtain bank charters so that they could receive direct loans from the Fed's discount window. The Fed even provided short-term emergency financing arrangements for nonfinancial firms such as Caterpillar, Inc. and Toyota. Even though the Fed had engaged in none of these varied forms of credit policy activities prior to 2008, *today more than $1 trillion, or 40 percent, of the Fed's asset holdings relate to its conduct of credit policy*.

In recent years, the Fed has slowed its extension of credit to institutions and firms. Nevertheless, many of the debts that it purchased from banks and other firms have long *maturities*—periods of time before full repayments are due. This situation is quite different from the situation prior to 2008, when only a small portion of the Fed's assets had lengthy maturities.

Furthermore, a number of the debts the Fed has purchased from private institutions are based on mortgage obligations of dubious value. Consequently, the Fed faces considerable risk that at least some of the debts will never be fully repaid. This state of affairs is also quite different from the situation in preceding years, when the bulk of the Fed's assets, about 80 percent of which were U.S. government securities, offered very low risks of loss.

How the Fed Finances the Credit It Extends

In an important sense, the Fed's credit policy results in its activities more closely resembling those of a private bank than a central bank. Like a private banking institution, the Fed extends credit by lending out funds that it obtains from depositors. Unlike private banks, however, the Fed collects the bulk of its deposits from banking institutions instead of from households and firms. These deposits consist of the reserve deposits that banks hold with Federal Reserve banks.

To engage in its active and substantial credit policy, the Fed must induce private banks to maintain substantial reserve deposits with the Federal Reserve banks. A key inducement is the interest rate the Fed pays on reserves. Even though the Fed has paid a very low interest rate of about 0.25 percent on reserve deposits since 2008, throughout most this period, the market clearing federal funds rate has been even lower. Thus, banks have earned more by setting funds aside in reserve deposit accounts at Federal Reserve banks than by lending to other banks in the federal funds market. This means that the Fed essentially has paid banks a per-unit *subsidy* to keep hundreds of billions of dollars on deposit with the Fed.

All such funds held at Federal Reserve banks do not remain idle, though. Just as private banks can use the deposits of households and firms to fund loans and purchases of securities, the Fed can use the reserve deposits of private banks to fund its own lending and securities-buying activities. Since 2008, reserve deposits at Federal Reserve banks have risen from less than $50 billion to more than $1.5 *trillion*. These funds have financed the Fed's credit policy—lending to domestic and foreign banks, nonfinancial companies, and central banks and buying risky, longer-term mortgage obligations.

How has payment of interest on banks' *excess* reserves constituted a subsidy?

POLICY EXAMPLE

Interest on Excess Reserves as a Subsidy

To induce banks to hold the more than $1.5 trillion in funds desired by the Fed to finance its credit policy, in 2008 the Fed began paying interest on excess as well as required reserves. Receipt of these interest payments gave banks an incentive to borrow funds from other sources (at a lower interest rate) to hold on reserve at the Fed. These sources of funds were the government-sponsored housing finance institutions—the Federal National Mortgage Association (FNMA) and the Federal Home Loan Mortgage Corporation (FHLMC).

Banks thereby borrow from FNMA and FHLMC to add to their excess reserves holdings with the Fed at a slightly higher interest rate. In this way, the Fed effectively pays interest on reserves that banks split with FNMA and FHLMC. As a result, the Fed's policy of paying interest on excess reserves effectively grants an estimated $1 billion per year in subsidies to banks and to these two government-sponsored housing finance institutions.

FOR CRITICAL THINKING

How does interest on excess reserves reduce bank lending to households and firms?

Arguments in Favor of the Fed's Credit Policy

Three arguments support the Federal Reserve's credit policy:

1. ***Giving Banks Time to Recover from the Financial Meltdown.*** The original rationale for initiating the credit policy was to address the deteriorating condition of the U.S. banking industry that began in 2007. As more and more banks weakened during 2008 and 2009, the Fed created an array of lending programs aimed at countering the fact that institutions were less willing to lend to one another in private markets. These new Fed lending programs made banks much more liquid than they would have been otherwise, which ensured their ability to withstand bank runs. The Fed's lending programs also succeeded in keeping many otherwise insolvent banks—those for which the value of assets dropped below the value of liabilities—afloat until they could become more economically viable. A few large institutions ultimately could not continue as stand-alone banks, and hundreds of smaller community banks failed. Nevertheless, the programs provided "breathing space" until other financial institutions could acquire those banks and their lower-valued assets.

2. ***Making Financial Markets and Institutions More Liquid and Solvent.*** The Fed's purchases of debt securities also helped make financial markets and institutions more liquid and solvent. At the height of the financial crisis, the Fed's purchases of debt securities from companies such as Ford Motor Company and Harley & Davidson, Inc. ensured that these otherwise profitable and solvent firms remained liquid. The Fed's later purchases of mortgage-obligation debt securities removed many high-risk assets from banks' balance sheets and thereby improved the banks' longer-term solvency prospects.

3. ***Contributing to International Financial Liquidity.*** Finally, the credit extended by the Fed to foreign private banks and central banks enabled these institutions to maintain holdings of U.S. dollars. This credit policy action helped ensure liquidity in international financial markets.

Thus, the Fed's credit policy activities did much to help prevent banks, firms, and financial markets from becoming illiquid, which undoubtedly forestalled possible bank runs in 2008 and 2009. Its credit policy actions also prevented a number of bank failures.

Arguments Against the Fed's Credit Policy

Critics of the Fed's credit policy have offered three arguments against it.

1. ***Providing an Incentive for Institutions to Operate Less Efficiently.*** Critics point out that the Fed is capable of creating as much liquidity as desired via open market purchases. These critics worry that the Fed encourages institutions to which it directs credit to operate with less attention to minimizing operating costs than they would otherwise.

2. ***Reducing Incentives to Screen and Monitor in Order to Limit Asymmetric Information Problems.*** Critics of the Fed argue that preventing insolvencies via this credit policy interferes with the functions of private institutions and markets in identifying and addressing asymmetric information problems (see Chapter 15). If banks know the Fed will bail them out, critics suggest, banks will do poorer jobs of screening and monitoring borrowers. Hence, in the longer term, the Fed's credit policy could broaden the scope of asymmetric information problems.

3. ***Making Monetary Policy Less Effective.*** Critics suggest that the Fed has pursued its credit policy so vigorously that its performance in the realm of monetary policy has worsened. They point out that while the Fed was providing credit to many individual institutions and firms, difficulties in predicting how these actions would affect the money supply contributed to substantial swings in monetary aggregates. In fact, although quantitative-easing policies when the interest rate was near zero raised bank reserves by more than $1.5 trillion, the Fed's credit policies induced banks to hold those reserves idle at Federal Reserve banks. Thus, the reserve ratio increased, and the money multiplier fell. On net, therefore, the money supply failed to grow very much in response to the Fed's quantitative easing. Indeed, over some intervals the money supply even declined.

WHAT IF... the Fed responded to a future financial meltdown by buying up *all* bad debts?

In principle, the Fed possesses authority to buy IOUs from anyone in the event of an emergency. If the Fed were to respond to a future financial meltdown by buying up *all* bad debts, its actions technically would prevent *any* failures from occurring and effectively "bail out" the entire U.S. financial system. Purchasing all bad debts would increase the Fed's assets considerably. Because the Fed's total assets equal its total liabilities, the Fed's liabilities, including reserves of banks, would also increase by a significant amount. The result would be a multiplier effect on the money supply. Consequently, the quantity of money in circulation would rise substantially, which likely would contribute to higher annual inflation rates.

QUICK QUIZ See page 369 for the answers. Review concepts from this section in MyEconLab.

At present, the policy strategy of the Federal Open Market Committee (FOMC) focuses on aiming for a target value of the __________ __________ rate, which the FOMC seeks to achieve via __________ __________ __________ that alter the supply of reserves to the banking system.

The FOMC outlines the Fed's general monetary policy strategy in the FOMC __________, which it transmits to the Trading Desk of the Federal Reserve Bank of __________ __________ for implementation.

Since 2008, the Fed has implemented __________ policy, under which it has extended __________ directly to selected financial institutions and has purchased debt securities that have lost much of their market value.

Advantages of the Fed's __________ policy are that it has provided institutions with more liquidity, has helped to limit the number of bank __________, and has provided more dollars for use in international markets. Disadvantages include reduced incentives for banks to minimize operating costs and to screen and to __________ borrowers and potential conflicts of __________ policy with the Fed's monetary policy responsibilities.

YOU ARE THERE

Applying the Quantity Theory of Money and Prices to a Universe of Star Systems

Eyjolfur Gudmundsson is the central banker for a universe of 7,000 star systems traversed by more than 300,000 starship pilots. The stars and pilots are located in cyberspace, scattered among hundreds of thousands of computers worldwide.

Gudmundsson determines the supply of money used in exchange by players ("starship pilots") who participate in a multiplayer Internet-based game called Eve Online. Gudmundsson has learned that when Eve Online's general level of prices—tabulated from a consumer price index based on game items such as asteroid-mining gear and laser guns—begins to tick upward, a policy response is required. In Eve Online's economy, Gudmundsson has determined, reducing the inflation rate requires decreasing the rate of growth of the quantity of money in circulation. He brings about a lower money growth rate by reducing the amount of new game currency transmitted to players whenever they succeed in certain tasks required to move to different levels within the game. In this way, Gudmundsson conducts monetary policy based on the quantity theory of money and prices.

Critical Thinking Questions

1. How would Gudmundsson respond if Eve Online's economy experiences deflation?
2. If Eve Online's real GDP and income velocity of money remain unchanged, what determines the rate of inflation experienced by its "starship pilots"?

ISSUES & APPLICATIONS

While Credit Policy Gives, Monetary Policy Takes Away

CONCEPTS APPLIED

- Credit Policy
- Federal Funds Rate
- Money Balances

Since the Fed began implementing credit policy alongside traditional monetary policy in 2008, it has struggled to coordinate these two forms of policymaking. A consequence has been greater variability in the money supply and in the real interest rate.

Increased Money Supply Variability during the Recession

Panel (a) of Figure 16-9 on the following page shows the M2 measure of the money supply since 2001. As you can see, aside from some intermittent and very brief dips, the money supply generally rose at a steady pace until 2008.

When the Fed first began its credit policy programs in 2008, the M2 measure of aggregate money balances dipped and did not grow for several months. Throughout the rest of 2008, M2 grew rapidly. Then M2 steadily *decreased* during the middle part of 2009 before very slightly increasing during 2010.

Thus, just as the economic downturn began in 2008, the Fed allowed money supply growth to drop. Moreover, just as a recovery began in 2009 and 2010, the Fed again allowed the money supply to decline. Both actions reduced aggregate demand.

A "Low" Nominal Federal Funds Rate but a Volatile Real Rate

Panel (b) displays the nominal federal funds rate and the estimated real federal funds rate—the nominal rate minus the estimated expected inflation rate. Until 2008, the nominal and estimated real values of the federal funds rate moved in tandem.

During 2008, the Fed acted to keep the nominal federal funds rate very close to zero. Through its credit policy programs, the Fed extended loans to selected institutions at very low nominal rates of interest. After the Fed allowed money growth to falter in 2008, a significant decrease in inflation occurred. (Indeed, there was a short period of deflation.) As a consequence, although the nominal federal funds rate remained close to zero after 2008, the estimated real federal funds rate rose in 2008, and again during 2009 and 2010 following the second dip in money growth during 2009.

MyEconLab Real-time data

FIGURE 16-9

M2 and Nominal and Estimated Real Federal Funds Rates since 2001

Panel (a) shows that M2 generally increased until 2008. Its level dropped early that year and again during 2009. As indicated in panel (b), even though the nominal federal funds rate has been very low since 2008, the real federal funds rate increased in 2008 and again during 2009 and 2010 following the declines in M2.

Source: Board of Governors of the Federal Reserve System.

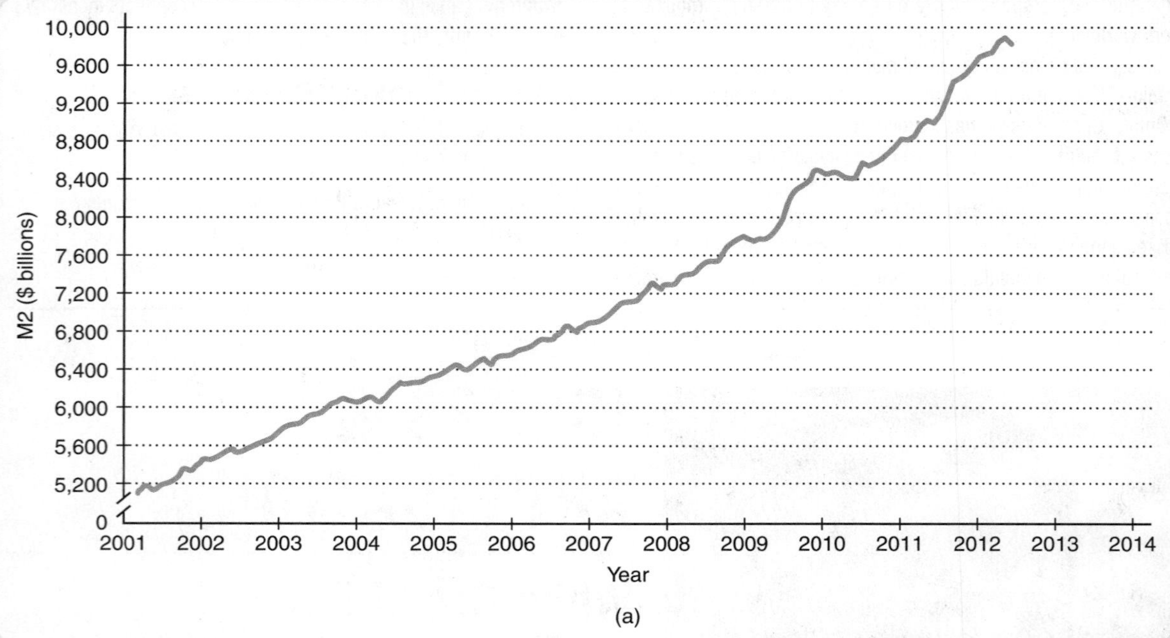

(a)

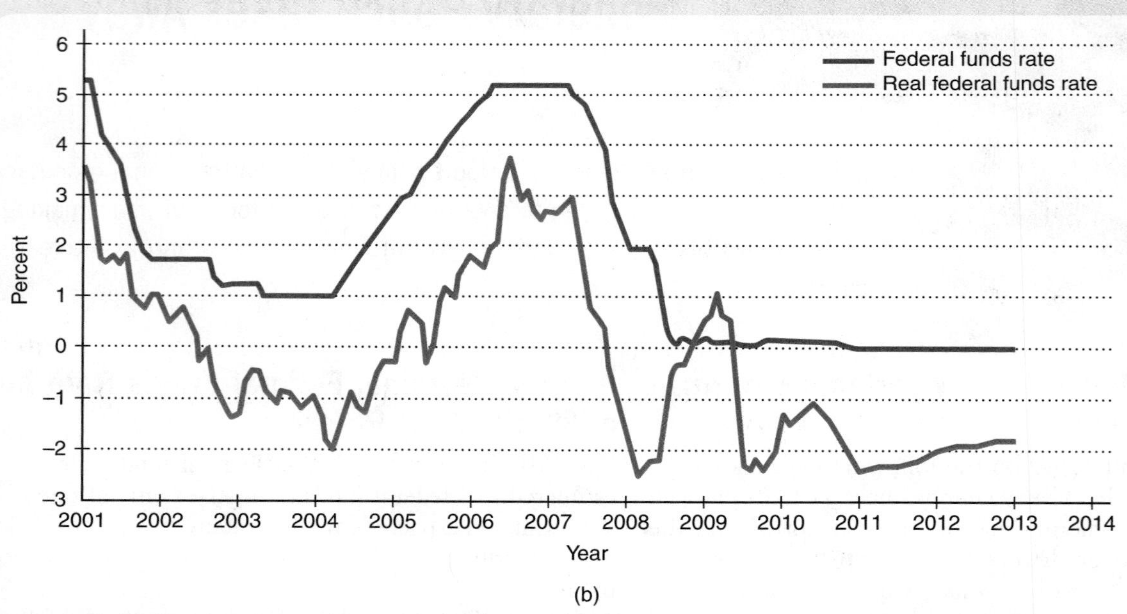

(b)

The Fed sought to support its credit policy with a near-zero nominal interest rate after 2008, but volatility in aggregate money balances contributed to variable real interest rates. Higher real interest rates raised real borrowing costs in 2009 and again in 2010 even as the Fed perceived that its credit policy was helping to keep borrowing costs low. Thus, the Fed failed to implement a consistently counter-recessionary monetary policy in conjunction with its credit policy.

For Critical Thinking

1. Why did decreases in inflation follow the drops in the money supply?
2. How does deflation raise real interest expenses for borrowers?

Web Resources

1. Take a look at recent values of M2 at **www.econtoday.com/chap16**.
2. Track the nominal federal funds rate at **www.econtoday.com/chap16**.

MyEconLab

For more questions on this chapter's Issues & Applications, go to MyEconLab. In the Study Plan for this chapter, select Section N: News.

MyEconLab

Here is what you should know after reading this chapter. MyEconLab will help you identify what you know, and where to go when you need to practice.

WHAT YOU SHOULD KNOW		WHERE TO GO TO PRACTICE
Key Factors That Influence the Quantity of Money That People Desire to Hold People desire to hold more money to make transactions when nominal GDP increases. In addition, money is a store of value that people may hold alongside bonds, stocks, and other interest-earning assets. The opportunity cost of holding money as an asset is the interest rate, so the quantity of money demanded declines as the market interest rate increases.	money balances, 347 transactions demand, 347 precautionary demand, 347 asset demand, 348 **Key Figure** Figure 16-1, 348	• MyEconLab Study Plan 16.1
How the Federal Reserve's Open Market Operations Influence Market Interest Rates When the Fed sells U.S. government bonds, it must offer them for sale at a lower price to induce buyers to purchase the bonds. The market price of existing bonds and the prevailing interest rate in the economy are inversely related, so the market interest rate rises when the Fed sells bonds.	**Key Figure** Figure 16-2, 349	• MyEconLab Study Plan 16.2 • Animated Figure 16-2
How Expansionary and Contractionary Monetary Policies Affect Equilibrium Real GDP and the Price Level in the Short Run An expansionary monetary policy action increases the money supply and causes a decrease in market interest rates. The aggregate demand curve shifts rightward, which can eliminate a short-run recessionary gap in real GDP. In contrast, a contractionary monetary policy action reduces the money supply and causes an increase in market interest rates. This results in a leftward shift in the aggregate demand curve, which can eliminate a short-run inflationary gap.	quantitative easing 351 **Key Figures** Figure 16-3, 351 Figure 16-4, 352	• MyEconLab Study Plan 16.3 • Animated Figures 16-3, 16-4

MyEconLab *continued*

WHAT YOU SHOULD KNOW		WHERE TO GO TO PRACTICE
The Equation of Exchange and the Quantity Theory of Money and Prices The equation of exchange states that the quantity of money times the average number of times a unit of money is used in exchange—the income velocity of money—must equal the price level times real GDP. The quantity theory of money and prices assumes that the income velocity of money is constant and real GDP is relatively stable. Thus, a rise in the quantity of money leads to an equiproportional increase in the price level.	equation of exchange, 354 income velocity of money (V), 354 quantity theory of money and prices, 355	• MyEconLab Study Plan 16.3
The Interest-Rate-Based Transmission Mechanism of Monetary Policy The interest-rate-based approach to the monetary policy transmission mechanism operates through effects of monetary policy actions on market interest rates, which bring about changes in desired investment and thereby affect equilibrium real GDP via the multiplier effect. At present, the Fed uses an interest rate target, which is the federal funds rate. Some economists favor selecting the federal funds rate target using a Taylor rule, which specifies an equation for the federal funds rate target based on an estimated long-run real interest rate, the current deviation of actual inflation from the Fed's inflation goal, and the gap between actual real GDP and a measure of potential real GDP.	federal funds market, 357 federal funds rate, 357 discount rate, 358 FOMC Directive, 358 Trading Desk, 358 Taylor rule, 358 **Key Figures** Figure 16-6, 356 Figure 16-7, 357 Figure 16-8, 359	• MyEconLab Study Plans 16.3, 16.4, 16.5 • Animated Figures 16-6, 16-7, 16-8
The Use of Credit Policy by Today's Fed Since the late 2000s, the Federal Reserve has used credit policy, which involves direct lending to financial and nonfinancial firms. Today, more than \$1.5 trillion, or 40 percent, of the Fed's asset holdings are related to the conduct of credit policy. The Fed's payment of an interest subsidy on reserves provides banks with an incentive to hold the reserves the Fed requires to obtain the funds that it lends. Arguments favoring the Fed credit policy are that it has helped banks recover from the financial meltdown, has contributed to liquidity and solvency of financial markets and institutions, and has made global financial markets more liquid. Arguments against the policy are that it contributes to lower efficiency of the banking system, has reduced bank incentives to screen and monitor in order to reduce asymmetric information problems, and has reduced the effectiveness of monetary policy.	credit policy, 359	• MyEconLab Study Plans 16.5, 16.6, 16.7

PROBLEMS

All problems are assignable in MyEconLab; *exercises that update with real-time data are marked with* . *Answers to odd-numbered problems appear at the back of the book.*

16-1. Let's denote the price of a nonmaturing bond (called a *consol*) as P_b. The equation that indicates this price is $P_b = I/r$, where I is the annual net income the bond generates and r is the nominal market interest rate. (See pages 349–350.)

a. Suppose that a bond promises the holder $500 per year forever. If the nominal market interest rate is 5 percent, what is the bond's current price?

b. What happens to the bond's price if the market interest rate rises to 10 percent?

16-2. On the basis of Problem 16-1, imagine that initially the market interest rate is 5 percent and at this interest rate you have decided to hold half of your financial wealth as bonds and half as holdings of non-interest-bearing money. You notice that the market interest rate is starting to rise, however, and you become convinced that it will ultimately rise to 10 percent. (See pages 347–350.)

a. In what direction do you expect the value of your bond holdings to go when the interest rate rises?

b. If you wish to prevent the value of your financial wealth from declining in the future, how should you adjust the way you split your wealth between bonds and money? What does this imply about the demand for money?

16-3. You learned in Chapter 11 that if there is an inflationary gap in the short run, then in the long run a new equilibrium arises when input prices and expectations adjust upward, causing the short-run aggregate supply curve to shift upward and to the left and pushing equilibrium real GDP per year back to its long-run value. In this chapter, however, you learned that the Federal Reserve can eliminate an inflationary gap in the short run by undertaking a policy action that reduces aggregate demand. (See page 352.)

a. Propose one monetary policy action that could eliminate an inflationary gap in the short run.

b. In what way might society gain if the Fed implements the policy you have proposed instead of simply permitting long-run adjustments to take place?

16-4. You learned in Chapter 11 that if a recessionary gap occurs in the short run, then in the long run a new equilibrium arises when input prices and expectations adjust downward, causing the short-run aggregate supply curve to shift downward and to the right and pushing equilibrium real GDP per year back to its long-run value. In this chapter, you learned that the Federal Reserve can eliminate a recessionary gap in the short run by undertaking a policy action that increases aggregate demand. (See page 352.)

a. Propose one monetary policy action that could eliminate the recessionary gap in the short run.

b. In what way might society gain if the Fed implements the policy you have proposed instead of simply permitting long-run adjustments to take place?

16-5. Suppose that the economy currently is in long-run equilibrium. Explain the short- and long-run adjustments that will take place in an aggregate demand–aggregate supply diagram if the Fed expands the quantity of money in circulation. (See page 352.)

16-6. Explain why the net export effect of a contractionary monetary policy reinforces the usual impact that monetary policy has on equilibrium real GDP per year in the short run. (See page 353.)

16-7. Suppose that, initially, the U.S. economy was in an aggregate demand–aggregate supply equilibrium at point A along the aggregate demand curve AD in the diagram below. Now, however, the value of the U.S. dollar suddenly appreciates relative to foreign currencies. This appreciation happens to have no measurable effects on either the short-run or the long-run aggregate supply curve in the United States. It does, however, influence U.S. aggregate demand. (See page 353.)

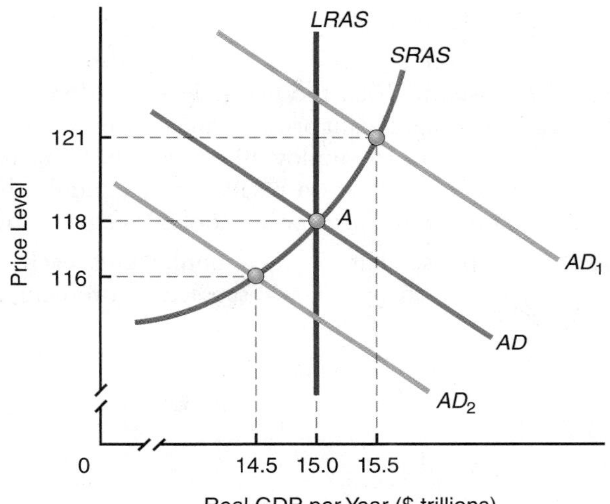

a. Explain in your own words how the dollar appreciation will affect net export expenditures in the United States.

b. Of the alternative aggregate demand curves depicted in the figure—AD_1 versus AD_2—which could represent the aggregate demand effect of the U.S. dollar's appreciation? What effects does the appreciation have on real GDP and the price level?

c. What policy action might the Federal Reserve take to prevent the dollar's appreciation from affecting equilibrium real GDP in the short run?

16-8. Suppose that the quantity of money in circulation is fixed but the income velocity of money doubles. If real GDP remains at its long-run potential level, what happens to the equilibrium price level? (See page 354.)

16-9. Suppose that following adjustment to the events in Problem 16-8, the Fed cuts the money supply in half. How does the price level now compare with its value before the income velocity and the money supply changed? (See page 354.)

16-10. Consider the following data: The money supply is \$1 trillion, the price level equals 2, and real GDP is \$5 trillion in base-year dollars. What is the income velocity of money? (See page 354.)

16-11. Consider the data in Problem 16-10. Suppose that the money supply increases by \$100 billion and real GDP and the income velocity remain unchanged. (See pages 354–355.)

a. According to the quantity theory of money and prices, what is the new equilibrium price level after full adjustment to the increase in the money supply?

b. What is the percentage increase in the money supply?

c. What is the percentage change in the price level?

d. How do the percentage changes in the money supply and price level compare?

16-12. Assuming that the Fed judges inflation to be the most significant problem in the economy and that it wishes to employ all of its policy instruments except interest on reserves, what should the Fed do with its three policy tools? (See page 357.)

16-13. Suppose that the Fed implements each of the policy changes you discussed in Problem 16-12. Now explain how the net export effect resulting from these monetary policy actions will reinforce their effects that operate through interest rate changes. (See page 353.)

16-14. Imagine working at the Trading Desk at the New York Fed. Explain whether you would conduct open market purchases or sales in response to each of the following events. Justify your recommendation. (See page 353.)

a. The latest FOMC Directive calls for an increase in the target value of the federal funds rate.

b. For a reason unrelated to monetary policy, the Fed's Board of Governors has decided to raise the differential between the discount rate and the federal funds rate. Nevertheless, the FOMC Directive calls for maintaining the present federal funds rate target.

16-15. To implement a credit policy intended to expand liquidity of the banking system, the Fed desires to increase its assets by lending to a substantial number of banks. How might the Fed adjust the interest rate that it pays banks on reserves in order to induce them to hold the reserves required for funding this credit policy action? What will happen to the Fed's liabilities if it implements this policy action? (See pages 359–362.)

16-16. Suppose that to finance its credit policy, the Fed pays an annual interest rate of 0.25 percent on bank reserves. During the course of the current year, banks hold \$1 trillion in reserves. What is the total amount of interest the Fed pays banks during the year? (See pages 359–362.)

16-17. During an interval between mid-2010 and early 2011, the Federal Reserve embarked on a policy it termed "quantitative easing." Total reserves in the banking system increased. Hence, the Federal Reserve's liabilities to banks increased, and at the same time its assets rose as it purchased more assets—many of which were securities with private market values that had dropped considerably. The money multiplier declined, so the net increase in the money supply was negligible. Indeed, during a portion of the period, the money supply actually declined before rising near its previous value. Evaluate whether the Fed's "quantitative easing" was a monetary policy or credit policy action. (See pages 351 and 359–362.)

ECONOMICS ON THE NET

The Fed's Policy Report to Congress Congress requires the Fed to make periodic reports on its recent activities. In this application, you will study recent reports to learn about what factors affect Fed decisions.

Title: Monetary Policy Report to the Congress

Navigation: Go to www.econtoday.com/chap16 to view the Federal Reserve's Monetary Policy Report to the Congress (formerly called the Humphrey-Hawkins Report).

Application Read the report; then answer the following questions.

1. According to the report, what economic events were most important in shaping recent monetary policy?
2. Based on the report, what are the Fed's current monetary policy goals?

For Group Study and Analysis Divide the class into "domestic" and "foreign" groups. Have each group read the past four monetary policy reports and then explain to the class how domestic and foreign factors, respectively, appear to have influenced recent Fed monetary policy decisions. Which of the two types of factors seems to have mattered most during the past year?

ANSWERS TO QUICK QUIZZES

p. 348: (i) demand; (ii) transactions . . . precautionary . . . asset; (iii) opportunity . . . downward

p. 350: (i) lower . . . higher; (ii) inverse; (iii) decrease . . . increase . . . increase . . . decrease

p. 352: (i) direct; (ii) indirect . . . reduction . . . lower

p. 354: (i) exports; (ii) negative . . . more . . . more; (iii) fewer . . . decrease . . . increase

p. 356: (i) equation . . . exchange; (ii) true . . . spent . . . received; (iii) money supply . . . price level

p. 362: (i) federal funds . . . open market operations; (ii) Directive . . . New York; (iii) credit . . . loans; (iv) credit . . . failures . . . monitor . . . credit

APPENDIX E

Monetary Policy: A Keynesian Perspective

According to the traditional Keynesian approach to monetary policy, changes in the money supply can affect the level of aggregate demand only through their effect on interest rates. Moreover, interest rate changes act on aggregate demand solely by changing the level of real planned investment spending. Finally, the traditional Keynesian approach argues that there are plausible circumstances under which monetary policy may have little or no effect on interest rates and thus on aggregate demand.

Figure E-1 below measures real GDP per year along the horizontal axis and total planned expenditures (aggregate demand) along the vertical axis. The components of aggregate demand are real consumption (C), investment (I), government spending (G), and net exports (X). The height of the schedule labeled $C + I + G + X$ shows total real planned expenditures (aggregate demand) as a function of real GDP per year. This schedule slopes upward because consumption depends positively on real GDP. All along the line labeled $Y = C + I + G + X$, real planned spending equals real GDP per year. At point Y^*, where the $C + I + G + X$ line intersects this 45-degree reference line, real planned spending is consistent with real GDP.

At any real GDP level less than Y^*, spending exceeds real GDP, so real GDP and thus spending will tend to rise. At any level of real GDP greater than Y^*, real planned spending is less than real GDP, so real GDP and thus spending will tend to decline. Given the determinants of C, I, G, and X, total spending (aggregate demand) will be Y^*.

FIGURE E-1

An Increase in the Money Supply

An increase in the money supply increases real GDP by lowering interest rates and thus increasing investment from I to I'.

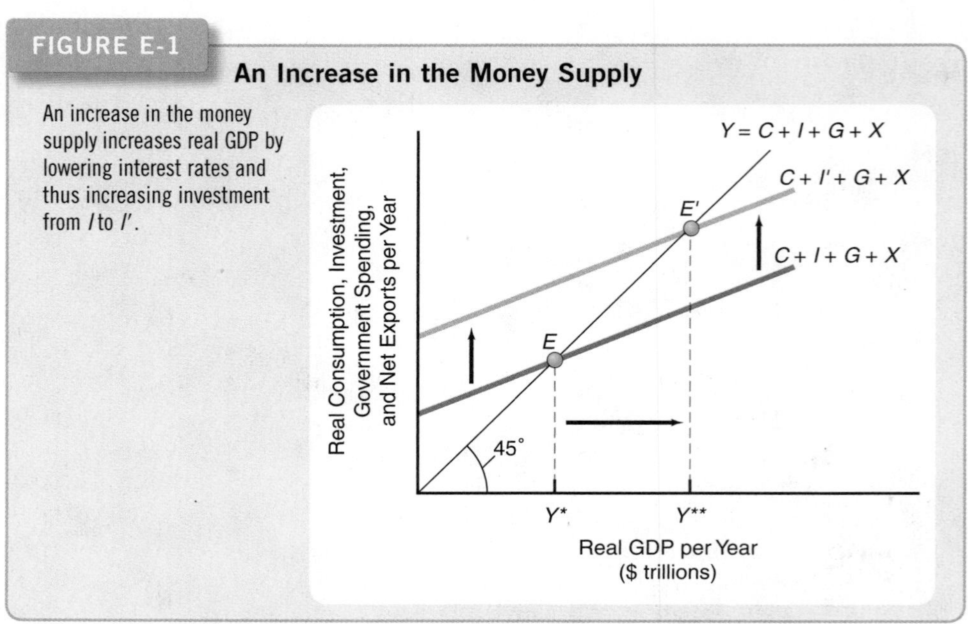

Increasing the Money Supply

According to the Keynesian approach, an increase in the money supply pushes interest rates down. This induces firms to increase the level of investment spending from I to I'. As a result, the $C + I + G + X$ line shifts upward in Figure E-1 on the facing page by the full amount of the rise in investment spending, thus yielding the line $C + I' + G + X$. The rise in investment spending causes real GDP to rise, which in turn causes real consumption spending to rise, further increasing real GDP. Ultimately, aggregate demand rises to Y^{**}, where spending again equals real GDP. A key conclusion of the Keynesian analysis is that total spending rises by *more* than the original rise in investment spending because consumption spending depends positively on real GDP.

Decreasing the Money Supply

Not surprisingly, contractionary monetary policy works in exactly the reverse manner. A reduction in the money supply pushes interest rates up. Firms respond by reducing their investment spending, and this pushes real GDP downward. Consumers react to the lower real GDP by scaling back on their real consumption spending, which further depresses real GDP. Thus, the ultimate decline in real GDP is larger than the initial drop in investment spending. Indeed, because the change in real GDP is a multiple of the change in investment, Keynesians note that changes in investment spending (similar to changes in government spending) have a *multiplier* effect on the economy.

Arguments Against Monetary Policy

It might be thought that this multiplier effect would make monetary policy a potent tool in the Keynesian arsenal, particularly when it comes to getting the economy out of a recession. In fact, however, many traditional Keynesians argue that monetary policy is likely to be relatively ineffective as a recession fighter.

According to their line of reasoning, although monetary policy has the potential to reduce interest rates, changes in the money supply have little *actual* impact on interest rates. Instead, during recessions, people try to build up as much as they can in liquid assets to protect themselves from risks of unemployment and other losses of income. When the monetary authorities increase the money supply, individuals are willing to allow most of it to accumulate in their bank accounts. This desire for increased liquidity thus prevents interest rates from falling very much, which in turn means that there will be almost no change in investment spending and thus little change in aggregate demand.

PROBLEMS

All problems are assignable in MyEconLab. *Answers to odd-numbered problems appear at the back of the book.*

E-1. Suppose that each 0.1-percentage-point decrease in the equilibrium interest rate induces a $10 billion increase in real planned investment spending by businesses. In addition, the investment multiplier is equal to 5, and the money multiplier is equal to 4. Furthermore, every $20 billion increase in the money supply brings about a 0.1-percentage-point reduction in the equilibrium interest rate. Use this information to answer the following questions under the assumption that all other things are equal. (See page 370–371.)

a. How much must real planned investment in crease if the Federal Reserve desires to bring about a $100 billion increase in equilibrium real GDP?

b. How much must the money supply change for the Fed to induce the change in real planned investment calculated in part (a)?

c. What dollar amount of open market operations must the Fed undertake to bring about the money supply change calculated in part (b)?

E-2. Suppose that each 0.1-percentage-point increase in the equilibrium interest rate induces a $5 billion decrease in real planned investment spending by businesses. In addition, the investment multiplier is equal to 4, and the money multiplier is equal to 3. Furthermore, every $9 billion decrease in the money supply brings about a 0.1-percentage-point increase in the equilibrium interest rate. Use this information to answer the following questions under the assumption that all other things are equal. (See pages 370–371.)

a. How much must real planned investment decrease if the Federal Reserve desires to bring about an $80 billion decrease in equilibrium real GDP?

b. How much must the money supply change for the Fed to induce the change in real planned investment calculated in part (a)?

c. What dollar amount of open market operations must the Fed undertake to bring about the money supply change calculated in part (b)?

E-3. Assume that the following conditions exist (see pages 370–371):

a. All banks are fully loaned up—there are no excess reserves, and desired excess reserves are always zero.

b. The money multiplier is 3.

c. The planned investment schedule is such that at a 6 percent rate of interest, investment is $1,200 billion; at 5 percent, investment is $1,225 billion.

d. The investment multiplier is 3.

e. The initial equilibrium level of real GDP is $12 trillion.

f. The equilibrium rate of interest is 6 percent.

Now the Fed engages in expansionary monetary policy. It buys $1 billion worth of bonds, which increases the money supply, which in turn lowers the market rate of interest by 1 percentage point. Determine how much the money supply must have increased, and then trace out the numerical consequences of the associated reduction in interest rates on all the other variables mentioned.

E-4. Assume that the following conditions exist (see pages 370–371):

a. All banks are fully loaned up—there are no excess reserves, and desired excess reserves are always zero.

b. The money multiplier is 4.

c. The planned investment schedule is such that at a 4 percent rate of interest, investment is $1,400 billion. At 5 percent, investment is $1,380 billion.

d. The investment multiplier is 5.

e. The initial equilibrium level of real GDP is $13 trillion.

f. The equilibrium rate of interest is 4 percent.

Now the Fed engages in contractionary monetary policy. It sells $2 billion worth of bonds, which reduces the money supply, which in turn raises the market rate of interest by 1 percentage point. Determine how much the money supply must have decreased, and then trace out the numerical consequences of the associated increase in interest rates on all the other variables mentioned.

Stabilization in an Integrated World Economy

17

LEARNING OBJECTIVES

After reading this chapter, you should be able to:

- Explain why the actual unemployment rate might depart from the natural rate of unemployment
- Describe why there may be an inverse relationship between the inflation rate and the unemployment rate, reflected by the Phillips curve
- Evaluate how expectations affect the actual relationship between the inflation rate and the unemployment rate
- Understand the rational expectations hypothesis and its implications for economic policymaking
- Distinguish among alternative modern approaches to strengthening the case for active policymaking

MyEconLab helps you master each objective and study more efficiently. See end of chapter for details.

For more than 50 years, many economists have used an inverse relationship between the unemployment rate and real GDP as a guide to macroeconomic policymaking. Since 2009, however, this relationship appears to have broken down. Now some economists are suggesting that the inverse relationship may not return for a long time—or perhaps never. If these economists are correct, the case for discretionary policymaking is weaker than it was prior to 2009. Studying this chapter will help you understand why such a policy implication follows if the inverse relationship between the unemployment rate and real GDP has indeed broken down.

? DID YOU KNOW THAT... analysis of prices posted on Internet Web sites and processed by automatic scanners in brick-and-mortar stores verifies that by far the most common ending number in a price for an item priced as high as $11 is "9"? In addition, prices ending in the number "9" change less often than prices ending in other numbers. When prices ending in the number "9" *do* change, though, the price changes typically are larger than those from prices ending in numbers other than "9." Some economists who study these and other data relating to how firms price their goods and services suggest that these facts contribute to "price stickiness"—that is, a generalized tendency for prices to adjust sluggishly over time.

In this chapter, you will learn about possible consequences of widespread price stickiness. Among these is that sticky prices may help to make macroeconomic policies aimed at stabilizing the economy more potent.

Active versus Passive Policymaking

If it is true that monetary and fiscal policy actions aimed at exerting significant stabilizing effects on overall economic activity are likely to succeed, then this would be a strong argument for **active (discretionary) policymaking.** This is the term for actions that monetary and fiscal policymakers undertake in reaction to or in anticipation of a change in economic performance. On the other side of the debate is the view that the best way to achieve economic stability is through **passive (nondiscretionary) policymaking,** in which there is no deliberate stabilization policy at all. Policymakers follow a rule and do not attempt to respond in a discretionary manner to actual or potential changes in economic activity.

Active (discretionary) policymaking
All actions on the part of monetary and fiscal policymakers that are undertaken in response to or in anticipation of some change in the overall economy.

Passive (nondiscretionary) policymaking
Policymaking that is carried out in response to a rule. It is therefore not in response to an actual or potential change in overall economic activity.

Recall from Chapter 13 that there are lags between the time when the national economy enters a recession or a boom and the time when that fact becomes known and acted on by policymakers. Proponents of passive policy argue that such time lags often render short-term stabilization policy ineffective or, worse, procyclical.

To take a stand on this debate concerning active versus passive policymaking, you first need to know the potential trade-offs that policymakers believe they face. Then you need to see what the data actually show. The most important policy trade-off appears to be between price stability and unemployment. Before exploring that, however, we need to look at the economy's natural, or long-run, rate of unemployment.

The Natural Rate of Unemployment

Recall from Chapter 7 that there are different types of unemployment: frictional, cyclical, structural, and seasonal. *Frictional unemployment* arises because individuals take the time to search for the best job opportunities. Much unemployment is of this type, except when the economy is in a recession or a depression, when cyclical unemployment rises.

Note that we did not say that frictional unemployment was the *sole* form of unemployment during normal times. *Structural unemployment* is caused by a variety of "rigidities" throughout the economy. Structural unemployment results from factors such as these:

1. Government-imposed minimum wage laws, laws restricting entry into occupations, and welfare and unemployment insurance benefits that reduce incentives to work

2. Union activity that sets wages above the equilibrium level and also restricts the mobility of labor

All of these factors reduce individuals' abilities or incentives to choose employment rather than unemployment.

Consider the effect of unemployment insurance benefits on the probability of an unemployed person's finding a job. When unemployment benefits run out, according to economists Lawrence Katz and Bruce Meyer, the probability of an unemployed person's finding a job doubles. The conclusion is that unemployed workers are more serious about finding a job when they are no longer receiving such benefits.

Frictional unemployment and structural unemployment both exist even when the economy is in long-run equilibrium—they are a natural consequence of costly information (the need to conduct a job search) and the existence of rigidities such as those noted above. Because these two types of unemployment are a natural consequence of imperfect and costly information and rigidities, they are components of what economists call the **natural rate of unemployment.** As we discussed in Chapter 7, this is defined as the rate of unemployment that would exist in the long run after everyone in the economy fully adjusted to any changes that have occurred. Recall that real GDP per year tends to return to the level implied by the long-run aggregate supply curve (*LRAS*). Thus, whatever rate of unemployment the economy tends to return to in long-run equilibrium can be called the natural rate of unemployment.

Natural rate of unemployment The rate of unemployment that is estimated to prevail in long-run macroeconomic equilibrium, when all workers and employers have fully adjusted to any changes in the economy.

How has the natural rate of unemployment changed over the years?

EXAMPLE

The U.S. Natural Rate of Unemployment

In 1982, the unemployment rate was nearly 10 percent. By the late 2000s and early 2010s, it was at this level once again. These two nearly matching unemployment rates prove nothing by themselves. But look at Figure 17-1 below. There you see not only what has happened to the unemployment rate since 1950 but an estimate of the natural rate of unemployment. The line labeled "Natural rate of unemployment" is produced by averaging unemployment rates from five years earlier to five years later at each point in time (except for the end period, which is estimated). This computation reveals that until the late 1980s, the natural rate of unemployment was rising. Then it trended downward until the late 2000s, when it began to rise once more, to nearly 8 percent by 2013.

FOR CRITICAL THINKING

Why does the natural rate of unemployment differ from the actual rate of unemployment?

FIGURE 17-1

MyEconLab Real-time data

Estimated Natural Rate of Unemployment in the United States

As you can see, the actual rate of unemployment has varied widely in the United States in recent decades. If we generate the natural rate of unemployment by averaging unemployment rates from five years earlier to five years later at each point in time, we get the line so labeled. It rose from the 1950s until the late 1980s and then declined until the late 2000s, when it began to rise again.

Sources: Economic Report of the President; Economic Indicators, various issues; author's estimates.

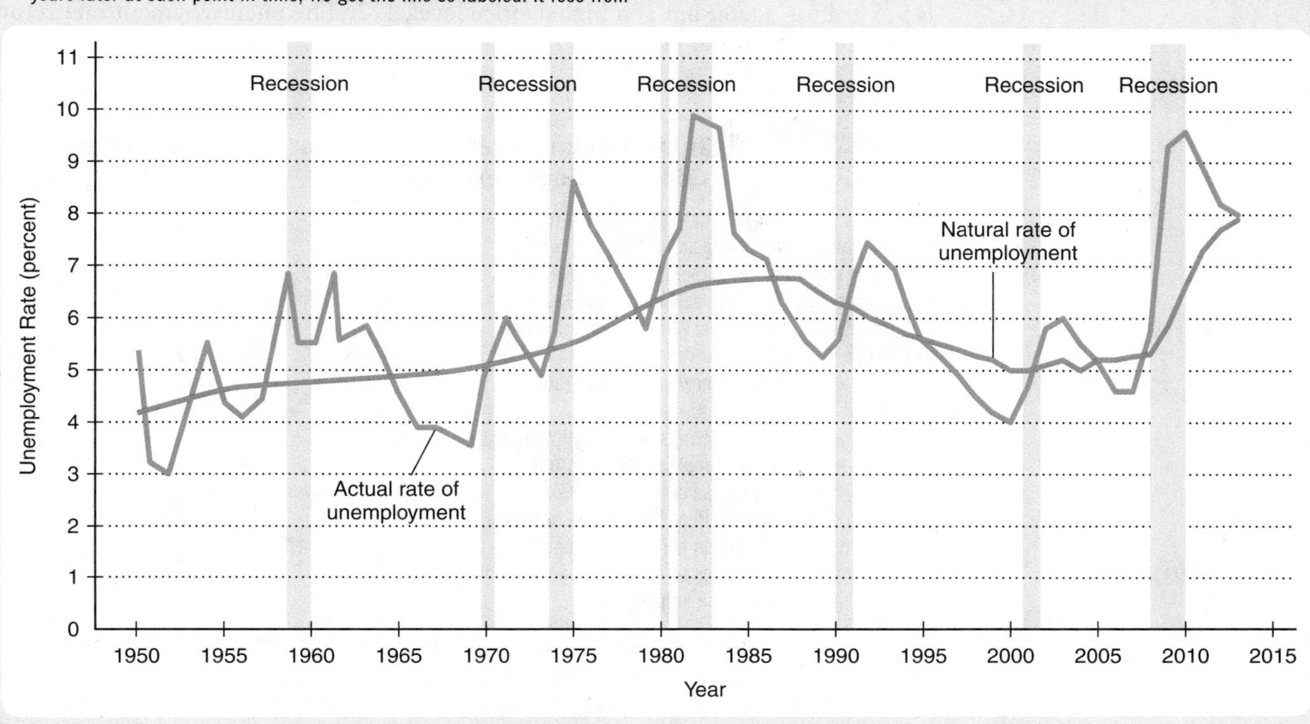

Departures from the Natural Rate of Unemployment

Even though the unemployment rate has a strong tendency to stay at and return to the natural rate, it is possible for other factors, such as changes in private spending or fiscal and monetary policy actions, to move the actual unemployment rate away from the natural rate, at least in the short run. Deviations of the actual unemployment rate from the natural rate are called *cyclical unemployment* because they are observed over the course of nationwide business fluctuations. During recessions, the overall unemployment rate exceeds the natural rate, so cyclical unemployment is positive. During periods of economic booms, the overall unemployment rate can go below the natural rate. At such times, cyclical unemployment is negative.

To see how departures from the natural rate of unemployment can occur, let's consider two examples. In Figure 17-2 below, we begin in equilibrium at point E_1 with the associated price level 117 and real GDP per year of $15 trillion.

YOU ARE THERE

To learn more about the extent to which active fiscal policy stabilizes employment in the dampened economy, take a look at **Active Policies Can Raise Employment—At a Substantial Cost** on page 390.

THE IMPACT OF EXPANSIONARY POLICY Now imagine that the government decides to use fiscal or monetary policy to stimulate the economy. Further suppose, for reasons that will soon become clear, that this policy surprises decision makers throughout the economy in the sense that they did not anticipate that the policy would occur.

As shown in Figure 17-2, the expansionary policy action causes the aggregate demand curve to shift from AD_1 to AD_2. The price level rises from 117 to 120. Real GDP, measured in base-year dollars, increases from $15 trillion to $15.4 trillion.

In the labor market, individuals find that conditions have improved markedly relative to what they expected. Firms seeking to expand output want to hire more workers. To accomplish this, they recruit more actively and possibly ask workers to work overtime, so individuals in the labor market find more job openings and more possible hours they can work. Consequently, as you learned in Chapter 7, the average duration of unemployment falls, and so does the unemployment rate.

The *SRAS* curve does not stay at $SRAS_1$ indefinitely, however. Input owners, such as workers and owners of capital and raw materials, revise their expectations. The short-run aggregate supply curve shifts to $SRAS_2$ as input prices rise. We find ourselves at a new equilibrium at E_3, which is on the *LRAS*. Long-run real GDP per year is $15 trillion again, but at a higher price level, 122. The unemployment rate returns to its original, natural level.

FIGURE 17-2

Impact of an Increase in Aggregate Demand on Real GDP and Unemployment

Point E_1 is an initial short-run and long-run equilibrium. An expansionary monetary or fiscal policy shifts the aggregate demand curve outward to AD_2. The price level rises from 117 to 120 at point E_2, and real GDP per year increases to $15.4 trillion in base-year dollars. The unemployment rate is now below its natural rate at the short-run equilibrium point E_2. As expectations of input owners are revised, the short-run aggregate supply curve shifts from $SRAS_1$ to $SRAS_2$ because of higher prices and higher resource costs. Real GDP returns to the *LRAS* level of $15 trillion per year, at point E_3. The price level increases to 122. The unemployment rate returns to the natural rate.

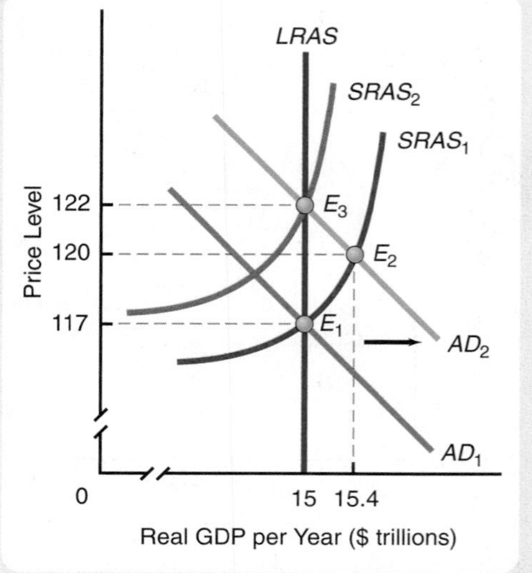

WHAT IF... the government were to boost economic expansion by offering people more food stamps?

In recent years, some U.S. government officials have claimed that surging use of the Supplemental Nutrition Assistance (food stamp) Program and various other transfer programs has helped contribute to increases in total planned expenditures. Indeed, Agriculture Secretary Tom Vilsack has referred to the food stamp program as an "economic stimulus." According to the secretary, "every dollar of food stamp benefits generates $1.84 in the economy in terms of economic activity." By definition, however, the food stamp program is a transfer program. That is, the program *transfers* a portion of income earned by some people during a given year to other people without influencing the *aggregate* income flow. Hence, higher food stamp benefits—as well as increases in any other forms of transfer payments—have virtually no effects on total planned expenditures, aggregate demand, or equilibrium real GDP.

THE CONSEQUENCES OF CONTRACTIONARY POLICY Instead of expansionary policy, the government could have decided to engage in contractionary (or deflationary) policy. As shown in Figure 17-3 below, the sequence of events would have been in the opposite direction of those in Figure 17-2 on the facing page.

Beginning from an initial equilibrium E_1, an unanticipated reduction in aggregate demand puts downward pressure on both prices and real GDP. The price level falls from 120 to 118, and real GDP declines from $15 trillion to $14.7 trillion. Fewer firms are hiring, and those that are hiring offer fewer overtime possibilities. Individuals looking for jobs find that it takes longer than predicted. As a result, unemployed individuals remain unemployed longer. The average duration of unemployment rises, and so does the rate of unemployment.

The equilibrium at E_2 is only a short-run situation, however. As input owners change their expectations about future prices, $SRAS_1$ shifts to $SRAS_2$, and input prices fall. The new long-run equilibrium is at E_3, which is on the long-run aggregate supply curve, *LRAS*. In the long run, the price level declines farther, to 116, as real GDP returns to $15 trillion. Thus, in the long run the unemployment rate returns to its natural level.

The Phillips Curve: A Rationale for Active Policymaking?

Let's recap what we have just observed. In the short run, an *unexpected increase* in aggregate demand causes the price level to rise and the unemployment rate to fall. Conversely, in the short run, an *unexpected decrease* in aggregate demand causes the

FIGURE 17-3

Impact of a Decline in Aggregate Demand on Real GDP and Unemployment

Starting from equilibrium at E_1, a decline in aggregate demand to AD_2 leads to a lower price level, 118, and real GDP declines to $14.7 trillion. The unemployment rate will rise above the natural rate of unemployment. Equilibrium at E_2 is temporary, however. At the lower price level, the expectations of input owners are revised. $SRAS_1$ shifts to $SRAS_2$. The new long-run equilibrium is at E_3, with real GDP equal to $15 trillion and a price level of 116. The actual unemployment rate is once again equal to the natural rate of unemployment.

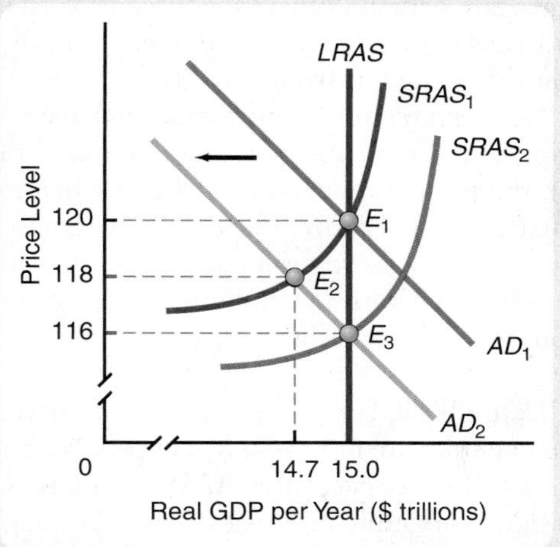

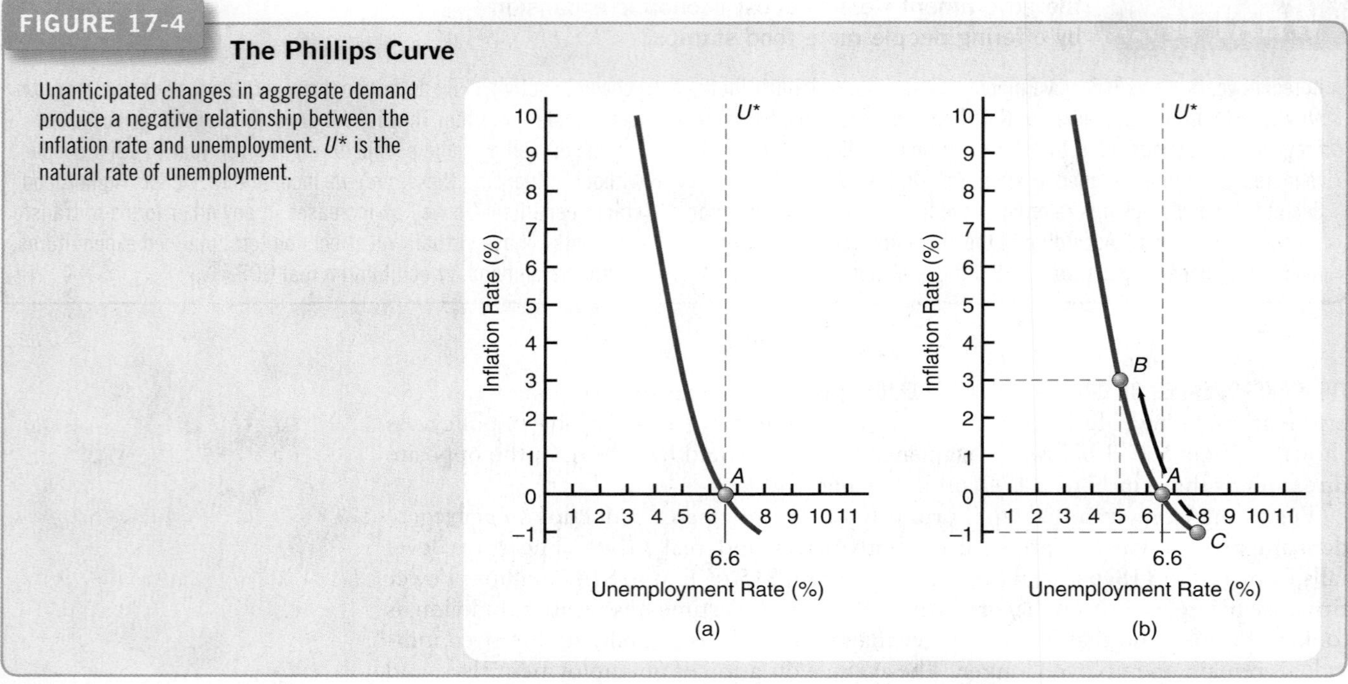

FIGURE 17-4

The Phillips Curve

Unanticipated changes in aggregate demand produce a negative relationship between the inflation rate and unemployment. *U** is the natural rate of unemployment.

price level to fall and the unemployment rate to rise. Moreover, although not shown explicitly in either diagram, two additional points are true:

1. The greater the unexpected increase in aggregate demand, the greater the amount of inflation that results in the short run, and the lower the unemployment rate.

2. The greater the unexpected decrease in aggregate demand, the greater the deflation that results in the short run, and the higher the unemployment rate.

THE NEGATIVE SHORT-RUN RELATIONSHIP BETWEEN INFLATION AND UNEMPLOYMENT Figure 17-4 above summarizes these findings. The inflation rate (*not* the price level) is measured along the vertical axis, and the unemployment rate is measured along the horizontal axis. Panel (a) shows the unemployment rate at a sample natural rate, *U**, that is assumed to be 6.6 percent at point *A*. At this point, the actual inflation rate and anticipated inflation rate are both equal to 0 percent. Panel (b) of Figure 17-4 depicts the effects of unanticipated changes in aggregate demand. In panel (b), an unexpected increase in aggregate demand causes the price level to rise—the inflation rate rises to 3 percent—and causes the unemployment rate to fall to 5 percent. Thus, the economy moves upward to the left from *A* to *B*.

Conversely, in the short run, unexpected decreases in aggregate demand cause the price level to fall and the unemployment rate to rise above the natural rate. In panel (b), the price level declines—the *deflation* rate is –1 percent—and the unemployment rate rises to 8 percent. The economy moves from point *A* to point *C*. If we look at both increases and decreases in aggregate demand, we see that high inflation rates tend to be associated with low unemployment rates (as at *B*) and that low (or negative) inflation rates tend to be accompanied by high unemployment rates (as at *C*).

Phillips curve
A curve showing the relationship between unemployment and changes in wages or prices. It was long thought to reflect a trade-off between unemployment and inflation.

IS THERE A TRADE-OFF? The apparent negative relationship between the inflation rate and the unemployment rate shown in panels (a) and (b) of Figure 17-4 has come to be called the **Phillips curve,** after A. W. Phillips, who discovered that a similar relationship existed historically in Great Britain. Although Phillips presented his findings only as an empirical regularity, economists quickly came to view the relationship as representing a *trade-off* between inflation and unemployment. In particular, policymakers who favored active policymaking believed that they could *choose* alternative combinations of unemployment and inflation. Thus, it seemed that a government that disliked unemployment could select a point like *B* in panel (b) of Figure 17-4 on the facing page, with a positive inflation rate but a relatively low unemployment rate. Conversely, a government that feared inflation could choose a stable price level at *A*, but only at the expense of a higher associated unemployment rate. Indeed, the Phillips curve seemed to suggest that it was possible for discretionary policymakers to fine-tune the economy by selecting the policies that would produce the exact mix of unemployment and inflation that suited current government objectives. As it turned out, matters are not so simple.

The Importance of Expectations

The reduction in unemployment that takes place as the economy moves from *A* to *B* in Figure 17-4 occurs because the wage offers encountered by unemployed workers are unexpectedly high. As far as the workers are concerned, these higher *nominal* wages appear, at least initially, to be increases in *real* wages. It is this perception that induces them to reduce the duration of their job search. This is a sensible way for the workers to view the world if aggregate demand fluctuates up and down at random, with no systematic or predictable variation one way or another. But if activist policymakers attempt to exploit the apparent trade-off in the Phillips curve, according to economists who support passive policymaking, aggregate demand will no longer move up and down in an *unpredictable* way.

THE EFFECTS OF AN UNANTICIPATED POLICY Consider, for example, Figure 17-5 below. If the Federal Reserve attempts to reduce the unemployment rate to 5 percent, it must increase the rate of growth of the money supply enough to produce an inflation rate of 3 percent. If this is an unexpected one-shot action in which the rate of growth of the money supply is first increased and then returned to its previous level, the inflation rate will temporarily rise to 3 percent, and the unemployment rate will temporarily fall to 5 percent. Proponents of passive policymaking contend that past experience with active policies indicates that after the money supply stops growing, the inflation

FIGURE 17-5

A Shift in the Phillips Curve

When there is a change in the expected inflation rate, the Phillips curve (*PC*) shifts to incorporate the new expectations. PC_0 shows expectations of zero inflation. PC_3 reflects a higher expected inflation rate, such as 3 percent.

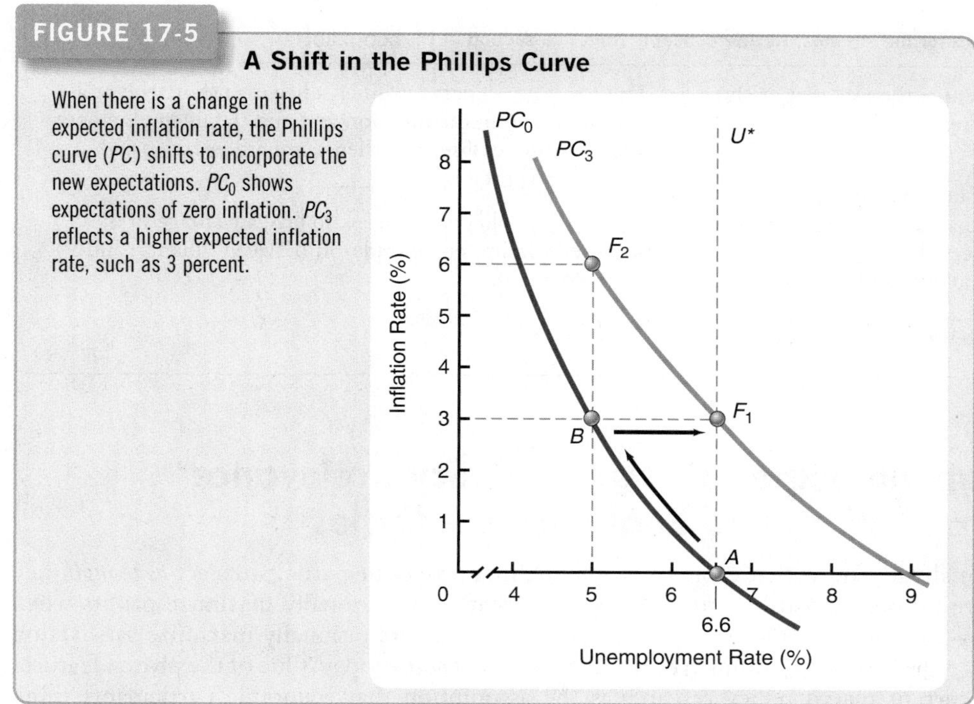

rate will soon return to zero and unemployment will return to 6.6 percent, its natural rate. Thus, an unexpected temporary increase in money supply growth will cause a movement from point A to point B, and the economy will move on its own back to A.

ADJUSTING EXPECTATIONS AND A SHIFTING PHILLIPS CURVE Why do those advocating passive policymaking argue that variations in the unemployment rate from its natural rate typically are temporary? If activist authorities wish to prevent the unemployment rate from returning to $U^* = 6.6$ percent in Figure 17-5 on the previous page, they will conclude that the money supply must grow fast enough to keep the inflation rate up at 3 percent. But if the Fed does this, argue those who favor passive policymaking, all of the economic participants in the economy—workers and job seekers included—will come to *expect* that inflation rate to continue. This, in turn, will change their expectations about wages.

To try out the "biz/ed" Web site's virtual economy and use the Phillips curve as a guide for policymaking in the United Kingdom, go to www.econtoday.com/chap17.

For example, when the expected inflation rate was zero, a 3 percent rise in nominal wages meant a 3 percent expected rise in real wages, and this was sufficient to induce some individuals to take jobs rather than remain unemployed. It was this expectation of a rise in real wages that reduced search duration and caused the unemployment rate to drop from $U^* = 6.6$ percent to 5 percent. But if the expected inflation rate becomes 3 percent, a 3 percent rise in nominal wages means *no* rise in *real* wages. Once workers come to expect the higher inflation rate, rising nominal wages will no longer be sufficient to entice them out of unemployment. As a result, as the *expected* inflation rate moves up from 0 percent to 3 percent, the unemployment rate will move up also.

In terms of Figure 17-5, as authorities initially increase aggregate demand, the economy moves from point A to point B. If the authorities continue the stimulus in an effort to keep the unemployment rate down, workers' expectations will adjust, causing the unemployment rate to rise. In this second stage, the economy moves from B to point F_1. The unemployment rate returns to the natural rate, $U^* = 6.6$ percent, but the inflation rate is now 3 percent instead of zero. Once the adjustment of expectations has taken place, any further changes in policy will have to take place along a curve such as PC_3, say, a movement from F_1 to F_2. This new schedule is also a Phillips curve, differing from the first, PC_0, in that the actual inflation rate consistent with a 5 percent unemployment rate is higher, at 6 percent, because the expected inflation rate is higher.

QUICK QUIZ See page 395 for the answers. Review concepts from this section in MyEconLab.

The **natural rate of unemployment** is the rate that exists in __________-run equilibrium, when workers' __________ are consistent with actual conditions.

Departures from the natural rate of unemployment can occur when individuals encounter unanticipated changes in fiscal or monetary policy. An unexpected __________ in aggregate demand will reduce unemployment below the natural rate, whereas an unanticipated __________ in aggregate demand will push unemployment above the natural rate.

The __________ curve exhibits a negative short-run relationship between the inflation rate and the unemployment rate that can be observed when there are *unanticipated* changes in aggregate __________.

__________ policymakers seek to take advantage of a proposed Phillips curve trade-off between inflation and unemployment.

Rational Expectations, the Policy Irrelevance Proposition, and Real Business Cycles

You already know that economists assume that economic participants act *as though* they were rational and calculating. We assume that firms rationally maximize profits when they choose today's rate of output and that consumers rationally maximize satisfaction when they choose how much of what goods to consume today. One of the pivotal features of current macro policy research is the assumption that economic participants think rationally about the future as well as the present. This relationship was developed by Robert Lucas, who won the Nobel Prize in 1995 for his work. In particular, there is widespread agreement among many macroeconomics researchers that the **rational expectations hypothesis** extends our understanding of the behavior of the macroeconomy. This hypothesis has two key elements:

Rational expectations hypothesis A theory stating that people combine the effects of past policy changes on important economic variables with their own judgment about the future effects of current and future policy changes.

1. Individuals base their forecasts (expectations) about the future values of economic variables on all readily available past and current information.
2. These expectations incorporate individuals' understanding about how the economy operates, including the operation of monetary and fiscal policy.

In essence, the rational expectations hypothesis holds that Abraham Lincoln was correct when he said, "You can fool all the people some of the time. You can even fool some of the people all of the time. But you can't fool *all* of the people *all* the time."

If we further assume that there is pure competition in all markets and that all prices and wages are flexible, we obtain what many call the *new classical* approach to evaluating the effects of macroeconomic policies. To see how rational expectations operate in the new classical perspective, let's take a simple example of the economy's response to a change in monetary policy.

Flexible Wages and Prices, Rational Expectations, and Policy Irrelevance

Consider Figure 17-6 below, which shows the long-run aggregate supply curve (*LRAS*) for the economy, as well as the initial aggregate demand curve (AD_1) and the short-run aggregate supply curve ($SRAS_1$). The money supply is initially given by $M_1 = \$10$ trillion, and the price level and real GDP are equal to 110 and \$15 trillion, respectively. Consequently, point *A* represents the initial long-run equilibrium.

Suppose now that the money supply is unexpectedly increased to $M_2 = \$11$ trillion, thereby causing the aggregate demand curve to shift outward to AD_2. Given the location of the short-run aggregate supply curve, this increase in aggregate demand

FIGURE 17-6

Responses to Anticipated and Unanticipated Increases in Aggregate Demand

A \$1 trillion increase in the money supply causes the aggregate demand curve to shift rightward. If people anticipate the increase in the money supply, then workers will insist on higher nominal wages, which causes the short-run aggregate supply curve to shift leftward immediately, from $SRAS_1$ to $SRAS_2$. Hence, there is a direct movement, indicated by the green arrow, from point *A* to point *C*. In contrast, an unanticipated increase in the money supply causes an initial upward movement along $SRAS_1$ from point *A* to point *B*, indicated by the black arrow. Thus, in the short run, real GDP rises from \$15 trillion to \$15.3 trillion. In the long run, workers recognize that the price level has increased and demand higher wages, causing the *SRAS* curve to shift leftward, resulting in a movement from point *B* to point *C*.

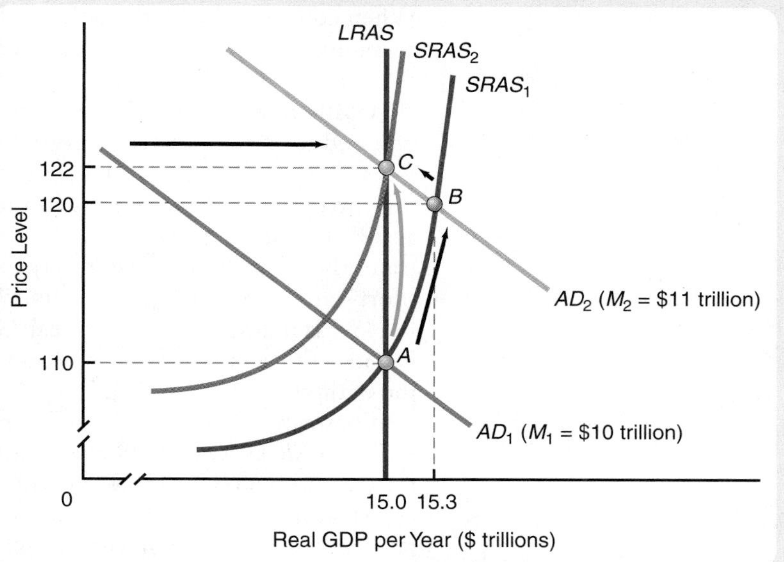

will cause the price level and real GDP to rise to 120 and $15.3 trillion, respectively. The new short-run equilibrium is at *B*. Because real GDP is *above* the long-run equilibrium level of $15 trillion, unemployment must be below long-run levels (the natural rate), and so workers will soon respond to the higher price level by demanding higher nominal wages. This will cause the short-run aggregate supply curve to shift upward vertically. As indicated by the black arrow, the economy moves from point *B* to a new long-run equilibrium at *C*.

The price level thus continues its rise to 122, even as real GDP declines back down to $15 trillion (and unemployment returns to the natural rate). So, as we have seen before, even though an increase in the money supply can raise real GDP and lower unemployment in the short run, it has no effect on either variable in the long run.

ANTICIPATED POLICY AND THE POLICY IRRELEVANCE PROPOSITION What if people *anticipate* the policy action discussed above? Let's look again at Figure 17-6 on the previous page to consider the answer to this question. In the initial equilibrium at point *A* of the figure, the short-run aggregate supply curve $SRAS_1$ corresponds to a situation in which the expected money supply and the actual money supply are equal. When the money supply changes in a way that is anticipated by economic participants, the aggregate supply curve will shift to reflect this expected change in the money supply. The new short-run aggregate supply curve $SRAS_2$ reflects this. According to the rational expectations hypothesis, the short-run aggregate supply curve will shift upward *simultaneously* with the rise in aggregate demand. As a result, the economy will move directly from point *A* to point *C*, without passing through *B*, as depicted by the green arrow in Figure 17-6.

The *only* response to the rise in the money supply is a rise in the price level from 110 to 122. Neither output nor unemployment changes at all. This conclusion—that fully anticipated monetary policy is irrelevant in determining the levels of real variables—is called the **policy irrelevance proposition:**

Policy irrelevance proposition
The conclusion that policy actions have no real effects in the short run if the policy actions are anticipated and none in the long run even if the policy actions are unanticipated.

Under the assumption of rational expectations on the part of decision makers in the economy,* anticipated *monetary policy cannot alter either the rate of unemployment or the level of real GDP. Regardless of the nature of the anticipated policy, the unemployment rate will equal the natural rate, and real GDP will be determined solely by the economy's long-run aggregate supply curve.

Another Challenge to Policy Activism: Real Business Cycles

When confronted with the policy irrelevance proposition, many economists began to reexamine the first principles of macroeconomics with fully flexible wages and prices.

THE DISTINCTION BETWEEN REAL AND MONETARY SHOCKS Some economists argue that real, as opposed to purely monetary, forces might help explain aggregate economic fluctuations. These shocks may take various forms such as technological advances that improve productivity, changes in the composition of the labor force, or changes in availability of a key resource. Consider Figure 17-7 on the facing page, which illustrates the concept of *real business cycles*. We begin at point E_1 with the economy in both short- and long-run equilibrium, with the associated supply curves, $SRAS_1$ and $LRAS_1$. Initially, the level of real GDP is $15 trillion, and the price level is 118. Because the economy is in long-run equilibrium, the unemployment rate must be at the natural rate.

A permanent reduction in the supply of a key productive resource, such as oil, causes both the *SRAS* and *LRAS* curves to shift to the left, to $SRAS_2$ and $LRAS_2$, because fewer goods will be available for sale due to the reduced supplies. In the short run, two adjustments begin to occur simultaneously. First, the prices of oil and petroleum-based products begin to rise, so the overall price level rises to 121. Second, the higher costs

FIGURE 17-7

Effects of a Reduction in the Supply of Resources

The position of the *LRAS* depends on our endowments of all types of resources. Hence, a permanent reduction in the supply of one of those resources, such as oil, causes a reduction—an inward shift—in the aggregate supply curve from $LRAS_1$ to $LRAS_2$. In addition, there is a rise in the equilibrium price level and a fall in the equilibrium rate of real GDP per year.

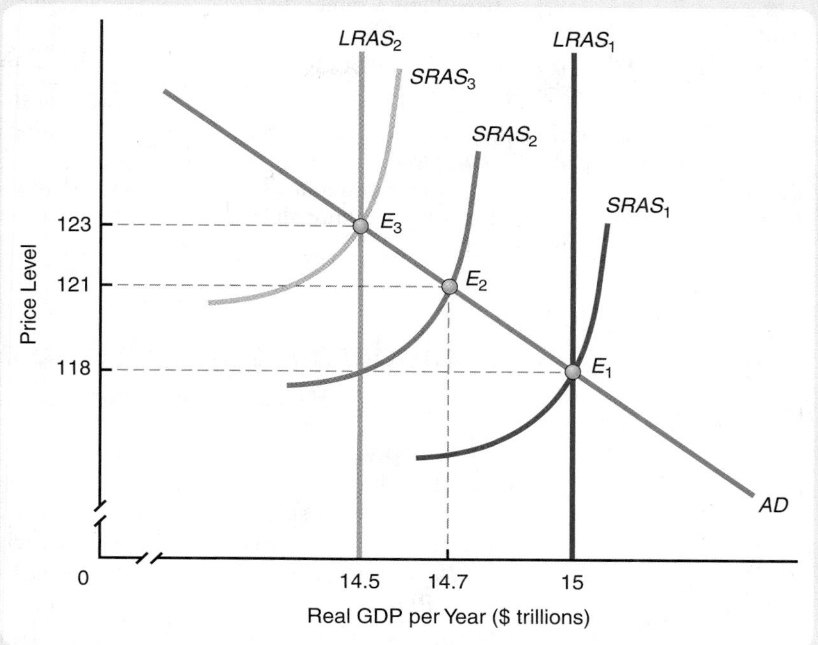

of production occasioned by the rise in oil prices induce firms to cut back production, so real GDP falls to $14.7 trillion in the short run. The new temporary short-run equilibrium occurs at E_2, with a higher price level (121) and a lower level of real GDP ($14.7 trillion).

This is not the full story, however. Owners of nonoil inputs, such as labor, are also affected by the reduction in oil supplies. For instance, as the real wage falls as a result of the higher price level, some workers who were willing to continue on the job at lower real wages in the short run will eventually decide to switch from full-time to part-time employment or to drop out of the labor force altogether. Thus, there will be a fall in the supply of nonoil inputs, reflected in an upward shift in the *SRAS* curve from $SRAS_2$ to $SRAS_3$. This puts additional upward pressure on the price level and exerts a downward force on real GDP. Thus, the final long-run equilibrium occurs at point E_3, with the price level at 123 and real GDP at $14.5 trillion.

STAGFLATION Notice that in the example depicted in Figure 17-7 above, real GDP declines over the same interval that the price level increases. This decline in real GDP is associated with lower employment and a higher unemployment rate. At the same time, there is higher inflation. Such a situation involving lower real GDP and increased inflation is called **stagflation.**

Stagflation
A situation characterized by lower real GDP, lower employment, and a higher unemployment rate during the same period that the rate of inflation increases.

The most recent prolonged periods of stagflation in the United States occurred during the 1970s and early 1980s. One factor contributing to stagflation episodes during those years was sharp reductions in the supply of oil, as in the example illustrated in Figure 17-7. In addition, Congress enacted steep increases in marginal tax rates and implemented a host of new federal regulations on firms in the early 1970s. All these factors together acted to reduce long-run aggregate supply and hence contributed to stagflation. Increases in oil supplies, cuts in marginal tax rates, and deregulation during the 1980s and 1990s helped to prevent stagflation episodes from occurring after the early 1980s.

QUICK QUIZ See page 395 for the answers. Review concepts from this section in MyEconLab.

The __________ __________ hypothesis assumes that individuals' forecasts incorporate all readily available information, including an understanding of government policy and its effects on the economy.

If the **rational expectations hypothesis** is valid, there is pure competition, and all prices and wages are flexible, then the __________ __________ proposition follows: Fully anticipated monetary policy actions cannot alter either the rate of unemployment or the level of real GDP.

Even if all prices and wages are perfectly flexible, aggregate __________ shocks such as sudden changes in technology or in the supplies of factors of production can cause national economic fluctuations. To the extent that these __________ __________ cycles predominate as sources of economic fluctuations, the case for active policymaking is weakened.

Modern Approaches to Justifying Active Policymaking

The policy irrelevance proposition and the idea that real shocks are important causes of business cycles are major attacks on the desirability of trying to stabilize economic activity with activist policies. Both criticisms of activist policies arise from combining the rational expectations hypothesis with the assumptions of pure competition and flexible wages and prices. It should not be surprising, therefore, to learn that economists who see a role for activist policymaking do not believe that market clearing models of the economy can explain business cycles. They contend that the "sticky" wages and prices assumed by Keynes in his major work (see Chapter 11) remain important in today's economy. To explain how aggregate demand shocks and policies can influence a nation's real GDP and unemployment rate, these economists, who are sometimes called *new Keynesians*, have tried to refine the theory of aggregate supply.

Small Menu Costs and Sticky Prices

One approach to explaining why many prices might be sticky in the short run supposes that much of the economy is characterized by imperfect competition and that it is costly for firms to change their prices in response to changes in demand. The costs associated with changing prices are called *menu costs*. These include the costs of renegotiating contracts, printing price lists (such as menus), and informing customers of price changes.

Small menu costs
Costs that deter firms from changing prices in response to demand changes—for example, the costs of renegotiating contracts or printing new price lists.

Many such costs may not be very large, so economists call them **small menu costs.** Some of the costs of changing prices, however, such as those incurred in bringing together business managers from points around the nation or the world for meetings on price changes or renegotiating deals with customers, may be significant.

What are the estimated magnitudes of small menu costs?

EXAMPLE

Just How "Small" Are Small Menu Costs?

Economists have developed two ways of gauging small menu costs experienced by sellers. One method is to try to measure the average dollar amount of menu cost per change in each item's price. Such a cost includes the average expense that a firm incurs in expending managerial resources to decide on a price change, as well as costs of printing new menus or attaching updated price tags. Estimates of per-unit menu costs across a number of industries and types of products range from as low as about 50 cents to as high as several dollars.

Another approach to estimating menu costs is to try measuring them in relation to firms' revenues. According to this approach, most estimates indicate that menu costs range between about 0.2 percent and 1 percent of the total revenues of firms. Thus, with menu costs as high as 1 percent of revenues, it does not pay for firms to change prices unless they anticipate the resulting increase in total revenues to be at least 1 percent.

FOR CRITICAL THINKING

If the average menu cost of changing the per-unit price of an item is $1, how much must revenues per item increase for the price change to be profitable?

Real GDP and the Price Level in a Sticky-Price Economy

According to the new Keynesians, sticky prices strengthen the argument favoring active policymaking as a means of preventing substantial short-run swings in real GDP and, as a consequence, employment.

NEW KEYNESIAN INFLATION DYNAMICS To see why the idea of price stickiness strengthens the case for active policymaking, consider panel (a) of Figure 17-8 below. If a significant portion of all prices do not adjust rapidly, then in the short run the aggregate supply curve effectively is horizontal, as assumed in the traditional Keynesian theory discussed in Chapter 11. This means that a decline in aggregate demand, such as the shift from AD_1 to AD_2 shown in panel (a), will induce the largest possible decline in equilibrium real GDP, from \$15 trillion to \$14.7 trillion at E_2. When prices are sticky, economic contractions induced by aggregate demand shocks are as severe as they can be.

As panel (a) shows, in contrast to the traditional Keynesian theory, the new Keynesian sticky-price theory indicates that the economy will find its own way back to a long-run equilibrium. The theory presumes that small menu costs induce firms not to change their prices in the short run. In the long run, however, the profit gains to firms from reducing their prices to induce purchases of more goods and services cause them to cut their prices. Thus, in the long run, the price level declines in response to the decrease in aggregate demand. As firms reduce their prices, the horizontal aggregate supply curve shifts downward, from $SRAS_1$ to $SRAS_2$, and equilibrium real GDP returns to its former level at E_3, other things being equal.

Of course, an increase in aggregate demand would have effects opposite to those depicted in panel (a) of Figure 17-8. A rise in aggregate demand would cause real GDP to rise in the short run. In the long run, firms would gain sufficient profits from raising

FIGURE 17-8

Short- and Long-Run Adjustments in the New Keynesian Sticky-Price Theory

Panel (a) shows that when prices are sticky, the short-run aggregate supply curve is horizontal, here at a price level of 118. As a consequence, the short-run effect of a fall in aggregate demand from AD_1 to AD_2 generates the largest possible decline in real GDP, from \$15 trillion at point E_1 to \$14.7 trillion at point E_2. In the long run, producers perceive that they can increase their profits sufficiently by cutting prices and incurring the menu costs of doing so. The resulting decline in the price level implies a downward shift of the *SRAS* curve, so that the price level falls to 116 and real GDP returns to \$15 trillion at point E_3. Panel (b) illustrates the argument for active policymaking based on the new Keynesian theory. Instead of waiting for long-run adjustments to occur, policymakers can engage in expansionary policies that shift the aggregate demand curve back to its original position, thereby shortening or even eliminating a recession.

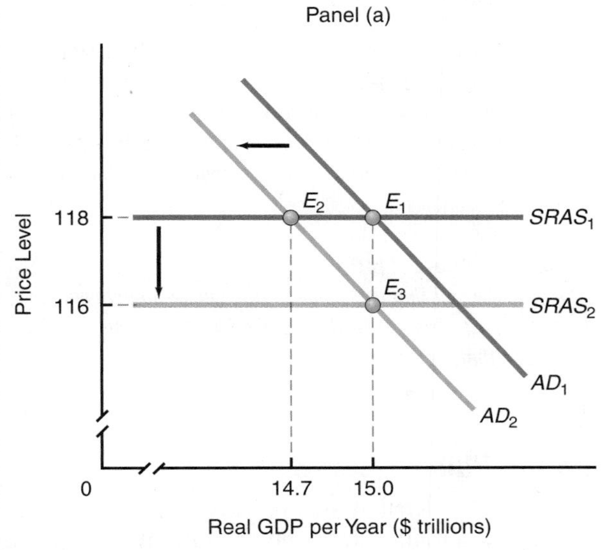

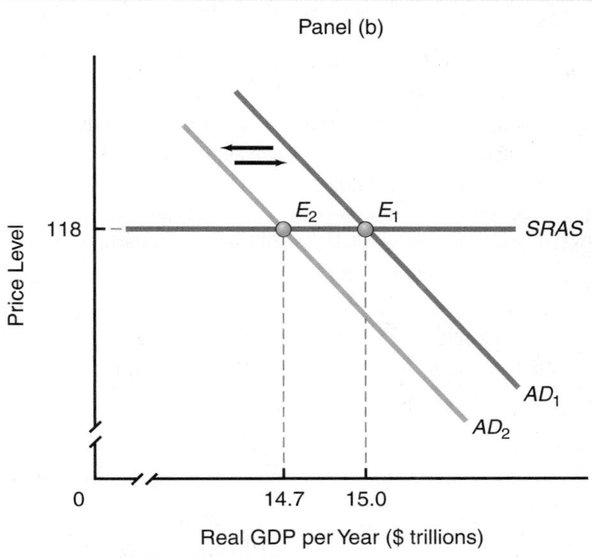

their prices to compensate for incurring menu costs, and the short-run aggregate supply curve would shift upward. Consequently, an economy with growing aggregate demand should exhibit so-called **new Keynesian inflation dynamics:** initial sluggish adjustment of the price level in response to aggregate demand increases followed by higher inflation later on.

New Keynesian inflation dynamics
In new Keynesian theory, the pattern of inflation exhibited by an economy with growing aggregate demand—initial sluggish adjustment of the price level in response to increased aggregate demand followed by higher inflation later.

WHY ACTIVE POLICYMAKING CAN PAY OFF WHEN PRICES ARE STICKY To think about why the new Keynesian sticky-price theory supports the argument for active policymaking, let's return to the case of a decline in aggregate demand illustrated in panel (a) of Figure 17-8 on the previous page. Panel (b) shows the same decline in aggregate demand as in panel (a) and the resulting maximum contractionary effect on real GDP.

Monetary and fiscal policy actions that influence aggregate demand are as potent as possible when prices are sticky and short-run aggregate supply is horizontal. In principle, therefore, all that a policymaker confronted by the leftward shift in aggregate demand depicted in panel (b) must do is to conduct the appropriate policy to induce a rightward shift in the *AD* curve back to its previous position. Indeed, if the policymaker acts rapidly enough, the period of contraction experienced by the economy may be very brief. Active policymaking can thereby moderate or even eliminate recessions.

Is There a New Keynesian Phillips Curve?

A fundamental thrust of the new Keynesian theory is that activist policymaking can promote economic stability. Assessing this implication requires evaluating whether policymakers face an *exploitable* relationship between the inflation rate and the unemployment rate and between inflation and real GDP. By "exploitable," economists mean a relationship that is sufficiently predictable (for policymakers only) and long-lived to allow enough time for policymakers to reduce unemployment or to push up real GDP when economic activity falls below its long-run level.

According to the new Keynesian theory, how much active policymaking speeds up the stabilization process relative to a longer-term self-adjustment by natural economic forces depends on how quickly firms adjust prices. What is the evidence on the speed of overall U.S. price adjustment?

POLICY EXAMPLE

How Fast Do U.S. Firms Change Their Prices?

During the late 1990s and early 2000s, a number of studies by new Keynesian economists estimated that it took U.S. companies an average of two years to alter the prices of their products. These estimates suggested considerable time was available for active policymaking to reduce unemployment and boost real GDP whenever the pace of economic activity fell below its long-run trend.

Critics of these early studies argued that they were biased by reliance on studying changes in the GDP deflator, which tends to exhibit smooth changes over time, instead of examining changes in prices of individual items sold by U.S. firms. The critics also maintained that the initial studies' use of aggregate measures of U.S. firms' costs was inappropriate and that data on firms' *actual* costs should be used instead. Making these measurement changes reduces estimates of the average time it takes U.S. firms to adjust their prices to as low as four months. If the latter estimate is correct, active policymaking must be employed very rapidly if it is to provide clear-cut stabilization benefits for the U.S. economy.

FOR CRITICAL THINKING

How does the fact that estimated average price-adjustment intervals for Europe almost always exceed 1½ years affect the case for active policymaking in that region?

The U.S. Experience with the Phillips Curve

For more than fifty years, economists have debated the existence of a policy-exploitable Phillips curve relationship between the inflation rate and the rate of unemployment. In separate articles in 1968, the late Milton Friedman and Edmond Phelps published pioneering studies suggesting that the apparent trade-off suggested by the Phillips curve could *not* be exploited by activist policymakers. Friedman and Phelps both argued that any attempt to reduce unemployment by boosting inflation would soon be thwarted by the incorporation of the new higher inflation rate into the public's expectations. The Friedman-Phelps research thus implies that for any given unemployment rate, *any* inflation rate is possible, depending on the actions of policymakers.

Figure 17-9 below appears to provide support for the propositions of Friedman and Phelps. It clearly shows that in the past, a number of inflation rates have proved feasible at the same rates of unemployment.

The New Keynesian Phillips Curve

Today's new Keynesian theorists are not concerned about the lack of an apparent long-lived relationship between inflation and unemployment revealed by Figure 17-9. From their point of view, the issue is not whether a relationship between inflation and unemployment or between inflation and real GDP breaks down over a period of years. All that matters for policymakers, the new Keynesians suggest, is whether such a relationship is exploitable in the near term. If so, policymakers can intervene in the economy as soon as actual unemployment and real GDP vary from their long-run levels. Appropriate activist policies, new Keynesians conclude, can dampen cyclical fluctuations and make them shorter-lived.

EVALUATING NEW KEYNESIAN INFLATION DYNAMICS To assess the predictions of new Keynesian inflation dynamics, economists seek to evaluate whether inflation is closely related to two key factors that theory indicates should determine the inflation rate. The first of these factors is anticipated future inflation. The new Keynesian theory implies that menu costs reduce firms' incentive to adjust their prices. When some

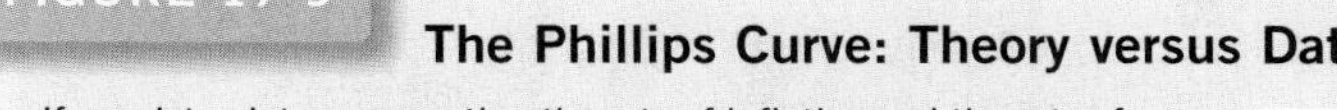

FIGURE 17-9
The Phillips Curve: Theory versus Data

If we plot points representing the rate of inflation and the rate of unemployment for the United States from 1953 to the present, there does not appear to be any trade-off between the two variables.
Sources: Economic Report of the President; Economic Indicators, various issues.

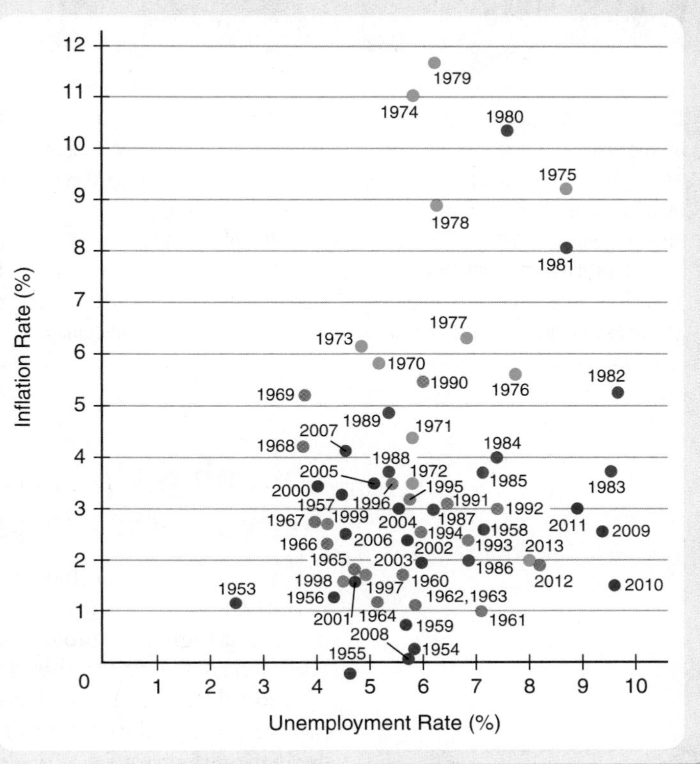

firms *do* adjust their prices, however, they will seek to set prices at levels based on expected future positions of demand curves for their products. The expected future inflation rate signals to firms how much equilibrium prices are likely to increase during future months, so firms will take into account the expected future inflation rate when setting prices at the present time.

The second key factor that new Keynesian theory indicates should affect current inflation is the average inflation-adjusted (real) per-unit costs that firms incur in producing goods and services. Thus, new Keynesians propose a positive relationship between inflation and an aggregate measure of real per-unit costs faced by firms throughout the economy. If firms' average inflation-adjusted per-unit costs increase, the prediction is that there will be higher prices charged by that portion of firms that do adjust their prices in the current period and, hence, greater current inflation.

Empirical evidence does indicate that increases in expected future inflation and greater real per-unit production costs are indeed associated with higher observed rates of inflation. In light of this support for these key predictions of the new Keynesian theory, the theory is exerting increasing influence on U.S. policymakers. For instance, media reports commonly refer to Fed officials' careful attention to changes in inflation expectations and firms' production costs that they interpret as signals of altered inflationary pressures.

JUST HOW EXPLOITABLE IS THE NEW KEYNESIAN PHILLIPS CURVE? Not all economists are persuaded that the new Keynesian theory is correct. They point out that new classical theory already indicates that when prices are *flexible*, higher inflation expectations should reduce short-run aggregate supply. Such a decline in aggregate supply should, in turn, contribute to increased inflation.

Even if one were convinced that new Keynesian theory is correct, a fundamental issue is whether the new Keynesian theory has truly identified *exploitable* relationships. At the heart of this issue is just how often firms adjust their prices.

How might difficulties that people experience in processing large volumes of information help to explain real-world macroeconomic phenomena?

EXAMPLE

Are Households and Firms "Rationally Inattentive"?

A fundamental drawback of most new Keynesian sticky-price theories is their prediction that decreases in inflation will have expansionary effects on the economy. In reality, reductions in inflation induced by declines in aggregate demand typically lead to business-cycle contractions. A theory of *rational inattention* based on bounded rationality (see page 9) has shown promise of better matching this real-world observation.

The rational-inattention theory assumes that households and firms have limitations on their abilities to process information. Therefore, stickiness in setting prices naturally increases as a result of presumed menu costs. In rational-inattention models, consumers and businesses are slow to recognize decelerations in aggregate demand that reduce inflation and generate a business contraction. With these new models, economists may be able to make more accurate predictions.

FOR CRITICAL THINKING

Why do you think that it is difficult to develop a theory that matches every observed pattern in economywide business fluctuations?

Summing Up: Economic Factors Favoring Active versus Passive Policymaking

To many people who have never taken a principles of economics course, it seems apparent that the world's governments should engage in active policymaking aimed at achieving high and stable real GDP growth and a low and stable unemployment rate. As you have learned in this chapter, the advisability of policy activism is not so obvious.

Several factors are involved in assessing whether policy activism is really preferable to passive policymaking. Table 17-1 on the facing page summarizes the issues involved in evaluating the case for active policymaking versus the case for passive policymaking.

TABLE 17-1

Issues That Must Be Assessed in Determining the Desirability of Active versus Passive Policymaking

Economists who contend that active policymaking is justified argue that for each issue listed in the first column, there is evidence supporting the conclusions listed in the second column. In contrast, economists who suggest that passive policymaking is appropriate argue that for each issue in the first column, there is evidence leading to the conclusions in the third column.

Issue	Support for Active Policymaking	Support for Passive Policymaking
Phillips curve inflation–unemployment trade-off	Stable in the short run; perhaps predictable in the long run	Varies with inflation expectations; at best fleeting in the short run and nonexistent in the long run
Aggregate demand shocks	Induce short-run and perhaps long-run effects on real GDP and unemployment	Have little or no short-run effects and certainly no long-run effects on real GDP and unemployment
Aggregate supply shocks	Can, along with aggregate demand shocks, influence real GDP and unemployment	Cause movements in real GDP and unemployment and hence explain most business cycles
Pure competition	Is not typical in most markets, where imperfect competition predominates	Is widespread in markets throughout the economy
Price flexibility	Is uncommon because factors such as small menu costs induce firms to change prices infrequently	Is common because firms adjust prices immediately when demand changes
Wage flexibility	Is uncommon because labor market adjustments occur relatively slowly	Is common because nominal wages adjust speedily to price changes, making real wages flexible

The current state of thinking on the relative desirability of active or passive policymaking may leave you somewhat frustrated. On the one hand, most economists agree that active policymaking is unlikely to exert sizable long-run effects on any nation's economy. Most also agree that aggregate supply shocks contribute to business cycles. Consequently, it is generally agreed that there are limits on the effectiveness of monetary and fiscal policies. On the other hand, a number of economists continue to argue that there is evidence indicating stickiness of prices and wages. They argue, therefore, that monetary and fiscal policy actions can offset, at least in the short run and perhaps even in the long run, the effects that aggregate demand shocks would otherwise have on real GDP and unemployment.

These diverging perspectives help explain why economists reach differing conclusions about the advisability of pursuing active or passive approaches to macroeconomic policymaking. Different interpretations of evidence on the issues summarized in Table 17-1 above will likely continue to divide economists for years to come.

QUICK QUIZ See page 395 for the answers. Review concepts from this section in MyEconLab.

Some new Keynesian economists suggest that __________ __________ costs inhibit many firms from making speedy changes in their prices and that this price stickiness can make the short-run aggregate supply curve __________. Variations in aggregate demand have the largest possible effects on real GDP in the short run, so policies that influence aggregate demand also have the greatest capability to stabilize real GDP in the face of aggregate demand shocks.

Even though there is little evidence supporting a long-run trade-off between inflation and unemployment, new Keynesian theory suggests that activist policymaking may be able to stabilize real GDP and employment in the __________ run. This is possible, according to the theory, if stickiness of __________ adjustment is sufficiently great that policymakers can exploit a __________-run trade-off between inflation and real GDP.

YOU ARE THERE

Active Policies Can Raise Employment—At a Substantial Cost

James Feyrer and Bruce Sacerdote of Dartmouth College have just completed a study of the effects on U.S. employment exerted by active fiscal policy actions implemented under the American Recovery and Reinvestment Act (ARRA) of 2009. One conclusion that Feyrer and Sacerdote have reached is that the number of new jobs attributable to ARRA varied considerably across different forms of discretionary fiscal expenditures. Federal spending directed to states for infrastructure projects, such as road construction and bridge repair, definitely led to new positions. In contrast, no jobs resulted from government grants for education.

Feyrer and Sacerdote conclude that ARRA made a significant contribution to the number of jobs available to about 2 million U.S. residents who were able to find new positions after losing jobs in 2008 and 2009. They have trouble reaching firm conclusions regarding the net effect of ARRA on aggregate employment, given that about 6 million people have not yet found positions to replace lost jobs. They are, however, certain that the jobs "created" by ARRA had a substantial cost to taxpayers. They estimate this cost as somewhere between $170,000 and $400,000 per position.

Critical Thinking Questions

1. Why might one argue that ARRA's policy activism helped stabilize employment?
2. How could someone argue that ARRA failed to help stabilize employment?

ISSUES & APPLICATIONS

A "Law" for Guiding Active Policymaking Breaks Down

CONCEPTS APPLIED

- Active (Discretionary) Policymaking
- Passive (Nondiscretionary) Policymaking
- Phillips Curve

Ever since an economist named Arthur Okun proposed in 1962 the existence of a stable relationship, known as "Okun's law," economists have suggested that it can help guide active policymaking. Okun's law describes an inverse empirical relationship between deviations of the unemployment rate from its long-run trend value and the gap between actual real GDP and potential real GDP. Keeping the unemployment rate close to its long-run trend level, active-policy proponents suggest, requires policies to reduce the gap between actual real GDP and potential real GDP.

Okun's Law Breaks Down

Figure 17-10 on the facing page displays observed pairings between unemployment rate deviations and output gaps for the United States. Consistent with Okun's law, most of these observations cluster along a downward-sloping line.

Dots predate late 2009; and square points follow that date with 2009i denoting the first three-month interval in 2009, and so on. Clearly, since the end of 2009, Okun's law appears to have broken down. The unemployment rate has remained high even though the output gap has declined.

Alternative Views of Implications of the Breakdown

Proponents of active policymaking argue that the breakdown of Okun's law is temporary. The unemployment rate

FIGURE 17-10

An Altered Relationship between Unemployment Deviations from Trend and the Percentage "Output Gap"

Traditionally, a stable relationship existed between deviations of the unemployment rate from its long-term trend value and the percentage gap between actual real GDP and potential real GDP. The succession of square points for the most recent three-month intervals indicates that this relationship has not been stable since early 2009, however.

Sources: Bureau of Labor Statistics; Congressional Budget Office: author's estimates.

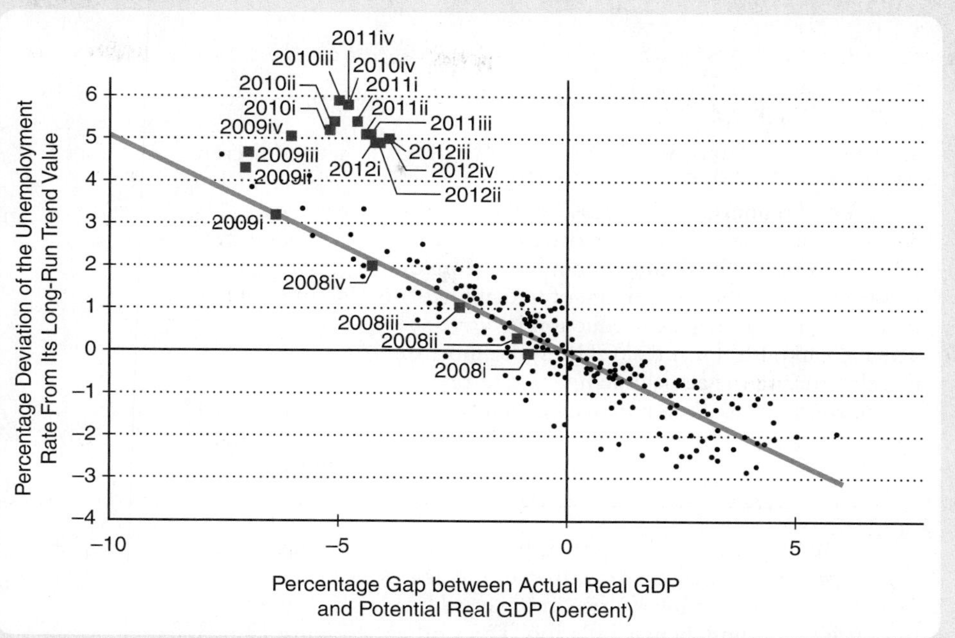

eventually will drop toward its long-run trend value, they contend, as the output gap shrinks in response to discretionary policies.

Those who support passive policymaking argue that the breakdown in Okun's law likely will be much more persistent, just as breakdowns in the theory of a downward-sloping Phillips curve (see page 387) often have lasted for lengthy periods. Proponents of passive policymaking contend that extended unemployment benefits have given people incentives not to look as intensively for new jobs and that new government regulations have reduced labor demand by firms. According to this perspective, active policies aimed at reducing the gap between actual real GDP and potential real GDP will not necessarily generate a lower unemployment rate.

For Critical Thinking

1. Would a breakdown in the Okun's law relationship strengthen or weaken the case for active policymaking?
2. Do Okun's law and the short-run Phillips curve appear to be related concepts?

Web Resources

1. Learn more about Okun's law at **www.econtoday.com/chap17**.
2. For a discussion of the applicability of Okun's law around the globe during the recent economic downturn, go to **www.econtoday.com/ch17**.

MyEconLab

For more questions on this chapter's Issues & Applications, go to MyEconLab. In the Study Plan for this chapter, select Section N: News.

MyEconLab

Here is what you should know after reading this chapter. MyEconLab will help you identify what you know, and where to go when you need to practice.

WHAT YOU SHOULD KNOW		WHERE TO GO TO PRACTICE
Why the Actual Unemployment Rate Might Depart from the Natural Rate of Unemployment An unexpected increase in aggregate demand can cause real GDP to rise in the short run, which results in a reduction in the unemployment rate below the natural rate of unemployment. Likewise, an unanticipated reduction in aggregate demand can push down real GDP in the short run, thereby causing the actual unemployment rate to rise above the natural unemployment rate.	active (discretionary) policymaking, 374 passive (nondiscretionary) policymaking, 374 natural rate of unemployment, 375 **Key Figures** Figure 17-1, 375 Figure 17-2, 376 Figure 17-3, 377	• MyEconLab Study Plans 17.1, 17.2 • Animated Figures 17-1, 17-2, 17-3
The Phillips Curve An unexpected increase in aggregate demand that causes a drop in the unemployment rate also induces a rise in the equilibrium price level and, hence, inflation. Thus, other things being equal, there should be an inverse relationship between the inflation rate and the unemployment rate. This downward-sloping relationship is called the Phillips curve.	Phillips curve, 378 **Key Figures** Figure 17-4, 378 Figure 17-5, 379	• MyEconLab Study Plan 17.2 • Animated Figures 17-4, 17-5
How Expectations Affect the Actual Relationship between the Inflation Rate and the Unemployment Rate A Phillips curve relationship will exist only when expectations are unchanged. If people anticipate policymakers' efforts to exploit the Phillips curve trade-off via inflationary policies aimed at pushing down the unemployment rate, then input prices such as nominal wages will adjust more rapidly to an increase in the price level. As a result, the Phillips curve will shift outward, and the economy will adjust more speedily toward the natural rate of unemployment.		• MyEconLab Study Plan 17.2
Rational Expectations, Policy Ineffectiveness, and Real-Business-Cycle Theory The rational expectations hypothesis suggests that people form expectations of inflation using all available past and current information and an understanding of how the economy functions. If pure competition prevails, wages and prices are flexible, and people completely anticipate the actions of policymakers, so real GDP remains unaffected by anticipated policy actions. Technological changes and labor market shocks such as variations in the composition of the labor force can induce business fluctuations, called real business cycles, which weaken the case for active policymaking.	rational expectations hypothesis, 381 policy irrelevance proposition, 382 stagflation, 383 **Key Figures** Figure 17-6, 381 Figure 17-7, 383	• MyEconLab Study Plan 17.3 • Animated Figures 17-6, 17-7

MyEconLab *continued*

WHAT YOU SHOULD KNOW		WHERE TO GO TO PRACTICE
Modern Approaches to Bolstering the Case for Active Policymaking New Keynesian approaches suggest that firms may be slow to change prices in the face of variations in demand. Thus, the short-run aggregate supply curve is horizontal, and changes in aggregate demand have the largest possible effects on real GDP in the short run. If prices and wages are sufficiently inflexible in the short run that there is an exploitable trade-off between inflation and real GDP, discretionary policy actions can stabilize real GDP.	small menu costs, 384 new Keynesian inflation dynamics, 386	• MyEconLab Study Plans 17.4, 17.5, 17.6

Log in to MyEconLab, take a chapter test, and get a personalized Study Plan that tells you which concepts you understand and which ones you need to review. From there, MyEconLab will give you further practice, tutorials, animations, videos, and guided solutions. For more information, visit www.myeconlab.com

PROBLEMS

All problems are assignable in MyEconLab. *Answers to odd-numbered problems appear at the back of the book.*

17-1. Suppose that the government altered the computation of the unemployment rate by including people in the military as part of the labor force. (See page 374.)

a. How would this affect the actual unemployment rate?

b. How would such a change affect estimates of the natural rate of unemployment?

c. If this computational change were made, would it in any way affect the logic of the short-run and long-run Phillips curve analysis and its implications for policymaking? Why might the government wish to make such a change?

17-2. The natural rate of unemployment depends on factors that affect the behavior of both workers and firms. Make lists of possible factors affecting workers and firms that you believe are likely to influence the natural rate of unemployment. (See pages 374–375.)

17-3. Suppose that more unemployed people who are classified as part of frictional unemployment decide to stop looking for work and start their own businesses instead. What is likely to happen to each of the following, other things being equal? (See pages 375–379.)

a. The natural unemployment rate

b. The economy's Phillips curve

17-4. Suppose that people who previously had held jobs become cyclically unemployed at the same time the inflation rate declines. Would the result be a movement along or a shift of the short-run Phillips curve? Explain your reasoning. (See pages 376–379.)

17-5. Suppose that people who previously had held jobs become structurally unemployed due to establishment of new government regulations during a period in which the inflation rate remains unchanged. Would the result be a movement along or a shift of the short-run Phillips curve? Explain your reasoning. (See pages 376–379.)

17-6. Suppose that the greater availability of online job placement services generates a reduction in frictional unemployment during an interval in which the inflation rate remains unchanged. Would the result be a movement along or a shift of the short-run Phillips curve? Explain your reasoning. (See pages 376–379.)

17-7. Consider a situation in which a future president has appointed Federal Reserve leaders who conduct monetary policy much more erratically than in past years. The consequence is that the quantity of money in circulation varies in a much more unsystematic and, hence, hard-to-predict manner. According to the policy irrelevance proposition, is it more or less likely that the Fed's policy actions will cause real GDP to change in the short run? Explain. (See pages 379–380.)

17-8. People called "Fed watchers" earn their living by trying to forecast what policies the Federal Reserve will implement within the next few weeks and months. Suppose that Fed watchers discover that the current group of Fed officials is following very systematic and predictable policies intended to reduce the unemployment rate. The Fed watchers then sell this information to firms, unions, and others in the private sector. If pure competition prevails, prices and wages are flexible, and people form rational expectations, are the Fed's policies enacted after the information sale likely to have their intended effects on the unemployment rate? (See pages 379–381.)

17-9. Suppose that economists were able to use U.S. economic data to demonstrate that the rational expectations hypothesis is true. Would this be sufficient to demonstrate the validity of the policy irrelevance proposition? (See page 381.)

17-10. Evaluate the following statement: "In an important sense, the term *policy irrelevance proposition* is misleading because even if the rational expectations hypothesis is valid, economic policy actions can have significant effects on real GDP and the unemployment rate." (See page 381.)

17-11. Consider the diagram below, which is drawn under the assumption that the new Keynesian sticky-price theory of aggregate supply applies. Assume that at present, the economy is in long-run equilibrium at point *A*. Answer the following questions. (See page 385.)

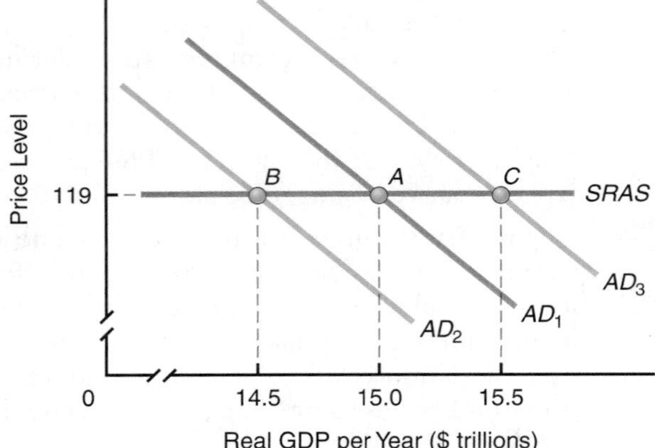

a. Suppose that there is a sudden increase in desired investment expenditures. Which of the alternative aggregate demand curves—AD_2 or AD_3—will apply after this event occurs? Other things being equal, what will happen to the equilibrium price level and to equilibrium real GDP in the *short run*? Explain.

b. Other things being equal, after the event and adjustments discussed in part (a) have taken place, what will happen to the equilibrium price level and to equilibrium real GDP in the *long run*? Explain.

17-12. Both the traditional Keynesian theory discussed in Chapter 11 and the new Keynesian theory considered in this chapter indicate that the short-run aggregate supply curve is horizontal. (See page 385.)

a. In terms of their *short-run* implications for the price level and real GDP, is there any difference between the two approaches?

b. In terms of their *long-run* implications for the price level and real GDP, is there any difference between the two approaches?

17-13. The real-business-cycle approach attributes even short-run increases in real GDP largely to aggregate supply shocks. Rightward shifts in aggregate supply tend to push down the equilibrium price level. How could the real-business-cycle perspective explain the low but persistent inflation that the United States experienced until 2007? (See pages 382–383.)

17-14. Normally, when aggregate demand increases, firms find it more profitable to raise prices than to leave prices unchanged. The idea behind the small-menu-cost explanation for price stickiness is that firms will leave their prices unchanged if their profit gain from adjusting prices is less than the menu costs they would incur if they change prices. If firms anticipate that a rise in demand is likely to last for a long time, does this make them more or less likely to adjust their prices when they face small menu costs? (See page 384. Hint: Profits are a flow that firms earn from week to week and month to month, but small menu costs are a one-time expense.)

17-15. The policy relevance of new Keynesian inflation dynamics based on the theory of small menu costs and sticky prices depends on the exploitability of the implied relationship between inflation and real GDP. Explain in your own words why the average time between price adjustments by firms is a crucial determinant of whether policymakers can actively exploit this relationship to try to stabilize real GDP. (See page 386.)

ECONOMICS ON THE NET

The Inflation–Unemployment Relationship According to the basic aggregate demand and aggregate supply model, the unemployment rate should be inversely related to changes in the inflation rate, other things being equal. This application allows you to take a direct look at unemployment and inflation data to judge for yourself whether the two variables appear to be related.

Title: Bureau of Labor Statistics: Economy at a Glance

Navigation: Go to **www.econtoday.com/ch17** to visit the Bureau of Labor Statistics Economy at a Glance home page.

Application Perform the indicated operations, and then answer the following questions.

1. Click on the "back data" box next to *Consumer Price Index*. Has the U.S. economy consistently experienced inflation since 2008? Was there consistently inflation prior to 2008?
2. Back up to *Economy at a Glance*, and now click on the "back data" box next to *Unemployment Rate*. Was the unemployment rate lower or higher before 2008? Do you note any appearance of an inverse relationship between the unemployment rate and the inflation rate?

For Group Study and Analysis Divide the class into groups, and have each group search through the *Economy at a Glance* site to develop an explanation for the key factors accounting for the recent behavior of the unemployment rate. Have each group report on its explanation. Is there any one factor that best explains the recent behavior of the unemployment rate?

ANSWERS TO QUICK QUIZZES

p. 380: (i) long . . . expectations; (ii) increase . . . decrease; (iii) Phillips . . . demand; (iv) Activist

p. 384: (i) rational expectations; (ii) policy irrelevance; (iii) supply . . . real business

p. 389: (i) small menu . . . horizontal; (ii) short . . . price . . . short

18 Policies and Prospects for Global Economic Growth

For years, a large portion of Mongolia's capital equipment, including drills and excavating machines, has lain idle, and operations of key industries such as mining have ebbed about as often as they have flowed. Brief intervals of meager economic growth have been followed by lengthy periods during which the nation's per capita real GDP has remained stagnant. Suddenly, however, Mongolia's longer-term economic situation appears brighter. The catalyst for change has been a government plan to issue shares of ownership in future returns derived from the mining of newly discovered coal and copper deposits. Mongolian capital investment has exploded, and the nation's economic growth rate has more than doubled. After reading this chapter, you will understand why the granting of private ownership shares in mining operations has had such a significant impact on economic growth in Mongolia.

LEARNING OBJECTIVES

After reading this chapter, you should be able to:

- Explain why population growth can have uncertain effects on economic growth
- Understand why the existence of dead capital retards investment and economic growth in much of the developing world
- Describe how government inefficiencies have contributed to the creation of relatively large quantities of dead capital in the world's developing nations
- Discuss the sources of international investment funds for developing nations and identify obstacles to international investment in these nations
- Identify the key functions of the World Bank and the International Monetary Fund
- Explain the problems faced by policymakers at the World Bank and the International Monetary Fund and discuss some proposals for dealing with these problems

MyEconLab helps you master each objective and study more efficiently. See end of chapter for details.

? DID YOU KNOW THAT...

92 percent of Egypt's residents do not hold official legal title to the properties in which they reside and conduct their business affairs? The estimated value of all of these not-legally-owned capital assets is more than 30 times the value of private assets that people formally own. Furthermore, about 43 percent of Egyptian residents are employed by businesses that have no official legal standing on which to operate.

Economists' understanding of the determinants of economic growth suggests that in light of the above figures it is not surprising that the long-run average rate of economic growth is much lower in Egypt than in most of the rest of the world. After reading this chapter, you will be equipped to undertake your own evaluation of the prospects for global economic growth.

Labor Resources and Economic Growth

You learned in Chapter 9 that the main determinants of economic growth are the growth of labor and capital resources and the rate of increase of labor and capital productivity. Human resources are abundant around the globe. Currently, the world's population increases by more than 70 million people each year. This population growth is not spread evenly over the earth's surface. Among the relatively wealthy nations of Europe, women bear an average of just over one child during their lifetimes. In the United States, a typical woman bears about 1.5 children. But in the generally poorer nations of Africa, women bear an average of six children.

Population growth does not necessarily translate into an increase in labor resources in the poorest regions of the world. Many people in poor nations do not join the labor force. Many who do so have trouble obtaining employment.

A common assumption is that high population growth in a less developed nation hinders the growth of its per capita GDP. Certainly, this is the presumption in China, where the government has imposed an absolute limit of one child per female resident. In fact, however, the relationship between population growth and economic growth is not really so clear-cut.

Basic Arithmetic of Population Growth and Economic Growth

Does a larger population raise or lower per capita real GDP? If a country has fixed borders and an unchanged level of aggregate real GDP, a higher population directly reduces per capita real GDP. After all, if there are more people, then dividing a constant amount of real GDP by a larger number of people reduces real GDP per capita.

This basic arithmetic works for growth rates too. We can express the growth rate of per capita real GDP in a nation as

$$\frac{\text{Rate of growth of}}{\text{per capita real GDP}} = \frac{\text{rate of growth}}{\text{in real GDP}} - \frac{\text{rate of growth}}{\text{of population}}$$

Hence, if real GDP grows at a constant rate of 4 percent per year and the annual rate of population growth increases from 2 percent to 3 percent, the annual rate of growth of per capita real GDP will decline, from 2 percent to 1 percent.

HOW POPULATION GROWTH CAN CONTRIBUTE TO ECONOMIC GROWTH The arithmetic of the relationship between economic growth and population growth can be misleading. Certainly, it is a mathematical fact that the rate of growth of per capita real GDP equals the difference between the rate of growth in real GDP and the rate of growth of the population. Economic analysis, however, indicates that population growth can affect the rate of growth of real GDP. Thus, these two growth rates generally are not independent.

Recall from Chapter 9 that a higher rate of labor force participation by a nation's population contributes to increased growth of real GDP. If population growth is also accompanied by growth in the rate of labor force participation, then population growth can positively contribute to *per capita* real GDP growth. Even though population growth by itself tends to reduce the growth of per capita real GDP, greater labor force participation by an expanded population can boost real GDP growth sufficiently to more than compensate for the increase in population. On balance, the rate of growth of per capita real GDP can thereby increase.

WHETHER POPULATION GROWTH HINDERS OR CONTRIBUTES TO ECONOMIC GROWTH DEPENDS ON WHERE YOU LIVE On net, does an increased rate of population growth detract from or add to the rate of economic growth? Table 18-1 below indicates that the answer depends on which nation one considers. In some nations that have experienced relatively high rates of population growth, such as Egypt, Indonesia, and Malaysia, and, to a lesser extent, Chile and China, economic growth has accompanied population growth. In contrast, in nations such as the Congo Democratic Republic, Liberia, and Togo, there has been a negative relationship between population growth and per capita real GDP growth. Other factors apparently must affect how population growth and economic growth ultimately interrelate.

The Role of Economic Freedom

Economic freedom
The rights to own private property and to exchange goods, services, and financial assets with minimal government interference.

A crucial factor influencing economic growth is the relative freedom of a nation's residents. Particularly important is the degree of **economic freedom**—the rights to own private property and to exchange goods, services, and financial assets with minimal government interference—available to the residents of a nation.

Go to www.econtoday.com/chap18 to review the Heritage Foundation's evaluations of the degree of economic freedom in different nations.

Approximately two-thirds of the world's people reside in about three dozen nations with governments unwilling to grant residents significant economic freedom. The economies of these nations, even though they have the majority of the world's population, produce less than 20 percent of the world's total output. Some of these countries have experienced rates of economic growth at or above the 1.2 percent annual average for the world's nations during the past 30 years, but many are growing much more slowly. More than 30 of these countries have experienced negative rates of per capita income growth.

Only 17 nations, with 17 percent of the world's people, grant their residents high degrees of economic freedom. These nations together account for 81 percent of total world output. All of the countries that grant considerable economic freedom have experienced positive rates of economic growth, and most are close to or above the world's average rate of economic growth.

TABLE 18-1

Population Growth and Growth in Per Capita Real GDP in Selected Nations since 1970

Country	Average Annual Population Growth Rate (%)	Average Annual Rate of Growth of Per Capita Real GDP (%)
Central African Republic	2.5	−1.2
Chile	1.5	2.8
China	1.2	7.1
Congo Democratic Republic	3.1	−3.3
Egypt	2.3	3.4
Haiti	1.8	0.0
Indonesia	1.8	4.1
Liberia	2.4	−1.3
Madagascar	2.9	−0.4
Malaysia	2.3	4.7
Togo	3.0	−1.0
United States	1.0	1.8

Source: Penn World Tables, International Monetary Fund.

Why is per capita real GDP growth lower in Jamaica than in Singapore?

INTERNATIONAL POLICY EXAMPLE

A Tale of Diverging Economic Growth Rates in Two Island Nations

During the first half of the 1960s, two island countries with nearly identical levels of per capita real GDP—about $2,700—and the same populations—just over 1,700,000 at that time—became independent nations. One was Jamaica, and the other was Singapore. Since that time, Jamaica's population has grown to 2,700,000 people. Singapore's population has grown to 3,500,000. Today, Jamaica's per capita real GDP is about $4,800. In contrast, Singapore's per capita real GDP exceeds $31,000.

Why has Jamaica's per capita real GDP grown so much less than Singapore's, even though Singapore's population has increased at a faster pace? The fundamental answer is that people in Jamaica have considerably less economic freedom. In contrast to Singapore, which has business taxation and regulations rated among the least burdensome in the world, tax rates and regulatory rules in Jamaica rank among the most oppressive. As a consequence, rates of growth of saving, investment, and productivity—and, hence, per capita real GDP—in Jamaica have been far below corresponding growth rates in Singapore.

FOR CRITICAL THINKING

In Jamaica, the cost of registering a business is 13 percent of the value of a firm's capital, as compared with less than 0.2 percent in Singapore. In which country would you guess that more new companies are started each year?

The Role of Political Freedom

Interestingly, *political freedom*—the right to openly support and democratically select national leaders—appears to be less important than economic freedom in determining economic growth. Some countries that grant considerable economic freedom to their citizens have relatively strong restrictions on their residents' freedoms of speech and the press.

When nondemocratic countries have achieved high standards of living through consistent economic growth, they tend to become more democratic over time. This suggests that economic freedom tends to stimulate economic growth, which then leads to more political freedom.

QUICK QUIZ

See page 413 for the answers. Review concepts from this section in MyEconLab.

For a given rate of growth of aggregate real GDP, higher population growth tends to __________ the growth of per capita real GDP.

To the extent that increased population growth also leads to greater __________ __________ participation that raises the growth of total real GDP, a higher population growth rate can potentially __________ the rate of growth in per capita real GDP.

In general, the extent of __________ freedom does not necessarily increase the rate of economic growth. A greater degree of __________ freedom, however, does have a positive effect on a nation's growth prospects.

Capital Goods and Economic Growth

A fundamental problem developing countries face is that a significant portion of their capital goods, or manufactured resources that may be used to produce other items in the future, is what economists call **dead capital,** a term coined by economist Hernando de Soto. This term describes a capital resource lacking clear title of ownership. Dead capital may actually be put to some productive purpose, but individuals and firms face difficulties in exchanging, insuring, and legally protecting their rights to this resource. Thus, dead capital is a resource that people cannot readily allocate to its *most efficient* use. As economists have dug deeper into the difficulties confronting residents of the world's poorest nations, they have found that dead capital is among the most significant impediments to growth of per capita incomes in these countries.

Dead capital
Any capital resource that lacks clear title of ownership.

Dead Capital and Inefficient Production

Physical structures used to house both business operations and labor resources are forms of capital goods. Current estimates indicate that unofficial, nontransferable physical structures valued at more than $10 trillion are found in developing nations around the world. Because people in developing countries do not officially own this huge volume of capital goods, they cannot easily trade these resources. Thus, it is hard for many of the world's people to use capital goods in ways that will yield the largest feasible output of goods and services.

Consider, for instance, a hypothetical situation faced by an individual in Cairo, Egypt, a city in which an estimated 95 percent of all physical structures are unofficially owned. Suppose this person unofficially owns a run-down apartment building but has no official title of ownership for this structure. Also suppose that the building is better suited for use as a distribution center for a new import-export firm. The individual would like to sell or lease the structure to the new firm, but because he does not formally own the building, he is unable to do so. If the costs of obtaining formal title to the property are sufficiently high relative to the potential benefit—as they apparently are at present for more than 9 out of every 10 Cairo businesses and households—this individual's capital resource will likely not be allocated to its highest-valued use.

This example illustrates a basic problem of dead capital. People who unofficially own capital goods are commonly constrained in their ability to employ them in their most productive uses. As a result, large quantities of capital goods throughout the developing world are inefficiently employed.

Dead Capital and Economic Growth

Recall from Chapter 2 that when we take into account production choices over time, any society faces a trade-off between consumption goods and capital goods. Whenever we make a choice to produce more consumption goods today, we incur an opportunity cost of fewer goods in the future. This means that when we make a choice to aim for more future economic growth to permit consumption of more goods in the future, we must allocate more resources to producing capital goods today. This entails incurring an opportunity cost today because society must allocate fewer resources to the current production of consumption goods.

This growth trade-off applies to any society, whether in a highly industrialized nation or a developing country. In a developing country, however, the inefficiencies of dead capital greatly reduce the rate of return on investment by individuals and firms. The resulting disincentives to invest in new capital goods can greatly hinder economic growth.

GOVERNMENT INEFFICIENCIES, INVESTMENT, AND GROWTH A major factor contributing to the problem of dead capital in many developing nations is significant and often highly inefficient government regulation. Governments in many of the world's poorest nations place tremendous obstacles in the way of entrepreneurs interested in owning capital goods and directing them to profitable opportunities.

In addition to creating dead capital, overzealously administered government regulations that impede private resource allocation tend to reduce investment in new capital goods. If newly produced capital goods cannot be easily devoted to their most efficient uses, there is less incentive to invest. In a nation with a stifling government bureaucracy regulating the uses of capital goods, newly created capital will all too likely become dead capital.

Thus, government inefficiency can be a major barrier to economic growth. Figure 18-1 on the facing page depicts the relationship between average growth of per capita incomes and index measures of governmental inefficiency for various nations. As you can see, the economies of countries with less efficient governments tend to grow at relatively slower rates. The reason is that bureaucratic inefficiencies complicate private individuals' efforts to direct capital goods to their most efficient uses.

FIGURE 18-1

Bureaucratic Inefficiency and Economic Growth

Inefficiencies in government bureaucracies reduce the incentive to invest and thereby detract from economic growth.

Sources: International Monetary Fund; World Bank.

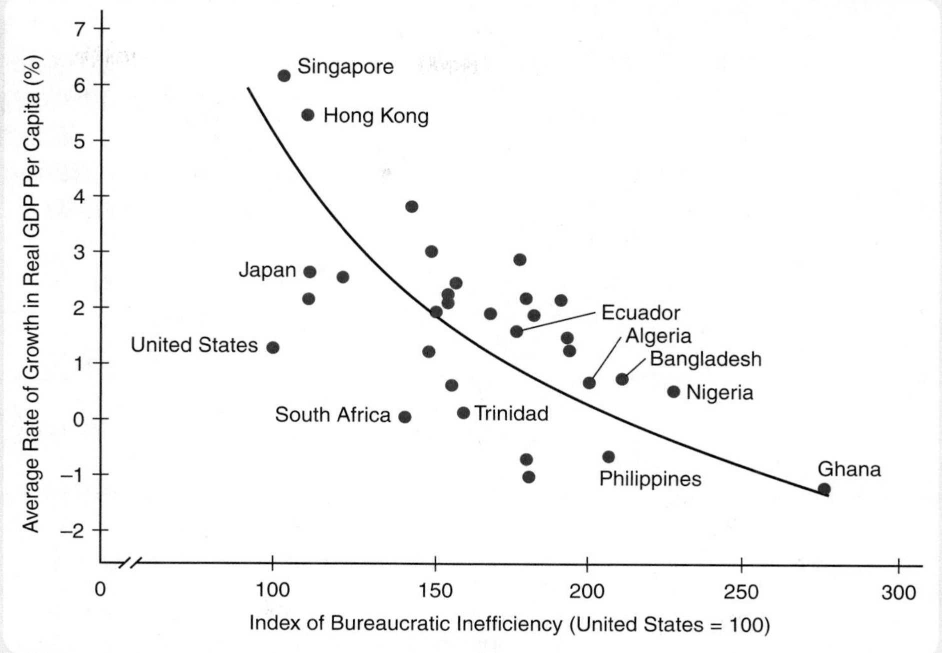

ACCESS TO CREDIT MATTERS The 2006 Nobel Peace Prize went to Muhammad Yunus of Bangladesh. Yunus contends that access to private credit is vital for promoting economic growth in poverty-stricken countries, where, in his view, present credit arrangements are inadequate. Yunus received the Nobel Peace Prize for his efforts to operate a *microlender*—a banking institution that specializes in making very small loans to entrepreneurs seeking to lift themselves up from the lowest rungs of poverty.

How are microlenders attracting deposit funds to lend to entrepreneurs in developing nations?

YOU ARE THERE

To contemplate some of the complications entailed in providing banking services in developing areas of the world, take a look at **Generating New Saving on a Floating Amazon River Bank Branch** on page 408.

INTERNATIONAL EXAMPLE

Mobile Microsaving Enables Microlending in Africa

To be able to extend small loans to entrepreneurs in developing nations, microlenders must obtain funds from savers. In sub-Saharan Africa, people who have accounts with microlenders can transmit securely encrypted funds as attachments to cell phone messages. In this way, individuals can submit small deposits to microlenders as they receive income payments—often via cell phones. Cell phone–to–cell phone deposits are one of the fastest-growing sources of saving in sub-Saharan Africa, and the resulting growth of deposits is creating increased microlending in that part of the world.

FOR CRITICAL THINKING

Why are rates of interest that microlenders pay to their depositors related to rates of interest that microlenders earn on the credit that they extend to borrowers?

Private lenders such as microlenders, Yunus suggests, are more likely to grant loans if borrowers can provide marketable collateral in the form of capital assets that lenders can obtain if a borrower defaults. Loan applicants cannot offer as collateral capital assets that they do not officially own, however. Even if an applicant has legal title to capital assets, a lender is unlikely to accept them as collateral if government rules and inefficiencies inhibit the marketability of those assets in the event that the borrower defaults.

FIGURE 18-2

The Ratio of Private Credit to GDP in Selected Nations

This figure displays the top five and bottom five nations of the world ranked according to ratios of private credit to GDP.

Source: Federal Reserve Bank of St. Louis.

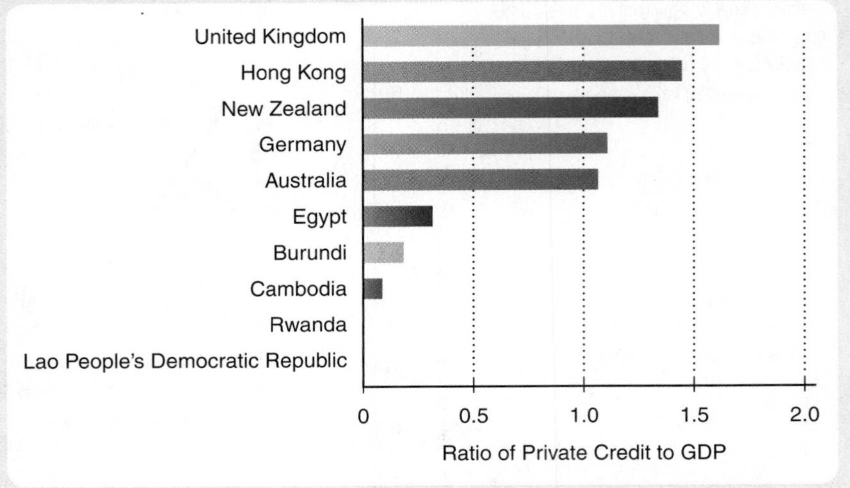

Figure 18-2 above displays both the top five and the bottom five nations of the world ranked by their ratios of private credit to GDP. Common features of the bottom five nations are significant stocks of informally used but officially unowned capital goods and very inefficient government bureaucracies. Access to credit in these nations is very limited, so ratios of private credit to GDP are low.

In some of the poorest nations in which microlending activities are beginning to flourish, tens of millions of people are obtaining access to credit for the first time in their lives. As a consequence, ratios of private credit to GDP are climbing.

WHAT IF... governments force more saving to be channeled to microfinance, with the goal of enhancing economic growth?

Successful microfinance institutions typically arise to fill niches in private markets and thereby lead to higher rates of saving and investment by lower-income people, more capital formation, and greater economic growth. When a nation's government requires a portion of the existing flow of saving to be shifted from its current use in financing investment to microfinance, the result is primarily a redistribution of resources. To be sure, lower-income people often are made better off when they receive the shifted saving as loans that help finance new entrepreneurial activities. Nevertheless, saving shifted away from previous uses generates lower capital investment in other sectors of a nation's economy. Overall capital accumulation remains virtually unaffected, so that the economic growth effects of the forced redistribution of national saving are negligible.

QUICK QUIZ

See page 413 for the answers. Review concepts from this section in MyEconLab.

Dead capital is a capital resource without clear title of __________. It is difficult for a buyer to trade, insure, or maintain a right to use dead capital.

The inability to put dead capital to its most efficient use contributes to __________ economic growth, particularly in __________ nations, where dead capital can be a relatively large portion of total capital goods.

Inefficient government __________ contribute to the dead capital problem, which reduces the incentive to invest in additional capital goods.

Private International Financial Flows as a Source of Global Growth

Given the large volume of inefficiently employed capital goods in developing nations, what can be done to promote greater global growth? One approach is to rely on private markets to find ways to direct capital goods toward their best uses in most nations. Another is to entrust the world's governments with the task of developing and implementing policies that enhance economic growth in developing nations. Let's begin by considering the market-based approach to promoting global growth.

Private Investment in Developing Nations

Between 1995 and 2007, at least $150 billion per year in private funds flowed to developing nations in the form of loans or purchases of bonds or stock. Of course, in some years, international investors stop lending to developing countries or sell off government-issued bonds and private-company stocks of those countries. When these international outflows of funds are taken into account, the *net* flows of funds to developing countries have averaged just over $80 billion per year since 1995. This is nearly 5 percent of the annual net investment within the United States.

Nearly all the funds that flow into developing countries do so to finance investment projects in those nations. Economists group these international flows of investment funds into three categories. One is loans from banks and other sources. The second is **portfolio investment,** or purchases of less than 10 percent of the shares of ownership in a company. The third is **foreign direct investment,** or the acquisition stocks to obtain more than a 10 percent share of a firm's ownership.

Portfolio investment
The purchase of less than 10 percent of the shares of ownership in a company in another nation.

Foreign direct investment
The acquisition of more than 10 percent of the shares of ownership in a company in another nation.

Figure 18-3 below displays percentages of each type of international investment financing provided to developing nations since 1981. As you can see, three decades ago, bank loans accounted for the bulk of international funding of investment in the world's less developed nations. Today, direct ownership shares in the form of portfolio investment and foreign direct investment together account for most international investment financing.

Obstacles to International Investment

There is an important difficulty with depending on international flows of funds to finance capital investment in developing nations. The markets for loans, bonds, and stocks in developing countries are particularly susceptible to problems relating to

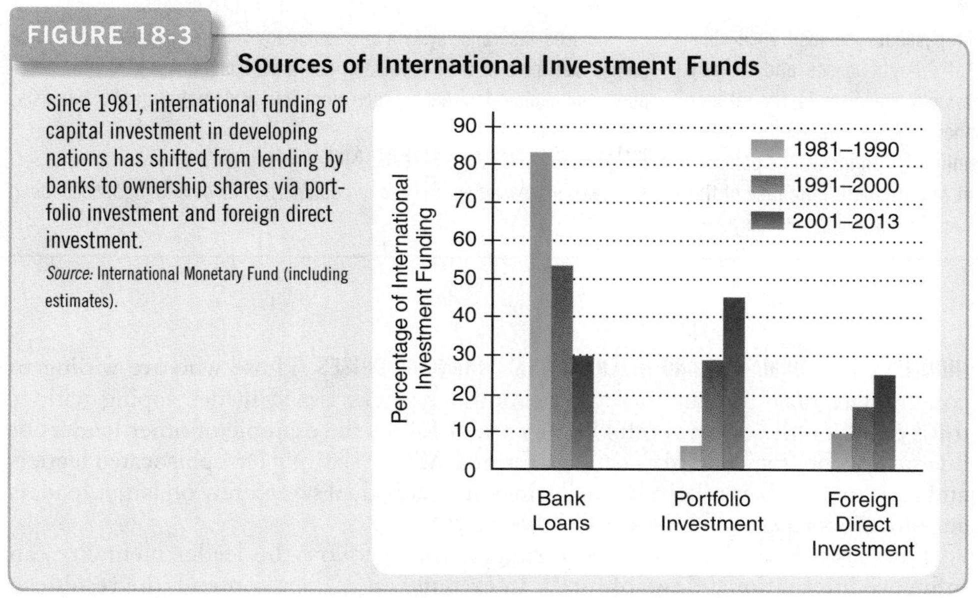

FIGURE 18-3 Sources of International Investment Funds

Since 1981, international funding of capital investment in developing nations has shifted from lending by banks to ownership shares via portfolio investment and foreign direct investment.

Source: International Monetary Fund (including estimates).

For a link to an Asian Development Bank analysis of the effects of foreign direct investment on developing nations, go to www.econtoday.com/chap18.

asymmetric information (see Chapter 15). International investors are well aware of the informational problems to which they are exposed in developing nations, so many stand ready to withdraw their financial support at a moment's notice.

ASYMMETRIC INFORMATION AS A BARRIER TO FINANCING GLOBAL GROWTH Recall from Chapter 15 that asymmetric information in financial markets exists when institutions that make loans or investors who hold bonds or stocks have less information than those who seek to use the funds. *Adverse selection* problems arise when those who wish to obtain funds for the least worthy projects are among those who attempt to borrow or issue bonds or stocks. If banks and investors have trouble identifying these higher-risk individuals and firms, they may be less willing to channel funds to even creditworthy borrowers. Another asymmetric information problem is *moral hazard.* This is the potential for recipients of funds to engage in riskier behavior after receiving financing.

In light of the adverse selection problem, anyone thinking about funding a business endeavor in any locale must study the firm carefully before extending financial support. The potential for moral hazard requires a lender to a firm or someone who has purchased the firm's bonds or stock to continue to monitor the company's performance after providing financial support.

By definition, financial intermediation is still relatively undeveloped in less advanced regions of the world. Consequently, individuals interested in financing potentially profitable investments in developing nations typically cannot rely on financial intermediaries based in these countries. Asymmetric information problems may be so great in some developing nations that very few private lenders or investors will wish to direct their funds to worthy capital investment projects. In some countries, therefore, concerns about adverse selection and moral hazard can be a significant obstacle to economic growth.

How are farmers in Kenya using cell phones to overcome asymmetric information problems, obtain insurance, and produce and sell larger grain harvests?

INTERNATIONAL EXAMPLE

Insuring Crops and Increased Harvests in Kenya

In years past, Kenyan farmers, who have always feared destruction of their crops by periodic droughts, cut their costs by using substandard seeds. This practice reduced harvests and lowered their quality.

Today, firms that sell high-quality crop seeds use insurance contracts to reduce Kenyan farmers' risks of drought losses and thereby boost sales of "good" seeds. When farmers buy these seeds, the retailer scans a barcode on each farmer's cell phone. The phone sends a message to the seed seller, which pays a premium for an insurance policy to cover the farmer's seed costs in the event of a drought. Purchase of the seeds also automatically connects the farmer's cell phone with a system of 30 weather stations. If this system determines that the farmer's crop will not be viable because of insufficient moisture, the farmer is entitled to an insurance payment covering the initial seed expense.

The seed-insurance system has benefited everyone involved. Seed companies sell more of their products, insurance companies earn more revenues, and insured farmers produce more bountiful, higher-quality harvests.

FOR CRITICAL THINKING

How does increased agricultural productivity contribute to higher economic growth?

INCOMPLETE INFORMATION AND INTERNATIONAL FINANCIAL CRISES Those who are willing to contemplate making loans or buying bonds or stocks issued in developing nations must either do their own careful homework or follow the example of other lenders or investors whom they regard as better informed. Many relatively unsophisticated lenders and investors, such as relatively small banks and individual savers, rely on larger lenders and investors to evaluate risks in developing nations.

International financial crisis The rapid withdrawal of foreign investments and loans from a nation.

This has led some economists to suggest that a follow-the-leader mentality can influence international flows of funds. In extreme cases, they contend, the result can be an **international financial crisis.** This is a situation in which lenders rapidly withdraw loans made to residents of developing nations and investors sell off bonds and stocks issued by firms and governments in those countries.

An international financial crisis began in 2008. Unlike the crisis that started in 1997 and radiated outward from Southeast Asia, Central Asia, and Latin America, the more recent crisis began in the United States. It then spread to Europe before adversely affecting most developing nations. Although economies of several Asian nations have weathered the crisis relatively well so far, the world economy shrank for the first time in decades. Undoubtedly, this has contributed to a decline in flows of private funds to developing nations.

QUICK QUIZ See page 413 for the answers. Review concepts from this section in MyEconLab.

The three main categories of international flows of investment funds are loans by __________, __________ investment that involves purchasing less than 10 percent of the shares of ownership in a company, and __________ __________ investment that involves purchasing more than 10 percent of a company's ownership shares.

On net, an average of about $__________ billion in international investment funds flows to developing nations each year. In years past, bank loans were the source of most foreign funding of investment in developing countries, but recently __________ investment and __________ __________ investment have increased.

Obstacles to private financing of capital accumulation and growth in developing nations include __________ __________ and __________ __________ problems caused by asymmetric information, which can restrain and sometimes destabilize private flows of funds.

International Institutions and Policies for Global Growth

There has long been a recognition that adverse selection and moral hazard problems can both reduce international flows of private funds to developing nations and make these flows relatively variable. Since 1945, the world's governments have taken an active role in supplementing private markets. Two international institutions, the World Bank and the International Monetary Fund, have been at the center of government-directed efforts to attain higher rates of global economic growth.

The World Bank

The **World Bank** specializes in extending relatively long-term loans for capital investment projects that otherwise might not receive private financial support. When the World Bank was first formed in 1945, it provided assistance in the post–World War II rebuilding period. In the 1960s, the World Bank broadened its mission by widening its scope to encompass global antipoverty efforts.

World Bank
A multinational agency that specializes in making loans to about 100 developing nations in an effort to promote their long-term development and growth.

Today, the World Bank makes loans solely to about 100 developing nations containing roughly half the world's population. Governments and firms in these countries typically seek loans from the World Bank to finance specific projects, such as better irrigation systems, road improvements, and better hospitals.

The World Bank is actually composed of five separate institutions: the International Development Association, the International Bank for Reconstruction and Development, the International Finance Corporation, the Multinational Investment Guarantee Agency, and the International Center for Settlement of Investment Disputes. These World Bank organizations each have between 144 and 186 member nations, and on their behalf, the approximately 10,000 people employed by World Bank institutions coordinate the funding of investment activities undertaken by various governments and private firms in developing nations. Figure 18-4 on the following page displays the current regional distribution of about $20 billion yearly in World Bank lending. Governments of the world's wealthiest countries provide most of the funds that the World Bank lends each year, although the World Bank also raises some of its funds in private financial markets.

FIGURE 18-4

Distribution of World Bank Lending since 1990

Currently, about 40 percent of the World Bank's loans go to developing nations in the East Asia/Pacific and Africa regions.

Source: World Bank.

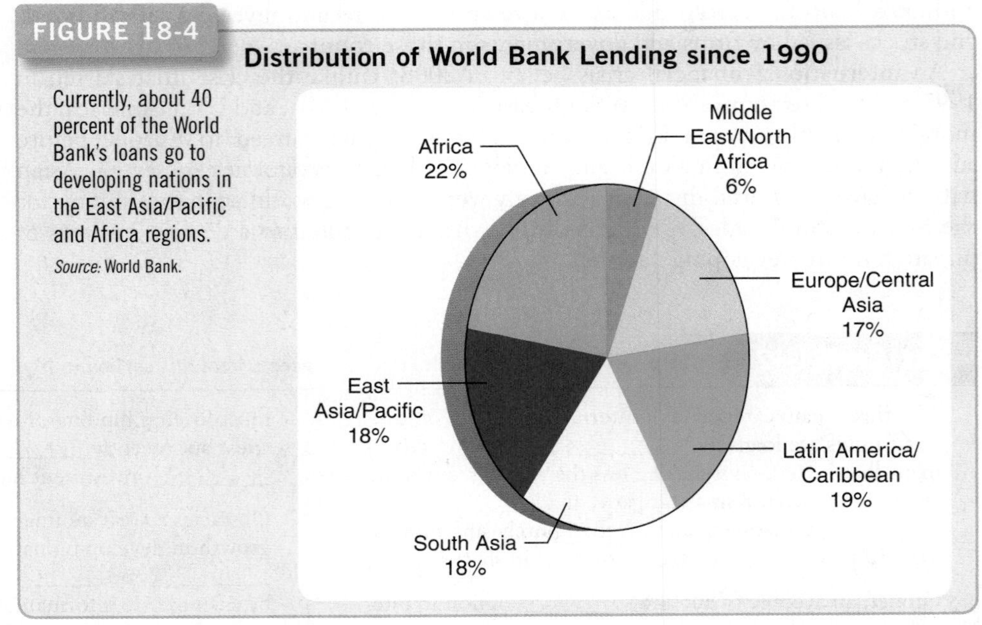

The International Monetary Fund

International Monetary Fund (IMF) A multinational organization that aims to promote world economic growth through more financial stability.

Quota subscription A nation's account with the International Monetary Fund, denominated in special drawing rights.

The **International Monetary Fund (IMF)** is an international organization that aims to promote global economic growth by fostering financial stability. Currently, the IMF has more than 180 member nations.

When a country joins the IMF, it deposits funds to an account called its **quota subscription.** These funds are measured in terms of an international unit of accounting called *special drawing rights (SDRs)*, which have a value based on a weighted average of a basket of four key currencies: the euro, the pound sterling, the yen, and the dollar. At present, one SDR is equivalent to just over $1.50.

The IMF assists developing nations primarily by making loans to their governments. Originally, the IMF's primary function was to provide short-term loans, and it continues to offer these forms of assistance.

After the 1970s, however, nations' demands for short-term credit declined, and the IMF adapted by expanding its other lending programs. It now provides certain types of credit directly to poor and heavily indebted countries, either as long-term loans intended to support growth-promoting projects or as short- or long-term assistance aimed at helping countries experiencing problems in repaying existing debts. Under these funding programs, the IMF seeks to assist any qualifying member experiencing an unusual fluctuation in exports or imports, a loss of confidence in its own financial system, or spillover effects from financial problems originating elsewhere.

The World Bank and the IMF: Problems and Proposals

Among the World Bank's client nations, meager economic growth in recent decades shows up in numerous ways. The average resident in a nation receiving World Bank assistance lives on less than $2 per day. Hundreds of millions of people in nations receiving its financial support will never attend school, and tens of thousands of people in these countries die of preventable diseases every day. Thus, there is an enormous range of areas where World Bank funds might be put to use.

The International Monetary Fund also continues to deal with an ongoing string of major international financial crisis situations. Countries most notably involved in such crises have included Mexico in 1995; Thailand, Indonesia, Malaysia, and South Korea in 1997; Russia in 1998; Brazil in 1999 and 2000; Turkey in 2001; Argentina in 2001 and 2002; and Greece, Spain, and other European nations since 2008.

ASYMMETRIC INFORMATION AND THE WORLD BANK AND IMF Like any other lenders, the World Bank and IMF encounter adverse selection and moral hazard problems. In an effort to address these problems, both institutions impose conditions that borrowers must meet to receive funds.

Officials of these organizations do not publicly announce all terms of lending agreements, however, so it is largely up to the organizations to monitor whether borrower nations are wisely using funds donated by other countries. In addition, the World Bank and IMF tend to place very imprecise initial conditions on the loans they extend. They typically toughen conditions only after a borrowing nation has violated the original arrangement. By giving nations that are most likely to try to take advantage of vague conditions a greater incentive to seek funding, this policy worsens the adverse selection problem the World Bank and IMF face.

RETHINKING LONG-TERM DEVELOPMENT LENDING Since the early 1990s, one of the main themes of development economics has been the reform of market processes in developing nations. Markets work better at promoting growth when a developing nation has more effective institutions, such as basic property rights, well-run legal systems, and uncorrupt government agencies.

Hence, there is considerable agreement that a top priority of the World Bank and the IMF should be to identify ways to put basic market foundations into place by guaranteeing property and contract rights. Doing so would require constructing legal systems that can credibly enforce laws protecting these rights. Another key requirement is simplifying the processes for putting capital goods to work most efficiently in developing countries.

ALTERNATIVE INSTITUTIONAL STRUCTURES FOR LIMITING FINANCIAL CRISES In recent years, economists have advanced a wide variety of proposals on the appropriate role for the International Monetary Fund in anticipating and reacting to international financial crises. Many of these proposals share common features, such as more frequent and in-depth releases of information both by the IMF and by countries that borrow from this institution. Nearly all economists also recommend improved financial and accounting standards for those receiving funds from the World Bank and the IMF, as well as other changes that might help reduce moral hazard problems in such lending.

To learn about the International Monetary Fund's view on its role in international financial crises, go to www.econtoday.com/chap18.

Nevertheless, proposals for change diverge sharply. The IMF and its supporters have suggested maintaining its current structure but working harder to develop so-called early warning systems of financial crises so that aid can be provided to head off crises before they develop. Some economists have proposed establishing an international system of rules restricting capital outflows that might threaten international financial stability.

Other economists call for more dramatic changes. For instance, one proposal suggests creating a board composed of finance ministers of member nations to be directly in charge of day-to-day management of the IMF. Another recommends providing government incentives, in the form of tax breaks and subsidies, for increased private-sector lending that would supplement or even replace loans now made by the IMF.

QUICK QUIZ

See page 413 for the answers. Review concepts from this section in MyEconLab.

The **World Bank** is an umbrella institution for __________ international organizations, each of which has more than 140 member nations, which coordinate __________-term loans to governments and private firms in developing nations.

The **International Monetary Fund** is an organization with more than 180 member nations. It coordinates mainly __________-term and some longer-term financial assistance to developing nations in an effort to __________ international flows of funds.

Like other lenders, the World Bank and the IMF confront __________ __________ and __________ __________ problems. Recently, there have been suggestions for restructuring the operations of both institutions, but so far there is little agreement about how to do so.

YOU ARE THERE

Generating New Saving on a Floating Amazon River Bank Branch

Luzia Moraes faces different problems than most bank branch managers confront—she must watch out for rainstorms and leaks in her bank branch's hull. Moraes takes in saving and extends loans from a boat along Brazil's Amazon River. Every two weeks, her "branch" begins a nine-day trip on a 125-foot boat called the *Voyager III*. Her bank branch offers financial services to hundreds of customers who live along the river. While *Voyager III* is moored, Moraes continues to provide services on canoes and rafts to customers along smaller Amazon tributaries. Most of Moraes's customers seek access to her bank branch's interest-bearing deposit accounts. Other customers desire loans to buy capital goods, such as structures suitable for small businesses.

Several Brazilian banks now have floating branches such as the one operated by Moraes. Bank branches established in some of Brazil's poorest regions since the 1990s have generated a tripling of that nation's savings accounts and a substantial increase in the national saving rate. There has been a corresponding growth in lending to finance capital investment throughout the Brazilian countryside. The upsurge in saving and investment helps to explain how Brazil's real GDP per capita has risen by more than 60 percent since the late 1990s.

Critical Thinking Questions

1. Why is saving an important contributor to Brazil's economic growth?
2. How does an increase in the rate of capital investment boost economic growth?

ISSUES & APPLICATIONS

A New Mongol Hoard Raises Investment and Growth

CONCEPTS APPLIED

- Economic Freedom
- Foreign Direct Investment
- Dead Capital

Most rankings of all the world's nations based on their levels of economic freedom place Mongolia near the middle. Recently, however, the country took a major step toward improving its economic freedom rating, increasing capital investment, and raising its rate of economic growth.

Stock Shares of a Mining Boom

Geologists have found substantial new deposits of coal and copper in Mongolia. The government has arranged for foreign companies to assist in constructing mines to extract these minerals. The companies' capital investments in these mining operations constitute foreign direct investment.

Foreign firms provide the Mongolian government with guaranteed rights to future returns on their mining operations. The government, in turn, transferred these rights to each Mongolian resident in the form of shares of stock. The initial dollar value of each resident's shares was equal to nearly \$360—about 10 percent of the nation's per capita real GDP at the time of the rights transferal.

Previously Dead Capital Livens Up

The mining industry had already been an important part of Mongolia's economy prior to the discovery of even more mineral deposits. In past years, however, the government's partial share of the ownership in mining equipment created uncertainty about managing the capital equipment, thereby rendering a large portion of the equipment dead capital. The government's transferal of rights to future returns from mining to the nation's residents immediately shifted most existing equipment out of this category. The action also moved Mongolia up a number of places on the economic freedom list.

Other consequences of the government's rights transferal have been significant upswings in capital investment and in the rate of economic growth. The year that the

Mongolian government announced its plans to transfer the rights to mining returns to its residents, the nation's economic growth rate rose from below 5 percent per year to about 10 percent. During the first two years following the transferal, Mongolia's annual economic growth rate jumped to above 20 percent per year.

For Critical Thinking

1. How might freeing up dead capital have helped to increase Mongolia's rate of economic growth?
2. What type of investment would foreign residents undertake if they were to purchase a small fraction of the shares of stocks owned by Mongolia's residents?

Web Resources

1. View a video discussing the Mongolian government's mining rights transferal at **www.econtoday.com/chap18**.
2. Learn about how the government transmitted shares to future returns from mineral mines to the country's residents at **www.econtoday.com/chap18**.

MyEconLab

For more questions on this chapter's Issues & Applications, go to MyEconLab. In the Study Plan for this chapter, select Section N: News.

MyEconLab

Here is what you should know after reading this chapter. MyEconLab will help you identify what you know, and where to go when you need to practice.

WHAT YOU SHOULD KNOW		WHERE TO GO TO PRACTICE
Effects of Population Growth on Economic Growth Increased population growth has contradictory effects on economic growth. On the one hand, for a given growth rate of real GDP, increased population growth tends to reduce growth of per capita real GDP. On the other hand, if increased population growth is accompanied by higher labor productivity and participation, the growth rate of real GDP can increase.	economic freedom, 398	• MyEconLab Study Plan 18.1
Why Dead Capital Deters Investment and Slows Economic Growth Relatively few people in less developed countries establish legal ownership of capital goods. Unofficially owned resources are known as dead capital. Inability to trade, insure, and enforce rights to dead capital makes it difficult to employ these resources most efficiently, and this tends to limit economic growth.	dead capital, 399	• MyEconLab Study Plan 18.2
Government Inefficiencies and Dead Capital in Developing Nations In many developing nations, government regulations and red tape impose very high costs on those who officially register capital ownership. The dead capital problem that these government inefficiencies create reduces investment and growth.	**Key Figure** Figure 18-1, 401	• MyEconLab Study Plan 18.2 • Animated Figure 18-1

MyEconLab *continued*

WHAT YOU SHOULD KNOW		WHERE TO GO TO PRACTICE
Sources of International Investment Funds and Obstacles to Investing in Developing Nations International flows of funds to developing nations promote global economic growth. Asymmetric information problems, such as adverse selection and moral hazard problems, hinder international flows of funds and thereby slow economic growth in developing nations.	portfolio investment, 403 foreign direct investment, 403 international financial crisis, 404 **Key Figure** Figure 18-3, 403	• MyEconLab Study Plan 18.3 • Animated Figure 18-3
The Functions of the World Bank and the International Monetary Fund Adverse selection and moral hazard problems faced by private investors can both limit and destabilize international flows of funds to developing countries. The World Bank finances capital investment in countries that have trouble attracting funds from private sources. The International Monetary Fund attempts to stabilize international financial flows by extending loans to countries caught up in international financial crises.	World Bank, 405 International Monetary Fund (IMF), 406 quota subscription, 406	• MyEconLab Study Plan 18.4
Problems Faced by Policymakers at the World Bank and IMF Both the World Bank and the IMF face adverse selection and moral hazard problems that may be worsened by the imprecise initial conditions they impose on the loans they extend. Development economists generally agree that both institutions should emphasize reforms such as basic property rights that give domestic residents more incentive to invest.		• MyEconLab Study Plan 18.4

Log in to MyEconLab, take a chapter test, and get a personalized Study Plan that tells you which concepts you understand and which ones you need to review. From there, MyEconLab will give you further practice, tutorials, animations, videos, and guided solutions. For more information, visit www.myeconlab.com

PROBLEMS

All problems are assignable in MyEconLab; *exercises that update with real-time data are marked with* [real-time data icon]. *Answers to odd-numbered problems appear at the back of the book.*

18-1. A country's real GDP is growing at an annual rate of 3.1 percent, and the current rate of growth of per capita real GDP is 0.3 percent per year. What is the population growth rate in this nation? (See page 397.)

18-2. A nation's current annual rate of growth of per capita real GDP is 3.0 percent, and its annual rate of population growth is 3.4 percent. What is the nation's annual rate of growth of real GDP? (See page 397.)

18-3. Currently, the rate of growth of real GDP in a nation is 1.3 percent per year. Its population growth rate is 2.7 percent per year. What is the nation's annual rate of growth of per capita real GDP? (See page 397.)

18-4. The annual rate of growth of real GDP in a developing nation is 0.3 percent. Initially, the country's population was stable from year to year. Recently, however, a significant increase in the nation's birthrate has raised the annual rate of population growth to 0.5 percent. (See page 397.)

a. What was the rate of growth of per capita real GDP before the increase in population growth?

b. If the rate of growth of real GDP remains unchanged, what is the new rate of growth of per capita real GDP following the increase in the birthrate?

18-5. A developing country has determined that each additional $1 billion of net investment in capital goods adds 0.01 percentage point to its long-run average annual rate of growth of per capita real GDP. (See pages 399–400.)

a. Domestic entrepreneurs recently began to seek official approval to open a range of businesses employing capital resources valued at $20 billion. If the entrepreneurs undertake these investments, by what fraction of a percentage point will the nation's long-run average annual rate of growth of per capita real GDP increase, other things being equal?

b. After weeks of effort trying to complete the first of 15 stages of bureaucratic red tape necessary to obtain authorization to start their businesses, a number of entrepreneurs decide to drop their investment plans completely, and the amount of official investment that actually takes place turns out to be $10 billion. Other things being equal, by what fraction of a percentage point will this decision reduce the nation's long-run average annual rate of growth of per capita real GDP from what it would have been if investment had been $20 billion?

18-6. Consider the estimates that the World Bank has assembled for the following nations:

Country	Legal Steps Required to Start a Business	Days Required to Start a Business	Cost of Starting a Business as a Percentage of Per Capita GDP
Angola	14	146	838%
Bosnia-Herzegovina	12	59	52%
Morocco	11	36	19%
Togo	14	63	281%
Uruguay	10	27	47%

Rank the nations in order starting with the one you would expect to have the highest rate of economic growth, other things being equal. Explain your reasoning. (See pages 399–400.)

18-7. Suppose that every $500 billion of dead capital reduces the average rate of growth in worldwide per capita real GDP by 0.1 percentage point. If there is $10 trillion in dead capital in the world, by how many percentage points does the existence of dead capital reduce average worldwide growth of per capita real GDP? (See page 400.)

18-8. Assume that each $1 billion in net capital investment generates 0.3 percentage point of the average percentage rate of growth of per capita real GDP, given the nation's labor resources. Firms have been investing exactly $6 billion in capital goods each year, so the annual average rate of growth of per capita real GDP has been 1.8 percent. Now a government that fails to consistently adhere to the rule of law has come to power, and firms must pay $100 million in bribes to gain official approval for every $1 billion in investment in capital goods. In response, companies cut back their total investment spending to $4 billion per year. If other things are equal and companies maintain this rate of investment, what will be the nation's new average annual rate of growth of per capita real GDP? (See page 400.)

18-9. During the past year, several large banks extended $200 million in loans to the government and several firms in a developing nation. International investors also purchased $150 million in bonds and $350 million in stocks issued by domestic firms. Of the stocks that foreign investors purchased, $100 million were shares that amounted to less than a 10 percent interest in domestic firms. This was the first year this nation had ever permitted inflows of funds from abroad. (See page 403.)

a. Based on the investment category definitions discussed in this chapter, what was the amount of portfolio investment in this nation during the past year?

b. What was the amount of foreign direct investment in this nation during the past year?

18-10. Last year, $100 million in outstanding bank loans to a developing nation's government were not renewed, and the developing nation's government paid off $50 million in maturing government bonds that had been held by foreign residents. During that year, however, a new group of banks participated in a $125 million loan to help finance a major government construction project in the capital city. Domestic firms also issued $50 million in bonds and $75 million in stocks to foreign investors. All of the stocks issued gave the foreign investors more than 10 percent shares of the domestic firms. (See page 403.)

a. What was gross foreign investment in this nation last year?

b. What was net foreign investment in this nation last year?

18-11. Identify which of the following situations currently faced by international investors are examples of adverse selection and which are examples of moral hazard. (See pages 404–405.)

a. Among the governments of several developing countries that are attempting to issue new bonds this year, it is certain that a few will fail to collect taxes to repay the bonds when they mature. It is difficult, however, for investors considering buying government bonds to predict which governments will experience this problem.

b. Foreign investors are contemplating purchasing stock in a company that, unknown to them, may have failed to properly establish legal ownership over a crucial capital resource.

c. Companies in a less developed nation have already issued bonds to finance the purchase of new capital goods. After receiving the funds from the bond issue, however, the company's managers pay themselves large bonuses instead.

d. When the government of a developing nation received a bank loan three years ago, it ultimately repaid the loan but had to reschedule its payments after officials misused the funds for unworthy projects. Now the government, which still has many of the same officials, is trying to raise funds by issuing bonds to foreign investors, who must decide whether or not to purchase them.

18-12. Identify which of the following situations currently faced by the World Bank or the International Monetary Fund are examples of adverse selection and which are examples of moral hazard. (See pages 404–405.)

a. The World Bank has extended loans to the government of a developing country to finance construction of a canal with a certain future flow of earnings. Now, however, the government has decided to redirect those funds to build a casino that may or may not generate sufficient profits to allow the government to repay the loan.

b. The IMF is considering extending loans to several nations that failed to fully repay loans they received from the IMF during the past decade but now claim to be better credit risks. Now the IMF is not sure in advance which of these nations are unlikely to fully repay new loans.

c. The IMF recently extended a loan to a government directed by democratically elected officials that would permit the nation to adjust to an abrupt reduction in private flows of funds from abroad. A coup has just occurred, however, in response to newly discovered corruption within the government's elected leadership. The new military dictator has announced tentative plans to disburse some of the funds in equal shares to all citizens.

18-13. For each of the following situations, explain which of the policy issues discussed in this chapter is associated with the stance the institution has taken. (See pages 405–407.)

a. The World Bank offers to make a loan to a company in an impoverished nation at a lower interest rate than the company had been about to agree to pay to borrow the same amount from a group of private banks.

b. The World Bank makes a loan to a company in a developing nation that has not yet received formal approval to operate there, even though the government approval process typically takes 15 months.

c. The IMF extends a loan to a developing nation's government, with no preconditions, to enable the government to make already overdue payments on a loan it had previously received from the World Bank.

18-14. For each of the following situations, explain which of the policy issues discussed in this chapter is associated with the stance the institution has taken. (See pages 405–407.)

a. The IMF extends a long-term loan to a nation's government to help it maintain publicly supported production of goods and services that the government otherwise would have turned over to private companies.

b. The World Bank makes a loan to companies in an impoverished nation in which government officials typically demand bribes equal to 50 percent of companies' profits before allowing them to engage in any new investment projects.

c. The IMF offers to make a loan to banks in a country in which the government's rulers commonly require banks to extend credit to finance high-risk investment projects headed by the rulers' friends and relatives.

18-15. Answer the following questions concerning proposals to reform long-term development lending programs currently offered by the IMF and World Bank. (See pages 406–407.)

a. Why might the World Bank face moral hazard problems if it were to offer to provide funds to governments that promise to allocate the funds to major institutional reforms aimed at enhancing economic growth?

b. How does the IMF face an adverse selection problem if it is considering making loans to governments in which the ruling parties have already shown predispositions to try to "buy" votes by creating expensive public programs in advance of elections? How might following an announced rule in which the IMF cuts off future loans to governments that engage in such activities reduce this problem and promote increased economic growth in nations that do receive IMF loans?

ECONOMICS ON THE NET

The International Monetary Fund The purpose of this exercise is to evaluate the IMF's role in promoting global economic growth.

Title: International Monetary Fund

Navigation: Go to the home page of the IMF on the Web at **www.econtoday.com/chap18**.

Application Read each entry, and then answer the question.

1. Click on the link on the Web page titled *Our Work*. Which of the IMF's purposes are most directly related to promoting a higher rate of global economic growth? Are any related more indirectly to this goal?
2. Click on *Surveillance*. Based on this discussion, what type of asymmetric information problem does IMF surveillance attempt to address?
3. Click on *Lending*, and then click on *Main Lending Facilities*. Which IMF lending "facilities" appear to be aimed at maintaining stability of international flows of funds? Which appear to be longer-term loans similar to those extended by the World Bank?

For Group Study and Analysis The full reading at the *Lending* link, titled "Lending by the IMF," discusses terms of lending that the IMF imposes on different groups of nations. What are the likely rationales for charging some nations lower interest rates than others? Are there any potential problems with this policy? (Hint: Consider the adverse selection and moral hazard problems faced by the IMF.)

ANSWERS TO QUICK QUIZZES

p. 399: (i) reduce; (ii) labor force . . . increase; (iii) political . . . economic

p. 402: (i) ownership; (ii) lower . . . developing; (iii) bureaucracies

p. 405: (i) banks . . . portfolio . . . foreign direct; (ii) 80 . . . portfolio . . . foreign direct; (iii) adverse selection . . . moral hazard

p. 407: (i) five . . . long; (ii) short . . . stabilize; (iii) adverse selection . . . moral hazard

32 Comparative Advantage and the Open Economy

In 2001, the U.S. government slashed *tariffs*—taxes on imported items—that it imposed on goods and services imported into the United States from countries located along the Andes mountain range in South America. From that year through the early 2010s, the dollar value of U.S. imports of cut flowers from the Andean nation of Colombia grew by about 400 percent, while Californian production and sale of cut flowers declined considerably. California flower growers responded by successfully lobbying Congress to increase tariff rates on Andean products to previous levels, and Colombian cut-flower imports promptly plummeted. To understand how tariffs affect volumes of imports and, ultimately, prices in markets in which imported goods and services are traded, you must learn about the economics of international trade, which is the subject of this chapter.

LEARNING OBJECTIVES

After reading this chapter, you should be able to:

- Discuss the worldwide importance of international trade
- Explain why nations can gain from specializing in production and engaging in international trade
- Understand common arguments against free trade
- Describe ways that nations restrict foreign trade
- Identify key international agreements and organizations that adjudicate trade disputes among nations

MyEconLab helps you master each objective and study more efficiently. See end of chapter for details.

DID YOU KNOW THAT... since 2011, more oil-based fuels have been exported each year from the United States than have been imported? Thus, recent years represent the first time since 1949 that international trade statistics have classified the United States as a "net exporter" of fossil fuels. Current projections indicate that it likely will remain a net fuel exporter for many years to come. In this chapter, you will learn about the fundamental economic determinants of whether a nation's residents become net exporters or importers of particular goods and services.

The Worldwide Importance of International Trade

Look at panel (a) of Figure 32-1 below. Since the end of World War II, world output of goods and services (world real gross domestic product, or world real GDP) has increased almost every year. It is now about 10 times what it was then. Look at the top line in panel (a) of Figure 32-1. Even taking into account its recent dip, world trade has increased to about 26 times its level in 1950.

FIGURE 32-1

The Growth of World Trade

In panel (a), you can see the growth in world trade in relative terms because we use an index of 100 to represent real world trade in 1950. By the early 2010s, that index had exceeded 2,500. At the same time, the index of world real GDP (annual world real income) had gone up only about 1,000. Thus, generally world trade has been on the rise. In the United States, both imports and exports, expressed as a percentage of annual national income (GDP) in panel (b), generally rose after 1950 and recovered following the 2008–2009 recession.

Sources: Steven Husted and Michael Melvin, *International Economics*, 3rd ed. (New York: HarperCollins, 1995), p. 11, used with permission; World Trade Organization; Federal Reserve System; U.S. Department of Commerce.

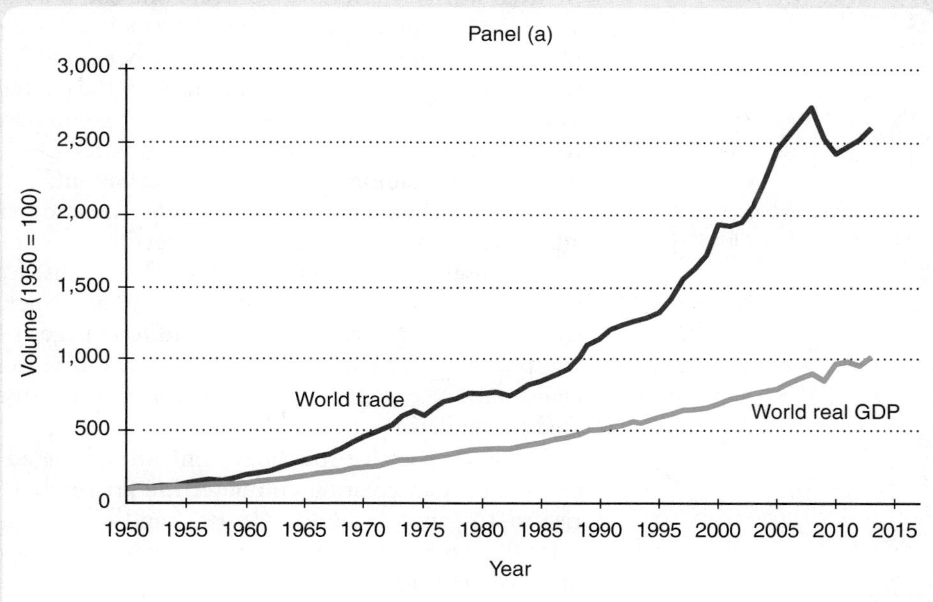

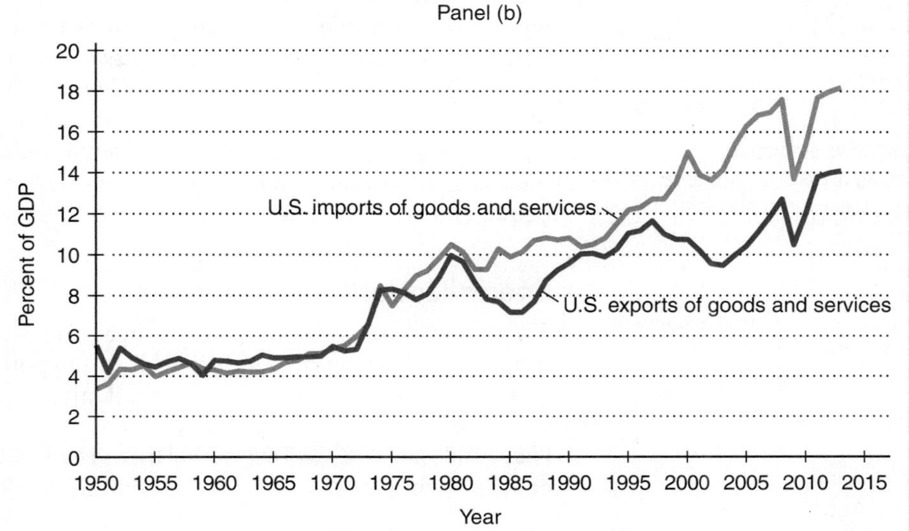

Go to www.econtoday.com/chap32 for the World Trade Organization's most recent data on world trade.

The United States has figured prominently in this expansion of world trade. In panel (b) of Figure 32-1 on page 705, you see imports and exports expressed as a percentage of total annual yearly income (GDP). Whereas imports amounted to barely 4 percent of annual U.S. GDP in 1950, today they account for more than 18 percent. International trade has become more important to the U.S. economy, and it may become even more so as other countries loosen their trade restrictions.

Why We Trade: Comparative Advantage and Mutual Gains from Exchange

You have already been introduced to the concept of specialization and mutual gains from trade in Chapter 2. These concepts are worth repeating because they are essential to understanding why the world is better off because of more international trade. The best way to understand the gains from trade among nations is first to understand the output gains from specialization between individuals.

The Output Gains from Specialization

Suppose that a creative advertising specialist can come up with two pages of ad copy (written words) an hour or generate one computerized art rendering per hour. At the same time, a computer art specialist can write one page of ad copy per hour or complete one computerized art rendering per hour. Here the ad specialist can come up with more pages of ad copy per hour than the computer specialist and seemingly is just as good as the computer specialist at doing computerized art renderings. Is there any reason for the ad specialist and the computer specialist to "trade"? The answer is yes because such trading will lead to higher output.

Go to www.econtoday.com/chap32 for data on U.S. trade with all other nations of the world.

Consider the scenario of no trading. Assume that during each eight-hour day, the ad specialist and the computer whiz devote half of their day to writing ad copy and half to computerized art rendering. The ad specialist would create eight pages of ad copy (4 hours × 2) and four computerized art renderings (4 × 1). During that same period, the computer specialist would create four pages of ad copy (4 hours × 1) and four computerized art renderings (4 × 1). Each day, the combined output for the ad specialist and the computer specialist would be 12 pages of ad copy and eight computerized art renderings.

If the ad specialist specialized only in writing ad copy and the computer whiz specialized only in creating computerized art renderings, their combined output would rise to 16 pages of ad copy (8 × 2) and eight computerized art renderings (8 × 1). Overall, production would increase by four pages of ad copy per day with no decline in art renderings.

Note that this example implies that to create one additional computerized art rendering during a day, the ad specialist has to sacrifice the creation of two pages of ad copy. The computer specialist, in contrast, has to give up the creation of only one page of ad copy to generate one more computerized art rendering. Thus, the ad specialist has a comparative advantage in writing ad copy, and the computer specialist has a comparative advantage in doing computerized art renderings. **Comparative advantage** is simply the ability to produce something at a lower *opportunity cost* than other producers, as we pointed out in Chapter 2.

Comparative advantage
The ability to produce a good or service at a lower opportunity cost than other producers.

Specialization among Nations

To demonstrate the concept of comparative advantage for nations, let's consider a simple two-country, two-good world. As a hypothetical example, let's suppose that the nations in this world are India and the United States.

PRODUCTION AND CONSUMPTION CAPABILITIES IN A TWO-COUNTRY, TWO-GOOD WORLD In Table 32-1 on the facing page, we show maximum feasible quantities of high-performance

TABLE 32-1

Maximum Feasible Hourly Production Rates of Either Digital Apps or Tablet Devices Using All Available Resources

This table indicates maximum feasible rates of production of digital apps and tablet devices if all available resources are allocated to producing either one item or the other. If U.S. residents allocate all resources to producing a single good, they can produce either 90 digital apps per hour or 225 tablets per hour. If residents of India allocate all resources to manufacturing one good, they can produce either 100 apps per hour or 50 tablets per hour.

Product	United States	India
Digital apps	90	100
Tablet devices	225	50

commercial digital apps (apps) and tablet devices (tablets) that may be produced during an hour using all resources—labor, capital, land, and entrepreneurship—available in the United States and in India. As you can see from the table, U.S. residents can utilize all their resources to produce either 90 apps per hour or 225 tablets per hour. If residents of India utilize all their resources, they can produce either 100 apps per hour or 50 tablets per hour.

COMPARATIVE ADVANTAGE Suppose that in each country, there are constant opportunity costs of producing apps and tablets. Table 32-1 above implies that to allocate all available resources to production of 50 tablets, residents of India would have to sacrifice the production of 100 apps. Thus, the opportunity cost in India of producing 1 tablet is equal to 2 apps. At the same time, the opportunity cost of producing 1 app in India is 0.5 tablet.

In the United States, to allocate all available resources to production of 225 tablets, U.S. residents would have to give up producing 90 apps. This means that the opportunity cost in the United States of producing 1 tablet is equal to 0.4 app. Alternatively, we can say that the opportunity cost to U.S. residents of producing 1 app is 2.5 tablets (225 ÷ 90 = 2.5).

The opportunity cost of producing a tablet is lower in the United States than in India. At the same time, the opportunity cost of producing apps is lower in India than in the United States. Consequently, the United States has a comparative advantage in manufacturing tablets, and India has a comparative advantage in producing apps.

PRODUCTION WITHOUT TRADE Table 32-2 on the following page tabulates two possible production choices in a situation in which U.S. and Indian residents choose not to engage in international trade. Let's suppose that in the United States, residents choose to produce and consume 30 digital apps. To produce this number of apps requires that 75 fewer tablets (30 apps times 2.5 tablets per app) be produced than the maximum feasible tablet production of 225 tablets, or 150 tablets. Thus, in the absence of trade, 30 apps and 150 tablets are produced and consumed in the United States.

Table 32-2 indicates that during an hour's time in India, residents choose to produce and consume 37.5 tablets. Obtaining this number of tablets entails the production of 75 fewer apps (37.5 tablets times 2 apps per tablet) than the maximum of 100 apps, or 25 apps. Hence, in the absence of trade, 37.5 tablets and 25 apps are produced and consumed in India.

Finally, Table 32-2 displays production of apps and tablets for this two-country world, given the nations' production (and, implicitly, consumption) choices in the absence of trade. In an hour's time, U.S. app production is 30 units, and Indian app production is 25 units, so the total apps produced and available for consumption worldwide

TABLE 32-2

U.S. and Indian Production and Consumption without Trade

This table indicates two possible hourly combinations of production and consumption of digital apps and tablet devices in the absence of trade in a "world" encompassing the United States and India. U.S. residents produce 30 apps, and residents of India produce 25 apps, so the total apps that can be consumed worldwide is 55. In addition, U.S. residents produce 150 tablets, and Indian residents produce 37.5 tablets, so worldwide production and consumption of tablets amount to 187.5 tablets per hour.

Product	United States	India	Actual World Output
Digital apps (per hour)	30	25	55
Tablet devices (per hour)	150	37.5	187.5

is 55. Hourly U.S. tablet production is 150 tablets, and Indian tablet production is 37.5 tablets, so a total of 187.5 tablets per hour is produced and available for consumption in this two-country world.

SPECIALIZATION IN PRODUCTION More realistically, residents of the United States will choose to specialize in the activity for which they experience a lower opportunity cost. In other words, U.S. residents will specialize in the activity in which they have a comparative advantage, which is the production of tablet devices, which they can offer in trade to residents of India. Likewise, Indian residents will specialize in the manufacturing industry in which they have a comparative advantage, which is the production of digital apps, which they can offer in trade to U.S. residents.

By specializing, the two countries can gain from engaging in international trade. To see why, suppose that U.S. residents allocate all available resources to producing 225 tablets, the good in which they have a comparative advantage. In addition, residents of India utilize all resources they have on hand to produce 100 apps, the good in which they have a comparative advantage.

CONSUMPTION WITH SPECIALIZATION AND TRADE U.S. residents will be willing to buy an Indian digital app as long as they must provide in exchange no more than 2.5 tablet devices, which is the opportunity cost of producing 1 app at home. At the same time, residents of India will be willing to buy a U.S. tablet as long as they must provide in exchange no more than 2 apps, which is their opportunity cost of producing a tablet.

Suppose that residents of both countries agree to trade at a rate of exchange of 1 tablet for 1 app and that they agree to trade 75 U.S. tablets for 75 Indian apps. Table 32-3 on the facing page displays the outcomes that result in both countries. By specializing in tablet production and engaging in trade, U.S. residents can continue to consume 150 tablets. In addition, U.S. residents are also able to import and consume 75 apps produced in India. At the same time, specialization and exchange allow residents of India to continue to consume 25 apps. Producing 75 more apps for export to the United States allows India to import 75 tablets.

GAINS FROM TRADE Table 32-4 on the facing page summarizes the rates of consumption of U.S. and Indian residents with and without trade. Column 1 displays U.S. and Indian app and tablet consumption rates with specialization and trade from Table 32-3, and it sums these to determine total consumption rates in this two-country world. Column 2 shows U.S., Indian, and worldwide consumption rates without international trade from Table 32-2 above. Column 3 gives the differences between the two columns.

TABLE 32-3

U.S. and Indian Production and Consumption with Specialization and Trade

In this table, U.S. residents produce 225 tablet devices, and no digital apps and Indian residents produce 100 digital apps and no tablets. Residents of the two nations then agree to a rate of exchange of 1 tablet for 1 app and proceed to trade 75 U.S. tablets for 75 Indian apps. Specialization and trade allow U.S. residents to consume 75 apps imported from India and to consume 150 tablets produced at home. By specializing and engaging in trade, Indian residents consume 25 apps produced at home and import 75 tablets from the United States.

Product	U.S. Production and Consumption with Trade		Indian Production and Consumption with Trade	
Digital apps (per hour)	U.S. production	0	Indian production	100
	+Imports from India	75	−Exports to U.S.	75
	Total U.S. consumption	75	Total Indian consumption	25
Tablet devices (per hour)	U.S. production	225	Indian production	0
	−Exports to India	75	+Imports from U.S.	75
	Total U.S. consumption	150	Total Indian consumption	75

Table 32-4 below indicates that by producing 75 additional tablets for export to India in exchange for 75 apps, U.S. residents are able to expand their app consumption from 30 to 75. Thus, the U.S. gain from specialization and trade is 45 apps. This is a net gain in app consumption for the two-country world as a whole, because neither country had to give up consuming any tablets for U.S. residents to realize this gain from trade.

In addition, without trade residents of India could have used all resources to produce and consume only 37.5 tablets and 25 apps. By using all resources to specialize in producing 100 apps and engaging in trade, residents of India can consume 37.5 *more* tablets than they could have produced and consumed alone without reducing their app consumption. Thus, the Indian gain from trade is 37.5 tablets. This represents a worldwide gain in tablet consumption, because neither country had to give up consuming any tablets for Indian residents to realize this gain from trade.

TABLE 32-4

National and Worldwide Gains from Specialization and Trade

This table summarizes the consumption gains experienced by the United States, India, and the two-country world. U.S. and Indian app and tablet consumption rates with specialization and trade from Table 32-3 above are listed in column 1, which sums the national consumption rates to determine total worldwide consumption with trade. Column 2 shows U.S., Indian, and worldwide consumption rates without international trade, as reported in Table 32-2 on the facing page. Column 3 gives the differences between the two columns, which are the resulting national and worldwide gains from international trade.

Product	(1) National and World Consumption with Trade		(2) National and World Consumption without Trade		(3) Worldwide Consumption Gains from Trade	
Digital apps (per hour)	U.S. consumption	75	U.S. consumption	30	Change in U.S. consumption	+45
	+Indian consumption	25	+Indian consumption	25	Change in Indian consumption	+0
	World consumption	100	World consumption	55	**Change in world consumption**	**+45**
Tablet devices (per hour)	U.S. consumption	150	U.S. consumption	150	Change in U.S. consumption	+0
	+Indian consumption	75	+Indian consumption	37.5	Change in Indian consumption	+37.5
	World consumption	225	World consumption	187.5	**Change in world consumption**	**+37.5**

SPECIALIZATION IS THE KEY This example shows that when nations specialize in producing goods for which they have a comparative advantage and engage in international trade, considerable consumption gains are possible for those nations and hence for the world. Why is this so? The answer is that specialization and trade enable Indian residents to obtain each tablet device at an opportunity cost of 1 digital app instead of 2 apps and permit U.S. residents to obtain each app at an opportunity cost of 1 tablet instead of 2.5 tablets.

Indian residents effectively experience a gain from trade of 1 app for each tablet purchased from the United States, and U.S. residents experience a gain from trade of 1.5 tablets for each app purchased from India. Thus, specializing in producing goods for which the two nations have a comparative advantage allows both nations to produce more efficiently. As a consequence, worldwide production capabilities increase. This makes greater worldwide consumption possible through international trade.

Of course, not everybody in our example is better off when free trade occurs. In our example, the U.S. app industry and Indian tablet industry have disappeared. Thus, U.S. app makers and Indian tablet manufacturers are worse off.

Some people worry that the United States (or any country, for that matter) might someday "run out of exports" because of overaggressive foreign competition. The analysis of comparative advantage tells us the contrary. No matter how much other countries compete for our business, the United States (or any other country) will always have a comparative advantage in something that it can export. In 10 or 20 years, that something may not be what we export today, but it will be exportable nonetheless because we will have a comparative advantage in producing it. Consequently, the significant flows of world trade shown in Figure 32-2 below will continue because the United States and other nations will retain comparative advantages in producing various goods and services.

FIGURE 32-2

World Trade Flows

International merchandise trade amounts to nearly $20 trillion worldwide. The percentage figures show the proportion of trade flowing in the various directions throughout the globe.

Sources: World Trade Organization and author's estimates (data are for 2013).

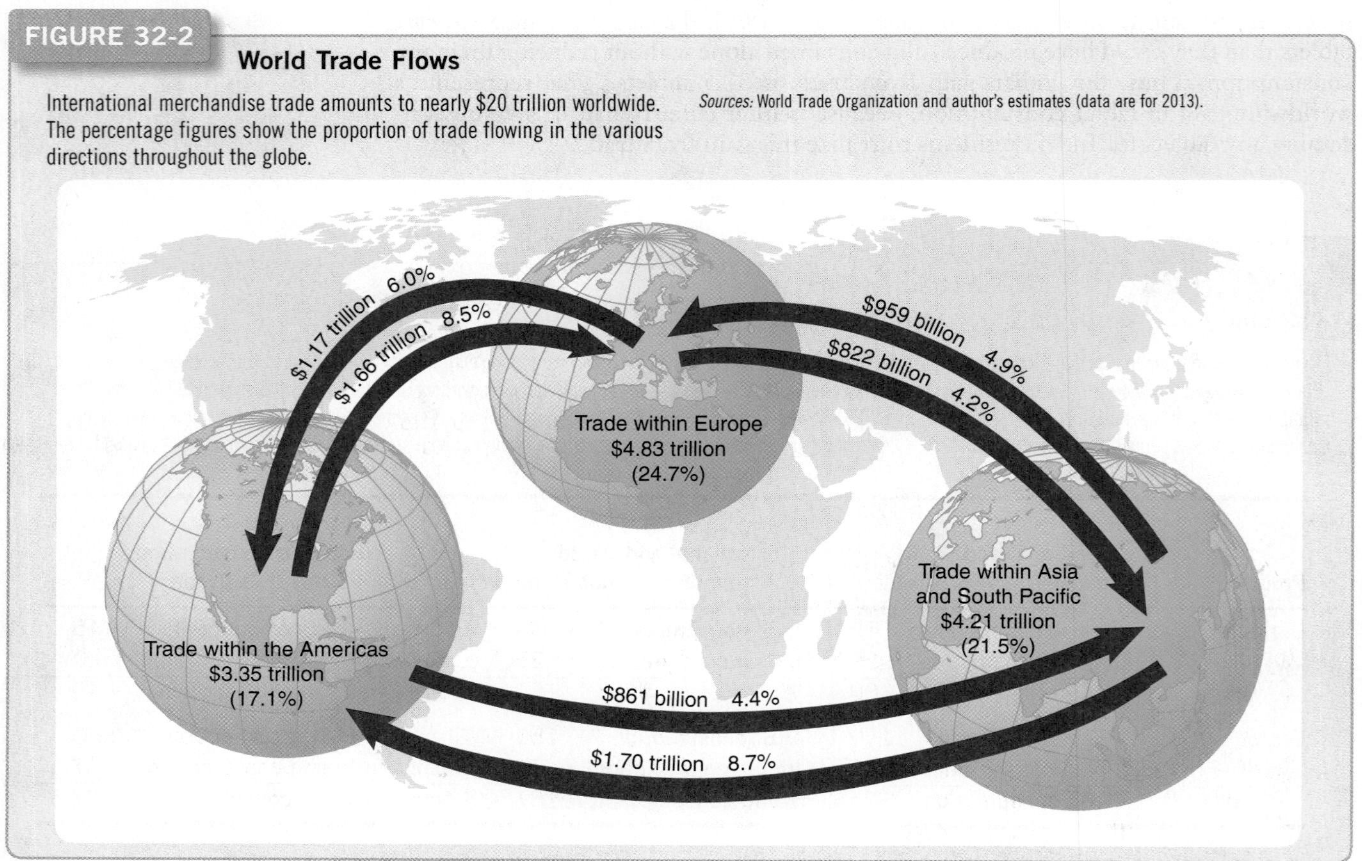

What accounts for the fact that the bulk of the world's linen fabrics are produced within a very small area on the earth's surface?

INTERNATIONAL EXAMPLE

Comparative Advantage and Specialization in European Linens

The production of linen requires twice as much land and labor as the production of an equivalent amount of cotton. Nevertheless, linen is a staple material utilized in designer clothing, such as women's blazers and dresses with prices exceeding $2,000, men's trench coats that sell for more than $1,500, and wedding gowns priced above $5,500.

Two-thirds of the world's linen is derived from a fiber called flax that is harvested within a narrow belt of farmland stretching from northern France into the Netherlands. The European coastal climate provides alternating sunshine and rain that contribute to development of a fungus that grows on the flax stems. The fungus breaks down the stems so that the linen fibers can be more readily separated from the plants. Thus, farmers residing this area are able to produce flax at a lower opportunity cost, in terms of forgone production of other goods, than almost anywhere else on the planet. This fact explains why this region of Europe has a comparative advantage in growing flax and specializes in the production of linen.

FOR CRITICAL THINKING

Why do you think that linen production generates gains from trade for European producers of flax and linen, even though cotton-based fabrics can be produced at lower absolute *cost in many other parts of the world?*

Other Benefits from International Trade: The Transmission of Ideas

Beyond the fact that comparative advantage results in an overall increase in the output of goods produced and consumed, there is another benefit to international trade. International trade also aids in the transmission of ideas. According to economic historians, international trade has been the principal means by which new goods, services, and processes have spread around the world. For example, coffee was initially grown in Arabia near the Red Sea. Around AD 675, it began to be roasted and consumed as a beverage. Eventually, it was exported to other parts of the world, and the Dutch started cultivating it in their colonies during the seventeenth century and the French in the eighteenth century. The lowly potato is native to the Peruvian Andes. In the sixteenth century, it was brought to Europe by Spanish explorers. Thereafter, its cultivation and consumption spread rapidly. Finally, it became part of the North American agricultural scene in the early eighteenth century.

New processes have also been transmitted through international trade. An example is the Japanese manufacturing innovation that emphasized redesigning the system rather than running the existing system in the best possible way. Inventories were reduced to just-in-time levels by reengineering machine setup methods.

In addition, international trade has enabled *intellectual property* to spread throughout the world. New music, such as rock and roll in the 1950s and 1960s and hip-hop in the 1990s and 2000s, has been transmitted in this way, as have the digital devices applications and application tools that are common for online and wireless users everywhere.

The Relationship between Imports and Exports

The basic proposition in understanding all of international trade is this:

In the long run, imports are paid for by exports.

The reason that imports are ultimately paid for by exports is that foreign residents want something in exchange for the goods that are shipped to the United States. For the most part, they want U.S.-made goods. From this truism comes a remarkable corollary:

Any restriction of imports ultimately reduces exports.

This is a shocking revelation to many people who want to restrict foreign competition to protect domestic jobs. Although it is possible to "protect" certain U.S. jobs by restricting foreign competition, it is impossible to make *everyone* better off by imposing import restrictions. Why? The reason is that ultimately such restrictions lead to a reduction in employment and output—and hence incomes—in the export industries of the nation.

WHAT IF... the government saved U.S. jobs from foreign competition by prohibiting all imports?

In the long run, U.S. imports are paid for by U.S. exports. Shutting out all imports of goods and services from abroad certainly would protect U.S. firms from competition and hence would protect many U.S. workers' jobs with those firms. A prohibition on all imports additionally would lead to an eventual halt in all purchases of U.S. firms' exports by residents of other nations, however. The consequence would be a reduction in production and sales by U.S. exporting firms, which would respond by eliminating positions for U.S. workers. Ultimately, therefore, a prohibition on U.S. imports would not really "save" jobs for U.S. workers.

International Competitiveness

"The United States is falling behind." "We need to stay competitive internationally." Statements such as these are often heard when the subject of international trade comes up. There are two problems with such talk. The first has to do with a simple definition. What does "global competitiveness" really mean? When one company competes against another, it is in competition. Is the United States like one big corporation, in competition with other countries? Certainly not. The standard of living in each country is almost solely a function of how well the economy functions *within that country*, not relative to other countries.

Another point relates to real-world observations. According to the Institute for Management Development in Lausanne, Switzerland, the United States is among the top ten nations in overall productive efficiency. According to the report, the relatively high ranking of the United States over the years has been due to widespread entrepreneurship, economic restructuring, and information-technology investments. Other factors include the open U.S. financial system and large investments in scientific research.

QUICK QUIZ See page 724 for the answers. Review concepts from this section in MyEconLab.

A nation has a **comparative advantage** when its residents are able to produce a good or service at a __________ opportunity cost than residents of another nation.

Specializing in production of goods and services for which residents of a nation have a __________ __________ allows the nation's residents to __________ more of all goods and services.

__________ from trade arise for all nations in the world that engage in international trade because specialization and trade allow countries' residents to __________ more goods and services without necessarily giving up consumption of other goods and services.

Arguments against Free Trade

Numerous arguments are raised against free trade. These arguments focus mainly on the costs of trade. They do not consider the benefits or the possible alternatives for reducing the costs of free trade while still reaping benefits.

The Infant Industry Argument

A nation may feel that if a particular industry is allowed to develop domestically, it will eventually become efficient enough to compete effectively in the world market. Therefore, the nation may impose some restrictions on imports in order to give domestic producers the time they need to develop their efficiency to the point where they can compete in the domestic market without any restrictions on imports. In graphic terminology, we would expect that if the protected industry truly does experience improvements in production techniques or technological breakthroughs toward greater efficiency in the future, the supply curve will shift outward to the right so that the domestic industry can produce larger quantities at each and every price. National policymakers often assert that this **infant industry argument** has some merit in the short run. They have used it to protect a number of industries in their infancy around the world.

Infant industry argument
The contention that tariffs should be imposed to protect from import competition an industry that is trying to get started. Presumably, after the industry becomes technologically efficient, the tariff can be lifted.

Such a policy can be abused, however. Often the protective import-restricting arrangements remain even after the infant has matured. If other countries can still produce more cheaply, the people who benefit from this type of situation are obviously the stockholders (and specialized factors of production that will earn economic rents—see pages 463–465 in Chapter 21) in the industry that is still being protected from world competition. The people who lose out are the consumers, who must pay a price higher than the world price for the product in question. In any event, because it is very difficult to know beforehand which industries will eventually survive, it is possible, perhaps even likely, that policymakers will choose to protect industries that have no reasonable chance of competing on their own in world markets. Note that when we speculate about which industries "should" be protected, we are in the realm of *normative economics*. We are making a value judgment, a subjective statement of what *ought to be*.

Countering Foreign Subsidies and Dumping

Another common argument against unrestricted foreign trade is that a nation must counter other nations' subsidies to their own producers. When a foreign government subsidizes its producers, our producers claim that they cannot compete fairly with these subsidized foreign producers. To the extent that such subsidies fluctuate, it can be argued that unrestricted free trade will seriously disrupt domestic producers. They will not know when foreign governments are going to subsidize their producers and when they are not. Our competing industries will be expanding and contracting too frequently.

How do government credit subsidies promote international trade by some U.S. industries while assisting foreign competitors of another industry?

POLICY EXAMPLE

A U.S. Agency Subsidizes U.S. Exports—and Also Foreign Firms

The U.S. Export-Import (Ex-Im) Bank regularly extends about $100 billion in subsidized loans to foreign buyers of U.S.-manufactured products, including aircraft, hair-care products, and construction equipment. The Ex-Im Bank's extensions of taxpayer-subsidized credit to companies in other nations gives these foreign firms incentives to buy U.S. exports.

Airlines based in the United States are not enthused about aircraft-loan subsidies to competitors based in other nations, however. The U.S. airlines argue that the Ex-Im Bank's low-interest loans to foreign carriers provide a cost advantage that enables the foreign airlines to compete at lower expense in the international air transportation market. Thus, from the U.S. airlines' point of view, U.S. taxpayers are subsidizing their foreign competitors.

FOR CRITICAL THINKING

Why do you suppose that some U.S. makers of hair-care products and certain U.S. construction contractors that bid for work in other nations have lodged complaints similar to those of the U.S. airlines?

The phenomenon called *dumping* is also used as an argument against unrestricted trade. **Dumping** is said to occur when a producer sells its products abroad below the price that is charged in the home market or at a price below its cost of production. Often, when a foreign producer is accused of dumping, further investigation reveals that the

Dumping
Selling a good or a service abroad below the price charged in the home market or at a price below its cost of production.

foreign nation is in the throes of a recession. The foreign producer does not want to slow down its production at home. Because it anticipates an end to the recession and doesn't want to hold large inventories, it dumps its products abroad at prices below home prices. U.S. competitors may also allege that the foreign producer sells its output at prices below its full costs to be assured of covering variable costs of production.

Protecting Domestic Jobs

Perhaps the argument used most often against free trade is that unrestrained competition from other countries will eliminate jobs in the United States because other countries have lower-cost labor than we do. (Less restrictive environmental standards in other countries might also lower their private costs relative to ours.) This is a compelling argument, particularly for politicians from areas that might be threatened by foreign competition. For example, a representative from an area with shoe factories would certainly be upset about the possibility of constituents' losing their jobs because of competition from lower-priced shoe manufacturers in Brazil and Italy. But, of course, this argument against free trade is equally applicable to trade between the states within the United States.

Economists David Gould, G. L. Woodbridge, and Roy Ruffin examined the data on the relationship between increases in imports and the unemployment rate. They concluded that there is no causal link between the two. Indeed, in half the cases they studied, when imports increased, the unemployment rate fell.

Another issue involves the cost of protecting U.S. jobs by restricting international trade. The Institute for International Economics examined the restrictions on foreign textiles and apparel goods. The study found that U.S. consumers pay $9 billion a year more than they would otherwise pay for those goods to protect jobs in those industries. That comes out to $50,000 *a year* for each job saved in an industry in which the average job pays only $20,000 a year. Similar studies have yielded similar results: Restrictions on imports of Japanese cars have cost $160,000 *per year* for every job saved in the auto industry. Every job preserved in the glass industry has cost $200,000 each and every year. Every job preserved in the U.S. steel industry has cost an astounding $750,000 per year.

Emerging Arguments against Free Trade

In recent years, two new antitrade arguments have been advanced. One of these focuses on environmental and safety concerns. For instance, many critics of free trade have suggested that genetic engineering of plants and animals could lead to accidental production of new diseases and that people, livestock, and pets could be harmed by tainted foods imported for human and animal consumption. These worries have induced the European Union to restrain trade in such products.

Another argument against free trade arises from national defense concerns. Major espionage successes by China in the late 1990s and 2000s led some U.S. strategic experts to propose sweeping restrictions on exports of new technology.

Free trade proponents counter that at best these are arguments for the judicious regulation of trade. They continue to argue that, by and large, broad trade restrictions mainly harm the interests of the nations that impose them.

QUICK QUIZ See page 724 for the answers. Review concepts from this section in MyEconLab.

The __________ industry argument against free trade contends that new industries should be __________ against world competition so that they can become technologically efficient in the long run.

Unrestricted foreign trade may allow foreign governments to subsidize exports or foreign producers to engage in __________, or selling products in other countries below their cost of production. Critics claim that to the extent that foreign export subsidies and __________ create more instability in domestic production, they may impair our well-being.

Ways to Restrict Foreign Trade

International trade can be stopped or at least stifled in many ways. These include quotas and taxes (the latter are usually called *tariffs* when applied to internationally traded items). Let's talk first about quotas.

Quotas

Under a **quota system,** individual countries or groups of foreign producers are restricted to a certain amount of trade. An import quota specifies the maximum amount of a commodity that may be imported during a specified period of time. For example, the government might allow no more than 200 million barrels of foreign crude oil to enter the United States in a particular month.

Quota system
A government-imposed restriction on the quantity of a specific good that another country is allowed to sell in the United States. In other words, quotas are restrictions on imports. These restrictions are usually applied to one or several specific countries.

Consider the example of quotas on textiles. Figure 32-3 below presents the demand and supply curves for imported textiles. In an unrestricted import market, the equilibrium quantity imported is 900 million yards at a price of $1 per yard (expressed in constant-quality units). When an import quota is imposed, the supply curve is no longer *S*. Instead, the supply curve becomes vertical at some amount less than the equilibrium quantity—here, 800 million yards per year. The price to the U.S. consumer increases from $1.00 to $1.50.

Clearly, the output restriction generated by a quota on foreign imports of a particular item has the effect of raising the domestic price of the imported item. Two groups benefit. One group is importers that are able to obtain the rights to sell imported items domestically at the higher price, which raises their revenues and boosts their profits. The other group is domestic producers. Naturally, a rise in the price of an imported item induces an increase in the demand for domestic substitutes. Thus, the domestic prices of close substitutes for the item subject to the import restriction also increase, which generates higher revenues and profits for domestic producers.

YOU ARE THERE

To consider why domestic producers often desire protection from competing foreign products, read **A French Family Bookshop Seeks Protection from U.S. E-Books** on page 720.

FIGURE 32-3

The Effect of Quotas on Textile Imports

Without restrictions, at point E_1, 900 million yards of textiles would be imported each year into the United States at the world price of $1.00 per yard. If the federal government imposes a quota of only 800 million yards, the effective supply curve becomes vertical at that quantity. It intersects the demand curve at point E_2, so the new equilibrium price is $1.50 per yard.

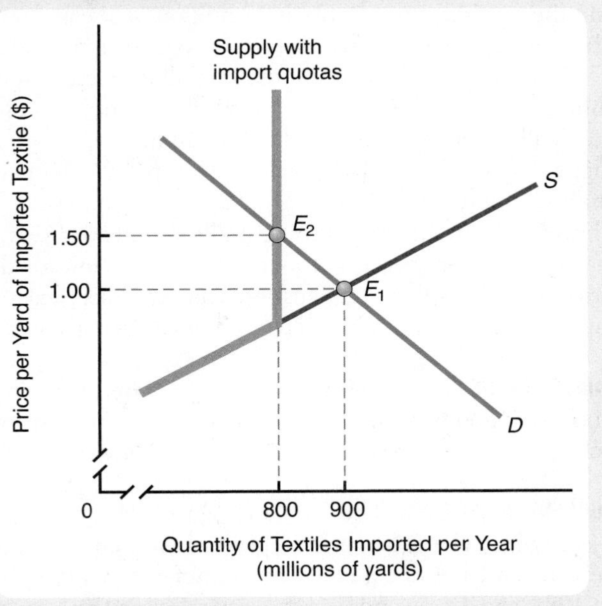

Why did U.S. government agents recently conduct a raid on a U.S. guitar manufacturer?

POLICY EXAMPLE

Gibson Guitars Confronts a Very Particular Import Quota

One of the most famous U.S. guitar makers is Gibson Guitars, which places a "Made in the U.S.A." label on each instrument it sells. Recently, federal agents raided the company's corporate offices and its two guitar factories. The agents seized 24 pallets of rosewood and ebony imported from India, which Gibson had planned to use in making fingerboards for its guitars.

The company, the U.S. government alleged, had run afoul of an international trade quota on unfinished rosewood and ebony products. Finished rosewood or ebony, though, had no U.S. trade quota. Hence, if Indian workers had finished the rosewood and ebony prior to shipment, instead of Gibson's U.S. workers finishing the materials following shipment. Gibson would not have violated any U.S. trade quotas.

FOR CRITICAL THINKING

Gibson presumably violated an environmental protection law. Why does this trade quota have the same economic effects as laws designed to protect domestic firms from foreign competition?

Voluntary restraint agreement (VRA)
An official agreement with another country that "voluntarily" restricts the quantity of its exports to the United States.

Voluntary import expansion (VIE)
An official agreement with another country in which it agrees to import more from the United States.

VOLUNTARY QUOTAS Quotas do not have to be explicit and defined by law. They can be "voluntary." Such a quota is called a **voluntary restraint agreement (VRA).** In the early 1980s, Japanese automakers voluntarily restrained exports to the United States. These restraints stayed in place into the 1990s. Today, there are VRAs on machine tools and textiles.

The opposite of a VRA is a **voluntary import expansion (VIE).** Under a VIE, a foreign government agrees to have its companies import more foreign goods from another country. The United States almost started a major international trade war with Japan in 1995 over just such an issue. The U.S. government wanted Japanese automobile manufacturers to voluntarily increase their imports of U.S.-made automobile parts. Ultimately, Japanese companies did make a token increase in their imports of U.S. auto parts.

Tariffs

Go to www.econtoday.com/chap32 to take a look at the U.S. State Department's reports on economic policy and trade practices.

We can analyze tariffs by using standard supply and demand diagrams. Let's use as our commodity laptop computers, some of which are made in Japan and some of which are made domestically. In panel (a) of Figure 32-4 on the facing page, you see the demand for and supply of Japanese laptops. The equilibrium price is $500 per constant-quality unit, and the equilibrium quantity is 10 million per year. In panel (b), you see the same equilibrium price of $500, and the *domestic* equilibrium quantity is 5 million units per year.

Now a tariff of $250 is imposed on all imported Japanese laptops. The supply curve shifts upward by $250 to S_2. For purchasers of Japanese laptops, the price increases to $625. The quantity demanded falls to 8 million per year. In panel (b), you see that at the higher price of imported Japanese laptops, the demand curve for U.S.-made laptops shifts outward to the right to D_2. The equilibrium price increases to $625, and the equilibrium quantity increases to 6.5 million units per year. So the tariff benefits domestic laptop producers because it increases the demand for their products due to the higher price of a close substitute, Japanese laptops. This causes a redistribution of income from Japanese producers and U.S. consumers of laptops to U.S. producers of laptops.

TARIFFS IN THE UNITED STATES In Figure 32-5 on the facing page, we see that tariffs on all imported goods have varied widely. The highest rates in the twentieth century occurred with the passage of the Smoot-Hawley Tariff in 1930.

CURRENT TARIFF LAWS The Trade Expansion Act of 1962 gave the president the authority to reduce tariffs by up to 50 percent. Subsequently, tariffs were reduced by about 35 percent. In 1974, the Trade Reform Act allowed the president to reduce tariffs further. In 1984, the Trade and Tariff Act resulted in the lowest tariff rates ever. All such trade agreement obligations of the United States were carried out under the auspices of the

FIGURE 32-4

The Effect of a Tariff on Japanese-Made Laptop Computers

Without a tariff, the United States buys 10 million Japanese laptops per year at an average price of $500, at point E_1 in panel (a). U.S. producers sell 5 million domestically made laptops, also at $500 each, at point E_1 in panel (b). A $250 tariff per laptop will shift the Japanese import supply curve to S_2 in panel (a), so that the new equilibrium is at E_2 with price increased to $625 and quantity sold reduced to 8 million per year. The demand curve for U.S.-made laptops (for which there is no tariff) shifts to D_2, in panel (b). Domestic sales increase to 6.5 million per year, at point E_2.

Panel (a)
Panel (b)
$250
tariff
S2
S1
S
Price per Laptop ($)
625
500
E2
E1
D
D2
D1
0
8
10
5.0
6.5
Japanese-Made Laptops (millions)
U.S.-Made Laptops (millions)

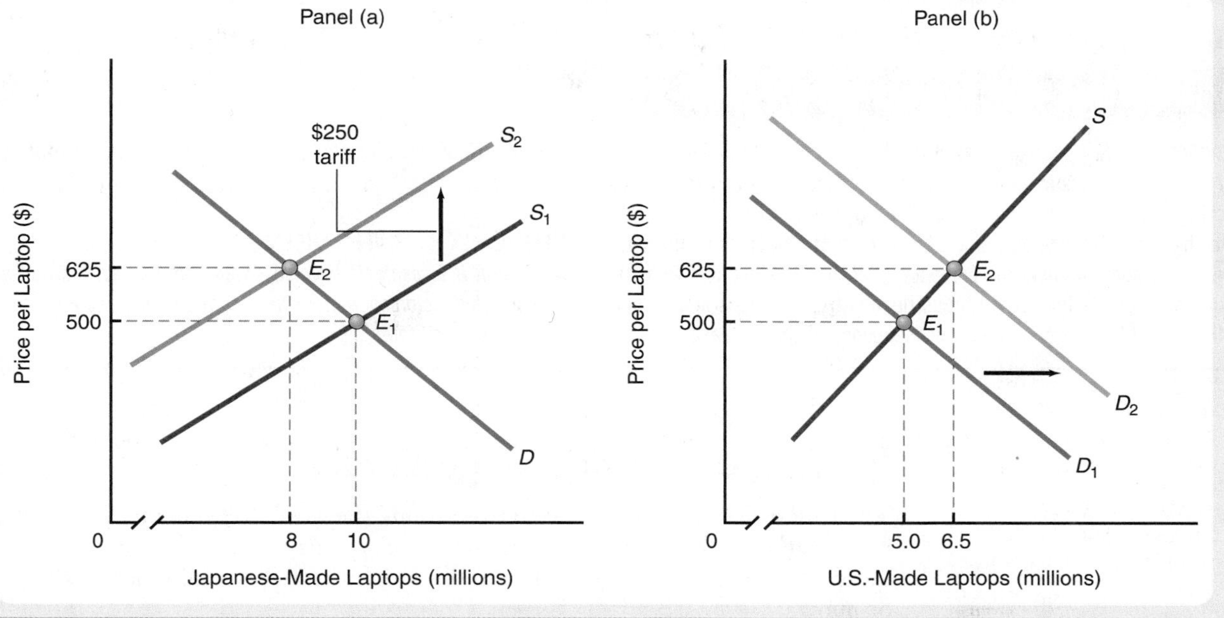

FIGURE 32-5

Tariff Rates in the United States Since 1820

Tariff rates in the United States have bounced around like a football. Indeed, in Congress, tariffs are a political football. Import-competing industries prefer high tariffs. In the twentieth century, the highest tariff was the Smoot-Hawley Tariff of 1930, which was about as high as the "tariff of abominations" in 1828.

Source: U.S. Department of Commerce.

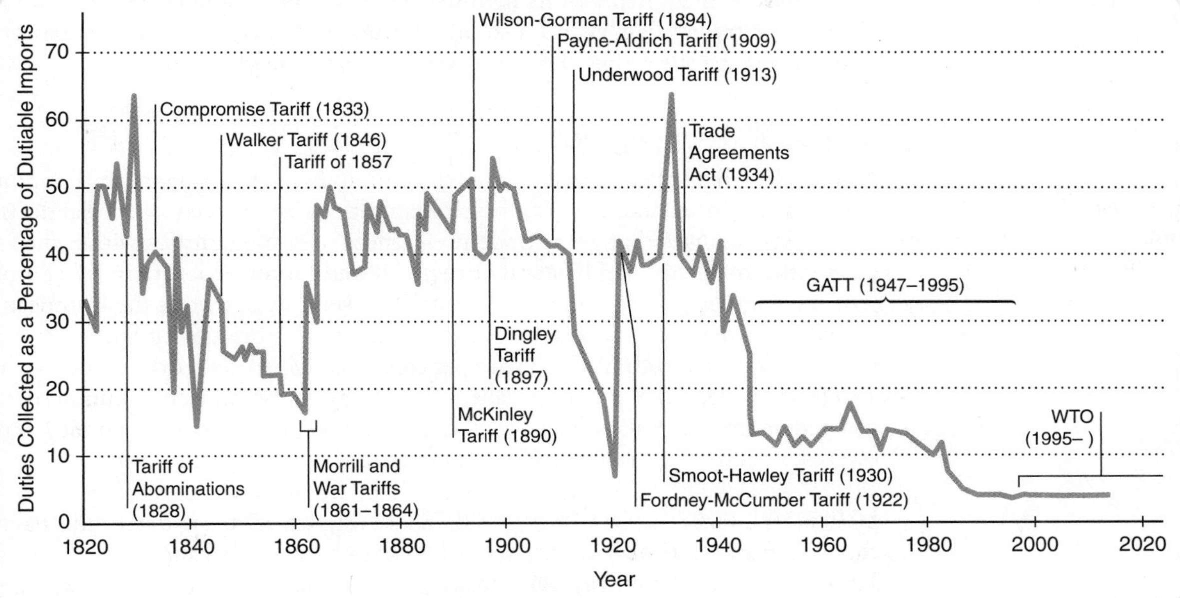

Duties Collected as a Percentage of Dutiable Imports
70
60
50
40
30
20
10
0
Wilson-Gorman Tariff (1894)
Payne-Aldrich Tariff (1909)
Underwood Tariff (1913)
Compromise Tariff (1833)
Walker Tariff (1846)
Tariff of 1857
Trade Agreements Act (1934)
GATT (1947–1995)
Dingley Tariff (1897)
McKinley Tariff (1890)
WTO (1995–)
Tariff of Abominations (1828)
Morrill and War Tariffs (1861–1864)
Smoot-Hawley Tariff (1930)
Fordney-McCumber Tariff (1922)
1820
1840
1860
1880
1900
1920
1940
1960
1980
2000
2020
Year

General Agreement on Tariffs and Trade (GATT)
An international agreement established in 1947 to further world trade by reducing barriers and tariffs. The GATT was replaced by the World Trade Organization in 1995.

General Agreement on Tariffs and Trade (GATT), which was signed in 1947. Member nations of the GATT account for more than 85 percent of world trade. As you can see in Figure 32-5 on the previous page, U.S. tariff rates have declined since the early 1960s, when several rounds of negotiations under the GATT were initiated.

How have recently reduced barriers to trade with the United States affected nations in Africa?

INTERNATIONAL POLICY EXAMPLE

African Nations Benefit from Lower U.S. Trade Barriers

In 2000, the U.S. Congress passed the African Growth and Opportunity Act, which reduced substantially the tariffs faced by African companies seeking to export goods and services to the United States. African-U.S. trade has risen considerably since. Earnings that African companies derive from exports are now 500 percent higher than in 2001. Furthermore, estimates indicate that export industries in African nations now employ 300,000 additional workers as a consequence of the increased volume of trade. Thus, slashing trade barriers has generated welfare gains for African residents.

FOR CRITICAL THINKING

How might U.S. residents have benefited from the fact that African countries granted reciprocal reductions in tariffs on imports into their nations from the United States?

International Trade Organizations

The widespread effort to reduce tariffs around the world has generated interest among nations in joining various international trade organizations. These organizations promote trade by granting preferences in the form of reduced or eliminated tariffs, duties, or quotas.

The World Trade Organization (WTO)

World Trade Organization (WTO)
The successor organization to the GATT that handles trade disputes among its member nations.

The most important international trade organization with the largest membership is the **World Trade Organization (WTO),** which was ratified by the final round of negotiations of the General Agreement on Tariffs and Trade at the end of 1993. The WTO, which as of 2012 had 157 member nations and included 30 observer governments, began operations on January 1, 1995. The WTO has fostered important and far-reaching global trade agreements. There is considerable evidence that since the WTO was formed, many of its member nations have adopted policies promoting international trade. The WTO also adjudicates trade disputes between nations in an effort to reduce the scope of protectionism around the globe.

Regional Trade Agreements

Regional trade bloc
A group of nations that grants members special trade privileges.

Numerous other international trade organizations exist alongside the WTO. Sometimes known as **regional trade blocs,** these organizations are created by special deals among groups of countries that grant trade preferences only to countries within their groups. Currently, more than 475 bilateral or regional trade agreements are in effect around the globe. Examples include groups of industrial powerhouses, such as the European Union, the North American Free Trade Agreement, and the Association of Southeast Asian Nations. Nations in South America with per capita real GDP nearer the world average have also formed regional trade blocs called Mercosur and the Andean Community. Less developed nations have also formed regional trade blocs, such as the Economic Community of West African States and the Community of East and Southern Africa.

DO REGIONAL TRADE BLOCS SIMPLY DIVERT TRADE? Figure 32-6 on the facing page shows that the formation of regional trade blocs, in which the European Union and the United States are often key participants, is on an upswing. An average African nation participates in four separate regional trading agreements. A typical Latin American country belongs to eight different regional trade blocs.

FIGURE 32-6

The Percentage of World Trade within Regional Trade Blocs

As the number of regional trade agreements has increased since 1990, the share of world trade undertaken among nations that are members of regional trade blocs—involving the European Union (EU), the United States, and developing nations—has also increased.

Source: World Bank.

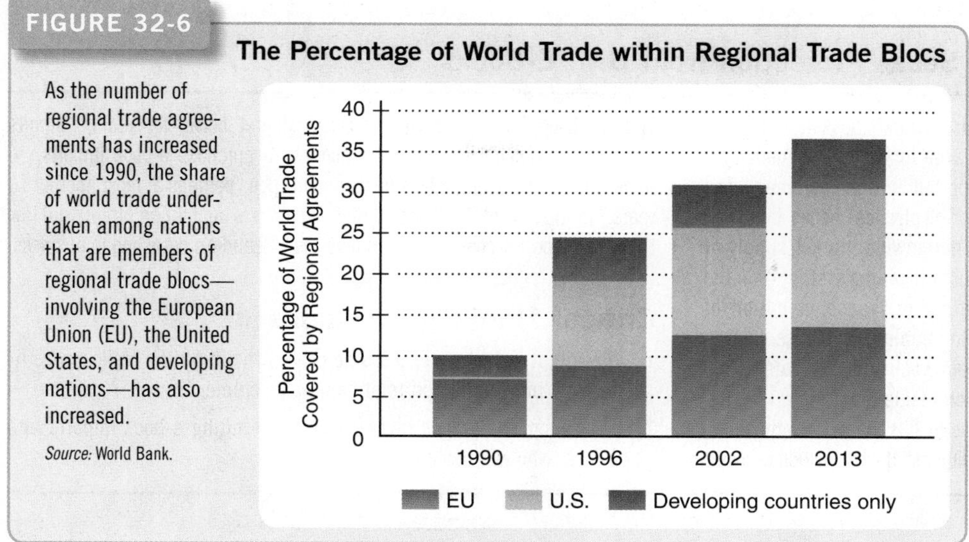

In the past, economists worried that the formation of regional trade blocs could mainly result in **trade diversion,** or the shifting of trade from countries outside a regional trade bloc to nations within a bloc. Indeed, a study by Jeffrey Frankel of Harvard University found evidence that some trade diversion does take place. Nevertheless, Frankel and other economists have concluded that the net effect of regional trade agreements has been to boost overall international trade, in some cases considerably.

Trade diversion
Shifting existing international trade from countries outside a regional trade bloc to nations within the bloc.

THE TRADE DEFLECTION ISSUE Today, the primary issue associated with regional trade blocs is **trade deflection.** This occurs when a company located in a nation outside a regional trade bloc moves goods that are not quite fully assembled into a member country, completes assembly of the goods there, and then exports them to other nations in the bloc. To try to reduce incentives for trade deflection, regional trade agreements often include **rules of origin,** which are regulations carefully defining categories of products that are eligible for trading preferences under the agreements. Some rules of origin, for instance, require any products trading freely among members of a bloc to be composed mainly of materials produced within a member nation.

Trade deflection
Moving partially assembled products into a member nation of a regional trade bloc, completing assembly, and then exporting them to other nations within the bloc, so as to benefit from preferences granted by the trade bloc.

Rules of origin
Regulations that nations in regional trade blocs establish to delineate product categories eligible for trading preferences.

Proponents of free trade worry, however, about the potential for parties to regional trade agreements to use rules of origin to create barriers to trade. Sufficiently complex rules of origin, they suggest, can provide disincentives for countries to utilize the trade-promoting preferences that regional trade agreements ought to provide. Indeed, some free trade proponents applaud successful trade deflection. They contend that it helps to circumvent trade restrictions and thus allows nations within regional trade blocs to experience additional gains from trade.

QUICK QUIZ

See page 724 for the answers. Review concepts from this section in MyEconLab.

One means of restricting foreign trade is an import quota, which specifies a __________ amount of a good that may be imported during a certain period. The resulting increase in import prices benefits domestic __________ that receive higher prices resulting from substitution to domestic goods.

Another means of restricting imports is a **tariff,** which is a __________ on imports only. An import tariff __________ import-competing industries and harms consumers by raising prices.

The main international institution created to improve trade among nations was the General Agreement on Tariffs and Trade (GATT). The last round of trade talks under the GATT led to the creation of the __________ __________ __________.

__________ __________ agreements among numerous nations of the world have established more than 475 bilateral and __________ __________ blocs, which grant special trade privileges such as reduced tariff barriers and quota exemptions to member nations.

YOU ARE THERE

A French Family Bookshop Seeks Protection from U.S. E-Books

For more than three decades, Thierry Meaudre's family bookshop in Paris has been protected from competition with large foreign booksellers by a French law restricting the distribution of imported "printed volumes." The legislation effectively constrains the number of physical books imported into the country and thereby restrains the nationwide market supply of books, which raises book prices. This enables Meaudre's store and the other 3,000 independent bookstores operating in France, a nation of 65 million people, to earn sufficient profits to remain in business. By way of comparison, fewer than 2,000 independent bookstores operate in the United States, a country with over 300 million residents.

The advent of low-priced U.S. e-book imports fills Meaudre with dread, because the existing law's limits of "printed volumes" do not include e-books.

"I have been having nightmares about digital books for years," admits Meaudre. If French consumers are allowed to purchase e-book imports, he thinks that his store might be able to remain open "perhaps at most another 10 years." In the face of the e-book threat, Meaudre is supporting a proposed law that would boost e-book prices and help keep Meaudre's bookshop in business.

Critical Thinking Questions

1. Why might imports of e-books be more difficult for the French government to limit than imports of "physical volumes"?
2. If the proposed French law succeeds in limiting e-book imports into France, who will pay higher e-book prices?

ISSUES & APPLICATIONS

U.S. Flower Growers Induce Congress to Snip Foreign Imports

CONCEPTS APPLIED

- Regional Trade Bloc
- Tariffs
- Subsidies

When the U.S. Congress passed the 1991 Andean Trade Promotion Act, it established a regional trade bloc encompassing the United States and several South American nations located along the Andes mountain range. This law slashed tariff rates on goods imported into the United States from Andean nations.

Budding Colombian Imports of Cut Flowers Ultimately Blossom

Among the imported items for which the 1991 legislation sharply reduced U.S. tariff rates were Colombian cut flowers. The Colombian climate is superior to that of the western United States for growing most flowers, and Colombian farm labor costs are much lower. Thus, within a few years after the reduction in tariffs, Colombian flower growers had established a network for selling cut flowers in California. Furthermore, in 2010, the Colombian firms opened a large distribution center in Los Angeles to increase the flow of cut-flower imports into the United States.

As Figure 32-7 on the facing page indicates, Colombian flower growers' efforts led to a substantial increase in U.S. flower imports from that nation during the 2000s. By 2010, U.S. imports of Colombian cut flowers were nearly 400 percent greater than the 2002 level.

California Flower Growers Lobby for Protection

As Colombian flower imports into California bloomed, the sales of cut flowers by California growers shriveled. When Congress passed the Andean Trade Promotion Act, there were 450 Californian flower farms. By 2010, there were 250.

In response to the upsurge in competition from Colombia, the California Cut Flower Commission, a trade association, successfully lobbied to delay congressional approval of a renewal of the Andean regional trade pact. The consequence

FIGURE 32-7
U.S. Imports of Cut Flowers from Colombia since 2002

The dollar value of cut flowers imported from Colombia increased substantially during the 2000s but plummeted after California flower growers succeeded in delaying renewal of the Andean Trade Promotion Act.

Sources: U.S. International Trade Commission; author's estimates.

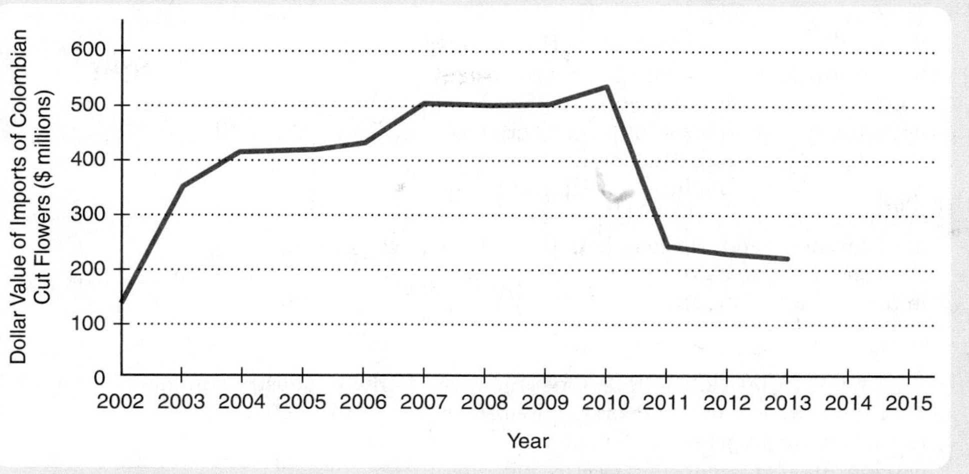

was a reimposition in 2011 of tariffs on Colombian flower growers, whose tariff payments increased sharply. As shown in Figure 32-7 above, this significant tariff increase resulted in a considerable reduction in cut-flower imports from Colombia. As a consequence, the foreign supply of cut flowers in California decreased, and the demand for Californian cut flowers increased, which pushed up U.S. prices of cut flowers. Even as California flower growers' earnings flourished, they began lobbying for U.S. government subsidies to enable them to establish their own cut-flower distribution center to compete with Colombia's.

For Critical Thinking

1. Which region appears to have a comparative advantage in producing cut flowers: Colombia or California? Explain.
2. How have U.S. consumers of cut flowers been affected by the cutback in Colombian imports?

Web Resources

1. Find out more about the Andean Trade Promotion Act at **www.econtoday.com/chap32**.
2. Learn about the Colombian flower industry at **www.econtoday.com/chap32**.

MyEconLab

For more questions on this chapter's Issues & Applications, go to MyEconLab. In the Study Plan for this chapter, select Section N: News.

MyEconLab

Here is what you should know after reading this chapter. MyEconLab will help you identify what you know, and where to go when you need to practice.

WHAT YOU SHOULD KNOW		WHERE TO GO TO PRACTICE
The Worldwide Importance of International Trade Total trade among nations has been growing faster than total world GDP. The growth of U.S. exports and imports relative to U.S. GDP parallels this global trend. Today, exports constitute more than 14 percent of total national production. In some countries, trade accounts for a much higher share of total economic activity.	**Key Figure** Figure 32-1, 705	• MyEconLab Study Plan 32.1 • Animated Figure 32-1

MyEconLab *continued*

WHAT YOU SHOULD KNOW		WHERE TO GO TO PRACTICE
Why Nations Can Gain from Specializing in Production and Engaging in Trade A country has a comparative advantage in producing a good if it can produce that good at a lower opportunity cost, in terms of forgone production of a second good, than another nation. Both nations can gain by specializing in producing the goods in which they have a comparative advantage and engaging in trade. Together, they can consume more than they would have in the absence of specialization and trade.	comparative advantage, 706 **Key Figure** Figure 32-2, 710	• MyEconLab Study Plan 32.2 • Animated Figure 32-2
Arguments against Free Trade One argument against free trade is that temporary import restrictions might permit an "infant industry" to develop. Another argument concerns dumping, in which foreign firms allegedly sell some of their output in domestic markets at prices below the prices in their home markets or even below their costs of production. In addition, some environmentalists support restrictions on foreign trade to protect their nations from exposure to environmental hazards. Finally, some contend that countries should limit exports of technologies that could pose a threat to their national defense.	infant industry argument, 713 dumping, 713	• MyEconLab Study Plans 32.3, 32.4, 32.5
Ways That Nations Restrict Foreign Trade One way to restrain trade is to impose a quota, or a limit on imports of a good. This action restricts the supply of the good in the domestic market, thereby pushing up the equilibrium price of the good. Another way to reduce trade is to place a tariff on imported goods. This reduces the supply of foreign-made goods and increases the demand for domestically produced goods, thereby bringing about a rise in the price of the good.	quota system, 715 voluntary restraint agreement (VRA), 716 voluntary import expansion (VIE), 716 General Agreement on Tariffs and Trade (GATT), 718 **Key Figures** Figure 32-3, 715 Figure 32-4, 717	• MyEconLab Study Plan 32.6 • Animated Figures 32-3, 32-4
Key International Trade Agreements and Organizations From 1947 to 1995, nations agreed to abide by the General Agreement on Tariffs and Trade (GATT), which laid an international legal foundation for relaxing quotas and reducing tariffs. Since 1995, the World Trade Organization (WTO) has adjudicated trade disputes that arise between or among nations. Now there are also more than 475 bilateral and regional trade blocs, including the North American Free Trade Agreement and the European Union, that provide special trade preferences to member nations.	World Trade Organization, 718 regional trade bloc, 718 trade diversion, 719 trade deflection, 719 rules of origin, 719 **Key Figure** Figure 32-5, 717	• MyEconLab Study Plan 32.7 • Animated Figure 32-5

Log in to MyEconLab, take a chapter test, and get a personalized Study Plan that tells you which concepts you understand and which ones you need to review. From there, MyEconLab will give you further practice, tutorials, animations, videos, and guided solutions. For more information, visit www.myeconlab.com

PROBLEMS

All problems are assignable in MyEconLab. *Answers to the odd-numbered problems appear at the back of the book.*

32-1. To answer the questions below, consider the following table for the neighboring nations of Northland and West Coast. The table lists maximum feasible hourly rates of production of pastries if no sandwiches are produced and maximum feasible hourly rates of production of sandwiches if no pastries are produced. Assume that the opportunity costs of producing these goods are constant in both nations. (See page 707.)

Product	Northland	West Coast
Pastries (per hour)	50,000	100,000
Sandwiches (per hour)	25,000	200,000

a. What is the opportunity cost of producing pastries in Northland? Of producing sandwiches in Northland?

b. What is the opportunity cost of producing pastries in West Coast? Of producing sandwiches in West Coast?

32-2. Based on your answers to Problem 32-1, which nation has a comparative advantage in producing pastries? Which nation has a comparative advantage in producing sandwiches? (See page 707.)

32-3. Suppose that the two nations in Problems 32-1 and 32-2 choose to specialize in producing the goods for which they have a comparative advantage. They agree to trade at a rate of exchange of 1 pastry for 1 sandwich. At this rate of exchange, what are the maximum possible numbers of pastries and sandwiches that they could agree to trade? (See page 708.)

32-4. Residents of the nation of Border Kingdom can forgo production of digital televisions and utilize all available resources to produce 300 bottles of high-quality wine per hour. Alternatively, they can forgo producing wine and instead produce 60 digital TVs per hour. In the neighboring country of Coastal Realm, residents can forgo production of digital TVs and use all resources to produce 150 bottles of high-quality wine per hour, or they can forgo wine production and produce 50 digital TVs per hour. In both nations, the opportunity costs of producing the two goods are constant. (See pages 707–708.)

a. What is the opportunity cost of producing digital TVs in Border Kingdom? Of producing bottles of wine in Border Kingdom?

b. What is the opportunity cost of producing digital TVs in Coastal Realm? Of producing bottles of wine in Coastal Realm?

32-5. Based on your answers to Problem 32-4, which nation has a comparative advantage in producing digital TVs? Which nation has a comparative advantage in producing bottles of wine? (See page 708.)

32-6. Suppose that the two nations in Problem 32-4 decide to specialize in producing the good for which they have a comparative advantage and to engage in trade. Would residents of both nations find a rate of exchange of 4 bottles of wine for 1 digital TV potentially agreeable? Why or why not? (See pages 708–709.)

To answer Problems 32-7 and 32-8, refer to the following table, which shows possible combinations of hourly outputs of modems and flash memory drives in South Shore and neighboring East Isle, in which opportunity costs of producing both products are constant.

South Shore		East Isle	
Modems	Flash Drives	Modems	Flash Drives
75	0	100	0
60	30	80	10
45	60	60	20
30	90	40	30
15	120	20	40
0	150	0	50

32-7. Consider the above table and answer the questions that follow. (See pages 707–709.)

a. What is the opportunity cost of producing modems in South Shore? Of producing flash memory drives in South Shore?

b. What is the opportunity cost of producing modems in East Isle? Of producing flash memory drives in East Isle?

c. Which nation has a comparative advantage in producing modems? Which nation has a comparative advantage in producing flash memory drives?

32-8. Refer to your answers to Problem 32-7 when answering the following questions. (See page 709.)

a. Which *one* of the following rates of exchange of modems for flash memory drives will be acceptable to *both* nations: (i) 3 modems for 1 flash drive; (ii) 1 modem for 1 flash drive; or (iii) 1 flash drive for 2.5 modems? Explain.

b. Suppose that each nation decides to use all available resources to produce only the good for which it has a comparative advantage and to engage in trade at the single feasible rate of exchange you identified in part (a). Prior to specialization and trade, residents of South Shore chose to produce and consume 30 modems per hour and 90 flash drives per hour, and residents of East Isle chose to produce and consume 40 modems per hour and 30 flash drives per hour. Now, residents of South Shore agree to export to East Isle the same quantity of South Shore's specialty good that East Isle residents were consuming prior to engaging in international trade. How many units of East Isle's specialty good does South Shore import from East Isle?

c. What is South Shore's hourly consumption of modems and flash drives after the nation specializes and trades with East Isle? What is East Isle's hourly consumption of modems and flash drives after the nation specializes and trades with South Shore?

d. What consumption gains from trade are experienced by South Shore and East Isle?

32-9. Critics of the North American Free Trade Agreement (NAFTA) suggest that much of the increase in exports from Mexico to the United States now involves goods that Mexico otherwise would have exported to other nations. Mexican firms choose to export the goods to the United States, the critics argue, solely because the items receive preferential treatment under NAFTA tariff rules. What term describes what these critics are claiming is occurring with regard to U.S.-Mexican trade as a result of NAFTA? Explain your reasoning. (See pages 718–719.)

32-10. Some critics of the North American Free Trade Agreement (NAFTA) suggest that firms outside NAFTA nations sometimes shift unassembled inputs to Mexico, assemble the inputs into final goods there, and then export the final product to the United States in order to take advantage of Mexican trade preferences. What term describes what these critics are claiming is occurring with regard to U.S.-Mexican trade as a result of NAFTA? Explain your reasoning. (See page 719.)

32-11. How could multilateral trade agreements established for all nations through the World Trade Organization help to prevent both trade diversion and trade deflection that can occur under regional trade agreements, thereby promoting more overall international trade? (See page 719.)

ECONOMICS ON THE NET

How the World Trade Organization Settles Trade Disputes A key function of the WTO is to adjudicate trade disagreements that arise among nations. This application helps you learn about the process that the WTO follows when considering international trade disputes.

Title: The World Trade Organization: Settling Trade Disputes

Navigation: Go to **www.econtoday.com/chap32** to access the WTO's Web page titled *Dispute Settlement.* Under "Introduction to dispute settlement in the WTO," click on *How does the WTO settle disputes?*

Application Read the article. Then answer the following questions.

1. As the article discusses, settling trade disputes often takes at least a year. What aspects of the WTO's dispute settlement process take the longest time?
2. Does the WTO actually "punish" a country it finds has broken international trading agreements? If not, who does impose sanctions?

For Group Study and Analysis Go to the WTO's main site at **www.econtoday.com/chap32**, and click on *The WTO*. Divide the class into groups, and have the groups explore this information on areas of WTO involvement. Have a class discussion of the pros and cons of WTO involvement in these areas. Which are most important for promoting world trade? Which are least important?

ANSWERS TO QUICK QUIZZES

p. 712: (i) lower; (ii) comparative advantage . . . consume; (iii) Gains . . . consume

p. 714: (i) infant . . . protected; (ii) dumping . . . dumping

p. 719: (i) maximum . . . producers; (ii) tax . . . benefits; (iii) World Trade Organization; (iv) Regional trade . . . regional trade

Exchange Rates and the Balance of Payments

33

LEARNING OBJECTIVES

After reading this chapter, you should be able to:

- Distinguish between the balance of trade and the balance of payments
- Identify the key accounts within the balance of payments
- Outline how exchange rates are determined in the markets for foreign exchange
- Discuss factors that can induce changes in equilibrium exchange rates
- Understand how policymakers can go about attempting to fix exchange rates

MyEconLab helps you master each objective and study more efficiently. See end of chapter for details.

Every few months, a U.S. media story reports on the substantial gap between U.S. imports of physical goods from China and U.S. exports of goods to China. Typically, media commentators follow up with complaints that U.S. residents are thoughtlessly paying prices for Chinese imports that effectively transfer a portion of U.S. residents' incomes to people in China. Does every dollar that you pay for a Chinese-manufactured item translate into an income transfer from the United States to China? Before you can answer this question, you must learn how economists use an accounting system called the *balance of payments* to track flows of spending on goods and services exported from and imported into the United States.

DID YOU KNOW THAT... the annual dollar value of trading in *foreign exchange markets*—markets in which people buy and sell national currencies, such as the U.S. dollar, European euro, Japanese yen, or Chinese yuan—exceeds $4 trillion? Thus, the total value of exchanges of the world's currencies during a given year amounts to more than one-fourth of the value of exchanges for all goods and services produced per year in the United States. By the time you have completed this chapter, you will understand why people desire to obtain so many currencies of other nations in foreign exchange markets scattered around the globe. First, however, you must learn how we keep track of flows of payments across a country's borders.

The Balance of Payments and International Capital Movements

Governments typically keep track of each year's economic activities by calculating the gross domestic product—the total of expenditures on all newly domestic-produced final goods and services—and its components. A summary information system has also been developed for international trade. It covers the balance of trade and the balance of payments. The **balance of trade** refers specifically to exports and imports of physical goods, or merchandise, as discussed in Chapter 32. When international trade is in balance, the value of exports equals the value of imports. When the value of imports exceeds the value of exports, we are running a deficit in the balance of trade. When the value of exports exceeds the value of imports, we are running a surplus.

Balance of trade
The difference between exports and imports of physical goods.

The **balance of payments** is a more general concept that expresses the total of all economic transactions between a nation and the rest of the world, usually for a period of one year. Each country's balance of payments summarizes information about that country's exports and imports of services as well as physical goods, earnings by domestic residents on assets located abroad, earnings on domestic assets owned by residents of foreign nations, international capital movements, and official transactions by central banks and governments. In essence, then, the balance of payments is a record of all the transactions between households, firms, and the government of one country and the rest of the world. Any transaction that leads to a *payment* by a country's residents (or government) is a deficit item, identified by a negative sign (−) when the actual numbers are given for the items listed in the second column of Table 33-1 on the facing page. Any transaction that leads to a *receipt* by a country's residents (or government) is a surplus item and is identified by a plus sign (+) when actual numbers are considered. Table 33-1 provides a list of the surplus and deficit items on international accounts.

Balance of payments
A system of accounts that measures transactions of goods, services, income, and financial assets between domestic households, businesses, and governments and residents of the rest of the world during a specific time period.

Accounting Identities

Accounting identities—definitions of equivalent values—exist for financial institutions and other businesses. We begin with simple accounting identities that must hold for families and then go on to describe international accounting identities.

Accounting identities
Values that are equivalent by definition.

If a family unit is spending more than its current income, the family unit must necessarily be doing one of the following:

1. Reducing its money holdings or selling stocks, bonds, or other assets
2. Borrowing
3. Receiving gifts from friends or relatives
4. Receiving public transfers from a government, which obtained the funds by taxing others (a transfer is a payment, in money or in goods or services, made without receiving goods or services in return)

We can use this information to derive an identity: If a family unit is currently spending more than it is earning, it must draw on previously acquired wealth, borrow, or receive either private or public aid. Similarly, an identity exists for a family unit that is

TABLE 33-1

Surplus (+) and Deficit (−) Items on the International Accounts

Surplus Items (+)	Deficit Items (−)
Exports of merchandise	Imports of merchandise
Private and governmental gifts from foreign residents	Private and governmental gifts to foreign residents
Foreign use of domestically operated travel and transportation services	Use of foreign-operated travel and transportation services
Foreign tourists' expenditures in this country	U.S. tourists' expenditures abroad
Foreign military spending in this country	Military spending abroad
Interest and dividend receipts from foreign entities	Interest and dividends paid to foreign individuals and businesses
Sales of domestic assets to foreign residents	Purchases of foreign assets
Funds deposited in this country by foreign residents	Funds placed in foreign depository institutions
Sales of gold to foreign residents	Purchases of gold from foreign residents
Sales of domestic currency to foreign residents	Purchases of foreign currency

currently spending less than it is earning: It must be increasing its money holdings or be lending and acquiring other financial assets, or it must pay taxes or bestow gifts on others. When we consider businesses and governments, each unit in each group faces its own accounting identities or constraints. Ultimately, *net* lending by households must equal *net* borrowing by businesses and governments.

DISEQUILIBRIUM Even though our individual family unit's accounts must balance, in the sense that the identity discussed previously must hold, sometimes the item that brings about the balance cannot continue indefinitely. *If family expenditures exceed family income and this situation is financed by borrowing, the household may be considered to be in disequilibrium because such a situation cannot continue indefinitely.* If such a deficit is financed by drawing on previously accumulated assets, the family may also be in disequilibrium because it cannot continue indefinitely to draw on its wealth.

Eventually, the family will find it impossible to continue that lifestyle. (Of course, if the family members are retired, they may well be in equilibrium by drawing on previously acquired assets to finance current deficits. This example illustrates that it is necessary to understand all circumstances fully before pronouncing an economic unit in disequilibrium.)

EQUILIBRIUM Individual households, businesses, and governments, as well as the entire group of all households, businesses, and governments, must eventually reach equilibrium. Certain economic adjustment mechanisms have evolved to ensure equilibrium. Deficit households must eventually increase their income or decrease their expenditures. They will find that they have to pay higher interest rates if they wish to borrow to finance their deficits. Eventually, their credit sources will dry up, and they will be forced into equilibrium. Businesses, on occasion, must lower costs or prices—or go bankrupt—to reach equilibrium.

AN ACCOUNTING IDENTITY AMONG NATIONS When people from different nations trade or interact, certain identities or constraints must also hold. People buy goods from people in other nations. They also lend to and present gifts to people in other nations. If residents of a nation interact with residents of other nations, an accounting identity ensures a balance (but not necessarily an equilibrium, as will soon become clear). Let's look at the three categories of balance of payments transactions: current account transactions, capital account transactions, and official reserve account transactions.

Current Account Transactions

Current account
A category of balance of payments transactions that measures the exchange of merchandise, the exchange of services, and unilateral transfers.

During any designated period, all payments and gifts that are related to the purchase or sale of both goods and services constitute the **current account** in international trade. Major types of current account transactions include the exchange of merchandise, the exchange of services, and unilateral transfers.

MERCHANDISE TRADE EXPORTS AND IMPORTS The largest portion of any nation's balance of payments current account is typically the importing and exporting of merchandise. During 2013, for example, as shown in lines 1 and 2 of Table 33-2 below, the United States exported an estimated $1,609.7 billion of merchandise and imported $2,404.5 billion. The balance of merchandise trade is defined as the difference between the value of merchandise exports and the value of merchandise imports. For 2013, the United States had a balance of merchandise trade deficit because the value of its merchandise imports exceeded the value of its merchandise exports. This deficit was about $794.8 billion (line 3).

SERVICE EXPORTS AND IMPORTS The balance of (merchandise) trade involves tangible items—things you can feel, touch, and see. Service exports and imports involve invisible or intangible items that are bought and sold, such as shipping, insurance, tourist expenditures, and banking services. Also, income earned by foreign residents on U.S. investments and income earned by U.S. residents on foreign investments are part of service imports and exports. As shown in lines 4 and 5 of Table 33-2, in 2013, estimated service exports were $564.6 billion, and service imports were $416.8 billion. Thus, the balance of services was about $147.8 billion in 2013 (line 6). Exports constitute receipts or inflows into the United States and are positive. Imports constitute payments abroad or outflows of money and are negative.

When we combine the balance of merchandise trade with the balance of services, we obtain a balance on goods and services equal to −$647.0 billion in 2013 (line 7).

TABLE 33-2

U.S. Balance of Payments Account, Estimated for 2013 (in billions of dollars)

Current Account		
(1) Exports of merchandise goods	+1,609.7	
(2) Imports of merchandise goods	−2,404.5	
(3) Balance of merchandise trade		−794.8
(4) Exports of services	+564.6	
(5) Imports of services	−416.8	
(6) Balance of services		+147.8
(7) Balance on goods and services [(3) + (6)]		−647.0
(8) Net unilateral transfers	−159.3	
(9) Balance on current account		−806.3
Capital Account		
(10) U.S. private capital going abroad	−299.2	
(11) Foreign private capital coming into the United States	+665.3*	
(12) Balance on capital account [(10) + (11)]		+366.1
(13) Balance on current account plus balance on capital account [(9) + (12)]		−440.2
Official Reserve Transactions Account		
(14) Official transactions balance		+440.2
(15) Total (balance)		0

Sources: U.S. Department of Commerce, Bureau of Economic Analysis; author's estimates.

*Includes an approximately $28 billion statistical discrepancy, probably uncounted capital inflows, many of which relate to the illegal drug trade.

UNILATERAL TRANSFERS U.S. residents give gifts to relatives and others abroad, the federal government makes grants to foreign nations, foreign residents give gifts to U.S. residents, and in the past some foreign governments have granted funds to the U.S. government. In the current account, we see that net unilateral transfers—the total amount of gifts given by U.S. residents and the government minus the total amount received from abroad by U.S. residents and the government—came to an estimated −\$159.3 billion in 2013 (line 8). The minus sign before the number for unilateral transfers means that U.S. residents and the U.S. government gave more to foreign residents than foreign residents gave to U.S. residents.

BALANCING THE CURRENT ACCOUNT The balance on current account tracks the value of a country's exports of goods and services (including income on investments abroad) and transfer payments (private and government) relative to the value of that country's imports of goods and services and transfer payments (private and government). In 2013, it was estimated to be −\$806.3 billion (line 9).

Go to www.econtoday.com/chap33 for the latest U.S. balance of payments data from the Bureau of Economic Analysis.

If the sum of net exports of goods and services plus net unilateral transfers plus net investment income exceeds zero, a* current account surplus *is said to exist. If this sum is negative, a* current account deficit *is said to exist. A current account deficit means that we are importing more goods and services than we are exporting. Such a deficit must be paid for by the export of financial assets.

WHAT IF... all governments attempted to require their nations to have current account surpluses?

By definition, a current account surplus arises in a nation when its residents export more goods and services than they import. The only way for some nations to have current account surpluses, though, is for others to operate with current account deficits. That is, residents of some countries must import more goods and services than they export in order for other nations to be able to export more goods and services than they import. Thus, if all governments were to require that their countries have current account surpluses, their efforts would be doomed to failure.

Capital Account Transactions

In world markets, it is possible to buy and sell not only goods and services but also financial assets. These international transactions are measured in the **capital account.** Capital account transactions occur because of foreign investments—either by foreign residents investing in the United States or by U.S. residents investing in other countries. The purchase of shares of stock in British firms on the London stock market by a U.S. resident causes an outflow of funds from the United States to Britain. The construction of a Japanese automobile factory in the United States causes an inflow of funds from Japan to the United States. Any time foreign residents buy U.S. government securities, there is an inflow of funds from other countries to the United States. Any time U.S. residents buy foreign government securities, there is an outflow of funds from the United States to other countries. Loans to and from foreign residents cause outflows and inflows.

Capital account
A category of balance of payments transactions that measures flows of financial assets.

Line 10 of Table 33-2 on the facing page indicates that in 2013, the value of private capital going out of the United States was an estimated −\$299.2 billion, and line 11 shows that the value of private capital coming into the United States (including a statistical discrepancy) was \$665.3 billion. U.S. capital going abroad constitutes payments or outflows and is therefore negative. Foreign capital coming into the United States constitutes receipts or inflows and is therefore positive. Thus, there was a positive net capital movement of \$366.1 billion into the United States (line 12). This net private flow of capital is also called the balance on capital account.

There is a relationship between the current account balance and the capital account balance, assuming no interventions by the finance ministries or central banks of nations.

In the absence of interventions by finance ministries or central banks, the current account balance and the capital account balance must sum to zero. Stated differently, the current account deficit must equal the capital account surplus when governments or central banks do not engage in foreign exchange interventions. In this situation, any nation experiencing a current account deficit, such as the United States, must also be running a capital account surplus.

This basic relationship is apparent in the United States, as you can see in Figure 33-1 below. As the figure shows, U.S. current account deficits experienced since the early 1980s have been balanced by private capital inflows and *official reserve transactions*, to which we now turn our attention.

Official Reserve Account Transactions

The third type of balance of payments transaction concerns official reserve assets, which consist of the following:

1. Foreign currencies
2. Gold
3. **Special drawing rights (SDRs)**, which are reserve assets that the **International Monetary Fund** created to be used by countries to settle international payment obligations
4. The reserve position in the International Monetary Fund
5. Financial assets held by an official agency, such as the U.S. Treasury Department

Special drawing rights (SDRs)
Reserve assets created by the International Monetary Fund for countries to use in settling international payment obligations.

International Monetary Fund
An agency founded to administer an international foreign exchange system and to lend to member countries that had balance of payments problems. The IMF now functions as a lender of last resort for national governments.

To consider how official reserve account transactions occur, look again at Table 33-2 on page 728. The surplus in the U.S. capital account was \$366.1 billion. But the deficit in the U.S. current account was −\$806.3 billion, so the United States had a net deficit

MyEconLab Real-time data

FIGURE 33-1

The Relationship between the Current Account and the Capital Account

The current account balance is the mirror image of the sum of the capital account balance and the official transactions balance. We can see this in years since 1970. When the current account balance was in surplus, the sum of the capital account balance and the official transactions balance was negative. When the current account balance was in deficit, the sum of the current account balance and the official transactions balance was positive.

Sources: International Monetary Fund; *Economic Indicators.*

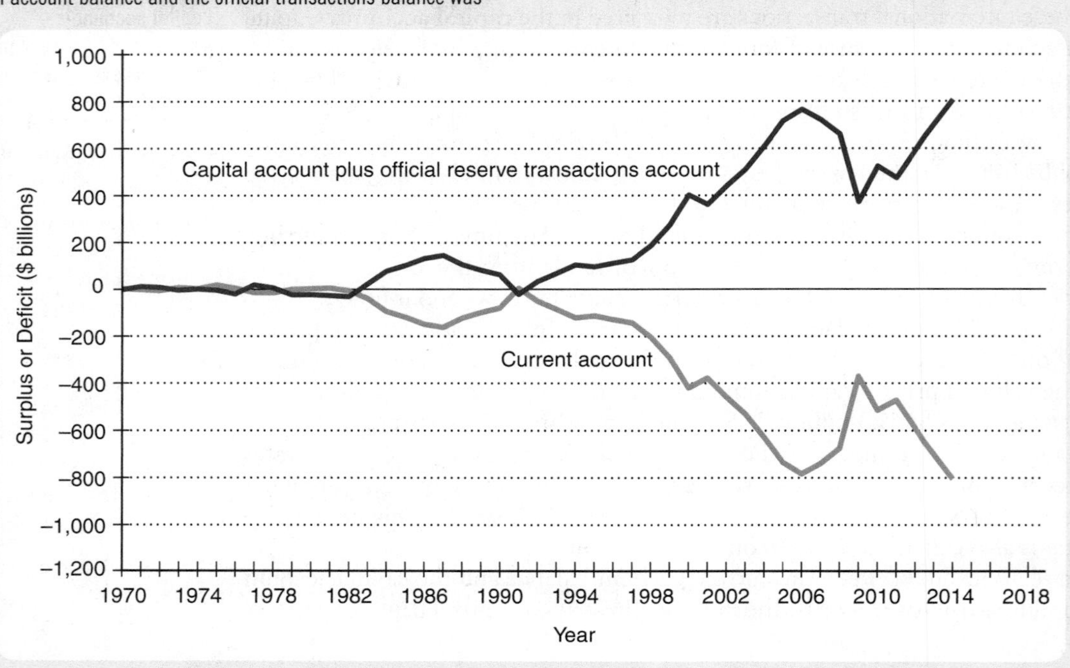

on the combined accounts (line 13) of −$440.2 billion. In other words, the United States obtained less in foreign funds in all its international transactions than it used. How is this deficiency made up? By foreign central banks and governments adding to their U.S. funds, shown by the +$440.2 billion in official transactions on line 14 in Table 33-2 on page 728. There is a plus sign on line 14 because this represents an *inflow* of foreign exchange in our international transactions.

The U.S. balance of payments deficit is measured by the official transactions figure on line 14. The balance (line 15) in Table 33-2 is zero, as it must be with double-entry bookkeeping. Hence, as shown in Figure 33-1 on the facing page, the current account balance is a mirror image of the sum of the capital account balance and the official reserve transactions account.

What Affects the Distribution of Account Balances within the Balance of Payments?

A major factor affecting the distribution of account balances within any nation's balance of payments is its rate of inflation relative to that of its trading partners. Assume that the rates of inflation in the United States and in the European Monetary Union (EMU)—the nations that use the euro as their currency—are equal. Now suppose that all of a sudden, the U.S. inflation rate increases. EMU residents will find that U.S. products are becoming more expensive, and U.S. firms will export fewer of them to EMU nations. At the current dollar-euro exchange rate, U.S. residents will find EMU products relatively cheaper, and they will import more. Other things being equal, the reverse will occur if the U.S. inflation rate suddenly falls relative to that of the EMU. All other things held constant, whenever the U.S. rate of inflation exceeds that of its trading partners, we expect to see a larger deficit in the U.S. balance of merchandise trade and in the U.S. current account balance. Conversely, when the U.S. rate of inflation is less than that of its trading partners, other things being constant, we expect to see a smaller deficit in the U.S. balance of merchandise trade and in the U.S. current account balance.

Another important factor that sometimes influences account balances within a nation's balance of payments is its relative political stability. Political instability causes *capital flight*. Owners of capital in countries anticipating or experiencing political instability will often move assets to countries that are politically stable, such as the United States. Hence, the U.S. capital account balance is likely to increase whenever political instability looms in other nations in the world.

QUICK QUIZ See page 746 for the answers. Review concepts from this section in MyEconLab.

The __________ of __________ reflects the value of all transactions in international trade, including goods, services, financial assets, and gifts.

The merchandise trade balance gives us the difference between exports and imports of __________ items.

Included in the __________ account along with merchandise trade are service exports and imports relating to commerce in intangible items, such as shipping, insurance, and tourist expenditures. The __________ account also includes income earned by foreign residents on U.S. investments and income earned by U.S. residents on foreign investments.

__________ __________ involve international private gifts and federal government grants or gifts to foreign nations.

When we add the balance of merchandise trade and the balance of services and take account of net unilateral transfers and net investment income, we come up with the balance on the __________ account, a summary statistic.

There are also __________ account transactions that relate to the buying and selling of financial assets. Foreign capital is always entering the United States, and U.S. capital is always flowing abroad. The difference is called the balance on the __________ account.

Another type of balance of payments transaction concerns the __________ __________ assets of individual countries, or what is often simply called official transactions. By standard accounting convention, official transactions are exactly equal to but opposite in sign from the sum of the current account balance and the capital account balance.

Account balances within a nation's balance of payments can be affected by its relative rate of __________ and by its __________ stability relative to other nations.

Determining Foreign Exchange Rates

When you buy foreign products, such as European pharmaceuticals, you have dollars with which to pay the European manufacturer. The European manufacturer, however, cannot pay workers in dollars. The workers are European, they live in Europe, and they must have euros to buy goods and services in nations that are members of the European Monetary Union (EMU) and use the euro as their currency. There must therefore be a way to exchange dollars for euros that the pharmaceuticals manufacturer will accept. That exchange occurs in a **foreign exchange market,** which in this case involves the exchange of euros and dollars.

Foreign exchange market
A market in which households, firms, and governments buy and sell national currencies.

Exchange rate
The price of one nation's currency in terms of the currency of another country.

The particular **exchange rate** between euros and dollars that prevails—the dollar price of the euro—depends on the current demand for and supply of euros and dollars. In a sense, then, our analysis of the exchange rate between dollars and euros will be familiar, for we have used supply and demand throughout this book. If it costs you $1.20 to buy 1 euro, that is the foreign exchange rate determined by the current demand for and supply of euros in the foreign exchange market. The European person going to the foreign exchange market would need about 0.83 euro to buy 1 dollar.

Now let's consider what determines the demand for and supply of foreign currency in the foreign exchange market. We will continue to assume that the only two regions in the world are Europe and the United States.

Demand for and Supply of Foreign Currency

You wish to purchase European-produced pharmaceuticals directly from a manufacturer located in Europe. To do so, you must have euros. You go to the foreign exchange market (or your U.S. bank). Your desire to buy the pharmaceuticals causes you to offer (supply) dollars to the foreign exchange market. Your demand for euros is equivalent to your supply of dollars to the foreign exchange market.

> ***Every U.S. transaction involving the importation of foreign goods constitutes a supply of dollars and a demand for some foreign currency, and the opposite is true for export transactions.***

In this case, the import transaction constitutes a demand for euros.

In our example, we will assume that only two goods are being traded, European pharmaceuticals and U.S. tablet devices. The U.S. demand for European pharmaceuticals creates a supply of dollars and a demand for euros in the foreign exchange market. Similarly, the European demand for U.S. tablet devices creates a supply of euros and a demand for dollars in the foreign exchange market. Under a system of **flexible exchange rates,** the supply of and demand for dollars and euros in the foreign exchange market will determine the equilibrium foreign exchange rate. The equilibrium exchange rate will tell us how many euros a dollar can be exchanged for—that is, the euro price of dollars—or how many dollars a euro can be exchanged for—the dollar price of euros.

Flexible exchange rates
Exchange rates that are allowed to fluctuate in the open market in response to changes in supply and demand. Sometimes called *floating exchange rates.*

The Equilibrium Foreign Exchange Rate

Go to **www.econtoday.com/chap33** for recent data from the Federal Reserve Bank of St. Louis on the exchange value of the U.S. dollar relative to the major currencies of the world.

To determine the equilibrium foreign exchange rate, we have to find out what determines the demand for and supply of foreign exchange. We will ignore for the moment any speculative aspect of buying foreign exchange. That is, we assume that there are no individuals who wish to buy euros simply because they think that their price will go up in the future.

The idea of an exchange rate is no different from the idea of paying a certain price for something you want to buy. Suppose that you have to pay about $1.50 for a cup of coffee. If the price goes up to $2.50, you will probably buy fewer cups. If the price goes down to 50 cents, you will likely buy more. In other words, the demand curve for cups of coffee, expressed in terms of dollars, slopes downward following the law of demand. The demand curve for euros slopes downward also, and we will see why.

Let's think more closely about the demand schedule for euros. If it costs you $1.10 to purchase 1 euro, that is the exchange rate between dollars and euros. If tomorrow you have to pay $1.25 for the same euro, the exchange rate would have changed. Looking at such a change, we would say that there has been an **appreciation** in the value of the euro in the foreign exchange market. But another way to view this increase in the value of the euro is to say that there has been a **depreciation** in the value of the dollar in the foreign exchange market. The dollar used to buy almost 0.91 euro, but tomorrow the dollar will be able to buy only 0.80 euro at a price of $1.25 per euro.

Appreciation
An increase in the exchange value of one nation's currency in terms of the currency of another nation.

Depreciation
A decrease in the exchange value of one nation's currency in terms of the currency of another nation.

If the dollar price of euros rises, you will probably demand fewer euros. Why? The answer lies in the reason you and others demand euros in the first place.

APPRECIATION AND DEPRECIATION OF EUROS Recall that in our example, you and others demand euros to buy European pharmaceuticals. The demand curve for European pharmaceuticals follows the law of demand and therefore slopes downward. If it costs more U.S. dollars to buy the same quantity of European pharmaceuticals, presumably you and other U.S. residents will not buy the same quantity. Your quantity demanded will be less. We say that your demand for euros is *derived from* your demand for European pharmaceuticals. In panel (a) of Figure 33-2 on the following page, we present the hypothetical demand schedule for packages of European pharmaceuticals by a representative set of U.S. consumers during a typical week. In panel (b) of Figure 33-2, we show graphically the U.S. demand curve for European pharmaceuticals in terms of U.S. dollars taken from panel (a).

AN EXAMPLE OF DERIVED DEMAND Let us assume that the price of a package of European pharmaceuticals in Europe is 100 euros. Given that price, we can find the number of euros required to purchase 500 packages of European pharmaceuticals. That information is given in panel (c) of Figure 33-2. If purchasing one package of European pharmaceuticals requires 100 euros, 500 packages require 50,000 euros. Now we have enough information to determine the derived demand curve for euros. If 1 euro costs $1.20, a package of pharmaceuticals would cost $120 (100 euros per package × $1.20 per euro = $120 per package). At $120 per package, the representative group of U.S. consumers would, we see from panel (a) of Figure 33-2, demand 500 packages of pharmaceuticals.

From panel (c), we see that 50,000 euros would be demanded to buy the 500 packages of pharmaceuticals. We show this quantity demanded in panel (d). In panel (e), we draw the derived demand curve for euros. Now consider what happens if the price of euros goes up to $1.25. A package of European pharmaceuticals priced at 100 euros in Europe would now cost $125. From panel (a), we see that at $125 per package, 300 packages of pharmaceuticals will be imported from Europe into the United States by our representative group of U.S. consumers. From panel (c), we see that 300 packages of pharmaceuticals would require 30,000 euros to be purchased. Thus, in panels (d) and (e), we see that at a price of $1.25 per euro, the quantity demanded will be 30,000 euros.

YOU ARE THERE

To consider how an appreciation of Brazil's currency has affected Brazilian spending on U.S. goods and services, take a look at **An Exchange-Rate-Induced U.S. Shopping *Bagunça* for Brazilians** on page 742.

We continue similar calculations all the way up to a price of $1.30 per euro. At that price, a package of European pharmaceuticals with a price of 100 euros in Europe would have a U.S. dollar price of $130, and our representative U.S. consumers would import only 100 packages of pharmaceuticals.

DOWNWARD-SLOPING DERIVED DEMAND As can be expected, as the price of the euro rises, the quantity demanded will fall. The only difference here from the standard demand analysis developed in Chapter 3 and used throughout this text is that the demand for euros is derived from the demand for a final product—European pharmaceuticals in our example.

SUPPLY OF EUROS Assume that European pharmaceutical manufacturers buy U.S. tablet devices. The supply of euros is a derived supply in that it is derived from the European demand for U.S. tablet devices. We could go through an example similar to the one for pharmaceuticals to come up with a supply schedule of euros in Europe. It slopes upward.

Panel (a)
Demand Schedule for Packages of European Pharmaceuticals in the United States per Week

Price per Package	Quantity Demanded
$130	100
125	300
120	500
115	700

Panel (b)
U.S. Demand Curve for European Pharmaceuticals

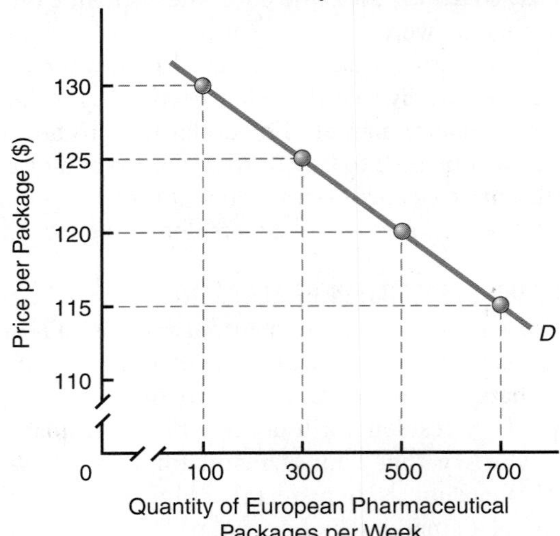

Panel (c)
Euros Required to Purchase Quantity Demanded (at P = 100 euros per package of pharmaceuticals)

Quantity Demanded	Euros Required
100	10,000
300	30,000
500	50,000
700	70,000

Panel (d)
Derived Demand Schedule for Euros in the United States with Which to Pay for Imports of Pharmaceuticals

Dollar Price of One Euro	Dollar Price of Pharmaceuticals	Quantity of Pharmaceuticals Demanded	Quantity of Euros Demanded per Week
$1.30	$130	100	10,000
1.25	125	300	30,000
1.20	120	500	50,000
1.15	115	700	70,000

FIGURE 33-2

Deriving the Demand for Euros

In panel (a), we show the demand schedule for European pharmaceuticals in the United States, expressed in terms of dollars per package of pharmaceuticals. In panel (b), we show the demand curve, *D*, which slopes downward. In panel (c), we show the number of euros required to purchase up to 700 packages of pharmaceuticals. If the price per package of pharmaceuticals is 100 euros, we can now find the quantity of euros needed to pay for the various quantities demanded. In panel (d), we see the derived demand for euros in the United States in order to purchase the various quantities of pharmaceuticals given in panel (a). The resultant demand curve, D_1, is shown in panel (e). This is the U.S. derived demand for euros.

Panel (e)
U.S. Derived Demand for Euros

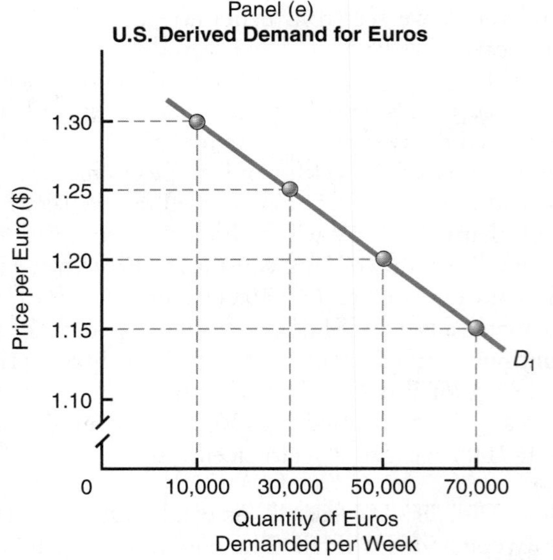

Obviously, Europeans want dollars to purchase U.S. goods. European residents will be willing to supply more euros when the dollar price of euros goes up, because they can then buy more U.S. goods with the same quantity of euros. That is, the euro would be worth more in exchange for U.S. goods than when the dollar price for euros was lower.

FIGURE 33-3

The Supply of Euros

If the market price of a U.S.-produced tablet device is $200, then at an exchange rate of $1.20 per euro, the price of the tablet to a European consumer is 167.67 euros. If the exchange rate rises to $1.25 per euro, the European price of the tablet falls to 160 euros. This induces an increase in the quantity of tablets demanded by European consumers and consequently an increase in the quantity of euros supplied in exchange for dollars in the foreign exchange market. In contrast, if the exchange rate falls to $1.15 per euro, the European price of the tablet rises to 173.91 euros. This causes a decrease in the quantity of tablets demanded by European consumers. As a result, there is a decline in the quantity of euros supplied in exchange for dollars in the foreign exchange market. Hence, the euro supply curve slopes up.

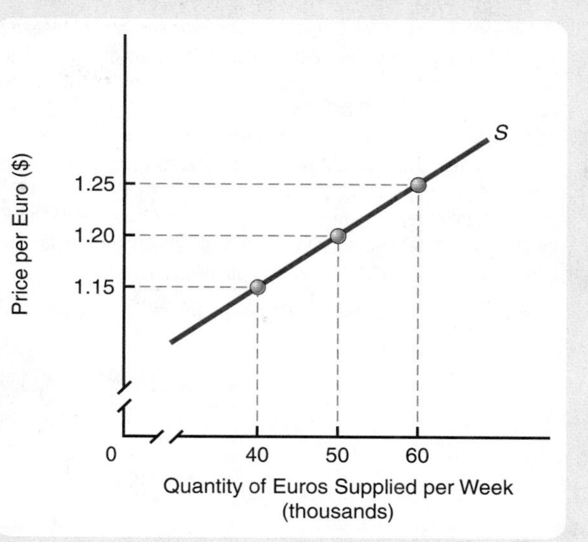

AN EXAMPLE Let's take an example. Suppose a U.S.-produced tablet device costs $200. If the exchange rate is $1.20 per euro, a European resident will have to come up with 166.67 euros ($200 ÷ $1.20 per euro = 166.67 euros) to buy one tablet. If, however, the exchange rate goes up to $1.25 per euro, a European resident must come up with only 160 euros ($200 ÷ $1.25 per euro = 160 euros) to buy a U.S. tablet. At this lower price (in euros) of U.S. tablets, Europeans will demand a larger quantity.

In other words, as the price of euros goes up in terms of dollars, the quantity of U.S. tablets demanded will go up, and hence the quantity of euros supplied will go up. Therefore, the supply schedule of euros, which is derived from the European demand for U.S. goods, will slope upward, as seen in Figure 33-3 above.

TOTAL DEMAND FOR AND SUPPLY OF EUROS Let us now look at the total demand for and supply of euros. We take all U.S. consumers of European pharmaceuticals and all European consumers of U.S. tablet devices and put their demands for and supplies of euros together into one diagram. Thus, we are showing the total demand for and total supply of euros. The horizontal axis in Figure 33-4 on the following page represents the quantity of foreign exchange—the number of euros per year. The vertical axis represents the exchange rate—the price of foreign currency (euros) expressed in dollars (per euro). The foreign currency price of $1.25 per euro means it will cost you $1.25 to buy 1 euro. At the foreign currency price of $1.20 per euro, you know that it will cost you $1.20 to buy 1 euro. The equilibrium, *E*, is again established at $1.20 for 1 euro.

In our hypothetical example, assuming that there are only representative groups of pharmaceutical consumers in the United States and tablet consumers in Europe, the equilibrium exchange rate will be set at $1.20 per euro.

This equilibrium is not established because U.S. residents like to buy euros or because Europeans like to buy dollars. Rather, the equilibrium exchange rate depends on how many tablet devices Europeans want and how many European pharmaceuticals U.S. residents want (given their respective incomes, their tastes, and, in our example, the relative prices of pharmaceuticals and tablet devices).

A SHIFT IN DEMAND Assume that a successful advertising campaign by U.S. pharmaceutical importers causes U.S. demand for European pharmaceuticals to rise. U.S. residents demand more pharmaceuticals at all prices. Their demand curve for European pharmaceuticals shifts outward to the right.

FIGURE 33-4

Total Demand for and Supply of Euros

The market supply curve for euros results from the total European demand for U.S. tablet devices. The demand curve, *D*, slopes downward like most demand curves, and the supply curve, *S*, slopes upward. The foreign exchange price, or the U.S. dollar price of euros, is given on the vertical axis. The number of euros is represented on the horizontal axis. If the foreign exchange rate is \$1.25—that is, if it takes \$1.25 to buy 1 euro—U.S. residents will demand 20 billion euros.

The equilibrium exchange rate is at the intersection of *D* and *S*, or point *E*. The equilibrium exchange rate is \$1.20 per euro. At this point, 30 billion euros are both demanded and supplied each year.

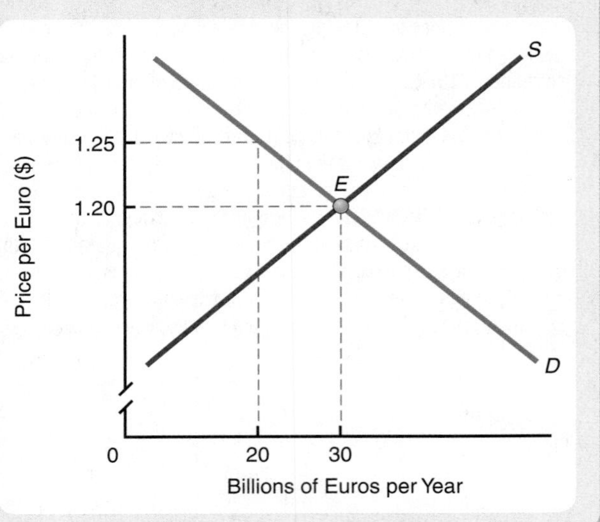

The increased demand for European pharmaceuticals can be translated into an increased demand for euros. All U.S. residents clamoring for European pharmaceuticals will supply more dollars to the foreign exchange market while demanding more euros to pay for the pharmaceuticals. Figure 33-5 below presents a new demand schedule, D_2, for euros. This demand schedule is to the right of the original demand schedule. If Europeans do not change their desire for U.S. tablet devices, the supply schedule for euros will remain stable.

A new equilibrium will be established at a higher exchange rate. In our particular example, the new equilibrium is established at an exchange rate of \$1.25 per euro. It now takes \$1.25 to buy 1 euro, whereas formerly it took \$1.20. This will be translated into an increase in the price of European pharmaceuticals to U.S. residents and into a decrease in the price of U.S. tablet devices to Europeans. For example, a package of European pharmaceuticals priced at 100 euros that sold for \$120 in the United States will now be priced at \$125. Conversely, a U.S. tablet priced at \$200 that previously sold for 166.67 euros will now sell for 160 euros.

FIGURE 33-5

A Shift in the Demand Schedule

The demand schedule for European pharmaceuticals shifts to the right, causing the derived demand schedule for euros to shift to the right also. We have shown this as a shift from D_1 to D_2. We have assumed that the supply schedule for euros has remained stable—that is, European demand for U.S. tablet devices has remained constant. The old equilibrium foreign exchange rate was \$1.20 per euro.

The new equilibrium exchange rate will be E_2. It will now cost \$1.25 to buy 1 euro. The higher price of euros will be translated into a higher U.S. dollar price for European pharmaceuticals and a lower euro price for U.S. tablet devices.

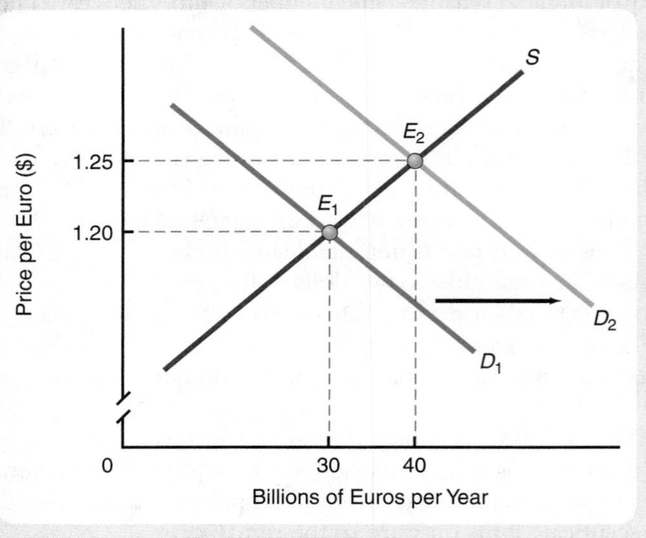

FIGURE 33-6

A Shift in the Supply of Euros

There has been a shift in the supply curve for euros. The new equilibrium will occur at E_1, meaning that $1.15, rather than $1.20, will now buy 1 euro. After the exchange rate adjustment, the annual amount of euros demanded and supplied will increase from 30 billion to 60 billion.

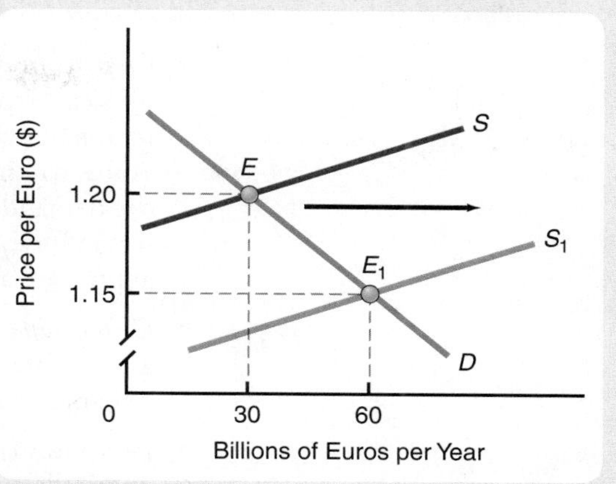

A SHIFT IN SUPPLY We just assumed that the U.S. demand for European pharmaceuticals shifted due to a successful ad campaign. The demand for euros is derived from the demand by U.S. residents for pharmaceuticals. This change in pharmaceuticals demand is translated into a shift in the demand curve for euros. As an alternative exercise, we might assume that the supply curve of euros shifts outward to the right. Such a supply shift could occur for many reasons, one of which is a relative rise in the European price level. For example, if the prices of all European-manufactured tablets went up 20 percent in euros, U.S. tablets would become relatively cheaper. That would mean that European residents would want to buy more U.S. tablets. But remember that when they want to buy more U.S. tablets, they supply more euros to the foreign exchange market.

Thus, we see in Figure 33-6 above that the supply curve of euros moves from S to S_1. In the absence of restrictions—that is, in a system of flexible exchange rates—the new equilibrium exchange rate will be $1.15 equals 1 euro. The quantity of euros demanded and supplied will increase from 30 billion per year to 60 billion per year. We say, then, that in a flexible international exchange rate system, shifts in the demand for and supply of foreign currencies will cause changes in the equilibrium foreign exchange rates. Those rates will remain in effect until world supply or demand shifts.

Which national currencies are most actively traded in global foreign exchange markets?

INTERNATIONAL EXAMPLE

The Most Traded Currencies in Foreign Exchange Markets

On a given day, the U.S. dollar is involved in more than 80 percent of trades of one currency for another in the world's foreign exchange markets. Thus, the dollar is utilized more than twice as often in exchange for other currencies as the second most commonly traded currency, the European euro. The dollar is involved in currency exchanges more than four times as often as either the Japanese yen or the British pound, the third and fourth most commonly exchanged currencies.

FOR CRITICAL THINKING

In light of the fact that the dollar valuation of all currency trades during a given year is $4 trillion, about how many U.S. dollars circulate within foreign exchange markets within a given year?

Market Determinants of Exchange Rates

The foreign exchange market is affected by many other variables in addition to changes in relative price levels, including the following:

- *Changes in real interest rates*. Suppose that the U.S. interest rate, corrected for people's expectations of inflation, increases relative to the rest of the world. Then international investors elsewhere seeking the higher returns now available in the United States will increase their demand for dollar-denominated assets, thereby increasing the demand for dollars in foreign exchange markets. An increased demand for dollars in foreign exchange markets, other things held constant, will cause the dollar to appreciate and other currencies to depreciate.
- *Changes in consumer preferences*. If Germany's citizens, for example, suddenly develop a taste for U.S.-made automobiles, this will increase the derived demand for U.S. dollars in foreign exchange markets.
- *Perceptions of economic stability*. As already mentioned, if the United States looks economically and politically more stable relative to other countries, more foreign residents will want to put their savings into U.S. assets rather than in their own domestic assets. This will increase the demand for dollars.

QUICK QUIZ See page 746 for the answers. Review concepts from this section in MyEconLab.

The foreign __________ __________ is the rate at which one country's currency can be exchanged for another's.

The __________ for foreign exchange is a derived __________, which is derived from the demand for foreign goods and services (and financial assets). The __________ of foreign exchange is derived from foreign residents' demands for U.S. goods and services.

The demand curve of foreign exchange slopes __________, and the supply curve of foreign exchange slopes __________. The equilibrium foreign exchange rate occurs at the intersection of the demand and supply curves for a currency.

A __________ in the demand for foreign goods will result in a shift in the __________ for foreign exchange, thereby changing the equilibrium foreign exchange rate. A shift in the supply of foreign currency will also cause a change in the equilibrium exchange rate.

The Gold Standard and the International Monetary Fund

The current system of more or less freely floating exchange rates is a relatively recent development. In the past, we have had periods of a gold standard, fixed exchange rates under the International Monetary Fund, and variants of the two.

The Gold Standard

Until the 1930s, many nations were on a gold standard. The value of their domestic currency was fixed, or *pegged*, in units of gold. Nations operating under this gold standard agreed to redeem their currencies for a fixed amount of gold at the request of any holder of that currency. Although gold was not necessarily the means of exchange for world trade, it was the unit to which all currencies under the gold standard were pegged. And because all currencies in the system were pegged to gold, exchange rates between those currencies were fixed.

Two problems plagued the gold standard, however. One was that by fixing the value of its currency in relation to the amount of gold, a nation gave up control of its domestic monetary policy. Another was that the world's commerce was at the mercy of gold discoveries. Throughout history, each time new veins of gold were found, desired domestic expenditures on goods and services increased. If production of goods and services failed to increase proportionately, inflation resulted.

Bretton Woods and the International Monetary Fund

On December 27, 1945, the world's capitalist countries, which in 1944 had sent representatives to meetings in Bretton Woods, New Hampshire, created a new permanent institution, the International Monetary Fund (IMF). The IMF's task was to lend to member countries for which the sum of the current account balance and the capital account balance was negative, thereby helping them maintain an offsetting surplus in their official reserve transactions accounts. Governments that joined the Bretton Woods system agreed to maintain the value of their currencies within 1 percent of the declared **par value**—the officially determined value. The United States, which owned most of the world's gold stock, was similarly obligated to maintain gold prices within a 1 percent margin of the official rate of $35 an ounce. Except for a transitional arrangement permitting a one-time adjustment of up to 10 percent in par value, members could alter exchange rates thereafter only with the approval of the IMF.

Par value
The officially determined value of a currency.

On August 15, 1971, President Richard Nixon suspended the convertibility of the dollar into gold. On December 18, 1971, the United States officially devalued the dollar—that is, lowered its official value—relative to the currencies of 14 major industrial nations. Finally, on March 16, 1973, the finance ministers of the European Economic Community (now the European Union) announced that they would let their currencies float against the dollar, something Japan had already begun doing with its yen. Since 1973, the United States and most other trading countries have had either freely floating exchange rates or managed ("dirty") floating exchange rates, in which their governments or central banks intervene from time to time to try to influence world market exchange rates.

Fixed versus Floating Exchange Rates

The United States went off the Bretton Woods system of fixed exchange rates in 1973. As Figure 33-7 below indicates, many other nations of the world have been less willing to permit the values of their currencies to vary in the foreign exchange markets.

Fixing the Exchange Rate

How did nations fix their exchange rates in years past? How do many countries accomplish this today? Figure 33-8 on the following page shows the market for dinars, the currency of Bahrain. At the initial equilibrium point E_1, U.S. residents had to give up $2.66 to obtain 1 dinar. Suppose now that there is an increase in the supply of dinars for dollars, perhaps because Bahraini residents wish to buy more U.S. goods.

FIGURE 33-7

Current Foreign Exchange Rate Arrangements

Today, 21 percent of the member nations of the International Monetary Fund have an independent float, and 24 percent have a managed float exchange rate arrangement. Another 12 percent of all nations use the currencies of other nations instead of issuing their own currencies. The remaining 43 percent of countries have fixed exchange rates.

Source: International Monetary Fund.

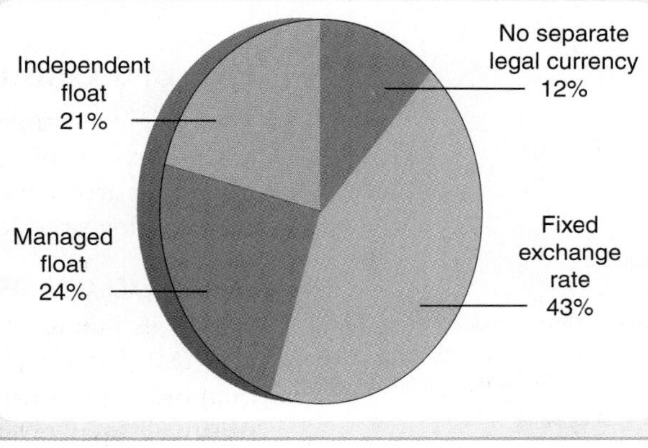

FIGURE 33-8

A Fixed Exchange Rate

This figure illustrates how the Central Bank of Bahrain could fix the dollar-dinar exchange rate in the face of an increase in the supply of dinars caused by a rise in the demand for U.S. goods by Bahraini residents. In the absence of any action by the Central Bank of Bahrain, the result would be a movement from point E_1 to point E_2. The dollar value of the dinar would fall from $2.66 to $2.00. The Central Bank of Bahrain can prevent this exchange rate change by purchasing dinars with dollars in the foreign exchange market, thereby increasing the demand for dinars. At the new equilibrium point, E_3, the dinar's value remains at $2.66.

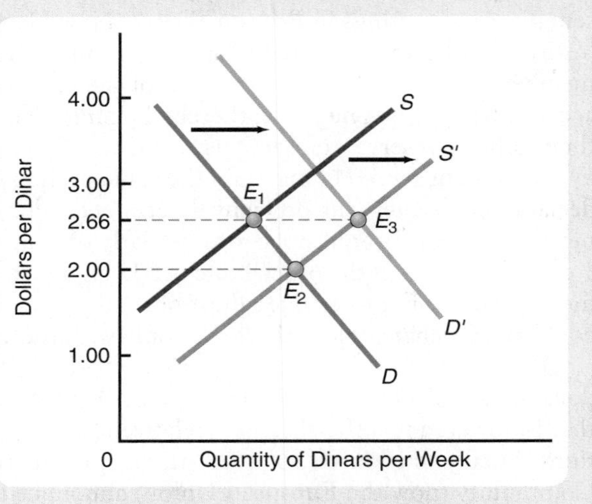

Other things being equal, the result would be a movement to point E_2 in Figure 33-8 above. The dollar value of the dinar would fall to $2.00.

To prevent a dinar depreciation from occurring, however, the Central Bank of Bahrain could increase the demand for dinars in the foreign exchange market by purchasing dinars with dollars. The Central Bank of Bahrain can do this using dollars that it has on hand as part of its *foreign exchange reserves*. All central banks hold reserves of foreign currencies. Because the U.S. dollar is a key international currency, the Central Bank of Bahrain and other central banks typically hold billions of dollars in reserve so that they can make transactions such as the one in this example.

Note that a sufficiently large purchase of dinars could, as shown in Figure 33-8, cause the demand curve to shift rightward to achieve the new equilibrium point E_3, at which the dinar's value remains at $2.66. Provided that it has enough dollar reserves on hand, the Central Bank of Bahrain could maintain—effectively fix—the exchange rate in the face of the rise in the supply of dinars.

The Central Bank of Bahrain has maintained the dollar-dinar exchange rate in this manner since 2001. This basic approach—varying the amount of the national currency demanded at any given exchange rate in foreign exchange markets when necessary—is also the way that *any* central bank seeks to keep its nation's currency value unchanged in light of changing market forces.

Central banks can keep exchange rates fixed as long as they have enough foreign exchange reserves to deal with potentially long-lasting changes in the demand for or supply of their nation's currency.

Pros and Cons of a Fixed Exchange Rate

Why might a nation such as Bahrain wish to keep the value of its currency from fluctuating? One reason is that changes in the exchange rate can affect the market values of assets that are denominated in foreign currencies. This can increase the financial risks that a nation's residents face, thereby forcing them to incur costs to avoid these risks.

Foreign exchange risk
The possibility that changes in the value of a nation's currency will result in variations in the market value of assets.

FOREIGN EXCHANGE RISK The possibility that variations in the market value of assets can take place due to changes in the value of a nation's currency is the **foreign exchange risk** that residents of a country face because their nation's currency value can vary. Suppose that companies in Bahrain have many loans denominated in dollars but earn nearly all their revenues in dinars from sales within Bahrain. A decline in the dollar value of the dinar would mean that Bahraini companies would have to allocate a larger portion of their earnings to make the same *dollar* loan payments as before. Thus, a fall in the dinar's value would increase the operating costs of these companies, thereby reducing their profitability and raising the likelihood of eventual bankruptcy.

Limiting foreign exchange risk is a classic rationale for adopting a fixed exchange rate. Nevertheless, a country's residents are not defenseless against foreign exchange risk. In what is known as a **hedge,** they can adopt strategies intended to offset the risk arising from exchange rate variations. For example, a company in Bahrain that has significant euro earnings from sales in Germany but sizable loans from U.S. investors could arrange to convert its euro earnings into dollars via special types of foreign exchange contracts called *currency swaps*. The Bahraini company could likewise avoid holdings of dinars and shield itself—*hedge*—against variations in the dinar's value.

Hedge
A financial strategy that reduces the chance of suffering losses arising from foreign exchange risk.

THE EXCHANGE RATE AS A SHOCK ABSORBER If fixing the exchange rate limits foreign exchange risk, why do so many nations allow the exchange rates to float? The answer must be that there are potential drawbacks associated with fixing exchange rates. One is that exchange rate variations can actually perform a valuable service for a nation's economy. Consider a situation in which residents of a nation speak only their own nation's language. As a result, the country's residents are very *immobile*: They cannot trade their labor skills outside their own nation's borders.

Now think about what happens if this nation chooses to fix its exchange rate. Imagine a situation in which other countries begin to sell products that are close substitutes for the products its people specialize in producing, causing a sizable drop in worldwide demand for that nation's goods. If wages and prices do not instantly and completely adjust downward, the result will be a sharp decline in production of goods and services, a falloff in national income, and higher unemployment. Contrast this situation with one which the exchange rate floats. In this case, a sizable decline in outside demand for the nation's products will cause it to experience a trade deficit, which will lead to a significant drop in the demand for that nation's currency. As a result, the nation's currency will experience a sizable depreciation, making the goods that the nation offers to sell abroad much less expensive in other countries. People abroad who continue to consume the nation's products will increase their purchases, and the nation's exports will increase. Its production will begin to recover somewhat, as will its residents' incomes. Unemployment will begin to fall.

This example illustrates how exchange rate variations can be beneficial, especially if a nation's residents are relatively immobile. It can be difficult, for example, for a Polish resident who has never studied Portuguese to move to Lisbon, even if she is highly qualified for available jobs there. If many residents of Poland face similar linguistic or cultural barriers, Poland could be better off with a floating exchange rate even if its residents must incur significant costs hedging against foreign exchange risk as a result.

How did having a separate currency and a floating exchange rate actually end up helping Poland in the early 2010s?

INTERNATIONAL POLICY EXAMPLE

Poland's Floating Exchange Rate Protects It from Euro Ills

During the 2000s, Estonia, Slovakia, and Slovenia rushed to adopt the euro as their currency, and other nations of Eastern Europe fixed their exchange rates in relation to the euro. In contrast, Poland retained its *zloty* currency and allowed its value to float in the foreign exchange market.

A European-wide economic slowdown that began during the early 2010s triggered downturns in Estonia, Slovakia, Slovenia, and other countries in Eastern Europe. When the Polish *zloty* depreciated sharply relative to the euro, Polish goods and services became cheaper for most Europeans. As a consequence, European spending on Polish merchandise exports rose sharply, and the Polish tourism industry boomed as more Europeans selected Poland as a less expensive vacation destination. By maintaining its own currency and a floating exchange rate, Poland thereby helped to insulate its economy from problems afflicting the rest of Europe. Thus, Poland was the only European Union nation to experience uninterrupted economic growth during the early 2010s.

FOR CRITICAL THINKING

Why do you suppose that the Polish unemployment rate remained stable during the early 2010s while unemployment rates elsewhere in Eastern Europe rose?

QUICK QUIZ See page 746 for the answers. Review concepts from this section in MyEconLab.

The International Monetary Fund was developed after World War II as an institution to maintain __________ exchange rates in the world. Since 1973, however, __________ exchange rates have disappeared in most major trading countries. For these nations, exchange rates are largely determined by the forces of demand and supply in global foreign exchange markets.

Central banks can fix exchange rates by buying or selling foreign __________ and thereby adding to or subtracting from their foreign exchange __________.

Although fixing the exchange rate helps protect a nation's residents from foreign exchange __________, this policy makes less mobile residents susceptible to greater volatility in income and employment.

YOU ARE THERE

An Exchange-Rate-Induced U.S. Shopping *Bagunça* for *Brazilians*

Ana Ligia Paladino has traveled 5,000 miles from her home in the southernmost part of Brazil to engage in a 10-day-long shopping spree in New York City. When Paladino emerges from her first morning of shopping at Macy's, the only words she can think of to describe her experience are, "It was a *bagunça*!"—that is, a combination of "mess" and "mayhem." During the year of her visit, Paladino is among 700,000 Brazilians to visit New York City, where Brazilians have spent more than $1.6 billion. Within the same year, Brazilians also have spent more than $2 billion in Florida. In both U.S. locations, Brazilians have outspent visitors from any other country in the world.

What has induced Paladino and so many other Brazilians to engage in spending in the United States is that the Brazilian currency, the *real,* can now buy a great deal more U.S. goods and services than was true previously. Indeed, during the two years prior to Paladino's visit, the *real* appreciated relative to the U.S. dollar by 25 percent. Thus, during her New York shopping *bagunça,* Paladino was able to buy about 25 percent more items in the United States than she could have bought 24 months earlier.

Critical Thinking Questions

1. What happened to the U.S. dollar's value in relation to the Brazilian *real* during the preceding two years?
2. Why do you suppose that more Brazilian students are now studying at U.S. colleges and universities than was true several years ago?

ISSUES & APPLICATIONS

Items "Made in China" Generate Income Elsewhere

CONCEPTS APPLIED

- Balance of Payments
- Merchandise Trade Deficit
- Balance on Goods and Services

In a typical year, the value of U.S. imports from China amounts to one-sixth of total U.S. import spending recorded in the nation's balance of payments. Expenditures on merchandise imported from China make up more than 70 percent of both the U.S. merchandise trade deficit and the U.S. balance on goods and services. These facts do not imply, however, that every dollar you spend as a consumer on an item "made in China" finds its way to people in China. In fact, less than half of each dollar you spend on Chinese merchandise actually reaches someone in China.

Only Part of the Price of a Chinese Import Is Chinese Income

Consider a toy action figure manufactured in China that has a price of $15 in the United States. A substantial portion of the U.S. retail price pays for transportation of the toy within the United States, rent for the U.S. retail outlet that sells the action figure, profits for the retailer's owners, and expenses incurred in marketing the toy. The latter expenses include the wages paid to managers and employees of the U.S. firms that marketed the action figure in the United States.

Alternatively, consider the iPhone, which earns substantial profits for U.S.-based Apple. iPhones are assembled in China from components that are made by and that generate revenues for firms located outside both the United States and China. Yet when an assembled iPhone is shipped from China for a U.S. consumer to purchase, that device is classified as a Chinese export and a U.S. import.

The U.S. Content of "Made in China"

Galina Hale and Bart Hoblin of the Federal Reserve Bank of San Francisco have calculated shares of spending on U.S. imports from China that flow to Chinese producers and to U.S. firms and their workers. They find that only 45 cents of each dollar U.S. consumers pay toward the price of a typical Chinese-imported good actually makes its way to China as income.

Thus, your spending on merchandise imported from China contributes dollar-for-dollar to the U.S. merchandise trade deficit, but fewer than half of the dollars that you spend on items "made in China" ultimately flow to that nation as income. The income that your spending generates is split among people who live in China, the United States, and sometimes—as in the case of iPhones—other nations.

For Critical Thinking

1. The United States is a net exporter of services to China. What does this imply about the magnitude of the deficit in the U.S. balance on goods and services with China compared with the size of the U.S. merchandise trade deficit with China?
2. Why does a portion of Chinese residents' expenditures on goods and services exported from the United States to China likely add to the earnings of Chinese firms and those firms' managers and workers?

Web Resources

1. To view key trade balance statistics for China, go to www.econtoday.com/chap33.
2. For a look at U.S. balance of payments data, go to www.econtoday.com/chap33.

MyEconLab

For more questions on this chapter's Issues & Applications, go to MyEconLab. In the Study Plan for this chapter, select Section N: News.

MyEconLab

Here is what you should know after reading this chapter. MyEconLab will help you identify what you know, and where to go when you need to practice.

WHAT YOU SHOULD KNOW		WHERE TO GO TO PRACTICE
The Balance of Trade versus the Balance of Payments The balance of trade is the difference between exports and imports of physical goods, or merchandise, during a given period. The balance of payments is a system of accounts for all transactions between a nation's residents and the residents of other countries of the world.	balance of trade, 726 balance of payments, 726 accounting identities, 726	• MyEconLab Study Plan 33.1

MyEconLab *continued*

WHAT YOU SHOULD KNOW		WHERE TO GO TO PRACTICE
The Key Accounts within the Balance of Payments There are three accounts within the balance of payments. The current account measures net exchanges of goods and services, transfers, and income flows across a nation's borders. The capital account measures net flows of financial assets. The official reserve transactions account tabulates exchanges of financial assets involving the home nation's and foreign nations' governments and central banks. Because each international exchange generates both an inflow and an outflow, the sum of the balances on all three accounts must equal zero.	current account, 728 capital account, 729 special drawing rights (SDRs), 730 International Monetary Fund, 730 **Key Figure** Figure 33-1, 730	• MyEconLab Study Plan 33.1 • Animated Figure 33-1
Exchange Rate Determination in the Market for Foreign Exchange From the perspective of the United States, the demand for a nation's currency by U.S. residents is derived largely from the demand for imports from that nation. Likewise, the supply of a nation's currency is derived mainly from the supply of U.S. exports to that country. The equilibrium exchange rate is the rate of exchange between the dollar and the other nation's currency at which the quantity of the currency demanded is equal to the quantity supplied.	foreign exchange market, 732 exchange rate, 732 flexible exchange rates, 732 appreciation, 733 depreciation, 733 **Key Figures** Figure 33-2, 734 Figure 33-3, 735 Figure 33-4, 736 Figure 33-5, 736	• MyEconLab Study Plan 33.2 • Animated Figures 33-2, 33-3, 33-4, 33-5
Factors That Can Induce Changes in Equilibrium Exchange Rates The equilibrium exchange rate changes in response to changes in the demand for or supply of another nation's currency. Changes in desired flows of exports or imports, real interest rates, tastes and preferences of consumers, and perceptions of economic stability affect the positions of the demand and supply curves in foreign exchange markets and induce variations in equilibrium exchange rates.	**Key Figure** Figure 33-6, 737	• MyEconLab Study Plan 33.2 • Animated Figure 33-6
How Policymakers Can Attempt to Keep Exchange Rates Fixed If the current price of the home currency in terms of another nation's currency starts to fall below the level where the home country wants it to remain, the home country's central bank can use reserves of the other nation's currency to purchase the home currency in foreign exchange markets. This raises the demand for the home currency and thereby pushes up the currency's value in terms of the other nation's currency.	par value, 739 foreign exchange risk, 740 hedge, 741 **Key Figure** Figure 33-8, 740	• MyEconLab Study Plans 33.3, 33.4 • Animated Figure 33-8

Log in to MyEconLab, take a chapter test, and get a personalized Study Plan that tells you which concepts you understand and which ones you need to review. From there, MyEconLab will give you further practice, tutorials, animations, videos, and guided solutions. For more information, visit www.myeconlab.com

PROBLEMS

All problems are assignable in MyEconLab; *exercises that update with real-time data are marked with* . *Answers to the odd-numbered problems appear at the back of the book.*

33-1. Suppose that during a recent year for the United States, merchandise imports were $2 trillion, unilateral transfers were a net outflow of $0.2 trillion, service exports were $0.2 trillion, service imports were $0.1 trillion, and merchandise exports were $1.4 trillion. (See pages 728–729.)

a. What was the merchandise trade deficit?

b. What was the balance on goods and services?

c. What was the current account balance?

33-2. Suppose that during a recent year for the United States, the current account balance was −0.2 trillion, the flow of U.S. private holdings of assets abroad was −$0.1 trillion, and the flow of foreign private assets held in the United States was +0.2 trillion. (See pages 729–730.)

a. What was the balance on the capital account during the year?

b. What was the change in official reserves during the year?

33-3. Over the course of a year, a nation tracked its foreign transactions and arrived at the following amounts:

Merchandise exports	500
Service exports	75
Net unilateral transfers	10
Domestic assets abroad (capital outflows)	−200
Foreign assets at home (capital inflows)	300
Changes in official reserves	−35
Merchandise imports	600
Service imports	50

What are this nation's balance of trade, current account balance, and capital account balance? (See pages 728–730.)

33-4. Identify whether each of the following items creates a surplus item or a deficit item in the current account of the U.S. balance of payments. (See page 726.)

a. A Central European company sells products to a U.S. hobby-store chain.

b. Japanese residents pay a U.S. travel company to arrange hotel stays, ground transportation, and tours of various U.S. cities, including New York, Chicago, and Orlando.

c. A Mexican company pays a U.S. accounting firm to audit its income statements.

d. U.S. churches and mosques send relief aid to Pakistan following a major earthquake in that nation.

e. A U.S. microprocessor manufacturer purchases raw materials from a Canadian firm.

33-5. Explain how the following events would affect the market for the Mexican peso, assuming a floating exchange rate. (See pages 735–737.)

a. Improvements in Mexican production technology yield superior guitars, and many musicians around the world buy these guitars.

b. Perceptions of political instability surrounding regular elections in Mexico make international investors nervous about future business prospects in Mexico.

33-6. Explain how the following events would affect the market for South Africa's currency, the rand, assuming a floating exchange rate. (See page 736.)

a. A rise in U.S. inflation causes many U.S. residents to seek to buy gold, which is a major South African export good, as a hedge against inflation.

b. Major discoveries of the highest-quality diamonds ever found occur in Russia and Central Asia, causing a significant decline in purchases of South African diamonds.

33-7. Suppose that the following two events take place in the market for China's currency, the yuan: U.S. parents are more willing than before to buy action figures and other Chinese toy exports, and China's government tightens restrictions on the amount of U.S. dollar–denominated financial assets that Chinese residents may legally purchase. What happens to the dollar price of the yuan? Does the yuan appreciate or depreciate relative to the dollar? (See pages 735–737.)

33-8. On Wednesday, the exchange rate between the Japanese yen and the U.S. dollar was $0.010 per yen. On Thursday, it was $0.009. Did the dollar appreciate or depreciate against the yen? By how much, expressed as a percentage change? (See page 730.)

33-9. On Wednesday, the exchange rate between the euro and the U.S. dollar was $1.20 per euro, and the exchange rate between the Canadian dollar and the U.S. dollar was U.S. $1.05 per Canadian dollar. What is the exchange rate between the Canadian dollar and the euro? (See page 730.)

33-10. Suppose that signs of an improvement in the Japanese economy lead international investors to resume lending to the Japanese government and businesses. How would this event affect the market for the yen? How should the central bank, the Bank of Japan, respond to this event if it wants to keep the value of the yen unchanged? (See pages 739–740.)

33-11. Briefly explain the differences between a flexible exchange rate system and a fixed exchange rate system. (See pages 738–739.)

33-12. Suppose that under a gold standard, the U.S. dollar is pegged to gold at a rate of $35 per ounce and the pound sterling is pegged to gold at a rate of £17.50 per ounce. Explain how the gold standard constitutes an exchange rate arrangement between the dollar and the pound. What is the exchange rate between the U.S. dollar and the pound sterling? (See pages 738–739.)

33-13. Suppose that under the Bretton Woods system, the dollar is pegged to gold at a rate of $35 per ounce and the pound sterling is pegged to the dollar at a rate of $2 = £1. If the dollar is devalued against gold and the pegged rate is changed to $40 per ounce, what does this imply for the exchange value of the pound in terms of dollars? (See page 739.)

33-14. Suppose that the People's Bank of China wishes to peg the rate of exchange of its currency, the yuan, in terms of the U.S. dollar. In each of the following situations, should it add to or subtract from its dollar foreign exchange reserves? Why? (See pages 739–740.)

a. U.S. parents worrying about safety begin buying fewer Chinese-made toys for their children.

b. U.S. interest rates rise relative to interest rates in China, so Chinese residents seek to purchase additional U.S. financial assets.

c. Chinese furniture manufacturers produce high-quality early American furniture and successfully export large quantities of the furniture to the United States.

ECONOMICS ON THE NET

Daily Exchange Rates It is easy to keep up with daily changes in exchange rates by using the Web site of Oanda.com. In this application, you will learn how hard it is to predict exchange rate movements, and you will get some practice thinking about what factors can cause exchange rates to change.

Title: Oanda Currency Converter

Navigation: Go to **www.econtoday.com/chap33** to visit the Oanda.com's currency converter home page. Click on *Foreign Exchange 12 PM Rates*.

Application Answer the following questions.

1. Choose a currency from the many available in the drop-down menu. How many dollars does it take to purchase a unit of the currency in the spot foreign exchange market?

2. For currency you chose in Question 1, keep track of its value relative to the dollar over the course of several days. Based on your tabulations, try to predict the value of the currency at the end of the week *following* your data collections. Use any information you may have, or just do your best without any additional information. How far off did your prediction turn out to be?

For Group Study and Analysis Divide the class into groups, and assign a currency to each group. Ask the group to track the currency's value over the course of two days and to determine whether the currency's value appreciated or depreciated relative to the dollar from one day to the next. In addition, ask each group to discuss what kinds of demand or supply shifts could have caused the change that occurred during this interval.

ANSWERS TO QUICK QUIZZES

p. 731: (i) balance . . . payments; (ii) physical; (iii) current . . . current; (iv) Unilateral transfers; (v) current; (vi) capital . . . capital; (vii) official reserve; (viii) inflation . . . political

p. 738: (i) exchange rate; (ii) demand . . . demand . . . supply; (iii) downward . . . upward; (iv) shift . . . demand

p. 742: (i) fixed . . . fixed; (ii) currencies . . . reserves; (iii) risk

Answers to Odd-Numbered Problems

CHAPTER 1

1-1. Economics is the study of how individuals allocate limited resources to satisfy unlimited wants.

a. Among the factors that a rational, self-interested student will take into account are her income, the price of the textbook, her anticipation of how much she is likely to study the textbook, and how much studying the book is likely to affect her grade.

b. A rational, self-interested government official will, for example, recognize that higher taxes will raise more funds for mass transit while making more voters, who have limited resources, willing to elect other officials.

c. A municipality's rational, self-interested government will, for instance, take into account that higher hotel taxes will produce more funds if as many visitors continue staying at hotels, but that the higher taxes will also discourage some visitors from spending nights at hotels.

1-3. Because wants are unlimited, the phrase applies to very high-income households as well as low- and middle-income households. Consider, for instance, a household with a low income and unlimited wants at the beginning of the year. The household's wants will still remain unlimited if it becomes a high-income household later in the year.

1-5. Sally is displaying rational behavior if all of these activities are in her self-interest. For example, Sally likely derives intrinsic benefit from volunteer and extracurricular activities and may believe that these activities, along with good grades, improve her prospects of finding a job after she completes her studies. Hence, these activities are in her self-interest even though they reduce some available study time.

1-7. The rationality assumption states that people do not intentionally make choices that leave them worse off. The bounded rationality hypothesis suggests that people are *almost*, but not completely, rational.

1-9. Suppose that a person faces a change in the environment, and the person adjusts to this change as predicted by the rationality assumption. If the new environment becomes predictable, then the individual who actually behaves as predicted by the traditional rationality assumption may settle into behavior that *appears* to involve repetitive applications of a rule of thumb.

1-11. **a.** Rationality assumption

b. Bounded rationality

c. Bounded rationality

1-13. **a.** The model using prices from the Iowa Electronic Market is more firmly based on the rationality assumption, because people who trade assets on this exchange that are based on poor forecasts actually experience losses. This gives them a strong incentive to make the best possible forecasts. Unpaid respondents to opinion polls have less incentive to give truthful answers about whether and how they will vote.

b. An economist would develop a means of evaluating whether prices in the Iowa Electronic Market or results of opinion polls did a better job of matching actual electoral outcomes.

1-15. **a.** Positive

b. Normative

c. Normative

d. Positive

APPENDIX A

A-1. **a.** Independent: price of a notebook; Dependent: quantity of notebooks

b. Independent: work-study hours; Dependent: credit hours

c. Independent: hours of study; Dependent: economics grade

A-3. **a.** Above x axis; to left of y axis

b. Below x axis, to right of y axis

c. On x axis; to right of y axis

A-5.

y	*x*
−20	−4
−10	−2
0	0
10	2
20	4

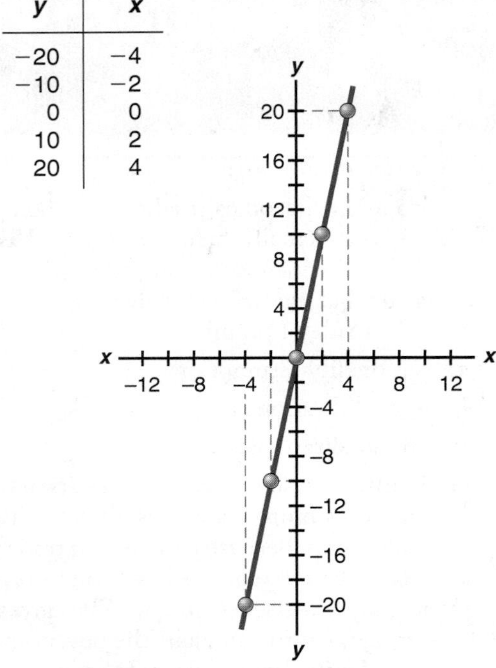

A-7. Each one-unit increase in *x* yields a 5-unit increase in *y*, so the slope given by the change in *y* corresponding to the change in *x* is equal to 5.

CHAPTER 2

2-1. The opportunity cost of attending a class at 11:00 a.m. is the next-best use of that hour of the day. Likewise, the opportunity cost of attending an 8:00 a.m. class is the next-best use of that particular hour of the day. If you are an early riser, it is arguable that the opportunity cost of the 8:00 a.m. hour is lower, because you will already be up at that time but have fewer choices compared with the 11:00 a.m. hour when shops, recreation centers, and the like are open. If you are a late riser, it may be that the opportunity cost of the 8:00 a.m. hour is higher, because you place a relatively high value on an additional hour of sleep in the morning.

2-3. The opportunity cost is the cost of the single, next-best forgone alternative to the \$100 spent on the concert ticket, which for your friend was a restaurant meal she otherwise could have purchased and which for you was movie downloads that you otherwise could have bought.

2-5. The bank apparently determined that the net gain anticipated from trying to sell the house to someone else, taking into account the opportunity cost of resources that the bank would have had to devote to renovating the house, was less than \$10.

2-7. If the student allocates additional study time to economics in order to increase her score from 90 to 100, her biology score declines from 50 to 40, so the opportunity cost of earning 10 additional points in economics is 10 fewer points in biology.

2-9.

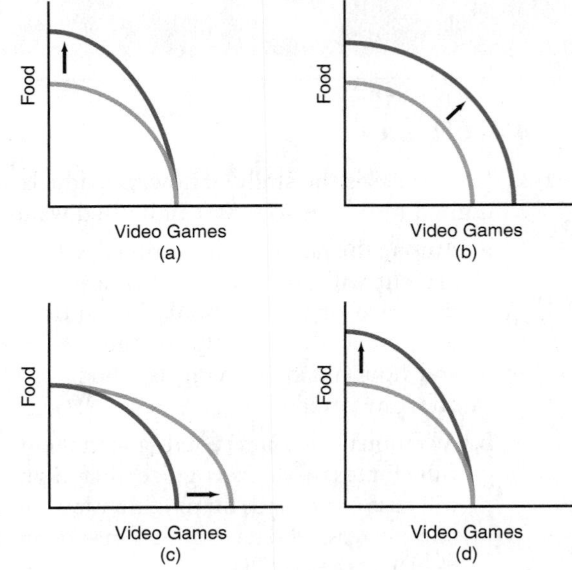

2-11. D

2-13. **a.** If the nation's residents increase production of consumption goods from 0 units to 10 units, the opportunity cost is 3 units of human capital forgone. If the nation's residents increase production of consumption goods from 0 units to 60 units, the opportunity cost is 100 units of human capital.

b. Yes, because successive 10-unit increases in production of consumption goods generate larger sacrifices of human capital, equal to 3, 7, 15, 20, 25, and 30.

2-15. Because it takes you less time to do laundry, you have an absolute advantage in laundry. Neither you nor your roommate has an absolute advantage in meal preparation. You require 2 hours to fold a basket of laundry, so your opportunity cost of folding a basket of laundry is 2 meals. Your roommate's opportunity cost of folding a basket of laundry is 3 meals. Hence, you have a comparative advantage in laundry, and your roommate has a comparative advantage in meal preparation.

2-17. It may be that the professor is very proficient at doing yard work relative to teaching and research activities, so in fact the professor may have a comparative advantage in doing yard work.

CHAPTER 3

3-1. The equilibrium price is \$410 per tablet device, and the equilibrium quantity is 80 million tablet devices. At a price of \$400 per tablet device, the quantity of tablet devices demanded is 90 million, and the quantity of tablet devices supplied is 60 million.

Hence, there is a shortage of 30 million tablet devices at a price of $400 per tablet device.

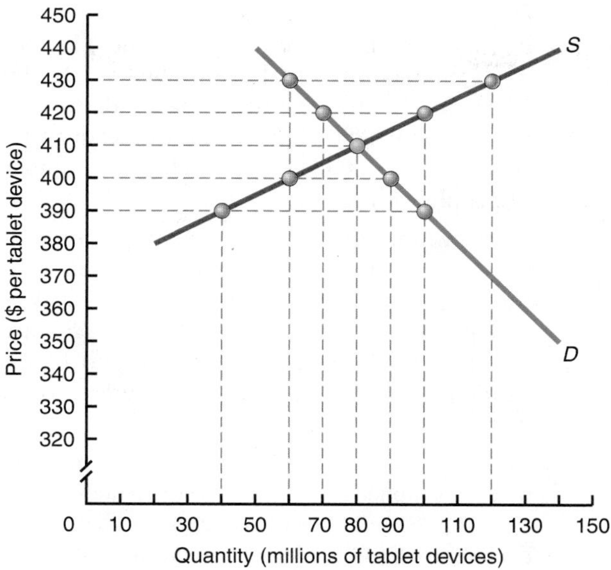

3-3. a. Wireless and cable Internet access services are substitutes, so a reduction in the price of wireless Internet access services causes a decrease in the demand for cable-based Internet access services.

b. A decrease in the price of cable-based Internet access services generates an increase in the quantity of these services demanded.

c. Cable-based Internet access services are a normal good, so a fall in the incomes of consumers reduces the demand for these services.

d. If consumers' tastes shift away from wireless Internet access services in favor of cable-based Internet services, then the demand for the latter services increases.

3-5. a. Complement: eggs; Substitute: sausage

b. Complement: tennis balls; Substitute: racquetball racquets

c. Complement: cream; Substitute: tea

d. Complement: gasoline; Substitute: city bus

3-7. b and d

3-9. a. At the $1,000 rental rate, the quantity of one-bedroom apartments supplied is 3,500 per month, but the quantity demanded is only 2,000 per month. Thus, the excess quantity of one-bedroom apartments supplied equals 1,500 apartments per month.

b. To induce consumers to lease unrented one-bedroom apartments, some landlords will reduce their rental rates. As they do so, the quantity demanded will increase. In addition, some landlords will choose not to offer apartments for rent at lower rates, and the quantity supplied will decrease. At the equilibrium rental rate of $800 per month, no excess quantity will be supplied.

c. At the $600 rental rate, the quantity of one-bedroom apartments demanded is 3,000 per month, but the quantity supplied is only 1,500 per month. Thus, the excess quantity of one-bedroom apartments demanded equals 1,500 apartments per month.

d. To induce landlords to make more one-bedroom apartments available for rent, some consumers will offer to pay higher rental rates. As they do so, the quantity supplied will increase. In addition, some consumers will choose not to try to rent apartments at higher rates, and the quantity demanded will decrease. At the equilibrium rental rate of $800 per month, no excess quantity will be demanded.

3-11 a. Because touchscreens are an input in the production of smartphones, a decrease in the price of touchscreens causes an increase in the supply of smartphones. The market supply curve shifts to the right, which causes the market price of smartphones to fall and the equilibrium quantity of smartphones to increase.

b. Machinery used to produce smartphones is an input in the production of these devices, so an increase in the price of machinery generates a decrease in the supply of smartphones. The market supply curve shifts to the left, which causes the market price of smartphones to rise and the equilibrium quantity of smartphones to decrease.

c. An increase in the number of manufacturers of smartphones causes an increase in the supply of smartphones. The market supply curve shifts rightward. The market price of smartphones declines, and the equilibrium quantity of smartphones increases.

d. The demand curve for smartphones shifts to the left along the same supply curve, so the quantity supplied decreases. The market price falls, and the equilibrium quantity declines.

3-13. Aluminum is an input in the production of canned soft drinks, so an increase in the price of aluminum reduces the supply of canned soft drinks (option c). The resulting rise in the market price of canned soft drinks brings about a decrease in the quantity of canned soft drinks demanded (option b). In equilibrium, the quantity of soft drinks supplied decreases (option d) to an amount equal to the quantity demanded. The demand curve does not shift, however, so option b does not apply.

CHAPTER 4

4-1. The ability to produce basic cell phones at lower cost and the entry of additional producers shift the supply curve rightward, from S_1 to S_2. At the same time, reduced prices of substitute smartphones result in a leftward shift in the demand for basic cell phones, from D_1 to D_2. Consequently, the equilibrium price of basic cell phones declines, from P_1 to P_2. The equilibrium quantity may rise, fall, or, as shown in the diagram, remain unchanged.

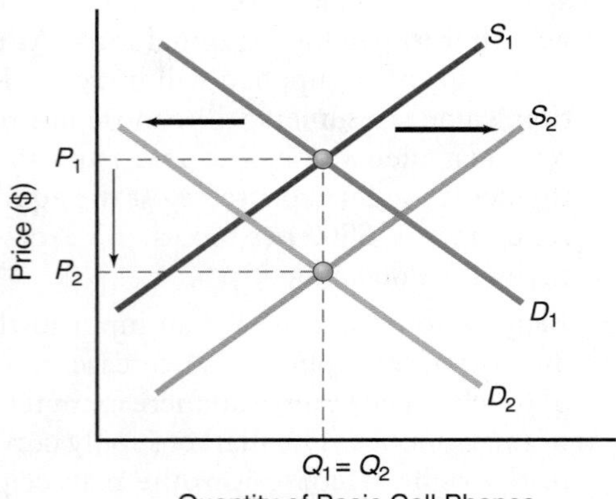

4-3. An increase in demand for GPS devices and an accompanying reduction in supply of GPS devices could result in an unambiguous increase in the market clearing price but with no change in the equilibrium quantity.

4-5. The market rental rate is $700 per apartment, and the equilibrium quantity of apartments rented to tenants is 2,000. At a ceiling price of $650 per month, the number of apartments students desire to rent increases to 2,500 apartments. At the ceiling price, the number of apartments that owners are willing to supply decreases to 1,800 apartments. Thus, there is a shortage of 700 apartments at the ceiling price, and only 1,800 are rented at the ceiling price.

4-7. The market price is $400, and the equilibrium quantity of seats is 1,600. If airlines cannot sell tickets to more than 1,200 passengers, then passengers are willing to pay $600 per seat. Normally, airlines would be willing to sell each ticket for $200, but they will be able to charge a price as high as $600 for each of the 1,200 tickets they sell. Hence, the quantity of tickets sold declines from 1,600, and the price of a ticket rises from $400 to as high as $600.

4-9. **a.** Consumers buy 10 billion kilograms at the support price of $0.20 per kilogram and hence spend $2 billion on wheat.

b. The amount of surplus wheat at the support price is 8 billion kilograms, so at the $0.20-per-kilogram support price, the government must spend $1.6 billion to purchase this surplus wheat.

c. Pakistani wheat farmers receive a total of $3.6 billion for the wheat they produce at the support price.

4-11. **a.** At the present minimum wage of $11 per hour, the quantity of labor supplied is 102,000 workers, and the quantity of labor demanded by firms is 98,000. There is an excess quantity supplied of 4,000 workers, which is the number of people who are unemployed.

b. At a minimum wage of $9 per hour, nothing would prevent market forces from pushing the wage rate to the market clearing level of $10 per hour. This $10-per-hour wage rate would exceed the legal minimum and hence would prevail. There would be no unemployed workers.

c. At a $12-per-hour minimum wage, the quantity of labor supplied would increase to 104,000 workers, and the quantity of labor demanded would decline to 96,000. There would be an excess quantity of labor supplied equal to 8,000 workers, which would then be the number of people unemployed.

4-13. **a.** The rise in the number of wheat producers causes the market supply curve to shift rightward, so more wheat is supplied at the support price.

b. The quantity of wheat demanded at the same support price is unchanged.

c. Because quantity demanded is unchanged while quantity supplied has increased, the amount of surplus wheat that the government must purchase has risen.

CHAPTER 5

5-1. In the absence of laws forbidding cigar smoking in public places, people who are bothered by the odor of cigar smoke will experience costs not borne by cigar producers. Because the supply of cigars will not reflect these costs, from society's perspective, the market cigar supply curve will be in a position too far to the right. The market price of cigars will be too low, and too many cigars will be produced and consumed.

5-3. Imposing the tax on pesticides causes an increase in the price of pesticides, which are an input in the production of oranges. Hence, the supply curve in the orange market shifts leftward. The market price of oranges increases, and the equilibrium quantity of oranges declines. Thus, orange consumers indirectly help to pay for dealing with the spillover costs of pesticide production by paying more for oranges.

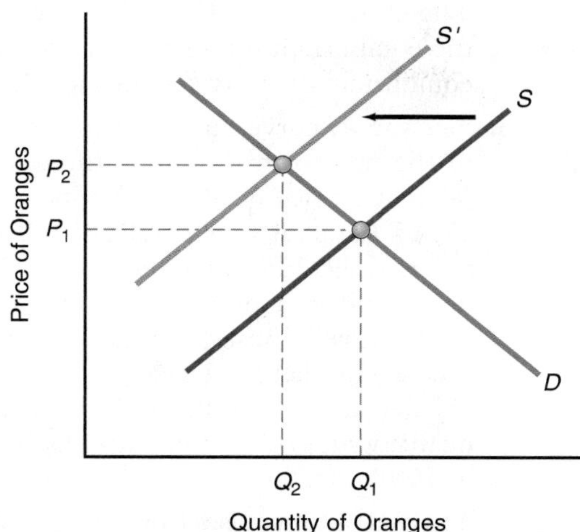

5-5. **a.** As shown in the figure below, if the social benefits associated with bus ridership were taken into account, the demand schedule would be D' instead of D, and the market price would be higher. The equilibrium quantity of bus rides would be higher.

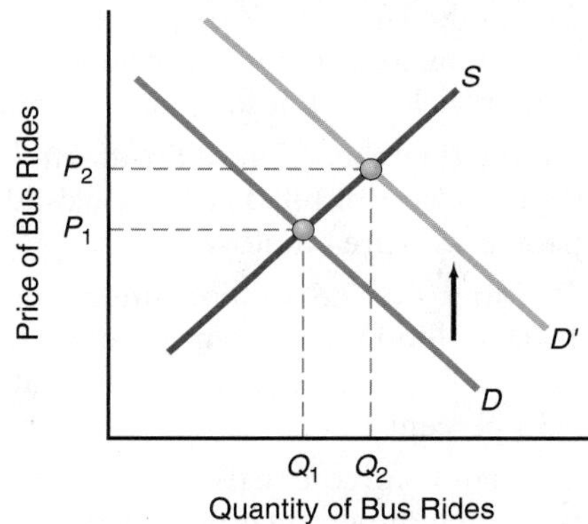

b. The government could pay commuters a subsidy to ride the bus, thereby shifting the demand curve outward and to the right. This would increase the market price and equilibrium number of bus rides.

5-7. If this nation's government does not provide people with property rights for a number of items and fails to enforce the property rights that it does assign for remaining items, externalities would be more common than in a country such as the United States. Any two parties undertaking transactions would experience no incentives to reduce or eliminate their transactions' spillover effects, resulting in widespread externalities.

5-9. At present, the equilibrium quantity of residences with Internet access is 2 million. To take into account the external benefit of Internet access and boost the quantity of residences with access to 3 million, the demand curve would have to shift upward by $20 per month at any given quantity, to D_2 from the current position D_1. Thus, the government would have to offer a $20-per-month subsidy to raise the quantity of residences with Internet access to 3 million.

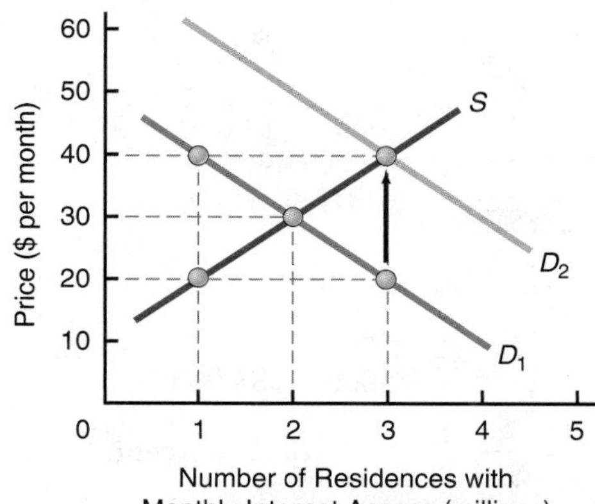

5-11. No, the outcome will be different. If the government had simply provided grants to attend private schools at the current market tuition rate, parents and students receiving the grants would have paid a price equal to the market valuation of the last unit of educational services provided. Granting a subsidy to private schools allows the private schools to charge parents and students a price less than the market price. Private schools thereby will receive a higher-than-market price for the last unit of educational services they provide. Consequently, they will provide a quantity of educational services in excess of the market equilibrium quantity. At this quantity, parents and students place a lower value on the services than the price received by the private schools.

5-13. **a.** $40 million

b. The effective price of a tablet device to consumers will be lower after the government pays the subsidy, so people will purchase a larger quantity.

c. $60 million

d. $90 million

5-15. **a.** $\$60 - \$50 = \$10$

b. Expenditures after the program expansion are $2.4 million. Before the program expansion, expenditures were $1 million. Hence, the increase in expenditures is $1.4 million.

c. At a per-unit subsidy of $50, the share of the per-unit $60 price paid by the government is 5/6, or 83.3 percent. Hence, this is the government's share of total expenditures on the 40,000 devices that consumers purchase.

CHAPTER 6

6-1. a. The average tax rate is the total tax of $40 divided by the $200 in income: $40/$200 = 0.2, or 20 percent.

b. The marginal tax rate for the last hour of work is the change in taxes, $3, divided by the change in income, $8: $3/$8 = 0.375, or 37.5 percent.

6-3. a. Christino's marginal tax rate is

$$\frac{\$300 - \$200}{\$2{,}000 - \$1{,}000} = \frac{\$400 - \$300}{\$3{,}000 - \$2{,}000} = \frac{\$100}{\$1{,}000} = 0.1, \text{ or 10 percent.}$$

b. Jarius's marginal tax rate is

$$\frac{\$400 - \$200}{\$2{,}000 - \$1{,}000} = \frac{\$600 - \$400}{\$3{,}000 - \$2{,}000} = \frac{\$200}{\$1{,}000} = 0.2, \text{ or 20 percent.}$$

c. Meg's marginal tax rate is

$$\frac{\$500 - \$200}{\$2{,}000 - \$1{,}000} = \frac{\$800 - \$500}{\$3{,}000 - \$2{,}000} = \frac{\$300}{\$1{,}000} = 0.3, \text{ or 30 percent.}$$

6-5. 2005: $300 million; 2007: $350 million; 2009: $400 million; 2011: $400 million; 2013: $420 million

6.7. a. The supply of tickets for flights into and out of London shifts upward by $154. The equilibrium quantity of flights into and out of London declines. The market clearing price of London airline tickets rises by an amount less than the tax.

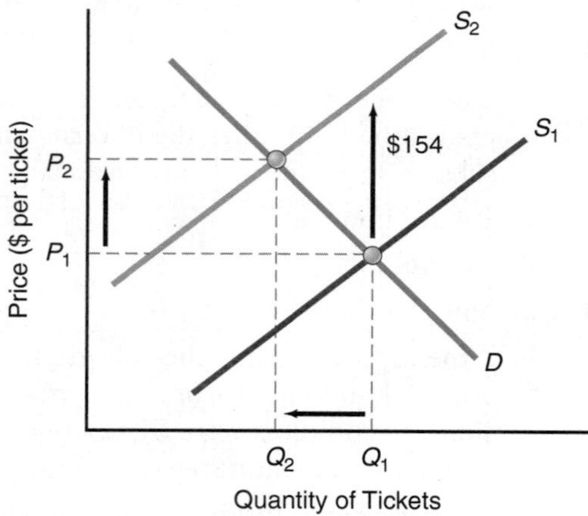

b. Tickets for flights into or out of London are substitutes for tickets for flights into and out of nearby cities. Thus, the demand for tickets for flights into and out of these cities will increase. This will cause an increase in the equilibrium quantities of these tickets and an increase in the market clearing prices.

6-9. a. The initial market price is $7 per unit, at which the equilibrium quantity demanded equals the equilibrium quantity supplied at 125 units.

b. The supply curve shifts upward by the amount of the tax, so in the table, the quantity supplied at a price of $6 is 50 units; at a price of $7, 75 units; at a price of $8, 100 units; at a price of $9, 125 units; at a price of $10, 150 units; and at a price of $11, 175 units. The demand relationship is unchanged. Hence, the new market price is $8, at which the quantity demanded of 100 units is equal to the new quantity supplied at this price that is also equal to 100 units.

c. The market price rises from $7 to $8, and this $1 price increase is half of the $2 tax. Consequently, consumers pay half of the tax, and producers pay the other half.

CHAPTER 7

7-1. a. Multiplying the fraction of people who participate in the labor force, 0.7, times the adult, noninstitutionalized, nonmilitary population of 200.0 million yields a labor force of 140.0 million.

b. Subtracting the 7.5 million unemployed from the labor force of 140.0 million yields 132.5 million people who are employed.

c. Dividing the 7.5 million unemployed by the 140.0 million in the labor force and multiplying by 100 yields an unemployment rate of about 5.36 percent.

7-3. a. The labor force equals the number employed plus the number unemployed, or 156 million + 8 million = 164 million. In percentage terms, therefore, the unemployment rate is 100 times 8 million/164 million, or 4.9 percent.

b. These 60 million people are not in the labor force. The labor force participation rate is, in percentage terms, 100 times 164 million/224 million, or 73.2 percent.

7-5. a. Four of the 100 people are always continuously unemployed because they are between jobs, so the frictional unemployment rate is $(4/100) \times 100 = 4$ percent.

b. Three of the 100 people are always unemployed as a result of government regulations, so the structural unemployment rate is $(3/100) \times 100 = 3$ percent.

c. The unemployment rate is the sum of the frictional and structural rates of unemployment, or 7 percent.

7-7. The overall unemployment rate is 8 percent, and the natural rate of unemployment is 5 percent.

7-9. In 2013, the value of the price index is $10,000/$10,000 × 100 = 100. In 2014, the value of the price index is $11,100/$10,000 × 100 = 111.

7-11. **a.** 2014

b. 10 percent

c. 10 percent

d. $1,800 in 2013; $3,000 in 2017

7-13. The expected rate of inflation is equal to 100 × [(99 − 90)/90] = 10 percent. Hence, the real interest rate equals the difference between the 12 percent nominal interest rate and the 10 percent anticipated inflation rate, or 2 percent.

7-15. **a.** The homeowner gains; the savings bank loses.

b. The tenants gain; the landlord loses.

c. The auto buyer gains; the bank loses.

d. The employer gains; the pensioner loses.

CHAPTER 8

8-1. As illustrated by the basic circular-flow diagram, the flow of the market value of final goods and services produced within a nation's borders during a given interval—that is, gross domestic product—is what generates the gross domestic income received by the nation's households during that interval, which they in turn spend in the nation's product markets. Consequently, the flows of gross domestic product and gross domestic income must be equivalent.

8-3. **a.** When Maria does all the work herself, only purchases of the materials in markets (magazines, texturing materials, paint brushes, and paints), which total $280 per year, count in GDP.

b. She must pay the market price of $200 for the texturing, so her contribution to annual GDP from this project, including the materials, is $480.

c. Because Maria now pays for the entire project via market transactions, her total contribution to GDP equals the sum of the $280 material purchases from part (a), $200 for the texturing from part (b), and $350 for the painting, or $830 per year.

8-5. **a.** GDP = $16.6 trillion; NDP = $15.3 trillion; NI = $14.5 trillion.

b. GDP in 2017 will equal $15.5 trillion.

8-7. **a.** Gross domestic income = $14.6 trillion; GDP = $14.6 trillion.

b. Gross private domestic investment = $2.0 trillion.

c. Personal income = $12.0 trillion; personal disposable income = $10.3 trillion.

8-9. **a.** Measured GDP declines.

b. Measured GDP increases.

c. Measured GDP does not change (the firearms are not newly produced).

8-11. **a.** The chip is an intermediate good, so its purchase in June is not included in GDP; only the final sale in November is included.

b. This is a final sale of a good that is included in GDP for the year.

c. This is a final sale of a service that is included in GDP for the year.

8-13. **a.** Nominal GDP for 2013 is $2,300; for 2017, nominal GDP is $2,832.

b. Real GDP for 2013 is $2,300; for 2017, real GDP is $2,229.

8-15. The price index is (2015 nominal GDP/2015 real GDP) × 100 = ($88,000/$136,000) × 100 = 64.7.

8-17. The $1 billion expended to pay for employees and equipment and the additional $1 billion paid to clean up the oil spill would be included in GDP, for a total of $2 billion added to GDP in 2015. The rise in oil reserves increases the stock of wealth but is not included in the current flow of newly produced goods and services. In addition, the welfare loss relating to the deaths of wildlife is also not measured in the marketplace and therefore is not included in GDP.

CHAPTER 9

9-1. **a.** Y

b. X

9-3. The nation will maintain its stock of capital goods at its current level, so its rate of economic growth will be zero.

9-5. A: $8,250 per capita; B: $4,500 per capita; C: $21,000 per capita

9-7. 1.77 times higher after 20 years; 3.16 times higher after 40 years

9-9. 5 years

9-11. In Mozambique, in 50 years the typical resident's annual real GDP per capita will equal $3,000 × 4.38 = $13,140. In China, a typical resident's real GDP per capita will equal $3,000 × 46.90 = $140,700, which is $127,560 per year greater than in Mozambique.

9-13. 4 percent

9-15. Per capita real GDP in 2014 was 10 percent higher than in 2013, or $2,200. The level of real GDP is $2,200 per person × 5 million people = $11 billion.

CHAPTER 10

10-1. The amount of unemployment would be the sum of frictional, structural, and seasonal unemployment.

10-3. The real value of the new full-employment level of nominal GDP is ($17.7 trillion/1.15) = $15.39 trillion, so the long-run aggregate supply curve has shifted rightward by $2.35 trillion, in base-year dollars.

10-5. **a.** A rightward shift of the *LRAS* curve coupled with a shift in the *AD* curve farther to the right

b. A leftward shift of the *LRAS* curve coupled with a leftward shift of the *AD* curve of the same magnitude

c. A rightward shift of the *LRAS* curve coupled with a rightward shift of the *AD* curve of the same magnitude

d. A leftward shift of the *LRAS* curve coupled with a shift of the *AD* curve farther to the left

10-7. This change implies a rightward shift of the long-run aggregate supply curve along the unchanged aggregate demand curve, so the long-run equilibrium price level will decline.

10-9. There are three effects. First, there is a real-balance effect, because the rise in the price level reduces real money balances, inducing people to cut back on their spending. In addition, there is an interest rate effect as a higher price level pushes up interest rates, thereby reducing the attractiveness of purchases of autos, houses, and plants and equipment. Finally, there is an open-economy effect as home residents respond to the higher price level by reducing purchases of domestically produced goods in favor of foreign-produced goods, while foreign residents cut back on their purchases of our home-produced goods. All three effects entail a reduction in purchases of goods and services, so the aggregate demand curve slopes downward.

10-11. **a.** At the price level P_2 above the equilibrium price level P_1, the total quantity of real goods and services that people plan to consume is less than the total quantity that is consistent with firms' production plans. One reason is that at the higher-than-equilibrium price level, real money balances are lower, which reduces real wealth and induces lower planned consumption. Another is that interest rates are higher at the higher-than-equilibrium price level, which generates a cutback in spending on consumer durables. Finally, at the higher-than-equilibrium price level P_2, people tend to cut back on purchasing domestic goods in favor of foreign-produced goods, and foreign residents reduce purchases of our domestic goods. As unsold inventories of output accumulate, the price level drops toward the equilibrium price level P_1, which ultimately causes planned consumption to rise toward equality with total production.

b. At the price level P_3 below the equilibrium price level P_1, the total quantity of real goods and services that people plan to consume exceeds the total quantity that is consistent with firms' production plans. One reason is that at the lower-than-equilibrium price level, real money balances are higher, which raises real wealth and induces higher planned consumption. Another is that interest rates are lower at the lower-than-equilibrium price level, which generates an increase in consumption spending. Finally, at the lower-than-equilibrium price level P_3, people tend to raise their purchases of domestic goods and cut back on buying foreign-produced goods, and foreign residents increase purchases of our domestic goods. As inventories of output are depleted, the price level begins to rise toward the equilibrium price level P_1, which ultimately causes planned consumption to fall toward equality with total production.

10-13. **a.** When the price level falls with deflation, there is a movement downward along the *AD* curve.

b. The decline in foreign real GDP levels reduces incomes of foreign residents, who cut back on their spending on our domestic exports. Thus, the domestic *AD* curve shifts leftward.

c. The fall in the foreign exchange value of the nation's currency makes our domestically produced goods and services less expensive to foreign residents, who increase their spending on our domestic exports. Thus, the domestic *AD* curve shifts rightward.

d. An increase in the price level causes a movement upward along the *AD* curve.

10-15. **a.** The aggregate demand curve shifts leftward along the long-run aggregate supply curve. The equilibrium price level falls, and equilibrium real GDP remains unchanged.

b. The aggregate demand curve shifts rightward along the long-run aggregate supply curve. The equilibrium price level rises, and equilibrium real GDP remains unchanged.

c. The long-run aggregate supply curve shifts rightward along the aggregate demand curve. The equilibrium price level falls, and equilibrium real GDP increases.

d. The aggregate demand curve shifts rightward along the long-run aggregate supply curve. The equilibrium price level rises, and equilibrium real GDP remains unchanged.

10-17. a. The income flows are mainly influencing relatives' consumption, so the main effect is on the aggregate demand curve.

b. A rise in aggregate demand will lead to an increase in the equilibrium price level.

CHAPTER 11

11-1. a. Because saving increases at any given interest rate, the desired saving curve shifts rightward. This causes the equilibrium interest rate to decline.

b. There is no effect on current equilibrium real GDP, because in the classical model, the vertical long-run aggregate supply curve always applies.

c. A change in the saving rate does not directly affect the demand for labor or the supply of labor in the classical model, so equilibrium employment does not change.

d. The decrease in the equilibrium interest rate generates a downward movement along the demand curve for investment. Consequently, desired investment increases.

e. The rise in current investment implies greater capital accumulation. Other things being equal, this will imply increased future production and higher equilibrium real GDP in the future.

11-3. False. In fact, an important distinction can be made. The classical model of short-run real GDP determination applies to an interval short enough that some factors of production, such as capital, are fixed. Nevertheless, the classical model implies that even in the short run the economy's short-run aggregate supply curve is the same as its long-run aggregate supply curve.

11-5. In the long run, the aggregate supply curve is vertical because all input prices adjust fully and people are fully informed in the long run. Thus, the short-run aggregate supply curve is more steeply sloped if input prices adjust more rapidly and people become more fully informed within a short-run interval.

11-7. To prevent a short-run decrease in real GDP from taking place after the temporary rise in oil prices shifts the *SRAS* curve leftward, policymakers should increase the quantity of money in circulation. This will shift the *AD* curve rightward and prevent equilibrium real GDP from declining in the short run.

11-9. An increase in total planned real expenditures by U.S. households in response to an increase in the quantity of money in circulation implies a rightward shift in the position of the aggregate demand curve along the short-run aggregate supply curve. The predicted effects are increases in both the equilibrium U.S. price level and the equilibrium U.S. real GDP. Keynesian theory indicates that a consequence would be a short-term inflationary gap between expenditures on real GDP in the short run and expenditures on real GDP that would be consistent with long-run equilibrium.

11-11. a. *E*: The union wage boost causes the *SRAS* curve to shift leftward, from $SRAS_1$ to $SRAS_3$. The reduction in incomes abroad causes import spending in this nation to fall, which induces a leftward shift in the *AD* curve, from AD_1 to AD_3.

b. *B*: The short-term reduction in production capabilities causes the *SRAS* curve to shift leftward, from $SRAS_1$ to $SRAS_3$, and the increase in money supply growth generates a rightward shift in the *AD* curve, from AD_1 to AD_2.

c. *C*: The strengthening of the value of this nation's currency reduces the prices of imported inputs that domestic firms utilize to produce goods and services, which causes the *SRAS* curve to shift rightward, from $SRAS_1$ to $SRAS_2$. At the same time, currency's strengthening raises the prices of exports and reduces the prices of imports, so net export spending declines, thereby inducing a leftward shift in the *AD* curve, from AD_1 to AD_3.

CHAPTER 12

12-1. a. Flow

b. Flow

c. Stock

d. Flow

e. Stock

f. Flow

g. Stock

12-3. a. The completed table follows (all amounts in dollars):

Real GDP	Consumption	Saving	Investment
2,000	2,000	0	1,200
4,000	3,600	400	1,200
6,000	5,200	800	1,200
8,000	6,800	1,200	1,200
10,000	8,400	1,600	1,200
12,000	10,000	2,000	1,200

MPC = 1,600/2000 = 0.8;

MPS = 400/2,000 = 0.2.

b. The graph appears on the next page.

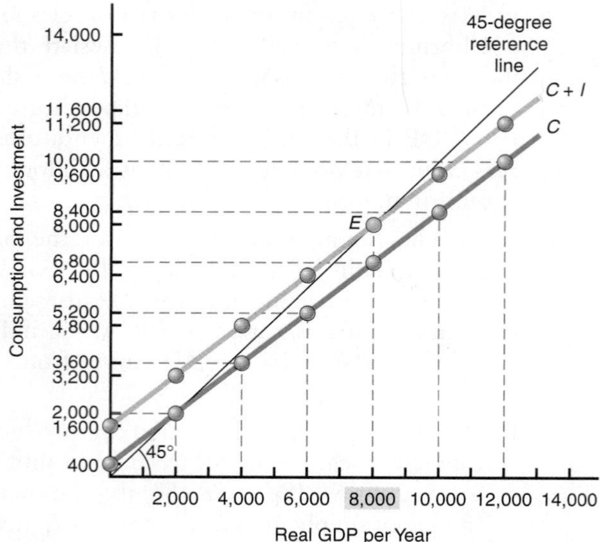

c. The graph appears below. Equilibrium real GDP on both graphs equals \$8,000 per year.

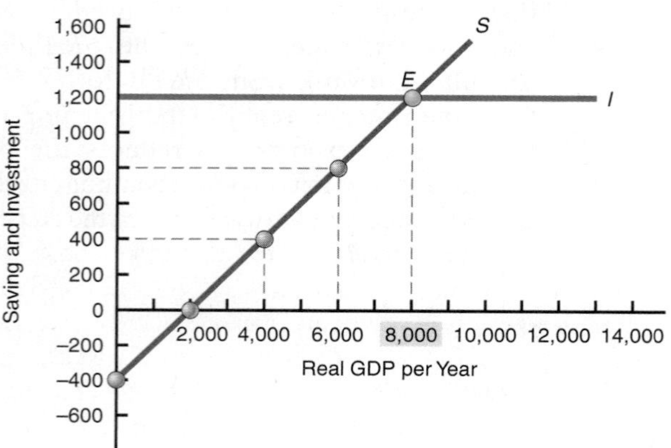

d. APS = \$1,200/\$8,000 = 0.15

e. The multiplier is 1/(1 − MPC) = 1/(1 − 0.8) = 1/0.2 = 5. Thus, if autonomous consumption were to rise by \$100, then equilibrium real GDP would increase by \$100 times 5, or \$500.

12-5. a. MPC = 0.95; MPS = 0.05

b. MPC = 0.90; MPS = 0.10

c. MPC = 0.875; MPS = 0.125

d. MPC = 0.80; MPS = 0.20

12-7. The multiplier is 1/(1 − MPC) = 4, so 1 − MPC = 0.25, which implies that MPC = 0.75. Thus, when real GDP equals \$15 trillion, consumption is \$1 trillion + (0.75 × \$15 trillion) = \$12.25 trillion.

12-9. The multiplier is 1/(1 − MPC) = 1/(1 − 0.75) = 4, so the increase in equilibrium real GDP is \$250 billion × 4 = \$1 trillion, and the level of real GDP at the new point on the aggregate demand curve is \$16 trillion per year.

12-11. a. The MPS is equal to 1/3.

b. \$0.1 trillion

CHAPTER 13

13-1. a. A key factor that could help explain why the actual effect may have turned out to be lower is the crowding-out effect. Some government spending may have entailed direct expenditure offsets that reduced private expenditures on a dollar-for-dollar basis. In addition, indirect crowding out may have occurred. Because the government did not change taxes, it probably sold bonds to finance its increased expenditures, and this action likely pushed up interest rates, thereby discouraging private investment. Furthermore, the increase in government spending likely pushed up aggregate demand, which may have caused a short-run increase in the price level. This, in turn, may have induced foreign residents to reduce their expenditures on U.S. goods. It also could have reduced real money holdings sufficiently to discourage consumers from spending as much as before. On net, therefore, real GDP rose in the short run, but not by the full amount predicted by the basic multiplier effect.

b. In the long run, as the increased spending raised aggregate demand, wages and other input prices likely increased in proportion to the resulting increase in the price level. Thus, in the long run the aggregate supply schedule was vertical, and the increase in government spending induced only a rise in the price level.

13-3. Because of the recognition time lag entailed in gathering information about the economy, policymakers may be slow to respond to a downturn in real GDP. Congressional approval of policy actions to address the downturn may be delayed; hence, an action time lag may also arise. Finally, there is an effect time lag, because policy actions take time to exert their full effects on the economy. If these lags are sufficiently long, it is possible that by the time a policy to address a downturn has begun to have its effects, equilibrium real GDP per year may already be rising. If so, the policy action may push real GDP up faster than intended, thereby making real GDP less stable.

13-5. Situation *b* is an example of indirect crowding out because the reduction in private expenditures takes place indirectly in response to a change in the interest rate. In contrast, situations *a* and *c* are examples of direct expenditure offsets.

13-7. Situation *b* is an example of a discretionary fiscal policy action because this is a discretionary action by Congress. So is situation *d* because the president uses discretionary authority. Situation *c* is an example of monetary policy, not fiscal policy, and situation *a* is an example of an automatic stabilizer.

13-9. There is a recessionary gap, because at point *A*, equilibrium real GDP of $15.5 trillion is below the long-run level of $16.0 trillion. To eliminate the recessionary gap of $0.5 trillion, government spending must increase sufficiently to shift the *AD* curve rightward to a long-run equilibrium, which will entail a price level increase from 115 to 120. Hence, the spending increase must shift the *AD* curve rightward by $1 trillion, or by the multiplier, which is $1/0.20 = 5$, times the increase in spending. Government spending must rise by $200 billion, or $0.2 trillion per year.

13-11. Because the MPC is 0.80, the multiplier equals $1/(1 - \text{MPC}) = 1/0.2 = 5$. Net of indirect crowding out, therefore, total autonomous expenditures must rise by $40 billion in order to shift the aggregate demand curve rightward by $200 billion. If the government raises its spending by $50 billion, the market interest rate rises by 0.5 percentage point and thereby causes planned investment spending to fall by $10 billion, which results in a net rise in total autonomous expenditures equal to $40 billion. Consequently, to accomplish its objective, the government should increase its spending by $50 billion.

13-13. A cut in the tax rate should induce a rise in consumption and, consequently, a multiple short-run increase in equilibrium real GDP. In addition, however, a tax-rate reduction reduces the automatic-stabilizer properties of the tax system, so equilibrium real GDP would be less stable in the face of changes in autonomous spending.

13-15. According to the logic of the permanent income hypothesis, these small, one-time payments did not raise people's average lifetime disposable incomes. Instead of using the funds to increase their consumption spending, people applied them toward paying down outstanding debts or to their savings. Hence, consumption spending did not rise in response to the temporary increase in real disposable income.

APPENDIX D

D-1. a. The marginal propensity to consume is equal to $1 - \text{MPS}$, or $6/7$.

b. The required increase in equilibrium real GDP is $0.35 trillion, or $350 billion. The multiplier equals $1/(1 - \text{MPC}) = 1/\text{MPS} = 1/(1/7) = 7$. Hence, investment or government spending must increase by $50 billion to bring about a $350 billion increase in equilibrium real GDP.

c. The multiplier relevant for a tax change equals $-\text{MPC}/(1 - \text{MPC}) = -\text{MPC}/\text{MPS} = -(6/7)/(1/7) = -6$. Thus, the government would have to cut taxes by $58.33 billion to induce a rise in equilibrium real GDP equal to $350 billion.

D-3. a. The aggregate expenditures curve shifts up by $1 billion; equilibrium real GDP increases by $5 billion per year.

b. The aggregate expenditures curve shifts down by the MPC times the tax increase, or by $0.8 \times \$1$ billion $= \$0.8$ billion; equilibrium real income falls by $4 billion per year.

c. The aggregate expenditures curve shifts upward by (1 − MPC) times $1 billion = $0.2 billion. Equilibrium real income rises by $1 billion.

d. No change; no change

CHAPTER 14

14-1. $0.4 trillion

14-3. A higher deficit creates a higher public debt.

14-5. The net public debt is obtained by subtracting government interagency borrowing from the gross public debt.

14-7. When foreign dollar holders hold more of our domestic government bonds issued to finance higher domestic government budget deficits, they purchase fewer of our domestic exports, so the domestic trade deficit rises, other things being equal.

14-9. As shown in the diagram below, the increase in government spending and/or tax reduction that creates the budget deficit also causes the aggregate demand curve to shift rightward, from *AD* to AD_2. Real GDP rises to its long-run equilibrium level of $15 trillion at point *B*. The equilibrium price level increases to a value of 130 at this point. As real GDP rises, the government's tax collections increase and benefit payouts fall, both of which will help ultimately reduce the deficit.

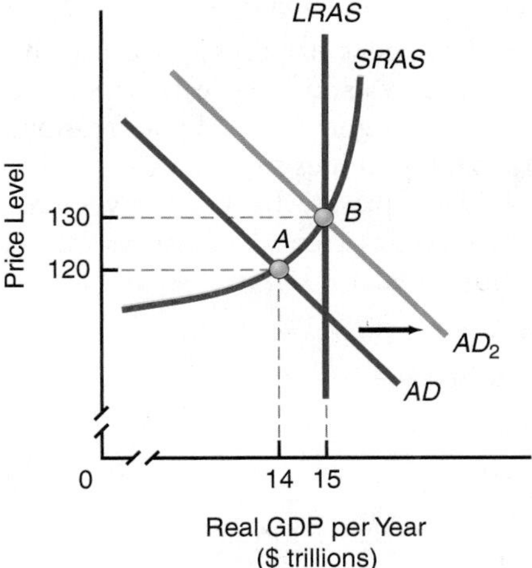

14-11. "The rich" are likely to respond to higher tax rates by reducing their activities that generate taxable income, so actual tax collections from "the rich" will not turn out to be as high as the politician suggests. In any event, as shown in Figure 14-5 on page 311, even imposing a 100 percent tax rate on the highest-income taxpayers could not raise sufficient tax revenues to eliminate the deficit.

14-13. These data indicate that tax revenues have been able to cover only about two-thirds—about 67 percent—of federal expenditures. Because more than 60 percent of all federal expenditures are entitlements, this implies that the federal government has been borrowing to pay for most discretionary spending.

CHAPTER 15

15-1. Medium of exchange; store of value; standard of deferred payment

15-3. Store of value; standard of deferred payment

15-5. M1 equals transactions deposits plus currency plus traveler's checks, or \$1,025 billion + \$1,050 billion + \$25 billion = \$2,100 billion; M2 equals M1 + savings deposits plus small-denomination time deposits plus money market deposit accounts plus retail (noninstitution) money market mutual funds, or \$2,100 billion + \$3,300 billion + \$1,450 billion + \$1,950 billion + \$1,900 billion = \$10,700 billion.

15-7. **a.** M1 and M2

b. Neither

c. M2 only

d. M1 and M2

e. M2 only

15-9. **a.** Moral hazard problem

b. Adverse selection problem

c. Moral hazard problem

15-11. The Fed provides banking services such as check clearing services and large-value payment services for other banks and for the U.S. Treasury, just as a private bank provides such services for its customers. Unlike a private bank, however, the Federal Reserve serves as a lender of last resort, a regulator, and a policymaker.

15-13. **a.** Asset

b. Liability

c. Asset

d. Asset

e. Asset

f. Liability

15-15. 9.09

15-17. 25 percent (or 0.25)

15-19. The maximum potential money multiplier is 1/0.01 = 100, so total deposits in the banking system will increase by \$5 million × 100 = \$500 million.

CHAPTER 16

16-1. **a.** \$500/0.05 = \$10,000

b. Its price falls to \$500/0.10 = \$5,000.

16-3. **a.** One possible policy action would be an open market sale of securities, which would reduce the money supply and shift the aggregate demand curve leftward. Others would be to increase the discount rate relative to the federal funds rate or to raise the required reserve ratio.

b. In principle, the Fed's action would reduce inflation more quickly.

16-5. The short-run effect is an upward movement along the short-run aggregate supply curve generated by an increase in aggregate demand. The equilibrium price level rises, and equilibrium real GDP increases. In the long run, input prices rise, and people anticipate a higher price level, which causes the short-run aggregate supply curve to shift upward and to the left. The equilibrium price level rises once more, and equilibrium real GDP falls back to its long-run equilibrium level.

16-7. **a.** The dollar appreciation will raise the prices of U.S. goods and services from the perspective of foreign residents, so they will reduce their spending on U.S. exports. It will reduce the prices of foreign goods and services from the perspective of U.S. residents, so they will increase their spending on foreign imports. Thus, net export expenditures per year will decline.

b. The fall in net export expenditures will bring about a decrease in U.S. aggregate demand, so the aggregate demand curve AD_2 will apply to this situation. In the short run, the equilibrium price level will fall from 118 to 116, and equilibrium real GDP, measured in base-year dollars, will fall from \$15.0 trillion to \$14.5 trillion per year.

c. The Federal Reserve could engage in a policy action, such as open market purchases, that increases aggregate demand to its original level.

16-9. The price level remains at its original value. Because $M_sV = PY$, V has doubled, and Y is unchanged, cutting M_s in half leaves P unchanged.

16-11. **a.** $M_sV = PY$, so $P = M_sV/Y$ = (\$1.1 trillion × 10)/\$5 trillion = 2.2.

b. \$100 billion/\$1 trillion = 0.1, or 10 percent.

c. 0.2/2 = 0.1, or 10 percent.

d. Both the money supply and the price level increased by 10 percent.

16-13. Any one of these contractionary actions will tend to raise interest rates, which in turn will induce international inflows of financial capital. This pushes up the value of the dollar and makes U.S. goods less attractive abroad. As a consequence, real planned total expenditures on U.S. goods decline even further.

16-15. To induce the banks to hold the reserves, the Fed would have to raise the interest rate it pays on the reserves. The increase in reserves owned by private banks would generate a rise in the Fed's liabilities equal to the expansion of the Fed's assets.

16-17. The money supply did not change, so this did not actually constitute a monetary policy action. Instead, the Fed only expanded its reserves and, hence, its liabilities, which corresponded to the increase in the Fed's holdings of privately issued assets. Consequently, the Fed's "quantitative easing" was primarily a credit policy action.

APPENDIX E

E-1. a. $20 billion increase

b. $40 billion increase

c. $10 billion open market purchase

E-3. Through its purchase of $1 billion in bonds, the Fed increased reserves by $1 billion. This ultimately caused a $3 billion increase in the money supply after full multiple expansion. The 1 percentage-point drop in the interest rate, from 6 percent to 5 percent, caused investment to rise by $25 billion, from $1,200 billion to $1,225 billion. An investment multiplier of 3 indicates that equilibrium real GDP rose by $75 billion, to $12,075 billion, or $12.075 trillion per year.

CHAPTER 17

17-1. a. The actual unemployment rate, which equals the number of people unemployed divided by the labor force, would decline, because the labor force would rise while the number of people unemployed would remain unchanged.

b. Natural unemployment rate estimates also would be lower.

c. The logic of the short- and long-run Phillips curves would not be altered. The government might wish to make this change if it feels that those in the military "hold jobs" and therefore should be counted as employed within the U.S. economy.

17-3. a. The measured unemployment rate when all adjustments have occurred will now always be lower than before, so the natural unemployment rate will be smaller.

b. The Phillips curve will shift inward.

17-5. Because the unemployment rate has increased as a consequence of a rise in structural unemployment while the inflation rate has remained unchanged, the short-run Phillips curve will tend to shift rightward, together with a rightward shift in the long-run Phillips curve as the natural rate of unemployment increases.

17-7. Because monetary policy is now harder for people to predict, the unsystematic variations in the quantity of money in circulation will tend to be more likely to generate changes in equilibrium real GDP. Inflation expectations will not change, and the short-run aggregate supply curve will remain in position as the aggregate demand curve shifts.

17-9. No. It could still be true that wages and other prices of factors of production adjust sluggishly to changes in the price level. Then a rise in aggregate demand that boosts the price level brings about an upward movement along the short-run aggregate supply curve, causing equilibrium real GDP to rise.

17-11. a. An increase in desired investment spending induces an increase in aggregate demand, so AD_3 applies. The price level is unchanged in the short run, and equilibrium real GDP rises from $15 trillion at point *A* to $15.5 trillion per year at point *C*.

b. Over time, firms perceive that they can increase their profits by adjusting prices upward in response to the increase in aggregate demand. Thus, firms eventually will incur the menu costs required to make these price adjustments. As they do so, the aggregate supply curve will shift upward, from *SRAS* to $SRAS_2$, as shown in the diagram below. Real GDP will return to its original level of $15 trillion per year, in base-year dollars. The price level will increase to a level above 119, such as 124.

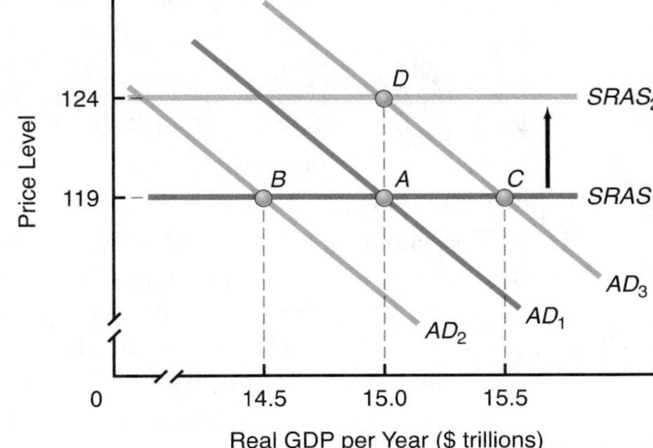

17-13. The explanation would be that aggregate demand increased at a faster pace than the rise in aggregate supply caused by economic growth. On net, therefore, the price level rose during those years.

17-15. If the average time between price adjustments by firms is significant, then the short-run aggregate supply curve could be regarded as horizontal, as hypothesized by the new Keynesian theorists. As a consequence, there would be a short-run trade-off between inflation and real GDP that policymakers potentially could exploit.

CHAPTER 18

18-1. Population growth rate = real GDP growth rate − rate of growth of per capita real GDP = 3.1 percent − 0.3 percent = 2.8 percent.

18-3. Rate of growth of per capita real GDP = rate of growth of real GDP − population growth rate = 1.3 percent − 2.7 percent per year = −1.4 percent.

18-5. **a.** 20 × 0.01 percent = 0.2 percent

b. 10 × 0.01 percent = 0.1 percent

18-7. \$10 trillion/\$0.5 trillion × 0.1 = 2 percentage points.

18-9. **a.** Portfolio investment is equal to \$150 million in bonds plus \$100 million in stocks representing ownership of less than 10 percent, or \$250 million. (Bank loans are neither portfolio investment nor foreign direct investment.)

b. Foreign direct investment is equal to \$250 million in stocks representing an ownership share of at least 10 percent. (Bank loans are neither portfolio investment nor foreign direct investment.)

18-11. **a.** Adverse selection

b. Adverse selection

c. Moral hazard

d. Adverse selection

18-13. **a.** The company had already qualified for funding at a market interest rate, so the World Bank is interfering with functioning private markets for credit. In addition, by extending credit to the company at a below-market rate, the World Bank provides an incentive for the company to borrow additional funds for less efficient investment.

b. In this situation, the World Bank effectively is tying up funds in dead capital. There is an associated opportunity cost, because the funds could instead be allocated to another investment that would yield more immediate returns.

c. In this case, the IMF contributes to a moral hazard problem, because the government has every incentive not to make reforms that will enable it to repay this and future loans it may receive.

18-15. **a.** An incentive exists for at least some governments to fail to follow through with reforms, even if those governments might have had good intentions when they applied for World Bank loans.

b. National governments most interested in obtaining funds to "buy" votes will be among those most interested in obtaining IMF loans. The proposed IMF rule could help reduce the number of nations whose governments seek to obtain funds to try to "buy" votes.

CHAPTER 32

32-1. **a.** The opportunity cost of pastries in Northland is 0.5 sandwich per pastry. The opportunity cost of sandwiches in Northland is 2 pastries per sandwich.

b. The opportunity cost of pastries in West Coast is 2 sandwiches per pastry. The opportunity cost of sandwiches in West Coast is 0.5 pastry per sandwich.

32-3. If Northland specializes in producing pastries, the maximum number of pastries it can produce and trade to West Coast is 50,000 pastries. Hence, the maximum number of units of each good that the two countries can trade at a rate of exchange of 1 pastry for 1 sandwich is 50,000.

32-5. Coastal Realm has a comparative advantage in producing digital TVs, and Border Kingdom has a comparative advantage in wine production.

32-7. **a.** The opportunity cost of modems in South Shore is 2 flash drives per modem. The opportunity cost of flash drives in South Shore is 0.5 modem per flash drive.

b. The opportunity cost of modems in East Isle is 0.5 flash drive per modem. The opportunity cost of flash drives in East Isle is 2 modems per flash drive.

c. Residents of South Shore have a comparative advantage in producing flash drives, and residents of East Isle have a comparative advantage in producing modems.

32-9. The critics are suggesting that Mexican exporters are shifting exports that would have gone to other nations to the United States, a nation within NAFTA, which would constitute trade diversion.

32-11. Diversion and deflection occur when nations within or outside a particular regional trade bloc try to benefit from preferences that exist only within the bloc. As long as the WTO agreements involve all nations equally, no diversion or deflection could occur.

CHAPTER 33

33-1 **a.** −\$0.6 trillion

b. −\$0.5 trillion

c. −\$0.7 trillion

33-3. The trade balance is merchandise exports minus merchandise imports, which equals 500 − 600 = −100, or a deficit of 100. Adding service exports of 75 and subtracting net unilateral transfers of 10 and service imports of 50 yields −100 + 75 − 10 − 50 = −85, or a current account balance of −85. The capital account balance equals the difference between capital inflows and capital outflows, or 300 − 200 = +100, or a capital account surplus of 100.

33-5. **a.** The increase in demand for Mexican-made guitars increases the demand for Mexican pesos, and the peso appreciates.

b. International investors will remove some of their financial capital from Mexico. The increase in the supply of pesos in the foreign exchange market will cause the peso to depreciate.

33-7. The demand for Chinese yuan increases, and the supply of yuan decreases. The dollar-yuan exchange rate rises, so the yuan appreciates.

33-9. The Canadian dollar–euro exchange rate is found by dividing the U.S. dollar–euro exchange rate by the U.S. dollar–Canadian dollar exchange rate, or (1.45 $U.S./euro)/(0.94 $U.S./$C) = 1.54 $C/euro, or 1.54 Canadian dollars per euro.

33-11. A flexible exchange rate system allows the exchange value of a currency to be determined freely in the foreign exchange market with no intervention by the government. A fixed exchange rate pegs the value of the currency, and the authorities responsible for the value of the currency intervene in foreign exchange markets to maintain this value.

33-13. When the dollar is pegged to gold at a rate of $35 and the pound is pegged to the dollar at $2 = £1, an implicit value between gold and the pound is established at £17.50 = 1 ounce of gold. If the dollar falls in value relative to gold, yet the pound is still valued to the dollar at $2 = £1, the pound become undervalued relative to gold. The exchange rate between the dollar and the pound will have to be adjusted to 2.29 $/£.

Glossary

A

Absolute advantage The ability to produce more units of a good or service using a given quantity of labor or resource inputs. Equivalently, the ability to produce the same quantity of a good or service using fewer units of labor or resource inputs.

Accounting identities Values that are equivalent by definition.

Accounting profit Total revenues minus total explicit costs.

Action time lag The time between recognizing an economic problem and implementing policy to solve it. The action time lag is quite long for fiscal policy, which requires congressional approval.

Active (discretionary) policymaking All actions on the part of monetary and fiscal policymakers that are undertaken in response to or in anticipation of some change in the overall economy.

***Ad valorem* taxation** Assessing taxes by charging a tax rate equal to a fraction of the market price of each unit purchased.

Adverse selection The tendency for high-risk projects and clients to be overrepresented among borrowers.

Age-earnings cycle The regular earnings profile of an individual throughout his or her lifetime. The age-earnings cycle usually starts with a low income, builds gradually to a peak at around age 50, and then gradually curves down until it approaches zero at retirement.

Aggregate demand The total of all planned expenditures in the entire economy.

Aggregate demand curve A curve showing planned purchase rates for all final goods and services in the economy at various price levels, all other things held constant.

Aggregate demand shock Any event that causes the aggregate demand curve to shift inward or outward.

Aggregate supply The total of all planned production for the economy.

Aggregate supply shock Any event that causes the aggregate supply curve to shift inward or outward.

Aggregates Total amounts or quantities. Aggregate demand, for example, is total planned expenditures throughout a nation.

Anticipated inflation The inflation rate that we believe will occur. When it does occur, we are in a situation of fully anticipated inflation.

Antitrust legislation Laws that restrict the formation of monopolies and regulate certain anticompetitive business practices.

Appreciation An increase in the exchange value of one nation's currency in terms of the currency of another nation.

Asset demand Holding money as a store of value instead of other assets such as corporate bonds and stocks.

Assets Amounts owned; all items to which a business or household holds legal claim.

Asymmetric information Information possessed by one party in a financial transaction but not by the other party.

Automatic, or built-in, stabilizers Special provisions of certain federal programs that cause changes in desired aggregate expenditures without the action of Congress and the president. Examples are the federal progressive tax system and unemployment compensation.

Autonomous consumption The part of consumption that is independent of (does not depend on) the level of disposable income. Changes in autonomous consumption shift the consumption function.

Average fixed costs Total fixed costs divided by the number of units produced.

Average physical product Total product divided by the variable input.

Average propensity to consume (APC) Real consumption divided by real disposable income. For any given level of real income, the proportion of total real disposable income that is consumed.

Average propensity to save (APS) Real saving divided by real disposable income. For any given level of real income, the proportion of total real disposable income that is saved.

Average tax rate The total tax payment divided by total income. It is the proportion of total income paid in taxes.

Average total costs Total costs divided by the number of units produced; sometimes called *average per-unit total costs*.

Average variable costs Total variable costs divided by the number of units produced.

B

Balance of payments A system of accounts that measures transactions of goods, services, income, and financial assets between domestic households, businesses, and governments and residents of the rest of the world during a specific time period.

Balance of trade The difference between exports and imports of physical goods.

Balance sheet A statement of the assets and liabilities of any business entity, including financial institutions and the Federal Reserve System. Assets are what is owned; liabilities are what is owed.

Balanced budget A situation in which the government's spending is exactly equal to the total taxes and other revenues it collects during a given period of time.

Bank run Attempt by many of a bank's depositors to convert transactions and time deposits into currency out of fear that the bank's liabilities may exceed its assets.

Barter The direct exchange of goods and services for other goods and services without the use of money.

Base year The year that is chosen as the point of reference for comparison of prices in other years.

Base-year dollars The value of a current sum expressed in terms of prices in a base year.

Behavioral economics An approach to the study of consumer behavior that emphasizes psychological limitations and complications that potentially interfere with rational decision making.

Bilateral monopoly A market structure consisting of a monopolist and a monopsonist.

Black market A market in which goods are traded at prices above their legal maximum prices or in which illegal goods are sold.

Bond A legal claim against a firm, usually entitling the owner of the bond to receive a fixed annual coupon payment, plus a lump-sum payment at the bond's maturity date. Bonds are issued in return for funds lent to the firm.

Bounded rationality The hypothesis that people are *nearly*, but not fully, rational, so that they cannot examine every possible choice available to them but instead use simple rules of thumb to sort among the alternatives that happen to occur to them.

Budget constraint All of the possible combinations of goods that can be purchased (at fixed prices) with a specific budget.

Bundling Offering two or more products for sale as a set.

Business fluctuations The ups and downs in business activity throughout the economy.

C

Capital account A category of balance of payments transactions that measures flows of financial assets.

Capital consumption allowance Another name for depreciation, the amount that businesses would have to put aside in order to take care of deteriorating machines and other equipment.

Capital gain A positive difference between the purchase price and the sale price of an asset. If a share of stock is bought for $5 and then sold for $15, the capital gain is $10.

Capital goods Producer durables; nonconsumable goods that firms use to make other goods.

Capital loss A negative difference between the purchase price and the sale price of an asset.

Capture hypothesis A theory of regulatory behavior that predicts that regulators will eventually be captured by special interests of the industry being regulated.

Cartel An association of producers in an industry that agree to set common prices and output quotas to prevent competition.

Central bank A banker's bank, usually an official institution that also serves as a bank for a nation's government treasury. Central banks normally regulate commercial banks.

***Ceteris paribus* [KAY-ter-us PEAR-uh-bus] assumption** The assumption that nothing changes except the factor or factors being studied.

***Ceteris paribus* conditions** Determinants of the relationship between price and quantity that are unchanged along a curve. Changes in these factors cause the curve to shift.

Closed shop A business enterprise in which employees must belong to the union before they can be hired and must remain in the union after they are hired.

Collective bargaining Negotiation between the management of a company and the management of a union for the purpose of reaching a mutually agreeable contract that sets wages, fringe benefits, and working conditions for all employees in all the unions involved.

Collective decision making How voters, politicians, and other interested parties act and how these actions influence nonmarket decisions.

Common property Property that is owned by everyone and therefore by no one. Air and water are examples of common property resources.

Comparative advantage The ability to produce a good or service at a lower opportunity cost than other producers.

Complements Two goods are complements when a change in the price of one causes an opposite shift in the demand for the other.

Concentration ratio The percentage of all sales contributed by the leading four or leading eight firms in an industry; sometimes called the *industry concentration ratio*.

Constant dollars Dollars expressed in terms of real purchasing power, using a particular year as the base or standard of comparison, in contrast to current dollars.

Constant returns to scale No change in long-run average costs when output increases.

Constant-cost industry An industry whose total output can be increased without an increase in long-run per-unit costs. Its long-run supply curve is horizontal.

Consumer optimum A choice of a set of goods and services that maximizes the level of satisfaction for each consumer, subject to limited income.

Consumer Price Index (CPI) A statistical measure of a weighted average of prices of a specified set of goods and services purchased by typical consumers in urban areas.

Consumer surplus The difference between the total amount that consumers would have been willing to pay for an item and the total amount that they actually pay.

Consumption Spending on new goods and services to be used up out of a household's current income. Whatever is not consumed is saved. Consumption includes such things as buying food and going to a concert.

Consumption function The relationship between amount consumed and disposable income. A consumption function tells us how much people plan to consume at various levels of disposable income.

Consumption goods Goods bought by households to use up, such as food and movies.

Contraction A business fluctuation during which the pace of national economic activity is slowing down.

Cooperative game A game in which the players explicitly cooperate to make themselves jointly better off. As applied to firms, it involves companies colluding in order to make higher than perfectly competitive rates of return.

Corporation A legal entity that may conduct business in its own name just as an individual does. The owners of a corporation, called shareholders, own shares of the firm's profits and have the protection of limited liability.

Cost-of-living adjustments (COLAs) Clauses in contracts that allow for increases in specified nominal values to take account of changes in the cost of living.

Cost-of-service regulation Regulation that allows prices to reflect only the actual average cost of production and no monopoly profits.

Cost-push inflation Inflation caused by decreases in short-run aggregate supply.

Craft unions Labor unions composed of workers who engage in a particular trade or skill, such as baking, carpentry, or plumbing.

Creative response Behavior on the part of a firm that allows it to comply with the letter of the law but violate the spirit, significantly lessening the law's effects.

Credence good A product with qualities that consumers lack the expertise to assess without assistance.

Credit policy Federal Reserve policymaking involving direct lending to financial and nonfinancial firms.

Cross price elasticity of demand (E_{xy}) The percentage change in the amount of an item demanded (holding its price constant) divided by the percentage change in the price of a related good.

Crowding-out effect The tendency of expansionary fiscal policy to cause a decrease in planned investment or planned consumption in the private sector. This decrease normally results from the rise in interest rates.

Current account A category of balance of payments transactions that measures the exchange of merchandise, the exchange of services, and unilateral transfers.

Cyclical unemployment Unemployment resulting from business recessions that occur when aggregate (total) demand is insufficient to create full employment.

D

Dead capital Any capital resource that lacks clear title of ownership.

Deadweight loss The portion of consumer surplus that no one in society is able to obtain in a situation of monopoly.

Decreasing-cost industry An industry in which an increase in output leads to a reduction in long-run per-unit costs, such that the long-run industry supply curve slopes downward.

Deflation A sustained decrease in the average of all prices of goods and services in an economy.

Demand A schedule showing how much of a good or service people will purchase at any price during a specified time period, other things being constant.

Demand curve A graphical representation of the demand schedule. It is a negatively sloped line showing the inverse relationship between the price and the quantity demanded (other things being equal).

Demand-pull inflation Inflation caused by increases in aggregate demand not matched by increases in aggregate supply.

Dependent variable A variable whose value changes according to changes in the value of one or more independent variables.

Depository institutions Financial institutions that accept deposits from savers and lend funds from those deposits out at interest.

Depreciation A decrease in the exchange value of one nation's currency in terms of the currency of another nation.

Depression An extremely severe recession.

Derived demand Input factor demand derived from demand for the final product being produced.

Development economics The study of factors that contribute to the economic growth of a country.

Diminishing marginal utility The principle that as more of any good or service is consumed, its *extra* benefit declines. Otherwise stated, increases in total utility from the consumption of a good or service become smaller and smaller as more is consumed during a given time period.

Direct expenditure offsets Actions on the part of the private sector in spending income that offset government fiscal policy actions. Any increase in government spending in an area that competes with the private sector will have some direct expenditure offset.

Direct marketing Advertising targeted at specific consumers, typically in the form of postal mailings, telephone calls, or e-mail messages.

Direct relationship A relationship between two variables that is positive, meaning that an increase in one variable is associated with an increase in the other and a decrease in one variable is associated with a decrease in the other.

Discount rate The interest rate that the Federal Reserve charges for reserves that it lends to depository institutions. It is sometimes referred to as the *rediscount rate* or, in Canada and England, as the *bank rate*.

Discounting The method by which the present value of a future sum or a future stream of sums is obtained.

Discouraged workers Individuals who have stopped looking for a job because they are convinced that they will not find a suitable one.

Diseconomies of scale Increases in long-run average costs that occur as output increases.

Disposable personal income (DPI) Personal income after personal income taxes have been paid.

Dissaving Negative saving; a situation in which spending exceeds income. Dissaving can occur when a household is able to borrow or use up existing assets.

Distribution of income The way income is allocated among the population based on groupings of residents.

Dividends Portion of a corporation's profits paid to its owners (shareholders).

Division of labor The segregation of resources into different specific tasks. For instance, one automobile worker puts on bumpers, another doors, and so on.

Dominant strategies Strategies that always yield the highest benefit. Regardless of what other players do, a dominant strategy will yield the most benefit for the player using it.

Dumping Selling a good or a service abroad below the price charged in the home market or at a price below its cost of production.

Durable consumer goods Consumer goods that have a life span of more than three years.

Dynamic tax analysis Economic evaluation of tax rate changes that recognizes that the tax base eventually declines with ever-higher tax rates, so that tax revenues may eventually decline if the tax rate is raised sufficiently.

E

Economic freedom The rights to own private property and to exchange goods, services, and financial assets with minimal government interference.

Economic goods Goods that are scarce, for which the quantity demanded exceeds the quantity supplied at a zero price.

Economic growth Increases in per capita real GDP measured by its rate of change per year.

Economic profits Total revenues minus total opportunity costs of all inputs used, or the total of all implicit and explicit costs.

Economic rent A payment for the use of any resource over and above its opportunity cost.

Economic system A society's institutional mechanism for determining the way in which scarce resources are used to satisfy human desires.

Economics The study of how people allocate their limited resources to satisfy their unlimited wants.

Economies of scale Decreases in long-run average costs resulting from increases in output.

Effect time lag The time that elapses between the implementation of a policy and the results of that policy.

Efficiency The case in which a given level of inputs is used to produce the maximum output possible. Alternatively, the situation in which a given output is produced at minimum cost.

Effluent fee A charge to a polluter that gives the right to discharge into the air or water a certain amount of pollution; also called a *pollution tax*.

Elastic demand A demand relationship in which a given percentage change in price will result in a larger percentage change in quantity demanded.

Empirical Relying on real-world data in evaluating the usefulness of a model.

Endowments The various resources in an economy, including both physical resources and such human resources as ingenuity and management skills.

Entitlements Guaranteed benefits under a government program such as Social Security, Medicare, or Medicaid.

Entrepreneurship The component of human resources that performs the functions of raising capital; organizing, managing, and assembling other factors of production; making basic business policy decisions; and taking risks.

Equation of exchange The formula indicating that the number of monetary units (M_s) times the number of times each unit is spent on final goods and services (V) is identical to the price level (P) times real GDP (Y).

Equilibrium The situation when quantity supplied equals quantity demanded at a particular price.

Exchange rate The price of one nation's currency in terms of the currency of another country.

Excise tax A tax levied on purchases of a particular good or service.

Expansion A business fluctuation in which the pace of national economic activity is speeding up.

Expenditure approach Computing GDP by adding up the dollar value at current market prices of all final goods and services.

Experience good A product that an individual must consume before the product's quality can be established.

Explicit costs Costs that business managers must take account of because they must be paid. Examples are wages, taxes, and rent.

Externality A consequence of a diversion of a private cost (or benefit) from a social cost (or benefit). A situation in which the costs (or benefits) of an action are not fully borne (or gained) by the decision makers engaged in an activity that uses scarce resources.

F

Featherbedding Any practice that forces employers to use more labor than they would otherwise or to use existing labor in an inefficient manner.

Federal Deposit Insurance Corporation (FDIC) A government agency that insures the deposits held in banks and most other depository institutions. All U.S. banks are insured this way.

Federal funds market A private market (made up mostly of banks) in which banks can borrow reserves from other banks that want to lend them. Federal funds are usually lent for overnight use.

Federal funds rate The interest rate that depository institutions pay to borrow reserves in the interbank federal funds market.

Fiduciary monetary system A system in which money is issued by the government and its value is based uniquely on the public's faith that the currency represents command over goods and services and will be accepted in payment for debts.

Final goods and services Goods and services that are at their final stage of production and will not be transformed into yet other goods or services. For example, wheat ordinarily is not considered a final good because it is usually used to make a final good, bread.

Financial capital Funds used to purchase physical capital goods, such as buildings and equipment, and patents and trademarks.

Financial intermediaries Institutions that transfer funds between ultimate lenders (savers) and ultimate borrowers.

Financial intermediation The process by which financial institutions accept savings from businesses, households, and governments and lend the savings to other businesses, households, and governments.

Firm A business organization that employs resources to produce goods or services for profit. A firm normally owns and operates at least one "plant" or facility in order to produce.

Fiscal policy The discretionary changing of government expenditures or taxes to achieve national economic goals, such as high employment with price stability.

Fixed costs Costs that do not vary with output. Fixed costs typically include such expenses as rent on a building. These costs are fixed for a certain period of time (in the long run, though, they are variable).

Fixed investment Purchases by businesses of newly produced producer durables, or capital goods, such as production machinery and office equipment.

Flexible exchange rates Exchange rates that are allowed to fluctuate in the open market in response to changes in supply and demand. Sometimes called *floating exchange rates*.

Flow A quantity measured per unit of time; something that occurs over time, such as the income you make per week or per year or the number of individuals who are fired every month.

FOMC Directive A document that summarizes the Federal Open Market Committee's general policy strategy, establishes near-term objectives for the federal funds rate, and specifies target ranges for money supply growth.

Foreign direct investment The acquisition of more than 10 percent of the shares of ownership in a company in another nation.

Foreign exchange market A market in which households, firms, and governments buy and sell national currencies.

Foreign exchange rate The price of one currency in terms of another.

Foreign exchange risk The possibility that changes in the value of a nation's currency will result in variations in the market value of assets.

45-degree reference line The line along which planned real expenditures equal real GDP per year.

Fractional reserve banking A system in which depository institutions hold reserves that are less than the amount of total deposits.

Free-rider problem A problem that arises when individuals presume that others will pay for public goods so that, individually, they can escape paying for their portion without causing a reduction in production.

Frictional unemployment Unemployment due to the fact that workers must search for appropriate job offers. This activity takes time, and so they remain temporarily unemployed.

Full employment An arbitrary level of unemployment that corresponds to "normal" friction in the labor market. In 1986, a 6.5 percent rate of unemployment was considered full employment. Today it is somewhat higher.

G

Gains from trade The sum of consumer surplus and producer surplus.

Game theory A way of describing the various possible outcomes in any situation involving two or more interacting individuals when those individuals are aware of the interactive nature of their situation and plan accordingly. The plans made by these individuals are known as *game strategies*.

GDP deflator A price index measuring the changes in prices of all new goods and services produced in the economy.

General Agreement on Tariffs and Trade (GATT) An international agreement established in 1947 to further world trade by reducing barriers and tariffs. The GATT was replaced by the World Trade Organization in 1995.

Goods All things from which individuals derive satisfaction or happiness.

Government budget constraint The limit on government spending and transfers imposed by the fact that every dollar the government spends, transfers, or uses to repay borrowed funds must ultimately be provided by the user charges and taxes it collects.

Government budget deficit An excess of government spending over government revenues during a given period of time.

Government budget surplus An excess of government revenues over government spending during a given period of time.

Government, or political, goods Goods (and services) provided by the public sector; they can be either private or public goods.

Government-inhibited good A good that has been deemed socially undesirable through the political process. Heroin is an example.

Government-sponsored good A good that has been deemed socially desirable through the political process. Museums are an example.

Gross domestic income (GDI) The sum of all income—wages, interest, rent, and profits—paid to the four factors of production.

Gross domestic product (GDP) The total market value of all final goods and services produced during a year by factors of production located within a nation's borders.

Gross private domestic investment The creation of capital goods, such as factories and machines, that can yield production and hence consumption in the future. Also included in this definition are changes in business inventories and repairs made to machines or buildings.

Gross public debt All federal government debt irrespective of who owns it.

H

Health insurance exchanges Government agencies to which the national health care program assigns the task of assisting individuals, families, and small businesses in identifying health insurance policies to purchase.

Hedge A financial strategy that reduces the chance of suffering losses arising from foreign exchange risk.

Herfindahl-Hirschman Index (HHI) The sum of the squared percentage sales shares of all firms in an industry.

Horizontal merger The joining of firms that are producing or selling a similar product.

Human capital The accumulated training and education of workers.

I

Implicit costs Expenses that managers do not have to pay out of pocket and hence normally do not explicitly calculate, such as the opportunity cost of factors of production that are owned. Examples are owner-provided capital and owner-provided labor.

Import quota A physical supply restriction on imports of a particular good, such as sugar. Foreign exporters are unable to sell in the United States more than the quantity specified in the import quota.

Incentive structure The system of rewards and punishments individuals face with respect to their own actions.

Incentives Rewards or penalties for engaging in a particular activity.

Income approach Measuring GDP by adding up all components of national income, including wages, interest, rent, and profits.

Income elasticity of demand (E_i) The percentage change in the amount of a good demanded, holding its price constant, divided by the percentage change in income. The responsiveness of the amount of a good demanded to a change in income, holding the good's relative price constant.

Income in kind Income received in the form of goods and services, such as housing or medical care. Income in kind differs from money income, which is simply income in dollars, or general purchasing power, that can be used to buy *any* goods and services.

Income velocity of money (V) The number of times per year a dollar is spent on final goods and services; identically equal to nominal GDP divided by the money supply.

Increasing-cost industry An industry in which an increase in industry output is accompanied by an increase in long-run per-unit costs, such that the long-run industry supply curve slopes upward.

Independent variable A variable whose value is determined independently of, or outside, the equation under study.

Indifference curve A curve composed of a set of consumption alternatives, each of which yields the same total amount of satisfaction.

Indirect business taxes All business taxes except the tax on corporate profits. Indirect business taxes include sales and business property taxes.

Industrial unions Labor unions that consist of workers from a particular industry, such as automobile manufacturing or steel manufacturing.

Industry supply curve The locus of points showing the minimum prices at which given quantities will be forthcoming; also called the *market supply curve*.

Inefficient point Any point below the production possibilities curve, at which the use of resources is not generating the maximum possible output.

Inelastic demand A demand relationship in which a given percentage change in price will result in a less-than-proportionate percentage change in the quantity demanded.

Infant industry argument The contention that tariffs should be imposed to protect from import competition an industry that is trying to get started. Presumably, after the industry becomes technologically efficient, the tariff can be lifted.

Inferior goods Goods for which demand falls as income rises.

Inflation A sustained increase in the average of all prices of goods and services in an economy.

Inflationary gap The gap that exists whenever equilibrium real GDP per year is greater than full-employment real GDP as shown by the position of the long-run aggregate supply curve.

Information product An item that is produced using information-intensive inputs at a relatively high fixed cost but distributed for sale at a relatively low marginal cost.

Informational advertising Advertising that emphasizes transmitting knowledge about the features of a product.

Innovation Transforming an invention into something that is useful to humans.

Inside information Information that is not available to the general public about what is happening in a corporation.

Interactive marketing Advertising that permits a consumer to follow up directly by searching for more information and placing direct product orders.

Interest The payment for current rather than future command over resources; the cost of obtaining credit.

Interest rate effect One of the reasons that the aggregate demand curve slopes downward: Higher price levels increase the interest rate, which in turn causes businesses and consumers to reduce desired spending due to the higher cost of borrowing.

Intermediate goods Goods used up entirely in the production of final goods.

International financial crisis The rapid withdrawal of foreign investments and loans from a nation.

International Monetary Fund An agency founded to administer an international foreign exchange system and to lend to member countries that had balance of payments problems. The IMF now functions as a lender of last resort for national governments.

Inventory investment Changes in the stocks of finished goods and goods in process, as well as changes in the raw materials that businesses keep on hand. Whenever inventories are decreasing, inventory investment is negative. Whenever they are increasing, inventory investment is positive.

Inverse relationship A relationship between two variables that is negative, meaning that an increase in one variable is associated with a decrease in the other and a decrease in one variable is associated with an increase in the other.

Investment Spending on items such as machines and buildings, which can be used to produce goods and services in the future. (It also includes changes in business inventories.) The investment part of real GDP is the portion that will be used in the process of producing goods *in the future*.

J

Job leaver An individual in the labor force who quits voluntarily.

Job loser An individual in the labor force whose employment was involuntarily terminated.

Jurisdictional dispute A disagreement involving two or more unions over which should have control of a particular jurisdiction, such as a particular craft or skill or a particular firm or industry.

K

Keynesian short-run aggregate supply curve The horizontal portion of the aggregate supply curve in which there is excessive unemployment and unused capacity in the economy.

L

Labor Productive contributions of humans who work.

Labor force Individuals aged 16 years or older who either have jobs or who are looking and available for jobs; the number of employed plus the number of unemployed.

Labor force participation rate The percentage of noninstitutionalized working-age individuals who are employed or seeking employment.

Labor productivity Total real domestic output (real GDP) divided by the number of workers (output per worker).

Labor unions Worker organizations that seek to secure economic improvements for their members. They also seek to improve the safety, health, and other benefits (such as job security) of their members.

Land The natural resources that are available from nature. Land as a resource includes location, original fertility and mineral deposits, topography, climate, water, and vegetation.

Law of demand The observation that there is a negative, or inverse, relationship between the price of any good or service and the quantity demanded, holding other factors constant.

Law of diminishing marginal product The observation that after some point, successive equal-sized increases in a variable factor of production, such as labor, added to fixed factors of production will result in smaller increases in output.

Law of increasing additional cost The fact that the opportunity cost of additional units of a good generally increases as people attempt to produce more of that good. This accounts for the bowed-out shape of the production possibilities curve.

Law of supply The observation that the higher the price of a good, the more of that good sellers will make available over a specified time period, other things being equal.

Leading indicators Events that have been found to occur before changes in business activity.

Lemons problem The potential for asymmetric information to bring about a general decline in product quality in an industry.

Lender of last resort The Federal Reserve's role as an institution that is willing and able to lend to a temporarily illiquid bank that is otherwise in good financial condition to prevent the bank's illiquid position from leading to a general loss of confidence in that bank or in others.

Liabilities Amounts owed; the legal claims against a business or household by nonowners.

Life-cycle theory of consumption A theory in which a person bases decisions about current consumption and saving on both current income and anticipated future income.

Limited liability A legal concept in which the responsibility, or liability, of the owners of a corporation is limited to the value of the shares in the firm that they own.

Liquidity The degree to which an asset can be acquired or disposed of without much danger of any intervening loss in *nominal* value and with small transaction costs. Money is the most liquid asset.

Liquidity approach A method of measuring the money supply by looking at money as a temporary store of value.

Long run The time period during which all factors of production can be varied.

Long-run aggregate supply curve A vertical line representing the real output of goods and services after full adjustment has occurred. It can also be viewed as representing the real GDP of the economy under conditions of full employment—the full-employment level of real GDP.

Long-run average cost curve The locus of points representing the minimum unit cost of producing any given rate of output, given current technology and resource prices.

Long-run industry supply curve A market supply curve showing the relationship between prices and quantities after firms have been allowed the time to enter into or exit from an industry, depending on whether there have been positive or negative economic profits.

Lorenz curve A geometric representation of the distribution of income. A Lorenz curve that is perfectly straight represents complete income equality. The more bowed a Lorenz curve, the more unequally income is distributed.

Lump-sum tax A tax that does not depend on income. An example is a $1,000 tax that every household must pay, irrespective of its economic situation.

M

M1 The money supply, measured as the total value of currency plus transactions deposits plus traveler's checks not issued by banks.

M2 M1 plus (1) savings deposits at all depository institutions, (2) small-denomination time deposits, and (3) balances in retail money market mutual funds.

Macroeconomics The study of the behavior of the economy as a whole, including such economywide phenomena as changes in unemployment, the general price level, and national income.

Majority rule A collective decision-making system in which group decisions are made on the basis of more than 50 percent of the vote. In other words, whatever more than half of the electorate votes for, the entire electorate has to accept.

Marginal cost pricing A system of pricing in which the price charged is equal to the opportunity cost to society of producing one more unit of the good or service in question. The opportunity cost is the marginal cost to society.

Marginal costs The change in total costs due to a one-unit change in production rate.

Marginal factor cost (MFC) The cost of using an additional unit of an input. For example, if a firm can hire all the workers it wants at the going wage rate, the marginal factor cost of labor is that wage rate.

Marginal physical product The physical output that is due to the addition of one more unit of a variable factor of production. The change in total product occurring when a variable input is increased and all other inputs are held constant. It is also called *marginal product*.

Marginal physical product (MPP) of labor The change in output resulting from the addition of one more worker. The MPP of the worker equals the change in total output accounted for by hiring the worker, holding all other factors of production constant.

Marginal propensity to consume (MPC) The ratio of the change in consumption to the change in disposable income. A marginal propensity to consume of 0.8 tells us that an additional $100 in take-home pay will lead to an additional $80 consumed.

Marginal propensity to save (MPS) The ratio of the change in saving to the change in disposable income. A marginal propensity to save of 0.2 indicates that out of an additional $100 in take-home pay, $20 will be saved. Whatever is not saved is consumed. The marginal propensity to save plus the marginal propensity to consume must always equal 1, by definition.

Marginal revenue The change in total revenues resulting from a one-unit change in output (and sale) of the product in question.

Marginal revenue product (MRP) The marginal physical product (MPP) times marginal revenue (MR). The MRP gives the additional revenue obtained from a one-unit change in labor input.

Marginal tax rate The change in the tax payment divided by the change in income, or the percentage of *additional* dollars that must be paid in taxes. The marginal tax rate is applied to the highest tax bracket of taxable income reached.

Marginal utility The change in total utility due to a one-unit change in the quantity of a good or service consumed.

Market All of the arrangements that individuals have for exchanging with one another. Thus, for example, we can speak of the labor market, the automobile market, and the credit market.

Market clearing, or equilibrium, price The price that clears the market, at which quantity demanded equals quantity supplied; the price where the demand curve intersects the supply curve.

Market demand The demand of all consumers in the marketplace for a particular good or service. The summation at each price of the quantity demanded by each individual.

Market failure A situation in which an unrestrained market operation leads to either too few or too many resources going to a specific economic activity.

Mass marketing Advertising intended to reach as many consumers as possible, typically through television, newspaper, radio, or magazine ads.

Medium of exchange Any item that sellers will accept as payment.

Microeconomics The study of decision making undertaken by individuals (or households) and by firms.

Minimum efficient scale (MES) The lowest rate of output per unit time at which long-run average costs for a particular firm are at a minimum.

Minimum wage A wage floor, legislated by government, setting the lowest hourly rate that firms may legally pay workers.

Models, or theories Simplified representations of the real world used as the basis for predictions or explanations.

Money Any medium that is universally accepted in an economy both by sellers of goods and services as payment for those goods and services and by creditors as payment for debts.

Money balances Synonymous with money, money stock, money holdings.

Money illusion Reacting to changes in money prices rather than relative prices. If a worker whose wages double when the price level also doubles thinks he or she is better off, that worker is suffering from money illusion.

Money multiplier A number that, when multiplied by a change in reserves in the banking system, yields the resulting change in the money supply.

Money price The price expressed in today's dollars; also called the *absolute* or *nominal price*.

Money supply The amount of money in circulation.

Monopolist The single supplier of a good or service for which there is no close substitute. The monopolist therefore constitutes its entire industry.

Monopolistic competition A market situation in which a large number of firms produce similar but not identical products. Entry into the industry is relatively easy.

Monopolization The possession of monopoly power in the relevant market and the willful acquisition or maintenance of that power, as distinguished from growth or development as a consequence of a superior product, business acumen, or historical accident.

Monopoly A firm that can determine the market price of a good. In the extreme case, a monopoly is the only seller of a good or service.

Monopsonist The only buyer in a market.

Monopsonistic exploitation Paying a price for the variable input that is less than its marginal revenue product; the difference between marginal revenue product and the wage rate.

Moral hazard The possibility that a borrower might engage in riskier behavior after a loan has been obtained.

Multiplier The ratio of the change in the equilibrium level of real GDP to the change in autonomous real expenditures. The number by which a change in autonomous real investment or autonomous real consumption, for example, is multiplied to get the change in equilibrium real GDP.

N

National income (NI) The total of all factor payments to resource owners. It can be obtained from net domestic product (NDP) by subtracting indirect business taxes and transfers and adding net U.S. income earned abroad and other business income adjustments.

National income accounting A measurement system used to estimate national income and its components. One approach to measuring an economy's aggregate performance.

Natural monopoly A monopoly that arises from the peculiar production characteristics in an industry. It usually arises when there are large economies of scale relative to the industry's demand such that one firm can produce at a lower average cost than can be achieved by multiple firms.

Natural rate of unemployment The rate of unemployment that is estimated to prevail in long-run macroeconomic equilibrium, when all workers and employers have fully adjusted to any changes in the economy.

Negative market feedback A tendency for a good or service to fall out of favor with more consumers because other consumers have stopped purchasing the item.

Negative-sum game A game in which players as a group lose during the process of the game.

Net domestic product (NDP) GDP minus depreciation.

Net investment Gross private domestic investment minus an estimate of the wear and tear on the existing capital stock. Net investment therefore measures the change in the capital stock over a one-year period.

Net public debt Gross public debt minus all government interagency borrowing.

Net wealth The stock of assets owned by a person, household, firm, or nation (net of any debts owed). For a household, net wealth can consist of a house, cars, personal belongings, stocks, bonds, bank accounts, and cash (minus any debts owed).

Network effect A situation in which a consumer's willingness to purchase a good or service is influenced by how many others also buy or have bought the item.

New entrant An individual who has never held a full-time job lasting two weeks or longer but is now seeking employment.

New growth theory A theory of economic growth that examines the factors that determine why technology, research, innovation, and the like are undertaken and how they interact.

New Keynesian inflation dynamics In new Keynesian theory, the pattern of inflation exhibited by an economy with growing aggregate demand—initial sluggish adjustment of the price level in response to increased aggregate demand followed by higher inflation later.

Nominal rate of interest The market rate of interest observed in contracts expressed in today's dollars.

Nominal values The values of variables such as GDP and investment expressed in current dollars, also called *money values;* measurement in terms of the actual market prices at which goods and services are sold.

Noncontrollable expenditures Government spending that changes automatically without action by Congress.

Noncooperative game A game in which the players neither negotiate nor cooperate in any way. As applied to firms in an industry, this is the common situation in which there are relatively few firms and each has some ability to change price.

Nondurable consumer goods Consumer goods that are used up within three years.

Nonincome expense items The total of indirect business taxes and depreciation.

Nonprice rationing devices All methods used to ration scarce goods that are price-controlled. Whenever the price system is not allowed to work, nonprice rationing devices will evolve to ration the affected goods and services.

Normal goods Goods for which demand rises as income rises. Most goods are normal goods.

Normal rate of return The amount that must be paid to an investor to induce investment in a business. Also known as the *opportunity cost of capital.*

Normative economics Analysis involving value judgments about economic policies; relates to whether outcomes are good or bad. A statement of *what ought to be*.

Number line A line that can be divided into segments of equal length, each associated with a number.

O

Oligopoly A market structure in which there are very few sellers. Each seller knows that the other sellers will react to its changes in prices, quantities, and qualities.

Open economy effect One of the reasons that the aggregate demand curve slopes downward: Higher price levels result in foreign residents desiring to buy fewer U.S.-made goods, while U.S. residents now desire more foreign-made goods, thereby reducing net exports. This is equivalent to a reduction in the amount of real goods and services purchased in the United States.

Open market operations The purchase and sale of existing U.S. government securities (such as bonds) in the open private market by the Federal Reserve System.

Opportunistic behavior Actions that focus solely on short-run gains because long-run benefits of cooperation are perceived to be smaller.

Opportunity cost The highest-valued, next-best alternative that must be sacrificed to obtain something or to satisfy a want.

Opportunity cost of capital The normal rate of return, or the available return on the next-best alternative investment. Economists consider this a cost of production, and it is included in our cost examples.

Optimal quantity of pollution The level of pollution for which the marginal benefit of one additional unit of pollution abatement just equals the marginal cost of that additional unit of pollution abatement.

Origin The intersection of the *y* axis and the *x* axis in a graph.

Outsourcing A firm's employment of labor outside the country in which the firm is located.

P

Par value The officially determined value of a currency.

Partnership A business owned by two or more joint owners, or partners, who share the responsibilities and the profits of the firm and are individually liable for all the debts of the partnership.

Passive (nondiscretionary) policymaking Policymaking that is carried out in response to a rule. It is therefore not in response to an actual or potential change in overall economic activity.

Patent A government protection that gives an inventor the exclusive right to make, use, or sell an invention for a limited period of time (currently, 20 years).

Payoff matrix A matrix of outcomes, or consequences, of the strategies available to the players in a game.

Perfect competition A market structure in which the decisions of *individual* buyers and sellers have no effect on market price.

Perfectly competitive firm A firm that is such a small part of the total *industry* that it cannot affect the price of the product it sells.

Perfectly elastic demand A demand that has the characteristic that even the slightest increase in price will lead to zero quantity demanded.

Perfectly elastic supply A supply characterized by a reduction in quantity supplied to zero when there is the slightest decrease in price.

Perfectly inelastic demand A demand that exhibits zero responsiveness to price changes. No matter what the price is, the quantity demanded remains the same.

Perfectly inelastic supply A supply for which quantity supplied remains constant, no matter what happens to price.

Permanent income hypothesis A theory of consumption in which an individual determines current consumption based on anticipated average lifetime income.

Personal Consumption Expenditure (PCE) Index A statistical measure of average prices that uses annually updated weights based on surveys of consumer spending.

Personal income (PI) The amount of income that households actually receive before they pay personal income taxes.

Persuasive advertising Advertising that is intended to induce a consumer to purchase a particular product and discover a previously unknown taste for the item.

Phillips curve A curve showing the relationship between unemployment and changes in wages or prices. It was long thought to reflect a trade-off between unemployment and inflation.

Physical capital All manufactured resources, including buildings, equipment, machines, and improvements to land that are used for production.

Planning curve The long-run average cost curve.

Planning horizon The long run, during which all inputs are variable.

Plant size The physical size of the factories that a firm owns and operates to produce its output. Plant size can be defined by square footage, maximum physical capacity, and other physical measures.

Policy irrelevance proposition The conclusion that policy actions have no real effects in the short run if the policy actions are anticipated and none in the long run even if the policy actions are unanticipated.

Portfolio investment The purchase of less than 10 percent of the shares of ownership in a company in another nation.

Positive economics Analysis that is *strictly* limited to making either purely descriptive statements or scientific predictions; for example, "If A, then B." A statement of *what is*.

Positive market feedback A tendency for a good or service to come into favor with additional consumers because other consumers have chosen to buy the item.

Positive-sum game A game in which players as a group are better off at the end of the game.

Potential money multiplier The reciprocal of the reserve ratio, assuming no leakages into currency. It is equal to 1 divided by the reserve ratio.

Precautionary demand Holding money to meet unplanned expenditures and emergencies.

Present value The value of a future amount expressed in today's dollars; the most that someone would pay today to receive a certain sum at some point in the future.

Price ceiling A legal maximum price that may be charged for a particular good or service.

Price controls Government-mandated minimum or maximum prices that may be charged for goods and services.

Price differentiation Establishing different prices for similar products to reflect differences in marginal cost in providing those commodities to different groups of buyers.

Price discrimination Selling a given product at more than one price, with the price difference being unrelated to differences in marginal cost.

Price elasticity of demand (E_p) The responsiveness of the quantity demanded of a commodity to changes in its price; defined as the percentage change in quantity demanded divided by the percentage change in price.

Price elasticity of supply (E_s) The responsiveness of the quantity supplied of a commodity to a change in its price—the percentage change in quantity supplied divided by the percentage change in price.

Price floor A legal minimum price below which a good or service may not be sold. Legal minimum wages are an example.

Price index The cost of today's market basket of goods expressed as a percentage of the cost of the same market basket during a base year.

Price searcher A firm that must determine the price-output combination that maximizes profit because it faces a downward-sloping demand curve.

Price system An economic system in which relative prices are constantly changing to reflect changes in supply and demand for different commodities. The prices of those commodities are signals to everyone within the system as to what is relatively scarce and what is relatively abundant.

Price taker A perfectly competitive firm that must take the price of its product as given because the firm cannot influence its price.

Principle of rival consumption The recognition that individuals are rivals in consuming private goods because one person's consumption reduces the amount available for others to consume.

Principle of substitution The principle that consumers shift away from goods and services that become priced relatively higher in favor of goods and services that are now priced relatively lower.

Prisoners' dilemma A famous strategic game in which two prisoners have a choice between confessing and not confessing to a crime. If neither confesses, they serve a minimum sentence. If both confess, they serve a longer sentence. If one confesses and the other doesn't, the one who confesses goes free. The dominant strategy is always to confess.

Private costs Costs borne solely by the individuals who incur them. Also called *internal costs*.

Private goods Goods that can be consumed by only one individual at a time. Private goods are subject to the principle of rival consumption.

Private property rights Exclusive rights of ownership that allow the use, transfer, and exchange of property.

Producer durables, or capital goods Durable goods having an expected service life of more than three years that are used by businesses to produce other goods and services.

Producer Price Index (PPI) A statistical measure of a weighted average of prices of goods and services that firms produce and sell.

Producer surplus The difference between the total amount that producers actually receive for an item and the total amount that they would have been willing to accept for supplying that item.

Product differentiation The distinguishing of products by brand name, color, and other minor attributes. Product differentiation occurs in other than perfectly competitive markets in which products are, in theory, homogeneous, such as wheat or corn.

Production Any activity that results in the conversion of resources into products that can be used in consumption.

Production function The relationship between inputs and maximum physical output. A production function is a technological, not an economic, relationship.

Production possibilities curve (PPC) A curve representing all possible combinations of maximum outputs that could be produced, assuming a fixed amount of productive resources of a given quality.

Profit-maximizing rate of production The rate of production that maximizes total profits, or the difference between total revenues and total costs. Also, it is the rate of production at which marginal revenue equals marginal cost.

Progressive taxation A tax system in which, as income increases, a higher percentage of the additional income is paid as taxes. The marginal tax rate exceeds the average tax rate as income rises.

Property rights The rights of an owner to use and to exchange property.

Proportional rule A decision-making system in which actions are based on the proportion of the "votes" cast and are in proportion to them. In a market system, if 10 percent of the "dollar votes" are cast for blue cars, 10 percent of automobile output will be blue cars.

Proportional taxation A tax system in which, regardless of an individual's income, the tax bill comprises exactly the same proportion.

Proprietorship A business owned by one individual who makes the business decisions, receives all the profits, and is legally responsible for the debts of the firm.

Public debt The total value of all outstanding federal government securities.

Public goods Goods for which the principle of rival consumption does not apply and for which exclusion of nonpaying consumers is too costly to be feasible. They can be jointly consumed by many individuals simultaneously at no additional cost and with no reduction in quality or quantity. Furthermore, no one who fails to help pay for the good can be denied the benefit of the good.

Purchasing power The value of money for buying goods and services. If your money income stays the same but the price of one good that you are buying goes up, your effective purchasing power falls.

Purchasing power parity Adjustment in exchange rate conversions that takes into account differences in the true cost of living across countries.

Q

Quantitative easing Federal Reserve open market purchases intended to generate an increase in bank reserves at a nearly zero interest rate.

Quantity theory of money and prices The hypothesis that changes in the money supply lead to equiproportional changes in the price level.

Quota subscription A nation's account with the International Monetary Fund, denominated in special drawing rights.

Quota system A government-imposed restriction on the quantity of a specific good that another country is allowed to sell in the United States. In other words, quotas are restrictions on imports. These restrictions are usually applied to one or several specific countries.

R

Random walk theory The theory that there are no predictable trends in securities prices that can be used to "get rich quick."

Rate of discount The rate of interest used to discount future sums back to present value.

Rate-of-return regulation Regulation that seeks to keep the rate of return in an industry at a competitive level by not allowing prices that would produce economic profits.

Rational expectations hypothesis A theory stating that people combine the effects of past policy changes on important economic variables with their own judgment about the future effects of current and future policy changes.

Rationality assumption The assumption that people do not intentionally make decisions that would leave them worse off.

Reaction function The manner in which one oligopolist reacts to a change in price, output, or quality made by another oligopolist in the industry.

Real disposable income Real GDP minus net taxes, or after-tax real income.

Real rate of interest The nominal rate of interest minus the anticipated rate of inflation.

Real values Measurement of economic values after adjustments have been made for changes in the average of prices between years.

Real-balance effect The change in expenditures resulting from a change in the real value of money balances when the price level changes, all other things held constant; also called the *wealth effect*.

Real-income effect The change in people's purchasing power that occurs when, other things being constant, the price of one good that they purchase changes. When that price goes up, real income, or purchasing power, falls, and when that price goes down, real income increases.

Recession A period of time during which the rate of growth of business activity is consistently less than its long-term trend or is negative.

Recessionary gap The gap that exists whenever equilibrium real GDP per year is less than full-employment real GDP as shown by the position of the long-run aggregate supply curve.

Recognition time lag The time required to gather information about the current state of the economy.

Reentrant An individual who used to work full-time but left the labor force and has now reentered it looking for a job.

Regional trade bloc A group of nations that grants members special trade privileges.

Regressive taxation A tax system in which as more dollars are earned, the percentage of tax paid on them falls. The marginal tax rate is less than the average tax rate as income rises.

Reinvestment Profits (or depreciation reserves) used to purchase new capital equipment.

Relative price The money price of one commodity divided by the money price of another commodity; the number of units of one commodity that must be sacrificed to purchase one unit of another commodity.

Relevant market A group of firms' products that are closely substitutable and available to consumers within a geographic area.

Rent control Price ceilings on rents.

Repricing, or menu, cost of inflation The cost associated with recalculating prices and printing new price lists when there is inflation.

Reserve ratio The fraction of transactions deposits that banks hold as reserves.

Reserves In the U.S. Federal Reserve System, deposits held by Federal Reserve district banks for depository institutions, plus depository institutions' vault cash.

Resources Things used to produce goods and services to satisfy people's wants.

Retained earnings Earnings that a corporation saves, or retains, for investment in other productive activities; earnings that are not distributed to stockholders.

Ricardian equivalence theorem The proposition that an increase in the government budget deficit has no effect on aggregate demand.

Right-to-work laws Laws that make it illegal to require union membership as a condition of continuing employment in a particular firm.

Rule of 70 A rule stating that the approximate number of years required for per capita real GDP to double is equal to 70 divided by the average rate of economic growth.

Rules of origin Regulations that nations in regional trade blocs establish to delineate product categories eligible for trading preferences.

S

Sales taxes Taxes assessed on the prices paid on most goods and services.

Saving The act of not consuming all of one's current income. Whatever is not consumed out of spendable income is, by definition, saved. *Saving* is an action measured over time (a flow), whereas *savings* are a stock, an accumulation resulting from the act of saving in the past.

Say's law A dictum of economist J. B. Say that supply creates its own demand. Producing goods and services generates the means and the willingness to purchase other goods and services.

Scarcity A situation in which the ingredients for producing the things that people desire are insufficient to satisfy all wants at a zero price.

Search good A product with characteristics that enable an individual to evaluate the product's quality in advance of a purchase.

Seasonal unemployment Unemployment resulting from the seasonal pattern of work in specific industries. It is usually due to seasonal fluctuations in demand or to changing weather conditions that render work difficult, if not impossible, as in the agriculture, construction, and tourist industries.

Secondary boycott A refusal to deal with companies or purchase products sold by companies that are dealing with a company being struck.

Secular deflation A persistent decline in prices resulting from economic growth in the presence of stable aggregate demand.

Securities Stocks and bonds.

Services Mental or physical labor or assistance purchased by consumers. Examples are the assistance of physicians, lawyers, dentists, repair personnel, housecleaners, educators, retailers, and wholesalers; items purchased or used by consumers that do not have physical characteristics.

Share of stock A legal claim to a share of a corporation's future profits. If it is *common stock*, it incorporates certain voting rights regarding major policy decisions of the corporation. If it is *preferred stock*, its owners are accorded preferential treatment in the payment of dividends but do not have any voting rights.

Share-the-gains, share-the-pains theory A theory of regulatory behavior that holds that regulators must take account of the demands of three groups: legislators, who established and oversee the regulatory agency; firms in the regulated industry; and consumers of the regulated industry's products.

Short run The time period during which at least one input, such as plant size, cannot be changed.

Shortage A situation in which quantity demanded is greater than quantity supplied at a price below the market clearing price.

Short-run aggregate supply curve The relationship between total planned economywide production and the price level in the short run, all other things held constant. If prices adjust incompletely in the short run, the curve is positively sloped.

Short-run break-even price The price at which a firm's total revenues equal its total costs. At the break-even price, the firm is just making a normal rate of return on its capital investment. (It is covering its explicit and implicit costs.)

Short-run economies of operation A distinguishing characteristic of an information product arising from declining short-run average total cost as more units of the product are sold.

Short-run shutdown price The price that covers average variable costs. It occurs just below the intersection of the marginal cost curve and the average variable cost curve.

Signals Compact ways of conveying to economic decision makers information needed to make decisions. An effective signal not only conveys information but also provides the incentive to react appropriately. Economic profits and economic losses are such signals.

Slope The change in the *y* value divided by the corresponding change in the *x* value of a curve; the "incline" of the curve.

Small menu costs Costs that deter firms from changing prices in response to demand changes–for example, the costs of renegotiating contracts or printing new price lists.

Social costs The full costs borne by society whenever a resource use occurs. Social costs can be measured by adding external costs to private, or internal, costs.

Special drawing rights (SDRs) Reserve assets created by the International Monetary Fund for countries to use in settling international payment obligations.

Specialization The organization of economic activity so that what each person (or region) consumes is not identical to what that person (or region) produces. An individual may specialize, for example, in law or medicine. A nation may specialize in the production of coffee, e-book readers, or digital cameras.

Stagflation A situation characterized by lower real GDP, lower employment, and a higher unemployment rate during the same period that the rate of inflation increases.

Standard of deferred payment A property of an item that makes it desirable for use as a means of settling debts maturing in the future; an essential property of money.

Static tax analysis Economic evaluation of the effects of tax rate changes under the assumption that there is no effect on the tax base, meaning that there is an unambiguous positive relationship between tax rates and tax revenues.

Stock The quantity of something, measured at a given point in time—for example, an inventory of goods or a bank account. Stocks are defined independently of time, although they are assessed at a point in time.

Store of value The ability to hold value over time; a necessary property of money.

Strategic dependence A situation in which one firm's actions with respect to price, quality, advertising, and related changes may be strategically countered by the reactions of one or more other firms in the industry. Such dependence can exist only when there are a limited number of major firms in an industry.

Strategy Any rule that is used to make a choice, such as "Always pick heads."

Strikebreakers Temporary or permanent workers hired by a company to replace union members who are striking.

Structural unemployment Unemployment of workers over lengthy intervals resulting from skill mismatches with position requirements of employers and from fewer jobs being offered by employers constrained by governmental business regulations and labor market policies.

Subsidy A negative tax; a payment to a producer from the government, usually in the form of a cash grant per unit.

Substitutes Two goods are substitutes when a change in the price of one causes a shift in demand for the other in the same direction as the price change.

Substitution effect The tendency of people to substitute cheaper commodities for more expensive commodities.

Supply A schedule showing the relationship between price and quantity supplied for a specified period of time, other things being equal.

Supply curve The graphical representation of the supply schedule; a line (curve) showing the supply schedule, which generally slopes upward (has a positive slope), other things being equal.

Supply-side economics The suggestion that creating incentives for individuals and firms to increase productivity will cause the aggregate supply curve to shift outward.

Surplus A situation in which quantity supplied is greater than quantity demanded at a price above the market clearing price.

Sympathy strike A work stoppage by a union in sympathy with another union's strike or cause.

T

Tariffs Taxes on imported goods.

Tax base The value of goods, services, wealth, or incomes subject to taxation.

Tax bracket A specified interval of income to which a specific and unique marginal tax rate is applied.

Tax incidence The distribution of tax burdens among various groups in society.

Tax rate The proportion of a tax base that must be paid to a government as taxes.

Taylor rule An equation that specifies a federal funds rate target based on an estimated long-run real interest rate, the current deviation of the actual inflation rate from the Federal Reserve's inflation objective, and the gap between actual real GDP per year and a measure of potential real GDP per year.

Technology The total pool of applied knowledge concerning how goods and services can be produced.

The Fed The Federal Reserve System; the central bank of the United States.

Theory of public choice The study of collective decision making.

Third parties Parties who are not directly involved in a given activity or transaction. For example, in the relationship between caregivers and patients, fees may be paid by third parties (insurance companies, government).

Thrift institutions Financial institutions that receive most of their funds from the savings of the public. They include savings banks, savings and loan associations, and credit unions.

Tie-in sales Purchases of one product that are permitted by the seller only if the consumer buys another good or service from the same firm.

Tit-for-tat strategic behavior In game theory, cooperation that continues as long as the other players continue to cooperate.

Total costs The sum of total fixed costs and total variable costs.

Total income The yearly amount earned by the nation's resources (factors of production). Total income therefore includes wages, rent, interest payments, and profits that are received by workers, landowners, capital owners, and entrepreneurs, respectively.

Total revenues The price per unit times the total quantity sold.

Trade deflection Moving partially assembled products into a member nation of a regional trade bloc, completing assembly, and then exporting them to other nations within the bloc, so as to benefit from preferences granted by the trade bloc.

Trade diversion Shifting existing international trade from countries outside a regional trade bloc to nations within the bloc.

Trading Desk An office at the Federal Reserve Bank of New York charged with implementing monetary policy strategies developed by the Federal Open Market Committee.

Transaction costs All of the costs associated with exchange, including the informational costs of finding out the price and quality, service record, and durability of a product, plus the cost of contracting and enforcing that contract.

Transactions approach A method of measuring the money supply by looking at money as a medium of exchange.

Transactions demand Holding money as a medium of exchange to make payments. The level varies directly with nominal GDP.

Transactions deposits Checkable and debitable account balances in commercial banks and other types of financial institutions, such as credit unions and savings banks. Any accounts in financial institutions from which you can easily transmit debit-card and check payments without many restrictions.

Transfer payments Money payments made by governments to individuals for which no services or goods are rendered in return. Examples are Social Security old-age and disability benefits and unemployment insurance benefits.

Transfers in kind Payments that are in the form of actual goods and services, such as food stamps, subsidized public housing, and medical care, and for which no goods or services are rendered in return.

Traveler's checks Financial instruments obtained from a bank or a nonbanking organization and signed during purchase that can be used in payment upon a second signature by the purchaser.

Two-sided market A market in which an intermediary firm provides services that link groups of producers and consumers.

U

Unanticipated inflation Inflation at a rate that comes as a surprise, either higher or lower than the rate anticipated.

Unemployment The total number of adults (aged 16 years or older) who are willing and able to work and who are actively looking for work but have not found a job.

Union shop A business enterprise that may hire nonunion members, conditional on their joining the union by some specified date after employment begins.

Unit elasticity of demand A demand relationship in which the quantity demanded changes exactly in proportion to the change in price.

Unit of accounting A measure by which prices are expressed; the common denominator of the price system; a central property of money.

Unit tax A constant tax assessed on each unit of a good that consumers purchase.

Unlimited liability A legal concept whereby the personal assets of the owner of a firm can be seized to pay off the firm's debts.

Util A representative unit by which utility is measured.

Utility The want-satisfying power of a good or service.

Utility analysis The analysis of consumer decision making based on utility maximization.

V

Value added The dollar value of an industry's sales minus the value of intermediate goods (for example, raw materials and parts) used in production.

Variable costs Costs that vary with the rate of production. They include wages paid to workers and purchases of materials.

Versioning Selling a product in slightly altered forms to different groups of consumers.

Vertical merger The joining of a firm with another to which it sells an output or from which it buys an input.

Voluntary exchange An act of trading, done on an elective basis, in which both parties to the trade expect to be better off after the exchange.

Voluntary import expansion (VIE) An official agreement with another country in which it agrees to import more from the United States.

Voluntary restraint agreement (VRA) An official agreement with another country that "voluntarily" restricts the quantity of its exports to the United States.

W

Wants What people would buy if their incomes were unlimited.

World Bank A multinational agency that specializes in making loans to about 100 developing nations in an effort to promote their long-term development and growth.

World Trade Organization (WTO) The successor organization to the GATT that handles trade disputes among its member nations.

X

***x* axis** The horizontal axis in a graph.

Y

***y* axis** The vertical axis in a graph.

Z

Zero-sum game A game in which any gains within the group are exactly offset by equal losses by the end of the game.

Index

J

K

L

MACROECONOMIC PRINCIPLES

Nominal versus Real Interest Rate

$$i_n = i_r + \text{expected rate of inflation}$$

where i_n = nominal rate of interest
i_r = real rate of interest

Marginal versus Average Tax Rates

$$\text{Marginal tax rate} = \frac{\text{change in taxes due}}{\text{change in taxable income}}$$

$$\text{Average tax rate} = \frac{\text{total taxes due}}{\text{total taxable income}}$$

GDP—The Expenditure and Income Approaches

$$GDP = C + I + G + X$$

where C = consumption expenditures
I = investment expenditures
G = government expenditures
X = net exports

$$GDP = \text{wages} + \text{rent} + \text{interest} + \text{profits}$$

Say's Law

Supply creates its own demand, or *desired* aggregate expenditures will equal *actual* aggregate expenditures.

Saving, Consumption, and Investment

Consumption + saving = disposable income

Saving = disposable income − consumption

Average and Marginal Propensities

$$APC = \frac{\text{real consumption}}{\text{real disposable income}}$$

$$APS = \frac{\text{real saving}}{\text{real disposable income}}$$

$$MPC = \frac{\text{change in real consumption}}{\text{change in real disposable income}}$$

$$MPS = \frac{\text{change in real saving}}{\text{change in real disposable income}}$$

The Multiplier Formula

$$\text{Multiplier} = \frac{1}{MPS} = \frac{1}{1 - MPC}$$

Multiplier × change in autonomous real spending = change in equilibrium real GDP

Relationship between Bond Prices and Interest Rates

The market price of existing (old) bonds is inversely related to "the" rate of interest prevailing in the economy.

Government Spending and Taxation Multipliers

$$M_g = \frac{1}{MPS}$$

$$M_t = -MPC \times \frac{1}{MPS}$$